Border Settlers of
Northwestern
Virginia

A Borderman of Northwestern Virginia

FROM A DRAWING MADE ESPECIALLY FOR THIS WORK BY
COLISTA M. DOWLING

For description of the border dress see pages 34, 145 and 244; also Note 8, Chapter I; Note 9, Chapter IX; Note 2, Chapter XII, and Note 6, Chapter XVIII.

THE BORDER SETTLERS OF NORTHWESTERN VIRGINIA
FROM 1768 TO 1795

EMBRACING

THE LIFE OF JESSE HUGHES

AND

OTHER NOTED SCOUTS OF THE GREAT WOODS OF THE TRANS-ALLEGHENY

WITH NOTES AND ILLUSTRATIVE ANECDOTES

By

LUCULLUS VIRGIL McWHORTER

LIFE MEMBER OF THE WISCONSIN STATE HISTORICAL SOCIETY; MEMBER OF THE WASHINGTON STATE UNIVERSITY HISTORICAL SOCIETY, AUTHOR OF "THE CRIME AGAINST THE YAKIMAS."

WITH PREFACE AND ADDITIONAL NOTES
By WILLIAM ELSEY CONNELLEY

AND

SKETCH OF THE AUTHOR
By J. P. MACLEAN, PH. D.

ILLUSTRATED

PUBLISHED FOR JUDGE J. C. McWHORTER

JANAWAY PUBLISHING
Santa Maria, California

Notice

In many older books, foxing (or discoloration) occurs and, in some instances, print lightens with wear and age. Reprinted books, such as this, often duplicate these flaws, notwithstanding efforts to reduce or eliminate them. The pages of this reprint have been digitally enhanced and, where possible, the flaws eliminated in order to provide clarity of content and a pleasant reading experience.

The Border Settlers of Northwestern Virginia from 1768 to 1795: Embracing the Life of Jesse Hughes and Other Noted Scouts of the Great Woods of the Trans-Allegheny

By:
Lucullus Virgin McWhorter

Copyright © 1915, J. C. McWhorter
Buckhannon, West Virginia

Originally published:
Hamilton, Ohio
1915

Reprinted by:

Janaway Publishing, Inc.
732 Kelsey Ct.
Santa Maria, California 93454
(805) 925-1038
www.JanawayGenealogy.com

2016

ISBN: 978-1-59641-380-1

Made in the United States of America

To the Memory of

Sabinus Bruce

BROTHER AND PLAYMATE OF GOLDEN CHILDHOOD IN THE MONONGAHELA HILLS; AND TO THE REDOLENT MEMORY OF SPRINGTIME WITH ITS NEW LIFE AND BIRD SONG AND THE CALL OF THE DISTANT "BOB-WHITE." OF SUMMER, WITH ITS SUNSHINE AND SHOWERS; AND THE "OLD OAKEN BUCKET" AND GREAT WILLOW TREE; AND THE TRACKS OF LITTLE BARE FEET IN THE DUST OF THE WINDING VALLEY ROAD: OF TRUANTS FISHING AND THE WEED-FRINGED "SWIMMING HOLE" IN THE VIOLET-SPANGLED MEADOW; OF THE ORCHARD AND THE COOL SHADOWS OF THE DEEP FOREST WITH ITS LEAPING, GAMBOLING SQUIRRELS, SKIPPING RABBITS AND DRUMMING OF THE PHEASANT'S WING: OF THE TWILIGHT GLOAMING AND THE CRY OF THE WHIP-POOR-WILL, AND THE CLOUDS SAILING THROUGH THE SILVERY MOONLIGHT. OF AUTUMN, WITH ITS DREAMY HAZE OF INDIAN SUMMER AND THE FLOATING, STREAMING COBWEBS AND THE WIND MOANING THROUGH THE GOLD AND CRIMSON WOOD-CRESTED HILLS; OF THE SCARLET, DROPPING LEAVES OF THE OLD "SUGAR CAMP;" AND THE CLIFF AND THE "BIG ROCK" WITH THE LICHEN MOSS AND THE BURROWING WOODCHUCKS: OF A LITTLE WOOD-WHEELED WAGON AND AN OAKEN-RUNNERED SLED; OF NUT GATHERING AND WILD GRAPE HUNTING: AND THE NIGHT SONG OF THE "KATY-DID" AND "MAJOR'S" DEEP BAYING IN THE DARKSOME WOODS, CHASING THE WILY 'COON. OF WINTER, WITH ITS NIGHTMARE "TERM" OF SCHOOL IN THE DISTANT "LOW GAP;" OF COASTING, AND OF NUT CRACKING AND "TELLING STORIES" AROUND THE EVENING HEARTH OF THE RADIANT WOOD FIRE; OF THE LOW TRUNDLE-BED AND THE HALLOWED PRAYERS OF DEVOTED PARENTS: IS THIS VOLUME AFFECTIONATELY DEDICATED BY ONE WHO EVER DREAMS OF HIS NATIVE HILLS AND OF THE HALCYON DAYS OF YOUTH.

TABLE OF CONTENTS

Chapter I

First Permanent Settlement in the Trans-Allegheny. Pringle Brothers of the Sycamore — Their History — Fugitives and Hunters — Employed by Simpson the Trapper — Brings Settlers to the Buckhannon Valley. Jesse Hughes the Indian Fighter — Nationality — Personal Appearance — Dress and Habits. Other Settlers, Hunters and Explorers — What Became of Them? — Military Records.

Notes — South Branch of the Potomac. — Indian Names: — Delaware, — Shawnee, — Iroquois. Monongahela, Meaning of. The Pringle Sycamore. The Hunting Shirt.

Chapter II

Dearth of the Written Record. *Withers'* Recognized Authority. Fragmentary Narrative. Who Wrote *Border Warfare?* — Authorship Disputed. Claim of William Hacker and William Powers — Were They Wronged of Title? Powers Commander of Scouts — His Ability as Chronicler — Achievements of Hacker — His Education. Partisan Writers Unjust to the Indian. Incidents in Modern Border Wars — Suppressing Facts.

Notes — The Hacker Family. Captivity of Mrs. Cunningham. Simon Girty. The Bonnetts as Indian Spies. Other Scouts. Military Records. Fraudulent Pension Claims.

Chapter III

Printed Record of Jesse Hughes — Sagacity as Scout — Fatal Ambuscade — Determining a Coward — Alone in the Wilderness — Kills an Indian — The Turkey Decoy — Is the Hughes Turkey Story a Myth?

Notes — Tragedies — Capt. Shaylor at Fort Jefferson.

Chapter IV

The Hughes Family — Birth Place — Traditions of Jesse — Father Killed — A Deadly Vow. Thomas Hughes Lieut. of Scouts — Bravery of — His Pathetic Death — A Country's Ingratitude. Other Hughes. Dogs in Indian Warfare. Marriage of Jesse — A Noble Wife — Settles on Hacker's Creek — Cabin in the Wilderness — A Dangerous Bed-fellow — Poisonous Reptiles — Jesse Shoots an Indian Hunter.

Notes — Woodson's Memoranda of the Hughes Family in Powhatan Co., Virginia. French Huguenots. Lowther Killed. The Washburn Family. Tragedies. Romance. Lewis Wetzel. McClellan the Ranger. Military Records. Singleton, Pension Agent — Unjust Ruling — Wages of Scouts — Land Laws — Tomahawk Claims — Unreliable Data of Settlements. Rattlesnakes.

Chapter V

Indian Settlements on Hacker's Creek. Discovery of Prehistoric Interest. Mysterious Finds: — Village Sites — Unusual Remains — Burial Grounds — Mounds — Ancient Art — Indian Fields — Ash Circles.

Notes — Superstitions — Buried Treasure — Ghost Stories.

TABLE OF CONTENTS

CHAPTER VI

Shawnee Towns on Hacker's Creek — Wi-ya-ni-pe, Birth Place of Tecumseh; Old Chillicothe. Shawnee Cist Burial. Tecumseh's Pipe — Wi-ya-ni-pe, the Indian's Paradise. Wild Fruits — Game — Fish. Alexander West, Scout and Hunter — Bear Fight in the Dark. Wild Boars. Hunting Stories — Dangerous Joke — A Fearful Tragedy. John Hacker First Settler — Chases Buffaloes — Exploration. Dearth of Bread — Pathetic Incident. Deadly Cold of the Mountains. Death of a Guide.—A Mountain Tragedy.

NOTES — Traditions of Mines. The Shawnees — Summary of History. Statesmen and Warriors. Descendants of Tecumseh.

CHAPTER VII

The Stroud Family Murdered by Shawnees. Delaware Settlement on Little Kanawha. Captain Bull Friend of the Whites — His Village and People Destroyed — Treachery of the Settlers — Names of the Murderers — Pathetic Story of Capt. Bull.

NOTES — Gaulouise the Trapper. The Delawares — Their Home — Tribal Status — Story of the "Woman." Renegade White Kills Indians — Shawnees not the Aggressors.

CHAPTER VIII

Terrible Culmination to the Bulltown Massacre — Unrestrained Fierceness of the Borderers — Jesse Hughes and Capt. William White Leaders — Indians Discovered at Indian Camp on the Buckhannon — The Surprise and Butchery — A Wounded Indian's Greeting — The Leaden Reply — Were the Victims Buried? An Aged Nimrod's Gruesome Find. Interesting Tradition. Abundance of Game — A Bear Shambles.

CHAPTER IX

John Cutright, Scout of the Buckhannon — An Indian Moccasin Maker — Confusion of Names — Indian Incursions — Shoots Indian Horse Thief — Wounded by an Indian — Primitive Surgery — Revolutionary Soldier — Declaration for Pension — Services as Scout and Soldier — Branded an Impostor — Honesty Proven — Ability as a Warrior — Errors Corrected — Personal Appearance of Cutright — Hatred for the Red Race — Attempts to Kill Indian in Time of Peace.

NOTES — Virginia Hard Pressed for Troops — Loss in Battle of Germantown — Appalling Destitution Among the State Soldiery. Disputed Boundary Between Virginia and Pennsylvania — Hauteur of the Virginia Minute Man — Efficiency in Indian Warfare — Unreliability in Open Battle.—British Estimate of the "Shirt Man."

CHAPTER X

Requisites of a Scout Leader — Capt. White, Chief of Buckhannon Spies — Ancestry — Associate of Col. Crawford — Kills Indians in the Glades — Imprisoned — Liberated by Mob — Status of Border Society — A Romance of the Wilderness — An Indian Runner — Cunning Ruse — Mysterious Captive — Insatiate Venom — Indian Camp Surprised — Desperate Chase — Sickening Scene — An Indian's Revenge — Death of Capt. White. John Fink Killed. Timothy Dorman, Renegade. Buckhannon Fort Abandoned. Jacob Bush, Scout and Soldier — In Clark's Campaign 1781. Incidents — Drink of Whiskey for Brain of a Deer. Descendants — Lieut. Jacob Westfall — Military Record — With Gen. Clark — Lochry's Defeat — Failure of Expedition. "Flight of 1770" — Doubtful Narrative — Shaver the Spy — Kaskaskie Campaign — Wounded in Battle — Suffered Injustice.

NOTES — Lieut. John White Killed. — Deserters or Indians? Outrages by Settlers Laid to Indians. Col. John Sevier. Capture of Capt. White and Petro —

Escape of White — Fate of Petro — Mrs. White Witnesses Killing of Husband. Monument to White and Fink. Treaty of Fort Stanwix. Indian Claims to the Trans-Allegheny.—Twenty Years War.

Chapter XI

Cause of Dunmore's War. Storm Brewing — Facts Perverted. Boone in Kentucky — Long Hunters — Indians Killed — Connolly's Warning.— Creasap's Declaration of War — Massacre of Logan's Family. Death of Bald Eagle — Killing of Cat Eye — Number of Friendly Indians Murdered — Indian Law of Reprisal. Storm Bursts on Virginia Border — Bloody Sequel — Murder of Cornstalk — Vengeful Shawnees. Jesse Hughes Defender of the Border — Hacker's Creek Invaded by Indians — West's Fort Besieged — Fort Abandoned.—Beech Fort — Hughes Memorable Night Run — Signal Cry from the Hill — Dangers of the Night Trail — Panthers — Wolves — A Daring Feat — Hughes Chased by Three Indians — Remarkable Endurance.

Notes — Character of the Kentucky Settlers. Franklin on War 1774 — Indians Murdered East of Mountains — Sympathy for Logan. David Sleeth the Scout — Accusation of Singleton. Jackson's Block House.

Chapter XII

Indian Raid in Tygart's Valley — Six Families Destroyed — Col. Lowther in Pursuit — Indians Surprised — A Deadly Volley — Capt. Bull Mortally Wounded. Jesse Hughes — Fiendish Deed — A Ghastly Joke. West and the "Yellow Boy" — Indian Horse Thieves — Two are Shot — Indian Idea of Justice — Retaliatory Vengeance — Martha Hughes Captured. Attack on the West Families. Leonard Schoolcraft, Renegade — Heartrending Scene. West in Clark's Expedition 1781 — Declaration for Bounty Lands — Personal Appearance.

Notes — Moccasin Making. Vision of the Red Doe. Story of a Forty Niner.—Poison for Indian Cattle Thieves. Gen. Clark — Difficulties Encountered in Procuring Troops — Contemplated Foray Against Moravian Indians. John Gibson.

Chapter XIII

The Schoolcraft Family — Its Fate — Five Brothers Swept into Captivity — Three Turn Indian — Career as Warriors — Two Unaccounted for — Mystery Solved — Schoolcraft the Hunter — The Phantom Deer. — Schoolcraft the Scout. — Services along the Ohio. Indian Ambuscade Near Wheeling.—Mason and Ogal Companies Wiped Out. Simon Girty. Wheeling Threatened — Village Burned. Col. Broadhead's Allegheny Expedition — Scouting in Monongahela County. Wheeling in the Revolution — Besieged by Indians and British — Col. Zane's Defense of His Cabin — Choice or Surprise? — Testimony of Jacob Scott — Swiftness of Indian Descent — Length of Siege. Scouting in Kentucky — Campaigning with Gen. Clark.

Notes — Superstitions of the Wilderness — The Silent Trailing Dog — Singular Song from the Darkness. Pigeon Roosts —- Slaughter of Birds. Last Great Flight. Col. Broadhead's Coshocton Expedition — Lawlessness of the Borderers — Executing Prisoners — Village Destroyed — Lewis Wetzel Tomahawks a Chief — Massacre of the Unarmed.

Chapter XIV

Jesse Hughes — Trapped by Two Indians — Cunning Ruse and Escape — Search for Lost Child — Kills Wounded Indian — Remarkable Fleetness of Indian Athlete — His Tragic Death. Indian Motives. Lone Indian Shot by West —

His Miserable Death. — Indian Rock — Indian Spring. Flat-boating on the Monongahela — Hughes Attempts to Kill Indian Child — Barbarity of Combatants.

NOTES — Conquest of Primitive Races — Similar Throughout World — Exterminating Australian Blacks.

CHAPTER XV

Buckhannon River — Name a Mystery — Conjecture of Writers. Indian Habitations — Village Near the Pringle Camp. Stream Named for Buckongahelas, Delaware War Chief — Name Corrupted — Indian Ghost Story — Character of Buckongahelas — Washington of His Tribe.

NOTES — Buckhannon River — Earliest Mention — John Buchannon Missionary. Ancient Remains — Mounds — Effigy Pipe. Indian Plurality of Names.

CHAPTER XVI

Frontier Posts — Construction — No Adequate Description. Buckhannon Fort — Size and Character — Ruins — Mill — Traces of Dam and Race — Burned by Indians. Invasion by Indians — Battle of the Narrows. — Hughes Kills Indian Leader. Cutright — New Shotpouch. The Regers as Scouts. John Bush Builder of Buckhannon Fort — Thrilling Adventures with Indians. Other Bushes — Confusion of Names — Desperate Encounter — Heroic Woman — Conflict with a Bear — Death of Bush.

NOTES — Intended Forays Revealed by Indians. The Reger Flint-Lock Rifle. Virginia Militia Regiments Revolutionary War — Field of Action. Size of Frontier Rifles. Bush Land Claims.

CHAPTER XVII

Capt. George Jackson — First Military Company of Buckhannon. Col. Wm. Darke's Emergency Regiment — British in Virginia — Siege of Yorktown — Jackson in Gen. Clark's Expedition — Col. of Militia — Memorable Night-Run — Col. Lowther's Rangers — Thomas and Elias Hughes Officers — Jesse Hughes Subaltern — Indian War Paths — Canoe Travel — Portage — Hughes and West — Scouting Tour — Bear in "Town" — A Great Hunt — The Spoils. Memorial Names — Joseph Hall. — In Dunmore's War — Old Camp Unearthed. Henry Jackson Surveyor — A Surveying Party — Camp Alarmed — Hughes Discovers Indians — Camp Abandoned — War Party Raids on Cheat River — Intercepted by Lowther's Rangers — Uncompleted Survey — Notable Land Suit — Settlements on West Fork River — The Halls. Wm. Strange — Lost in Mountains — Fruitless Quest — Gun and Skeleton Found — Traditions — Mrs. Strange — Twice Widowed by Tragedy — Marries Joseph Hall — Descendants. Mollohan Lost — Unsolved Mystery.

NOTES — The Jacksons — Streams Named by Scouts — Kanawha and Monongahela *Portage* — Indian Remains. Col. Duvall — Commander of Scouts — Available Military Force. Simon Girty in Settlements — Two Children Killed — Mythical Indian Town. Incident of Seneca Trail.

CHAPTER XVIII

Forts on the Ohio. Cattle Drover's Camp Attacked by Tecumseh — Account by *Withers* — By *Hildreth*. Death of Carpenter — Others Killed. Jesse Hughes' Narrow Escape — Rapid Flight — Indian Respect for Dead — Escape of Negro Captive — Hughes in Foot Race — Charging Gun while Speeding. Traditional Account of Carpenter Tragedy — Expedition of Revenge. — Shawnees Attacked on Shade River — Hughes Saves Indian Baby — Doubtful Narrative. Hunters Attacked — Death of Coleman.

Notes — Red Stone and Marietta Road — Tecumseh — First War Path — Abstinence from Food. Peter Waggoner Captive. Indian Dress Adopted by Bordermen.

Chapter XIX

Waggoner Massacre — Hughes Gives Alarm — Tecumseh — Prisoners Object of Raid — Indian Parental Love — Escape of Marauders — Eighty Miles without Food. Peter Waggoner — Captive Twenty Years — Found in Ohio — His Indian Family — Persuaded Home — Promised Return — Detained — Grows Restive — Despondent, Attempts Violence — More Strictly Guarded — Marries White Woman — Stories of Captivity — Traits — His Indian Wife Visits Settlements — Her Fate — Death of Peter — Captive Sisters.

Notes — Waggoner Family in Virginia. Chillicothe Destroyed by Kentuckians.

Chapter XX

Hughes Last Defense of Border. Carpenter Tragedy on Elk River. Folly of Adam O'Brien — The Big and Little Indian. — Superior Skill as Warriors — Cunning Ruse — Outwitted by Hughes and Killed — John Carpenter — Soldier of Revolution — In Battle of Guilford Court House — Border Scout — House Burned by Indians. Virginia Militia at Frontier Forts. Desertion. The Carpenters' in Dunmore's War.

Notes — Adam O'Brien — Type Virginia Bordermen — Love of Wilderness — Adventure — Companion Killed. Jeremiah Carpenter Captive of Shawnee. Pleasing Episode in Indian Life. Traditions — Omen of the *Red Deer*. Jesse Hughes Avenger. Carpenter's Gun. Bell Decoy. — Settlers Killed.

Chapter XXI

Wayne's Defeat of Indians. — Receding of the Border. — Jesse Hughes Grows Restive — Follows Indians to the Wabash — Adventure at Vincennes — Chills and Fever — Moves to Kentucky — Wanders Back to the Ohio — Settles in Jackson County (West) Virginia — Game and Fish — Was Hughes a Long Hunter? — Tradition of Morgan — Dead Indian Flayed — Hughes Kills Friendly Indians. War Paths — Haynes Cave — Concealed Rifles — Fate of Drunken Indians.

Notes — Remarkable Pioneer House — Defensive Features — One Hughes a Long Hunter — Character and Achievements of Long Hunters — Prominence of Hughes Family. David Morgan — Atrocious Deed — Morgan's Descendants in Oregon War — Hereditary Depravity — Mutilating Dead Body of Indian Chief — Facts Suppressed. — Debauchery of Northwestern Tribes. Description of Haynes' Cave — Indian Sagacity.

Chapter XXII

Closing Scenes in Life of Jesse Hughes — Review of Eventful Career — Judge Brown's Eulogy — Country's Ingratitude — Loss of Home — Dotage of Old Age — Hunts Imaginary Indians — Dies Alone in the Woods — Where is the Old Scout's Grave? — Irony of Fate — Jesse Hanshaw — Death of Mrs. Hughes — Relics of the Hughes.

Notes — Boone — Hughes — Kenton — Lives Compared. Drouillard, French Trader.

Table of Contents

Chapter XXIII

Genealogy of Hughes Family — Thomas, Sr. — Jesse — Thomas, Jr. — Elias — No Peers as Scouts on Virginia Border — Sudna — Marriage to Col. Lowther. Job — Bibbee's — Descendants of Jesse. — James Gandee — Descendants of Elias.

Notes — Hughes' Race of Warriors. Transformation of Names.

Chapter XXIV
(Biographical)

Elias *Alias* Ellis Hughes — In Battle of Point Pleasant — Who Was the Last Survivor? — Samuel Bonifield — Incidents of the Battle — Hughes Defender of Border — Career as Told in Declaration for Pension — Rare Unpublished History — Captain of Spies — No Equal as Leader — Captured Indian Ornaments — Gen. Wilson's Tribute — Marauding Indians Killed — Remarkable Elk Chase.

Notes — A Ghastly Tradition — Camp Site of Gen. Lewis Army — Historic Tree — Boy Homesteader.

Chapter XXV
(Biographical)

Elias Hughes Moves to Ohio — Career in Western Country — Printed Records — John Ratliff, Indian Fighter — Companion Hunters — Kills Two Indians — Builds Blockhouse — A Night of Peril — Interesting Unpublished History — "Last of Border Warriors" — Sketches — Thrilling Adventure — Lieut. War 1812 — Character — Personal Appearance — Traditions — Death — Burial Under Honors of War.

Notes — By Canoe to the Muskingum — On Foot to Licking River — Forty Mile Walk at Eighty — Record War 1812 — Death of Sons in War — Siege of Fort Meigs — Capt. Samuel Brady — Monument to Hughes.

Chapter XXVI
(Biographical)

Col. William Lowther of Nutter's Fort — Commander of Militia and Scouts — Residence — Descendant from Ancient Family — Nationality — Prowess in Days of Knighthood — Family Coat of Arms — Skill as Leader — Old Cabin — Exploration of Little Kanawha — Hardships of Wilderness Life — Touching Incident — A Mother's Tears — The "Starving Year" — "God Has Sent This" — Lowther in Clark's Expedition 1781 — Best Record not in Annals — Interesting Testimony — Companions in Arms. The Bonnetts. Jacob Bush. Sotha Hickman, Noted Scout and Hunter. Nutter Family — Builder of Nutter's Fort — Its Location.

Notes — Col. Lowther's Slaves — An Interesting Story — Wild Life of the Pioneer. — Education. Richards' Fort — Disputed Location — Stockades — The Richards as Settlers. Scarcity of Bread — Indian Pemmican.

Chapter XXVII
(Biographical)

Printed Record of Col. Lowther — Distribution of Scouts — Commissioned Captain of Militia — Charged with Misconduct — Senior Officer — Merits of the Scouts. Capt. Bogart. Capt. McCullock. Indians at Neal's Station. Arrest of Lieut. Biggs. Indians Kill Whites. Dearth of Ammunition — Scarcity of Rations. Scouts Unpaid — Pay Roll of Scouts. Descendants of Col. Lowther — Records War 1812 — Genealogy.

Notes — Charges Against Capt. McCullock. Alexander Lowther — Soldier War 1812.

Chapter XXVIII
(Biographical)

Henry McWhorter — Pioneer Millwright of West's Fort — Nationality and Clan Affinity — Three Noted Brothers — Remarkable Strength — Battle with Keel Boatmen — Henry a Minute Man Revolutionary War — Battle of White Plains — Building the Chevaux-de-frise Across the Hudson — Contractor Turns Tory — Pilots British Ships Through Gap — Battle of Fort Montgomery — Mud Fort — Barracks Burned. McWhorter Moves to Pennsylvania — Enlists Against Indians — Marries — Moves to Hampshire County, Virginia — To Hacker's Creek — The Old Cabin — Packing Salt Across Mountains — Comrade Freezing — Warmed with Beech Limb — Builds Mill — Capacity of a Mountain "Corn Cracker" — Act of Charity. Waggoner Tragedy. Death of Henry. John McWhorter — Boy Life in Wilderness — Eccentricity of Character — Hunting Deer with Bucket — Capt. War 1812 — Public Career — Amusing Anecdotes — A Scathing Rebuke. Other McWhorters — Incidents — Genealogy — Soldiers Civil War.

Notes — McWhorter — Modes of Spelling Name — The Family in New York — Minute Men — Obstructing the Hudson — Family in Pennsylvania — Soldiers Revolutionary War. Joseph Kester — Revolutionary Soldier.

Chapter XXIX
(Biographical)

The Regers — Early Pioneers — Nationality — Founder of Family in Virginia — Soldiers in Revolution — Wonderful Hunters — Terrible Conflict with a Bear — Scouting on the Monongahela — Bitten by Rattlesnake — Thrilling Combats with Bears — Carrying Eight Bushels Salt — Tossing Man in Air — The Hercules of the Border — Cowing a Bully — "Wallowing" Two Men at 80 — Descendants in War 1812-1861 — Battle with Indians — Entering Bear's Den — Notice of Bozarth Tragedy — Adventure with Wolves — Mysterious Quarry — Chasing the Devil — Superstitions — Occult Healing. Genealogy.

Notes — Col. Wm. Russel in Revolution — On the Border. Col. Silas Zane — Revolutionary Record. Siege of Fort Henry. Bozarth Children Captives — A "Brave Boy" — "Forenash Plantation." Ludicrous Incident — Kentucky "Col." Hunting Trouble — Hurled Over Rail Fence. — Hunter's Attachment for His Dog — A Touching Scene. Entering Den of Panthers — Gen. Putnam's Achievement Eclipsed. Bloody Run — Origin of Name.

Chapter XXX
(Biographical)

Jacob Brake Indian Captive — Life Among Northwestern Tribes — Pontiac's War — Return from Captivity — Knows of Copper Mime in Michigan — Company Formed to Develop Ore — Brake Pilots Party Through Wilderness — Arrives Near the Mine — Angered — Refuses to Reveal Location — Brake of Noble Birth — Father a German Baron. Tory Uprising on Wappatomaka — John Claypole Leader — Brake's Mill Rendezvous — Militia Overawed — Tories Scattered by Morgan's Riflemen — The Baron's Estate Destroyed — Returns to Germany. Genealogy.

Notes — Mary Harris Indian Captive. Brake Family. First Census of Virginia. Augusta County Militia on Border. Col. Paston's Appeal for Aid in Suppressing Tory Element.

Chapter XXXI
(Biographical)

Cozads — Settlers on Cheat River — Nationality — Different Forms of Name — Jacob Cozad, Sr., Moves to Hacker's Creek — Indian Incursion — Jacob, Jr., and Three Brothers Captured — Youngest Killed — Cozad Tree — Bark Inscription — Flight and Escape of Indians — Jacob's Alarm Halloo — Knocked Senseless with Rifle — Saved by Squaw — Brothers Freed at Treaty of Greenville — Jacob Remains Prisoner — Found by Brother. Incidents in Indian Life — Indian Superstition. — Jacob Rescues Child — A Mother's Gratitude. Battle of Fallen Timbers — Rage of Indians — Jacob Condemned to the Stake — Preparation for Death — Secreted by Strange Squaw — Spirited Away. Indian Nursery Song. Huntercraft. Hardships. Spartan Training of Boys. Jacob's After Life — Marriage — Settles on Hacker's Creek — Baptist Minister — Sweat Doctor. Comments. Indian Veneration for Rattlesnake — Serpent Worship — Pictographs — Petroglyphs.

NOTES — Indian Women Taking War Path — Modern Instances Cited. The Wah^k-puch of the Yakimas.

CHAPTER XXXII
(Biographical)

The Hursts' — Revolutionary Soldier Head of Family — Dies on Cheat River — Widow Moves to West Fork — Life in the Woods — John Hurst Soldier War 1812 — Antipathy for Reptiles — Den of Rattlesnakes — Narrow Escape — Panthers — Hair Whitened by Fright — Adventures — Price of Two Charges of Powder — Wolves — Dangerous Night Prowler — A Close Call. Daniel Hurst — Soldier 1812. Stock Driving Across Mountains — Slave Whipping — Taming a Slave Overseer.

NOTES — Poisonous Snakes — Fabulous Size of Rattler — Death from Bite — The Copperhead — Extermination.

CHAPTER XXXIII
(Biographical)

James Belt — Typical Mountaineer — Eccentricity of Character — Born Orator — Stickler for Truth — Midnight Lecture in Down-pour. Recreant Jack Condemned to Hang — Funeral Oration on Mountain — Timely Reprieve. Tanglefoot and Stump Speaking. Land of Milk and Honey. Soldier War 1812 — A Martinet — Traits of a Napoleon — Cat vs. Batrachian. Sam — War-horse of the Valley — "Pards" in the Fray — Charging the Enemy — An Army on the "Knob" — Peace to The "Pards."

CHAPTER XXXIV
(Witchcraft)

Witchcraft and Black Art — Superstitions of Early Settlers — Witch Spells — Gun and Shotpouch Effected — Witch Doctors — Status with Bordermen — Modern Belief in Occult — Human Steed — Strenuous Night Journey — Sumptuous Repast — Malicious Persecution — Destroying the Witch — Bewitched Sugar Orchard — Achievements of Elkany Roby — Potency of the Silver Bullet and Muttered "Spell."

CHAPTER XXXV
(Carnivora)

Carnivora of West Virginia — Present Range of Black Bear. The Timber Wolf — Early Practical Extinction — Former Packs Swarming the Great Woods — Cunning Ferocity. A Narrow Escape. Woman Pursued. Hunter Lost. The Panther — Sly Fierceness. Bozarth Stalked — Rescued by Dogs. Sleeping Baby Saved by a Fice. Unarmed Settler Attacked — Decisive Combat in the Dark. Heroic Woman. Mail Carrier's Thrilling Adventure — An Eye Dual — Lonely Ride — A Scream from the Darkness. The Masked Camp Fire — A Surprised

TABLE OF CONTENTS 15

Panther. A Scared Darkey — Lucky Knife Thrust. Hunter Pursued — Saved by Random Shot. A Startled Irishman. A Gamboling Panther Killed. The Last Bear. A Daring Woman. Humorous Bear Story. The First Buck. A Modern Nimrod.

NOTES — Ruse of Wolf in Securing Prey — Deer Herded by Wolves.

APPENDIX

APPENDIX 1

Draper Correspondence — Rare Collection of Letters on Border History of Upper Monongahela — Light on Disputed Points — Contribution by Col. Westfall — By David Smith — Authorship of *Border Warfare* — Hacker and Powers Letters — Jacksons as Pioneers.

NOTES — Stroud Tragedy — Battle of Point Pleasant — First Shot — Lieut. Frogg — *Withers* Account of Killing Capt. White — Other Incidents — John Hacker — Hezekiah Hess — Soldier Revolution — Descendants — Henry Hinzman — Record Revolutionary War — Genealogy — Rev. Wm. G. Hacker.

APPENDIX 2

Buffalo in Western Virginia — *Bibliography* by Draper — Additional Data — Distribution Throughout Trans-Allegheny — Last Buffalo and Elk in West Virginia — Gazetteer.

APPENDIX 3

Archaeological Examination of Indian Camp — Relics — Human Remains — Fire Hearths — Flint Implements — Ash Camp — Why Named — Legend of the Lost Mine — Ruins — Strange Rock Inscriptions — What are They? — Old Map — Mysterious Cave — Buried Treasure — The Swift Mines — Where Located? — Swift's Journal — The Judge Apperson Copy — Connelley's Letter.

NOTES — Tragedy of Powell's Mountain. Civil War.

APPENDIX 4

Concerning Tory Uprising on Wappatomaka — Petitions for Executive Clemency for John Claypole — Jacob Brake and Others — Brake's Mill — Baron John Brake.

House Occupied by Author,
Just After Marriage to Miss Ardelia Swisher

PREFACE

Jesse Hughes was a pioneer in Northwestern Virginia, that region so designated in early annals and now principally included in the State of West Virginia. It was, at the time he came into it, a wilderness. It was a country of hills and clear streams and magnificent forests. It abounded in beautiful valleys, precipitous bluffs, rugged cliffs, and rolling uplands stretching away to greater elevations, ending finally in some watershed composed of steep and lofty ranges, outlying flankers of the Alleghenies. These ranges are spread out without regularity or order. They are ever-present. They are formed, fashioned and separated by the swift streams flowing by their bases to the larger tributaries of the Ohio. Trees cover them to their summits. Sometimes the country bears a park-like appearance; and again it becomes choked with thickets of bushes, brambles, vines and enormous greenbriers. Often the tops of the ranges are covered with immense masses of sandstone, from which innumerable fragments have scattered over both mountain and valley. It is a country of moods. In winter, when the trees are stripped and their branches bare, groan and creak in the north wind, it has a bleak and savage aspect. In summer it is full-leaved, delicately-lined, and lies blushing and plentifully-promising in a flood of sunshine. In autumn it is glowing, gorgeous, magnificently colored, sublime. The changing hues of the land create an environment which begets the spirit of mystery. The dweller therein is lifted above himself — charmed. Something akin to worship rises in his heart as he views from some mountain-top his native land lying spread below him robed in colors more varied and beautiful than queen or princess ever wore. The mountaineer who wanders from this land may see vast plains covered with waving harvests, and a thousand hills covered with grazing cattle; he may live where rolls old ocean; he may prosper in the riches of this world; he may attain fame and greatness and power; but his heart is in the romantic hills and enchanted valleys stretching down from the Alleghenies toward the great river which flows out to lose itself in roaring breakers and washing tides, and which so fitly typifies human life.

When Jesse Hughes and those who came with him arrived in this mystic wilderness, it was a solitude well-nigh tenantless. Indian tribes claimed it for a hunting-ground. They roamed over it in quest of game. They hunted through its mazes for the settler who dared defile it with axe and plow. In the contest for the land Jesse Hughes bore a part far beyond that of the average settler. He was one of those woodsmen in whom was concentrated the hardihood, the daring, the fierce and uncontrollable spirit of our barbarous ancestors in the fens and on the swamp shores of Northwestern Europe. The wild life of the great woods appealed to him. It suited his rancorous humor. It was in accord with the fountains of his life. He gloried in it. It was war, danger, adventure. His life was forfeit every minute, but the knowledge of this fact stimulated him like wine. The hunt for those who would slay him became his ruling passion, the sole end for which he lived. On the trail of the wild Indian his soul hardened to iron and his nature grew more savage than that of the man he hunted. He was grim, cruel, relentless, and bloodthirsty. But he was the product of the age in which he lived. Nature makes no mistakes. Every emergency produces the men to cope with it. In the conquest of the great valley of the Mississippi such men were a necessity, and they were developed by the westward migration of the white man. They were the warriors of our advancing lines — heroes now and evermore.

WILLIAM ELSEY CONNELLEY.

TO THE READER

The friends of Mr. McWhorter, who are acquainted with his work among the Indians and his researches into the archives of Virginia, as well as his explorations in the field of archaeology, urged upon him that it was simple justice to the reader that a personal sketch should be included in the present volume. Having been acquainted with the author for over twenty years, knowing his venerated father, and more or less familiar with the sturdy and honorable characteristics of the family, the pleasure of writing this sketch devolved upon me. The reader should realize what one may accomplish when the mind is willing though obstacles may intervene.

Mr. McWhorter is an unassuming man, without scholastic learning, thoroughly honest in purpose and always willing to listen to others. When his mind is decisively made up he acts without any thought of reward or encomium. In the services he rendered the Indians of the State of Washington he incurred the enmity of one of the most thoroughly organized gangs of land robbers in the history of this country, whose territories were strongly entrenched in the Indian Department. Single-handed he coped with them. His only guide being that of simple justice. In every move he outwitted all, though some of the shrewdest lawyers were at work. While his movements were silent, he did not disguise the fact he had determined to stand between them and the Indian. However, it is better for the narrative to reveal the truth.

Lucullus Virgil, son of Rev. J. M. McWhorter, M. D., was born in a log cabin built by his great uncle, Thomas McWhorter, on the ancestral home, on McKinney's Run, a tributary of Hacker's Creek, in Harrison County, (West) Virginia, January 29, 1860. The following March his parents moved to Buckhannon Run, an upper branch of Hacker's Creek, in Upshur County. In this isolated little valley, with six brothers and two sisters he grew to manhood, inheriting all the mountaineer's love of freedom and clan affinity. Many of his habits were solitary. The hills, woods and limpid streams were inexhaustible sources of pleasure. He lamented the passing of the native forest with its indigene life.

His pro-primitive disposition and proneness for the wild, precluded the collegiate course and West Point Cadetship which were open to him. Four months of dreaded winter schooling until twenty-one years of age was all that his nature could endure. He chafed at restraint; and his distaste for text books was surpassed only by his infatuation for some of the poets, Indian and pioneer history, traditions and mountain folk-lore. He reveled in the legends of the wilderness. The hunter stories of the first settlers which he heard in childhood were never forgotten. The thrilling adventures of Jesse Hughes and his associates with the red warriors of the forest appealed to him as nothing else could. These tales of a past epoch eventually culminated in the pages of *Border Settlers*.

Unlike most of our pioneer annals, the reader will find this work strikingly non-partisan. The author has endeavored to give events without discriminating in favor of his own race. To him the aggressors in the Trans-Allegheny wars were too palpable to admit of controversy. Upon this point he is likely to be assailed, for he has crossed some recognized authorities; but his position is strongly entrenched with facts. Justly loyal to his own racial affinities, he has, from early childhood been noted for his Indian sympathies. While yet in his early teens he prevailed on his little sister to bore his ears, preparatory to a life with the red men. The culminating set-back to this utopian dream was when, in anticipation of a visit to the parental home of a noted preacher from Ohio, his more "civilized" brothers forcibly applied the shears to his flowing locks. As he grew older, filial duty alone stayed his nomadic proclivities; but with each recurring flight of the wild geese the inherent longing for the boundless open was almost unendurable. Indian Summer affected him inexplicably. The murky haze was from the smoke-flues of the invisible wigwams of the spirit Indians which haunt the Monongahela hills. The autumnal winds soughing in the trees scattering the crimson foliage, was a funeral dirge for the primitive life forever gone.

Early in life Mr. McWhorter read MacLean's: *The Mound Builders;* published in serial form in *The Star in the West;* which found its way into his mountain home. The reading of this work had a very marked effect on his future career. Those old *Stars* were treasured for years and from their perusal a new world was unfolded, and there came a longing for delving into the past.

Other archaeological authors were studied, which in time led to a practical examination of the various Indian remains in the Hacker's Creek valley, with a correct tabulation of all data obtained. Graves, mounds, stone-heaps and village sites were explored and their history revealed. No antiquities in the valley that he did not visit and note. Caves and aboriginal rock-shelters in other localities were investigated and their secrets wrested from them. But in all these excavations his veneration for the ancient was such that even the most lowly grave was invariably left restored to its former state. None could accuse him of undue desecration or vandalism. He became an expert on flint and stone implements. Thousands of relics were collected with accurate history of their finding; constituting the finest aggregation of antiquarian objects ever secured in central West Virginia; a region not rich in ancient remains. These in later years were placed intact and permanently in the Museum of *The West Virginia Historical and Antiquarian Society,* Charleston; since created *The Department of State Archives and History.* In 1893 he was one of three who originated and published *The Archaeologist,* an illustrated journal intended to meet the primary needs of the archaeological student. This publication was suspended three years later.

In 1897, the home farm was disposed of and the author soon after settled near the historic Fort Jefferson, in Darke County, Ohio. In the spring of 1903, he consummated his life-long desire to "go west," by moving with his family to North Yakima, Washington; where he continued for a time in the live stock business, which he had previously been following. His delight was Devon cattle. His father and himself brought the first of this active breed into Central West Virginia. He held to them in Ohio, and selected the cream of seven different herds and took them to Washington. He and his two sons had, when they disposed of their business, the nucleus of the best herd in the United States. They exhibited throughout the Northwest and the Pacific Slope.

In his new home, situated only a few miles from the Yakima Indian Reservation, he found opportunity for the field study of ethnology, which he had combined with archaeology. He soon won the friendship of the tribe. He joined in their social gatherings and festivities. He camped with them in the mountains, participating in their feats of strength and testing the splendid efficiency of the sweat-house and the icy river bath. He mingled with them in their primitive worship, for which he has inherent respect. He has been instructed in the mystic rites of the "medicine dance," and the touching simplicity of the "feast of the new food;" a ceremony of invocation and thanksgiving to Me-yäy'-wäh, the Supreme. He has been welcomed at the "funeral feast," where

the grief and respect for the memory of the dead is attested by wailing and the distribution of presents. Looked upon as one of their number, they have sought his counsel. As one aged warrior expressed it "He has ears and he hears straight. He has but one tongue and he talks from his heart." So great was their confidence in him, that *Yöŏm-tee-bee*, "bitten by a grizzly bear," a strong clan Chieftain, adopted him into his tribe; conferring upon him all the honors of a councilman, under the name of a deceased sub-chief: *He-mène-Ka'-wan*, "Old Wolf." This name in Klickitat, a tribe amalgamated with the Yakimas, is *Häl-ish Ho-sat*. At a later day, *Too-skas-Pot-thah'-nook*, "Seven Mountains," the last surviving son of the great War Chief, *Owhi*, adopted him in lieu of a deceased brother, *Ko-täh'-wi-nat*, "rain falling from a passing cloud," a noted warrior of his day.

Chief Yöömteebee's newly made clansman soon became aware that his people were being systematically looted; that their right to the reservation streams for irrigation purposes, without which their lands are worthless, had been appropriated by the white settlers; and that later this wrong had been arbitrarily sanctioned by an unfair ruling of the Secretary of the Interior, leaving the Indians entirely unprovided for. Also that through Congressional legislation, steered by local "promoters" and land grabbers, three-fourths of all allotments within a large area were to be sold under a law that was equivalent to confiscation; permitting the allottees to hold twenty acres each only, for which they were to pay for a water right on such terms and at such price as the Secretary of the Interior might provide. This appalling robbery, which if consummated meant ruin for the victims, he saw hanging over the Yakimas. Acting upon his own volition and without legal advice, he went secretly into the fight with the determination that if the game could not be defeated, he would in any event expose the conspiracy which he surmised to be far-reaching and powerful. His conjecture proved true and the odds against him were heavy. But casting his lot with that of Yöömteebee, the "leader of the hostiles," and enjoying the full confidence of that determined, primitive-minded Chieftain, he well knew what danger lurked ahead should he fail to break the mighty combine and the tribesmen be driven to the "last ditch." He kept his own counsel, but when the time came for the Indians to be approached by the Government officials for the purpose of securing the contracts necessary for the consummation of the crime, he acted promptly. Mounted on *Wild Eye*, "The Grey Cayuse," he struck the Reservation trails night and day; warning his red brothers against signing any papers that might be presented to them. Chief Yöömteebee sent out other runners and soon the entire tribe was awake to the impending danger. They refused to sign, and the pet scheme to ensnare the Yakimas was foiled, nor did the despoilers know for a time from whence came the blow.

The first skirmish had been won and the lines of the enemy thrown into confusion. This, however, only augmented the ominous menace of an actual tragedy should the tide turn. On March 10, 1910, Chief Yoomteebee died of pneumonia, leaving the tribe in mourning and the "hostiles" without an aggressive leader. New measures, covert and subtile were launched by the opposition and the fight continued. *Wild Eye*, an integral factor in the battle, covered hundreds of miles, traversing obscure trails in the darkness of night; and on one such occasion crossing a swollen reservation stream on a rude Indian bridge of round poles, the loose timbers half floating on the flood, giving at every step of the faithful steed. Often for days and nights the rider did not remove his clothes, eating when he could and sleeping when and wherever weariness demanded a rest. He was always welcomed at the Indian's lowly home, but many times his bed was a blanket and a pile of straw in the open or the bare ground. The haunting appeal of Chief Yoomteebee, "You are now my brother. You must always stand by my people and help them," ever urged him on. During the thickest gloom of the trouble, Rev. Stwire G. Waters, who had been elected Head Chief of the Tribe, said, "I have been praying that the Lord would send a good man to help us, and he has heard me."

For three years, single-handed he kept up the struggle, balking every effort of the "system." He then successfully invoked the aid of the Indian Rights Association. Mr. Brosius, the agent for this powerful, philanthropic body, entered the contest with spirit. He looked to the legal and strategic feature at the National Capitol, while Mr. McWhorter kept guard on the Reservation. Judge Carroll B. Graves, an eminent attorney of Seattle, was employed, and in the end a victory was won, insofar as recovering free water for one-half of the land involved and preventing the jeopardizing of any part of the allotments in question. Mr. Brosius said that if it had not been for "The Grey Cayuse" and rider, the Yakimas would have been despoiled of water rights to the value of several millions of dollars. The most effective and characteristic of the tribal petitions were drafted by Mr. McWhorter.

The white owners of 20,000 acres of deeded Indian lands

shared equally with the tribesmen in the fruits of this triumph, but strange to say they blindly stood in with the opposition, or held aloof until the last stages of the struggle. Mr. McWhorter did this work, ignoring alike intimidating threats and warnings of social ostracism; spending months of time and considerable money without any expectation of compensation or reward; nor did he ever solicit or receive a dollar for the sacrifice which left him financially crippled.

In 1913, Mr. McWhorter published his "Crime Against the Yakimas," a strongly written pamphlet of fifty-six pages, illustrated, setting forth the flagrant wrongs heaped upon this tribe and the strenuous fight made by the chief men for tardy justice. It is a fearful exposure of an attempt at despoiling the *Nation's Wards;* wherein Government officials, speculators and political cohorts under the cloak of philanthropic motives were combined to deliver the final *coup de maitre* to a helpless remnant of a race upon whose neck the heel of the conqueror has ground for the last four centuries. In the introduction, by Mr. William E. Johnson, known and dreaded by the lawless whiskey vendors who haunt the western Indian reservations as "Pussie Foot," in part, says:

"Years ago McWhorter began mingling with the Yakima Indians. He earned their confidence. He fought their battles. He aired their wrongs in public. He spent his time and money in efforts to secure for them a square deal. He was formally adopted into their tribe by Chief Yöom-tee-bee, and is known among them as He-mene Ka-wan (Old Wolf). And, while he is an adopted member of their tribe and has participated in tribal affairs as a member of their council, he has never sought or received one dollar of benefit from such membership.

"Four years ago, when I began operations in Washington, suppressing the liquor traffic among Indians, as chief officer of the Indian service, I first crossed this man McWhorter's trail. I found him stirring them up to protest against the issuing of saloon license at Toppenish. I found the Indians under his influence, protesting against the issuing of saloon licenses at Wapato, at Parker and other places. I found him stirring up the Yakimas to petition the Secretary of the Interior, asking for the removal of the white man's saloon from their midst.

"In March, 1911, a bill was introduced into the Washington senate to destroy the splendid state law against selling liquor to

Indians. The news came to me immediately over the wire and I telegraphed to many persons of influence in that state, asking assistance in defeating the infamous proposal. It was L. V. McWhorter who played the card that defeated the liquor grafters. He rode the Yakima Reservation for two days. The result was, that, representing five hundred Indians, he sent a telegram to the sponsor of the bill protesting and imploring that it be withdrawn. And it was withdrawn, as the hundreds of scoundrels who have since been convicted under this law can testify.

"Because of my interest in my own race as well as my interest in the Indian, I rejoice that the following pages have been written, and written by one so well qualified to tell the sordid story as Mr. McWhorter. If the remainder of the white race were like him, there would be no 'Indian problems.'"

During these years of friendly contact with the Yakimas, McWhorter obtained many of their traditions and folk-lore stories, to which he is constantly adding. These, with much obscure tribal history, because of the native eloquence of oratory which he carefully preserves, will, if ever published, constitute a valuable contribution to our Indian literature. Not the least interesting of his manuscripts is the personal narratives of a number of the warriors of Chief Joseph's Band, Nez Perce War, 1877. Some of these cover previous tribal wars, and the thrilling experiences of the grim fighters, told in their own way, reveals the Indian character as seldom found in border history. The lack of money alone has prevented the completion of these researches and their publication in book form.

J. P. MACLEAN.

Franklin, Ohio.
February 22, 1915.

PRELUDE

Border Settlers, begun in 1896, has been written under adversity during such time as could be spared from keeping the traditional wolf from the door. The volume is a growth from an original design to write a biography of Jesse Hughes, the great Indian Scout of Western Virginia. Whatever its merits, it is the product of an incentive to place in tangible form some of the unpublished records, history and traditions of the pioneers of the most interesting region of our entire western border. In some instances widely scattered authorities have been drawn from, in the belief that a complete, though condensed history so far as practicable, was desirable. Comparatively, the printed record is meagre; but the field was found rich in unchronicled lore.

Nowhere in the Anglo-Saxon conquest of the New World is there a territory so fraught with dramatic tragedy, personal prowess and adventure, as the Trans-Allegheny. For more than twenty years, embracing the Revolutionary struggle, amid the dark mazes of this mighty wilderness, the Red and the White warriors met in deadly conflict. It was a warfare cruel, fierce and unrelenting; where mutual wrongs and implacable race hatred ever whetted anew the murderous scalping knife and rendered unerring the aim of the deadly rifle. The sombre dales of the Monongahela and the deep glens of the Kanawhas' witnessed many a tragic scene. The set purpose to found new homes in the wilderness was met with a grim determination to maintain those homes long established to the westward, by holding, if *possible*, this natural barrier against the invader.

By instinct and training the contestants stood fairly matched. Baring the torture stake, the status of the "Advance guard of civilization," was scarce above that of the Red guard of barbarism. The isolation of the settlers' cabins was responsible for the many dreadful massacres of innocence; while the segregation of the Indians alone secured them from the ravages of a like warfare. When the opportunity afforded, entire families, bands and villages were ruthlessly destroyed. The wolf and the vulture ever hovered in the wake of the Red and the White forayer. The war whoop and the border yell were alike synonymous of death: — a call for the carrion creatures to assemble in feast.

The antipathy of the Indian for the "Long Knives" was well founded. Nowhere in the early annals can we find such reckless dare-devil bravery as displayed by the Virginia frontiersman; where every settler was a warrior. And nowhere has the chronicler dealt more unfairly with the memory of the forest ranger. If zeal in the extirpation of the Indian is to be considered a virtue, then many of these bordermen were entitled to canonization. Jesse Hughes and his two noted brothers: — the peers of Boone, Brady, Kenton, the McColloughs', Wetzels' and the Zanes', have but small space in the annals, while the names of others of scarce less ability are practically unknown. In the present work, many of the deeds of these scouts are, for the first time, made public.

Pathos and tragedy are the component parts of the early history of this region. Domestic life held but little cheer. The warrior-settler engaged so constantly in scouting and the chase, was not only necessarily improvident, but his meagre wages for military services were often in arrears. On the wife and the mother devolved the heavier burden of providing for the family. It was not enough that she spin and manufacture clothing, but the "corn patch" and the "truck patch" were usually the product of her toil, aided, perhaps, by the children. Unceasing danger and hardships were her portion, and her worth has never been appreciated.

A descendant of one of the oldest and most noted pioneer families of the upper Monongahela, writes me.

"In writing the record of the wilderness heroes, do not forget that it was our old grandmothers who cooked for all the people around open wood fires when they attended church in their cabin homes: that there were as many noble women as there were noble men, true heroines, who with but few pleasures to mitigate the monotony of their hard, arduous lives; they toiled without murmur or complaint. Their courage, industry, patience and self-denial, were the beautiful as well as the pathetic side of the pioneer life in those trying days. They were the real foundations of the great civilization of our land. Do not forget our grandmothers."

This is true; and the historian has failed to recognize the actual part of these grandmothers in the settlement and development of the Trans-Allegheny. When life in the boundless woods threatened to revert husband, father and son to hopeless barbarism, it was their influence which checkmated the seductive "call of the wild." PEACE TO THEIR MEMORY.

MEMORANDA

The following is a list of the names of men for whose military records search was made among the archives of the War Department, and the Pension Office, Washington, D. C. With the exception of a few soldiers of the War of 1812, which are so designated, all were for services during the Revolutionary War, either Continental Troops or State Militia; which latter included frontier scouts or rangers. Many of these never applied for pension; some dying before the pension laws covering their case were enacted. The prospect of a record through the widow's claim was an incentive for the examination. I am indebted to Laura Gertrude Rogers, of Washington City, for the splendid results obtained, which are fully set forth in the course of this volume. It was found that not a few of the bravest defenders of the border were left entirely without the pale of any pensioning legislation.

Baily, Capt. Minter; Bent, Belt or Broadbelt, James (War 1812); Biggs, Lieut. Joseph; Bonnett, Jacob; Bonnett, Lewis; Bonnett, Peter; Bozarth, Cap. John (War 1812); Bozarth, George (War of 1812); Brake, Jacob; Brown, John; Bush, Jacob; Bush, John; Butcher, Paulcene.

Carpenter, Christopher; Carpenter, Jesse; Carpenter, John; Connells, Col. John (War 1812); Cotteral, Thomas; Cutright, John; Cutright, Benjamin; Cutright, Peter.

Davisson, Hezekiah; Dorman, Timothy; Drennen, Thomas; Duval, John P.

Flesher, Adam; Flesher, Henry; Forenash, Jacob.

Green, George; Gregory, Capt. Joseph.

Hacker, John; Hacker, William; Hall, Joseph; Hess, Hezekiah (1776-1812); Hicks, Sotha; Hinzman, Henry; Hughes, Jesse (for widow's claim); Hughes, Elias; Hughes, Thomas; Hughes, Job; Hughes, Charles; Hughes, Charles (War of 1812); Hughes, David (War of 1812); Hughes (any name Volunteer from Licking Co., Ohio. War 1812); Hurst, William; Hurst (any name); Hurst, John (War of 1812); Hurst, Daniel (War of 1812); Hurst, William (War of 1812).

Jackson, John; Jackson, George; Jackson, Edward; Jackson, Henry; Jenkins, Bartholomew.

Kester, Joseph; King, Col. William (3rd U. S. Rifles, War of 1812).

Lowther, William; Lowther, Robert; Lowther (any name); Lowther, Alexander (War of 1812); Lowther (any name, War of 1812); Lynn, John.

Martin, Stephen; McCan, Paterick; McColloch, or McCullough, Major John; McWhorter, Henry; McWhorter, Alexander (Knox Artillery Brigade); McWhorter, Capt. John (War of 1812); McWhorter, James; McWhorter, John; McWhorter, Gilbert; McWhorter, Robert; McWhorter, William — New York, New Jersey and Pennsylvania, War 1776; McWhorter (any name); Morgan, (any name); Morrison, James.

Nutter, Christopher; Nutter, Capt. Thomas.

O'Brien, Adam.

Powers, William; Powers, John; Pringle, Capt. Samuel; Pringle, John.

Radcliff, William; Radcliff, John; Reeder, ——; Reger, Anthony; Reger, Philip; Reger, Jacob; Reger, John; Robinson, Major Benjamin; Runner, Elijah; Ryan, John; Ryan, ——.

Schoolcraft, John (mentioned by *Withers*); Schoolcraft, John (scout about Wheeling); Scott, Andrew; Scott, Jacob; Scott, Robert; Sevier, Col. John; Shaver, Paul; Sleeth, David; Smith, David.

Waggoner, John; Waggoner, William; West, Alexander; West, Edmund; West, Joseph; Westfall, Jacob; White, Capt. William (for widow's claim); Wilson, Col. Benjamin.

Zane, Col. Ebenezer; Zane, Col. Silas.

It is with pleasure that I acknowledge valuable assistance from Mr. William Elsey Connelley, the late lamented Prof. Virgil A. Lewis, Hon. Hu Maxwell, Hon. W. B. Cutright, Mr. Henry Haymond, Dr. J. P. MacLean, Judge Wm. S. O'Brien, Miss Minnie Kendall Lowther, Prof. H. R. McIlwain of the Virginia State Library; and Dr. R. G. Thwaites and Miss Annie A. Nunns, of Wisconsin State Historical Society. Aside from the preface and notes written by Mr. Connelley, his counsel and suggestions were invaluable in the final arrangement of material. Second only to Mr. Connelley in this respect was Mr. J. Scott McWhorter, Attorney, Lewisburg, W. Va. Other sources of help are duly credited where given.

LUCULLUS VIRGIL MCWHORTER.

North Yakima, Wash., May, 1914.

Photograph of The Pringle Sycamore, March, 1915

COURTESY OF MR. AND MRS. U. I. JENKINS

CHAPTER I

The first permanent settlers to enter the Trans-Allegheny of Western Virginia, came from the Wappatomaka, (1) and were led by Samuel Pringle. Samuel and his younger brother John were soldiers in the British garrison at Fort Pitt, which they, with William Childers and Joseph Linsey deserted in 1761. (2) They fled first to the wilds of the Monongahela, but subsequently sought the glades at the head of the Youghiogheny, where they encamped about one year. In 1762 they ventured to the Looney's Creek settlement but almost immediately Childers and Linsey were arrested. The Pringles escaped to their old haunts where they remained in the employment of John Simpson, a trapper, until some time in 1764.

As the glades were now being invaded by hunters from the Wappatomaka, the trio resolved to retreat further west. By such move Simpson would find better hunting and the Pringles would be more secure from detection and arrest. While executing this resolution and after crossing the Cheat River at the Horse Shoe (bend) the trapper and the fugitives parted company as a result of a disagreement. Simpson proceeded to the mouth of Elk Creek, near the present site of Clarksburg, where he erected a camp and continued until permanent settlements were made on the western waters. He then disappeared, in all probability going to Kentucky. He appears to have been a man of fierce temperament. One Cottral, or Cottrell, met death at his hands in an altercation over two gallons of salt. The Cottrals were, however, known for their great fighting qualities.

The Pringles kept up Tygart's Valley, and reached the Buckhannon River (1764), where they took up residence in a hollow sycamore tree at the mouth of Turkey Run. (3) Here they resided until late in the autumn of 1767, when they had remaining but two charges of powder. Leaving these with Samuel, John recrossed the mountains for a supply of ammunition. While there he learned that peace had been declared with both French and Indian, and that they now could return in safety to the settlements. After some delay he hastened back to the wilderness camp to find his brother reduced to the verge of

---
(1) See page 415. (2) p. 415. (3) p. 416.

despair. One charge of powder Samuel had lost in a vain endeavor to kill a buck, but with the other he brought down a fine buffalo; otherwise he must have succumbed to the ravages of hunger. The continued absence of John had induced the belief that he had been apprehended and imprisoned.

The brothers, no longer fugitives, now determined to return to the Wappatomaka. The sequel was the rapid colonization of the Trans-Allegheny. Subsequently John settled in Kentucky. The time of his removal to the Blue Grass region is not known, but it was at an early date. No mention of him is found in connection with the settlements of the upper Monongahela after 1768; nor is it believed that he ever took up actual residence after abandoning the camp in the Sycamore.

One John Pringle was a settler on Chaplin's Fork, Kentucky, in 1780. He came with a fleet of three boats from the Wappatomaka, and in an encounter with the Indians, led by Simon Girty, Pringle's boat alone escaped. He married Rebecca Simpson, a sister to a John Simpson, from whom she inherited slaves in 1825. (4)

Samuel Pringle settled permanently on the Buckhannon, and was prominent in the border wars. From sworn statements preserved in the Government Pension Office, it would appear that Samuel Pringle was at one time during the Revolution, captain of a band of scouts, but as no claim for pension on account of his Revolutionary service was made, we find no actual record of his military career. (5) His wife, Charity Cutright, was the daughter of Benjamin Cutright, and a sister of John Cutright, Jr., the noted scout of the Buckhannon. A family tradition has it that Samuel and Charity were married before the fugitive brothers made residence in the Sycamore, where Mrs. Pringle joined her husband in 1767, guided by a path blazed by John when he first sought the settlements. Another account says they were not married until after the return of the brothers to the Wappatomaka, although a warm attachment had sprung up between the young couple, while the deserters were at Looney's Creek in 1762. It is more than probable that the marriage was consummated during the brief stay of Pringle at Looney's Creek, and that the devoted wife actually traversed the wilderness path to her absent husband.

The children of Samuel and Charity were William, John, Samuel, Elizabeth and another daughter whose name is not

(4) See page 416. (5) p. 416.

recalled. Their descendants are numerous in the Buckhannon country, while some are scattered through sections of Ohio and Indiana. (6)

The claim that the Pringles, as soldiers in the Royal Army, only came to America during the French and Indian wars, can not be accepted as fact. It is not probable that such men would have deserted and fled to a wilderness fraught with known dangers with which they were unqualified to cope. Border Colonial troops, as in the Patriot Army of the Revolution, chafed at restraint and discipline, and often deserted. The Pringles evinced a consummate skill in woodcraft, not attributable to the raw European soldier.

It is a remarkable coincidence that a William Pringle resided in Philadelphia, who had two sons named John and Samuel, born in 1728 and 1731 respectively.

It is not improbable that this family removed to the Virginia border and that the sons were identical with those of later renown.

Momentous events were destined to follow in the wake of these wilderness refugees. In the autumn of 1768, several adventurous and prospective settlers under the guidance of Samuel, visited the region of the Pringle refuge, and so well pleased were they, that the following spring they returned, selected lands, cleared small fields, planted crops and built cabins preparatory to bringing their families. After the crops were "laid by," the men returned to the settlements, and in the fall when they came back to harvest their corn, they found it entirely destroyed by buffaloes. This delayed the removal of the families, or at least a greater part of them, until the winter of 1770.

With Pringle's band of prospectors of 1769, came a youth of about nineteen — Jesse Hughes. He was of Welsh extraction, slight in his proportions, and light and active in his movements. He possessed a form as erect as that of an Indian, and had endurance and fleetness of limb that no man of his day surpassed. His height was about five feet and nine inches, and his weight never exceeded one hundred and forty-five pounds. He had thin lips, a narrow chin, a nose that was sharp and inclined to the Roman form, little or no beard, light hair, and eyes of that indefinable color that one person would pronounce grey, another blue, but which was both — and neither. They were piercing, cold, fierce, and as penetrating and restless as those of the mountain panther.

---
(6) See page 416.

Said one who knew him: "Hughes had eyes like a rattlesnake." It has been averred, and without contradiction, that Jesse Hughes, like the famed "Deaf Smith" of Texas, could detect the presence of an Indian at a considerable distance by the mere sense of smell. He was of an irritable, vindictive, and suspicious nature, and his hatred, when aroused, knew no bounds. Yet it is said that he was true to those who gained his friendship. Such was Jesse Hughes in character and appearance when he arrived in that country destined to become his future home, and where he became the noted hunter, the great scout and famous Indian fighter of Northwestern Virginia.

In an interview with an intelligent and reputable lady, now deceased, who, in her childhood, had known Jesse Hughes, and had been intimately acquainted with some of his family, I was given this vivid description of the characteristics and personal appearance of the great Indian fighter:

"Hughes' countenance was hard, stern and unfeeling; his eyes were the most cruel and vicious I ever saw. He was profane and desperately wicked. He was very superstitious, and a firm believer in witchcraft. (7) He told horrible stories of how witches would crawl like spiders over the naked bodies of babies, causing them to cry out from pain and misery; and he would conjure to counteract the witches, and offer incantations to overcome their evil influence. His temper was fierce and uncontrollable, often finding vent in the abuse of his family. In a drunken brawl near West's Fort, he and a Mr. Stalnaker nearly killed Ichabod Davis, his neighbor, leaving the unconscious victim for dead. Hughes fled from the settlement, but returned after Davis recovered. He never worked, but spent his time in hunting and scouting. His clothing was colored in the ooze made from the bark of the chestnut oak; he would wear no other color, this shade harmonizing with the forest hues and rendering him less conspicuous to game and Indians. When scouting, his dress consisted only of the long hunting shirt, (8) belted at the waist, open leggins, moccasins, and a brimless cap; or a handkerchief bound about his head. Thus dressed, he was ever ready for the chase, or the trail of the Indian foe." (9)

When further questioned as to his traits of character, the lady bluntly closed the interview by saying, "I would not tell all I know about Jesse Hughes for this much gold," designating the amount she could hold in her doubled-hands. "There are," she continued, "too many of his descendants living about here." Nor could she be induced to speak further on the subject.

His mode of dress, as above described, has been amply verified from other sources. When Indian incursions were expected,

(7) See page 416. (8) p. 416. (9) p. 417.

Jesse Hughes wore his hunting shirt both day and night, without regard to weather.

Mrs. Catharine Simms-Allman remembered that when she was a little girl, Jesse Hughes came to her father's house on Hacker's Creek, one mile below West's Fort, early one morning, and ordered them to run to the fort. Upon that occasion his dress consisted of the hunting shirt and moccasins only. He was riding a pony without a saddle, and mounted her mother behind him, and with one of the children in his arms, galloped to the fort. This incident occurred while Hughes lived at the mouth of Jesse's Run.

At the end of his cabin, Hughes erected a "lean-to," where at all times he kept his pony ready for instant use in case of an Indian alarm.

Of the pioneers who came with Pringle into the Buckhannon country, *Withers* says:

"The others of the party (William Hacker, Thomas and Jesse Hughes, John and William Radcliff and John Brown) appear to have employed their time exclusively in hunting, neither of them making any improvement of land for his own benefit. Yet they were of considerable service to the new settlement. Those who had commenced clearing land, were supplied by them with an abundance of meat, while in their hunting excursions through the country, a better knowledge of it was obtained, than could have been acquired, had they been engaged in making improvements.

"In one of these expeditions they discovered and gave name to Stone Coal Creek, which flowing westwardly, induced the supposition that it discharged itself directly into the Ohio. Descending this creek, to ascertain the fact, they came to its confluence with a river, which they then called, and has since been known as the West Fork. After having gone some distance down the river, they returned by a different route to the settlement, better pleased with the land on it and some of its tributaries, than with that on Buckhannon." (10)

The hunters evidently returned to the settlement by way of Hacker's Creek. The Indian name for this stream signifies "Muddy Water."

The Pringles had never crossed the divide, to any of the waters falling into the West Fork, and knew nothing of the topography of the country. Of the six who comprised this band of explorers, the three first named became prominent in the border annals. The Radcliffs settled on Hacker's Creek, (11) and we find that William Ratliff (Radcliff) claimed land there prior to 1781. John subsequently gained notoriety for murdering Indians on the Ohio frontier, (12) but we find nothing definite concerning

---
(10) See page 418. (11) p. 418. (12) p. 418.

the later life of William. One William Radcliff was a pensioner of the Revolutionary War, whose certificate for eighty dollars per year was issued May 16, 1833, at which time he was a resident of Lewis County, Virginia. His original declaration for pension is missing, and the only narrative of his services that we find is from Special Pension Agent, W. G. Singleton, in his report to the Commissioner of Pensions, after a re-examination of Radcliff in 1834.

Singleton's Report:

"In a conversation between Radcliff and Weeden Hoffman, Radcliff states that he only served six months in the war and that he only claimed six months' service in his declaration.

"On July 30th I saw Radcliff and received from him the following narrative of his services in the Revolutionary War. In his sixteenth or seventeenth year of age, he served as substitute in the place of Adam Harpole for two months, and marched from Hardy County, Virginia, under he don't recollect whom nor where to, and immediately after the defeat of Cornwallis at Little Fort, Virginia, he marched from Hardy County to Winchester, Virginia, under Capt. James Stephanson, and served under him at latter place for two months, guarding the British prisoners. Capt. Stephanson's company, except five or six men including himself, were discharged at the end of two months, at which time Capt. Jas. Berry came to Winchester with a company. Himself and the four or five men above mentioned were attached to Capt. Joseph Berry's company and served under him, guarding the prisoners for two months. Then Capt. Berry's company (except the five or six men including himself above mentioned) was discharged; then the five or six men including himself were attached to Capt. James Simeral's company and served under him two months. A Colonel Kennedy commanded at Winchester thinks he went to Winchester about October 1st and got his discharge about May 20th, which was signed by Col. Joseph Holm's captain. Wamsley with his declaration expects that the narrative now given is the same given to Wamsley by contract. Wamsley was to have the half of the first pay drawn."

(Signed) His
Witnesses: WILLIAM X RADCLIFF.
NATHAN GOFF. Mark.

NOTE: "The statement of Radcliff is untrue in all particulars except as to the contract with Wamsley. This is one of the cases upon which suit has been instituted. The original papers are missing."

(Signed)
November 1, 1834. W. G. SINGLETON.

This pensioner could hardly have been the William Ratliff of the Buckhannon exploring party of 1769. According to his declaration to Singleton, he was only sixteen or seventeen at the time of Gen. Cornwallis' surrender in 1781. This would make him but twelve years old at the time of the exploration in question.

Nothing is known of the subsequent history of John Brown, a member of the exploring party. It has been surmised that both William Radcliff and Brown settled on the West Fork. (13) This is true of Radcliff, for Hacker's Creek is a branch of the West Fork, but I doubt if this supposition can be verified in Brown's case. No trace of his history can be found subsequent to his advent into the Buckhannon settlement in 1769. One John Brown was a resident on the waters of the West Fork, about the close of the Revolution, but his record precludes the inference that he was of the exploring party in question.

In the application for pension as a Revolutionary soldier, made in Lewis County, Aug. 7, 1833, it would appear that Brown was born in 1764, and was raised in Hardy County, Virginia. March 1st, 1781, he volunteered from Hampshire County, in the Virginia Militia under Capt. Michael Stump, and marched to Fredericksburg, Va., and from thence, under orders of Gen. George Weedon, to Richmond, where they encamped on the hill where the capitol now (1833) stands. He was in the command of Col. William Darke, under Gen. Porter Muhlenberg. They continued in camp about three weeks, when the enemy entered the city, and the Virginia troops retreated to Raccoon Ford, where they were joined by Gen. Anthony Wayne. The Americans then turned and drove the British back to Richmond. Wayne's army encamped for seven days near Bacon branch, preparing to make an attack, but on the morning of the intended assault, there was a dense fog, which enabled the enemy, whom Brown believed was commanded by Lord Cornwallis [correct], to escape towards New Kent Court House. The Americans pursued and came up with the enemy near New Kent, and the two armies skirmished for two days, alternately pursuing and retreating. Wayne was then joined by Gen. Lafayette, and the British retreated towards their fleet. The American forces went to Williamsburg, and later to Yorktown.

About October 1st, 1781, just prior to the surrender of Gen. Cornwallis, Brown received his discharge from Capt. Anderson, and returned home, having served seven months.

Brown then moved to (now) Lewis County, West Virginia, where he was still living in 1833. On November 1st, 1781, he was ordered out as an Indian spy by Col. Benjamin Wilson, under Capt. Christopher Carpenter, and spied in that part of Virginia,

---
(13) See page 418.

which in 1833 comprised Wood, Nicholas, Harrison and Lewis counties. He continued under Carpenter until August, 1782, when he left his company, and was commissioned an Ensign of Spies under Colonels Lowther and Wilson, and was in command of Indian spies from August 1st, 1782, to June 1st, 1783, when he ceased to act as an Ensign. Brown was allowed $146.66 per year.

Subsequently, there were doubts as to Brown's integrity and his right to a pension; and adverse testimony was taken by W. G. Singleton, U. S. District Attorney, Virginia, Nov. 4, 1834.

John Waggoner, of Lewis County, had known Brown all his life. They had, when young, resided in Hardy County, and afterwards were neighbors in Lewis County. He (Waggoner) had never heard of Brown doing service as a soldier in the Revolution, nor did he believe that he did. Henry Flesher, of Harrison County, stated that Brown came to western Virginia after the close of the Revolution, at which time he was not quite grown. Flesher was of the opinion that Brown had been a soldier. Isaac Washburn, of Harrison County, had known Brown from his earliest recollection. Brown and himself had been posted or stationed at Brown's Fort (built by Brown's father) after the close of the Revolution. Brown was then a young man of twenty years or more. Edward, a younger brother of John Brown, stated "That his brother John was in service as a soldier of the Revolution for three months, but he thinks not longer."

The testimony most damaging to the claimant was that of William Powers. Mr. Powers was a man of integrity, and his statement is interesting. It reveals the military and social status of the Trans-Allegheny during the Revolution.

I quote as reported by Singleton.

"Wm Powers resided in w. Va. now Harrison Co. all the time except 1 year during the Rev. war Knew Brown in Hardy county in 1778-1779. he Powers was at school there at that time. Brown settled in w. Va. where he now [1834] lives in 1785 removed from Hardy county in that year, knows nothing of Browns Rev. service. Brown was an Indian spy after his removal to the west in 1785 as before stated. Brown was not in the settlement (w. Va) in 1782, 1783, 1784 as stated by him he could not have been without his (Powers) knowledge, there were but few in the settlement at that period. every man engaged in defending the country was known to each other. Powers knew every man able to bear arms, and almost every woman and child, the settlement to which he refers is embraced in the present limits of Harrison, Tyler, Lewis and the n. part of Kenhawhas co. having heard Browns statement read Mr Powers states confidently that Brown is mistaken.

"Capt. Copelaw also argues browns statements are false. * * * *

(Signed)

W. G. SINGLETON
Nov. 4, 1834."

Mr. Singleton in transmitting this testimony, spoke derogatory of Brown's character, and adversely to his right to a pension. He also submitted a statement from Brown of his military services, which were at variance, in some respects with his first declaration.

CHAPTER II

It is astonishing when we realize how little there is recorded of the actual border life of Jesse Hughes, and other noted scouts of Northwestern Virginia. Especially is this true when we remember that Mr. Withers wrote his *Chronicles of Border Warfare* in the midst of the very scenes of some of the most daring escapades and bloody achievements of border strife; and this, too, while many of the principal actors in the tragedies were still living. It is but natural that we should expect a reasonably complete record of local events; but, unfortunately, we find the record as preserved for us woefully deficient. A careful perusal of the excellent work in question, reveals the fact that a greater part of that section of it which deals with local affairs is not so complete, nor are the events so carefully portrayed, as is that part which treats of the matters pertaining to more distant localities. It cannot be denied that the first part of the volume, which sets out the general history of the more distant settlements, is more complete, more concise, and far more minutely written than the latter portion, which deals with events largely local. Dr. Thwaites recognized this deficiency. In the *Editor's Preface* to the revised edition he says:

"The weakness of the traditional method is well exemplified in Withers' work. His treatment of many of the larger events on the border may now be regarded as little else than a thread on which to hang annotations; * * *" (1)

There must have been a cause for this deficiency, which becomes very apparent when we read Dr. Lyman C. Draper's *Memoir of Withers*, and the letter from Mr. Bond set out below. Dr. Draper tells us that:

"* * * Mr. Withers got nothing whatever for his diligence and labor in producing it [*Border Warfare*], save two or three copies of the work itself. He used to say that had he published the volume himself, he would have made it much more complete, and better in every way; for he was hampered, limited and hurried—often correcting proof of the early, while writing the later chapters." (2)

The letter from Mr. Bond is in response to an inquiry, and is as follows:

---
(1) See page 418. (2) p. 418.

"Lost Creek, W. Va., January 23, 1898."

Mr. L. V. McWhorter,
   Mason, Ohio.

Dear Sir:

"Your letter received, and in reply will say; I am a grandson of William Powers, one of the men who got up Border Warfare; William Hacker (3) was the other. This work lay dormant in their hands for many years. Hacker passed away first. Powers purchased Hacker's interest in the work, and it lay in his hands until 1831, when Joseph Israel, an editor in Clarksburg, bought the manuscript and arranged for its publication by employing Alexander Scott Withers to prepare it for the press. Accordingly Mr. Withers took up the work, and after he had it about half completed some friend told him that he was likely to get nothing for his labor, and that Israel was poor and could not raise the amount of money agreed upon. Mr. Withers did not want to leave the work in that condition and said, 'I will dispose of it in some shape.' So he ran through the most notable and prominent features, leaving the balance entirely out.

"Now from this time on you and all others will see that the second part of *Border Warfare* is rather incomplete and scattered as compared to the first part of the volume.

"This is the history that my grandfather gave me of the work from his own lips. My grandfather lived on a farm adjoining Jane Lew [West Fort], about three miles from Withers' office, and was there several times while Withers was preparing the work, and he told me these things himself.

"I am the only man that can give this history, as I am the only one living who took any account of these things. I am now in my eighty-second year.

"In regard to Jesse Hughes, my grandfather told me that they had hunted Indians together, and were in the volunteer company pursuing the Indians on the Little Kanawha, when John Bonnett was killed; that Jesse was the best trailer among the whites and could trail with any Indian on the border. Jesse's brother Ellis was also a noted scout. While he could not trail with Jesse, he was the greater with the rifle, and could hit an Indian under any and all circumstances within the range of his rifle. He was a dead shot. (4)

"When hunting, Ellis could get more game than Jesse at long range, but at the end of the day Jesse would have as much, but he would get it by slipping upon it unawares. In this, as in trailing Indians, he had no equal."

Yours truly,
Levi Bond.

Here, then, we have the solution to the mystery of the incomplete and defective character of the history in question. This very apparent fault is lamentable. It is the incidental details that give interest to local history. There is little wonder that Mr. Withers became discouraged and lost interest in his noble but arduous task. A less energetic and patriotic man would have dropped the work entirely when it became apparent that there would be no compensation for his labor. All honor to Mr. Withers!

---

(3) See page 418. (4) p. 418.

Yet, William Hacker and William Powers, the true authors of that part of the history in question, have never received the recognition and credit due them for the invaluable service they rendered in the preservation of this record. To them we are indebted for most of the narrative of border strife in and about Clarksburg, West's Fort, Buckhannon and adjacent settlements. The character of Mr. Bond is above question, and his account of the origin of *Border Warfare* has long been an open secret with many of the older inhabitants of that region. (5)

William Powers was born in Frederick County, Virginia, November 9, 1765. He came with his father, John Powers, to Simpson's Creek, a tributary of the West Fork, where, in 1781, a certificate of homestead entry was granted "John Powers, 400 acres on Simpson's Creek, adjoining lands of James Anderson, to include his settlement made in 1772." William Powers at a very early age became a scout of prominence. In March, 1781, when but fifteen years old, he enlisted for nine months (during the scouting season) in Captain Joseph Gregory's Company of Indian spies; place of enlistment, Monongalia County, Virginia. March 2, 1782, he re-enlisted for the same length of time, in the same company. During this time, he was stationed at Power's Fort (probably named for his father) on Simpson's Creek, and was engaged in spying from that fort to the Ohio River and over the territory that afterwards comprised the counties of Ohio, Tyler, Wood, Lewis, Harrison, and Randolph. In March, 1783, he was made ensign of a company of scouts until the first day of September, following. During this enlistment he was engaged in scouting throughout Monongalia County. It is singular that Withers has not even mentioned William Powers' name in connection with a single incident of the frontier. This, however, is true of other deserving pioneers, and is much to be regretted. Powers was one of the scouts who searched for the marauding Indians that desolated the home of Thomas Cunningham (6) on Bingamon Creek in 1785; and was with Colonel Lowther's party in pursuit of Indians on the Little Kanawha, in 1787, which resulted so fatally to John Bonnett.

He was also with Colonel Lowther in 1781, in his pursuit and attack on the Indian Camp on the Hughes River, when the Leading Creek captives were rescued. These events will be more fully treated elsewhere in this volume.

(5) See page 418. (6) p. 418.

Powers was connected with many other thrilling occurrences of border strife.

It was within a few days after Powers' first enlistment, 1781, that the Indians came near Booth's Creek and killed Capt. John Thomas, wife, and six of their children, carrying off the remaining child, a small boy, prisoner. (7)

Powers, in his declaration for pension, October 1st, 1833, states that it was in 1781 that John Owens and John Juggins were killed by Indians on Booth's Creek, in (now) Harrison County. *Withers* says that this tragedy occurred in June, 1780. (8) Powers also states that it was in 1782, that the Indians killed James Owens, and took prisoner Gilbert Hostead (Hustead) in the same region. This is again in contradiction of Withers, who gives the dates of these transactions as 1778. (9).

In March, 1783, he enlisted for the third time, and was elected Ensign, or Second Lieutenant of scouts, by his company. On April 4th he marched from Powers Fort to the mouth of Bingamon Creek, in now Harrison County, where he "stationed part of his men on the site of an old Indian town;" the remaining ones he stationed "at the mouth of Jones Run, a branch of Ten Mile Creek, about thirty miles from Bingamon Creek." These men he left to make regular scouting tours, while he traveled from station to station in the capacity of commander. During this season Indians came to the neighborhood of Simpson Creek and stole several horses belonging to Major Benjamin Robinson, who with others made a fruitless pursuit of the marauders. This was evidently the Major Robinson mentioned by *Withers*. (10) Powers disbanded his men in September, 1783.

Powers' discharge papers, with his commission of Ensign, were all misplaced, or lost in a fire which destroyed his house with its contents. John Brown and John Schoolcraft both testified to the good character and veracity of William Powers, who also gave as reference Alexander West and Adam Flesher. Powers was granted a pension, but in April, 1840, John H. Hays, of McWhorter's Mills, Lewis County, Virginia, contrived to have it stopped by reporting to the Pension Office that Powers was not entitled to a pension. In his protest Hays mentions the "Messrs. Bonnetts, (11) Adam Flesher, Hezekiah Hess and several others" who had been granted pensions for services similar to those of Mr. Powers,

---
(7) See page 419. (8) p. 419. (9) p. 419. (10) p. 419. (11) p. 419.

but later their names had been dropped from the list, and they required to refund the amounts paid them.

Notwithstanding Hays had declared to the Pension Office his ability and intention of proving his charges by affidavits, only one, that of Phoebe Cunningham, was submitted. Her testimony was "that she was acquainted with William Powers since the close of the Revolutionary War and believes that he was about thirteen years of age." Sworn to April 1st, 1840, before James Malone, Justice of the Peace for Lewis County, Virginia. In October of the same year, in response to an inquiry, Powers received official notice that his pension was stopped, but it seems he took no immediate steps to have his name restored.

On the 16th of December, 1846, the following testimony in behalf of Powers was forwarded from Weston, Lewis County, Va., to the Commissioner of Pensions:

Sir:
"I have been acquainted with William Powers for more than 30 years. He has acted as Sheriff for Lewis County, Va., and has discharged the duties of a Justice of the Peace in Harrison and Lewis counties for more than 30 years. He stands well before the community where he is acquainted, as an honest and upright man and I believe that any statement he would make under oath or otherwise would be believed by those who are acquainted with him. I will add that John H. Hays is a man of bad character and not to be relied on."

(Signed) J. McWhorter. (12)

A similar letter was signed by Weedon Hoffman, Minter Bailey, Levi Maxwell, William I. Bland, John Lorentz, and Thomas Bland, all men of unquestionable repute. At length the case was referred to the Secretary of the Interior with the following result:

"Department of the Interior
October 28, 1850.

J. L. Edwards, Esq.,
    Commissioner of Pensions.
Sir:
"I herewith return the papers in the case of William Powers, Esq., of Lewis County, Va., and I am of the opinion that his name should be restored to the Pension roll under the Act of June 7, 1732, at $80.00 per annum from the period when he was last paid.

"From examination of papers I can find no ground for the action of the Pension Office, but on the contrary the U. S. District Attorney for the Western District of Virginia who was especially charged with an examination of the case, reported in writing that Mr. Powers was entitled to his pension, and recommended his con-

---
(12) See page 420.

tinuance, whilst the individual who was instrumental in his being stricken from the roll is shown by the records of Lewis County to have committed crime for which he was indicted by the Grand Jury, and is returned by the Sheriff as a fugitive from justice. I am, very respectfully

      Your obedient servant,

         ALEX. H. H. STUART, *Secy.*"

 Thus, after a period of ten years, the name of William Powers was restored to the pension roll. The offense for which Hays was indicted was forgery, committed August 1st, 1841. He moved to the Northwest and was never apprehended. It is probable that he located on Military Bounty Lands, for it is found that in 1841 he was negotiating for 4000 acres due Captain John Baily, or heirs, as a Revolutionary soldier, Virginia Line.

 My father, who is still living,(13) was well acquainted with William Powers, and testifies to his good character and veracity. He recalls the trouble that Powers had with his pension and its final adjustment. Hays, he says, was a man of very bad repute, and fled to the then remote Northwest. His place of refuge was never known.

 William Powers was well educated for his day, and his wide experience on the frontier, where he "knew every man able to bear arms," and practically every woman and child in the upper Monongahela settlements, well qualified him for the role of local historian. He was sometimes called "Major" Powers, but if he was entitled to that distinction, it was doubtless as major of militia at a later day, as no mention of such rank is found in the early records. The "Major Power" referred to by *Withers* (14) was evidently the Major Powers who settled in (now) Barbour County, West Va., in 1776.

 William Powers was about five feet six inches in height, well built, spare and very erect, even at eighty-nine. His complexion was light with dark hair. He married Hannah Stout, a sister of Dr. Hezekiah Stout, and settled near West's Fort. He died June 6, 1856, and was buried under the honors of war in the Broad Run Cemetery, Lewis County, West Va. His wife is also buried there. Their children were:

 Thomas, married Millie Hart; John, married Percella Chenverout; Ezekiel, married Miss —— Jones; Benjamin, married Miss —— Stout; William, Jr., married Charity Paxton, second wife, Miss —— Lightburn, sister to Gen. Joseph Lightburn;

---
(13) See page 420. (14) p. 420.

Sarah, married Abel Bond; Prudence, married Richard Bond; Margaret, married Eli Vanhorne.

Abel and Richard Bond were brothers; sons of Richard Bond, a son of Samuel Bond, native of England, and whose descent can be traced to the nobility of knighthood. Levi Bond, whose letter appears in the first part of this chapter, is a son of Abel Bond and Sarah Powers. He was born April 3, 1817. A shoemaker by trade, on his ninety-seventh birthday he nailed the soles on a pair of boots without experiencing any material fatigue. He is, at the writing of this paragraph, October 10th, 1914, still living and bids fair to pass the one-hundred milestone.

His younger brother, Augustine P. Bond, born in 1832, went west with his parents in 1845. Settling in Wisconsin, he crossed the plains in the Spring of 1864, and spent the Summer in a mining camp at now Virginia City, Montana. With a fleet of flat boats he returned in the Fall, fighting Indians for seven hundred and fifty miles down the Yellow Stone and Missouri Rivers, to Yankton, Dakota. His experience on the western frontier has been similar to that of his noted grandfather of the Trans-Allegheny.

Touching the Grigsby tragedy mentioned by *Withers*, (15) Mr. Bond writes me: "Bettie, the wife of Charles Grigsby, whose home was raided on Grigsby's Run, a branch of Rooting Creek, June, 1777, was buried with her infant where killed near the top of the ridge on Lost Creek, opposite the village of that name. The grave was never marked. I stood by the side of her grave in June, 1898, — 121 years after her death — and it was then just as it was seventy years ago when I first saw it; a slight depression in the ground. Her little child had been dead some time when the mother was killed, but she still carried it in her arms."

William Hacker, Jr., it is claimed, was the first white child born on Hacker's Creek, but I am inclined to believe that his birth occurred on the Wappatomaka, just prior to the parents settling on the Western waters. In either event, he grew to maturity amid the tumult of border forays, and doubtless participated in the defense of the settlements during the later years of Indian hostility. He was a man of more than ordinary ability, and considering his environments, was well educated. He was schoolteacher, minister and magistrate, and in the discharge of these diversified duties throughout the settlements, he had unsurpassed facilities for collecting historical data.

(15) See page 420.

Equipped as these men were for their task, it is reasonable to suppose that their work would be replete and thorough, but necessarily biased by partisanism.

While it is evident that Mr. Withers cast aside some of the material placed at his disposal, we are not to infer that he came into possession of every event of historic interest. The darker side of the border story, as seen from the standpoint of the Indian, was perhaps never revealed to him. When we remember that Mr. Powers was an active scout and Indian hunter, and that one of the Hackers, at least, was notorious for his murder of peaceable Indians (16) and that both were associates of others who were engaged in deeds of shocking barbarity, we need no longer wonder that so little was chronicled touching certain events that appear in their best light when buried in the blackness of oblivion. The same motive that prompted the good old lady to declare that "not for a handful of gold" would she speak further, was more patent in the earlier days than at the present time.

The partisan writer cannot give just treatment to those who are opposed to his own conception of right and wrong; nor is it to be expected that the hand that wields the sword will pen an unbiased version of the fray. Charity, the one potent element of impartiality, is never found in the acrimonious flow of "gun powder ink," and unfortunate are the people who must depend upon the enemy of their race for a true chronicling of their grievances.

Our border annals have all been recorded by white men. Strong racial affinity, animosity and hatred of the Indian have colored the record and prevented a fair statement of the facts. The Indian, hardly regarded by the early settlers as human, has ever been presented in the most terrible and hideous character that imagination could conceive. As thus pictured, his supremest passions were murder, plunder, torture and revenge. On the other hand, his white foe, often equally savage and more cruel, has been extolled as a hero moved with a holy zeal to protect home and country against "savage" incursions and to advance civilization and Christianity. His acts of revolting barbarity have been excused, obscured, suppressed, and the result is a partial and one-sided history. From Plymouth Rock to the Golden Gate this has been true. The "Custer Massacre" and the "Battle (?)

(16) See page 420.

of Wounded Knee" are modern incidents illustrative of this point. When in 1876, General Custer and his command were annihilated in a square up and down fight on the Little Big Horn by the strategic Sioux, and this too, when the challenge had been given by Custer himself the event was heralded abroad as a horrible Indian massacre by Sitting Bull's horde of merciless savages. The fact that the patriotic Sioux were in reality fighting for their homes and the right to even exist was not considered, or at least, was thought of as a matter of minor importance.

On the field of the Wounded Knee in 1890, United States soldiers having the advantage in numbers of more than four to one, and of rapid-fire machine guns, shot to death more than ninety men and boys, fifty women and young girls, and eighteen helpless children, several of them infants. This event was proclaimed to the world as a "Great Indian Battle," despite the fact that the Sioux had surrendered and were hemmed in by a cordon of troops who had partly disarmed them before the firing began. All the ghastly details will never be known. I have it from good authority, from one who was present when the outbreak occurred, that when the action began, all the Indians save not to exceed forty-five had surrendered their guns. Many were sitting on the ground smoking. They were without a leader. Their Chief, Big Foot, at the time lay dying in his tepee with pneumonia. At the first crash of the guns, the dying chieftain feebly raised himself on his couch, only to fall back riddled by a score of bullets. Here is one of the incidents that went to make up the "great battle."

A mounted soldier pursued a little Indian boy. Perhaps the lad was five or six years old. Seeing that he could not escape by running, he made frantic and piteous efforts to conceal his little body in the sand. The soldier fired at him but missed. Another trooper came to his assistance, dismounted, kneeled, and shot the little fellow through the hips! The troopers rode away in pursuit of other "hostiles." When the relief party came the dying boy was found and carried to the agency buildings. The story leaked out. Some time afterwards a large red-haired cavalryman was discovered at the edge of the camp stabbed through the heart. He was the soldier who had shot the Indian boy.

During the Bannock uprising in 1878, a party of United States soldiers pursued a band of hostiles into a canyon on Snake River and indiscriminately slaughtered them all, men, women, and children, including babes in arms. A soldier fatally shot a Bannock warrior; he sprang from his horse and with a savage sweep of his knife disemboweled the dying Indian. Then seizing the scalp-lock and placing his foot on the Indian's neck, proceeded, with the help of his knife, to tear the scalp from the head of his writhing victim. After the battle (?) some of the soldiers found an Indian baby yet unharmed, perhaps placed in some shelter by its mother before stricken to death in that charnal glen. This babe, which could scarce sit alone, was placed on a boulder at some distance for target practice. While the soldiers were discussing among themselves as to who should have the first shot, an Indian armed only with a "pepper-box" pistol was discovered hiding in a nearby thicket. The infant was left for a time, and an attempt made to dislodge the warrior. With his antiquated weapon he killed one of his assailants, deterring the others from rushing upon him. Then a howitzer heavily charged with grapeshot was turned upon this lone Indian and the discharge tore him into fragments, which the soldiers carried out one by one. These brave soldiers of a civilized and Christian nation, again turned their attention to the "hostile" upon the boulder. No less than a half dozen rifle balls one after another were sent tearing through its tender body. The officer in charge of these troops "could not see very well," consequently "knew not what was being done."

A late ex-soldier of repute said to me "I was a private in a West Virginia Regiment, Federal Army during the Civil War, and at the close of that struggle, my term of enlistment not being expired, was sent with others to fight Indians on the Kansas frontier. One day we captured five warriors, members of a band which had been committing depredations, and our commandant determined to treat them to a severe death. Rude frames were constructed by nailing four poles together. In these the prisoners were laid, their feet and hands extended and securely tied to the side timbers. The frames were then set up and braced, leaving the victims suspended by the lashings. They were given neither food nor drink and at the end of three days all were dead. No, they made no outcry, not even a moan, but died like sullen dogs. As a warning to other Indians, the frames with their ghastly settings were left standing."

Jim Walsie, a Warm Springs Indian of integrity, gave me the following incident: "Long time ago [in the sixties] I was scout for government in war with Snake Injuns. One day troops found small party Snakes in Blue Mountains, Oregon. Our commander, Captain John, a white man, says: 'Snakes bad people, kill um all. Kill Snake man, Snake woman, little gal, little boy and little papoose.' Then soldiers surround Snakes and shoot all dead. Then they scalp Snakes; and one man say I scalp a woman. It is a lie; I no scalp woman."

For actions like the above there was no excuse; but our occupancy of the country was a conquest which meant the destruction of the Indian tribes to whom the soil by right belonged. Every act, however cruel and unjust, which tended to hasten that result was supposed to be in the interest of the white man. These deeds were justified by a large element on the frontiers, and if any man raised his voice in protest he was accused of being against his race and its known policy. For these reasons, the revolting actions of the white men were modified in the accounts of them, and when possible they were kept secret. Much of what we have has been distorted by the historian. True accounts of many incidents of border history have been lost or never written because those who condemned them feared the vengeance of the more savage scouts. Life on the border tried men's souls. It gave to some the outlet for a venomous passion for blood. Many deeds were too dark for the printed page. These were held in the memory, related around the cabin-hearth and the hunter's camp-fire with bated breath, and thus became the tradition of the border days. The record is incomplete, and it is now impossible ever to make it complete.

On the other hand, atrocities committed by the Indians were occasionally suppressed. The motive was merciful, that the family of the victim be spared unnecessary anguish.

John Harper was a soldier of the Revolution, and served seven years as a private, Virginia troops. He came to the Northwestern Territory in 1800, and settled on Mill Creek, near Cincinnati. His son, James Harper, was born in Berkley County, Virginia, 1786. He enlisted for the war of 1812, and served on the Northwestern frontier with General Harrison. In company with fourteen other soldiers, he was sent with a dispatch to an outlying post, with strict orders not to fire on Indians, if any were met, unless attacked. While en route a few Indians presented themselves, and were fired upon, when they fled. The soldiers pursued, and fell into an ambuscade. Only a few escaped. Harper, when last seen by his companions, was captured with one or more Indian scalps at his belt. He was carried to some point on the Lakes and burned at the stake. Through commiseration for his parents, the tragedy was never made public.

This story was given me by Mr. John Delaplane of Fort Jefferson, Ohio, an immediate descendant of the Harper family, and is here published for the first time.

CHAPTER III

There is considerable mention of Jesse Hughes in the annals of the early settlement of Northwestern Virginia, particularly in those portions relating to the Indian wars of the period. But taken all together there is not enough to give the reader any accurate idea of Hughes and the important part he played in the settlement of the central regions of the present State of West Virginia. It will, however, aid the reader much when combined with what has been preserved herein and published for the first time. For this reason I have decided to reproduce in this chapter the extended reference to him found in the *History of the Early Settlement and Indian Wars of Western Virginia*, by Dr. Willis DeHass, Wheeling, 1851. Another reason for this quotation is that this work is so very rare that it cannot be consulted by the average reader. It is a work of high order and has been an authority for more than half a century. A few references to Hughes from other sources will be found in this chapter.

JESSE HUGHES

"One of the most active, daring and successful Indian hunters in the mountain region of Virginia, was Jesse Hughes. He has not inappropriately been styled the Wetzel of that portion of the state, and in many respects, certainly was not undeserving of that distinctive appellation. Jesse Hughes possessed in an imminent degree the rare constituents of courage and energy. These qualities, so essential in those days of savage warfare, gained for him the confidence of the sturdy men by whom he was surrounded, and often induced them to select him for the post of leader in their various expeditions against the enemy. Many are the tales of adventure which the people of West Fork and Little Kanawha relate of this notable personage. A few of these we have collected and now give.

"Hughes was a native of the region to which his operations were chiefly confined. He was born on the headwaters of the Monongahela, and grew to manhood amid the dangers and privations which the people of that section of Virginia endured during the long years of a border warfare. Early learning that the rifle and tomahawk were his principal means of maintenance and defense, he became an adept in their use and refused to acknowledge a superior anywhere. Passionately devoted to the wood, he became invaluable to the settlements as hunter and scout. A man of delicate frame, but an iron constitution, he could endure more fatigue than any of his associates, and thus was enabled to remain abroad at all seasons without inconvenience or detriment. Many were the threatened blows which his vigilance averted, and numerous lives of helpless settlers his strong arm reached forth to save. The recollection of his services and devotion is still cherished with a lively feeling of admiration by the people of the region with which his name is so intimately associated.

"The following incidents illustrative of his career, we derive from sources entitled to every credit. The one which immediately follows is from an old and intimate friend of Hughes (Mr. Renick of Ohio), to whom it was communicated by the hero himself, and afterwards confirmed by Mr. Harness, who was one of the expedition. The time of the incident was about 1790.

"No Indian depredations had recently occurred in the vicinity of Clarksburg, and the inhabitants began to congratulate themselves that difficulties were finally at an end.

"'One night a man hearing the fence of a small lot, he had a horse in, fall, jumped up and running out saw an Indian spring on the horse and dash off. The whole settlement was alarmed in an hour or two, a company of twenty-five or thirty men were paraded, ready to start by daylight. They took a circle outside of the settlement, and soon found the trail of apparently eight or ten horses, and they supposed, about that many Indians. The captain (chosen before Hughes joined the company) called a halt, and held a council to determine in what manner to pursue them. The captain and a majority of the company were for following on their trail: Hughes was opposed, and he said he could pilot them to the spot where the Indians would cross the Ohio, by a nearer way than the enemy could go, and if they reached there before the Indians, could intercept them and be sure of success. But the commander insisted on pursuing the trail. Hughes then tried another argument: he pointed out the danger of trailing the Indians: insisted that they would waylay their trail, in order to know if they were pursued, and would choose a situation where they could shoot two or three and set them at defiance; and alarming the others, the Indians would out-travel them and make their escape. The commander found that Hughes was like to get a majority for his plan, in which event he (the captain) would lose the honor of planning the expedition. Hughes, by some, was considered too wild for the command, and it was nothing but jealousy that kept him from it, for in most of the Indian excursions, he got the honor of the best plan, or did the best act that was performed. The commander then broke up the council by calling aloud to the men to follow him and let the cowards go home, and dashed off full speed, the men all following. Hughes knew the captain's remark was intended for him, and felt the insult in the highest degree, but followed on with the rest. They had not gone many miles until the trail ran down a ravine where the ridge on one side was very steep, with a ledge of rock for a considerable distance. On the top of this cliff two Indians lay in ambush, and when the company got opposite they made a noise of some kind, that caused the men to stop: that instant two of the company were shot and mortally wounded. They now found Hughes' prediction fully verified, for they had to ride so far round before they could get up the cliff, that the Indians with ease made their escape.

"'They all now agreed that Hughes' plan was the best, and urged him to pilot them to the river where the Indians would cross. He agreed to do it; but was afraid it might be too late, for the Indians knew that they were pursued and would make a desperate push. After leaving some of the company to take care of the wounded men, they put off for the Ohio river, at the nearest point, and got there the next day shortly after the Indians had crossed. The water was still muddy, and the rafts that they crossed on were floating down the opposite shore. The men were now unanimous for returning home. Hughes soon got satisfaction for the insult the captain had given him: he said he wanted to find out who the cowards were; that if any of them would go, he would cross the river and scalp some of the Indians. They all refused. He then said if one man would go with him, he would undertake it; but none would consent. Hughes then said *he* would go and take one of their scalps, or leave his own.

"'The company now started home, and Hughes went up the river three or four miles, keeping out of sight of it, for he expected the Indians were watching them to see if they would cross. He there made a raft, crossed the river, and encamped for the night. The next day he found their trail, and pursued it very cautiously, and about ten miles from the Ohio found their camp. There was but one Indian in it, the rest were out hunting. The Indian left to keep camp, in order to pass away the time, got to playing the fiddle on some bones that they had for the purpose. Hughes crept up and shot him, took his scalp and made the best of his way home.

"The following characteristic anecdote goes far to illustrate the great discernment and instantaneous arrangement of plans of this shrewd and skillful Virginia hunter.

"It is a general belief that the Indian is exceedingly cunning; unrivalled in the peculiar knowledge of the woods, and capable, by the extraordinary imitative faculties which he possesses, to deceive either man, beast or fowl. This is true to a certain extent; but still, with all his natural sagacity and quick perception of a native woodman, the Indian warrior falls short of the acquired knowledge of a well trained hunter, as the following case serves to illustrate. Jesse Hughes was more than a match at any time for the most wary savage in the forest. In his ability to anticipate all their artifices, he had but few equals, and fewer still, superiors. But, to the incident.

"At a time of great danger from the incursions of the Indians, when the citizens of the neighborhood were in a fort at Clarksburg, Hughes one morning, observed a lad very intently fixing his gun. 'Jim', said he, 'what are you doing that for?' 'I am going to shoot a turkey that I hear gobbling on the hillside,' said Jim. 'I hear no turkey,' said the other. 'Listen,' said Jim: 'there, didn't you hear it? Listen again.' 'Well,' says Hughes, after hearing it repeated, 'I'll go and kill it.' 'No you won't, said the boy, 'it is my turkey; I heard it first.' 'Well,' said Hughes, 'but you know I am the best shot. I'll go and kill it, and give you the turkey.' The lad demurred but at length agreed. Hughes went out of the fort on the side that was farthest from the supposed turkey, and passing along the river, went up a ravine and cautiously creeping through the bushes behind the spot, came in whence the cries issued, and, as he expected, espied a large Indian sitting on a chestnut stump, surrounded by sprouts, gobbling, and watching if any one would come from the fort to kill the turkey. Hughes shot him before the Indian knew of his approach, took off the scalp, and went into the fort, where Jim was waiting for his prize. 'There now,' says Jim, 'you have let the turkey go. I would have killed it if I had gone.' 'No,' says Hughes, 'I didn't let it go;' and, taking out the scalp, threw it down. 'There take your turkey, Jim, I don't want it.' The lad was overcome, and nearly fainted to think of the certain death he had escaped, purely by the keen perception and good management of Jesse Hughes.' (1)

(1) See page 420.

"Jesse Hughes, as we have already stated, was often of invaluable service to the settlements along the upper Monongahela, by advising them of the approach of Indians. On one occasion, a considerable body of the common enemy attacked a fort near Clarksburg, and but for the energy and fearlessness of Hughes might have reduced the frail structure, and massacred every one within it. This daring man boldly went forth for succor, and succeeded in reaching a neighboring station in safety. Immediately a company of men left to relieve the besieged, when the Indians, fearing the superior numbers, retreated in haste. (2)

"Hughes' scouting expeditions were not always confined to the extreme upper regions of the Monongahela. He often visited the stations lower down, and spent much of his time at Prickett's fort, also at the stockade where Morgantown now stands, and many other settlements in the neighborhood. He was a great favorite, and no scouting party could be complete, unless Jesse Hughes had something to do with it. We regret that our limits will not allow us to give more incidents in his very eventful life."

Mr. Luther Haymond, who is still living at Clarksburg, says that William Powers, while on his death-bed, told him that the incident of Hughes and the turkey never occurred at Clarksburg; that he knew the settlement from the beginning, and that the story was a mistake. Powers had an impression that he had heard a similar story as occurring east of the mountains. Mr. Haymond says that Powers was well posted on events happening on the frontier after his arrival.

Mr. James Stanley Gandee, a son of Jesse's daughter Massie, often heard both his mother and his Aunt Rachel Cottrell tell the Hughes turkey story. There never was any doubt about its authenticity. As related by them, the occurrence was substantially the same as recorded by *DeHass*, but the place was West's Fort, instead of Clarksburg. The lad who first heard the turkey and who was preparing to go shoot it, was James Tanner, a brother to Jesse's wife, and was then some fourteen or fifteen years of age.

I was told by Mrs. Mary Straley, of Hacker's Creek, who had known Jesse Hughes and some of his family, that the boy who figured in the turkey story was Jim McCullough. Mrs. Straley seemed to have no doubts regarding the credibility of the story, but did not state where it occurred. She was well informed on the early history of the Hacker's Creek settlement, and was a woman of high integrity.

It must be borne in mind that Jesse Hughes never took up a residence at Clarksburg, although he spent much of his time about the fort there. His scouting expeditions extended all over the Virginia border and western Pennsylvania.

---

(2) See page 421.

That William Powers should have heard a similar story east of the mountains cannot militate against the authenticity of the Hughes' story. Border lore abounds in such incidents. (3)

J. Lewis Peyton (4) gives the following on Jesse Hughes, evidently epitomized from *DeHass:*

> "One of the most active, daring and successful Indian hunters in the mountain region of Virginia was Jesse Hughes—sometimes styled the Wetzel of his portion of the State. He was born on the headwaters of the Monongahela, Va., about 1768, and early became skilled in the use of the rifle and tomahawk. He was a man of iron constitution, and could endure extraordinary privations and fatigue. Many anecdotes are told of his encounters with the red men and of the invaluable services he rendered to the white settlements on the Monongahela. Jesse Hughes was more than a match at any time for the most wary savage in the forest. In his ability to anticipate all their artifices, he had few equals and no superiors. He was a great favorite, and no scouting party could be complete unless Jesse Hughes had something to do with it."

Jesse Hughes is mentioned frequently in *Withers' Chronicles of Border Warfare,* referred to hereinbefore, and which will be duly noticed in the course of this history.

CHAPTER IV

In *Doniphan's Expedition*, by William E. Connelley, there is a biographical sketch of Colonel John Taylor Hughes, a member of the expedition of Colonel Alexander W. Doniphan in the Mexican War. Colonel Hughes became the historian of the expedition. He was a gallant soldier, and was killed at the battle of Independence, Missouri, in the Civil War. Of Colonel Hughes, the biographical sketch says:

"His father was Samuel Swan Hughes, the descendant of Stephen Hughes and his wife Elizabeth Tarlton Hughes. Stephen Hughes came to Maryland from Wales, probably from Carnarvonshire, but possibly from Glamorganshire. The date of his arrival in America has not been preserved. His son Absalom moved to Powhatan County, Virginia, where he intermarried with the daughter of a planter whose name was also Hughes, and whose Christian name was either David or Jesse—most probably Jesse. He lived on Hughes Creek, in that county, and was a man of character and influence; many of his descendants live yet in Virginia and West Virginia, and some of them live in other parts of the United States. Joseph, the son of Absalom Hughes, married Sarah Swan. He moved to Kentucky about the year 1790, and settled in Woodford County. There his son, Samuel Swan Hughes, married Nancy Price, daughter of Colonel William Price, a Virginia soldier of the Revolution."

Jesse Hughes, who lived on the stream then known as Hughes Creek, in Powhatan County, Virginia, was related by blood to Stephen Hughes, and had preceded him from Wales to America. The Hughes and Swan families were pioneer families in Virginia, and in their migrations they kept well together, members of them often intermarrying. And from the intermarriage of Stephen Hughes with his kinswoman, the daughter of Jesse Hughes, in Powhatan County, Virginia, Jesse Hughes, the famous pioneer and woodsman of Western Virginia, was probably descended. (1)

The date of the birth of Jesse Hughes is not known to be of record, and cannot be fixed with accuracy; and the place is also uncertain. *DeHass* and *Peyton* agree as to the place; but *Peyton* alone gives the date. Evidently they are both in error. The citation heretofore made to the work of *Withers* shows that Jesse Hughes was an active hunter in the Buckhannon settlement in 1769. This was the first permanent settlement established on the waters of the upper Monongahela, and we find him there but

---
(1) See page 421.

one year later than the date given by *Peyton* as that of his birth. It is well nigh impossible that he should have been born on the waters of the Monongahela. The Blue Ridge marked the western frontier of Virginia as late as 1763. (2) The few settlements scattered beyond that boundary towards the Ohio, the westernmost of which was on Looney Creek, a tributary of the James, (3) were not permanent, and were almost all destroyed by the conspiracy of Pontiac.

Jesse Hughes was born about the year 1750. It might have been a year earlier or later, though it is not probable that it could vary a year either way from that date. As to the place of his birth, the evidence at hand indicates that it was east of the Allegheny Mountains, perhaps on the waters of the Wappatomaka of the Potomac. Susan Turner Hughes, the widow of George W. Hughes, a descendant of Jesse Hughes, told William E. Connelley, October 6, 1902, at Henry, Grant County, West Virginia, that: "Old Jesse Hughes was born right over here on Jackson's River, close to the Greenbrier county-line. I have passed the place myself, in company with my husband, who pointed out the place, which is in a fine river bottom. He was born in the winter, and the wolves were starving in the woods because of the deep snow. The night he was born they came into the yard and fought the dogs and ran them under the house and fought them there, and were only driven out by burning gunpowder on the hearth." Mrs. Hughes could not give the date of his birth, but said he was "A right smart chunk of a lad at the time of Braddock's battle."

Hughes Coat of Arms

If Mrs. Hughes was right, Jesse Hughes must have been born in Allegheny County, Virginia. Complete reliance cannot, however, be placed upon the information given by her; for some things which she related of Jesse Hughes, while they may be the local traditions of the country, could not be reconciled with known facts. Her description of the man and his cruel and bloodthirsty course towards the Indians coincides perfectly with what is known to be true. She said: "Old Jesse Hughes had eyes like a painter [panther] and could see at night almost as well as one. He could hear the slightest noise made in the forest at a great distance,

---

(2) See page 422. (3) p. 422.

and he was always disturbed by any noise he could not account for. He knew the ways of every animal and bird in the woods, and was familiar with the sounds and cries made by them. Any unusual cry or action of an animal or bird, or any note or sound of alarm made by either, caused him to stop and look about until he knew the cause. He could go through the woods, walking or running, without making any noise, unless the leaves were very dry, and then he made very little. He was as stealthy and noiseless as a painter, and could creep up on a deer without causing it any fright. And he could outrun any Indian that ever prowled the forest. He was as savage as a wolf, and he liked to kill an Indian better than to eat his dinner."

If Jesse Hughes was born on Jackson's River, the shiftings common on the disturbed border must have caused his parents to move to the Wappatomaka settlements, for he came into western Virginia with hunters from that region. Thomas Hughes, who was killed on Hacker's Creek by the Indians in April, 1778, (4) was Jesse's father; but no record or tradition indicating that he had settled on this stream, has ever been found. In 1781 a certificate was granted "Edmund West, assignee to Thomas Hughes, Senr., 400 acres on Sicamore Lick run, a branch of the West Fork [Harrison County] opposite Thomas Heughs [Hughes] Junr's land, to include his settlement made in 1773, with a pre-emption to 1,000 acres adjoining." This is the earliest record that I have found regarding the settling of Thomas Hughes, Sr., on the upper Monongahela waters. With some of the Radcliffs he settled on Elk Creek near Clarksburg, and his family still resided there in the fall of 1793. A family tradition has it that when the Indians ambushed and killed their father, who was then "quite old and bald-headed," Jesse and Elias solemnly pledged themselves "to kill Injuns as long as they lived and could see to kill them." Most terribly was that awful pledge redeemed. It will be seen, however, that both had killed Indians before the tragic death of their father, which event intensified, if possible, their hatred of the Indians, but was not the cause in which this hatred originated. (5)

I have not been able to find any printed record showing that Jesse Hughes was an enrolled Spy or Ranger on the border.

An inquiry to the Bureau of Pensions, Washington, D. C., elicited the reply that "a careful search of the Revolutionary War

---

(4) See page 422. (5) p. 424.

pension rolls fails to show a claim for any Jesse Hughes other than Survivor's File No. 9594." This was the Jesse Hughes, of Fluvanna County, Virginia, mentioned further on in this chapter.

Jesse Hughes, the scout, died prior to the Act of Congress, June 4, 1832, pensioning the soldiers of the Revolution, and if his services were pensionable, his widow, who survived him several years, never applied for same.

An inquiry made to the War Department failed to disclose any record of military enlistment by our Jesse Hughes. This, however, is true of others who were contemporary with Jesse, and who were known to have regularly enlisted in some branch of the military.

To a like inquiry to the Virginia State Library, Richmond, came the responses that, "neither the Muster Rolls of the State troops, nor the claims for Bounty Lands of that period, contain any record of the Jesse Hughes in question."

The Thomas Hughes who accompanied Pringle's Band of settlers to the Buckhannon, in 1769, was Jesse's younger brother, born about 1754. His inordinate passion for sport and adventure lured him to this Eldorado of the hunter. He afterwards settled on the West Fork River, and was the same Thomas Hughes whom we find on Hacker's Creek, and who hastened to the rescue of the Flesher family when they were attacked by the Indians in 1784, near where the town of Weston (6) now stands.

The homestead register of Monongalia County shows that in 1781, Thomas Hughes was granted a certificate for "400 acres on the West Fork, adjoining lands of Elias Hughes, to include his settlement made in 1773." The records of 1780 show that Thomas Hughes assigned to Thomas John (?) his claim to 250 acres on Ten Mile Creek (Harrison County), "to include his settlement made in the year 1772." Whether this assignor was the senior or junior Thomas Hughes, is not known, but the logical inference is that it was the latter. The date of the assignment is not of record.

Although Thomas Hughes, Jr., was one of the most capable and persistent scouts on the Virginia frontier, the only reference that we find to him in history, is his connection with the Flesher occurrence in 1784.

In 1833 or 1834, Hughes applied for a pension, and we have a glimpse of his border life in the meagre record preserved in the

---
(6) See page 424.

Government Pension Office at Washington. Hughes was illiterate and his name always appears with the customary "X." His original application, or declaration with accompanying papers, has been destroyed, but from the fragmentary record we learn that he was a resident on the West Fork of the Monongahela in 1774, and from that year until 1779 he was, every year, actively engaged in scouting from the West Fork to the Ohio River, under Captain William Lowther. His consummate skill in woodcraft, his bravery and caution, soon won for him a subaltern leadership. He was subsequently commissioned a Lieutenant of Indian Spies in Capt. Lowther's Company, a trust he did not resign until the spring of 1784. After this, he continued on ranging excursions to the different forts until the close of the Indian War in 1795. During this service, he was stationed at West's Fort, and at Richards' Fort on the West Fork.

In 1780, Lieutenant Hughes was riding a pathway about midway between the West and Richards' Forts, when he discovered an Indian mounted on a horse, recognized to be that of Adam O'Brien's. (7) The Lieutenant sprang from his horse and fired at the Indian wounding him, when he fled. Hughes was determined if possible to recapture the stolen horse, and in company with Alexander West pursued the Indian, tracking him by the blood. They found the tracks of several Indians, but lost the trail entirely at the West Fork River. It was supposed that the wounded Indian, perhaps dying, had been sunk in the river by his comrades.

In the affidavit of John Cartwright (Cutright), who in 1834 testified for Hughes, it would appear that Hughes was in some regular military expedition against the Indians, from which he returned in 1784. Cutright declares that after this, although he was stationed at the Buckhannon Fort, he and Hughes went spying and ranging together until 1795, and that Lieutenant Hughes lost much property through Indians.

William Powers, Alexander West and Adam Flesher also testified for Hughes in his claim for pension, while John McWhorter, J. P., vouched for the integrity of these witnesses.

W. G. Singleton, Special Pension Agent, who investigated Hughes' claim for pension, reported under date of January 2nd, 1835, "I understand from Hughes' Agent, James M. Camp, that his (Hughes) mind is entirely gone, and from other sources that

---
(7) See page 424.

he is a maniac and has been confined for years. Christopher Nutter, William Powers and others tell me that he did good service, but was in no regular service, so therefore is not entitled to pension." Hughes was refused a pension on the grounds that his service was rendered in the Indian Wars, and not in the War of the Revolution. (8)

The munificence of an appreciative and "grateful country" is pitifully portrayed in its sentiment toward this time-wrecked veteran of twenty years of incessant warfare. As a scout Lieutenant Thomas Hughes was surpassed only by his two renowned brothers. The life of the wilderness spy was arduous, and fraught with constant danger. His wages were meagre (9) and those who were thus employed throughout the long border wars, seldom laid up a sustenance for old age.

Lieutenant Hughes died in October, 1837, in Jackson County, West Virginia, where he moved, perhaps, soon after the treaty of Greenville in 1795. Mrs. Hughes died three months previous to the death of her husband. They left only one child, Thomas, whom it appears was still living in 1854, aged seventy-one years.

There is no family tradition that connects Charles Hughes (10) who was engaged in the repulse of the Indians at West's Fort on Hacker's Creek in 1778, with the family of Jesse Hughes, though they were together in that engagement. It is quite probable that two Hughes families, closely related, were represented in the pioneers who settled on Hacker's Creek, and the name seems to have disappeared from the settlement in that beautiful valley at an early date.

In 1781, a certificate was granted "William McCleery, assignee to James Hughes, for 400 acres on Spring Creek [tributary to the Little Kanawha] to include his settlement made in 1774." I know nothing of the antecedents of this James Hughes.

In an early day one Edward Hughes, then a boy, came with some men from the Greenbrier settlements to the mouth of Morris Creek, since known as Hughes Creek, on the Great Kanawha. I know nothing of this lad's parentage. He seems to have been the only one of the name who came from Greenbrier with the party, who apparently were hunters. They built a small fort on a cliff by the creek, where they could reach the water by letting down a gourd with a grapevine. The boy experienced many hardships. At one time he was left alone for several days at the fort,

(8) See page 424. (9) p. 425. (10) p. 425.

and subsisted on parched corn, and a few fish that he caught in the creek. He was captured by the Indians while fishing on Peters Creek, a tributary of the Gauley River, now in Nicholas County, and was carried to the Indian towns on the Muskingum. He remained with his captors for more than two years, during which time he learned their language. He ascertained that the Great Kanawha joined the Ohio somewhere below where they then were, and determined to escape. He secreted a quantity of dried venison, and waited for a full moon. He then fled to the Ohio River, where he constructed a raft of dry timber, and floated down to the mouth of the Great Kanawha. During the voyage he never approached the shore, but when tired nature demanded a rest, he anchored his raft in mid-stream with a stone attached to a grape-vine.

He abandoned his raft, and following up the Kanawha, and after much suffering reached the little fort on the cliff. When he left the Indians he took with him a coat neatly made from a bear skin. The fore-legs formed the arms, and the neck and head formed the collar and head-covering. It was soft, pliable, and comfortable in the most stormy weather. Edward Hughes married and settled near where Summersville, in Nicholas County, now is. He never used intoxicants, and was devotedly Christian. He was buried on the mountain side, overlooking the site of the little fort in which he had spent so many of his solitary days. (11)

In 1770, a Thomas Hughes, born in 1753, and who married Elizabeth Swan, settled on the west side of the Monongahela, near the mouth of Muddy Creek, (12) now Carmichaels, Green County, Pa.; but he was of another family, though perhaps a blood relation of Jesse's father. Thomas Hughes, of Carmichaels, had a brother John, who was a Captain of the Pennsylvania Rangers during the Revolution. He was killed by the Indians near Louisville, Kentucky, in 1780. This family also hailed from Virginia.

A Thomas Hughes resided in now Kanawha County, West Virginia, in 1791.

A Thomas Hughes was Paymaster of the 7th Virginia Regiment from January 1, 1777, to May 1, 1778. He received a military land bounty in 1783.

It may be of interest to note that the Jesse Hughes of Fluvanna County, Virginia, previously referred to, in the spring of 1776,

(11) See page 425. (12) p. 425.

at the age of twenty, enlisted as a private in Roger Thompson's company of minute men, which was attached to Meredith's Regiment in eastern Virginia, and then to Morgan's riflemen in western Virginia. In the fall of 1776, Hughes enlisted in William Pierce's Company of Harrison's artillery. He fought at Monmouth and Newport, was stationed at Providence, and was discharged in 1779. He volunteered as a lieutenant in Joseph Hayden's Company in 1780 and was at the battle of Camden. In 1781 he was drafted as a lieutenant of militia, but was seized with smallpox and did not join the army until the day after Cornwallis' surrender. He was, no doubt, closely related to the ancestors of Jesse Hughes of pioneer fame, for the locality from which he enlisted is very near the ancestral home of the Hughes family.

The Muster Rolls in the War Department at Washington show that one Jesse Hughes served as a matross in Captain William Pierce's Company, First Artillery Regiment, Continental Troops, commanded by Colonel Charles Harrison. He was enlisted December 31, 1776, for three years, and was discharged December 20, 1779. Neither his residence nor the place of his enlistment is of record. This matross was the Jesse Hughes of Fluvanna County. In 1837, he was allowed a Bounty Land Warrant for three years' service as private in Continental line. The First Continental Artillery Regiment was assigned to the State of Virginia by Act of Congress approved October 3, 1780.

In 1778, a Jesse Hughes, a matross in Col. Charles Harrison's Virginia and Maryland Regiment of Artillery, Company No. I, was returned as "sick in Virginia," along with Sergeant John Hughes of the same company. (13) There were several other Hughes among the Virginia troops, but they have no place in this story.

John Hughes, of Lancaster, Pa., under date of July 11, 1763, wrote to Colonel Bouquet an elaborate and detestable plan for hunting down the Indians with savage dogs, in the true Spanish way. (14) While this man was perhaps no relation to our hero, the two would probably have been in complete accord on the manner of procedure in dealing with the Indian question.

In 1770 or 1771, Jesse Hughes was married to Miss Grace Tanner, and settled on Hacker's Creek, about one mile above where West's Fort was afterwards built, and at the mouth of a

---
(13) See page 425. (14) p. 425.

stream which has since been known as Jesse's Run. Here he built his cabin on the site of an old Shawnee village. This was embraced in a homestead certificate, issued in 1781 to "Jesse Hughes for 400 acres on Hacker's Creek, adjoining lands of Edmund West to include his settlement made in 1770." (15)

In this lonely cabin, standing, as it did, on the western outskirts of the most western (16) and remote settlement on the Virginia frontier, this young couple experienced many thrilling adventures incident to border life in the virgin wilderness. The wife possessed the sterling qualities of rugged and noble womanhood. Endowed with that fearlessness and energy of character which a life of constant peril on the border engendered, she was admirably fitted for the companionship of her half-wild, yet renowned husband, whose savage temper was not conducive to domestic happiness. It was in this cabin that they had a thrilling experience with a rattlesnake.

One night Jesse was awakened from a sound sleep by feeling a living creature trying to work its way upward between his throat and the close-fitting collar of his homespun shirt. The contact of a cold, whip-like body with his own, caused him to suspect instantly the nature of his bed-fellow, and fully aroused him to a sense of his danger. With that rare self-control and presence of mind that served him so well in more than one instance of deadly peril, he softly spoke to his wife, waking, and telling her of the threatened danger, and directing her to get out of bed with their child, and remove the bed-clothing. This she did so gently that the restless intruder, who was still endeavoring to force its broad flat head under the obdurate shirt-collar, was not disturbed. The covering removed, with a single lightning-like movement, Jesse bounded to the floor several feet away. A huge yellow rattlesnake fell at his feet. With an angry whir-r-r-r it threw itself into the attitude of battle, but was soon dispatched. The next morning Jesse went prospecting for snakes, and found in the end of a hollow log which was built into his cabin, five copperheads and one rattlesnake. (17)

From his advent into the Buckhannon settlement in 1769 to the year 1778, we find no mention of the name of Jesse Hughes in border annals.

But it is not to be supposed that so restless and daring a man would remain inactive while such scenes of bloodshed were being

---
(15) See page 425. (16) p. 426. (17) p. 427.

enacted about him. His insatiate passion for Indian blood precludes this idea, and investigation proves the fallacy and adds strength to the statement of Mr. Bond, that the chronicle of *Withers* is but a partial and fragmentary history.

While living on Hacker's Creek, and within rifle-shot of his own door, Jesse consummated a deed, which, for needless and unprovoked treachery, was scarcely surpassed by the Indians in all their ravages of the Virginia border. He arranged a meeting with a friendly Indian for the ostensible purpose of spending a day in hunting. To reach the place of rendezvous the Indian had to cross Hacker's on a "foot-log," a tree felled across the stream to form a means of crossing. The time of meeting was appointed for an hour when the sun should reach a certain point above the tree-tops. Long before that time Jesse stealthily repaired to the spot and concealed himself in a position which commanded an unobstructed view of the foot-log, and there awaited the coming of his unsuspecting victim. At the appointed hour the Indian issued from the deep tangle of the valley forest. An eye gleamed along the barrel of the deadly rifle, the Indian reached the middle of the log, a report of the rifle reverberated through the valley, and the lifeless body of the Indian fell forward into the stream.

Hughes claimed that the Indian approached in a suspicious manner, wary and watchful, and that he felt justified in killing him. It is not at all probable that an Indian brought up amid the dangers of the wilderness, would traverse a forest path other than with every faculty alert to hidden danger. His very training would preclude this and his caution was no evidence that he intended treachery. Had he meditated evil, he would more likely have followed the course pursued by Hughes.

Not only did Hughes engage in Indian killings not chronicled by *Withers*, but he was a leader in the terrible massacre of the Bulltown Indians, an account of which must form a separate chapter of this narrative.

CHAPTER V

At no very remote period prior to the advent of the white man into the Trans-Allegheny region, Hacker's Creek had been the seat of an Indian population of no mean magnitude. Indeed the evidence of a very ancient occupation of this valley by man is not wanting. In the present work it is impossible to enter as deeply into this interesting subject as would be desired, or as personal observation might warrant; but as it is expedient that the reader have some idea of the condition of this valley in its primitive state, brief mention on the most salient points of what is known on the subject will be made here.

About the year 1896, Samuel Alkire, a great-grandson of Jesse Hughes, in the line of his daughter Martha, excavated a well for stock-water on his home farm some three miles below the village of Berlin. The well was dug in a broad, sloping draw, near the base of the hill bordering on the right of the valley. At the depth of twenty feet the workman, Charley Tenny, of Jane Lew, came upon a perfectly sound and well preserved spruce, or pine pole, to which some of the bark still adhered. This pole, about three feet in length, was firmly imbedded in a strata of blue clay, and with it was a quantity of pine cones, twigs and other debris of the forest, which, at some remote period, had been lodged there by the action of water. In removing the pole from its bed the workman, with his mattock, severed it near the middle. Mr. Alkire was present and saw the pole and cones taken out. One fragment was claimed by Mr. Tenny, but the other, together with several of the cones, was carefully preserved by Mr. Alkire, who believed them of scientific value. These he kindly placed at my disposal, and upon examining the timber, was astounded to find that it showed several distinct and well-defined knots where small limbs had been severed with some kind of cutting tool. These protuberances were smoothly trimmed and of uniform ridge-shape, like that produced by severing a limb with sloping cuts from two opposite sides. The end showed similar cuts where it had been dissevered in much the same way. It was impossible without the aid of a glass to determine the character of the incisions; whether made by a flint or a steel implement. Yet, owing to the texture of the wood in a young growth of this kind, time and other potent factors would have a tendency to smooth away and obliterate any slight irregularity or uneven surface left by the edged tool; or they may have been polished away by the ancient artisan; in which case a glass would have proved of little or no value in determining the primary nature of the marks in question. Be this as it may, it is unfortunate that within a few hours after this very interesting relic came into my possession, and before it could be given a crucial examination, it fell into the hands of some thoughtless boys who forever destroyed its archaeological value by whittling away every vestige of the traces left by the cutting implement of the unknown workman. The pole was partly carbonized and hardened; and was flattened to an oval shape, attesting to both age and the enormous pressure to which it had been subjected. When first found it was about the size of the fore-arm, but in drying had shrunk to nearly half its original size.

Owing to the location of this draw, where naturally we should expect a rapid accumulation of drift and soil washed from the hillside by every rain, the depth at which these objects were found would have slight weight in computing their age. But the fact that nowhere in this valley or its tributaries does there grow pine timber of any kind, nor does there exist any evidence that such trees ever did grow there, makes this find important. The mere finding of the limb would in itself signify little, as it might have been transported from other regions in quite recent times; but the discovery of pine cones in quantity, evidently washed there from a forest growing contiguous, is indeed puzzling. It is vain to speculate as to the time required for the passing of one variety of forest trees and the production of an entirely different species in its place, even if such was the case in this instance. Are we to take the discovery of this mysterious relic with its interesting surroundings as proof that in this valley man antedated, by vast ages, the primitive forest with which it was so densely clothed when the white man first set foot in its sylvan beauty? Or shall we accept Mr. Alkire's humorous solution of the riddle — "that some old codger, living here at some time, had planted evergreen shade trees about his domicile, and had trimmed a branch from one of them for a bean-pole, and that the well had been sunk in the old man's bean-patch." This theory would appear as logical and rational as those often advanced by archaeologists in support of their pet hobbies. Let the deduction be as it may, importance is attached to the discovery, and the loss of the relic is greatly deplored. Facts outweigh theory, and quite often what seems of no consequence proves of greatest value to the archaeologist in arriving at truth. But sometimes objects of recent origin are found under circumstances indicating great antiquity.

On Kinchelo Creek, Lewis County, West Virginia, several years ago in sinking a well, a fragment of pine board having wrought-iron nails driven into it was found at a depth of twenty-one feet from the surface. The location of this well was not at the foot of a hill or near any existing water-way, where a rapid burial would be insured by either landslides or the accumulation of flood sediment. How it came there is a mystery. I examined a fragment of this relic, and certainly no one could claim for it a remote origin.

Nearly one hundred years ago, while a well was being sunk at the old Henry McWhorter cabin, then occupied by his son Thomas, on McKinney's Run, (1) two and one-half miles from Jane Lew, at a depth of six feet below the surface was found a six- or eight-pound solid-shot cannon ball. It is scarcely necessary to comment on the probale age or history of this find, further than to say that there was no military post in that region, and the early settlers possessed no artillery of any kind. The fact that the relic was found within one-half mile of the old Indian village site on the Davis farm would suggest that it had been carried there by Indians from some distant post prior to the settlement of the country. It is not known what became of the ball; it disappeared several years ago.

Scattered through the valley of Hacker's Creek and its tributaries are to be met evidences of former Indian occupation. On every hill and in every glen are found those mysteriously pitted "cup-stones" that have been given so much notice by archaeologists. In addition to the isolated graves and numerous ancient camps, the valley is dotted over with sites of old abandoned villages, with their contiguous burial grounds. Because of their superior location and the absence of timber, these village grounds, or "Indian fields," were favorite places for homes with the first settlers. In the main valley of Hacker's Creek there are no less than seven Indian village sites; and there is one on McKinney's Run, and one on Jesse's Run. That on Jesse's Run is not of very

---
(1) See page 427.

great extent. The one on McKinney's Run is quite large and occupies a "flat" or second bottom. This old site is on the farm of Rev. Samuel Davis and in connection with it there is quite an extensive Indian burial ground. To secure this city of the dead from vandalism, Mr. Davis has planted a cherry tree on each separate grave.

Numerous stone relics have been picked up on this field. In an early day, Samuel Stalnaker discovered the skeleton of an Indian in the crevice of a small ledge of rock on the border of this field, and near a drain which flows between the Davis and the old McWhorter farms. The bones were never disturbed, and the spot has long since grown over with grass and obliterated. On a high point, or ridge, on the last named farm, two or three graves were found. One of them examined by my father, contained two skeletons, that of a very large man, and a girl about twelve years of age. Both were in sitting posture. The man's jaw had, several years previous to his death, been broken, but was neatly healed. No relics were found, and the remains were replaced, and the graves filled.

West's Fort, now the present site of the residence of Minor C. Hall, was once an Indian village. On a beautiful elevation, or second bottom, at the mouth of Jesse's Run, was an extensive village, and perhaps the very last in the valley that was occupied by the Indians. It was here, in a little dell which ran through this village ground, that Jesse Hughes built his cabin.

Another Indian village was located on a promontory-like flat, which extends out into the valley, on the farm of the late John Alkire. Here settled Samuel Bonnett, brother to John Bonnett who was killed on the Little Kanawha, hereafter noted. His old hewn-log house is still standing, though it is rapidly crumbling to decay. Just up the valley, on the opposite side of the creek, on a fine elevated bottom was another village of considerable proportions. Here can still be seen the remains of one of those mysterious earth-wall enclosures met with in the Ohio Valley. This earthwork, in former years, was reverently preserved by the then owner of the land, Mr. David Smith, who has been referred to elsewhere in this volume. When he transferred the title to other parties, with commendable sentiment he stipulated that this pre-historic work should never be desecrated or disturbed. But in time the estate fell into the hands of those whose sole incentive was money, and as this ancient monument stood in the way of crops, it was sacrificed. Its encircling moat was filled with logs and its walls leveled by the plow. It was the most portentious aboriginal remains in the valley.

Near here stood "Miller's Fort," a strongly constructed dwelling, built near the close of Indian hostilities, and which never figured in the defense of the border. With no place in the annals, the structure lives in tradition only.

On an elevation south or southeast of where the village with its mysterious monument stood, is an Indian burial ground of considerable magnitude. In one of the graves opened there in 1890, was found a small fragment of bright blue home-spun woolen cloth, which had been interred with the dead body of the Indian. This points to the occupation of the valley within historic times, and a comparatively recent burial. Unfortunately, this cloth was lost. Another grave yielded a fine stone bird-head pipe, and a polished slate gorget; and another, a well-made celt, slightly damaged on the poll. In a grave which I opened and where "bundle burial" had been resorted to, there was found a clay pipe and a broken clay vessel with the usual rounded bottom, which contained the fragment of a turtle, or tortoise shell, brittle from decay, and evidently the remains of a food-offering to the dead. Both pipes are of ancient type.

Next comes the Indian village ground where John Hacker, the first settler on the creek, built his cabin. (2) It is the most

SITE OF JOHN HACKER'S RESIDENCE
Photographed 1910

Old well and foundation of chimney. (Modern barn in background.)

(2) See page 427.

beautiful section of the valley, and about one mile, or over, below the present village of Berlin.

Many interesting relics have been picked up in the "Indian fields" on the old Hacker farm. When a boy, I often rode horseback to a corn mill near this place, and soon learned to watch for "flints" along the clay banks of the road. The fragment of an engraved sandstone tablet, a fine "chungky" stone, and a small copper pendant were, among other things, in the hands of nearby farmers, who refused to part with them. Grooved stone relics were seldom met with in any part of the valley.

Marked traces of an aboriginal occupation are found on the high creek bottom, on the old Cozad farm, now occupied by Mr. George Lawson. Not only stone implements, but iron or steel tomahawks have been found there. This farm was made historic by an Indian raid in 1794. (3)

Several miles up the creek, just below the mouth of Rover's Run, (4) and where Mr. William Kelly now resides, was another Indian village. On a high ridge above this village, and contiguous to the valley, was a stone-heap, perhaps three by eight feet, eighteen inches high, and enclosed with a curbing of rude slabs of sandstone planted on edge. With Mr. T. A. Law, I examined this interesting stone-heap, and found a small bed of ashes one foot below the original surface, and near the center of the enclosure. In the ash-bed was a flint spear-head, which showed traces of the heat to which it had been subjected. Over the ash-bed was a sandstone slab about twelve inches square and one inch thick, which had been broken into fragments by the fire.

Two other curbed stone-heaps were examined, apparently of the same age and of about the same dimensions as the first described. One of these was on the ridge dividing Jesse's Run from Hacker's Creek, on the farm of George Goodwin, and contained nothing. The other was at Berlin, on the farm of Mr. E. H. Bonnett, on the "flat" just above the old Hebron Church. This one was carefully opened by Professor G. F. Queen, and yielded nothing save a few flint chips and some charcoal. Most of the stone of this mound had previously been removed and used in repairing the public road. At no other place in America have similar remains been found, and it is lamentable that they have not been preserved.

Far up the mountain on the left-hand side of Rover's Run,

---
(3) See page 427. (4) p. 427.

and adjacent to Bear Knob, several years prior to these investigations, I examined an interesting effigy-like figure of Indian origin. It consisted of a single boulder, weighing perhaps three hundred pounds, lying on the surface, with a short row of small stones extending not unlike the arms of a rude cross from about the middle on either side. The stones were removed and an excavation of six feet failed to reveal any sign that the earth had ever been disturbed. (5)

A few miles up the creek from where stood the village last mentioned, and on the farm of my maternal grandfather, the late John W. Marple, is the trace of an Indian habitation of extraordinary import. It occupies a second bottom on the right-hand side of the valley, at the mouth of a small run which flows down from the hills and enters the creek on the south. On the west looms Bear Knob seven hundred and fifty feet above this old village ground. Here can still be seen the outlines of a great ash-circle. It is perfect in contour, save on the northeast side, where gently sloping ground has caused the ashes to work down the incline and thus broaden the circle slightly. Where normal, it is one hundred and eighty feet in diameter. A belt of dark ashes sixty feet wide, encircles a clear inner space sixty feet in diameter. This circle was thickly strewn with fragments of bone, mussel shell, flint chips, scraps of pottery, perfect and broken arrow points and stone relics. I saw this field plowed during the '80s, at which time the measurements were made. The arrow points then secured were mostly of rude workmanship. The fragment of a "chunkey" stone was picked up; but not of the least historic import was the finding of a clay pipe stem, of Caucasian origin.

The field on which this ash-circle is located was cleared about the year 1821, by Mr. John Warner and a companion. It was then covered with a growth of young sugar-trees measuring some twelve inches in diameter; which would denote that the occupancy by the Indians had been comparatively recent. There were but two large trees on it, one a yellow poplar and the other a black walnut; each measuring five feet "across the stump." One stood in the north part of the field and the other in the south part. Both were outside of the circle. Mr. Warner informed me that when they cleared this "Indian Field," he could have picked up a bushel of broken arrow points, which were sometimes used as gun flints,

---
(5) See page 428.

and that the ground was literally covered with fragments of bone and mussel shell. Also that there were numerous remnants of stone implements, but not many in perfect condition. Pieces of pottery were abundant. Many years afterwards, among other things, he found in an adjoining field a finely carved stone pipe, slightly broken. The material was hard, compact, brown sandstone highly polished. It is not known what became of this pipe. Some forty years later a perfect steatite "banner stone," perforated, was plowed up near the same place.

Stone filled graves are found along the rocky base of the hill west of the "Indian Field," and near where these last relics were found. North of these graves, a small mound was located in the first bottom. This mound I opened in 1880; and a flint spear head, a broken arrow point, a small piece of steatite paint-stone and a single bit of charcoal was all that was obtained. These, with the "banner stone" and hundreds of other interesting relics were collected from the village sites and burial grounds of the Hacker's Creek Valley and various parts of the State. (6)

There is said to be an ash-circle similar to the one described, on Rooting Creek, a branch of Elk Creek, (7) only a few miles north. These circles are unusual in American, or Old World antiquities. Locally, they are associated with past strange religious rites and occult practices. (8)

ANCIENT STONE PIPE

Found in a ploughed field near Willow Grove, Jackson County, West Virginia. In the McWhorter Collection, Museum of Archives and History, Charleston, W. Va. See The West Virginia Historical Magazine, 1901, Vol. I, No. 4.

---

(6) See page 428. (7) p. 428. (8) p. 428.

CHAPTER VI

The tradition that Tecumseh was born on Hacker's Creek, so briefly alluded to in a note supplied by me for the late edition of *Chronicles of Border Warfare*, is as follows:

Sometime after the Treaty of Greenville, so the story goes, Tecumseh was in the settlements of the Upper Monongahela and visited Hacker's Creek. While there, in a conversation with a Miss Mitchel, Tecumseh declared that he was born on this creek; either at the village where Jesse Hughes afterwards settled, or at the one where John Hacker, the pioneer, located. He was also authority for the statement that the Indian name for Hacker's Creek signified "muddy water." In Shawnee *wiya-kakami* is muddy water, as applied to a lake or pond; while *wiya-nipe* designates flowing muddy water, or river; and if Tecumseh was rightly reported, his tribe called this romantic stream *Wiya-nipe*. The same cognomen applies to the West Fork of the Monongahela, of which Hacker's Creek is an important tributary. Doubtless, the name, primarily, applied to the larger stream and extended to the smaller with some differentiating term.

Tecumseh was born about the year 1768, just one year preceding the Pringle colonization of the Upper Monongahela. The village at the mouth of Jesse's Run was occupied by Indians within historic times, as attested by the fact that brass buttons of an old style, and other objects of European manufacture, have been found intermixed with various Indian relics. After heavy rains large quantities of lead bullets have been picked up on a clay bank near where stood the cabin of Jesse Hughes. Tradition says that when the Indians wanted to clean their rifles they discharged them against this bank, or at marks placed there. The early settlers resorted thither for their lead. There is also a tradition that there resided near West's Fort, a hermit-like hunter who knew of a lead mine on a small stream that enters Hacker's Creek from the south, in what is now the Alkire settlement above the mouth of Jesse's Run. This grizzled nimrod obtained all the lead he required from this "mine," but he would never divulge its location to his fellow-countrymen. Dressed in buckskins and the traditional moccasins, his step was light and trackless. Cunning as a fox, he was often traced to the high ridge south of the creek, where he would disappear. Later he would return with a supply of lead. (1) Traditions of lead mines were current in nearly every Virginia settlement. In all probability the mysterious hunter obtained his lead from some such source as the claybank deposit, and was loth to share his failing store with his neighbors.

It is known that the Ohio Indians frequented this region as hunters after the white settlers came, and it is not improbable

TECUMSEH—THE GREATEST OF SHAWNEES

From a pencil sketch made about 1812. There is no true portrait of Chief Tecumseh in existence. Courtesy of the Smithsonian Institution.

that Tecumseh was born here while his people were on one of those excursions. *Drake* says that Tecumseh was born on the Scioto River, near where is now Chillicothe. (2) Other authorities state that he was born on Mad River, a few miles north of Old Chillicothe, claiming that his parents and relatives were on a hunting expedition at the time, and were encamped on Mad River. *Col. Hatch* contends that Tecumseh was born near the mouth of Clearwater, on the upper point of its junction with the Great Miami River. (3)

The Chillicothe, "Chi-la-ka-tha" one of the four divisions of the Shawnee tribe, (4) always occupied a village of the same name.

(1) See page 429. (2) p. 430. (3) p. 430. (4) p. 430.

As the Shawnees retreated westward before the whites, several villages of this name were successfully occupied. (5) To designate Tecumseh's birthplace as "Old Chillicothe" is misleading. There was an Old Chillicothe in each of the following counties in Ohio: — Ross, Pickaway, Clark, Green and Miami.

Old Chillicothe in Ross County, was the capitol of the Shawnees at the time of Tecumseh's birth, and it was evidently the home of his family. Such being the case, historians would suppose that he was born there; and in the absence of definite information, give that town the honor of his birthplace, though he may have been born at some distant and transient hunting camp. The Indians were, then, as they are now, accompanied by their women even when going to remote localities to hunt.

At the two villages on Hacker's Creek mentioned by Tecumseh, there have been found the stone cist graves believed to be of Shawnee origin. Such graves are located in the midst of, or contiguous to these village sites, while those constituting the burial grounds on the hillsides and the ridges, are the common stone-filled graves of a different tribe. The summit of Buck Knob (6) which overlooked the villages on McKinney's Run and at the mouth of Jesse's Run, is such a burial ground. Without entering into a discussion as to the probability of which of these tribes were the last to abandon a continuous occupancy of the valley, or whether they were contemporaneous, summing up the facts, I regard this claim of Hacker's Creek to the honor of being the birthplace of Tecumseh, supported as it is by his own statement, worthy of consideration and probably correct. Let Virginia then add to the long list of her warriors, patriots and statesmen, the name of Tecumseh; really Tikamthi, or Tecumtha, the "meteor" or "shooting-star;" the "crouching panther," "I cross the path, or way." Even if born at Old Chillicothe or on Mad River, Tecumseh was still a Virginian; for all that part of the territory Northwest of the Ohio River belonged to Virginia until after the Revolution.

There was a tradition on Hacker's Creek which declared that Tecumseh in one of his incursions into the valley, lost his pipe — usually an adjunct to the Indian Warrior's equipment — and with it much of his prestige as a war chief. He and his followers spent many moons in a fruitless search for the missing talisman. I remember that more than thirty years ago there was found on

---
(5) See page 430. (6) p. 432.

Jesse's Run a stone pipe of "strange and peculiar workmanship." This revived the old story of Tecumseh and his missing pipe; and many supposed that the pipe found was the one lost by this renowned chief. It is not known what became of the pipe.

A HACKER'S CREEK PAWPAW THICKET
Photographed September, 1914, by Master Joe Reger McWhorter.
(*Fruit of the Gods.*)

Primitive Wiya-nipe must have been a veritable paradise for the red man. Beyond doubt it is today the garden spot of central West Virginia. It has a milder winter climate than the Buckhannon region and the high mountain sections of the State. The soil from the creek bed to the summit of the surrounding hills is generally fertile and productive. The first settlers found the valley clothed with a heavy growth of timber. Here the nut-producing varieties: — the chestnut, shell-bark hickory, black and white walnut, the beech and white oak, grew to perfection on both bottom and hillside. The fruit was of superior size and quality. The hazel nut grew in abundance, while the uplands were covered with the persimmon; the service, or june-berry; the black and red haw, the mulberry and wild cherry. Plums of a most excellent flavor flourished along the banks of every stream and favored localities of the higher altitudes. Crabapples were also plentiful. The less fertile portions of the ridges were covered with the shrubs of the wild gooseberry and the huckleberry, beneath which was often found patches of the aromatic wintergreen. On every variety of soil of the uplands grew mountain grapes of varied size and flavor; while the low marsh and swamp lands were canopied with a matted tangle of the fox grape, large and luscious. A small winter grape, rather acrid and less palatable, was also found on the lowlands. The pawpaw, the fruit of the gods, attained to perfection and superabundance in this valley of valleys. Blackberries, raspberries and elderberries flourished in open and fertile ground, usually among the fallen timber. Occasionally wild strawberries were met with on the high ridges and points where the timber was scattering; but they were not plentiful. The sugar tree, whose sweet-producing qualities were so universally made use of by the Indian, stood dark and thick over most of the bottom land and the rich north coves. Sassafras, and spice, the root-bark of the one and the twig of the other, used in preparing food drinks were plentiful. Medicinal barks and herbs were multitudinous. A fragrant variety of plant used in the preparation of kinnikinick, or Indian smoking tobacco, was in abundance. Its leaves, when brewed, produce a drink scarce inferior to the best of imported teas.

The forest teemed with all the game native to the Ohio Valley, while the waters swarmed with excellent fish, turtles, frogs and mussels. The following incident will illustrate the profusion of the finny tribe in this stream at the time of the settlement of the valley.

One evening Henry McWhorter, the pioneer millwright of West's Fort, and his two oldest boys, prepared faggots or torches from slivers of dry wood and went "fish-gigging." Walter, a small lad, having no gig, did not go with them. After they had gone, from a board he fashioned a rude paddle — a poor substitute for a gig — and taking a torch went into the ripple below the mill dam. He said afterwards that had the fish been stones he could have walked across the creek on them, so plentiful and of such good size were they. He soon secured all the fish that he could carry — more than was caught by his father and brothers.

Even at a much later date this creek afforded superior fishing grounds. Walter, when grown, and his son, my father, then a lad, went gigging below the bridge at Jane Lew. Walter was an expert at spearing fish and prided himself as such. He saw what he supposed was a "chunk" of water-soaked wood lying in the ripple and lightly set his gig on it as he was passing by. What was his surprise and chagrin, when with a splash the supposed "chunk" flashed from under the spear and was off like a shot for deep water. The fisherman could never get over the loss of that fish, which he estimated to be not less than four feet in length.

Buffalo, elk, deer, bear and innumerable small game abounded throughout this region. One old hunter whom I remember seeing, declared that in traversing less than one mile of the dividing ridge between Bridge Run and the left-hand fork of Buckhannon Run, starting at the head of the latter stream, he secured five deer. Many are the tales of hunting adventures that have been handed down from the early settlers of this valley, and a few of them are here given.

Alexander West shot an elk on Hacker's Creek, but the shot did not prove fatal, and the elk made off. West followed, finding that the animal often lay down. His better plan would have been to let it lie, but he expected to find it dead. It continued to get up and travel, however, and West followed it to the present site of West Milford, on the West Fork River, where he killed it. He dressed the meat and hung it on trees out of the reach of wolves, and returned home. The next day he went with a pack horse and brought it in.

West was "coon hunting" on the right-hand fork of McKinney's Run, when his dogs engaged a bear down in a very deep hollow. West soon heard his favorite dog howling with pain, and like the true hunter he started at once to the rescue. With drawn knife he plunged into the depths of the narrow gorge, the sides of which reverberated with the fierce snarls and deep growls of the savage combatants. It was very dark, and West could distinguish nothing but a white spot on one of his dogs. He fearlessly approached the struggling mass and felt for the shaggy coat of the bear. Feeling along its side he located the fatal spot over the heart, and buried the long blade of his hunting-knife between its ribs, which ended the fray.

Bears frequently made forays upon the herds of swine belonging to the settlers. Knowing the fighting qualities of the full-grown boar, the pioneer always had one at the head of his herd. These long tusked savage brutes seldom came out of a battle with a bear with any serious injury. One night West heard a commotion among his hogs and went out to investigate. He found that a two-year-old bear had attacked the pigs, and in turn had been set upon and killed by the old boar. The pigs were unhurt. Hogs were turned loose in the woods and were semi-wild, ofttimes entirely so and were very dangerous. When in defense of young broods, or molested when in bands, they would not hesitate to attack man; and frequently hunters and ginsengers experienced thrilling adventures with them.

West was a great hunter and often led the settlers in the annual hunts for the purpose of securing their winter's meat. On one of these occasions a company of several men went into the Mountains of Randolph County. The party pitched camp, and early in the hunt killed two fine elk. That night the "marrow-bones" were cut out and roasted for supper. After the repast and while sitting around the camp fire, one of the men in a spirit of hilarity, pulled a large tick from one of the dogs and wrapping it in a "wad" of tobacco, handed it to a companion, a large athletic fellow, "ter chaw." The unsuspecting victim did "chaw," but soon found that the "quid" contained something not altogether "terbacker." Upon learning the nature of the rude joke that had been played on him, he seized one of the heavy marrow-bones and would have brained the thoughtless joker, had not West interfered and prevented the fight.

Alexander West related an occurrence near his father's house on Hacker's Creek. Some boys one Sunday, stealing out an old musket, went in quest of adventure. In a nearby cornfield they shot and killed a bear. This bear was dressed and as usual, the meat divided among the settlers. Soon there was a savory "bear-pork" simmering over the glowing fires in the great open chimneys of more than one cabin home. The dogs gnawing at the offal, shook from the maw the mangled fingers of a human hand. Notice of the ghastly find was at once given out, and the partly cooked meat thrown away. A search was instituted, and in another part of the field was found the half-eaten body of a man. All around was the evidence of a fearful conflict. Most of the corn on an acre of ground had been trampled down in a terrific life-and-death struggle. The victim was an eccentric fellow, of powerful build and strength, who often spent days and nights in the woods. On this occasion he had been absent several days but nothing was thought of it.

Of buffalo on Hacker's Creek, there is but one mention by

the early chroniclers. *Withers*, (7) in speaking of the first settlers on the Buckhannon River, and the stream in question, says:

"At the close of the working season of 1769 some of these adventurers, went to their families on the South Branch; and when they returned to gather their crops in the fall, found them entirely destroyed. In their absence the buffaloes, no longer awed by the presence of man, had trespassed on their enclosures, and eaten their corn to the ground—this delayed the removal of their families 'till the winter of 1770."

It has been noted in the preceding chapter that John Hacker, the first settler on the creek bearing his name, was one whose crop was destroyed. This occurred during his absence on the Wappatomaka for his family, and is history; but the sequel is tradition. There are few now living who have ever heard of Hacker's long pursuit of the destroyers of his sole means of bread; but the landmarks of that chase will remain indefinitely. I am indebted to Mr. John Strange Hall, of Walkersville, West Va., for the following account of the hunt, as given him in manuscript by Mr. Jackson Arnold, who got it direct from Hacker's children.

"As soon as Hacker had installed his family in their new home, with the usual equipment of a hunter he took up the trail of the buffaloes. It was a small herd, two full grown and a young calf. Buffalo and elk were not numerous on the upper waters of the Monongahela, and were never found in large droves. They, however, gave names to numerous licks and streams. (8)

"The band which Hacker followed, was moving leisurely south for the winter, and ranging up and down the streams. It consumed time to find the various crossings; hence the short marches and many camps made by the huntsman. All the waters crossed, or followed by trail, with the licks and camps were so accurately described that subsequent hunters easily recognized them. Hacker's first camp was at the mouth of (now) Curtis Run, a branch of Little Skin Creek, where he dined on a turkey. The second was 'Crane Camp,' on a tributary of the West Fork. Here in addition to the deer killed at a lick where the buffalo had halted, Hacker shot a crane; hence the name of camp and stream.

"The trail followed the right-hand branch of the river to its source, and Hacker was, so far as known, the first white man to look upon the upper waters of the Little Kanawha, known at its mouth as the first great tributary of the Ohio below Fort Pitt. In the glades above the falls of the creek, he met with more abun-

---

(7) See page 433. (8) p. 433.

dant and fresher signs of buffalo. In addition to the grass, the crab apples and thorn berries attracted the game.

"The third camp was noted for its durability. A rain storm coming up, the hunter sought shelter in a dry and comfortable cave in a cliff, where he again regaled himself on a fine turkey killed on the river bottom. This cave, or rock-shelter, has since been known as Hacker's Camp, and was subsequently occupied by hunters and ginseng diggers. The stream is known as Hacker's Branch.

"The fourth camp was at Buffalo Lick, where Hacker shot and crippled a buffalo cow. She had just come up from the lick where the others were, and all fled over a well-beaten path toward a gap in the mountain. The trail was followed but a short distance, when evening coming on, the hunter returned to the lick. It was at the source of a ravine, circular in form, rock bottom and about two rods in diameter. Several small springs issued from the bluffs, differing in taste, but none of them palatable. Here the sign of buffalo, elk and deer surpassed all that Hacker had ever seen. The brackish, or saline properties of the water allured the animals from a great distance.

"Buffalo Fork, an affluent of the Back Fork, or Right Fork of Little Kanawha, and Buffalo Lick are names given by Hacker. Following the trail through the gap, a scene of rugged grandeur opened to the hunter's view. A boisterous stream rushed through the deeply wooded canyon. From the trend of the mountains, he rightly conjectured that it did not belong to the system on which he had been traveling, which proved to be the Little Kanawha. He had dropped onto the waters of Elk, a tributary of the Great Kanawha.

"A few miles up the stream, the mountains receded, enclosing a beautiful valley. Here Hacker secured the cow previously wounded. She was standing in a clump of bushes near a lick. The sound of the rifle startled the others, now joined by another herd, and all fled towards the great Buffalo Lick at the forks of Elk River, which is now a noted health resort, the Webster Salt Sulphur Springs. The arduous chase was ended. The grim hunter's wrath was appeased and he prepared to return with the spoils. The robe was removed and a small amount of choice parts selected and cured by the fire to carry home as jerk.

"Hacker made a 'tomahawk-entry' at the lick where the

cow was killed, embracing the bottom land. For years it was known as Hacker's Lick, but in time the lick lost its value and now the locality with its village bears the name of Hacker's Valley. This is a branch of the Holly River, so named by Hacker from the groves of this evergreen which adorned its banks.

"The return trip was by short stages, the camps being at the mouth of Buffalo Fork, Crane Camp, and Little Skin Creek, at each of which Hacker made a 'tomahawk-entry.' The latter was the only one to which he secured a title. Here, early in the last century his son Jonathan became the first settler of Skin Creek. After several years he sold the place to Rev. John Hardman, and moved to Crane Camp. He soon learned that he had no title to the land, it being covered by a large patent. The abandoned cabin in the wilderness became the abode of spooks."

It is noteworthy that Mr. Hall places the removal of Hacker's family to their new home in the autumn of 1769. From all evidence this is correct, but it is very probable that they subsequently returned to the Wappatomaka, and that their permanent removal to Hacker's Creek was not until the following fall, or even later.

Hacker reported the existence of the artificial earth mounds at the mouth of Buffalo, where the village of Cleveland now stands in Webster County. There were ten or twelve of these, the largest in quite recent years measured about five feet in height and some twenty feet in diameter. He attributed them to Indian origin, which is doubtless correct. This pursuit of the buffalo stands unique, and has no rival in geographical discovery made in a single chase for game on the western waters. The incentive was revenge.

A pathetic story illustrative of the hardships incident to a life on the border has been handed down by the older settlers of this region. A few years after his settlement on Hacker's Creek, John Hacker returned to the Wappatomaka for salt and other necessary articles, and upon his departure for home his friends prepared provisions for his return journey. He saved some biscuits from his food and upon his arrival home gave one to his little boy, William, who was then about five years old. The child examined it closely and then began rolling it over the rough puncheon floor of the cabin. The little fellow had never seen bread other than that made from the coarse meal of Indian corn crushed in the rude mortar, and he imagined that in the strange object he possessed a new toy. It is said that Hacker wept over the incident.

Hacker, in one of his trips across the mountains for salt, was caught in a bitter storm on the bleak and cold Alleghenies. He made camp for the night, but from some cause was unable to kindle a fire with his flint and steel. His case was most desperate, and realizing the danger in which he stood, he had recourse to a most ingenious method of keeping warm. Standing his two pack horses side by side, he lashed them securely together. Then wrapping his blankets about him and stretching himself upon their backs, he spent the night in warmth and comfort.

The inadequacy of the flint and steel as a fire-producer undoubtedly resulted in more than one tragedy in the early settlement of the country. Hacker was fortunate in possessing means by which to avert death by freezing. Not all were so fortunate, as is shown by the following occurrence in the same range of mountains nearly one hundred years later. It also evidences with what astonishing tenacity the simple, contented hunter folk of this vast mountain region held to the primitive customs of their forefathers. The incident was told me in a hunter's cabin on the Greenbrier River in Pocahontas County in 1877, near the scene of the tragedy, which happened only a short time before.

A hunter had guided a party across the mountains. Winter was at hand. There was the appearance of snow, and a snowstorm in those mountains is accompanied with a humid cold that penetrates to the marrow and kills, unless fire can be had at once. The hardy guide, against the protests of friends, started on foot alone to return by the unfrequented trail through that wilderness. A terrible and blinding snowstorm swept the mountains, followed by the most intense cold. The poor guide became bewildered, wandered from the path, and was soon lost in the vast, desolate forest. His only means of producing fire was the flint and steel. These failed, and after hours, no one will ever know how long, he sat down at the root of a tree with his rifle resting between his knees and his arms folded across his breast. In this position a rescuing party, one of whom was Robert Carr, who told the story, several days later found him with bowed head, in frozen slumber. The poor fellow's knuckles on both hands were badly cut by the flint in his unavailing attempt to strike fire.

CHAPTER VII

The Stroud family, living on Gauley River a few miles south of Bull Town, was murdered by a band of Shawnees from Ohio, in June, 1772. (1) Bull Town was an Indian village at a salt spring on the Little Kanawha, about a mile and a quarter below the present Bull Town postoffice in Braxton County, West Virginia. It was a Delaware (2) settlement, consisting of five families, colonized from the Unadilla River, New York, about 1768, by Captain Bull, a Delaware chief, the chief man and ruler of the village. These Indians "were in habits of social and friendly intercourse with the whites on Buckhannon and on Hacker's Creek; frequently hunting and visiting with them." (3) Adam Stroud was absent from home at the time of the murder of his family. The Shawnees drove off his cattle, taking a trail that led in the direction of the Delaware settlement, though there never was any evidence that the Shawnees went to Captain Bull's village. The trail leading towards the village was discovered by the white settlers, which was eagerly taken as proof that the Delawares were guilty of the murder. William White, William Hacker, John Cutright, Jesse Hughes, (4) and one other whose name is now forgotten, five of the most desperate men in the Buckhannon and Hacker's Creek settlements, set out for the Delaware village to avenge the death of the Strouds. (5) There are no known circumstances that justified the acts of the settlers at Bull Town, and there is every proof at hand to show that it was murder committed in treachery and cold blood. The fact that the trail of the Stroud murderers "led in the direction of Bull Town" cannot be taken as evidence of the guilt of the hapless Delawares. If they were the perpetrators of the crime, what became of the Stroud cattle? So far as history or tradition tells, the cattle were never found. If the destroyers of the friendly Delawares "found clothing and other things known to have belonged to the Stroud family," (6) in their possession, why did they not bring some of those articles to view in the "remonstrating settlement" in vindication of their honor, and to convince the people that just retribution at their hands had fallen upon the guilty parties?

Men capable of such crimes on the border were clever in

(1) See page 433. (2) p. 433. (3) p. 435. (4) p. 435. (5) p. 435. (6) p. 436.

framing excuses to justify their actions. Their unsupported statement that such articles were found at Bull Town, in the absence of the articles, which should have been brought to the settlements and exhibited, cannot be accepted. And if such articles had been found and carried to the settlements, and there exposed to public view, the circumstances would have fallen far short of proving the guilt of the Delawares. They might have been obtained by barter or by gift. Or the Shawnees might have desired to cast suspicion on the friendly Delawares, and this supposition may account for their taking a trail in the direction of their village. This would enable them to escape suspicion and make their escape, leaving the Delawares to bear the consequences of a crime of which they were innocent and ignorant. Friendly Indians were always in more or less disrepute with both the settlers and their own people. The slaughter of the unfortunate Moravian Indians at Gnadenhutten ten years later is a case in point.

Just how the village of Bull Town became such an easy prey to the fury of the bordermen is not known. Circumstances connected with the outrage strengthens the belief that they, like their unfortunate relatives at Gnadenhutten, were the victims of craven treachery. Notwithstanding the supposition that there had been some fighting between these men and the Indians, it is now known that there was no fight. Christopher T. Cutright, commonly known as Uncle Stuffle Cutright, a son of John Cutright, one of the men of the expedition, gave me personally an account of the tragedy and its awful sequel at Indian Camp. He told the story as revealed to him by his father. It conforms strongly with the traditional account given by the Hacker family. (7) While not going into the minute details of the massacre, it was stated explicitly, as a fact, that there had been no fight, and that the Indians, one and all, were put to death, their bodies thrown into the river, and their homes desolated.

It has been conceded by historians that Captain Bull was killed in the general destruction of his people. But such was not the case; if the word of John Cutright, previously quoted, and one of the principals in the massacre, is to be regarded as reliable. To his positive testimony a verifying traditional account is still current among the old settlers of that region.

Mr. Cutright's statement was, that sometime prior to the massacre, death entered the lowly hut of Captain Bull and

---
(7) See page 436.

robbed him of his little child. The body was tenderly buried somewhere in the deep shades of the primeval forest. The parental affection in the Indian bosom is strong, and the grief of the stricken parents was most poignant. From their white neighbors came no show of respect, no condolence or expression of sympathy. So keenly was felt this heartless indifference, that Captain Bull despaired of ever living in harmony and social friendship with the usurpers of his country, and in bitter anguish and desolation of spirit the chieftain exhumed the body of his child, and with his immediate family rejoined his tribe in the country north of the Ohio. (8) The other five families remained, and were all sacrificed.

We shall find Capt. Bull again on the Virginia border, but not as a peaceful village builder.

CHAPTER VIII

Against the avowed purpose to kill the Bull Town Indians, a "remonstrance of the settlement generally," says *Withers*, was made. (1) Evidently this "remonstrance" was formal and feeble. No concerted action was taken to enforce order or to stay this the most deliberate and fiendish crime ever enacted on the border of the Upper Monongahela. A not altogether groundless dread of incurring the wrath of the five bordermen, who would likely brook no interference with their plans, may have justified to some small extent the indifference manifested by the settlers. But both the sequel and previous circumstances point an accusing finger, and the investigator is constrained to believe that the settlers generally were in direct sympathy with the acts of the merciless five, and felt little or no concern for the safety of their red friends on the Kanawha, or how they fared at the hands of the murderous foe.

While at Bull Town, the whites learned from the Delawares, that there was at that time a party of thirteen Indians, a hunting-party from beyond the Ohio, at Indian Camp, fourteen miles above the fort at Buckhannon. It is not probable that this information could have been obtained had not the settlers professed friendship and hidden their intentions for a time after their arrival at the village. Having secured this information, and their passions aroused by the scenes of their inhuman blood-letting at the Delaware town, they returned to the settlement and made rapid and grim preparations for the slaughter of the unsuspecting party at Indian Camp Rock. The sympathy (?) expressed for the Bull Town Indians found no utterance in behalf of the doomed thirteen at Indian Camp. These were unconscious of treachery, and were enjoying the solitude of their ancient rock camp in the wilderness of the Buckhannon. Yet they were marked as the next victims of the fierce bordermen.

Before marching against this new camp, the settlers were reinforced by volunteers who must have been acquainted with their intentions. Among these were Samuel Pringle, James Strange and John Truby, from the Buckhannon settlement, and several others whose names are unknown at this day. Truby's son had been killed by Indians some years before. With their

---
(1) See page 436.

force thus augmented, the company, under the leadership of White, set out for the Indian camp, and arrived in the immediate vicinity in the night, perhaps a short time before the break of day.

Indian Camp is situated on Indian Camp Run, in an amphitheatre-like valley on the land now owned by Lothrop Phillips in

INDIAN CAMP
Photographed by Professor G. F. Queen, 1892

an outcropping of carboniferous sandstone. This rock camp is of natural origin. The entrance is some fifty feet wide by about twelve in height, and it has a cavity or room running back a distance of twenty-six feet. The roof slopes uniformly from the front to the rear, and it is from four to six feet in height at the back of the cave. It faces east, and the first rays of the sun penetrate its inmost depths. This cave, or "rockhouse," as such overhanging rocks were called by the early settlers, is so sheltered that the fiercest storms lodge neither snow nor rain beneath the roof. It would be difficult to conceive a more perfect, natural shelter from the weather, and it is not surprising that it was a favorite resort of the Indians, and became such for the white pioneer scouts and hunters. An early settler lived therein with his family one entire summer, while he was erecting his cabin. Large congregations assembled there for public worship in post-pioneer days. In later years it has been put to the more ignoble use of a stable for domestic animals.

The entrance to the camp is flanked on both sides by huge fragments of sandstone, about which grew tangled thickets of laurel, vines and brush; much of which still remained when I last visited the locality in 1893. This afforded an effective covering for an ambushing foe. Within the immediate entrance there is a large block of stone bearing some resemblance to a rude altar. From this point the ground falls in a gentle slope to Indian Camp Run, several rods to the east.

It was at this stream that the settlers halted, while Captain White and Jesse Hughes stealthily reconnoitered the camp. After observing the position of the Indians and noting the best mode of attack, they returned to the company and prepared for the assault. The men were divided into two bands, one of them headed by White and the other by Hughes. These approached the camp from opposite sides, in the uncertain light of early dawn, and soon found the Indians astir, preparing their morning meal. White was in position first, and Hughes was to give a whistle, the signal of attack; to be answered by White. It seems that the light was too uncertain to aim with accuracy, and at the risk of discovery they awaited the tardy approach of day. They had command of the entire entrance, and there was no escape for the Indians.

As the shadows dispersed before the broadening rays of morning, the stillness was suddenly broken by a shrill whistle, and:

> "Wild as the scream of the curlew,
> From crag to crag the signal flew."

The recesses of the cavern and the adjacent cliffs and forest resounded with the roar of heavy riflery and the exultant yells of the bordermen as they sprang forward to complete the work of death. But there was little need for the knife or tomahawk. So deadly had been the volley that but one Indian, unarmed and badly wounded, escaped from that grotto of death. He was scarce able to hobble to the sheltering pit of an uprooted tree near by, where his relentless pursuers soon followed him. He greeted them with a friendly and supplicating "How." To this amicable salutation Captain White replied: "Damn you: you want powder and lead," and having reloaded, he dispatched his victim with another shot.

Thus perished this band of friendly Indians, in time of peace and without provocation. Their destruction was the blackest of crimes.

The number of settlers engaged in this massacre is not known, but the fact that every Indian was either killed or disabled at the first fire would indicate that the "remonstrating settlement"

Ash Camp
(Queen, 1892)

must have been represented by many of its best riflemen. The victims were left where they fell, to gorge the voracious wolf, and the carrion birds of the air. John Cutright's statement was to the effect that the dead Indians were left unburied, but others said that they were interred in the loose debris of the camp floor.

An aged nimrod, born in 1801, who resorted to this camp during the first quarter of the century, related to me the following story:

"Game of all kinds was most abundant in the wilderness region surrounding both the Indian, and Ash Camps. These camps were favorite rendezvous for the hunter. In a season's hunt of about one month, at Ash Camp, I killed seventy deer alone, to say nothing of the bear and turkey secured. I killed eleven bear around Indian Camp in one day. Hunting throughout that country was superb; but my associations with the latter camp was not of a continued pleasant nature. When I first visited it, there was a low, mound-like ridge some fifteen feet in length and eighteen inches high, near the center of the room, and immediately back of the large block of sandstone which stands at the entrance. I sometimes pillowed my head against the sloping base of the mound, wholly unconscious of the gruesome objects hidden beneath.

"One day a pouring rain prevented hunting, and in idle curiosity I began removing the dirt from one end of the mound, and was soon startled to find the skeleton feet of a human body. My interest was aroused and I continued the excavation, and discovered that the mound was full of human bones, representing, as I estimated, no less than eighteen bodies. They had been buried on a level with the original floor of the camp. In this bone-heap, I found numerous fragments of crockery, and a finely polished, hard stone "bleater." This bleater was perfect, and beautifully made. It was used by the Indian hunter to imitate the bleat of a fawn, and was evidently of Indian manufacture. With it I could mimic the cry of a fawn to perfection. It was afterwards broken and lost through accident. I prized it highly."

The "fragments of crockery" alluded to by the old hunter, was evidently that of steatite vessels, pieces of which were found there in after years. Shreds of crude Indian pottery were strewn all through the floor accumulation of the camp.

It is hardly probable that so many bodies could have been interred in the manner described and escaped the ravages of wild animals. It was a custom of some of the tribes to bury only the bones of their dead in a common, or final resting place. This manner of sepulcher, known as "bundle burial," is sometimes met with in this region. If the find in question was not of this nature, which I am inclined to believe is the case, then it was evidently the bones of the slain Indians, inhumed by the whites in later years. (2)

The discovery of these skeletons was regarded as proof of the tradition that during the border wars, a band of thirteen Indians returning from a raid in Tygart's Valley late one season, were snowbound at Indian Camp, and starved to death. The great abundance of game in that region would have been a guarantee against such a tragedy, even if it were probable that an unprecedented storm should have occurred at the time of year that we

---
(2) See page 436.

know the Indian incursions took place. The deep snow would have facilitated, rather than retard the success of the hunter. I knew a hunter in the Cheat Mountain, who, with a comrade, during a remarkably heavy snow and within a few days' time killed forty deer, many of which were clubbed to death. The animals are helpless in the snow, while the men properly equipped, travel easily over the surface.

Not only were deer plentiful, but this region was a favorite wintering quarters for bear; nor were they usually hard to locate. "Bear Den" rocks are located at the mouth of Indian Camp Run. In 1893, a middle-aged gentleman who was raised near Indian Camp, told me that when a boy he knew his father to have at one time sixteen bears in his cabin thawing them out so he could skin them and dress the meat. As bear hunters the woods Indians have always excelled. Evidently the starvation story originated with those who engaged in the killing at Indian Camp, and was told for the purpose of covering up their crime.

CHAPTER IX

The memories associated with John Cutright, the scout, more than any other of his companions, are inseparably connected with the region around Buckhannon and Indian Camp. He was at an early age a hunter of renown, and the Indians occasionally sought his companionship. Soon after the massacres narrated in foregoing chapters, Cutright one day was plowing corn in a field adjoining the forest; when an Indian suddenly appeared on the summit of a large rock at the edge of the woods, apparently alone and unarmed. As Cutright approached him, he held up to view an unfinished pair of moccasins. In broken English he said, "How! Injun no hurt white man. Injun make him white man moccasin. Good Injun. Good white man. White man big hunter. Injun big hunter. White man go with Injun, hunt. Get heap deer, heap bear. Ugh!" But Cutright having no desire for Indian companionship and fearing treachery, declined the invitation and continued his plowing. The Indian remained on the rock industriously at work completing the moccasins, and continued to importune the noted hunter by repeatedly ejaculating "Good Injun; good white man! Go hunt." Cutright at last became alarmed at the persistence of the strange moccasin-maker, and unhitched his horse from the plow, mounted its back and galloped home. The Indian disappeared as silently as he came.

In 1781, a certificate was granted "John Cutright, Sen., 400 acres at the mouth of Cutright's Run, to include his Settlement made in 1770, with a preemption of 1000 acres adjoining."

It has been supposed generally that this settler was John Cutright, the scout, which is error. *Withers*, in speaking of the emigrants who arrived under the guidance of Samuel Pringle, says, "Among them were John and Benjamin Cutright, who settled on the Buckhannon, where John Cutright the younger, now [1831] lives." (1)

"John Cutright, the younger," was the scout; and a son of Benjamin. The settlement was made at the mouth of Cutright's Run, and it was here that the scout was accosted by the friendly moccasin-maker. Cutright's Run empties into the Buckhannon River, some four miles above the present town of Buckhannon.

---
(1) See page 436.

By the side of a large stone near the mouth of the run, charred corn is still turned by the plow. This was burned by the Indians on one of their incursions into the settlement.

Local tradition says that one night the Indians stole a horse from John Cutright, Junior. Following the trail next day Cutright found the horse tied to a sugar tree on Cutright's Run, about three miles from Buckhannon. Not caring to venture too close until he learned something of the location of the enemy, he secreted himself at a distance. He soon saw an Indian running across the valley. Taking careful aim, he fired and the Indian fell. Cutright dashed to his horse, sprang upon its back, and with a whoop of defiance, galloped away. This tree was still standing in 1894, and was often pointed out to the traveler by Cutright's descendants.

At another time, Cutright and a companion had been hunting on French Creek and were on their way home. Cutright was mounted, with a deer slung across the pommel of his saddle. While crossing a stream, they halted to let the horse drink, and were fired on by two Indians. Cutright was severely wounded, the ball entering his breast, and coming out through his back, striking in its passage, however no vital point. He spurred up his horse and fled toward the fort, while his companion in the retreat held the Indians back. After a short running fight, one of the Indians was killed, and the other then abandoned the pursuit. When Cutright had ridden some distance, he grew faint and found it was impossible to retain his position in the saddle, and so dismounted and stretched himself on the ground, where his companion soon after found him. From the bullet hole the blood was pouring, and to stop it a small sour-gum was cut and stripped of its bark. Over the end of this a handkerchief was placed and forced into the wound. The stick was then withdrawn, leaving the handkerchief in place. This stopped the hemorrhage, and Cutright was placed on his horse, his companion mounting behind and supporting him in the saddle. In this manner, they made their way in safety to the fort.

The two foregoing stories may have had their origin in an occurrence set forth in Col. Westfall's letter, (2) this volume. But evidently Cutright was wounded during some excursion with William Hacker, who dressed his wound in the way described. Owing to Hacker's skill in rude surgery, he was known in the settlements as "Surgeon Hacker." (3)

(2) See page 436. (3) p. 436.

John Cutright developed into one of the most daring scouts on the Virginia border. He was also a soldier of the Revolutionary War. In his original declaration for pension made August 7, 1832, in Lewis County (Virginia), it would appear that he was born near Moorefield, Hampshire (now Hardy County, Virginia), in 1754, but he had no record of his age. In May, 1778, he volunteered for a term of eighteen months as private in Capt. James Boothe's Company of Indian Spies, at West's Fort on Hacker's Creek. He spied throughout most of (then) Monongalia County, until Capt. Boothe was killed on Boothe's Creek June, 1779. (4) After the death of Capt. Boothe he continued spying under the Company's Lieutenant, Edmund Freeman, until November, 1779, when his term of enlistment expired. Lieutenant Freeman left for Kentucky without officially discharging any of the Company.

"The Indian hostilities continuing, Capt. George Jackson was required to raise a company to spy in the same territory of country which Capt. Boothe's Company had been spying." Cutright joined this company as a private, a few days after his service under Capt. Boothe and Lieutenant Freeman had expired. Jacob Brake, an ex-Indian captive, (5) was Lieutenant of this company, and the afterwards notorious Timothy Dorman was Ensign. Cutright continued in the service until the latter part of 1781, and was in "several skirmishes with the Indians." David W. Sleeth, who was in service with Cutright, testified that he once saw Cutright wounded by an Indian. Jacob Cozard [Cozad], a clergyman, and Alexander West, the scout, both testified in behalf of Cutright. His claim was allowed and on May 18, 1833, a certificate was issued granting him eighty dollars a year, dating from March 4, 1831, including back pay.

Cutright was afterwards examined by Special Pension Agent Singleton, who sent the following report to the Commissioner of Pensions:

"July 3, 1834. Saw Cutright at his home, and received from him the statement here following: Says he will be 79 years old in August next, born on south branch of Potomac; was brought west of the Alleghany mountains when 8 years old and settled on the place where he now lives. He enlisted under Capt. Booth for twelve months. Joined his company at Nutter's Fort in the Spring; in the Fall removed to West's Fort. Remained there until his time expired. That was in the year in which Capt. Booth was killed, *and before the war of the Revolution had commenced.* After the commencement of the war of the Rev. and whilst residing at Buckhannon Fort (Lewis Co.) he was drafted for an 18 mos. tour. He

(4) See page 436. (5) p. 436.

refused to go. A Col. Wilson who then resided in Tiger's Valley sent a guard of men after him, caught him, tied him and marched him to Staunton. (6) A Sergeant Lack commanded the guard. On reaching Staunton, he enlisted under a Capt. Matthews for two years. Matthews enlisted 6 men including himself. They were sent on under Sergeant Samuel Warner to join Washington's main army then at the White Plains. They set out from Staunton in the summer, went through Winchester, Reading, Philadelphia; on getting to Phil. rested 4 days in the Barracks, set out again and pushed on without stopping until they joined the main army at the White Plains. The original number 6 was neither increased or diminished on the march above mentioned. Joined the main army in July. The army marched from the White Plains to West Point and from there to Middlebrook where it went into winter quarters. Remained there till warm weather. When part of the army (himself included) about 100 in number went up the North river as a guard. Gone at least 2 weeks. Can't recollect who commanded the guard *nor the name of any officer that was along on that occasion*. On returning was sent to a bridge on the North river where a colonel's (don't recollect his name) baggage had been broken down as a guard, remained there about a month. Think there were 10 or 12 of them. They were under the command of Sergeant Campbell. The main army marched from Middlebrook but can't recollect where. It got back to West Point where his time expired and where he got his discharge and returned home. His discharge was signed by a Colonel, whose name he don't recollect. On his way home met General Washington who also signed his discharge. Can't recollect the years in which the service above described was done.

"I have been unable to procure any evidence in reference to this man. Comparing his statement here given with his declaration it may be readily discerned whether or not he is an imposter.

W. G. SINGLETON, S. A."

Owing to the marked discrepancies between his original declaration and his statement to Singleton, Cutright's name was stricken from the pension roll, along with several others, from Lewis County, who were not entitled to pensions. (7) Subsequent investigation evoked the fact that Cutright had never enlisted in Capt. Jackson's Company of Scouts. Mr. Johnson F. Nowlan, Neulan or Naulon (name uncertain), who was Cutright's agent or attorney, visited him at his home and drew up his declaration for pension, and unknown to the scout, who could neither read nor write, and for the purpose of strengthening his case, added that part of it which alleges service with Capt. Jackson. For this work, Cutright was forced to pay to the unscrupulous attorney, eighty dollars from the first money drawn.

It now devolved upon Cutright to substantiate his Revolutionary record, as it had developed that those who served as border scouts alone were not entitled to pension.

---

(6) See page 436. (7) p. 438.

On August 20, 1835, Solomon Ryan testified in behalf of Cutright, corroborating the statement of the old soldier to Singleton. The following testimony is of historic interest, and I give it unabridged:

"LEWIS COUNTY VA.

"Susanna Stalnaker, in the 70th year of her age appeared before me the subscribed, one of the Commonwealth's Justice of the Peace for said county, and being sworn as the law directs, sayeth that she believes that it was about the year 1778, John Cutright was taken from the fort on Buckhannon, where she then lived, as a soldier draughted from Capt. Samuel Pringle's Company for a term of 18 months against the British, and to the best of her recollection it was 2 years before he returned, and the next spring after his return he was wounded by the Indian, (8) when on pursuit of them when they had committed depredations near the place where they were then posted. She also remembers hearing some one that returned from taking them to Staunton say that the above mentioned Cutright being dissatisfied with his officers, he enlisted for two years' service, at (9) Staunton, Augusta Co. (Va.)

(Signed) SUSANNA X STALNAKER
Her Mark

Sworn to August 1835.   WILLIAM POWERS, J. P."

Cutright was restored to the pension roll, but at the reduced rate of $43.33 per year from March 4, 1834, until his death, March 8, 1850.

It will be noted that Cutright could not recall the years in which his service in the army occurred, nor is it probable that the date can at this time be fixed. Washington had his headquarters at White Plains during the summer and autumn of 1778, and seven brigades of the American Army were quartered at Middlebrook the winter of 1779-80. (10) During a part of this period, Cutright, according to his original declaration, was an enlisted spy on the border. It is possible that he was with some contingent of the American Army wintered at Middlebrook in the later years of the war. Comfortable log cabins were built for the soldiers during the previous encampment, and they may have been in use afterwards.

In a statement made in July, 1838, Cutright was under the impression that his company was commanded by Capt. John Lewis, under Col. Matthews, whose given name he could not recall. With a view of possibly determining the exact date of Cutright's Revolutionary service, and the regiment to which he was attached, a search was made of the Revolutionary Muster

---

(8) See page 438. (9) p. 438. (10) p. 439.

Rolls of the Virginia State troops, preserved in the Virginia State Library, Richmond, with negative results. To an inquiry to the War Department, Washington, came the reply:

"The records show that one John Cutright served as a private in Captain Machen Boswell's Company, 2nd Virginia State Regiment, commanded by Colonel Gregory Smith, Revolutionary War. The date of his enlistment has not been found of record, but his name appears on the muster rolls of the company covering the period from September, 1778, to February, 1779. He was discharged March 6, 1779. The company to which he belonged was at various times commanded by Captain John Lewis. No record has been found of any other man of the same or similar name as a member of any Virginia military organization in service in the war of the Revolution."

Gregory Smith was commissioned Captain in Seventh Virginia Regiment, February 7, 1776, and resigned 28th November, 1776. He was made Colonel of the Second Virginia Regiment from 1777 to 1778. Machen Boswell was commissioned First Lieutenant Second Virginia Regiment, 6th October, 1777, and was promoted Captain 15th September, 1778, and served to February, 1781.

While there is much confusion in the dates and records, a close study of Cutright's narratives precludes a logical inference of any premeditated attempt at deception. The discrepancies reveal a faulty judgment, but not the willful prevaricator. His rating at the Pension Office for veracity was *first-class*. In his first declaration, no mention is made of his career in the main army, nor did he at any time allude to the important fact that he had been wounded while on duty as a spy. When compared with the actual events in his life, the scout's narrative is one of commendable modesty. Profoundly illiterate, his capabilities were measured solely in his skill as woodsman, scout, and warrior. His faculty for delineation was limited, and his conception of dates most vague. He could narrate the incidents in his career, but could not intelligently connect them with contemporary events. He was a maker of history, but not a chronicler, and more eloquent with his rifle than with his tongue.

I am inclined to believe that there were two John Cutrights from the Western border who served with the Virginia troops in the Revolution, and that it was not John Cutright, the scout, who enlisted under Col. Gregory Smith, but was perhaps, his uncle,

John Cutright, Sr., who also fought in the battle of Point Pleasant. (11)

We find a certificate of marriage of John Cutright and Deborah Osborn in Randolph County, Virginia, in 1799, but whether this was a later marriage of the Senior Cutright is not known. There is a tradition current among the Cutrights on the Buckhannon River that there were two branches of the family in that region, and that John Cutright and Deborah Osborn were the grandparents of Enoch Cutright, who, it is averred, had Indian blood in him. There was a Peter Cutright in a skirmish with the Indians on Hacker's Creek in 1780, (12) but I know nothing of his antecedents. He was, in all probability, of the same family.

Error has crept into history regarding Cutright's age, and the year of his death. Both *Border Warfare*, and *History of Upshur County, W. Va.*, state that he died in 1852, at the age of 105 years. According to Cutright's own declaration, he was born in 1755. In the testimony of John Lemmons in behalf of Rebecca Cutright, widow of John Cutright, when she applied for her husband's pension, we find that John Cutright died (Friday) March 8th, 1850. The widow at the time was too infirm to appear in court. Mrs. Cutright was a daughter of John Truby, and married John Cutright January 2, 1788. Isaac Edwards, D. D., was the officiating minister.

Hon. W. C. Carper, of Buckhannon, West Va., is perhaps the only man now living, (1908) who remembers seeing John Cutright. It was in 1838 when Mr. Carper was about twelve years of age that Cutright came to the Carper homestead on Turkey Run. Mr. Carper writes me: "The old scout came upon the porch, when he and I were alone for a short time, and I distinctly remember his appearance. He was about five feet nine inches high and heavily built, complexion dark, eyes dark, and his hair was then white. He told me that he once stopped under a walnut tree near where Point Pleasant Church now stands on the head of French Creek, 'to crack walnuts, and then a damned Injun shot me.' He showed me where the ball had entered under his arm, and glanced around the ribs and came out under the arm on the other side. Cutright added, 'I stuck a chaw terbacker in the bullet hole.' At this juncture of the conversation, my father came up and began to talk to Cutright on the subject of religion. The veteran Indian fighter seemed averse to this topic and abruptly

---
(11) See page 439. (12) p. 439.

said, 'Ad, quit talking about religion; it is all damned nonsense.' "This," concluded Mr. Carper, "is the only time I ever saw Cutright, and the above subjects all that I ever heard him talk about."

Christopher Cutright, when interviewed by me, in commenting on the deeds of his father and associates, said, "When Billy [William] White and Jesse Hughes went on an Indian killing they killed all with whom they came in contact, not even sparing women and children." When asked which of these two noted scouts was the most desperate and cruel in his forays against the Indians, came the laconic reply, "It was about buck up." "And," mused the old man, "my father was about as bad as they were, and Samuel Pringle, of the sycamore tree, who married my father's sister, was scarce better."

He then related an incident of the Pringle brothers. While living in the sycamore, they went in a canoe to an Indian village some miles below them on the river, and stole a bag of jerked buffalo. He gave the details of their narrow escape from detection and pursuit. Then again referring to his father's animosity towards the Indians, he told the following story:

Many years after the last Indian depredation in that country, a solitary Indian passed through the settlement late one evening and was seen by his father. Despite the fact that the scout was so aged and infirm that he could only walk with the assistance of a cane, his old-time hatred was aroused to that degree that he hobbled to the gun rack and took down his ancient flint-lock, and would have shot the Indian had not his family restrained him. That night the old gun was secreted and its owner closely guarded until the Indian disappeared from the neighborhood. (13)

---

(13) See page 439.

CHAPTER X

In the early settlement of our country, each community, blockhouse or fort had its recognized chief or headman, who was counsellor and advisor in threatened danger, and leader in all movements against the common foe. These men attained their places because of their superior wisdom and cool judgment in those emergencies constantly arising on an exposed and dangerous frontier. The matter of right or wrong weighed little in the events connected with the Indians. He was fittest to lead, who had the strongest determination to avenge an outrage upon the community, especially if it had been perpetrated by the Indians. The Buckhannon settlement possessed these requisites in the person of Captain William White, who came from Cedar Creek, Frederick County, Virginia. Reference to Captain White in border annals is meagre, and nothing is known positive of his antecedents further than that he was a descendant of Dr. White, of Frederick County, who was the ancestor of the White family of that region. Major John White and Major Robert White, also of Frederick County, were prominent in the defense of the border. (1) From the best information to be had, they all were of the same family. (2)

It is not known how Capt. William White came by his military title, but he bore it in 1768 and was ever after distinguished by it. A search of the Muster Rolls on file in the War Department (which are, however, very incomplete) and of the records of the Bureau of Pensions, Washington, failed to show any history of enlistment or military service of Captain William White, of the Buckhannon, in the Revolution. An inquiry to the Virginia State Library, Richmond, elicited the reply: "The Revolutionary Muster Rolls here on file reveal no enlistment of the William White in question." Usually, each settlement elected its own captain, and in this way White may have come by his title. Such an election was being held at Bush's Fort when the Schoolcraft family were massacred in 1779. These elections were not always confirmed by commissions.

Captain White and Colonel William Crawford were personal friends, and White was identified with many expeditions conducted by that famous officer against the Indians. He was also

---
(1) See page 439. (2) p. 439.

in the battle of Point Pleasant under Colonel Sevier. (3) With his experience in the field was coupled the superior skill of the scout, the spy and the woodsman. Back of these qualities was a strong constitution, a fearless nature and a relentless hatred for "everything Injun." The red flame of war had no terrors for him, neither had the white wing of peace any restraint for his insatiate thirst for Indian blood. Captain White's schooling was savage, and he proved an apt scholar. Just prior to Dunmore's War, he killed a peaceable Indian on the Wappatomaka. For this, he was imprisoned at Winchester, but an armed mob of his infuriated friends soon set him at liberty. (4)

While visiting Colonel Crawford at "The Meadows," in the Alleghenies in 1768, White in company with an Irishman went hunting in the glades, where they found two Indians. According to the story of White and his companion, the Indians, "the moment they discovered the two white men, flew behind trees and prepared for battle." The Indians were both killed, for which White and the Irishman were arrested and placed in the Winchester jail. Immediately, Captain Fry at the head of an armed mob of fifty-five or sixty men, urged on by a throng of cheering spectators, forced the jailor at the muzzle of a loaded rifle to surrender the prison keys. The door was thrown open and the prisoners liberated. (5)

It is not at all probable that the two Indians killed by White and the Irishman were at the time on the warpath. It must be said that most of the victims of murder on the border, from the close of Pontiac's War to the Dunmore War of 1774, were Indians. Nor do we find that any of the murderers ever received just punishment. The stories of the two releases of Captain White from the Winchester jail are two accounts of the same transaction. They portray most vividly the character of the man and the sentiment of the people. The work of the mob was only a repetition of the one that had previously released from the same prison, for a like crime, the red-handed Judah, (6) and was an emphatic approval and endorsement of the crimes which led to Dunmore's War. In these and like occurrences, we have an unconscious portrayal of the true status of border society.

The exact date of White's arrival in the Buckhannon settlement cannot be determined, but it was sometime between 1769 and 1771. Nor did he come unknown. Most, if not all, of the

---

(3) See page 439. (4) p. 440. (5) p. 440. (6) p. 440.

settlers had been his associates on the "Branch" and they recognized his superior ability in woodcraft. He was the ideal frontiersman and woodsman, and although I have been unable to find where he ever served as captain in the Buckhannon settlement, he was the recognized head scout of the colony. It would appear, however, from the declaration of Jacob Bush and Jacob Westfall that White was a lieutenant in Captain George Jackson's Company of Volunteer Militia, 1781. (7)

It is to the indefatigable efforts of Colonel Henry F. Westfall, a grandson of Captain White, that we are indebted for much of the heretofore unwritten history of this renowned scout on the western Virginia border. Colonel Westfall got his information direct from John Cutright and others who were boon companions and asscciates of Captain White.

By *Withers* he is mentioned four times; the first, in the incident of his imprisonment and release; second, his part in the murder of the Bull Town Indians; third, his capture by the Indians on the Little Kanawha, and his escape and return to the settlements; fourth, his death at the hands of the Indians near Buckhannon Fort, in 1782. Even in these accounts there are very indefinite statements, especially as to the identity of Captain White as the man who was captured on the Little Kanawha. It would be inferred that the captive was a resident of Tygart's Valley, (8) but at that time he was a member of the Buckhannon settlement.

White's ability to detect the presence of Indians had no equal in the settlement. He once discovered two Indians hiding under the river bank near the fort, and succeeded in killing one of them. At another time, while White was temporarily absent, an Indian entered the settlement under the following circumstances:

It was at the time of the Revolution, and a young lady of the settlement had a lover in the person of an officer in the British army. These young people became acquainted during a brief visit of the officer to that region just prior to the war. The object of his visit is not known, but it was evidently in the interest of the military. During his short stay a warm friendship sprang up between the officer and Captain White, and when the time arrived for the guest to depart for Fort Pitt, the Captain accompanied him. On their way they saw a bear, and White, through deference, permitted his young friend, who was a novice in hunt-

(7) See page 440. (8) p. 440.

ing, to have the first shot. The ball disabled the bear but did not kill it. White withheld his shot and urged his now excited companion to reload quickly and kill the bear before it recovered sufficiently to make an attack or to escape. He did so, but when he again attempted to recharge his rifle, he found that his ramrod was missing. Thinking that in his hurry he had dropped it, he looked about but could not find it. The discomfited hunter became puzzled, when White, who had been regarding him with amusement, laughingly pointed to the now lifeless body of the bear, from the side of which protruded the end of the splintered ramrod; showing that it had not been withdrawn before he made the second shot. From a young hickory, White deftly shaped a new ramrod for his friend, who begged that the incident be kept from his companions at the fort.

After the breaking out of the war, the young officer was assigned duty on the Canadian border, but ready means for communicating with the forest belle was at hand. An active young Indian warrior agreed to carry an exchange of letters, the compensation to be ten gallons of rum. After receiving a description of the young woman, he fastened the letter securely to his person and started fully armed on his long journey to the south. Arriving in the Buckhannon settlement, and knowing the dangers that beset him, he lurked and hid for two or three days, watching for an opportunity to deliver the letter.

One morning the girl had occasion to go from the fort to a nearby cabin, the path leading through a stretch of wood. After proceeding a short distance, she was startled to see a half-naked Indian step suddenly from behind a tree, immediately in front of her. In his belt hung a tomahawk and scalping knife, his left hand grasped a long rifle, while his right hand, which was extended to her, held a sealed package. Before she could recover from her fright sufficiently to utter a cry, the warrior, with a peaceful gesture and friendly "How!" handed her the package and in broken English said, "Squaw be no fraid. Injun no hurt. Me come from white chief. Him send good talk. Me come get squaw's talk when moon wake up," pointing to the brow of the eastern hill. He then glided into the thicket and was lost to view.

It happened that day that some men who were scouting about the woods, discovered the presence of the Indian and gave immediate pursuit. The warrior proved very athletic and soon outstripped his pursuers. He disappeared over the river bank just below the mill dam, where all trace of him was lost. After an exhaustive search of several hours the pursuit was abandoned. The Indian, it was supposed, despairing of escape, and for the purpose of saving his scalp, had plunged into the river and was drowned.

In the meantime, the young woman had prepared her communication, keeping the mission of the Indian secret. She was sorely grieved when she learned of his fate, for he was the only one by whom a letter could be forwarded. Night came on, and most anxiously did she await the appointed time of meeting. Just as the moon gleamed over the brow of the wood-crested hill, she stealthily repaired to the tryst. Like a wraith the Indian glided from the shadow of the thicket and came silently to her side. She handed him the package containing her "talk," also a small bag filled with jerked venison and parched corn. With a grunt expressive of appreciation, the warrior turned and started on his journey to the distant north. In due time he reached his destination, delivered the letter and received the promised rum, on which he and his friends became "gloriously drunk." Of the sequel to this story, nothing is known.

The next day, when Captain White returned to the fort and was told of the Indian and his mysterious disappearance, he chided the men, and declared that if they would go with him to the river he would show them "whar th' Injun was hid." Proceeding to the river bank, White pointed to the sheet of water pouring over the mill dam, and exclaimed, "If yo' had looked behind thar' yo' would have found yer Injun." An examination of the premises proved that his judgment was correct. The wily Indian, hard-pressed, had darted through the cataract of water, where he rested in safety on the apron or platform of timbers built at the foot of the dam.

There is a tradition in that country, handed down through the descendants of Captain White and the Cutrights, to the effect that in the early years of the settlement there were captured near the fort at Buckhannon an Indian and a Frenchman, who were loitering about the country. They were held in captivity. The Frenchman was of a morose disposition and very melancholy. He would not bathe, but took great pride in dressing his hair, which was very long and abundant. He refused food and died of starvation. Nothing could be learned of his past history, but it is supposed that he was a renegade from the Northwestern wilderness. As to the fate of the Indian, the tradition is silent. He was probably put to death.

About the death of Captain White there hovers a tinge of romance. There is also revealed a trait of Indian character not often met with in our border annals. With the Indian the spirit of retaliation was an unqualified principle, an inherent right; but it mattered not on whom the avenging hatchet fell. The life forfeited by an innocent member of the offending tribe or family was regarded as a just compensation for a life taken. This mode of warfare was honorable with the Indian. With the settlers the principle was regarded just, so long as Indian met Indian, if they themselves did the shooting; but when waged by the Indian against the border it was held in utter detestation and horror. While the Indian however, was content with the reprisal of scalp for scalp, the venom of the average borderer was insatiate.

Under no circumstances was Captain White ever known to show mercy to an Indian. With some of his associates he was hunting, when they surprised a small body of Indians. They fired and killed several, while a few escaped by flight. One active young warrior fled with White in hot pursuit, tomahawk in hand. The fugitive was driven to a precipice, over which he leaped. White jumped after him, both sinking to their waists in a quagmire, from which they were unable to extricate themselves. The young Indian, who was wholly unarmed made frantic efforts to escape, while White made strenuous attempts to strike him with his tomahawk. In the struggle the warrior inadvertently flung out his arm towards White, who seized his hand, and drawing his helpless victim within reach, sank the hatchet in his head.

That heartless blow sealed the doom of Captain White. The father of the victim was among those who escaped, and he seems to have sworn vengeance against the murderer of his son. For several years this stern warrior lurked about the settlement, trailing White with the relentless tenacity of a sleuth-hound. Finally, on Friday evening, the 8th of March, 1782, he shot White within sight of the fort, and in the presence of several of its inmates. (9) The avenger attempted to secure the scalp of his victim, but was prevented by the rescue party that hurried from the fort. This was one case where an Indian was satisfied with the death of the

(9) See page 440.

guilty party only. That White "was tomahawked, scalped and lacerated in a most frightful manner," is a mistake. (10) The facts are given here. The upturned roots of the tree under which it is said that White was shot is still to be seen. This tree stood on the opposite side of the river from the fort.

The death of Captain White, coupled with the capture by the Indians at the same time of Timothy Dorman, a degenerate renegade of whom the settlers stood in dread, resulted in the temporary abandonment of the Buckhannon settlement. (11)

There is strong evidence that White was betrayed or lured to death by Timothy Dorman, and that the latter was not captured, in the true sense of the word, but went willingly with the Indians.

SCENE OF CAPTAIN WILLIAM WHITE'S DEATH
Miss Josephine MacAvoy, Photographer, 1909

Looking east across the Buckhannon River from where the fort stood. Tradition has it that Capt. White was killed either in the low gap where the prostrate tree lies, or to the left under the high ridge, where can be seen the stump of an upturned tree. Both are indicated by **X**. *In either case, he evidently succeeded in reaching a point near the river before falling from his horse, where he was met by the rescue party from the fort. See Col. Westfall's letter, Appendix 1, this Volume.*

(10) See page 441. (11) p. 441.

Captain White was buried in what is now the Heavner Cemetery at Buckhannon, and by the grave of John Fink, (12) who was killed by Indians the preceding February. Capt. White's grave is marked by a rude flagstone, which bears his name without dates or other inscription. According to *Withers*, Fink was killed February 8, (Friday) 1782. The rough sandstone at his grave is inscribed with this legend:

"Here lieth the bo— John Fink who was killed by Indens in 1782, Feb. the —th"

Where the dash occurs after "bo," the stone is broken and missing. The inscription evidently read "body of." Part of the inscription is very dim and almost illegible, the date of the month being entirely so.

Col. Westfall, several years ago, endeavored to induce the citizens of Buckhannon to erect a block of granite over the neglected graves of Capt. White and John Fink. The Colonel did not live to realize his cherished hopes. (13)

The Capt. White and Fink Monument.

This cut was contributed by the Elizabeth Zane Chapter D. A. R. With its transmission, Mrs. Clara DuMont Heavner, Regent, writes me.

"It is owing to the patriotism of a little boy that the last resting place of Capt. White and Fink can now be identified. Elias Heavner, was born in Pendleton County, Va., April 9, 1805; and came with his father, Nicholas Heavner, 2nd, who in 1815 settled on 400 acres purchased of George Jackson, on the Buckhannon River, including the site of Bush's Fort. When but eleven years old, Elias, impressed with the story of the killing of these pioneers, unassisted procured from the river bed, irregular flag stones and with childish simplicity carved in rude lettering. "KILLED BY THE INDENS" along with additional legends which you already have, and set them up at the neglected graves; which until then were unmarked. Some of the inscriptions were defaced during the Civil War by relic hunters. These stones we have cemented to the base of the monument." Elias Heavner died October 10, 1884. He was the father of Maj. J. W. and Clark W. Heavner, of Buckhannon, West Va.

(12) See page 441. (13) p. 441.

THE CAPTAIN WHITE AND FINK MONUMENT

ILLUSTRATION CONTRIBUTED BY THE ELIZABETH ZANE CHAPTER, D. A. R.

Jacob Bush, referred to earlier in this chapter in connection with Jacob Westfall, was a brother of John Bush, who built the fort at Buckhannon. It is not known at what time he came to the settlements, but is supposed to be the same Jacob Bush, who in 1781 received a grant for "400 acres on the West Fork, about two miles below the main fork of said river, to include his improvement made in 1777." He was a man of intelligence and veracity, and his declaration is of historic value. It is here given in full:

"VA. LEWIS COUNTY

"On November 7, 1832, personally appeared in open court, etc., Jacob Bush who makes the following statement: That he entered the U. S. service under the following named officers and served as herein stated. In the spring of 1778 (does not recollect the precise time), he volunteered in Capt. Samuel Pringle's company of Indians spies, he joined the company of Capt. Pringle at the Buckhannon Ft. then in the county of Monongalia, Va. and continued in the service as an Indian spy under Capt. Pringle until in the fall of 1779 when he was discharged. While under Capt. Pringle he was engaged in spying from the Buchannon Fort, then in the county of Monongalia, now in the county of Lewis, to the headwaters of the West Fork and the Little Kanawha rivers, and frequently witnessed the massacre of the Indians, and was required to pursue the savages to the Ohio River; his lieutenant's name he thinks was Westfall, he thinks Capt. Pringle's Co. belonged to Col.-Morgan, Regiment of militia in Monongalia Co., Va., he thinks Capt. Pringle gave him a discharge but cannot be confident, if he did it is lost; he was in the service under Capt. Pringle as an Indian spy about eighteen months; when he entered the service under Capt. Pringle he resided on Buchannon river in Monongalia Co., Va. In April or May, 1781, according to his present recollection but cannot be confident, as a substitute for his brother John Bush at the Buchannon Fort in Monongalia Co., Va., he joined Capt. Jackson's Co. of militia, Wm. White was Lieut., the ensign's name he has forgotten. He was marched soon after from Buchannon Fort to the Fort at the mouth of Elk creek. Shortly after he was marched to Morgantown and there joined Col. Morgan's reg. and shortly after was marched to the "New Store" on Monongalia River about 15 miles from Pittsburg, and there joined General Roger Clarke's army; stayed there a considerable length of time preparing boats and provisions for the campaign, descended the river to Pittsburg where the whole army got in boats and went down the Ohio river to its Falls, Louisville, that in descending the river he was frequently required to act as a hunter. The hunting party he thinks was commanded by a Col. Green. One day while engaged as a hunter he discovered two deer on the north side of the Ohio river. (The hunters were advised not to hunt on that side of the river for fear they might be misled by the Indians.) Declarent however, persuaded the others to land him and he killed the 2 deer. Declarent presented Genl. Clarke with the brain of one and he received it with expressions of kindness and treated declarent to "whiskey." That he with Genl. Clarke's army arrived at the falls of the Ohio according to his recollection in August, 1781, and continued there some time. While near the Bear Grass Fort five officers were killed, three of whom he thinks were

Captains; when the news arrived at the fort about 30 men were ordered out to destroy the Indians responsible for the deed. He was one of the party. The party with 2 friendly Indian guides proceeded to the place and found the dead bodies. They pursued the Indians to a place where it crossed the Ohio about five miles above the Falls. The party there gave up the pursuit and went back for the bodies which they buried at the Falls. He with many others became sick with the fever and was unable to return home after he was discharged which was in the fall of 1781. He remained sick all winter and reached home sometime the following spring making his whole service two years and six months. He thinks he received a discharge for this last service, but if so it has been lost. He resided at the said Buckhannon Fort when he substituted for his brother in Capt. Jackson's Co.

                                                      His
                                            JACOB X BUSH."
                                              Mark

Alexander West and David Sleeth both testified for Jacob Bush and their affidavits are of more than casual interest.

"VA. LEWIS CO. — TO WIT:

"Alex. West, a man of unquestionable veracity, personally appeared before the subscribed Justice of the Peace in and for said County and made oath that in May, 1781, he with Jacob Bush of Lewis County joined Capt. George Jackson's Company, and knows that said Bush marched and joined General Clarke's Army and with it descended the Ohio River to its Falls and was there discharged, said Bush got sick at the Falls and when the Army was discharged was unable to return home; he thinks said Bush did not get home until sometime in the spring or early part of the summer of 1782.   His
                                        ALEXANDER X WEST.
                                        Mark

"Sworn to and subscribed before me this 5th day of November, 1832.
                              (Signed) JOHN McWHORTER, J. P."

"VA. LEWIS CO. — SS

"David W. Sleeth, a man of veracity and truth, personally appeared before the subscribed Justice of the Peace in and for said County and made oath that he recollected that Jacob Bush of Lewis County served as an Indian Spy under Capt. Samuel Pringle for a considerable time, from his knowledge of said Bush's services under said Capt. Pringle he supposed that he must have served under said Pringle about 18 months, is confident he was in said service upwards of a year. He also recollects that in the spring of 1781 said Bush substituted for his brother *John Bush* in Capt. George Jackson's Co. and was marched from the Buckhannon Fort, and it was understood joined Genl. Clarke's Army near Pittsburg and descended the Ohio River to its Falls; he recollects that said Bush did not return from said service until in the spring or early summer of 1782. He has known Bush for many years ever since about the year of 1776; he has always been esteemed a man of veracity and truth.

                                      (Signed) DAVID W. SLEETH.

"Sworn to and subscribed before me this 7th day of November, 1832.
                                        SAMUEL Z. JONES, J. P."

This affidavit is accompanied with a brief from Mr. Jones stating that "what Sleeth says is entitled to full confidence."

Jacob Bush was born in Hampshire County, Virginia, 1756. In the fall of 1782 he married Margaret Swan, on the South Branch, where they lived until the fall of 1785, then moved with their two oldest children, Peter and "Susan," to now Lewis County, West Virginia. Jacob Bush did not live to reap any benefits from the pension due him; but died Nov. 28, 1832.

The law required that the widow, to be entitled to pension, should have been married to the soldier prior to 1794. Mrs. Bush proved her marriage and was granted eighty dollars a year, to commence March 4, 1831. Margaret Bush died July 28, 1847, at the age of ninety or ninety-one years. Her surviving children who drew the money due their mother were Peter, born 1783, Henry, Jacob, John, George; Elizabeth married Stump; Margaret married Stump; Barbary married Fisher; Susannah married Simpson. Before her death another son, Michael Bush, died, leaving a widow and two children, Mary and Adam Bush.

DECLARATION OF LIEUTENANT JACOB WESTFALL.

Westfall stated on oath:

"That he entered the service of the U. S. under the following named officers and served as herein stated. General George Rodgers Clark, Commander in Chief. In the regiment of Col. Zecheriah Morgan, commanding a regiment of volunteers. Major William Louder (who became unhealthy and obtained leave to return home in about one month after he joined the regiment), Adjutant John Maughen, Captain George Jackson, first Lieut. Jacob Westfall, this applicant; 2nd Lieut. William Whight, Ensign Hezekiah Davidson who acted as Quartermaster Sergeant. Captains in said regiment William Breene (very eligible), Johnston, Whaley, Stewart. This applicant left home on June 20th, 1781, and he ——— at Morgantown on the 29th day of the same month and served a term of six months. The regiment to which applicant belonged marched from Morgan Town in the State of Virginia to the New Store (as it was then called) on the Monongalia river, and there served General Clark with Col. Crocket's regiment of regular troops. The applicant resided at the time he entered the service as above in Tigers Valley, Monongalia County, now Randolph County, Virginia. The object of this expedition as this applicant was informed by General Clark was to march to Detroit which was in the possession of the British, and if possible to take that place. The two regiments took water on board of boats at the New Store, the 20th of July, and descended the river and landed four miles below Fort Pitt and continued there for some days collecting provisions. After leaving the encampment below Fort Pitt, we did not land again until we arrived at Whiting when a council was held, the conclusion of which was to continue down the river to an island below the mouth of the Little Kenhaway river and wait the arrival of Col. Laughery who was expected on with 200 men. After landing on said island and remaining a few days, several men deserted and a council was held and the idea of marching to Detroit was abandoned, as the force was considered by us to be insufficient. It was then determined by the general and officers to continue down the river to Kentucky and raise an additional force of Kentucky militia and march out against some of the Indian towns. Major Cracroft was left with some men to guard some boats of provisions until Col. Laughery should arrive. Col. Laughery came on some time afterwards, and after descending the Ohio River about 15 miles below the mouth of the Great Miami river, he was discovered by the Indians with his boats between an island and the main land and the whole detachment was either killed or taken prisoners. Gen. Clark continued down the river to the Falls of the Ohio where a two [days'] council was held with the Regular Volunteer and Kentucky Militia officers, and it was then and there concluded that to raise a sufficient force and march against the Indian Towns, the season would be too far advanced for the volunteers to return home to the state of Va., the distance being too great. The applicant was not engaged in any battle, there being none fought during the campaign. The Indians killed several persons belonging to the Army outside of Col. Laughery's detachment. The applicant recollects the names of the following officers in Col. Crocket's Regiment of Regulars, to wit: Major Wales, Captains Tipton and Chapman (who were both killed by the Indians in Kentucky), Young, Carney and Chenny (or Chenry). The applicant has no documentary evidence of his claim, his commission having long since been lost, worn out or destroyed, and does not know the residence of anyone who served on said campaign who is now living.

(Signed) JACOB WESTFALL."

Lieutenant Jacob Westfall was born October 10, 1755. He was the builder of Westfall's Fort, Randolph County (West), Va., and was an active partisan during the border wars. His declaration for pension was executed September 1833, in Montgomery County, Ind., but he was then a resident of Putnam County, Ind. He was awarded $80.00 a year. Lieut. Westfall died March 5, 1835. He was married in Tygart's Valley, 1777; had one son, Cornelius. His widow, Mary Westfall, applied for pension from Boone County, Ind., November 13, 1838, aged 80 years.

Since the foregoing was written, Cutright's *History of Upshur County, West Va.*, has been published; from which the following wherein Capt. White and John Cutright figure prominently, is copied:

"FLIGHT OF 1770 AND PURSUIT OF INDIANS."

"Many of the most thrilling incidents in the pioneer settlement of the waters of the Buckhannon, are like unto the common laws of England, unwritten, traditional, handed from generation unto generations in fireside stories. Therefore, many must be the names of heroes lost in the oblivion of bygone years because no one cared, peradventure was not able, to enroll them on the annals of the past. Such a chapter is the following: We know it only through traditional sources. Paul Shaver tells it to Colonel Henry F. Westfall, in 1821, and he in turn converts it into notes and communicates it to older citizens now living.

"Soon after the first settlement of the year 1770 had been made on the Tygarts Valley, Buckhannon and West Fork Rivers and their tributaries, and before many inroads and invasions had been made by the merciless savages on these pioneers for the purpose of killing and scalping men, women, and children, or carrying them into captivity, arrangements were made by which spies or scouts were sent out to watch the movements and approach of the Indians, and to report same to the settlers. Indeed companies of these scouts or spies were organized and commanded by proper officials and were obliged to serve alternately by squads. Such military organizations were obtained in the summer of 1770, when a detachment of six men were sent out from Randolph County to spy on the maddened Indians. Four of this small company were, William White, Thomas Drennen, Paul Shaver and John Cutright, the other two are unknown.

"John Cutright was young, a mere boy, small of size, but not a drop of cowardly blood coursed his veins. The scouts went through the boundless forests following the meanderings of the Little Kanawha River to its conjunction with the Ohio. They descended this latter stream as far as the mouth of the Great Kanawha. After a season of inspection, scouting and spying near the famous battle grounds of Point Pleasant they began their homeward journey, passing through the trackless wilderness country now embraced in Mason, Jackson, Roane, Calhoun, Gilmer, Braxton and Lewis Counties. They reached the headwaters of the Little Kanawha River without having seen any trace of the savage. Game being bountiful along this river, they resolved to spend a few days on a hunt. They pitched their camp on Stewart's Creek. Indian Summer was now on and the weather was all that could be desired by our scouts (now turned hunters). They never forgot themselves so much as to neglect watching the trail, leading up the little river near where they were camping, and over to the settlement on the West Fork.

"One evening after having spent a full day hunting deer, several of which they had killed and the haunch of one they were now roasting in their camp fire, they heard a noise, at first supposed to be calling of turkeys going to roost. Cutright thinking that a variety of meat would be spice to their simple life, seized his gun saying he would get a turkey for supper. He walked very briskly toward where the turkey calling was heard; he had not gone far before the turkeys were answering each other in different directions. This fact appealed to the strong perceptive faculties of White and aroused his suspicion that all was not right. He called to Cutright to return and let him go and discover the roosting place of the turkeys. He went but a short distance before he returned with the thrilling news that they were nearly surrounded by a band of Indians. The situation was dangerous and the camp fire by means of which the savages had located them was put out. An escape must be now effected or in a short time the scouting party would be attacked. White was the leader, and the rest were his followers. They stole away and traveled at a rapid gait over rocks, hills, and small streams for four miles before a halt was made. On the summit of a ridge they stopped to reconnoiter and to ascertain whether they were pursued or not. Hearing and seeing no signs of the pursuing Indians they rested there for an hour, during which most of the party went to sleep. White alone being awake and on the lookout. Suddenly he called to his companions, the 'Indians are upon us.' He heard the whine of a dog. They took to their heels again until out of sight of danger then walked on for several miles until they came to a creek of considerable size (most probably Leading Creek). Knowing the keen scent of the Indian canine and the impossibility of being traced in water they waded up this stream a mile and a half or more, coming out on the same side they had entered the stream. They now ascended a hill some distance to its summit, then turned down the stream, keeping about a half mile from it and going about the same distance. Here they halted once more for the purpose of rest and observation. The Indians must have pursued them uncomfortably close, for soon White detected their approach again. This time they descended the hill, crossed the stream behind the Indians, ascended the opposite elevation and took a course along the ridge which led in the direction they wished to go to find the path leading over onto the West Fork. The path could not be found and White concluded that in the darkness they had missed it. They decided to wait the coming of day. To afford themselves the most advantages, they ascended a high bluff to await the action of the pursuers. Again they were driven from their resting place out into the darkness of the night and forced to travel until about sunrise, when they determined to stop, and if the Indians were not too many to give them battle. The most suitable position around them was selected and here they had to wait but for a short time before three Indians were seen on the neighboring hill. Seventeen others joined these three shortly afterwards and all seated themselves upon a fallen tree resting and talking and counseling. Presently they separated, twelve forming the pursuing party, eight returning. Six white men confronted by twelve red men ready for battle would be an easy proposition to wager money upon. Other things being equal superior numbers will win. Therefore our scouting party took themselves to flight rather than fight. Cutright being a mere boy and having traveled all day and night, now showed sign of great fatigue, but the others urged him on. White carried his gun and two others assisted him up the steepest hills, hoping thus to be able to bring him to the Buckhannon River where they thought the Indians would discontinue their pursuit. Cutright held out until the river was reached, when exhausted and crying he lay down and could not go farther. He said to his companions that he could welcome a natural death, but to be tomahawked and scalped by the savage was too hard to bear. 'Save yourselves by flight, but leave me to my fate,' was the answer to the urgent appeals of his companions to proceed. But White said, 'No John, we will never leave you; if one is left all will stay, fight and die together.' White being a man of wonderful strength and endurance gave his gun to one of his companions, took Cutright upon his back and bore him beyond the river. Two other companions carried him to the summit of the river hill opposite the mouth of a run which was then named Cutright's Run, and which afterwards was John Cutright's home. Here all the party fell asleep, but White and Drennen, who stood on guard watching to see the pursuers cross the river. Soon three Indians approached the river on the opposite side and began to cross the stream. A battle was imminent and necessary. Drennen rushed back and aroused his companions. All returned except Cutright, who was too exhausted to do anything. They took their position and waited orders from White to fire. At last the moment came. The three Indians were in a row. The report of the rifles rang out upon the air, two of the savages were killed and the third was anxious to retreat, but he was not to make his escape for White snatched the gun which had failed to fire and shot the Indian just as he leaped the bank of the river.

"Now for the first time it was known to a certainty why the Indians were able to follow the trail so well. They had a dog which went in advance of his red master. This dog fell into the hands of the victors and became the property of White, who used him to good account afterwards, for it is said that White exchanged the same dog and gun for the Heavner farm, upon which the Buckhannon or Bush Fort was afterwards erected."

I remember having seen a fragment of this narrative in the *Westfall Manuscript*. The date, 1770, is not compatible with the general supposition that there was peace on the border from the closing of Pontiac's War in 1765, to the breaking out of open hostilities in 1774. There was peace, but the wanton aggression and murdering propensities of the borderers kept the Indians in a foment of unrest. The settlements made on the Upper Monongahela, a region justly regarded by the Indians as their domain, and which should have been recognized as such by the Colonial Government, (14) was not unknown to the bordering tribes. There was never any serious attempt by the colonial or state authorities to prevent the settlement of the Trans-Allegheny in accordance with stipulated treaty agreements. The King's edict of 1763 warning settlers from the western waters, was not enforced. The proclamation of 1766 by Gov. Penn of Pennsylvania, and Gov. Faquier of Virginia, forbidding "His Majesty's subjects" from settling west of the mountains, may well be termed farcical. In 1769 the garrison at Fort Pitt "attempted" to remove all intruders to the eastern side of the mountains, but the soldiers were withdrawn, and the settlers returned without further molestation. Back of this pretense at justice, can be seen the set intentions of the colonials to gain speedy possession of this coveted domain. The *Ohio Company*, organized 1748, had for its object the settling of the Trans-Allegheny, and as early as 1750 their surveyor, Christopher Gist, had penetrated to the falls of the Ohio. The tribes beheld these encroachments with increasing alarm, and evidently scouts from their own towns kept close watch upon the movements of the aggressors. It may have been such a band with whom the whites on this occasion came in contact; or it may have been a hunting party only, who, finding the intruders so far from the settlements gave chase with disastrous

---
(14) See page 441.

results to themselves. But it can hardly be conceived that an organized body of scouts "were sent out from Randolph County to spy on the maddened Indians" in 1770; Randolph County was not formed until 1787, nor was this region at that time haunted by "maddened Indians." The strangest part of the story is that a "war" party of twenty Indians on the trail of six armed foemen, should of its own volition dwindle to three in number, and yet continue the pursuit. The narrative as a whole is not in accord with the known principles of Indian warfare.

That some such occurrence took place there can be no doubt. Col. Westfall was acquainted with both Paul Shaver and John Cutright, and possibly others of the bordermen. The narrative is interesting in more ways than one. Shaver, one of the actors, was, on his own declaration granted a pension as a soldier of the Revolutionary War, from 1776 to 1780, but was at the instance of W. G. Singleton, Special Pension Examiner, afterwards dropped from the pension roll as too young for military service during that struggle. If Singleton's charges are true, then it is hard to conceive how a man of Colonel Westfall's judgment could be so misled as to seriously consider Shaver a full fledged scout in 1770.

SHAVER'S DECLARATION.

"On this 12th day of Oct. 1833, personally etc., before me, James M. Camp, J. P. for Lewis County, Va., Paul Shaver, aged 74 years, makes the following statement. That in the year 1776 in April of that year he was ordered out as an Indian spy by Col. Warrick under Capt. Maxwell. He spied in Randolph Co. from April 1776, till Nov. 1776, himself and John Elliott detected the Indians at three different times during that summer and each time they retreated without making any attack, but once stole some horses and escaped with them, two of the horses belonged to Runyon. He was discharged in November 1776, having served more than six months in the service as an Indian spy (a private) in Capt. Maxwell's Company of Indian spies. Then in the spring of 1777 in April of that year he volunteered as a private in a company of Virginia Militia, most of whom were drafted, but declarent volunteered to make up a company under Captain Stuart for the defense of the Western Waters. When Capt. Stuart's Company was raised they were marched from what is now Randolph County to West's Fort in what is now Lewis County. There were ascertained a number of Indians in the neighborhood or distant about thirty miles on Salt Lick, some of whom in May 1777, appeared in the neighborhood of West's Fort and killed and scalped one woman, Mrs. Freeman. A few of Capt. Stuart's men in pursuit came in sight, wounded one Indian who got into thick woods with his fellows and prevented further pursuit. Capt. Stuart with his company marched to Salt Lick Creek, the Indians had dispersed. Capt. Stuart and company returned to West's Fort thence to Lowther's Fort, from that place, now Harrison County, 6 miles from where Clarksburg now stands,

Capt. Stuart detached declarent and 10 others as Indian spies to spy in what is now Lewis and Harrison till November, and then return to Westfall's Fort in Randolph, to which place he had marched with his other men. He spied in said tract of country till sometime in Nov. 1777. Then went to Westfall's Fort, from thence to Warrick's Fort where he joined his Captain & company and was in Nov. 1777 discharged, having served more than six months this tour as a private militia man and Indian spy. He then, in 1778, in the spring with several others migrated to what is now Kentucky, settled near where Louisville now stands. He was, in July 1778, drafted to go a tour of three months against the Indians in Illinois County as it was then called, was marched under Captain Andrew Kincaid. The whole under G. R. Clark did not succeed in bringing the Indians to a fight. Returned in the fall of 1778 to Louisville having served his draft of 3 months—was discharged. Then sometime in the winter of 1778 and 1779 Col. Clark conceived the notion of again marching against the Indians in the Illinois County as we then called it, declarent volunteered to go a tour of six months under Capt. Christy; they started, he thinks, Feb. or March 1779, [June 1778] from Louisville, marched to a place called Kaskaskias, there they completely surprised the garrison, he thinks, took the British General or Governor prisoner. Here declarent was stationed with other militia troops a short time whilst Gen. Clark prepared and sent some mounted men on horses taken at Kaskaskias higher up the county and took, as he then heard, three other Indian towns. Col. Clark understood by some means that a large force was concentrating, he stationed his militia and others, some at Kaskaskias and other towns. He soon drew in his troops to Kaskaskias and appealed to all to volunteer longer, declarent with the other troops did so. He was placed under his old Capt. Kincaid stationed at Kaskaskias as a private militia man agreed to stay till the war was settled in that quarter. Col. Clark with some men proceeded in Feb. (1780) as affiant thinks up the Wabash River to Fort Vincent as we then called it, but now Fort St. Vincent or Vincennes. He took that fort which was defended by Col. Hamilton and Indians and British. He, declarent, continued in that Illinois County as a volunteer militia (a private) under Capt. Kincaid, the summer of 1780 till November of that year, when he with other militia troops was marched to Louisville and discharged in November 1780. In this campaign he was more than eighteen months in service from February or March 1779 till November 1780. He received a wound in battle at a place called Andersontown which had healed up (in his right leg) now again broke out and so continues to this day. He served more than two and one-half years in the Revolutionary War. He lives more than thirty miles from Lewis County Court House, is too infirm to attend court, has no clergyman residing near him. He knows of no person whose testimony he can procure who can testify to his services as a soldier of the revolution.

His
Paul X Shaver."
Mark

Shaver stated that he was born in Pendleton County, Va., in the year 1759.

"Leaven Nichols, and David S. Cox both testify that Paul Shaver is believed in the neighborhood to have been a soldier in the Revolutionary War and that he has a good reputation and character.

(Signed) DAVID S. COX
His
LEAVEN X NICHOLS
Mark
(Signed) JAMES M. CAMP, J. P."

John Mitchell and Henry Flesher testified to W. S. Singleton July 1834, that Shaver was too young to have been in the war, and he was dropped from the pension roll as a fraud. From all the evidence gathered, Shaver certainly suffered an injustice at the hands of the over-zealous Pension Examiner. He evidently saw service on the border during the Revolution, but he could not have figured in the "Flight of 1770."

CHAPTER XI

Many prominent writers insist that Dunmore's War was inevitable; the actual beginning of the Revolution, and that hostilities were precipitated by the murdering propensities of the Indians alone. Not a few, however, charge that these conditions were created at the instance of Governor Dunmore and his lieutenant, John Connolly, who, for self-aggrandizement or as emissaries of the British Government, foreseeing the coming struggle, sought to engross the attention and resources of Virginia in a disastrous Indian War. Pages have been written in support of these accusations, and it would redound to the honor of the Virginias could they be verified. But it should be remembered that the conflict of 1774 was purely Virginia and Indian, waged on the Western Virginia border, and it is there that we are to look for the immediate, if not the primal, cause of the trouble. It is noteworthy that the long list of murders committed on peaceable tribesmen in the white settlements *east* of the mountains, prior to the outbreak, did not provoke the war. *Roosevelt* summarily settles the cause and *statu quo* of the Dunmore War in a single paragraph.

"Nor must we permit our sympathy for the foul wrongs of the two great Indian heroes (1) of the contest to blind us to the fact that the struggle was precipitated in the first place, by the outrages of the red men, not the whites; and that the war was not only inevitable, but was also in its essence just and righteous on the part of the borderers. Even the unpardonable and hideous atrocity of the murder of Logan's family, was surpassed in horror by many of the massacres committed by the Indians about the same time. The annals of the border are dark and terrible." (2)

This sweeping attempt at vindication of the borderers, reeking with acrimony for the Indians, might be convincing, did it contain a single instance of a "massacre committed by the Indians about the same time," that even approached in horror the murder of Logan's family. Our Indian conquests have *all* been "just and righteous" in the eyes of the average white man.

Prof. Maxwell in discussing this topic, says:

"* * * The first act of hostility was committed in 1773, not in West Virginia, but further south. A party of emigrants, under the leadership of a son of Daniel Boone, were on their way to Kentucky when they were set upon and several were

(1) See page 442. (2) p. 442.

killed, including young Boone. There can be no doubt that this attack was made to prevent or hinder the colonization of Kentucky. Soon after this, a white man killed an Indian at a horse race. This is said to have been the first Indian blood shed on the frontier of Virginia by a white man after Pontiac's War. In February 1774, the Indians killed six white men and two negroes; and in the same month, on the Ohio they seized a trading canoe, killed the men in charge and carried the goods to the Shawnee towns. Then the white men began to kill also. In March [1774] on the Ohio, a fight occurred between settlers and Indians, in which one was killed on each side, and five canoes were taken from the Indians. John Connolly wrote from Pittsburg on April 21, to the people of Wheeling to be on their guard, as the Indians were preparing for war. On April 26, two Indians were killed on the Ohio. On April 30, nine Indians were killed on the same river near Steubenville. On May 1, another Indian was killed. About the same time an old Indian named Bald Eagle was killed on the Monongahela River; and an Indian camp on the Little Kanawha, in the present county of Braxton, was broken up, and the natives were killed. This was believed to have been done by settlers on the West Fork, in the present county of Lewis. They were induced to take that course by intelligence from the Kanawha River that a family named Stroud, residing near the mouth of the Gauley River had been murdered, and the tracks of the Indians led toward the Indian camp on the Little Kanawha. When this camp was visited by the party of white men from the West Fork, they discovered clothing and other articles belonging to the Stroud family. Thereupon the Indians were destroyed. A party of white men with Governor Dunmore's permission destroyed an Indian village on the Muskingum River." (3)

Here is a sinister array of aggressive crime on the part of the Indians, with justified retaliation by the whites. Unfortunately for its object however, the events are not given in chronological order. The killing of young James Boone and five of his companions, emigrants under the leadership of the elder Boone, had been *preceded* in Kentucky by desultory fighting between adventurous white men and Indians. It is significant that John Findlay who was the first to enter the wilds of Kentucky, was never disturbed by the red man. It was not until Boone, in company with Findlay and four others, in 1769, repaired to that region, and after spending several months in killing game, were they molested. Boone and Stuart were surprised and captured. Many writers insist that during their captivity, the camp of Boone and Stuart was broken up by Indians, and their companions killed, scattered, or returned home. But it would appear from the investigations of others, among them *Dr. Thwaits*, that the returning prisoners found the camp and its occupants unmolested. In the meantime they were joined by Squire Boone and Alexander Neely, whom Squire had found on New (Great Kanawha) River. (4)

---

(3) See page 442. (4) p. 442.

The famous Long Hunters had already invaded this primeval wilderness and were slaughtering its teeming game by the thousands. This wasteful destruction of their sustenance, a gift from the Great Spirit, enraged the Indians, and in consequence the aggressors, hunters and explorers met with armed resistance. The Long Hunters shot buffalo, elk and deer for their skins, and Indians for their scalps.

Boone and his party were in reality Long Hunters. During the summer of 1770 while encamped on the Red River, Alexander Neely killed and scalped two Indians whom he found at a Shawnee village on a tributary creek. (5)

Stuart (also spelled Stewart) alone of the party was killed by the Indians, but whether prior or subsequent to the murder of the Shawnees by Neely, writers differ. *Roosevelt* declares that in the death of Stewart, "the Indians had wantonly shed the first blood." (6) But the elucidation by *Dr. Thwaits* is conclusive that Stuart was killed *after four of Boone's party had left for the settlement* and that "Neely, discouraged by his [Stuart's] fate, returned home." (7) This is positive evidence that Boone's party in reality "wantonly shed the first blood." It is obvious that Neely killed the two Shawnees *before* he "became discouraged and returned home."

The Indian killed at a horse race was a Cherokee, at Watauga, a settlement supposedly in Virginia, but located within the Cherokee lands, North Carolina. Watauga, like the early Trans-Allegheny settlements, was outlawed, so far as State or Colonial Government was concerned. The murder was committed at a friendly gathering of both Indians and whites, in celebrating the signing of a treaty between the Cherokees and the settlers of Watauga in 1772. (8) This crime has been excused on the grounds that the men implicated had lost a brother in the attack on Boone's emigrants in 1773. This is error, the friendly Cherokee was killed *a year previous to the Boone tragedy*. In the face of these facts, *who* were the aggressors in Kentucky? (9)

No serious trouble with the Cherokees resulted from the Watauga outrage; nor was that nation involved in Dunmore's War. It is averred, however, that the attack on Butler's trading canoe, near Wheeling, in February, 1774, containing three white men, in which one of the party was killed and another one wounded, was by a few outlaw Cherokees. If so, the act may have been provoked by the Watauga tragedy.

---

(5) See page 442. (6) p. 442. (7) p. 442. (8) p. 442. (9) p. 442.

The other occurrences cited by Mr. Maxwell are well known to the reader of border history. *Withers*, (10) states that the Bull Town Massacre occurred in the summer of 1772. The same authority fixes the death of Bald Eagle not only prior to this crime, but also to the Indian murder for which Capt. White was imprisoned at Winchester, and subsequently liberated by the infuriated populace. This last crime, as shown in Chapter X, of this volume, *Kercheval* states, occurred in 1768. This places the murder of Bald Eagle, according to *Withers*, (11) previous to the settling of the Upper Monongahela in 1769, which is error. The death of Bald Eagle evidently occurred between 1770 and the destruction of the Delaware Village on the Little Kanawha, in 1772, which was *two years previous* to the retaliatory and incipient outbreak of the few tribesmen on the Ohio. Then came the ill-timed warning of the fiery Connolly and the "planting of a new war post and a solemn declaration of war" by Creasap and his followers at Fort Henry. Immediately Creasap's band made two attacks on friendly Shawnees on the Ohio, killing three and wounding two others. The massacre of Logan's people swiftly followed, and the war was on.

West Virginia points with pride to the tenth of October, 1774, when at Point Pleasant was fought the "First Battle of the Revolution," wherein "was the first blood shed in defense of American Liberty," in a "just and righteous" war. This sounds well, but in reality the Dunmore War was one of conquest; its prelude a lurid chapter of aggressive wrong on the part of the whites which can reflect no halo of State or National glory. (12)

The brutal murder of Bald Eagle is deserving of more than a passing notice. His status, not only with his own race, but with the whites was high, and in his death is reflected the true character of the lawless ruffians who overran the Trans-Allegheny at this time. *Withers* says of this crime:

"The Bald Eagle was an Indian of notoriety, not only among his own nation, but also with the inhabitants of the North Western frontier; with whom he was in the habit of associating and hunting. In one of his visits among them, he was discovered alone, by Jacob Scott, William Hacker and Elijah Runner, who, reckless of the consequences, murdered him, solely to gratify a most wanton thirst for Indian blood. After the commission of this most outrageous enormity, they seated him in the stern of a canoe, and with a piece of journey-cake thrust into his mouth, set him afloat in the Monongahela. In this situation he was seen descending the river, by several, who supposed him to be as usual, returning from

---

(10) See page 442. (11) p. 442. (12) p. 442.

a friendly hunt with the whites in the upper settlements, and who expressed some astonishment that he did not stop to see them. The canoe floating near to the shore, below the mouth of George's Creek, was observed by a Mrs. Province, who had it brought to the bank, and the friendly, but unfortunate old Indian decently buried." (13)

Veech says that Bald Eagle was killed, perhaps, at the mouth of Cheat River; was found at Provance Bottom by Mrs. William Yard Provance, who had him buried on the Fayette (Pa.) shore. (14)

The murder of Bald Eagle had a parallel of which the particulars were never chronicled.

One Ryan and Eli Morgan, brother of David Morgan of border fame, killed an Indian named Cat Eye, and thrusting a corn cob into his mouth, propped him up in his canoe and sent him adrift on the Monongahela. This crime was evidently one of the many committed by John Ryan, told by *Withers:*

"At different periods of time, between the peace of 1765, and the renewal of hostilities in 1774, three Indians were unprovokedly killed by John Ryan, on the Ohio, Monongahela and Cheat Rivers. The first who suffered from the unrestrained licentiousness of this man, was an Indian of distinction in his tribe, and known by the name of Capt. Peter; the other two were private warriors. And but that Governor Dunmore, from the representations made to him, was induced to offer a reward for his apprehension, which caused him to leave the country, Ryan would probably have continued to murder every Indian, with whom he should chance to meet, wandering through the settlements." (15)

To this long list of recorded murders suffered by the friendly tribesmen at the hands of the borderers in the two years preceding Dunmore's War, must be added the massacre of the thirteen at Indian Camp, as depicted in a previous chapter of this volume. The summary is startling. If we allow but four to each of the five families destroyed at Bull Town, which is a very low estimate, then the grand total of peaceable Indians, including many women and children, who fell victims to white fury on the extreme western border of Virginia, from Bull Town to Wheeling in the time mentioned, is fifty-eight. This does not include those killed on the Wappatomaka by Judah, Harpold and others, nor the many slain throughout the settlements east of the mountains. (16) This number I have carefully computed from the meagre accounts at hand; but it is hardly possible that the Indian Camp Massacre was a solitary instance of unchronicled slaughtering by the whites. It is significant that in every instance noted by the historian of the

(13) See page 443. (14) p. 443. (15) p. 443. (16) p. 443.

day, the killing was so open and flagrant that concealment was impossible.

There could be but one sequel to this wanton, drunken saturnalia of crime. The ties of blood and clan are very strong in Indian systems of kinship and government, and the law of retaliation arises from these ties. In addition to murder, the white settlers were constantly making inroads upon the lands of the tribes in utter disregard of treaty stipulations. In view of these facts, it is a matter of wonder that hostilities were not commenced long before the outbreak actually occurred. Surely were the Indians "slow to anger."

But they were at last aroused; though not until their people had been wantonly murdered in plain view and under their own eyes in more than one instance by Greathouse and others. Logan, "the friend of the white man," lost his entire family. (17) Then the warriors took up the hatchet, and the Trans-Allegheny was compelled to drain the bitter cup of its own filling. For more than twenty years from the massacre of Logan's people, April 30, 1774, the border from Fort Pitt to the Falls of the Ohio suffered from Indian forays, (18) the most sanguinary of which fell upon the Virginia frontier. There were brief respites during this period, but no year went by without the striking of a blow — in most cases by the fierce Shawnee. This warlike tribe was rendered still more implacable by the betrayal and brutal murder of their mighty leader Cornstalk (Keigh-taugh-qua) and three of his chiefs, his son Ellinipsico; Red Hawk and another whose name is unknown, at Point Pleasant in the "bloody year," 1777; and for which his avenging warriors swept with fire the wilderness settlements. (19) In this long interval of strife, as usual in warfare, the innocent suffered far more than the guilty.

During this period, Jesse Hughes was the recognized chief of the Virginia scouts. He lived in the center of the field of the border strife; yet it was in the year 1778 that his name appears in the annals of this war for the first time. This, I believe, is the fault of the chroniclers rather than of inactivity on the part of Hughes. There is little or no doubt that he was constantly engaged in war-like enterprises during the whole of this period of the silence of the annals. A well-founded tradition says that he was in the Battle of Point Pleasant, which is more than probable. A man of his propensities would not ordinarily remain inactive at

---
(17) See page 443. (18) p. 443. (19) p. 443.

home while such an undertaking as the invasion of the Indian country was being executed. It is doubtful if any of the several expeditions against the Ohio Indians during the period mentioned was unaccompanied by Jesse Hughes.

An Indian alarm in June, 1778, sent the settlers on Hacker's Creek and the adjoining country into West's Fort. About the middle of that month, three women who were gathering greens in an adjacent field, were attacked by four Indians and a Mrs. Freeman was killed and scalped. The Indians fired but one shot, but this and the screams of the women brought the men from the Fort. Several ineffectual bullets were sent after the warrior who was scalping Mrs. Freeman. The Indians were driven off, and the firing gave warning to the men who were out of the fort at the time. Among the latter was Jesse Hughes, who for once, seemingly, was without his gun. The following account is from the work of *Withers:*

"Jesse Hughes and John Schoolcraft (who were out) in making their way to the fort, came very near two Indians standing by the fence looking towards the men at West's, so intently, that they did not perceive any one near them. They, however, were observed by Hughes and Schoolcraft who, avoiding them, made their way in, safely. Hughes immediately took up his gun, and learning the fate of Mrs. Freeman, went with some others to bring in the corpse. While there he proposed to go and shew them how near he had approached the Indians after the alarm had been given, before he saw them. Charles and Alexander West, Chas. Hughes, James Brown and John Steeth (20), went with him. Before they had arrived at the place, one of the Indians was heard to howl like a wolf; and the men with Hughes moved on in the direction from which the sound proceeded. Supposing that they were then near the spot, Jesse Hughes howled in like manner, and being instantly answered, they ran to a point of the hill, and looking over it, saw two Indians coming towards them. Hughes fired and one of them fell. The other took to flight. Being pursued by the whites, he sought shelter in a thicket of brush; and while they were proceeding to intercept him at his coming out, he returned by the way he had entered, and made his escape. The wounded Indian likewise got off. When the whites were in pursuit of the one who took to flight, they passed near to him who had fallen, and one of the men was for stopping and finishing him; but Hughes called to him, 'he is safe,—let us have the other,' and they all pressed forward. On their return, however, he was gone; and although his free bleeding enabled them to pursue his track readily for a while, yet a heavy shower of rain soon falling, all trace of him was quickly lost and could not be afterwards regained."

The chagrin which Hughes felt for his failure to secure at least one of the two scalps that were almost within his grasp may be conjectured. That his aim was not deadly, and his allowing

---
(20) See page 444.

the fallen Indian to escape because of his zeal to capture the fleeing Indian who baffled his pursuers by doubling on his track like a fox, was most humiliating to the pride of this renowned woodsman and his skilled companions. There was a superstition rife among the early settlers to the effect that if, in loading his rifle, the hunter accidentally let fall the bullet, and had to pick it up from the ground to put in his rifle, it would certainly miss the object shot at, no matter how careful and true his aim. This was a common belief in the woods of Virginia and Kentucky as recently as thirty years ago. Perhaps Jesse dropped his bullet.

Owing to its isolation and weakness, the Hacker's Creek settlement was a favorite point of attack by the Indians during this period. *Withers* says:

"The settlement on Hacker's Creek was entirely broken up in the spring of 1779—some of its inhabitants forsaking the country and retiring east of the mountains; while the others went to the fort on Buckhannon, and to Nutter's Fort, near Clarksburg, to aid in resisting the foe and in maintaining possession of the country." (21)

Again, speaking of the year 1780, he says:

"West's Fort on Hacker's Creek was also visited by the savages early in this year. The frequent incursions of the Indians into this settlement in the year 1778, had caused the inhabitants to desert their homes the next year, and shelter themselves in places of greater security; but being unwilling to give up the improvements which they had already made and commence anew in the woods, some few families returned to it during the winter, and on the approach of spring, moved into the fort. They had not been long here, before the savages made their appearance, and continued to invest the fort for some time. Too weak to sally out and give them battle, and not knowing when to expect relief, the inhabitants were almost reduced to despair, when Jesse Hughes resolved at his own hazard, to try to obtain assistance to drive off the enemy. Leaving the fort at night, he broke by their sentinels and ran with speed to the Buckhannon Fort. Here he prevailed on a part of the men to accompany him to West's, and relieve those who had been so long confined there. They arrived before day, and it was thought advisable to abandon the place once more, and remove to Buckhannon. On their way the Indians used every artifice to separate the party, so as to gain an advantageous opportunity of attacking them; but in vain. They exercised so much caution, and kept so well together, that every stratagem was frustrated, and they all reached the fort in safety." (22)

From the foregoing it would appear that West's Fort was abandoned not only in the fall of 1779, but also in the spring of 1780. It was during one of these abandonments, perhaps the last, that the fort was burned by the Indians, and the settlers then

(21) See page 445. (22) p. 445.

built a new fort, but not on the site of the old. It was located some five hundred yards or more from West's Fort, and about seventy-five yards east of where the Henry McWhorter house now stands. It was erected on a high bottom, or "flat," which at that time was rather marshy, and covered with beech trees. The building was constructed entirely of beech logs, and was locally known as "Beech Fort." (23)

THE HOME OF BLACK JEFF AND HIS MAMMY, "AUNT" EMELY
Photographed 1898, Kindness of Mr. Guy Alkire

This cabin stood on Jesse's Run, less than a mile from where Jesse Hughes settled in 1770 or 1771. During a heavy snow storm in 1899 or 1900 the roof of Jeff's cabin collapsed, burying himself and "Mammy" in its ruins. They were removed to the county infirmary, where they both soon afterwards died.

The daring feat of Jesse Hughes upon this occasion, so briefly alluded to by *Withers*, and doubtless referred to by *Dellass*, already quoted, was as follows:

A large force of Indians had invested the fort and gathered up all the live stock in the settlement. The despairing inmates could see the camp fires of the Indians, who, relying upon their superior numbers and the weakness of the garrison, failed to exercise that degree of vigilance and caution for which they are

(23) See page 445.

noted. However, they posted sentinels about the fort and the fords of the creek and other passes, while the main body of warriors regaled themselves around the camp fires. Hughes experienced great difficulty and much personal danger in breaking through the Indian investment. While gliding along a narrow path, he heard foot steps approaching. He stepped aside, when nine warriors passed in Indian file; "so close" said Hughes, "that I could have punched them with my ramrod."

When leaving the fort he told the inmates that if he succeeded in eluding the foe he would, upon gaining the hillside beyond the Indian encampment, "hoot like an owl." The hoot of the owl was a night signal in vogue with both Indian and scout. In crossing the creek Jesse was compelled to wade through a deep eddy about half-way between the fort and the mouth of Jesse's Run, near where he would strike the trail.

As time dragged, the forlorn and despairing band in the little fortress listened most eagerly for the signal of hope from the hillside. How they must have rejoiced when at last through the darkness from afar there came across the night-shrouded valley the melancholy cry of the bird of shadow and gloom. (24) To them it meant succor and speedy rescue; but to the wily Indian it was ominous of approaching danger, and during the night they broke camp and disappeared. When Hughes returned with the rescuing party not a warrior could be seen.

The difficulty of this achievement can be better understood when it is known that the distance between the two forts was not less than sixteen miles, all a dense forest; and as the Indians were in the settlement in force, he must have avoided to some extent the beaten trail, thus making the passage far more laborious and hazardous.

The frightful dangers that beset the path of Jesse Hughes on this heroic night-run were not confined to the hostile Indians alone. The stealthy panther, noted for its fierce nature and proneness to unprovoked attack on human beings, lurked among the dense thickets on every hand. Packs of gaunt gray wolves — huge timber wolves — the scourge of the wilderness, prowled the forest. The Buckhannon or Hacker's Creek mountain at the point traversed by Hughes was infested with these savage brutes long after this incident. (25)

Once during the Indian incursions into this region the settlers

---
(24) See page 445. (25) p. 445.

on Fink's Run, a tributary of the Buckhannon, took refuge in West's Fort. Why the settlers should, in this instance, have gone to West's Fort instead of the Buckhannon, (26) which was only three or four miles distant, cannot be surmised, unless it was after the latter fort had been abandoned in 1782, when Captain William White was killed. So precipitate had been their flight that they left some young calves penned from their dams. This was not discovered until they had reached the fort, which was at least twelve miles from their homes, and was liable to lead to calamity, for should the stock escape the wasting hands of the Indians, the calves would starve and the cows be hopelessly ruined from inflamed udders. In this dilemma, Jesse Hughes came to the rescue. He volunteered to go and liberate the calves. This was courting death, but he successfully accomplished it.

On his return to the fort he crossed the mountain previously referred to, to the waters of the right fork of Buckhannon Run, now on the farm of the late G. W. Swisher. Here seeing a deer, the instinct of the sportsman overcame the caution of the scout, and he shot and killed it. Proceeding to flay it, he had just completed that work, when the report of a rifle rang through the forest, and the bullet passed through the crown of his coon-skin cap, scarcely missing his head.

Snatching up his rifle and the reeking deerskin, he sped down the valley, towards the fort. Reaching Hacker's Creek proper, the trail left the lowlands and striking the hill to the right, passed around the head of a small stream known as Redlick Run, and along the meandering ridge between Hacker's Creek and Jesse's Run. Hughes did not slacken his pace until he reached the low gap in the ridge where Mr. Eben Post now lives. Here the woods were open, and he paused and glanced back over the trail. A quarter of a mile away three Indians were racing down the slope in hot pursuit. A very large warrior was in the lead. It was at this point in the race that Hughes first noticed that he was carrying the deerskin, showing that under certain circumstances the bravest may suffer from excitement and panic. The first impulse of Hughes was to secrete himself and shoot the big Indian when he came within range, for he felt he had nothing to fear from the remaining two. Being much more fleet of foot he could have reloaded and shot them at his leisure; for Jesse Hughes like his great contemporary, Lewis Wetzel, could load his rifle while

---
(26) See page 445.

running at full speed. This, however, was not an unusual feat among the Virginia bordermen. But fearing that the report of his rifle might draw others to the chase, and that he would be intercepted before he could reach the fort, he let discretion be the better part of valor, and again fled before his rapidly advancing pursuers. Out the long ridge like a hounded stag the scout stretched himself to the trail, followed by the grim avengers of a hundred wrongs.

> "Fate judges of the rapid strife;
> The forfeit, death—the prize is life."

There were yet several miles to be covered before the fugitive could hope to reach a refuge, and if other Indians should be lurking along the path his chances of escape were precarious in the extreme. Never before, perhaps, had the wonderful physical endurance of the veteran scout been put to such a test; and like the wild Seri, impervious to fatigue, onward he sped; and onward came his relentless pursuers. The hound-like tirelessness of the borderman enabled him to maintain the distance that was early established between him and the Indians. He gained the fort in safety, carrying the deerskin that had so nearly cost him his life.

The distance covered in this race for life was no less than nine miles, and it was over ground so rough that it must have taxed the endurance of the participants to the utmost. The course followed was an old Indian trail, which was also used as a bridle path by the pioneers. Few such races were run, even on the frontiers, and perhaps no other was so long and persistent; and winning it would alone entitle Jesse Hughes to a high rank in that host of pioneers who achieved fame on the border.

CHAPTER XII

In 1781, we find that Jesse Hughes and his brother Elias were members of Colonel Lowther's Company, which went in pursuit of the Indians who had captured Mrs. Alexander Roney and her son, and Daniel Dougherty, all of Leading Creek, Tygart's Valley. The history of this foray and the incidents immediately preceding the connection of Jesse Hughes therewith, I quote from *Withers:* (1)

"In the same month (April), as some men were returning to Cheat River from Clarksburg (where they had been to obtain certificates of settlement rights to their lands, from the commissioners appointed to adjust land claims in the counties of Ohio, Youghioghany and Monongalia) they, after having crossed the Valley River, were encountered by a large party of Indians, and John Manear, Daniel Cameron and a Mr. Cooper were killed—the others effected their escape with difficulty.

"The savages then moved on towards Cheat, but meeting with James Brown and Stephen Radcliff, and not being able to kill or take them, they changed their course, and passing over Leading creek (in Tygarts Valley), nearly destroyed the whole settlement. They there killed Alexander Roney, Mrs. Dougherty, Mrs. Hornbeck, and her children, Mrs. Buffington and her children, and many others; and made prisoners, Mrs. Roney and her son, and Daniel Dougherty. Jonathan Buffington and Benjamin Hornbeck succeeded in making their escape and carried the doleful tidings to Friend's and Wilson's forts. Col. Wilson immediately raised a company of men and proceeding to Leading Creek, found the settlement without inhabitants and the houses nearly all burned. He then pursued after the savages, but not coming up with them as soon as was expected, the men became fearful of the consequences which might result to their own families, by reason of this abstraction of their defense, provided other Indians were to attack them, and insisted on their returning. On the second day of the pursuit it was agreed that a majority of the company should decide whether they were to proceed farther or not. Joseph Friend, Richard Kettle, Alexander West and Col. Wilson were the only persons in favor of going on, and they consequently had to return.

"But though the pursuit was thus abandoned, yet did not the savages get off with their wonted impunity. When the land claimants, who had been the first to encounter this party of Indians, escaped from them, they fled back to Clarksburg, and gave the alarm. This was quickly communicated to the other settlements, and spies were sent out to watch for the enemy. By some of these, the savages were discovered on the West Fork, near the mouth of Isaac's creek, and intelligence of it was immediately carried to the forts. Col. Lowther collected a company of men, and going in pursuit, came in view of their encampment, awhile before night, on a branch of Hughes' River, ever since known as *Indian Creek*. Jesse and Elias Hughes—active, intrepid and vigilant men—were left to

(1) See page 446.

watch the movements of the savages, while the remainder retired a small distance to refresh themselves, and prepare to attack them in the morning.

"Before day Col. Lowther arranged his men in order of attack, and when it became light, on the preconcerted signal being given, a general fire was poured in upon them. Five of the savages fell dead and the others fled leaving at their fires, all their shot bags and plunder, and all their guns, except one. Upon going to their camp, it was found that one of the prisoners (a son of Alexander Roney who had been killed in the Leading creek massacre) was among the slain. Every care had been taken to guard against such an occurrence, and he was the only one of the captives who sustained any injury from the fire of the whites.

"In consequence of information received from the prisoners who were retaken (that a larger party of Indians was expected hourly to come up), Col. Lowther deemed it prudent not to go in pursuit of those who had fled, and collecting the plunder which the savages had left, catching the horses which they had stolen, and having buried young Roney, the party set out on its return march home—highly gratified at the success which had crowned their exertions to punish their untiring foe."

To the foregoing, *Withers* adds the following note:

"As soon as the fire was opened upon the Indians, Mrs. Roney (one of the prisoners) ran towards the whites rejoicing at the prospect of deliverance, and exclaiming, 'I am Ellick Roney's wife, of the Valley, I am Ellick Roney's wife, of the Valley, and a pretty little woman too, if I was well dressed.' The poor woman ignorant of the fact that her son was weltering in his own gore, and forgetting for an instant that her husband had been so recently killed, seemed intent only on her own deliverance from the savage captors.

"Another of the captives, Daniel Dougherty, being tied down, and unable to move, was discovered by the whites as they rushed towards the camp. Fearing that he might be one of the enemy and do them some injury if they advanced, one of the men, stopping, demanded who he was. Benumbed with cold, and discomposed by the sudden firing of the whites, he could not render his Irish dialect intelligible to them. The white man raised his gun and directed it towards him, calling aloud, that if he did not make known who he was, he should blow a ball through him, let him be white man or Indian. Fear supplying him with energy, Dougherty exclaimed, 'Loord Jasus! and am I to be killed by white people at last!' He was heard by Col. Lowther and his life saved."

Captain William White and John Cutright were with Colonel Lowther on this occasion. Christopher Cutright, son of John, gave me the following particulars of the affair, as received from his father.

The whites discovered the Indians in camp in the evening, and they hid in a ravine until the next morning. When it was about daylight, Mrs. Roney arose and replenished the fire, and at that moment the whites opened fire on the Indians, killing and mortally wounding seven of their number. Young Roney was killed, and Dougherty, in his frantic attempts to convey to the attacking party his identity, exclaimed, *"Can't ye sae that I'm a white mon?"* When the whites rushed upon the camp, one of the Indians struggling in the agonies of death was recognized as Captain Bull, the founder of Bull Town on the Little Kanawha. Jesse Hughes seized the dying chieftain and dragged him through the camp fire so recently replenished by Mrs. Roney, *"while he was yet kicking."* Not satisfied with this, he then flayed from the thigh of the dead chieftain pieces of skin, with which he repaired his own moccasins which had become badly worn during the pursuit. (2) "Upon the return of the company to the settlements," said Mr. Cutright, "Hughes, as a joke, threw his moccasins with their ghastly patches into my mother's lap."

The body of young Roney was sunk in the river, or creek, near the scene of his death, which occurred close where the Indian Creek schoolhouse now stands.

Colonel Lowther was accompanied on this expedition by one of his sons, a lad about sixteen years old, who assisted in the attack on the Indian camp and its subsequent massacre. Boys of those days had early schooling in the savage warfare of the border. (3)

On the evening before the Leading Creek settlement was destroyed, Alexander West was at Friend's Fort. Late in the evening, West and Joseph Friend were sitting on the porch and saw what West declared to be an Indian skulking near the fort. West started to get his gun, but Friend detained him and declared the figure to be one of his "yaller boys." "Yaller boy the mischief!" exclaimed West, "It's an Injun." West and Friend had each a very fierce dog, and not altogether satisfied as to the identity of the stranger, they attempted to set them on the slave boy or Indian. But the dogs flew at each other, and during the confusion that ensued, and while the men were engaged in separating the dogs, the unknown person whose mysterious movements had caused the uproar vanished into the nearby forest, and night coming on, the pursuit was abandoned.

West ever alert and cautious, wished to alarm the settlers that night, but Friend insisted there was no danger and that they wait until morning. West reluctantly acquiesced. That night or early the next morning occurred the Leading Creek massacre. Six families were destroyed. When the news of the disaster reached West he became furious, and condemned himself for not

(2) See page 446. (3) p. 446.

A TYPICAL PIONEER MILL

Photographed Feb. 16, 1910, Kindness of Mr. L. D. Wilmoth

This mill stands about sixteen miles north of Beverly on a small stream near its juncture with Leading Creek, Randolph County, W. Va., the scene of the Indian massacre in April, 1781. It was built in the first quarter of the last century by Jacob Slagele, and is now owned by Mr. R. B. Vanscoy. The burrs are from native stone found in Laurel Hill nearby. Originally, small grains as well as corn were ground, the flour and bran being separated with a small bolt turned by hand. Since the forest has been destroyed about the source of the stream, the acting upon his own judgment. If he had, it is probable that the tragedy would have been averted.

From the date of the Leading Creek massacre and the killing of Captain Bull on Indian Creek, to 1787, a period of six years, no mention is made of Hughes by the historians of his time.

In 1787, we find the Indians again in the Hacker's Creek settlement. The eldest daughter of Jesse Hughes was taken captive, and several of the settlers were killed. This tragedy was only the sequel of that which directly preceded it, and so closely are the incidents connected that I give them both as set out by *Withers*. (4)

"In September of this year, a party of Indians were discovered in the act of catching some horses on the West Fork above Clarksburg; and a company of men led on by Col. Lowther, went immediately in pursuit of them. On the third night the Indians and whites, unknown to each other, encamped not far apart; and in the morning the fires of the latter being discovered by Elias Hughes, the detachment which was accompanying him fired upon the camp, and one of the savages fell. The remainder taking to flight, one of them passed near to where Col. Lowther and the other men were, and the Colonel firing at him as he ran, the ball entering at his shoulder, perforated him and he fell. The horses and plunder which had been taken by the savages, were then collected by the whites, and they commenced their return home, in the confidence of false security. They had not proceeded far, when two guns were unexpectedly fired at them, and John Bonnett fell, pierced through the body. He died before he reached home. (5)

"The Indians never thought the whites justifiable in flying to arms to punish them for acts merely of rapine. They felt authorized to levy contributions of this sort, whenever an occasion served, viewing property thus acquired as (to use their own expression) the 'only rent which (6) they received for their lands;' and if when detected in secretly exacting them, their blood paid the penalty, they were sure to retaliate with tenfold fury, on the first favorable opportunity. The murder of these two Indians by Hughes and Lowther was soon followed by acts of retribution which are believed to have been, at least immediately, produced by them.

"On the 5th of December, a party of Indians and one white man (Leonard Schoolcraft) came into the settlement on Hacker's Creek, and meeting with a daughter of Jesse Hughes, took her prisoner. Passing on, they came upon E. West, Senr., carrying some fodder to the stable, and taking him likewise captive, carried him to where Hughes' daughter had been left in charge of some of their party. — Here the old gentleman fell upon his knees and expressed a fervent wish that they would not deal harshly by him. His petition was answered by a stroke of the tomahawk and he fell dead.

"They then went to the house of Edmund West, Jun., where were Mrs. West and her sister (a girl of eleven years old, daughter of John Hacker) and a lad of twelve, a brother of West. Forcing open the door, Schoolcraft and two of the savages entered, and one of them immediately tomahawked Mrs. West. The boy was taking some corn from under the bed, — he was drawn out by the feet and

(4) See page 446. (5) p. 446. (6) p. 446.

the tomahawk sank twice in his forehead, directly above each eye. The girl was standing behind the door. One of the savages approached and aimed at her a blow. She tried to evade it, but it struck on the side of her neck, though not sufficient force to knock her down. She fell however, and lay as if killed. Thinking their work of death accomplished here, they took from the press some milk, butter and bread, placed it on the table, and deliberately sat down to eat, — the little girl observing all that passed, in silent stillness. When they had satisfied their hunger, they arose, scalped the woman and boy, plundered the house, — even emptying the feathers to carry off the ticking, — and departed, dragging the little girl by the hair, forty or fifty yards from the house. They then threw her over the fence, and scalped her; but as she evinced symptoms of life, Schoolcraft observed *'that is not enough'*, when immediately one of the savages thrust a knife into her side, and they left her. Fortunately the point of the knife came in contact with a rib and did not injure her much.

"Old Mrs. West and her two daughters, who were alone when the old gentleman was taken, became uneasy that he did not return; and fearing that he had fallen into the hands of savages (as they could not otherwise account for his absence), they left the house and went to Alexander West's, who was then on a hunting expedition with his brother Edmund. They told of the absence of old Mr. West and their fears for his fate; and as there was no man here, they went over to Jesse Hughes' who was himself uneasy that his daughter did not come home. Upon hearing that West too was missing, he did not doubt but that both had fallen into the hands of the Indians; and knowing of the absence from home of Edmund West, Jun., he deemed it advisable to apprise his wife of danger, and remove her to his house. For this purpose and accompanied by Mrs. West's two daughters, he went on. On entering the door, the tale of destruction which had been done there was soon told in part. Mrs. West and the lad lay weltering in their blood but not yet dead. The sight overpowered the girls, and Hughes had to carry them off. Seeing that the savages had but just left them, and aware of the danger which would attend any attempt to move out and give the alarm that night, Hughes guarded his own house until day, when he spread the sorrowful intelligence, and a company were collected to ascertain the extent of the mischief and try to find those who were known to be missing.

"Young West was found, — standing in the creek about a mile from where he had been tomahawked. The brains were oozing from his head, yet he survived in extreme suffering for three days. Old Mr. West was found in the field where he had been tomahawked. Mrs. West was in the house; she probably lived but a few minutes after Hughes and her sisters-in-law had left there. — The little girl (Hacker's daughter) was in bed at the house of old Mr. West. She related the history of the transactions at Edmund West's, Jun., and said that she went to *sleep* when thrown over the fence and was awakened by the scalping. After she had been stabbed at the suggestion of Schoolcraft and left, she tried to recross the fence to the house, but as she was climbing up, again went to sleep and fell back. She then walked into the woods, sheltered herself as well as she could in the top of a fallen tree, and remained there until the cocks crew in the morning.

"Remembering that there was no person left alive at the house of her sister awhile before day she proceeded to old Mr. West's. She found no person at home, the fire nearly out, but the hearth warm and she laid down on it. The heat produced a sickly feeling, which caused her to get up and go to the bed, in which she was found. — She recovered, grew up, was married, gave birth to ten children, and died, as was believed, of an affection of the head, occasioned by the wound she received that night. Hughes' daughter was ransomed by her father the next year, and is yet living in sight of the theatre of those savage enormities."

Jesse Hughes and William Powers were also on the expedition with Colonel Lowther when Bonnett was killed. They followed the Indians to the Little Kanawha River, where the two Indians were slain. Bonnett, in utter disregard of West's remonstrance, had stepped aside from the party to a spring and had knelt there to get a drink. As he rose, he received the fatal shot. The return march of the party was necessarily slow, encumbered with a dying man. It is not likely that Bonnett was buried any great distance from where he was shot.

Mr. Levi Bond heard his grandfather, William Powers, tell the incidents of this tragedy as follows: Three of the Indians were killed. When they were fired upon in camp, only one of those who escaped had a gun. The whites felt that on their retreat some one of their number would be shot by this Indian, and that the victim would in all probability be the one in lead of the party. Bonnett declared that he had just as well die as any of them and stepped to the front. Powers was placed at some distance in the rear, to guard against pursuit. When he heard the gun report, he knew that some one of their party had been fired upon, and possibly killed. He saw the fleeing Indian, but at too great a distance for a shot, so he gave chase. Powers was a swift runner and gained on the warrior, who resorting to strategy, dodged and hid from his enemy. After peace was declared, an Indian told of his shooting the white man at the head of the party, and that he in turn was pursued by a "little white devil" and barely escaped. Powers said, that in this expedition, as in all others, Jesse Hughes led in the trailing.

The daughter of Hughes, who was captured at the time of the West tragedy, was his eldest child, Martha. She was then fourteen years old. When captured she was returning home from the house of John Hacker, where she had gone to get a pup. Hacker lived about four miles up the creek from where Hughes lived. *Withers* says she was "ransomed by her father the next year," but as a substance of fact she did not return home until 1790 and was a prisoner two years and nine months. Her father

secured her release at Sandusky Plains after the treaty of Fort
Harmer, January 9, 1789, which made it possible to secure the
release of Indian captives.

There is a tradition current among Jesse's descendants in
Jackson County, West Virginia, to the effect that another daughter,
Nancy, was captured by the Indians and held in captivity three
years. In this short time she became thoroughly Indianized, and
her father failed to recognize her when he went to bring her home.
Personal decoration, paint, rings on every finger and in her lip, a
complete Indian dress, so changed her appearance that only the
closest questioning in reference to the time and place of her capture enabled Hughes to determine her identity. This is merely
a distorted and fanciful version of Martha's capture. Hughes
recognized her as soon as he caught sight of her in the Indian
country.

The name of the Hacker girl, who figured in this tragedy was
Mary. Tradition says that she was stabbed seven times by an
Indian, who was afterwards killed; his body ripped open, filled
with sand and sunk in Hacker's Creek on the David Smith farm.
Mary Hacker married a Mr. Wolf and settled on Wolf's Run in
Lewis County. She never fully recovered from the effects of the
scalping and her death was caused from a nasal hemorrhage.

Barring a few burnings at the stake, there is hardly a more
pathetic tragedy in the annals of the border wars than the tomahawking at West's. The despairing appeal of the old man, who
with advancing age, had lost much of the nerve and energy of
hardy manhood, the utter helplessness of Mrs. West, the pulling
from beneath the bed of the little boy and his brutal tomahawking,
the ineffectual attempt of the little girl at concealment and her
instinctive efforts to evade the murderous blow — all this makes
a scene of pathetic woe. The long night of agony for the two
little children cannot be fully imagined. Contemplation of the
boy wandering aimlessly through the icy waters of the creek, with
skull bared from scalping, his brains oozing from the ghastly
wounds in his forehead, and chilled by the cold winds of December,
is most heartrending. The little girl dragged by the hair, falling
to "sleep" when thrown over the fence, her awakening from the
excruciating torture of the process of scalping, the relentless
thrust of the murderous knife, the feeble and unsuccessful attempt
to reach the house, the going to "sleep" the second time, the piteous

turning to the solitude of the woods for shelter, the arrival at the house and curling down upon the warm hearth, the sensation of sickness and the climbing into the lonely bed make up a story that fills the heart with sadness. It certainly must have been anything but comforting to Colonel Lowther, Elias Hughes and their followers, if they realized the situation, to reflect that to

THE HISTORIC BARN ON THE EDMUND WEST, SR., HOMESTEAD
(Queen, 1894)

their over-zeal in protecting a few miserable horses by shooting two fleeing Indians, was this awful tragedy due. And the greatest pity of all, retaliatory vengeance fell upon the innocent and helpless.

The Edmund West, Sr., homestead was covered by a grant issued in 1781 to "Edmund West, 400 acres on Hacker's Creek, adjoining lands of William Ratcliff, including his settlement made in 1773." This was the present Straley farm, about one mile above Jane Lew. The old barn, of which a cut is given, is still standing. The left room, or left end of this barn, was built by Edmund West, Sr., and is doubtless the stable referred to by *Withers*, where Mr. West was captured while "carrying fodder."

Tradition says that West's Fort was built by Edmund West's, Sr., two sons, Alexander and Edmund, Jr. This I believe to be a mistake. According to *Withers*, (7) the fort was standing in 1778. At that time Alexander West was but eighteen years old, and there is every reason to believe that the fort was built at the

---
(7) See page 447.

breaking out of Indian hostilities in 1774. Summing up the evidence at hand, Edmund West, Sr., was the builder of West's Fort.

Charles West, mentioned by *Withers*, (8) was also a son of Edmund West, Sr. The elder West and several of his family are buried near the old fort.

The appellation, "West's Fort" should never have been changed. The village that sprang up there was, in after years, known as "McWhorter's Mills." In 1829, Fields McWhorter was appointed Postmaster at McWhorter's Mills. (9) At a later day, Lewis Maxwell, a wealthy bachelor, who owned large tracts of realty in the immediate vicinity, contrived to have the name changed to its present form, *Jane Lew*, in honor of his mother, whose maiden name was Jane Lewis. This name is unhistoric and inappropriate.

Alexander West, who figured so prominently in the early history of Hacker's Creek, was born in Aconach County, Virginia, August 11, 1760. He came with his father, Edmund West, Sr., to Hacker's Creek just prior to Dunmore's War. In May, 1777, and before he was yet seventeen years old, he enlisted in Capt. James Booth's Company of Rangers and Spies, and served thirteen months as scout in (then) Monongalia County, Virginia. Before the term of enlistment had expired, Capt. Booth was killed by Indians near his own house on Booth's Creek, consequently none of the company were officially discharged.

In May, 1781, Alexander West volunteered in Capt. George Jackson's Company, which marched to Fort Pitt and joined General George Rogers Clark in his attempted expedition against Detroit. It had been Clark's intention to leave Fort Pitt in flat boats for the Falls of the Ohio about the middle of June, 1881, but disappointment in procuring men and supplies retarded the embarkation.

The invasion of Virginia by Lord Cornwallis prevented the acquisition of Virginia State troops as promised, and the success of the expedition eventually devolved upon new volunteers and raw *levies* from the more western counties of Virginia. This support, as the sequel shows, was precarious and unreliable. While clamorous for the reduction of that important post, which would in a measure insure peace to the harassed border, the settlers in the main were averse to engaging in an expedition which would take them so far from their homes, which were in constant need

(8) See page 447. (9) p. 447.

of protection. Consequently, accessions to Clark's army came in slowly. Drafts upon the several counties for men proved futile. The boundary line dispute between Virginia and Pennsylvania, was a prime hindrance to the acquisition of troops, either by enlistment or drafting. Gen. Clark and his methods were bitterly opposed by the Pennsylvania adherents. They impugned his right to forcibly take men from the controverted territory; and in some instances armed resistance was narrowly averted. The Virginia Volunteer Militia was not susceptible to strict military discipline, and could be held together only by "ties of confidence and affection to their leader." (10)

It was doubtless in the hope to escape these drafts, made on the ninth of the preceding February, that the settlers of Monongalia and Ohio Counties engaged in an expedition against the friendly Moravian towns on the Muskingum in the Spring of 1781. (11)

Finally, General Clark embarked with only four hundred men instead of two thousand as first intended. On the fourth of August, he was at Fort Henry, where he expected to be joined by one thousand militia from the East of the mountains. Only two hundred and fifty of this troop materialized, and half of these deserted after drawing a supply of guns, blankets and clothing. Those remaining were in a state of mutiny for several days. The expedition was abandoned at the Falls of the Ohio, where after a service of seven months West received a discharge signed by General Clark, and he returned home.

In his declaration for pension, made September 4, 1832, West states that his military discharge [paper] was torn to pieces by the Indians sometime in 1785, at which time they killed his father, brother and brother's wife and destroyed all their papers. *Withers* states that the West tragedy occurred December 5, 1787. This is evidently correct, for Edmund West, Jr., and Ann Hacker were not married until 1787, the year that the young wife was killed.

When applying for pension, Alexander West was vouched for by David W. Sleeth and Jacob Bush, and afterwards by John Talbot (clergyman) and Daniel Stringer. On July 18, 1833, he was granted a pension of $66.00 per annum. He also applied for "bounty lands" granted by Virginia to her state troops, but his claim was refused on the grounds that he had only served seven months in the military.

(10) See page 447. (11) p. 447.

In the Virginia State Library, Richmond, is preserved the following endorsements to West's claim for bounty land:

"ENDORSED. H. E. West and Alex. West, Rep. 29, Jan. 1833. March 5, 1833. Submitted to the council of State & advice required, John Floyd. Rejected March 24, 1833, J. F.

"HARRISON COUNTY VIRGINIA } TO WIT:

"This day Christopher Nutter appeared before Edward Stewart, a Justice of the Peace in and for Harrison County, and made Oath that Alexander West, a resident of Lewis County, volunteered under Capt. George Jackson sometime in May in the year 1781 and marched to fort Pitt. Was there attached to the army commanded by Gen.———Clark; from fort Pitt we descended the Ohio River to the falls thereof and served the whole campaign or the term of seven months.

"Given under my hand this 21st day of November, 1832.

CHRISTOPHER NUTTER

"Sworn to before me this day and year above written.

EDWARD STEWART, J. P."

"LEWIS COUNTY [VIRGINIA] } TO WIT:

"This day Jacob Bush appeared before John McWhorter, a Justice of the Peace in and for said county of Lewis, and made oath that Alexander West, a resident of the said county, volunteered under the command of Capt. George Jackson some time in May in the year 1781, in the county of Monongalia then, but now the county of Lewis, and marched in company with this affiant to fort Pitt. Was there attached to the army commanded by Genl. ———Clark. From fort Pitt we descended the Ohio river in boats to the falls thereof and served the whole Campaign under Genl. Clark, or the term of seven months. Given under my hand this 23rd day of November in the year 1832.

his
JACOB X BUSH.
mark

"Sworn to before me this day & year above written.

JOHN McWHORTER."

I have been unable to find anything further touching West's bounty land claim.

Alexander West was married twice, but no record of his first marriage has been found. His second wife was Mary Straley. They were married January 24, 1796, by Joseph Cheuront. They settled near the home of West's father.

When the Baptist church on Broad Run, Lewis County, was organized, West became a charter member. He was buried there, his death occurring in June, 1834. On April 12, 1851, a pension certificate was issued to his widow for $66.00 a year from March 4, 1848.

Regarding the personal appearance of West, Editor *Thwaites* gives the following note:

"Alexander West was prominent as a frontier scout. Rev. J. M. McWhorter, who saw him frequently, gives this description of him: 'A tall, spare-built man, very erect, strong, lithe, and active; dark-skinned, prominent Roman nose, black hair, very keen eyes; not handsome, rather raw-boned, but with an air and mien that commanded the attention and respect of those with whom he associated. Never aggressive, he lifted his arm against the Indians only in time of war.' West died in 1834. His house of hewed logs is, with its large barn, still standing and occupied by his relatives, about a mile east of the site of West's Fort." (12)

BARN BUILT BY ALEXANDER WEST
Photographed March, 1910

Hacker's Creek is seen on the right.

In addition to the foregoing, my father writes me under date June 28, 1899. "Some things that occurred when I was quite young were so vividly impressed upon my mind that time has never erased them; none more so than the sight of Alexander West. Long frame, broad across the shoulders, muscular with no surplus flesh. He wore the old-fashioned plain blue linsey hunting shirt, cape and belt and fringed in front of same color. His vest and pantaloons were of like material and he wore a black wool hat and moccasins. I remember the color of the horse that he rode. He and his wife stopped with my parents for dinner when on their

---
(12) See page 448.

way home from church held in an old log school house, where I got my first schooling. It was built before my earliest recollection. West was very fleet-footed and but few could outstrip him."

The log barn built by Alexander West is still standing, but his house, which stood on the present site of the residence of the late Lyman Straley, was torn down several years ago.

One Alexander West, was, in 1781, granted a certificate for "400 acres on the head of Brown's Creek, adjoining land claimed by Charles Wolf, to include his settlement made in 1772, with a preemption for 1000 acres adjoining."

If this settler was Alexander West the scout, he was, at the time of this "settlement," but twelve years old; which is not improbable. Many of these early "settlements" and "improvements" were made by mere boys, who were grown before it was possible to secure titles to homesteads on the western waters.

The earliest census of Virginia shows but one Alexander West in Monongalia County. In 1782 his family consisted of three; and in 1785 it numbered five persons. (13)

(13) See page 448.

CHAPTER XIII

The history of the Schoolcraft family, of which Leonard, who figured in the West tragedy was a member, forms a pathetic page.

It has been generally supposed that but one family of this name settled on the waters of the Upper Monongahela. This is an error, as evidenced by the record of homestead entries. In 1781, John Schoolcraft was granted a certificate for "400 acres on Stone Coal Run [creek] adjoining lands of Henry Flesher, to include his settlement made in 1775." In the same year, James Schoolcraft obtained certificate for "400 acres on the main fork of Fink Run, adjoining lands of John Schoolcraft, to include his settlement made in 1774." A certificate was also granted to Matthew Schoolcraft for "400 acres on Land Fork [evidently Sand Fork, in Lewis County] of the Monongahela, to include his settlement made in 1774."

Austin Schoolcraft was killed by Indians near the Buckhannon Fort in 1780, and his niece taken captive. (1)

The first notice that we have of the name is when John Schoolcraft and Jesse Hughes came in close contact with the Indians who killed Mrs. Freeman on Hacker's Creek in 1778. (2) The family of which John was the head, came from central New York, (3) and is supposed to have settled on Fink's Run, near the Buckhannon Fort, in 1774 or 1775. This supposition is strengthened by the knowledge that he owned, or claimed land on that stream, and that he was identified with the Buckhannon Fort. But evidently he was the same Schoolcraft who made the homestead entry adjoining the lands of Henry Flesher.

Fate seems to have been against this devoted family. In the spring of 1779, Leonard, a son sixteen years of age, was captured by the Indians near Buckhannon Fort and carried into captivity. In the autumn of the same year, the Indians surprised and killed Mrs. Schoolcraft and eight of her children, and carried two of the small boys away captives. In April, 1781, the last of the children, three boys, Matthias, Simon and Michael, visited a pigeon roost on Stone Coal Creek, where passenger pigeons congregated in vast numbers. (4) This was, perhaps, on a small stream, known as "Pigeon Roost," which, however, as claimed

(1) See page 448. (2) p. 448. (3) p. 448. (4) p. 448.

by a local resident, did not acquire its name until during the Civil War. While returning to the fort, they were fired upon by the Indians; Matthias was killed, and the other two were made prisoners. (5) Thus, within two years, this family of sixteen was entirely broken up. Nine of the children and the mother were killed, five boys were swept into captivity, while the father disappeared from the annals of the border. (6) There were many such instances on the frontier, and these were in a measure responsible for such characters as Jesse Hughes, William White, John Cutright, Lewis Wetzel and many others. According to *Withers*, Leonard "turned renegade," and eight years after his capture we find him in the Hacker's Creek settlement in the role of an Indian warrior. Prisoners who returned from the Indian country reported that three of the brothers had turned Indian and took part in the forays against the settlers. (7)

A local tradition worthy of credence accounts for the two brothers, John and Jacob, so completely lost sight of. They were carried away when the family was massacred and were held in captivity until nearly grown. Then they escaped under the following circumstances:

The lads took kindly to their forest life and often accompanied the Indians in their hunting expeditions. In time they were entrusted with guns and a limited amount of ammunition, for which they were required to account at the close of each day's hunt. After determining fully to attempt an escape they contrived occasionally to conceal a small quantity of ammunition. The vigilance of the Indians was such that after several weeks they had only a few bullets and charges of powder cached. To this they added a supply of jerk, and one morning they left the Indian encampment for the ostensible day's hunt, but going in a direction opposite to their cache, and intended retreat. They soon changed their course and after securing their hoarded supplies, set out on their long journey to the settlements, following a well-beaten Indian trail. All that day and night was spent in travel. The following morning found the fugitives so fatigued that rest was a necessity. That their escape had been discovered and they were being pursued was obvious, but the wary lads baffled their enemies by clever stratagem.

With an apparent design of concealing their trail, they entered a stream along which they had been traveling, and wading up its

---
(5) See page 448. (6) p. 448. (7) p. 449.

bed for some distance, then doubled and carefully passed down the creek and gained the shore far below where they had left it. In traveling up the stream they were careful to leave an occasional light footprint, or other signs by which they could be trailed, but when retracing they avoided everything whereby the ruse might be detected.

In a secluded place, they slept for several hours; then moved farther and secreted themselves in a cavern in a bluff commanding a good view of the trail, where they kept constantly on the lookout. Towards sundown, a small band of Indians passed in pursuit. The following evening, the baffled warriors repassed on their return home. That night the boys continued their flight, making a detour and striking the trail several miles ahead. During their entire journey they exercised the greatest caution, never camping near the path, nor did they kill any game.

In due time, they reached one of the settlements, supposedly West's Fort. As they approached, they narrowly escaped being fired upon by some of the settlers who mistook them for Indians. The lads held their reversed guns aloft and made other demonstrations of peace, when they were received. They made known the story of their captivity and escape, and afterwards proceeded to the Wappatomaka, where it seems that their father had gone sometime after the destruction of his family.

Nothing is known of John after his return from captivity. Leonard, Simon and Michael always remained with the Indians.

Jacob married a Miss Parsons, a daughter of Charles Parsons, who was killed by Indians while descending Shade River in Ohio. Their children were Aaron, James, John, Mary, Ann and Permelia. Aaron settled in Gilmer County, (West) Virginia, and was a noted hunter. He killed the last wolf seen in that region. This wolf, a lonely survivor of his race, had taken refuge in a secluded retreat known as "The Devil's Den," and had succeeded in eluding the best hunters and dogs of the surrounding country. Schoolcraft eventually outwitted the wary animal and took his scalp.

My father, when a boy and carrying the mail through Gilmer County in the early forties, witnessed a fight between this nimrod's two dogs and a yearling bear; which, being chased, had taken refuge in a tree. Schoolcraft, who was hunting his cattle, was without a gun, and he struck bruin with a rock, causing him to drop to the ground where he was immediately set upon by the dogs. They were well trained and knew their business. One seized the bear by the side of the head while the other fastened onto its ham; holding themselves in such position that the quarry could get at them with neither tooth nor paw. But Schoolcraft fearing that the bear might tear loose and disable the dogs, dispatched it with his knife. Aaron Schoolcraft moved to Spruce Creek, Ritchie County (West), Virginia, in 1852.

There was a William Schoolcraft on the Upper West Fork River in an early day. He was a son of one of the pioneer Schoolcrafts, and was a schoolteacher and a noted hunter. He had been trained in the superstitions of the border, and told weird stories of the woods. One was his own experience with the *"Phantom Deer."* This ghostly denizen of the Monongahela and Little Kanawha wilderness had often been seen and unwittingly fired at by the old hunters. I am indebted to Mr. John Strange Hall for the story.

Mr. Schoolcraft stated that while hunting one day, he saw a large buck standing on a point, or narrow ridge, beyond a deep gulch that separated him from it. The range was long, but there was no way of a closer approach without alarming the game. The hunter was a dead shot, and determined to fire from where he stood. He did so, and was surprised to find that the deer remained motionless. He repeated the shot, with the same result. Chagrined at his failure, he again took careful and deliberate aim, and at the report of his rifle, the deer vanished. Reloading his gun, he went to where the deer had stood, but the most careful search failed to reveal any signs of the game. The deep snow lay smooth and unbroken by track or trail. Thinking that he might be mistaken in the location, he went back to the place from which he had fired, and placing his feet in his former tracks, he could see his trail in the snow to where the deer had stood. He now knew that he had been firing at the *"Phantom Deer."* A strange uncanny feeling crept over the hunter; he hastened away, and hunted no more that day. (8)

The following is the declaration of one John Schoolcraft for pension as Revolutionary soldier: It covers some of the most stirring incidents in the border strife, and I give it unabridged.

{ "Lewis County
  Virginia

"On this 25th day of July, 1833, personally appeared in open court before the Justice of the County Court of Lewis Co., now sitting, John Schoolcraft a

(8) See page 449.

resident of Freeman's Cr., in Lewis Co., Va., aged 76 years, who being first duly sworn, etc.

"In the month of February near the last of that month in the year 1777, in the county of Ohio, he volunteered under Capt. Bilderbock as an Indian spy, and from Hollidays Fort he traversed the counties bordering on the Ohio r. from Wheeling fort to Ft. Pitt watching the approach of the savage enemy and notifying the garrisons at Bollings, Hollidays, Wheeling Ft. etc., of threatened danger of the Indians, but notwithstanding all the vigilance of the Indian spies, the frontier settlements in the counties of Yahogany, Ohio and Monongalia suffered severely by the desultory warfare of the Savages. About September 1 of this year a body of about 400 Indian warriors lay in ambush near Ft. Wheeling showing a few of their warriors only to the Garrison. A few men under Captain Mason and Ogal marched out from the Ft. to attack them and soon found themselves enclosed by a savage body of Indians and nearly every man perished except Capt. Mason and Capt. Ogal, the former of whom was badly wounded. The Indians led on by Simon Girty immediately after appeared before the Ft. threatening its destruction. Intelligence of this invasion soon reached Holliday and Bollings Forts and declarent under command of Capt. Bilderbock and Col. Swearingen with a few men who volunteered, embarked in a large canoe and proceeded during the night down the Ohio r. About daybreak [they] discovered the little village of Wheeling on fire. (9) After precautionary measures disembarked and finding the enemy had abandoned the siege proceeded to the ground where Mason and Ogal's companies were slain, found them cruelly mangled; buried them and soon after returned to Hollidays Ft. and resumed his business of spying through the counties aforesaid, which he continued until Dec. 1, 1777; was then dismissed having served nine mos. as an Indian spy under the immediate command of Capt. Bilderbock, subject to the orders of Col. Andrea Swearingen. During this year's service he became acquainted with Cols. Swearingen, Shepherd, and Gane (?) (10) who commanded at Ft. Pitt, and Col. David Williamson who commanded at Ft. Red Stone in Washington Co., Pa. In the spring he believes about the last of Feb. or Mar. 1 in the year 1778, he again volunteered as an Indian spy at the said Hollidays ft. under the command of the said Bilderbock, was engaged during the spring and summer and fall of this year in spying in the said country which now compose the counties of Ohio, Brooke and Washington. He also made several excursions on the n. w. side of the Ohio. An expedition was made under Genl. McIntosh into the Indian towns of Muskingdon and prevented them from carrying on their savage warfare as in the year '77. Genl. McIntosh this year built and garrisoned Ft. McIntosh at the mouth of Big Beaver Cr. and Fort Lawrence [Fort Laurens] on the Tuscarora [Tuscarawas] R., the latter visited in the beginning of winter in this year '78 found it garrisoned with a few hundred men commanded by Col. Gibson. Toward the last of December '78, the danger from incursions of the Indians ceasing, declarent was again dismissed, having served nine mos. as an Indian spy as a private. In the month of April, 1779, he again entered the service of the U. S. as an Indian spy by order of Col. Zane under command of Capt. Mason and from the fort at Wheeling spied through the whole country bordering on the Ohio, now Ohio, Brooke and Tyler Cos., and also on the opposite side of the Ohio, and on Nov. 30, 1779, was dismissed, served this year seven months as a private Indian spy. In June 1780 he again

(9) See page 450. (10) p. 450.

volunteered under Capt. Mason, marched from Wheeling to Ft. Pitt, there joined the regulars under Capt. Broadhead, was from thence marched up the Allegany r. to its fork, then up the North fork thereof to the Munsie Towns; destroyed their towns, their corn, and cut off a party of warriors that were on their march to Westmoreland Co., then retraced their steps to Ft. Pitt, from thence countermarched to Wheeling where he believes in the last of August a large force under Col. Broadhead, Col. Zane, and Col. Shepherd rendezvoused, soon afterwards marched toward the Indian villages in the forks of Muskingdon River, arrived at White [Eyes] plains towards the last of September, here discovered 2 Indians, fired at and wounded them, pushed on rapidly to Coshocton, took it by surprise, was in consequence of a great rise in the Coshocton prevented from penetrating farther into the Indian settlements, destroyed their village and corn and then returned to Wheeling where he arrived in November 1780. (11) Served in the campaign up the Allegheny to Coshocton under Capt. Mason and Col. Zane, was in Nov. discharged, having served five months as a private volunteered in the militia of Ohio Co.

"In the year 1781 declarent moved to Monongalia County. In the spring 1782 volunteered under Capt. Christopher Carpenter as an Indian spy, ranged the country from McCans Ft. on the west fork river, where he was stationed, to the Ohio through the country now composing the counties of Harrison, Lewis, Wood and Tyler, was on the last of Nov. 1782, dismissed, having served not less than seven mos. as a private Indian spy.

"In the spring 1783 he was engaged as an Indian spy, served under Capt. Carpenter at McCans Ft. until peace was declared and for many years afterwards, but which is not necessary here to mention. In the Rev. War he served as an Indian spy including the campaign to the Munsie and Coshocton villages more than three years. He has no documentary evidence by which to prove his services and knows of no person living whose testimony he can procure to prove same. He was born near Moorefield in Hampshire, now Hardy County, Va., on Feb. 13, 1757, lived there until the year 1774, when he moved to West Augusta, now Ohio [County], lived in Ohio [County] until the year 1781, then moved to the west fork of Monongahela r. in Monongalia, afterwards Harrison, now Lewis Co., Va., has lived in Lewis ever since.

his
(Signed) JOHN X SCHOOLCRAFT"
mark

Then followed a short statement vouching for Schoolcraft, signed by P. McCan and James Brown.

In 1834, W. G. Singleton, Special Pension Agent, investigated Schoolcraft's case and gave the following report:

"Christopher Nutter aged 74, John Reger aged 66, William Powers aged 70, John Neely and Nicholas Carpenter have all known John Schoolcraft from a boy and concur in saying, that he is too young by many years to have been in the war of the Rev. (12)

Respectfully reported,

July 1834. W. G. SINGLETON, S. *Agent.*"

(11) See page 450. (12) p. 451.

By referring to the border annals, it will be found that Schoolcraft is very correct in regard to the time and places of the events referred to in his declaration, which bears on its face the impress of truth. His dates are not so nearly confused as in many of the printed records.

Wheeling, or Fort Henry, played an important part in the Revolution. Of the two notable sieges which it withstood, unfortunately the greatest chaos prevails. There are fanciful descriptions of events connected with its investments which really never did occur. (13) *Withers,* as a recognized authority, is largely responsible for this; and now it appears as though he derived much of his information from traditions in the Zane family. The renowned defense of his cabin by Col. Ebenezer Zane and his few followers, and the "gun powder" exploit by Elizabeth Zane, or Molly Scott, or both, has been attributed to both of the sieges. The preference is with that of 1782. *DeHass, McKnight* and others favor this date, while *Albach* is only one of many who agrees with *Lossing* that these events took place in the siege of 1777. (14) Of the siege of 1782, which was the last engagement of the Revolution where the British flag was in evidence, *Withers,* (15) in part, says:

"In the first of September, John Lynn (a celebrated spy and the same who had been with Capt. Foreman at the time of the fatal ambuscade at Grave cr.), being engaged in watching the warriors paths, northwest of the Ohio, discovered the Indians marching with great expedition for Wheeling, and hastening to warn the inhabitants of the danger which was threatening them, swam the river, and reached the village, but a little while before the savage army made its appearance. The fort was at this time without any regular garrison, and depended for defense exclusively on the exertions of those who sought security within its walls. The brief space of time which elapsed between the alarm by Lynn, and the arrival of the Indians, permitted only those who were immediately present to retire into it, and when the attack was begun to be made, there were not within its palisades, twenty effective men to oppose the assault. The dwelling house of Col. Ebenezer Zane, standing about forty yards from the fort, contained the military stores which had been furnished by the government of Virginia; and as it was admirably situated as an outpost from which to annoy the savages in their onsets, he resolved on maintaining possession of it, as well to aid in the defense of the fort, as for the preservation of the ammunition. Andrew Scott, George Green, Mrs. Zane, Molly Scott and Miss McCullough, were all who remained with him. The kitchen adjoining was occupied by Sam (a negro belonging to Col. Zane) and Kate, his wife.—Col. Silas Zane commanded in the fort. * * *

"When Lynn gave the alarm that an Indian army was approaching, the fort for some time having been unoccupied by a garrison, and Col. Zane's house

(13) See page 451. (14) p. 451. (15) p. 451.

being used as a magazine, those who retired into the fortress had to take with them a supply of ammunition for its defense. The supply of powder, deemed ample at the time, by reason of the long continuance of the savages, and the repeated endeavors made by them to storm the fort, was almost entirely exhausted, a few loads only remaining. In this emergency it became necessary to replenish their stock from the abundance of that article in Col. Zane's house. * * * "

Withers' story of Elizabeth Zane's successful run from the fort to her brother's house to bring powder for the garrison, and the more plausible claim that the heroine was Molly Scott, whose family was in the Zane cabin, who ran to the fort to bring powder from the magazine store room, is here omitted as having no direct connection with the present narrative. (16) Although the descent of the Indian Army was swift, it would appear from the foregoing that Col. Zane with only three men and four women, including the slave man and his wife, remained in his cabin from choice; and that such action was necessary for the protection of the military supplies stored there. It is hard to conceive why an abundance of ammunition should be kept in this isolated and weakly garrisoned dwelling, while the fort was so scantily supplied with this most essential means of defense. It is not reasonable that such disposition was deliberately planned by men with the experience of the Zanes; but was rather the result of surprise. This view is strengthened when we consider that there were not to exceed twenty men at the fort, and that the Indian force was known to be great. About three o'clock that afternoon the trail of, supposedly, two hundred warriors had been discovered near the fort, and Capt. John Boggs was immediately sent to alarm the settlers and bring re-enforcements. Added to this the fact that the walls of the stockade were not in condition to withstand a heavy assault, it certainly appears very unmilitary to have divided the strength of the defense by retaining possession of the outstanding cabin. Capt. Boggs had not proceeded more than one mile and a half before he heard the boom of the fortress swivel gun and the sound of a rifle, attesting that the attack had begun. Soon after his departure, Ebenezer McColloch on his way from VanMeter's Fort on Short Creek, had reached within half a mile of Wheeling when he was deterred from venturing nearer by the heavy firing around that stockade. (17) The report of Col. Zane himself denotes with what rapidity the enemy moved.

(16) See page 451. (17) p. 451.

"WHEELING, SEPTEMBER 17, 1782.

SIR:—

"On the evening of the 11th instant, a body of the enemy appeared in sight of our garrison. They immediately formed their lines round the garrison, paraded British colors, and demanded the fort to be surrendered, which was refused. About twelve o'clock at night they rushed hard on the pickets in order to storm, but were repulsed. They made two other attempts to storm before day, but to no purpose.

"About 8 o'clock next morning, there came a negro from them to us and informed us that their force consisted of a British captain and forty regular soldiers and two hundred and sixty Indians. The enemy kept a continual fire the whole day. About ten o'clock at night, they made a fourth attempt to storm to no better purpose than the former. The enemy continued around the garrison until the morning of the 13th instant, when they disappeared. Our loss is none. Daniel Sullivan, who arrived here in the first of the action, is wounded in the foot.

"I believe they have driven the greatest part of our stock away, and might, I think, be soon overtaken."

(Col. Ebenezer Zane to Irvine.) (18)

But the strongest evidence that the inmates of Zane's cabin did not remain from choice, is that contained in the declaration for pension, of one of its defenders, Robert Scott. While Scott gives the date of the siege (as remembered) 1778, and the house that of "Lane," there can be no doubt that it was the siege in question, whether 1777, or 1782; and that *Lane* appears instead of *Zane*, through a misunderstanding of the recorder. Scott's declaration was given in Gallatin County, Kentucky, and is of such moment that I give it unabridged and in the original.

"On October 15, 1833, personally appeared before me, etc., Robert Scott aged 69 years, who upon oath makes the following statement: That he entered the U. S. service under the following named officers and served as herein stated, that is to say in very early times his father moved from Pa. where declarent was born, to the fort at Wheeling in Va. and carried declarent and family with him, that he continued at said fort until early in the spring of 1781, that whilst he was at the fort at Wheeling the Indians were very troublesome, and during the Rev. War the said fort was attacked whilst the declarent was there on two different occasions. Upon the last occasion, deponent thinks it was in 1778, there were only about 15 persons in this fort and declarent was in the house of Mr. Lanes with his family, just on the outside of the fort, and the descent of the Indians was so sudden and unexpected that the persons in the house were compelled to remain in it and make the best defense they could; he states he assisted in its defense actively and the siege of the house and fort continued about three days, and the Indians retired without taking either. That although he was quite a boy at the time, his services continued to be required to assist in defense of the place and frontier immediately adjoining until he moved from there in the spring 1781,—that he was not idle nor indeed could he be, for self-

(18) See page 451.

preservation required the utmost vigilance of all. He states that in Mar., 1781, as well as he remembers, having moved from Wheeling to Jefferson Co., Ky., he entered the service of the U. S. as a private volunteer soldier under Capt. Floyd at Floyd's station on Bear Grass in Jefferson Co., Ky., and he there remained as a part of the garrison of the fort at that place from the month of Mar. 1781 till Aug. 1781, embracing a period of five months, during all which time he served faithfully as a part of the garrison of that place and in scouting parties against the Indians.

"He further declares that in Aug. 1781, he again entered the U. S. service as a private volunteer soldier upon a tour of six months in Capt. Floyd's Company and joined Genl. Clarke at the Falls of the Ohio upon an expedition to Vincennes, that he marched with the troops upon said expedition and continued with them until his return, actively engaged in the service and upon the return of the expedition to the falls of Ohio he there was kept in garrison till the expiration of his said term of service; he then returned to Floyd's Station where he was again immediately enrolled under Capt. Floyd as a part of the garrison of that place where he continued under Capt. Floyd actively employed against the Indians until Dec., 1782, that he was engaged in many skirmishes and scouting parties against them during his service and encountered much hardship, difficulty and fatigue and danger, and that in the year 1782 he served as above named after the expiration of tour under Genl. Clarke no less than nine months. (19)

"He continued at the fort at Floyd's Station during the winter 1782 and spring 1783, and that in April 1783 he was again enrolled under Capt. Floyd as a volunteer soldier and continued at the said fort as a part of its garrison not less than six months ending in Oct. 1783, that there was not as much disturbance during the year 1783 from the Indians as there was the preceding year, but that his services were as unremittant during this year as any other year.

"He states that during the Revolution he was young and he is now old and his memory does not serve him in relation to the minute circumstances of his service, but he knows he did not serve as a private soldier against the Indians in the war of the Revolution less than 26 months, and for that service he claims pension. He states that he has no documentary evidence and that he knows of no person who can testify to his services.

(Signed) ROBERT SCOTT."

"John Foster and Frederick Coghill testified that Scott was reliable and believed by the neighborhood to have been in the Revolutionary War.

In all his enlistments Scott was a volunteer. After going to Kentucky, he lived in Jefferson County, in the midst of Indian troubles for about ten years and then moved to Henry County, same State, where he resided for about six years. Then he went to Gallatin County, where he still resided in 1833. He was granted a pension of $30.00 a year. Born in Pennsylvania, 1764.

---

(19) See page 452.

CHAPTER XIV

We come again to a period of several years, in which we hear nothing of Jesse Hughes. This, however, is true of many of his noted contemporaries during the same interval.

Jesse Hughes went hunting for service berries near his home on Hacker's Creek, and at the same time, two Indians were hunting for Jesse. Finding a tree loaded with berries, he was soon ensconced among its branches regaling himself with the delicious fruit; when suddenly two warriors appeared under the tree and exultingly exclaimed that they "had him," and laughing at his predicament, called to him to "come down, give up; Injun no hurt." Realizing that he was trapped, and in order to gain time to formulate some plan of escape, he effected a nonchalant air, and requested that they would allow him to eat a few more berries before descending. At the same time he began to break off small branches ladened with berries and toss them to his captors. The Indians, desiring to take him prisoner, and wishing to show their good intentions towards him, complied, and were soon enjoying the rich fruit. The tree stood on the brow of a steep bluff, or deep gully, and Jesse, with every faculty alert, cautiously and slowly drew the Indians away from the tree by skillfully dropping the branches further and further down the declivity. At last getting them as far away as possible or prudence would allow, he suddenly leaped from the tree, landing in an opposite direction. Before the astonished braves could fire upon him, Jesse had vanished like a flash over the brow of the bluff, and was soon lost to sight in the deep forest. The Indians, knowing from experience the utter futility of pursuit, made no attempt to recapture him.

A Mrs. Straley, who lived near West's Fort, related that when she was a little girl she went to hunt some sheep that had strayed from home, and getting lost on the West Fork, she remained all night alone in the wilderness. Next morning, getting her bearings, she started home, and met Jesse searching for her.

Somewhere on the waters of the West Fork River, two Indians were fired upon by the settlers, and one killed. The other badly wounded, made off. A party went in pursuit, and

INDIAN SPRING

Photographed by Mr. Percy E. Lawson, 1906

found him lying in a tangle of brush. As they approached, he greeted them kindly, and the men were inclined to mercy, but Jesse Hughes who came up a little later, tomahawked and scalped the helpless warrior, accompanying his work with many profane expletives. This was a distinct incident from the Morgan-Indian tragedy at Pricket's Fort in 1779, referred to elsewhere in this volume.

It was during this period that Jesse went very early one morning, to bring in a horse which had been in a pasture some distance from his cabin.

He arrived at the edge of the field just as day was breaking. Ever cautious, the wary scout paused to reconnoiter the premises before venturing into the open. Peering through his leafy screen, Jesse saw his horse, a spirited black, flying across the field pursued by a young Indian. The scout, who had on more than one occasion measured speed and endurance with fleet-footed warriors, was amazed and startled to see this Indian outstrip the frantic steed. But, owing to the dread in which the horse of the white man held Indians, this wild runner could not seize or fasten upon the coveted prize. It was yet too dark for Hughes to use his rifle with any degree of accuracy. So, from his place of concealment, he watched this chase in the dusk of the departing night. But the day grew, and soon the silence was broken by the crash of the scout's deadly rifle, and before the answering echoes had ceased to reverberate through the valley, the swiftest runner of the Monongahela was lying still in death.

One cannot but feel regret at the tragic death of this bronzed athlete, who was seemingly alone and bent on no bloody designs against the settlement. Like the untamed Highlander, he had merely come

> "To spoil the spoiler as we may,
> And from the robber rend the prey."

He was apparently trying to collect in his own way the poor tithe regarded as justly his from the robber-like usurpers of his country.

Indians sometimes came into the settlement alone. It was not uncommon for a young brave to go singly in quest of horses or scalps. If successful, his reputation as a warrior was assured. I have often heard the northwestern tribes narrate incidents of this nature. The one shot through the shoulder by West in the field just south of the old Henry McWhorter cabin, near "Beech Fort," (1) was a straggler of this kind. This Indian, badly wounded made off, and as was afterwards learned by following his trail, he stopped at a spring on the hillside, on what is now the Nicholas Alkire farm, about two miles up Hacker's Creek, near the mouth of Life's Run, and bathed his wound.

This spring has since been known as Indian Spring. After dressing his wound, the Indian went perhaps a mile further, and crept into a cleft in the rocks, where his dead body was afterwards found. This ridge-cliff, known as "Indian Rock," is on the farm now owned by Jesse Lawson, on Life's Run, a branch of Hacker's Creek.

Another View of Indian Spring
Photographed 1910

The settlers on the upper waters of the Monongahela often went in canoes and flat-boats to Fort Pitt, where they exchanged skins, furs, jerked venison, and other products of the wilderness for ammunition and necessaries. Jesse Hughes and Henry McWhorter made a trip together. One day they put ashore where a number of children were playing, among them a little Indian boy.

---

(1) See page 452.

The incident which followed I will give in McWhorter's own words.

"The instant that Jesse caught sight of the little Indian boy his face blazed with hatred. I saw the devil flash in his eye, as feigning great good humor, he called out, 'Children, don't you want to take a boat ride?' Pleased with a prospective glide over

INDIAN ROCK—LOOKING EAST
Photographed 1910

the still waters of the Monongahela, one and all came running towards the boat. Perceiving Hughes' cunning ruse to get the little Indian into his clutches, I picked up an oar, and gruffly ordering the children away, quickly shoved the boat from the bank. When safely away, I turned to Hughes and said, 'Now, Jesse, ain't you ashamed?' 'What have I done?' he sullenly asked. 'What have you done? why, you intended to kill that little Indian boy. I saw it in your every move and look, the moment you got sight of the little fellow.' 'Yes,' he said, 'I intended when we got into mid-stream to stick my knife in him and throw him overboard.' When I remonstrated with him about this, he said, 'Damn it, he's an Injun!'"

Brutal? Yes; but let us not deal too harshly with the memory of Jesse Hughes, whose only schooling was that acquired upon a bloody frontier. Naturally such a training was void of sentiment. It contained not the elements of charity or mercy. It was narrow, cramped and selfish. It saw only the smouldering ruins of the settler's cabin, its scalped inmates; the helpless swept into captivity, with visions of the gauntlet and the torture stake. The whites believed their own actions justifiable and in the interests of their civilization. The conquest of a country has always brought about the possibility of barbarous conditions, (2) and but comparatively few of our frontiersmen have possessed the sturdiness of purpose to avoid the inhuman actions prompted by them.

But there were two sides. The Indians were cruelly wronged. They were deceived, defrauded and treacherously dealt with. Their lands were encroached upon, in gross violation of solemn treaty rights. Their game was destroyed. Friendlies were shot down without provocation, and entire families and bands of hunters were murdered, in the fastnesses of their own domain. There were schemes promulgated, and I believe employed, by those high in authority, for the indiscriminate destruction of the Indians, far more hellish than those ever dreamed of by the (3) wilderness warrior. We should be just and place where they belong the various causes for the brutalities enacted on the border.

INDIAN ROCK—LOOKING WEST
Photographed 1910

(2) See page 452. (3) p 452

CHAPTER XV

The first permanent settlement on the Upper Monongahela was in 1769, on the Buckhannon River. This colony, from the earliest records that we find, has always borne the name of the stream on which it is located. The name is supposed to be that of some historic white person — but who? (1) There is no one of a similar name to be found in connection with the first years of the settlement. Records bearing the date of 1781 show that the river then bore practically the same name as at present. This has been spelled in various ways at different periods, some of the modes being *Buchanan, Buckanon, Buck-Hannan, Buchannon, Buckhannon.*

While a few of these forms may be due to carelessness or ignorance on the part of the writers, not all of them are so. There are no logical grounds for supposing the name to be that of a white person. The origin of most of the prominent topographical names of that region can be accounted for, but history is silent as to the source of the name of this stream. The fort at Buckhannon was built by John Bush in 1773, but it has usually been referred to by the early chroniclers as the "Buchannon Fort," or the "Fort at Buchannon." There can be but one conclusion — the river was named prior to or contemporary with the settlement made there in 1769. The only knowledge that we have of the origin of the name is contained in a statement left by John Cutright, the last surviving scout of western Virginia. Cutright secured his information directly from Pringles of the sycamore, the first known white men to enter the Buckhannon Valley.

"While the Pringles were domiciled in the mighty sycamore at the mouth of Turkey Run," said Cutright, "there was an Indian village located at or near the mouth of the river. The chief of the Indians of that village was Buck-on-go-ha-non, renowned in the border wars of the times. The first white settlers conferred the name of this chief to the beautiful stream on which he lived."

It has been conceded by historians generally, and maintained by pioneers universally, that in the region between the Allegheny Mountains and the Ohio River, in the present bounds of West Virginia, there were a few villages inhabited by bands of those

---

(1) See page 452.

tribes living principally north of the Ohio. Most of these villages were deserted upon the approach of the white settlements, and the inhabitants joined their people in the country northwest of the Ohio River. A few, however, remained until the settlements had grown numerous.

Withers says:

"Between the Allegheny mountains and the Ohio River, within the present limits of Virginia, there were some villages interspersed, inhabited by small numbers of Indians; the most of whom retired northwest of that river, as the tide of emigration rolled towards it. Some however remained in the interior, after settlements began to be made in their vicinity." (2)

The same writer in giving the causes that led to the destruction of the Tygart and Files settlements near Beverly in 1754, states:

"The difficulty of procuring bread stuffs for their families, their contiguity to an Indian village, and the fact that an Indian war path passed near their dwellings, soon determined them to retrace their steps." (3)

Again in depicting the imminent perils that constantly hovered around the lonely retreat of the Pringles:

"In the vicinity of a savage foe, the tomahawk and scalping knife were ever present to their imaginations."(4)

By some writers, however, these Indian habitations are termed "Mythical," but I find no good reasons for such inference. It is evident from personal observation, that there were Indian habitations of some magnitude in portions of this region, especially on Hacker's Creek, in quite recent historic times. This topic has been briefly noted in Chapters V and VI of this volume.

The summary by *Withers* does not necessarily denote a long continuous occupancy by Indians, (5) but it certainly is conclusive that there were resident Indians in that region contemporary with Tygart, Files and the Pringles. Not only were the latter in close proximity to an Indian village but, as shown in the ninth chapter of this volume, they even forayed against their red neighbors.

The distance from the Tygart and Files settlement to the mouth of the Buckhannon is only about thirty-five miles, and it is more than probable that somewhere in the lower part of this valley was located the village referred to by *Withers*, and was the same where the Pringles purloined the bag of dried buffalo meat. Evidently this settlement was transient, that of a periodical hunt-

---
(2) See page 453. (3) p. 453. (4) p. 453. (5) p. 453.

ing band, and was doubtless composed of Delawares living on the Miami and White Rivers in Ohio and Indiana, whose chief and head warrior was *Buckongahelas.* (6)

This chieftain was a fearless warrior, and tradition credits him with having led some of the war parties against the Virginia border. This may be true; he opposed the settling of the Trans-Allegheny, but nowhere can there be ascribed acts of cruelty in the warfare of this lofty-minded chieftain. With his ability as a warrior, was coupled a humane heart and a noble purpose. He sought not the injury of non-combatants, nor did he rejoice in the effusion of blood. He struck only in the defense of his outraged people. His prowess was felt in the French and Indian War of 1763. He assisted the British in the Revolution (7) and helped Little Turtle plan his attack on St. Clair. He was a signer of the Treaty of Greenville and other subsequent treaties. With the earlier exploits of this great warrior fresh in the minds of the settlers, and the fact that his village was pitched on the banks of the river, it was natural that this stream should have been given his name. From *Buckongahelas* to *Buckongehanon* and *Buckonhannon* would have been an easy transition for the uneducated and careless speaking pioneers. As time went on and new settlers came and records were made, it was an easy matter to still corrupt the fine old Indian name to the English *Buchannon, Buckhannan* and finally *Buckhannon.*

So deeply has the name of *Buckongahelas* become woven into the legends and traditions of the Virginia border, that to this day his name is mentioned in connection with a supernatural apparition which is said to occasionally startle the inhabitants of the Roaring Creek and Middle Fork countries. (8)

The following story has recently (1903) gone the rounds of the press. The reader will notice the slight variation in the name of the chief, and the usual exaggeration in the portrayal of Indian character:

"That most daring, vindictive and determined of Indian chiefs, Buch-on-ga-ha-la, whose violent and murderous bands alarmed, terrified and exterminated whole settlements through this state 125 years ago, on and after an occasion of a savage raid, like the destruction of the Bozarth family or the wholesale murder of all the whites on Files Creek, made his camp fires frequently on the waters of Roaring Creek and Middle Fork, where he said evil spirits dwelt. Middle Fork, a settlement near Belington, reports a very troublesome ghost. It appeared to a party of young folks who were out enjoying the fine sleighing the other evening

(6) See page 454. (7) p. 454. (8) p. 454.

and frightened ladies, gentlemen and horses out of their wits. This ghost has the right of way between the battle field of Rich Mountain and the bridge over the Middle Fork River. The nocturnal visits of this frightful unearthly apparition have occurred as far back as the oldest settler of Roaring Creek can remember. Buchongahela, the Indian chief who commanded the war parties from Ohio that made the raids on the settlements of Virginia, said that the evil Manitou inhabited the wilderness of Roaring Creek and Middle Fork."

It is hardly necessary to say that *Buckongahelas* could not have led the warriors who destroyed the Bozarth family. This chieftain, with his followers arrived at Greenville, June 21, 1795, and remained there, participating in the treaty that was made August 3, of that year. The Bozarth tragedy did not occur until mid-summer, and the raiding warriors returned only in time to deliver up their prisoners at that treaty. (9)

Buckongahelas was present, but did not sign the treaty made at Fort McIntosh, Pa., in 1785. He signed the treaty of June 7, 1803, at Fort Wayne, Indiana; and the treaty of August 18, 1804, at Vincennes, Indiana; with which his name disappears from the border annals. He is supposed to have died soon after the Treaty of Vincennes.

It is hard to conceive of a more lofty spirit than possessed by this proud, virtuous chieftain. At the Treaty of Fort McIntosh, he wholly ignored the other peace dignitaries, and stepping up to General Clark, took him by the hand and spoke:

"I thank the great spirit for having this day brought together two such great warriors as Buckongehelas and General Clark." * * *

"This man possessed all the qualifications of a hero; no Christian knight was ever more scrupulous in performing all his engagements than the renowned Buckongehelas." (10)

"Buckingehelas, a very distinguished war chief of the Delawares, lived some years subsequent to my agency for that nation, died on White River Indiana prior to the final removal of the tribe to the S. W. of Missouri. My impression is that this chief had no male descendants in a direct line living at the time of his decease. he probably had no superior as a warrior and orator. I first remember to have seen this chief about the year 1800 when on a visit to the President of the United States." (11)

"Buckingehelas is doubtless the same as quoted by Heckwelder by Broadhead and others, as we had but one Washington so the Delawares had but one Buckingehelas, a great warrior, chief and councillor, whose prowess in war and wisdom and actions in peace overshadowed that of all others, his name descended to no other." (12)

"Buckingehelas is said to have somewhat resembled Franklin in his physiog-

(9) See page 454. (10) p. 454. (11) p. 454. (12) p. 454.

nomy. He was about 5 feet 10 inches high, strong, & of powerful muscle. Universally esteemed & greatly lamented.

"Buckingehelas figured conspicuously in the French War of '63. About 80 when he died." (13)

Early in the eighteenth century, there was, among the Senecas, a very old warrior, whose name was Buck-in-je-hil-lish. He was a great councilor, and one day attended a war council, and declared that none but the ignorant made war, and the wise men and the warriors had to do the fighting. For this reflective speech, and because of his unprecedented age, and that he could give no good reason why he had not died, he was pronounced a witch, and sentenced to be tomahawked by a boy, which was immediately done. (14) This tragedy took place about the time that Buckongehelas, the *Washington of the Delawares*, was born; or when he was a very small lad.

---

(13) See page 454. (14) p. 454.

CHAPTER XVI

It is regrettable that so little is known in regard to the dimensions and characteristics of the forts erected on the Virginia border. Barring, perhaps, Fort Henry at Wheeling, it is doubtful if there is at this time sufficient data to insure a lucid reproduction of any one of the several forts which stood between the Alleghenies and the Ohio. The early historian evidently did not regard it of sufficient importance to give a minute description of those important places of defense. Constructed entirely of wood, they have long since crumbled to dust. So complete has been their demolition, that in most cases there remains not a vestige of their ruins.

John Bush built his fort at Buckhannon on land now owned by Major J. W. Heavner. It is not probable that it was more than a blockhouse when first constructed, but after the breaking out of Dunmore's War it was enclosed by a stockade. This stockade was of logs, one end planted firmly in the ground. Large quantities of stone once marked the site of this fort. Since owned by Major Heavner, not less than one hundred and fifty wagonloads have been hauled from its ruins, and it is not known how many were previously removed. For what purpose such quantities of stone were used, can only be conjectured. The stockade could not have been reinforced by a secondary, or interior, wall of earth and stone. It was not built to resist the assaults of artillery, for none were employed by either of the combatants along this region of the frontier.

In Chapter XXI reference is made to the vast amount of stone used in the chimney and in "chinking" the Tanner house near West's Fort. This fort-like house was erected for a private dwelling, yet was sufficiently strong to resist the assaults of the Indians. In the construction of a fort where it was expected at times that an entire settlement would take refuge, the building would be on a more colossal scale. If Bush's Fort was built with two such chimneys as that of the Tanner house — which is not improbable — it would be easy to account for this stone, to say nothing of that used for the foundation and chinking. It is to be regretted that the ruins of this fortress were not left inviolate to future generations.

Cut 1—Site of the Buckhannon Fort and Little Indian Knob*
Miss Josephine L. MacAvoy, Photographer, 1909

The fort stood on a slight eminence or flat on the north side of the valley, but the location could hardly be termed strategic. The palisade is supposed to have enclosed a half acre or more of ground, which would include the most of the flat. This flat is flanked on the north by "Little Indian Knob," shown in *Cut 1*. The foreground is the fort site, completely commanded by the knob.

The figure on the brow of "Little Indian Knob" (*Cut 1*) is that of a six-foot man. Just over the summit, on the east side of this knob, is still to be seen a slight depression where once grew a large poplar tree, behind which an Indian stood one morning, gently tinkling a bell taken from a cow for the purpose of decoying some one from the fort. A young girl went to bring the supposed cow, and escaped capture only by the opportune discovery of the ruse. From this incident the knob was named.

The party shown on the right (*Cut 1*) is standing in a depres-

---

*Owing to the loss of negatives (Cuts 1 and 2), it was impossible to give better illustrations. The party standing in the old well depression (Cut 1) is not visible.

sion which was evidently the fort well. A cellar some fourteen feet by twenty feet in size was located about twenty-eight feet southeast of the well. This cellar is supposed by some, not to have been within the stockade, and was the "outbuilding" where a few of the settlers were forced to take refuge from Timothy Dorman and the Indians after the fort was burned in 1782. (1) It is hard to conceive, however, why a store room of this class would be constructed without the enclosure. It was built in the side of the hill just below the brink of the flat, and walled with cobblestone. There is a graded entrance way on the south. The ruins of this cellar are shown in *Cut 3*. The location of the well is designated by a stake in the background, where the horse is standing.

There was a spring under the western flank of "Little Indian Knob," and about twenty-eight steps north of the center of the flat, or fort site. At present this spring is little more than a marsh, or wet bog.

Cut 2 taken from the same point as *Cut 1* (southwest part of the fort site) shows the Heavner Cemetery and "Big Indian Knob"

Cut 2—BIG INDIAN KNOB AND THE HEAVNER CEMETERY, LOOKING WEST FROM THE BUCKHANNON FORT
MacAvoy, 1909

1) See page 454.

to the west. This point, jutting out from the main ridge, commands a fine view of the entire country, and it was here that the Indians sometimes came to spy on the fort, hence the name.

The fort stood about two hundred and seventy-five paces from a point on the river where a mill was built, supposedly by Col. George Jackson. The date of its erection is not known to me. *Withers* speaks of a mill there in 1782. (2) The dam was

Cut 3—Ruins of the Old Cellar, Buckhannon Fort
MacAvoy, 1909

constructed of logs and stone, and within the memory of the present generation it was in a fair state of preservation. Traces of it are still seen at low water mark just below the Heavner Ford. Marks of the "race" are plainly visible in the north bank of the river. On the south side, the river sweeps the rocky base of a precipitous hill. This mill was evidently destroyed at an early day, probably immediately after the fort was burned, or as soon as the whites completely abandoned the settlement, after Capt. White was killed in 1782. It was not rebuilt, the settlers going to Nutter's Fort for their grinding until Henry McWhorter built his mill at

(2) See page 454.

West's Fort, about 1790. For many years the Buckhannon country patronized the McWhorter mill.

In the early nineties there was an occurrence of some magnitude at the Buckhannon Fort, which has never been chronicled. *Withers* declares that this settlement was exempt from Indian incursions from 1782 to 1795, when the Bozarths were killed. (3) This is a mistake. That the incident did occur is conclusive, and evidence of a trustworthy character places it near the close of Indian hostilities on the border. John Cutright, one of the actors, gave the facts to Colonel Henry Westfall, whose manuscript was destroyed by fire.

Through scouts, said the Westfall manuscript, word reached the settlements that a large body of Indians were advancing against the Hacker's Creek region, and a party left the Buckhannon Fort for the purpose of aiding West's Fort, where the settlers took refuge in case of an attack, or raid. When the party had reached the place now occupied by the Baptist Cemetery, about one and one-fourth miles below where the fort stood, they encountered a band of Indians. The meeting was a mutual surprise, and immediately all on both sides "treed." A sharp skirmish ensued, and two Indians were killed; one said to be the chief, was shot by Jesse Hughes. John Cutright was in this fight, sporting a brand-new shot-pouch, which was badly rent by a ball and its contents scattered on the ground. The Indians were routed, and in the short pursuit made by the whites, Cutright was left behind. When the party came back, he was sitting on a log stolidly mending his damaged shot-pouch, embellishing his crude work with an occasional emphatic expletive. None of the whites were killed. This anecdote of Cutright is similar to that reported by *DeHass*, of the German, Phouts. (4)

A tradition handed down in the Reger family, declares that it was Jacob Reger, Jr., a scout, who anticipated the Indians in this raid, and by his prowess and heroic exertion prevented what might have been a repetition of former tragedies. Through the kindness of Mrs. Lee A. Heavner, of Buckhannon, I am enabled to give this traditionary account of the fight, as found in a manuscript among the papers left by her father, Rev. John Reger, a grandson of John Reger, Sr., who was in the skirmish with the Indians.

"It was near the close of Indian hostilities on the border and in a time of comparative peace," says the tradition, "when Jacob Reger, Jr., who was scouting

(3) See page 455. (4) p. 455.

on the Ohio River, came one day upon the trail of a considerable body of Indians, who had but recently crossed to the Virginia side. This discovery aroused his suspicions to the highest pitch. Cautiously advancing, he came suddenly upon an Indian sitting with his back against a tree, sleeping, or given over to abandon and ease safe in false security. Reger was a man of most wonderful strength, backed with courage utterly devoid of fear. Prompted by the hope of learning the goal of the war party, as he believed it to be, he conceived the idea of capturing the recumbent warrior.

"Stealthily approaching, he sprang upon and securely fastened the astonished brave before he could make any resistance or outcry. Reger then made him understand that if he would reveal the destination of the Indians his life would be spared; if not his scalp would soon dangle at the white man's belt. With certain death hovering over him should he refuse to comply, the captive declared that the objective point of the party was the Buckhannon settlement. (5) Reger was endowed with the highest sense of honor, and not deigning to violate his compact to spare the life of his prisoner, he disarmed him, and covering him with his rifle, compelled him to swim to the Ohio side of the river.

"Reger then made rapid strides for the settlement, and on the evening of the second day arrived at West's Fort greatly exhausted. In consequence of recent heavy rains, the intervening rivers and creeks were flooded, and had to be crossed by swimming.

"Jesse Hughes volunteered to go on to the Buckhannon Fort that night and in the meantime West's Fort was put in the best possible state of defense. Upon the arrival of Hughes at the Buckhannon Fort, preparations were immediately made for a stout resistance. There were about thirty men soon gathered at the fort, including several from Clarksburg, among whom was Elias Hughes. A well within the stockade insured plenty of water, and the magazine was stocked with ammunition. Elias Hughes was chosen commander; and the scouts sent out soon reported that Indians, to the number of forty, were advancing by way of Brushy Fork Run. A hurried council of war was held, and it was determined to ambush the Indians, and the spot chosen was where a ravine or drain breaks into the river where the Baptist cemetery now is.

"A desperate conflict ensued, the result of which for a time hung in the balance, each party fighting from behind trees. An attempt by the Indians to flank their enemy under cover of the river bank was detected by Jesse Hughes, and frustrated. The Indian chief, in animating his warriors by personal bravery, exposed himself to Jesse's aim and he fell to rise no more. Jesse was most active in the fight, flitting from tree to tree like an evil bird of the woods; he seemed to anticipate every move of the enemy.

"John Reger, brother of Jacob, was also a conspicuous figure in this battle. Observing that with great regularity bullets from a certain point whistled uncomfortably near, he soon located his disagreeable neighbor, and silenced him with a shot. (6) When their chief fell, the warriors made a dash to recover his body, but were driven back and routed."

"This battle," concludes the tradition, "was the bloodiest fought on the Buckhannon, and the last attempt of the Indians against this fort."

(5) See page 455. (6) p. 455.

Evidently there is truth in this tradition, but in the lapse of time, error has crept in as to the magnitude of the affair, and the original point of attack as intended by the Indians. The narrative agrees with the manuscript version of Colonel Westfall, who got it from John Cutright, that there was a fight at the place mentioned, perhaps the only one of importance that ever took place in that settlement. It would be in keeping with the character of Jacob Reger to have spared the captive Indian, as alleged. He never shed human blood when it was possible to avoid it. (7)

THE PIFER MILL
Kindness of Dr. E. B. Alkire

Built on the Buckhannon River, six miles below Buckhannon, W. Va., about 1834. Was in use until the beginning of the present century. Dismantled in 1908 and rebuilt as a fishing camp near the original location.

But little is known of the life of John Bush, who gave his name to the fort at Buckhannon. In 1781 he received a certificate for 200 acres on the Buckhannon River to include his improvement made in 1773. *Withers* gives two incidents in connection with John Bush. In speaking of events when the Buckhannon settlement was broken up in 1782, (8) he says:

"While some of the inhabitants of that settlement were engaged in moving their property to a fort in Tygart's Valley (the others removing to Nutter's Fort

(7) See page 458. (8) p. 458.

and Clarksburg), they were fired upon by a party of savages, and two of them, Michael Hagle and Elias Paynter, fell. The horse on which John Bush was riding was shot through; yet Bush succeeded in extricating himself from the falling animal, and escaped though closely pursued by one of the savages. Several times the Indian following him, would cry out to him, '*Stop, and you shall not be hurt—if you do not, I will shoot you,*' and once Bush, nearly exhausted, and in despair of getting off, actually relaxed his pace for the purpose of yielding himself a prisoner, when turning round he saw the savage stop also, and commence loading his gun. This inspired Bush with fear for the consequences, and renewing his flight he made his escape. Edward Tanner, a mere youth was soon taken prisoner, and as he was being carried to their towns, met between twenty and thirty savages, headed by Timothy Dorman, proceeding to attack Buckhannon Fort. Learning from him that the inhabitants were moving from it, and that it would be abandoned in a few days, the Indians pursued their journey with so much haste, that Dorman had well nigh failed from fatigue. They arrived however, too late, for the accomplishment of their bloody purpose; the settlement was deserted, and the inhabitants safe within the walls of other fortresses." (9)

In dealing with occurrences on the border the spring following General Harmar's campaign against the Indians in September 1790, the same writer says:

"On the 24th of April, John Bush (living on Freeman's Creek), having very early sent two of his children to drive up the cattle, became alarmed by their screams, and taking down his gun, was proceeding to learn the cause of it, when he was met at the door by an Indian, who caught hold of the gun, forced it from his grasp, and shot him with it. Bush fell across the threshold, and the savage drew his knife to scalp him. Mrs. Bush ran to the assistance of her husband, and with an axe, aimed a blow at the Indian with such force that it fastened itself in his shoulder, and when he jumped back his exertion pulled the handle from her hand. She then drew her husband into the house and secured the door.

"In this time other of the savages had come up, and after endeavoring in vain to force open the door, they commenced shooting through it. Fortunately Mrs. Bush remained unhurt, although eleven bullets passed through her frock and some of them just grazing the skin. One of the savages observing an aperture between the logs thrust the muzzle of his gun thro' it. With another axe Mrs. Bush struck on the barrel so as to make it ring, and the savage on drawing it back, exclaimed '*Dern you.*' Still they were endeavoring to force an entrance into the house, until they heard what they believed to be a party of whites coming to its relief. It was Adam Bush, who living close by and hearing the screams of the children and the firing of the gun, had set off to learn what had given rise to them, and taking with him his dogs, the noise made by them in crossing the creek alarmed the savages, and caused them to retreat, taking off the two children as prisoners. A company of men were soon collected and went in pursuit of the Indians; but were unable to surprise them and regain the prisoners. They, however, came so nearly upon them, on the Little Kenhawa, that they were forced to fly precipitately, leaving the plunder and seven horses which they had taken from the settlement; these were retaken and brought back." (10)

---

(9) See page 458. (10) p. 458.

The hero in the first incident here related was undoubtedly John Bush of the Buckhannon; but the Freeman's Creek tragedy deals with another personage. *Cutright*, however, would have it differently.

"The same John Bush, after whom the fort on Buckhannon River was named, removed after some years of residence in this section to Freeman's Creek, Lewis County, and there on the 24th of April, 1791, met his death at the vile hands of the Indians." (11)

This unquestionably is error. There were two families of Bush's in the early settlements of the Upper Monongahela, one of which was small of stature, wiry and active, the other was of heavy build and less sprightly in movement. (12) John Bush of the Buckhannon was certainly of this first family. His desperate flight when pursued by the Indian, entitles him to the distinction of being fleet-footed. John Bush of Freeman's Creek belonged to the second family, very large and fleshy. He was not killed in the fight depicted. Abram Reger, referred to elsewhere in this volume, who was well acquainted with the facts and the parties, gave the following version of the occurrence to his grandson, Mr. J. S. Hall:

"Bush was a large, heavy built man, simple natured, but very passionate. The Indians came upon him while at work near the house, and before he was aware of their presence, one of them gained possession of his gun, which he had left only a few feet away. Before the Indian could shoot, Bush knocked him down, and ran for the house. As he neared the door, another Indian grappled him and the first warrior having recovered, came up and shot him through the hips. Mrs. Bush, a very muscular woman, ran out with an axe and split the head of the Indian who had hold of her husband, whom she then drew into the house and fastened the door. In the meantime an elderly lady in the room came running up, retarding the movements of Mrs. Bush, who threw her aside with such violence as to do her serious injury.

"The Indians fired several ineffectual shots through the door, and then with their tomahawks began chopping a hole through the shutter. They soon had an opening through which one of them thrust his head, and was instantly killed by Mrs. Bush with an axe. Another Indian shoved his rifle through a crevice in the cabin wall, but before he could fire Mrs. Bush struck the muzzle a heavy blow with her axe, and drove the breech of the gun against his shoulder with such force as to partly disable him.

"Bush was laid up for the winter, his wife gathering the crops and doing all the outdoor work. Meat was scarce in the cabin, owing to the husband's inability to hunt. With the opening of spring, Bush was able to go into the woods, where he shot a bear, which was lean and gaunt from its long winter fasting. The animal

(11) See page 458. (12) p. 458.

made off, and Bush followed in pursuit and came up with it in a ravine. He had no other bullet and approached the bank too closely, which giving way precipitated him to the bottom where the bear had laid down in a dying condition. The animal instantly seized him by the heel and notwithstanding he belabored it on the head with a heavy stone, it continued crunching his foot until dead. It is a noteworthy fact, that a bear when fighting only snaps with its teeth, unless in the last throes of death when it grapples and holds on until life is extinct. Bush was again disabled, but Mrs. Bush brought the bear home and dressed the meat."

The bullet which Bush received in the encounter with the Indian was never extracted. The wound healed, but broke out several years afterwards and finally resulted in his death.

CHAPTER XVII

George Jackson was captain of the first military company organized in the Buckhannon settlement. The date of this organization and its object has been a matter of conjecture. It is thought by some to have originated at the call of Col. William Darke, when he recruited his "Hampshire and Berkeley Regiment" in the Spring of 1781. This was an emergency regiment raised to oppose the invasion of Virginia by the British. This regiment was at the siege of Yorktown and the surrender of General Cornwallis in the following October, and was one of the guard which conducted a contingent of the vanquished army to the prison barracks near Winchester, Virginia.

It is not probable that Capt. Jackson participated in the campaign against Yorktown. He recruited a company from the settlements in May, 1781, and joined General Clark at Fort Pitt in his attempted expedition against Detroit.

The first military company at Buckhannon was a band of Indian spies, organized in 1779. George Jackson was Captain of this body. He is said subsequently to have had general command of the various bands of spies in the settlements, and was succeeded in this rank by Col. Lowther. Later, Jackson was a Colonel in the militia, and is inseparably connected with the early history of the Upper Monongahela. He is mentioned by *Withers* on several occasions, and his memorable night run from Buckhannon to Clarksburg for assistance when some of the settlers were besieged in an out-house in 1782, (1) was characteristic of the energy and daring courage that made him a leader among men.

He was a member of the First Virginia Assembly in 1788 which ratified the Federal Constitution. His long subsequent public career is of record and need not be repeated here. He was an associate of the Hughes, but could not vie with them in Indian woodcraft.

The two brothers of Jesse Hughes, Thomas and Elias, were both commissioned officers in Col. Lowther's Company of Rangers and Spies, and from the following story, which was gleaned from a source worthy of credence, it would appear that Jesse was also a subaltern officer in the same company.

---
(1) See page 458.

Sometime in the early nineties, Colonel Lowther ordered Jesse Hughes to take such men as he deemed necessary and scout from the Buckhannon Fort by way of French Creek and the headwaters of the West Fork to the falls of the Little Kanawha; from which point, if no Indian sign was discovered, he was to proceed to the mouth of Leading Creek, up which stream he was to return to the settlements by way of Polk Creek. Usually the scouts would strike the Ohio River near Wheeling, there construct a raft by which to descend the Ohio to the site of Parkersburg, examining all the Indian trails leading to the settlements. If signs of Indians were discovered, they would immediately strike for the settlements and give warning of the threatening danger, but if none were found they would scout over the Indian warpath that followed up the Little Kanawha and Leading Creek on their return home. This more northern territory, on the occasion of which I write, was doubtless patrolled by other efficient scouts residing on the Upper Monongahela. (2)

The route laid out for Jesse Hughes covered the several Indian trails leading from the Little Kanawha to the Upper Monongahela. The principal path was up Leading Creek and down Polk Creek (3) to the West Fork. There were, however, a few less frequented and more secluded paths among the labyrinth of small streams flowing from the divide between the headwaters of the Little Kanawha and the West Fork. One of these led up Oil Creek from the Kanawha and passed down the small stream known as "Indian Carrying Run" on the opposite side of the divide to the West Fork. The distance between the headings of these two tributaries is only a few hundred yards and was known as "Indian Carrying Place." This was the only point where the Indians "portaged," or "carried" between the Kanawha and the Monongahela, hence the name. The "Carrying Place" is on "Indian Farm," (4) where Arnold Station now is.

The war parties from Ohio, in their forays on the *western* Virginia border, never traveled by water. The topography of the country and the nature of its streams precluded the idea. By placing a few sentinels along the streams traversed, the settlers could have effectively guarded against surprise, and have easily intercepted the Indians in their flight. Canoe voyages were doubtless resorted to on some of these western streams by the Indians when raiding the settlements *east* of the Alleghenies, prior

---

(2) See page 458. (3) p. 458. (4) p. 459.

to the settling of the Upper Monongahela. At that period they were immune from pursuit *west* of the mountains, where the canoe would have been a safe and easy mode of travel. The Little Kanawha from its mouth to the "portage" referred to, afforded a direct highway of some fifty miles.

"Canoe Run," which flows into the West Fork about one-half mile below Roanoke, in Lewis County, derived its name from the scouts finding an Indian canoe moored under some willows in or near the mouth of this stream.

"Indian Cap Run," which enters the river from the east, between Jacksonville and Walkersville, took its name from an Indian cap, or head-dress, found on the western trail near its source.

In Walkersville, about one hundred and fifty yards from the forks of the river, and just above the road, a block of sandstone juts from the hillside, on which is carved "1780." The date is legible, though crudely executed. It was found there by the scouts, who attributed it to Simon Girty. But the handiwork could hardly be that of Simon Girty personally, who could neither read nor write. (5)

In the scouting expedition referred to, Jesse Hughes thought that a small party would be sufficient, and selected Alexander West to accompany him. They traversed the route designated without finding an Indian sign. They reported at Clarksburg, and in general council it was apparent that no Indians were lurking on the border. Winter was fast approaching, and there was but little probability of further hostilities that Fall. Colonel Lowther commended the scouts highly for their celerity and faithfulness, and dismissed them for the season. Colonel George Jackson, who was present, also praised their splendid work.

While out, the scouts had noted that the beech mast in the bottoms and low hills about the head of French Creek was heavy, and that the region was full of bear. A hunt was planned by the two scouts and the colonels. Hughes and West then proceeded to West's Fort, and sent a dispatch to notify the Buckhannon settlement of the result of their scouting. Within a few days they were joined at West's by the two officers, and the next day the company left for the hunting grounds. The first night they stayed at an old Indian camp, known to Hughes only, who had been there on previous occasions. Here they saw an abun-

---

(5) See page 459.

dance of deer, which at that time held no attraction for them. The next morning they crossed the divide to French Creek, where they found all the bear sign reported by the scouts. (6) The ground had been scratched over for miles, such as they had never seen before; but the sign was all old, and not a bear could be found. They had evidently gone to the rough mountainous regions of the Kanawha, the Holly, and the Buckhannon for winter quarters, as very few bear wintered in the more open hills of the West Fork.

Hughes and West desired to follow the bear, but it was necessary for Colonel Jackson to return home, and reluctantly they decided to accompany him. They recrossed the mountain and spent the night at their former camp. The deer, so unattractive the evening before, now engaged their attention, and they determined to spend the day shooting. They divided their party: Hughes and West were pitted against the two colonels. They were to hunt for a wager, the prize being all the deer skins taken. No fawns were to be counted, and if a shot failed to bring down the game it was to deduct one from the party who fired it. All bullets in the shot-pouches were counted, and for these the hunter must account at the close of the day. It was agreed that the two officers were to hunt below, while the scouts were to hunt above the camp.

Everything arranged, the hunt began, and in the evening when the game was tallied and the bullets all accounted for, the score stood nineteen for Hughes and West, and twenty-one for the colonels. The next morning the game was skinned, such vension selected as was desired, and the camp broken. It was then suggested that the stream, on a branch of which they were encamped, was yet unnamed, and it was unanimously agreed that it should be called "Skin Creek," in commemoration of their remarkable hunt. As Jesse Hughes had piloted them to the camp, and to him alone was known the sylvan retreat, they called this tributary "Hughes Fork." These names they still bear.

Afterwards, Joseph Hall, who came from England, and who was a corporal in Lord Dunmore's expedition in 1774, acquired title to a tract of land on Hughes Fork, including the camp site. Hall learned that Jesse Hughes also claimed this land by "tomahawk improvement." He met Hughes in Clarksburg and enquired regarding his claim, offering to pay him for any right he might hold to the land. Hughes replied, "I did have a claim to that land; I camped there two or three times, and had a great hunt. I marked some trees expecting to acquire a title to the land. But I have," he continued, "more of such claims than I have use for; and I hear, Joe, that you now have a wife, and will need the land." Hall told him that he not only had a wife, but also a little curly-headed boy. Hughes rejoined, "In that case, I would give the land to the boy if I had a patent for it." He then described the old Indian camp — a spring, and a beautiful location for a house.

Joseph Hall's son, Jonathan, settled on this land in 1820. Ten years later he cleared the site of the old camp, near which he built a new residence. The fire hearths of the camp, three in number, were unearthed by the plow. They were about two rods apart, and in the form of a triangle. They indicated long use, the ashes and burned stone extending considerably below the surface. Nearby were two dark spots in the soil, each about sixteen feet in diameter. These proved extremely fertile, the corn growing much more luxuriantly there than on the surrounding soil. The unearthing of the old camp was witnessed by Jonathan Hall's sons, the youngest of whom, John Strange Hall, is still living, and occupies the ancestral homestead. To Mr. Hall I am indebted for most of the particulars contained in this chapter.

Alexander West's son, Charles, settled on Hughes Fork of Skin Creek, on land said to have been "tomahawked" by his father during this hunt.

Some time prior to the close of Indian hostilities on the border, Henry Jackson, the great land surveyor, who executed several of the large surveys in (now) central West Virginia, received warrants for thirty-five thousand acres, to be laid off in five thousand acre tracts. This was the celebrated Bank's Survey, destined in after years, like many others of that day, to figure prominently in the courts.

A surveying party consisted of the surveyor, two chain-bearers, a "marker," and a cook, who helped as "packer;" also two hunters, who supplied the camp with meat and acted as scouts. Such an outfit was a recognized scouting party in time of Indian hostilities, and was often attended by regular Spies or Rangers employed by the State or Federal government.

Jackson selected a new field for his operations, and pitched camp on Leading Creek in (now) Gilmer County. He arrived there in the evening, and marked a black gum tree for a corner. He then set his compass and noted that the line determined on would cross the creek three times. After this he rested for the day. Supper over, Jesse Hughes, one of the hunters, announced that he and his comrade would go down the creek about two miles to a famous lick and kill a deer for breakfast. Before starting they heard the howl of a wolf. This was answered by another in the general direction of the lick, but apparently some distance apart. The calls were repeated occasionally and seemed to approach each other. Jackson declared these were Indian signals, and that they must return at once and alarm the settlements. Hughes rebelled. He would not "run from Injuns until he saw Injuns to run from." He then added that he could approach the lick from the bluff and see any object near it without danger of discovery. Jackson reluctantly permitted Hughes and his companion to go, but first exacted a promise that they would not fire, no odds how fair an Indian mark they might see. If the signals heard were from Indians it was evident that others were in the immediate vicinity, and it was of the utmost importance that the presence of the whites be kept secret. The scouts set out, and soon returned with the intelligence that two Indians were watching the lick, armed with bows and arrows. (7) The whites returned to West's Fort that night, and spread the alarm.

The Indians evidently discovered signs of the surveying party and its hasty retreat, for they passed by the immediate settlements and committed depredations on Cheat River, carrying off some plunder. Colonel Lowther had his scouts and rangers out watching, and succeeded in intercepting the Indians in their retreat, killed a few of them and recovered the stolen property.

Jackson never went back to complete his work. In due time, however, the Bank's Survey was properly returned, neatly plotted, and showing the crossings of the chief streams. It was forwarded to the Governor, who issued the patent. In later years Lewis Maxwell became owner of the Bank's Survey, and spent years in search of Jackson's beginning corner. Finally the place was located where the three crossings of the creek were visible, but no marks of survey were ever found there. However, in following one of Jackson's imaginary lines, a tree was found with an old "line mark." This, Maxwell claimed, had been placed by Jackson. In the meantime, later patents for the land had been dis-

') See page 460.

covered, and Maxwell brought suit for possession. The case was tried at Glenville, Gilmer County, and lasted two weeks, consuming the entire term of court. The main point involved was the identity of Jackson's beginning corner, although many other points were contested. The defense offered to prove that the mark found on "Jackson's line" was one of Jesse Hughes' tomahawk claims, antedating the Bank's Survey; but the Hughes' claim had never been carried into grant, and the court ruled against the introduction of such testimony. The case was decided for the defense.

Mr. J. S. Hall was present at the trial, and after the case was settled, Mr. Enoch Withers, an attorney for the defense, told Mr. Hall that there was an old veteran of Jackson's party still living, who could point out the exact spot of the gum tree corner, but it was not to the interest of the defense to divulge his name.

Henry Jackson told the particulars of the survey and scare by the Indians to his young nephew, George Jackson Arnold, (8) a grandson of Col. George Jackson, who figured in the Skin Creek hunt.

No actual settlements were made in the upper part of the West Fork Valley until after the treaty of Greenville in 1795. Col. Jackson was the first to enter this field. He secured a large boundary of land where Jacksonville now stands, in Lewis County; also a smaller tract at the forks of the river. In 1797, he settled four families by the name of Collins on his larger tract, giving each fifty acres of choice land. They were to remain until the colony was *permanent* and open a "Bridle Path" to the Flesher settlement, at Weston.

These settlers were hardy and gave their names to the township known as "Collins Settlement." The Collins were afterwards followed by the Bennetts: William, Joseph, Abram and Jacob, who came over the Seneca Trail (9) from the Upper Potomac. The Bennetts were fruit growers and propagated trees from seed brought from the Potomac. They left numerous descendants in the country.

The "Ireland Settlement" at the extreme head of the right-hand fork of the river, was named for Andrew Wilson, a son of Erin, who was the first settler there. He voted for James K. Polk for President when one hundred and fourteen years old, but died the following year.

---

(8) See page 460. (9) p. 460.

In 1781, a certificate was issued to "Joseph Hall, 400 acres on the east side of the West Branch of the Monongalia River, in the right of residence, to include his improvements made thereon in 1771, with a preemption right of 1000 acres adjoining."

Joseph did not settle on the West Fork of the Monongahela until several years after his "improvement" of 1771. He was born in England in the year 1745. His father, Jonathan Hall, was a land owner, or tenant proprietor, and like his ancestors, a farmer. Joseph was a younger son, and under the English laws could not inherit any of the ancestral acres, so he was educated for the mercantile business and entered the employment of an uncle.

In 1764, this uncle closed up business, and accompanied by Joseph, came to Alexandria, Virginia, and became one of the leading merchants of that place. In 1774, Joseph volunteered in Governor Dunmore's expedition against the Indians, and was made a corporal in Dunmore's division.

After the return of this wing of the army, the feeling against the Governor and the British Government became intense, and caused an estrangement between the merchant and his nephew. The former was favorable to opposing British interferences in colonial affairs, while Joseph advocated passive measures. As the Revolutionary storm thickened, patriot and loyalist parted company and Joseph rented a farm of Lord Fairfax on Patterson Creek, in now Mineral County, West Virginia, where with a partner he carried on farming for ten years. In the meantime, his views changed regarding governmental affairs, and he rejoiced in the downfall of the British rule.

In 1784, in company with Jacob Forenash and James Morrison, old comrades in Dunmore's War and who had worked for him, he came to Harrison County and purchased two hundred acres on Peor's Run, in now Upshur County, West Virginia. He employed Fecknash and Morrison to build a house and clear and cultivate this land under his supervision. For many years, Hall spent the most of his time at Clarksburg, assisting the Surveyor and the County Clerk. He entered numerous tracts of land, which involved him in lawsuits with but little compensation.

Among his early acquaintances at Clarksburg were three Englishmen, whose names were Hall, but they could trace no family relationship. One of these settled in now Marion County, one on Hughes River and the other on Elk Creek.

Some of the descendants of the latter intermarried with the Reger family. (10)

Joseph Hall was educated in advance of those around him, and was useful in imparting knowledge to his neighbors. He died in 1825.

In January 1796, Joseph Hall married Ann Strange, nee Hitt. Tragedy had twice widowed this woman. Her first husband, Joel Martin, a soldier of the Revolution, died at the siege of Yorktown, 1781. Her second husband, William Strange, was lost on a surveying expedition in the mountains and his skeleton only found a great many years afterward. The following is an account of this incident, as given by *Adkinson*:

Strange Creek.

"About the year 1790 a surveying party came from what is now Upshur County, to Elk and Holly Rivers, for the purpose of making a survey, which is known as the Budd Survey. Among their number was a man by the name of William Strange. Old Jerry Carpenter, who was the first adventurer in the upper Elk region, was employed to conduct the party. The lower line of the survey was to begin with the left-hand fork of Holly river, about six miles above its junction with main Holly river; thence in a southwesterly direction, crossing the mountains, to main Holly; thence over another mountain to Elk river, to a point near Carpenter's settlement. At that day there was no settlement in that section except Carpenter's, and they were obliged to carry their provisions and cooking utensils on a pack horse. Mr. Strange was a very indifferent woodsman, and to him was assigned the duty of taking the pack horse from one camping place to another. He was directed by the party to take the pack horse down the path on the left-hand fork to its mouth, then up main Holly river to a certain creek, where they met him the first night. They then directed him to go down Holly to its junction with Elk river, then up Elk to Carpenter's settlement, where they would meet him the second night. The path down Holly was on the left-hand side. About a half or three-quarters of a mile above its mouth the path forked, one path crossing the river and going up Elk, the other passing on down Holly for a short distance, and then bearing off to the right, ascending the mountain, passing through a long chestnut flat, and striking Elk some miles below. Owing to the dense growth of timber on his left, Strange, while passing by the ford on Holly, took the right-hand path, and failed to discover the junction of the rivers. A short distance below the junction, Elk came in view, and still believing it to be the Holly, he abandoned the path and attempted to follow the river shore. After having gone a short distance, he was unable to proceed further in consequence of impassable narrows, and was forced to retrace his steps to the path, which he followed down to the chestnut flat, where he became utterly confused, and tied his horse to a bush.

"The surveying party reached Carpenter's settlement that night, and as Strange's non-arrival created uneasiness among a portion of the party Carpenter

(10) See page 460.

immediately explained the mystery by stating that he had evidently been misled on account of their failure to inform him where he would have to cross the river. Early next morning they started in search of him, crossed Holly and followed the tracks of the horse until they found it tied to the bush before mentioned. Strange had wandered away from the horse, and while Carpenter was endeavoring to discover his trail one of the party fired his gun to let Strange know that they were near him. Carpenter reprimanded the party, and warned them against a repetition of the act; telling them that Strange, in his bewildered condition would take to flight, believing them to be Indians. After searching for some time, a few miles distant they found where he had been lying in the brush, and from the direction he had taken, he had evidently fled at the noise of the gun, as suggested by Mr. Carpenter, who was an experienced and adroit Indian hunter. They followed his trail for perhaps five or six miles below, where, in the wildness of the forest, they lost all traces of him.

"Nothing was heard of Mr. Strange for a number of years, when there was found, about forty miles below, on a branch of Elk, the bones of a man at the foot of a beech tree. The name of Strange and the following couplet had been cut in the bark of the tree:

> 'Strange is my name, and I'm on strange ground,
> And strange it is that I can't be found.'

"This branch, before that time known as Turkey Creek, from this incident, has ever since borne the name of Strange Creek. It is a few miles below Birch river, and is now the location of the Elk River Iron Works, in the County of Braxton, seventy miles from Charleston.

"It is also stated that the rifle of Mr. Strange, with his shot-pouch hanging on its ramrod, was found leaning against the tree at the root of which his bones were lying.

"I must conclude, from this remarkable circumstance, that 'Strange creek' was well and appropriately named." (11)

Adkinson errs in fixing the Strange tragedy in 1790, as attested by the birth record of two of his children given in a later paragraph of this chapter. Strange was lost in the autumn of 1795 subsequent to Wayne's Treaty with the Indians, of which the surveying party were wholly ignorant. This date is not only supported by family tradition, but it is coincident with a survey made in that year by Henry Jackson, for whom Strange was "cook and packer."

After a fruitless search for the missing man, Jackson returned home without completing the survey, but the imaginary lines were afterwards laid down and a patent secured covering the grant. Jackson, be it said, seldom ran all the lines of any of his surveys, but they were always properly patented; such was the case when he surveyed Joseph Hall's estate on Skin Creek, notwithstanding Hall was present.

---

(11) See page 460.

Upon the return of Jackson's party, others went in search of Strange, among them a Mr. Loudin, one of Jackson's hunters, and Philip Reger.

The beech tree bearing William Strange's name stood near the head of the creek, and was discovered by some hunters, who being familiar with the story of Strange, gave it his name. It is erroneously spoken of by some contemporaries as "Stranger's Creek." Mr. John Strange Hall, a grandson of Mrs. Strange, and well informed regarding his family history, in response to an inquiry, says:

"Mr. Fitzwater, the first settler on Big Buffalo, a tributary of the Elk River, found a gun under a shelving rock, with the stock so badly damaged that it fell to pieces when handled. Nothing was ever known touching the history of this gun, but it was supposed by many to have belonged to the unfortunate Strange, who placed it there before succumbing to death."

I am indebted to Mr. Giddeon M. Heavner of Buckhannon, West Virginia, for a traditional version of the tragedy:

"Mr. Strange was in the mountains with a Mr. Hall and a Mr. Reger," writes Mr. Heavner, "and was directed to take the pack horse to a certain gap, where they were to join him later. Perhaps Reger and Hall did not make the place of rendezvous as soon as expected, but when they came up the horse was found tied to a bush with the pack lying near, but Strange was not there. He had gone off in an opposite direction and a heavy snowstorm was raging, and his trail could be followed only a short distance. They searched during several days, but found no trace of the missing man. Many years after, about five miles from there, his remains were found by the side of a log with his gun at his side. On a beech tree near by were engraved these words:

'William Strange is my name,
And in these strange woods I must remain.'"

Mr. Heavner says that he has also understood that Strange tied the abandoned pack horse near where the town of Pickens, West Virginia, now stands, and that his remains were found on Sugar Creek, Braxton County.

The story was told Mr. Heavner by his mother, Mary, whose step-grandfather was Mr. Strange. She was the oldest child of Stephen, son of Joel Martin who died at Yorktown. Joel was not a regular enlisted soldier but when Virginia was invaded by the British under Gen. Cornwallis, he took his gun and went out with the patriot troops, never to return. His brother William was an enlisted soldier in the Revolution, and is said to have been killed at the siege of Yorktown. Joel Martin left two children, Joel, born July 26, 1778, Stephen, born April 14, 1781. Stephen never saw his father. This coupled with the fact that he pressed his hand into the throat of a dying wolf thereby hastening its death by suffocation gave him the power to cure the thrash in children, as more fully described in Chapter XXIX, this volume.

Doubtless the story as told by Heavner, that Strange was with Hall and Reger when last seen, originated in the following incident:

William Strange had a hunt with Jacob Reger, Sr., and Joseph Hall; and he got lost, but was near his home and there was no tragedy. Reger was too old to hunt at a distance and he proposed to Hall that they hunt the divide between Pecks Run and Turkey Run. This region was no longer the resort of the younger hunters who went far afield for game. William Strange's farm lay on their route and he joined them. As the latter had had but little experience in hunting, he was directed to take the ridge and upper benches to a "crossing" in a low gap where he was to watch for deer which might break cover, and where they would later join him.

Reger took the Pecks Run side while Hall crossed to the Turkey Run side, hunting on the lower benches and hollows, or ravines. After a time, Hall hearing the report of Reger's gun, recrossed the ridge and helped the old hunter hang up a large doe. They then proceeded together to the appointed rendezvous where they found Strange anxiously awaiting them. He had heard Reger's shot, and had succeeded in bringing down one of three deer which had been startled and broke for the accustomed pass. Strange had been tramping snow so long around the old oak where he was stationed, that he had decided that the other hunters had returned home and he was about to follow suit.

After a short rest, Strange picked up the fawn which he had killed and started to lead the company, but he took the path towards Turkey Run. When called back, he insisted that he was right and pointed to his recent tracks, showing that that was the direction from which he came. But as his comrades moved off in the opposite direction, he reluctantly followed, protesting that they were going wrong; and not until they reached Hall's farm and saw his house was he convinced of his error. Strange was joked about this until the tragedy in the wilderness a few years later when he was lost never again to be seen alive. Other stories of like nature were related of William Strange, attesting his utter lack of woodcraft.

William Strange was born in Fauquier County, Virginia. His children were:

Eliza, born September 22, 1784; James, born October 18, 1787; John, born November 15, 1789; Sarah, born July 26, 1792, married Enoch Hall, of the Elk Creek family of Halls; Margaret, born July 11th, 1794.

Mrs. Hall, nee Hitt, was an estimable woman, and her married life with Mr. Joseph Hall was ideal. She died in 1810 leaving two children by her last husband; Jonathan, born November 8, 1797, and David, born March 4, 1800. They inherited their father's estate on Skin Creek.

A unique feature of Joseph Hall's residence was the stairway, which was carved in one piece from a large poplar tree.

A tragedy not unlike that of Strange occurred about 1815.

George Mollohan who lived with his son, James, on Birch River, left one day to visit his son John, who resided about sixteen miles distant and near where Sutton now stands on the Little Kanawha; all within the present bounds of Braxton County.

About ten days after the old gentleman's departure, a settler from the Little Kanawha came to Birch River and James Mollohan inquired about his father. He was informed that Mr. Mollohan had not been at his son John's, nor had he, in coming over the path seen any trace of him. Moreover, John had requested the informant to tell his father to pay him a visit.

An unavailing search was immediately instituted for the missing man. The only trace ever found of him was his gloves placed in the forks of a bush, and, at no great distance, his horse feeding in the bottom lands. This incident is here given for the first time.

George Mollohan, settled in Greenbrier County, in 1780. (12)

CHAPTER XVIII

When forts were built along the Ohio, Indian incursions into Virginia became less frequent. The garrisons of these forts and the settlers who gathered about them created a demand on the settlements on the Western Monongahela for beef and milk cows. In 1791 we find Jesse Hughes with Nicholas Carpenter, in his ill-fated enterprise undertaken to supply this demand at Fort Harmer at the mouth of the Muskingum. The ensuing brief account of this occurrence is taken from *Withers*. (1)

"In the month of September, Nicholas Carpenter set off to Marietta with a drove of cattle to sell to those who had established themselves there; and when within some miles from the Ohio river, encamped for the night. (2) In the morning early, and while he and the drovers were yet dressing, they were alarmed by a discharge of guns, which killed one and wounded another of his party. The others endeavored to save themselves by flight; but Carpenter being a cripple (because of a wound received some years before) did not run far, when finding himself becoming faint, he entered a pond of water where he fondly hoped he should escape observation. But no! both he and a son who had likewise sought security there, were discovered, tomahawked and scalped. George Legget, one of the drovers, was never after heard of; but Jesse Hughes succeeded in getting off though under disadvantageous circumstances. He wore long leggins, and when the firing commenced at the camp, they were fastened at top to his belt, but hanging loose below. Although an active runner, yet he found that the pursuers were gaining and must ultimately overtake him if he did not rid himself of his incumbrance. For this purpose he halted somewhat and stepping on the lower part of his leggins, broke the strings which tied them to his belt; but before he accomplished this, one of the savages approached and hurled a tomahawk at him. It merely grazed his head, and he then again took flight and soon got off.

"It was afterwards ascertained that the Indians by whom this mischief was effected, had crossed the Ohio river near the mouth of the Little Kenhawa, where they took a negro belonging to Captain James Neal, and continued on towards the settlements on West Fork, until they came upon the trail made by Carpenter's cattle. Supposing that they belonged to families moving, they followed on until they came upon the drovers; and tying the negro to a sapling made an attack on them. The negro availed himself of their employment elsewhere, and loosening the bands which fastened him, returned to his master."

The following more elaborate description of the foregoing tragedy is given by *Hildreth*. (3)

"The year 1791 was more fruitful in tragical events than any other during the war, in the vicinity of Marietta. After that period the attention of the Indians

(1) See page 460. (2) p. 460. (3) p. 461.

was more occupied with the troops assembled on the borders of their own country, or already penetrating to the vicinity of their villages. The United States troops stationed at the posts within the new settlements, drew a considerable portion of their meat rations from the inhabitants of the western branches of the Monongahela, about Clarksburg, especially their fresh beef. Several droves had been brought from that region of the country in 1790 and '91 and sold to Paul Fearing, Esq., who had been appointed Commissary to the troops. A considerable number of cattle, especially milk cows, were also sold to the inhabitants of Marietta. Among those engaged in this employment was Nicholas Carpenter, a worthy, pious man, who had lived many years on the frontiers and was well acquainted with a forest life. He left Clarksburg the last of September, with a drove, accompanied by his little son, ten years old, and five other men, viz: Jesse Hughes, George Legit, John Paul, Barns, and Ellis. On the evening of the 3rd of October, they had reached a point six miles above Marietta, and encamped on a run half a mile from the Ohio, and since called 'Carpenter's run.' The cattle were suffered to range in the vicinity, feeding on the rich pea vines that then filled the woods, while the horses were hoppled, the leaves pulled out from around the clappers of their bells, and turned loose in the bottom. After eating their suppers, the party spread their blankets on the ground and lay down with their feet to the fire. No guard was set to watch the approach of an enemy. Their journey being so near finished, without discovering any signs of Indians, that they thought all danger was past.

"It so happened that not far from the time of their leaving home, a party of six Shawanese Indians, headed as was afterwards ascertained, by Tecumseh, (4) then quite a youth, but ultimately so celebrated for bravery and talents, had crossed the Ohio river near Bellville, on a marauding expedition in the vicinity of Clarksburg. From this place they passed over the ridges to 'Neil's Station,' on the Little Kenawha, one mile from the mouth, where they took prisoner a colored boy of Mr. Neil, about twelve years old, as he was out looking for the horses early in the morning. It was done without alarming the garrison, and they quietly proceeded on their route, doing no other mischief; pursuing their way up the Kenawha to the mouth of Hughes' river, and following the north fork, fell on to the trail from Clarksburg to Marietta. This took them about three days. There was no rain, and the leaves so dry that their rustling alarmed the deer, and they could kill no game for food. Their only nourishment for that period was a single tortoise, which they divided among them, giving Frank, the black boy, an equal share. (5) As he was much exhausted and discouraged, they promised him a horse to ride on their return. These circumstances were related by Frank after his escape.

"Soon after leaving the north fork of Hughes' river, they fell onto the trail of Carpenter's drove, and thinking it made by a caravan of settlers on their way to the Ohio, they held a short council. Giving up any further progress towards Clarksburg they turned with renewed energy and high spirits upon the fresh large trail, which they perceived had very recently been made. So broad was the track made by the cattle and four or five horses that they followed it without difficulty, at a rapid pace all night, and came in sight of the camp fire a little before daylight. Previous to commencing the attack, they secured Frank with leather thongs to a stout sapling on the top of an adjacent ridge. The trampling of the

(4) See page 461. (5) p. 461.

cattle and the noise of the horse bells greatly favored the Indians in their approach, but as there was no sentinel there was little danger of discovery. Tecumseh, with the cautious cunning that ever distinguished him, posted his men behind the trunk of a large fallen tree, a few yards from the camp, where they could watch the movements of their enemies.

"At the first dawn of day Mr. Carpenter called up the men, saying they would commence the day with the accustomed acts of devotion which he had long practiced. As the men sat around the fire, and he had just commenced reading a hymn, the Indians rose and fired, following the discharge with a terrific yell, and rushed upon their astonished victims with the tomahawk. Their fire was not very well directed, as it killed only one man, Ellis from Greenbrier, and wounded John Paul through the hand. Ellis instantly fell, exclaiming, 'O Lord, I am killed!' The others sprang to their feet, and before they could all get their arms which were leaning against a tree, the Indians were among them. Hughes who had been an old hunter and often in skirmishes with savages, in his haste seized on two rifles, Carpenter's and his own, and pushed into the woods, with two Indians in pursuit. He fired one of the guns, but whether with effect is not known, and threw the other away. Being partly dressed at the time of the attack, his long leggins (6) were only fastened to the belt around his waist and were loose below, entangling his legs, and greatly impeding his flight. To rid himself of this encumbrance he stopped for a moment, placed his foot on the lower end, and tore them loose from his belt, leaving his legs bare from the hips downward. This delay nearly cost him his life. His pursuer then within a few feet of him, threw his tomahawk so accurately as to graze his head. Freed from this impediment he soon left his foe far behind. Christopher Carpenter, the son of Nicholas, now living in Marietta, says he well remembers seeing the bullet holes in Hughes' hunting shirt after his return.

"In the race the competitors passed near the spot where Frank was concealed, who described it as one of the swiftest he had ever seen. John Paul, who had been in many engagements with the Indians, escaped by his activity in running. Burns, a stout, athletic man, but slow of foot, was slain near the camp after a stout resistance. When found a few days after his jack knife was still clasped in his hand, and the weeds trampled down for a rod or more around, showing he had resisted manfully for life. George Legit was pursued for nearly two miles, overtaken and killed. Mr. Carpenter, although a brave man, was without arms to defend himself, and being lame could not run rapidly. He therefore sought to conceal himself behind some willows in the bed of the run. He was soon discovered, with his little boy by his side. His captors conducted him to the spot where the black boy had been left, and killed both him and his son. What led to the slaughter, after they had surrendered, is not known. He was found wrapped in his blanket, with a pair of new Indian moccasins on his feet, and his scalp not removed. It is supposed that these marks of respect were shown him at the request of one of the Indians whose gun Carpenter had repaired at Marietta the year before, and had declined any compensation for the service. He was by trade a gunsmith. This circumstance was told to C. Carpenter, many years after, by one of the Indians who was present, at Urbana in Ohio. It is another proof of the fact, that an Indian never forgets an act of kindness, even in an enemy.

"Tecumseh and his men, after collecting the plunder of the camp, retreated

---

(6) See page 461.

in such haste, that they left all the horses, which had probably dispersed in the woods at the tumult of the attack. They no doubt feared a pursuit from the rangers at Marietta and Williams' station, who would be notified by the escape of their prisoner, Frank, who in the midst of the noise of the assault contrived to slip his hands loose from the cords, and hide himself in a thick patch of hazel bushes, from which he saw a part of the transactions. After the Indians had left the ground, he crept cautiously forth, and by good fortune took the right direction to Williams' station, opposite to Marietta. A party of men was sent out the next day, who buried the dead as far as they could then be found. Frank returned to his master, and died only a few years since."

Colonel Joseph Barker assisted in burying the bodies of Carpenter and his men. (7)

From the foregoing it would appear that Hughes had adopted the Indian mode of dress so popular with the half-wild hunters and scouts in the latter years of the Indian wars on the Virginia border. Tradition says that Hughes was surprised by the Indians near the Buckhannon Fort when entangled with loose leggins, and with difficulty effected his escape. Doubtless this story had its origin in the Carpenter occurrence.

A single instance illustrative of Hughes' wonderful fleetness and dexterity with his rifle will demonstrate to what a fearful strait he must have been reduced that he should in his flight cast aside a loaded gun. After he had moved from Hacker's Creek, and was an old man, he returned on a visit. A Mr. Bailey, of Freeman's Creek, then a lad, remembered seeing him and witnessing the feat at a house-raising on Broad Run, in what is now Lewis County. When the house was completed the assembled young men engaged in athletic sports, hopping, jumping and foot-racing, as was customary in those days. One athlete excelled all competitors in fleetness, and the old scout offered to run with him. The conditions of the race stipulated that Hughes with empty rifle in hand was to have ten paces the start of his adversary; and if successful in charging his piece before caught he was to be declared winner. Arrangements were accordingly made, and after the contestants had been properly placed, the signal was given and they sprang forward. One was an aged man, on whose visage the "shadows of the evening" were settling. The other, strong in the prime of youth, exulted in the mounting vigor of manhood. Swift was the race, but the chief of the Monongahela scouts proved himself. He charged his rifle, and whirling about, could easily have shot his rival before being caught.

(7) See page 461.

The following traditional sequel to the Carpenter tragedy is an extract from a manuscript by the late Mr. S. C. Shaw, of Parkersburg, West Virginia. Mr. Shaw spent considerable time in collecting traditions from old papers and the descendants of the border pioneers. He died only a few years ago.

"At the first volley from the guns of the Indians, Carpenter and three of his men fell dead. Hughes, the only one to escape death, was slightly wounded, but by his extraordinary activity and fleetness succeeded, after a long and at times close chase, in making his escape to Neal's blockhouse at the mouth of the Little Kanawha. The colored boy, Frank, whom the Indians had taken prisoner and tied to a tree with deer sinews during the attack, succeeded with his teeth in severing his bonds, and though closely pursued made his escape to the fort. When Hughes and the boy appeared at the blockhouse and told the story of savage cruelty and murder, Isaac Williams, (8) a noted scout, immediately took charge of a party which started in pursuit of the Indians. Arriving at the scene of the tragedy, they found the body of Carpenter and his three men lying by their camp fire, scalped and mutilated. They buried their dead, and struck the trail of the Shawnees leading towards the river. Owing to a heavy rain, they lost the trail somewhere near the point on which St. Mary's, the county seat of Pleasants County, now stands, and the pursuit was abandoned. Williams' party, consisting of Jesse Hughes, Malcomb Coleman, Elijah Pixley and James Ryan, now held a council of war and unanimously agreed to avenge the death of Carpenter and his party on the first Indians that fell in their way.

"Williams led his party of avengers across the Ohio at a ford near Willow Island and immediately took up their silent march towards the head of Shade River, where they learned from the scouts belonging to the Bellville blockhouse, a small party of Shawnees were encamped on a hunt. The scouts went into camp on the Little Hocking, early that evening, leaving one man on guard to be changed at midnight; and rested until two o'clock in the morning, when, after a hasty meal of dried venison and parched corn, they again took up the line of march. Arriving within three miles of where they had been told the Shawnees were camped, Williams and his party went into hiding beneath a mass of thick undergrowth lining a small stream between two wooded hills. Soon after being here ensconced, the report of fire arms nearby startled them. Peering through the branches of their bushy canopy the scouts silently listened and waited. A few minutes later a large buck broke cover on the hillside and came bounding down the slope in a straight line for the thicket in which they were concealed. The scouts supposed that the Indians were in pursuit, and were fearful that the buck would bring about their discovery. Fortunately for them, while the game was fifty yards away, a rifle rang out on the still morning air, and the buck sprang high and fell dead. An instant later three Indians ran down the hill, and began dressing the carcass. From their head dress and general appearance, the scouts recognized them as Shawnees, and knew that they were near the camp for which they were looking. The whites remained motionless and were undiscovered by the Indians, who, after completing their task, moved off with their spoils. The whites kept in hiding all day with one of their number constantly on the lookout.

(8) See page 461.

"On the banks of the Shade River, three miles distant from the hiding place of the whites, was a small creek which emptied into the larger stream. A huge rock stood back fifteen or twenty yards from the bank, and in front, and between it and the river, stood four brush wigwams. The Indians had brought three of their squaws with them to cure the meat, and with them three Indian lads, ranging from four to eleven years of age. The band of warriors or hunters consisted of four men. That night about midnight the scouts approached within two or three hundred yards of the Indian camp when Jesse Hughes went forward to ascertain their exact number and location. Hughes soon returned with the information given above, having arrived at this knowledge from the number of lodges and the equipment about the lodges. When Hughes reported, Williams divided his forces, sending Hughes with two men to follow under the bank of the creek until opposite the camp; and then followed by the remaining hunter, Williams cautiously crept up until he was directly behind the rock referred to. The cry of the whippoor-will was Hughes' signal that his force was in position, and a minute later Williams and Pixley crept from behind the rock and up to the nearest wigwam. So silent was their approach that even the keen-eared Shawnees had no suspicion that an enemy was near. The moon was in the full and even under the shade of the trees objects were plainly discernable. Williams and Pixley waited near the first wigwam until they saw Hughes, Coleman and Ryan close up to another, then raising his hand as a signal, dashed into the wigwam with a fearful yell, and before the sleeping Indians could spring to their feet, they were upon them. The scouts had rushed with tomahawk in hand, and almost in a second two Indian warriors and a squaw were tomahawked. While this tragedy was being enacted, Hughes and his companions were holding another carnival of death within a few yards. Yells and cries of pain rent the air, and instantaneously the remaining Indians were out of their wigwams with weapons in their hands. Heretofore the whites had refrained from using their rifles, but after they had exterminated the occupants of two wigwams first attacked, they sprang out with their rifles, and before the panic-stricken Indians could recover their presence of mind, the rifles of the whites began to crack, and at each shot an Indian fell. Nine of the party were killed. The remaining Shawnee yelled with terror and fled to the forest. Fearing an ambuscade, the scouts quickly reloaded their guns and then looked over the field of battle.

"One little Indian boy, not over four years old, was discovered concealed under a pile of furs and hides in a corner of one of the wigwams, where he had crawled when the whites made their attack.

"Although doubtless frightened at the sight of the first white faces and heavy beards he had ever seen, the boy did not so much as whimper when Pixley picked him up and was about to dash him against a tree. Hughes, near Pixley at the time, begged him to spare the boy; but Pixley, whose brother and son had been killed and scalped by the Shawnees several months before, at first refused to spare him, but after a good deal of persuasion Hughes at last succeeded in getting possession of the lad.

"Four horses, a large amount of fresh meat, a lot of furs and three good rifles were found and taken possession of. The dead Indians were scalped, the horses loaded with the captured plunder, and then fastening the Indian boy securely to the back of one of them, the scouts began their retreat. They followed the banks of the Shade River to its mouth, at what is today the town of Murrayville. From that point, they travelled several miles up the Ohio to a ford where they crossed, and arrived at the Bellville blockhouse. The little Indian prisoner was taken away a few days later by Jesse Hughes, and an old manuscript says that he lived many years among the whites in a settlement called Bulltown, dying at the age of nearly one hundred years, a devout Christian, greatly loved and respected in his community."

The date (1785) and some of the details as given in the original unabridged version of this tradition are so conflicting, and the story of Hughes saving the little boy, an act so foreign to his known nature, serve to cast doubt on the story. Some parts of it may be true; evidently much of it is untrue. It was published in the *Pittsburg Post* several years ago, and copied by the press, and is given for what it is worth.

It is said that the colored lad's name was Frank Wykoff, and that he was caught by the Indians one mile above Neal's Fort while fishing at the mouth of the Little Kanawha; that his captors tied his hands behind him, and packing a heavy load of food and utensils on his shoulders, compelled him to keep pace with them. But it is not probable that the Indians were encumbered with utensils or much food on a war expedition.

The companions of Jesse Hughes in this traditional expedition of revenge and plunder were well known on the Virginia frontier. In February, 1793, we find that Malcom Coleman, Elijah Pixley and James Ryan, accompanied by Coleman's son John, left the fort at Belleville, Ohio, in a canoe on a hunting trip up Big Mill Creek, in what is now Jackson County, West Virginia. They camped at or near where Cottageville now stands, and in a few days had all the venison and bear meat their canoe would carry. Their return home was delayed by the freezing of the creek. Pixley and young Coleman returned overland to the fort for a small supply of flour or meal and salt, expecting to return in the forenoon of the third day. On that fatal morning, the elder Coleman and Ryan rose early and prepared breakfast. While returning thanks at the beginning of the meal they were fired on by a band of Indians in ambush, and Coleman was instantly killed. Ryan was slightly wounded, but fled and in due time reached the fort. A party immediately returned to the camp, only to find Coleman scalped and stripped of his clothing and the camp plundered. (9) This occurrence was strangely coincident with the Carpenter tragedy.

(9) See page 461.

CHAPTER XIX

When the Waggoner family, (1) on Jesse's Run, was massacred in May, 1792, it was Jesse Hughes who carried the news of the tragedy to West's Fort and alarmed the settlers. Colonel John McWhorter, then a lad eight years of age, was out hunting the cows not far from his father's home near the fort, when hearing the rustling of underbrush and glancing up, he saw Jesse, rifle in hand, running towards the fort. As Jesse passed the astonished lad he ejaculated, "Heel it to the fort, ye' little devil; Injuns after ye'!" The little fellow did "heel it," endeavoring to keep pace with the scout, but to no purpose. The fleet-footed trailer disappeared as suddenly as he came to view.

This raid on the Waggoner family by Tecumseh and his two warriors, with its subsequent history, and the story of the tragedy as told by the Indians in after years, dimly reveals an incentive to these border forays not usually attributed to the Indian by the historian. That these incursions were primarily of a partisan and revengeful nature, cannot be gainsaid, but that occasionally they were prompted by motives of a different character is also certain. The carrying into captivity of small children over long and dangerous wilderness paths by the fierce warrior, is significant. I have elsewhere spoken of the strong parental feeling which sways the Indian bosom. The vacant seat at the fireside of the wigwam was as deeply mourned as in any home on earth. A longing to repair the broken circle, often led to the adoption of a stranger by the bereaved family or tribe. Preferably the adopted one was a child, although often grown or matured parties were acceptable. To fill these vacancies, young children of likely appearance were kidnaped from the settlements. (2) That these adoptions were successful, we need only refer to the pathetic scenes enacted at the several treaties where these captives were surrendered. Often it was necessary to force them from their foster parents. (3) The grief caused by these separations was always mutual. The running of the gauntlet by the prisoner before his adoption was, to use their own phraseology, "like how do you do," a hearty but rough initiation into Indian society. (4) The ceremony of adoption was serious, and assumed a religious

---
(1) See page 461. (2) p. 462. (3) p. 462. (4) p. 462.

phase. The eradication of every drop of white blood from the veins of James Smith when he was adopted by the Caughnewagos, was highly symbolical, and a beautiful portrayal of primitive simplicity and sincerity. (5)

In *Border Warfare*, (6) will be found a very concise account of the Waggoner tragedy, and reference here to the published account will be made only in connection with some of the incidents heretofore not of record.

The attack was made on Monday evening. The Indians, led by Tecumseh, in their flight passed over the bench land between Buck Knob and Jesse Hughes' cabin, near the present site of the old Tanner house. They crossed the small stream which heads towards McKinney's Run and flows between Jesse's cabin and the old Indian village site on the promontory, near where it empties into the creek. On the right and near the road now leading up this little vale, was in former years a spring, shaded by two beech trees. This was near the source of the stream. The Indians with their prisoners passed between these trees, against which they leaned their rifles while they quenched their thirst at the spring. I have been at this spot quite often. One of the trees is still standing; but the spring, it is said, has ceased to flow, except during the wet spring months. From here they crossed the little valley, and passed over the ridge onto McKinney's Run, on the farm lately owned by Rev. Mansfield McWhorter, a grandson of Henry McWhorter. There on the hillside, just under the brow of the ridge, finding that Mrs. Waggoner (who was in no condition to travel) and the two smallest children were an impediment to a necessarily rapid flight, the Indians tomahawked and scalped them.

In the meantime, Waggoner, who had escaped to Hardman's, a neighbor living about half a mile away, spread the alarm. Hardman lived about one and one-half miles from Jesse Hughes, the fleet-footed, who ran to the fort with the news. A rescue party immediately hastened to the Waggoner place, and started in pursuit of the Indians. The pursuers fully acquainted with the country, and under the skilled guidance of West and Hughes, pressed the Indians hard, and at one point nearly intercepted them. As subsequently learned, the red warriors, alert to the perils of their position, kept one of their number constantly scouting in advance. By a code of signals, this scout kept his two comrades informed

(5) See page 462. (6) p. 462.

of conditions ahead. At one time, they observed the scout coming towards them, making signals by an undulating or ducking posture of the body, in unison with the downward and outward sweep of the arm. They immediately stopped and the scout hurried towards them. They were being intercepted by the whites. A hasty council of war ensued, then changing their course, they made off at an increased rate of speed. The whites pursued them to the mouth of Kinchelo Creek, where night coming on and finding that the Indians were out-traveling them, the chase was abandoned. Henry McWhorter was one of the party, and helped to carry the dead to the fort. He often spoke of the appearance of the bodies where the tomahawking took place, but never mentioned that they were "mangled in the most barbarous and shocking manner" as stated by *Withers*.

Peter Waggoner, the only surviving boy, remained with the Indians more than twenty years, or until near the close of the War of 1812. He was then seen and recognized by Mr. Peter Booher, (6) with a band of friendly Indians, on Paint Creek, (7) a tributary of the Scioto River. Booher was a neighbor of Mr. Waggoner, and had gone to Ohio to take up land. He recognized the son by the strong resemblance to the father; and immediately communicated with him, telling of his discovery. Mr. Waggoner, in company with his neighbor Mr. Hardman, soon visited the Paint Creek Indians with the view of inducing his son to return home with him. While on Paint Creek, an old Indian, claiming to have been one of the raiding party, by signs and broken English gave Mr. Waggoner the following incidents of the destruction of his family.

The warrior first held up two fingers; pointed to the sun, and then to the western horizon, signifying that the sun was two hours high when they made the attack. He declared that it had been their intention to take the mother and all the children captives; and that the killing of the boy at the house was accidental. The warrior struck him for the purpose of rendering him senseless, and to prevent him from making an outcry; but the blow was too heavy, killing him instead. Mrs. Waggoner and the two smaller children were slain because it was learned that they were being pursued, and these captives could not travel as fast as was necessary to effect an escape. Tecumseh, who, it will be remembered, visited Hacker's Creek after the Treaty of Greenville, in conversation

---

(6) See page 462. (7) p. 462.

with a Miss Mitchell told practically the same story. He also declared that they had been watching the Waggoner family for some time, waiting until the children were large enough to travel. If we can place credence in any part of their words, and if we are to judge from all the circumstances connected with this unhappy affair, there was surely a motive back of the perpetration, not born of revenge.

Peter was married to an Indian woman and was the father of two children. He was very much attached to his little family and refused to leave them. His father pleaded that he go home, if only for a short visit. His wife opposed his going, saying that he would never return. Mr. Waggoner was obdurate and finally Peter agreed to accompany him and promised his wife that he would return in so many "moons." She was disconsolate, but when she found that he was determined to go she said in broken English, "Go, me no see you more." The poor woman's words were prophetic; Peter was doomed never to keep the promise so sincerely made.

When the time came for his return to his Indian home, he was zealously guarded by his relatives and friends, who allowed no opportunity for his escape. He became restive, and grew desperate in his determination to go. In an altercation with his father, who was sitting at the loom weaving, Peter suddenly drew his bow, it is said, and let fly an arrow with deadly aim. The missile struck the old man a glancing blow on the head, inflicting a scalp wound, and knocked him from the loom. Peter was now more closely confined, and after the allotted moons had passed, he was afraid to return, having failed to keep his word. Every influence possible was brought to wean him from his Indian attachments and in time he became more reconciled. His long hair was cut, and he was induced to discard his earrings and Indian garb for the habiliments of civilization. In 1814, he married Catherine Hyde, a widow, whose maiden name was Hardman, and raised a family of children; but he was always melancholy and often lamented having left his Indian family.

With the return of each succeeding "Indian Summer," Peter would languish for the wild free life of the wilderness. If ever the Great Spirit looked kindly upon his red children, it was at this season of the year, when all nature is indescribably dreamy, pleasant and sad. The ripening of wild grapes and nuts, the maturing of corn; the harvest and feast time of the Indian. The season of the great annual buffalo hunt, when this animal was in primest condition; all this, like a call from the past, appealed to Peter's primitive nature.

Of his Indian life, he was very reticent, and would seldom speak of it to his white friends. Occasionally however, he would become communicative with young boys, and getting a few of them together, he would relate to his eager listeners some wild hunter stories and tales of forest life. He once told of a fierce encounter that he had witnessed between a large panther and a bear. The panther would leap upon the bear and fight fiercely for a few minutes, and then spring up against the side of a tree, where it would cling and rest. Then it would again leap upon the bear and the deadly combat would rage until the panther, to escape the crushing embrace of his antagonist, would repeat its former tactics, and seek shelter of the tree. Thus the battle raged until both animals were badly torn and exhausted, then the bear walked away and the panther stayed in his tree.

At another time, he was with a hunting party, and becoming lost, wandered two days and a night in the wilderness before he was found. He had traveled in a zigzag course, often describing a complete circle. Peter was fearful lest the Indians should think that he was trying to escape and would deal harshly with him, but when he spoke to them about it, they only laughed and said, "No think lun 'way, him go too clooked. Him lun 'way, go stlate." Colonel James Smith had the same experience when a captive. (8) This coincidence is not remarkable, for it is well known that a person lost in the wilderness will usually travel in a circle. None would know this better than the Indians, hence practically the same comment by the red hunter's in each case.

Peter settled on Hacker's Creek, and in a measure adapted himself to his changed mode of life. He appears to have at first regarded the most arduous toil in the light of amusement. His first experience in plowing was in rooty ground with a "one-horse shovel plow." Most Virginia farmers know what this mode of plowing means both to muscle and temper; it is hardly conducive to pious reflection. But with Peter it was novel, and when the plow would strike a root, he would go lightly into the air with a long, loud *"who-o-op!"* He never lost his Indian mode of speech. His words were few, but expressive; and so strong is the law of

---
(8) See page 462.

PETER WAGGONER

From a ferrotype, 1876. Courtesy of Albert W. Swisher

heredity that many of his descendants to the third generation retain to a degree the short speech of their Indianized ancestor.

Owing to his long life with the primitive people, Peter was simple, honest and upright. He was not a warrior among his adopted people, but was a hunter of renown. When he first returned to the settlement, he was an expert with the bow, as well as the rifle. He often taught the boys of the neighborhood how to fashion the bow, and gave them lessons in the use of this primitive weapon. For many years there was among his descendants a small brass barrel pistol brought by him from Paint Creek. He could give the war-whoop of his tribe and emulate its several dances, although he could seldom be induced to perform them. He never lost the traits of alertness acquired in his forest life. When about his work he was watchful and prided himself on his ability to detect anyone attempting to approach him unawares.

One of his grandsons told me that he had often tried to surprise his grandfather when at work, but never succeeded. Once under favorable circumstances, he approached within a few rods of the old man before he was discovered. "Hey," he ejaculated, "tried to slip on me; didn't do it, though." Only once did anyone ever accomplish this feat, although it was constantly attempted.

When Peter was quite an old man, he was husking corn "on the stalk" against the hillside where the grain stood thick and luxuriant. A neighbor who was to help him, with great caution came upon him unawares, and placed his hand on his shoulder. The old man was startled and deeply humiliated. His Indian pride was touched; he felt disgraced. "Hey," he exclaimed, in a voice choked with emotion, "You slip on me. You first man ever slip on me." Waggoner all that day seemed not himself, but would at short intervals refer to the incident with such feeling that the joker regretted his thoughtless act.

A short time after Peter's return, an Indian woman passed through Hacker's Creek, inquiring for him. She could only speak imperfect English, and with difficulty made herself understood. She was Peter's Indian wife, who had come in search of him. None would tell of his whereabouts, nor was he ever informed of her presence in the settlements. She seemed partly demented, and sang wild, mournful melodies in her native tongue. At one place, where she was granted a night's lodging, she chanted and danced the greater part of the night. With the primitive Indian dancing, in such cases is an invocation, or worship, but not amusement. What became of this lone woman, no one ever knew. When last seen, she had passed beyond the settlement and was wending her steps eastward. Hints of a darker nature in time leaked out. It was said that she met death at the hands of some of Peter's relatives or friends. Whether such was her fate, or if in time she wandered back to her people, her story is a pathetic one. She was a young widow when Peter married her, the wife of a sub-chief of his tribe, who had died or fallen in battle. Peter was his adopted brother and, it was said, by a recognized tribal custom he married the widow. This may have been true, but at this day it is only tradition. Peter held some position of authority in his tribe, and as the chieftaincy is usually hereditary with the Indian, it is probable that the mantle of the deceased brother fell to him.

Let those who judge harshly of the capacity of the Indian bosom for love, think well of the desolation in this poor, faithful woman's heart. Let those who would approve of the forcible detention of that husband and father from wife and little ones, dependent on his rifle for meat and raiment, go learn their first lesson of charity at the shrine of Moloch.

Peter died at his home on Millstone Run, a branch of Hacker's Creek, February 26, 1879, in his ninety-third year. This would place his capture at six years of age, instead of eight, as *Withers* has it. He was buried in the Harmony Cemetery, near Jane Lew. He was the last survivor of tragedy on the Virginia border.

The two captive sisters, Mary and Lizzie Waggoner, were both older than Peter. Mary, the eldest soon escaped to the vicinity of Detroit and continued there until the Treaty of Greenville, August 3, 1795. Lizzie remained with the Shawnees until after the treaty, where her father in company with John Hacker and Jacob Cozad attended and brought her and other captives home.

Mary, in 1800, married Jacob Wolfe. She is buried on Polk Creek, in Lewis County, West Virginia. Lizzie married John Hardman. I do not know where she is buried.

CHAPTER XX

The last traditional account that we have of Jesse Hughes as defender of the border on the Upper Monongahela was in the fall of 1793. It was really the sequel of the following incident: (1)

"In the spring of 1793, a party of warriors proceeding towards the headwaters of the Monongahela river, discovered a marked way, leading a direction which they did not know to be inhabited by whites. It led to a settlement which had been recently made on Elk river, by Jeremiah and Benjamin Carpenter and a few others from Bath county, and who had been particularly careful to make nor leave any path which might lead to a discovery of their situation, but Adam O'Brien (2) moving into the same section of country in the spring of 1792, and being rather an indifferent woodsman, incautiously blazed the trees in several directions so as to enable him to readily find his home, when business or pleasure should have drawn him from it. It was upon one of these marked traces that the Indians chanced to fall; and pursuing it, came to the deserted cabin of O'Brien, he having returned to the interior, because of his not making a sufficiency of grain for the subsistence of his family. Proceeding from O'Brien's, they came to the house of Benjamin Carpenter, whom they found alone and killed. Mrs. Carpenter being discovered by them, before she was aware of their presence, was tomahawked and scalped, a small distance from the yard.

"The burning of Benjamin Carpenter's house, led to a discovery of these outrages; and the remaining inhabitants of that neighborhood, remote from any fort or populous settlement to which they could fly for security, retired to the mountains and remained for several days concealed in a cave. They then caught their horses and moved their families to the West Fork; and when they visited the places of their former habitancy for the purpose of collecting their stock and carrying it off with other property, scarce a vestige of them was to be seen—the Indians had been there after they left the cave, and burned the houses, pillaged their movable property, and destroyed the cattle and hogs."

The following traditional account is still preserved by the descendants of the Carpenters (3) on Elk River.

Jeremiah Carpenter was born at Big Bend, Jackson River, in Bath County, Virginia, and was there taken prisoner by a band of Shawnees when but nine years old. He lived with the tribe at Old Town, opposite the mouth of the Great Kanawha until he was eighteen, when he was exchanged and returned to Jackson River. From that place he moved to Elk River, in what is now Braxton County, West Virginia, settling about a quarter of a mile above Dry Run. Into that region the Indians came every spring.

Adam O'Brien had blazed a trail from the site of the present

---

(1) See page 462. (2) p. 462. (3) p. 463.

town of Sutton to the Salt Spring, the name by which the white people spoke of the Indian Bull Town. O'Brien went there to make salt. Bull Town being on the old Indian war trail, a party of two Shawnee warriors followed the blazed path made by O'Brien, to Elk River, and there saw chips floating down the stream, which to them was proof that settlers had erected buildings above. They followed the river. There were two brothers, Benjamin and Jeremiah Carpenter. Benjamin's cabin was lowest on the river, at the mouth of Holly, twelve miles above Sutton. The two Indians, one large and the other small, came first upon the cabin of Benjamin. At the time, he was across the river burning logs in his clearing, assisted by his mother and little sister, who had come that day to visit him. His wife was sick in bed, and the Indians tomahawked her, making no noise. The big Indian took Carpenter's gun from the rack over the door, and seated himself in the corner of the cabin, the little Indian concealing himself on a bank above the house. Carpenter came across the river to assist his wife if she should want any aid, and also to prepare dinner. But he stopped at the river bank, and took a deer skin from the water where it had been soaking in the process of dressing, and began work upon it. While about this business the little Indian shot at him and missed him. He ran to the house to get his gun, and as he reached up to take it down, the big Indian shot him in the side under the arm, and killed him. They then scalped Carpenter, took his gun, powder-horn and shot-pouch, and left that region. Carpenter's mother concealed her little girl in a hollow stump, and ran for her husband, but when he arrived at the cabin of his son, the Indians were gone.

The following fall, at a fort on the West Fork of the Monongahela, possibly at Clarksburg, the Indians killed and devoured a cow belonging to Jesse Hughes. They carried away with them a bell which the cow wore. One afternoon they rattled this bell in the woods on the mountain-side above the fort. Some said to Jesse Hughes that his cow was coming back. He knew, however, that she had been killed, and replied that he would "make that bell ring for something in the morning." That night he secreted himself in the woods on the mountain above the point where the bell had been heard the previous afternoon. As soon as it was light enough to shoot, he again heard the bell, and cautiously made his way towards it. He discovered two Indians, one large, the other small. The big Indian was standing up with his gun ready for instant use, and the little Indian was walking about on his hands and knees, with the bell on his neck, rattling it in imitation of a cow browsing in the woods. (4) Hughes shot the big Indian, and the small one ran. Jesse threw down his empty gun, seized that of the dead Indian, pursued and soon came up with the little Indian and shot him. The gun carried by the big Indian, and with which Hughes killed the little Indian, was the gun of Benjamin Carpenter. The gun, powder-horn and shot-pouch were returned to the Carpenter family.

The story of this occurrence, as told by the immediate descendants of Jesse Hughes, is as follows: Hughes was visiting his parents on Elk Creek, near Clarksburg. One evening the cow did not come home from the woods as usual, nor could she be found. The next morning Jesse's mother heard the bell in the woods, and told her daughter to go and bring the cow home. Jesse, hearing the order, stepped into the yard and listening attentively to the bell for a moment, told his sister that he would go and bring the cow. Taking his rifle, he went into the woods opposite to where the bell was still rattling, and making a circuit, came near the bell on the side furthest from the house. When getting near the object of his search, the odor of broiling meat was wafted to his nostrils. The Indians had killed the cow, and had been roasting the beef over the camp-fire. Cautiously advancing, he saw an Indian rattling the bell in such a manner as the noise produced by a belled cow when feeding. The Indians had gone some distance from their camp towards the house, and were waiting to see if anyone would come to get the cow. Hughes shot the Indian who was ringing the bell.

In this version no mention is made of Jesse killing more than one Indian, nor of the big and little Indian and Carpenter's gun. The last version is correct as to the place and circumstance of Jesse's exploit; but there is every reason to believe that the Carpenter version is correct in its relation to Carpenter and the two noted Indians.

Early in the nineties there were two Indians on the border who were well known to the rangers and scouts of Fort Harmer, and other posts on the frontier. *Hildreth*, (5) says of these famous warriors:

"There were among these Indians two whose footprints (6) were well known to the rangers. One of them left a track eleven inches long, the other not more

---

(4) See page 467. (5) p. 467. (6) p. 467.

than seven or eight. They were known as the big and little Indian. They were men of great subtlety and caution; often seen together by the spies, yet never but once within reach of their rifles. Joshua Fleehart, (7) a noted hunter, and as cautious and cunning as any savage, got a shot at the big Indian as the two lay in camp below Bellville. The ball cut loose his powder horn, which Joshua took as a prize, and wounded him in the side, but he escaped."

It is probable that these were the warriors killed by Hughes. No mention of them is found in the border strife after this time.

The killing of Carpenter was cunningly planned and executed and they would have succeeded in their decoy with the bell, but for the keen discernment of Hughes. Instead, they met a tragic death at the hands of this renowned scout of the Monongahela.

On file in the Bureau of Pensions, Washinton, is the brief military record of John Carpenter, a soldier of the Revolution and an Indian spy on the Virginia border. He was born in Botetourt County, Virginia, in 1764. In September, 1780, he enlisted from his native county for six months in Captain John Bowles' Rifle Company, Virginia Militia, and marched by way of Albemarle Court House, Virginia, to headquarters near Guilford Court House in North Carolina, where he joined the main army under General Green. Carpenter participated in the fiercely contested battle of Guilford, March 15, 1781, which was the principal event during the term of his enlistment. He was discharged in April, and in May of the same year, he enlisted as a private in Captain David May's Company, Virginia Militia, and was sent to various points, including Williamsburg, Richmond and Raccoon Ford on the Rappahannock River in Culpepper County, Virginia. There General Wayne joined forces with the Marquis LaFayette. Carpenter was at the siege of Yorktown and the surrender of Lord Cornwallis the following Autumn. He was a member of the guard which conducted a detachment of British prisoners to the Winchester Barracks, near Winchester, Frederick County, Virginia.

At the expiration of his term of service, he was discharged by his Lieutenant, Wallace Astre, or Aster (name illegible). He then returned home. In December, 1781, he enlisted for one year under Captain John McCoy to defend the Virginia frontier bordering the Ohio River, and was marched to West's Fort on Hacker's Creek under orders of Col. William Lowther. He became actively

---

(7) See page 467.

engaged in spying throughout the region embraced between the Upper Monongahela settlements and the Ohio River. He reported at Bush's Fort on the Buckhannon and at Neal's Station at the mouth of the Little Kanawha, as well as at West's Fort. He was not at all times under the immediate orders of Colonel Lowther, but was sometimes moved by orders from Colonel Wilson and other subaltern officers as occasion and country demanded. He was frequently engaged in recovering stolen property carried off by the Indians. In January, 1782, he was discharged by Colonel Lowther and returned home.

In March, 1783, he enlisted as a private Indian spy in Captain Peter Hull's Company and was sent to where Lewisburg now stands, in Greenbrier County, where he scouted throughout the adjacent country. At the expiration of his term, he received his discharge from Captain Hull. This ended his services as an enlisted militiaman, but subsequently performed many services of value to the frontier.

It is not known just when John Carpenter settled on Hacker's Creek, but he resided there in 1832, when he successfully applied for a pension as a Revolutionary soldier. He evidently was living on the Trans-Allegheny border in 1792, at which time he speaks of his house being burned by the Indians. It is very probable that he was at that time a resident of Hacker's Creek. That the State Militia east of the mountains was sometimes assigned to duty on the Upper Monongahela border is apparent from *Waddell*, who states that at a county court martial, held October 27, 1779, "Ensign James Steele reported the desertion of sundry men from their station on the west fork of Monongahela, they being substitutes for Augusta militiamen. Many other substitutes were returned on the same day by Ensign Robert Christian for deserting from his command at Buchanan Fort." (8)

This last desertion may or may not have been the fort at Buckhannon, but that reported by Ensign Steele must have occurred at West's Fort on Hacker's Creek, or Nutter's Fort at Clarksburg.

It is not known that John Carpenter, the scout, and the settlers on the Elk River were of the same family, but it is very probable that they were, as they hailed from the same region. Bath

---

(8) See page 467.

County was formed from Augusta, Botetourt and Greenbrier Counties in 1791.

Among the volunteer troops who served in Dunmore's War from Botetourt County, were Richard Willson Carpenter, Thomas Carpenter, Soloman Carpenter, Jeremiah Carpenter and John Carpenter, all privates. The name is given as Carpender. (9)

Thomas was wounded at the Battle of Point Pleasant.

---

(9) See page 467.

CHAPTER XXI

The border had receded: the frontier was no longer Trans-Allegheny; it was Trans-Ohio. Wayne's defeat of the Indians at Fallen Timbers in 1794 had effectually secured the Virginia settlements from Indian forays. The Twenty Years War, provoked by the white man, had closed; and a new era had dawned for the Trans-Allegheny. Peace fearfully bought had settled over the romantic Monongahela and the beautiful Kanawhas. The plumed warrior, the untutored patriot of the Northwestern wilderness, had succumbed to the inevitable, and was again facing the sunset. Life on the Upper Monongahela was now too tame for the sanguine spirit of Jesse Hughes, the pioneer, ranger, Indian fighter. He grew restive, and chafed under the inactive life forced upon him. With the dying echo of the last war-whoop of the painted warrior among the hills of Virginia, Jesse Hughes appears to have made preparations to follow him toward the west.

In the fall of 1797 or 1798, he sold his land to his brother-in-law, James Tanner, (1) and turning his back on the scenes of his many daring adventures and marvellous escapes, struck into the wilderness of the Northwest. With his family and live stock, he moved overland to or near Vincennes. But the child of the high forests of the Alleghenies could not flourish in the swamp woods of the Wabash. His family suffered from chills and fever, and this made him resolve to return again to his old paradise. Little is known of his life in that marsh country, and I can give but one occurrence of interest.

The Indians were in the habit of coming to the fort with furs and hides to barter for goods and rum. One day, a drunken Indian amused himself by approaching people unawares and biting them on the shoulder. Observing this, Jesse remarked "If that Injun bites me, he will never bite another man." Very soon the Indian came upon Hughes, and closed his teeth on the scout's shoulder. Hughes, whirling, struck the Indian, and at the same time kicked him in the stomach, knocking him from a high platform or porch, killing him instantly. The Indians said that the fall killed their brother, and they did not attempt to molest Hughes in the least.

(1) See page 467.

From Vincennes, Hughes moved by land to eastern Kentucky, where he remained until the spring of 1799 or 1800, when he moved again, overland, to what is now Jackson County, West Virginia. On this trip they camped at the mouth of Twelve Pole Creek, Wayne County, West Virginia, where, "setting his hooks," said his daughter Massie, then twelve years old, "my father caught the largest catfish I ever saw." He continued up the Ohio until he reached the mouth of Turkey Run, just above the present town of Ravenswood, Jackson County, West Virginia. Here he built a cabin and settled down for a few years. His main support, as in years past, was his rifle. Finding that the game was disappearing in that locality, and that it was more plentiful back from the Ohio River, he moved eight miles up Big Sandy Creek, and settled one mile north of where Sandyville is located. Here he entered a tract of land, built his last cabin, and seemingly settled to spend the remainder of his days in the seclusion of this sylvan retreat. But, as the sequel will show, he was doomed to disappointment.

The record of his career in this region is extremely meagre. No early history of Kentucky has ever been written, and the annals of the southwestern part of West Virginia is not so replete as the other portions of the State. The passing of the pioneer, and the great changes wrought in the latter section by the Civil War, which was followed by an inroad of strangers, has had much to do with the loss of traditions pertaining to the early days.

Tradition on the Big Sandy River says that in previous times, Jesse Hughes scouted and hunted all over eastern Kentucky; that he was an associate of Matthias Harman of Ingles' Ferry on the New River, and that he or his father was one of the famous "Long Hunters." (2) On one occasion he swam Red River, holding his rifle and shot-pouch high and dry in one hand. This was either a tributary of the Cumberland River in Tennessee or a small contingent of the Kentucky River in eastern Kentucky. Red River is spoken of by the "Long Hunters," who first came upon it in 1769. (3)

By his immediate descendants in Jackson County is preserved the following story of Jesse Hughes:

Among the associates of Hughes were one Morgan and one Straley. Morgan's two children were captured by five Indians in a cornfield. And Jesse and the father went in pursuit, and at

---
(2) See page 469. (3) p. 470.

night came upon the Indians and their captives, sleeping at the foot of a sycamore tree. They shot two of the warriors, and rushing in, tomahawked the other three before they could recover from their surprise or offer any resistance. One of the Indians they flayed, and tanning the skin, manufactured it into shot-pouches.

The scene of this incident is lost, but it could *not* have happened after Jesse left Hacker's Creek. The fact that Morgan and his two children were such conspicuous figures in the tragedy, gives strength to the inference that the story may have had its origin in the famous fight near Prickett's Fort, in 1779, between Morgan and two Indians in defense of his two children, and its ghoulish sequel. (4) As has been shown, Hughes was often at Prickett's Fort, and no doubt engaged in the stirring scenes enacted around that fortress. The revolting outrages perpetrated upon the bodies of the two dead warriors would have been in keeping with the savage instincts of Jesse and his border associates.

For Jesse Hughes the day of actual conflict had passed. The red warrior no longer haunted the Virginia wilderness, but desultory bands of friendly Indians, degraded by the vices of the white man's civilization (5) still lingered round their former homes and the graves of their people. These spent much of their time in wandering about through the white settlements and often indulged in drunken carousals. Against these beings, Jesse continued to glut his insatiate thirst for Indian blood. He had doubtless many opportunities for waylaying the unsuspecting tribesmen who occasionally passed over their primitive thoroughfares in this region, living as he did on the old Indian path, locally known as the "Interior Trail." This led from the Little Kanawha to the Salt Licks on the Great Kanawha, and crossed the warpath running from the Ohio up Sand Creek. This latter was a noted trail, which crossed from Sand Creek to the headwaters of Reedy Creek, Spring Creek and Henry's Fork, all tributary to the Little Kanawha; also Mill Creek flowing directly into the Ohio, and Pocotaligo and its tributaries feeding the Great Kanawha.

Jesse's awful vow of his younger days, "to kill Injuns as long as he lived and could see to kill them," was fearfully and savagely kept in the eventide of life. The laws for the protection of life were ineffective on the border and were seldom enforced when the victim was a "despised redskin." Too often have the minions of

---
(4) See page 470. (5) p. 472.

the law winked at, or shielded the blighting hand raised openly against the peaceable Indian. His daughter Massie used to tell that Hughes once killed three Indians and hid their bodies in a cave, since known as Haynes' Cave. (6)

Several years after Jesse settled on Sand Creek, he was visited by one of his former associates from Hacker's Creek. Accompanied by this friend, Jesse repaired to a secluded part of the forest and took from the cavity of a hollow beech tree eight rifles, the property of peaceable Indians whom he had secretly murdered. Another version of this tradition is that it was not Jesse, but his brother Elias, who displayed the hidden rifles as trophies of his prowess on the Licking River, in Ohio, where he settled in 1789. But some of Jesse's immediate descendants declared that Jesse alone was the founder and sole proprietor of the Beech Tree Museum. Elias Hughes, as hereafter shown, had a like collection of arms in a hollow sycamore.

At one time, Jesse Hughes, in company with a few companions, and at a rendezvous somewhere near the Ohio River, sat about a camp fire. They were joined by an Indian, who had a club foot. After carefully scrutinizing their visitor, Hughes remarked to one of the company: "I have tracked that old devil all over Northwestern Virginia." Subsequent conversation with the red hunter verified this statement, (7) it was evident that Hughes would not deal gently with the Indian, who with a deformed foot, had been so successful in evading him in the forest. The weary Indian accepted an invitation to spend the night with the hunters, and after partaking of food furnished him, wrapped himself in his blanket and lay down by the fire to sleep. The next morning when the party arose, Hughes was gone, and the lifeless body of the Indian was found to have a knife plunged to the hilt in his heart.

When an old man, Jesse spent much of his time fishing, always armed with his tomahawk, from which he was inseparable. Upon one occasion, he went fishing along the Ohio accompanied by one of his little grandchildren. In the afternoon, they came upon five Indians sleeping on the river bank, a tell-tale jug lying empty near them. Scanning the recumbent forms a moment, Hughes remarked, "They are drunk;" then went on with his fishing. But angling for the finny tribe no longer held charms for him. He became restless, going from place to place, yet ever

---

(6) See page 472. (7) p. 473.

hovering about the objects that had so roused his lagging propensities. He was the hereditary foe of the Indian in peace and in war, and the sight of these inebriated wretches had fanned to flame that hatred which ever rankled in his bosom.

Finally, as the day waned, he turned to his little companion and said: "Go along home. I will come soon." The lad wended his way homeward, leaving the old man still lingering near the sodden slumbering Indians. As the shades of night settled over the beautiful river and its forest-clad shores, Jesse Hughes returned home, but the five wretched Indians were never again seen or heard of. They had in some mysterious way disappeared; but what had been their fate? Had they aimlessly stumbled into the dark gliding Ohio, to be forever swallowed up by its murky tide? Charity for the memory of the grizzled scout would suggest as much, but the probability is that he first tomahawked his helpless victims, and then threw their bodies into the river. In fact, there is little doubt that this was the doom of these intoxicated friendlies.

CHAPTER XXII

We now come to the closing scenes of the turbulent career of Jesse Hughes. The swirling storms of threescore years had swept his path, leaving on his brow the heavy touch of time's relentless hand. His auburn locks were thin and grizzled. His lithe form was not so erect, nor his eagle eye so keen as in former years, when, daring the dangers and fearful privations incident to border life, he traversed the deep forests of the Monongahela wilds, meeting and challenging the skill and endurance of the most wily of his hereditary foes. He had laughed at danger's toils, and played "toss up and catch" with death in a hundred daring adventures, and always won. The great object of his life had been revenge. With death ever at his elbow, he had successfully run the grim gauntlet of war, striking down in his passage the warrior, the mother, and the child. And now, as the shadows were falling to the east, they thickened and became black, and the sunset of life was overcast with bitter disappointment, gloomy reflections, sorrow and despair. Touching the pathetic ending of the life of this remarkable borderman, Judge R. S. Brown, in his Centennial address delivered at Ravenswood, West Virginia, July 4, 1876, says:

"Jesse Hughes, brother of Thomas, before spoken of, was the son of Thomas Hughes who settled on the Monongahela River in 1776, and was soon after killed by the Indians, leaving a large and helpless family in the wilderness. (1) Jesse grew up in the school of hardship to be a brave, handsome, active man. The stories of the murder of his father and other kindred and friends embittered him against the Red Man, and terrible was the retribution he visited upon them.

"His name was a terror to the savage foe and a household word of comfort to the scattered settlers on the Buckhannon River, Hacker's Creek, and elsewhere where he visited with the brave and chivalrous spirit of the knight-errant to ward off the savage blow. Always on the alert and courting danger at every point, he pursued the savage with the pertinacity of a bloodhound and never stopped short of his prey. Hughes' River, a large navigable stream north of us, was so named in honor of his exploits. (2) He was justly regarded as the peer of the Zanes, McColloghs and Wetzels. A history of the deeds of this brave man in defense of his people would fill a volume. When the Indians fell back Jesse Hughes followed them, first to the Muskingum, and then to the Wabash, and only after their complete surrender to General Wayne did he make peace. (3)

"He came back here and settled on the Sandy (4) where Mr. J. S. Dilworth now lives near [Sandyville], where he obtained a patent for a piece of land, and

---

(1) See page 473. (2) p. 473. (3) p. 473. (4) 473.

made improvements. He was the first settler on that creek. He planted an orchard and cleared some land for a home in his old age; but after living there many years he found his land was long previously granted to John Allison, so Jesse Hughes, the hero of a hundred bloody battles in defense of his country and his race, like his great friends Simon Kenton and Daniel Boone, (5) was a homeless wanderer at the age of seventy-nine years. He went to live with his son-in-law, George W. Hanshaw, on the farm now owned by Mrs. W. S. Proctor. Worn out with toil and exposure and stung with the ingratitude of his countrymen, he wandered one day with his gun in the woods, and there, alone in a leafy grove, just on the run (6) near where we are met, he died. He was buried here on the bottom but no stone marks the spot where reposes the dust of the brave pioneer."

After the loss of their home, Jesse and his wife lived for a time with their son, Thomas, who resided on the Ohio just below Ravenswood. Afterwards they made their home with their daughter, Nancy Agnes Hanshaw, who lived at the mouth of Turkey Run, perhaps on the site of Jesse's former home. Here Jesse died, as narrated by Judge Brown in the last of September or the first of October, 1829.

In his old age he became very childish, and at every noise imagined that Indians were around. Then, taking down his rifle, he would go out and look for them. It was, perhaps, in one of these sallies against an imaginary enemy, that the old scout met death in the lonely, silent woods. His death was a fitting one. He had spent most of his career in the wilderness — a part of the wild savage life about him. Oft had he heard the reverberating echo of his deadly rifle answered by the moaning cadence of the sobbing wind, wailing in the gloomy forest a sad requiem over the dying warrior who had fallen a victim of his vengeance. Again had he listened in superstitious awe to the demoniacal shrieking of the mighty Manitou whirling and crashing in fury through the deep fastnesses of the sombre mountains, as if in protest against the withering hand of the pale-face lifted so unremorselessly against the red children of his wooded domain.

At last, in the beauteous mellow of the Southern autumn day — in the dreamy haze of the soft Indian summer — there alone under the trees he loved so well, death came to the old woodsman.

The grimness of the irony of fate is reflected in the closing career of this, the greatest of the pathfinders of western Virginia. Of all the vast regions that he had been so active and ruthless in wresting from the rightful owners, not an acre did he possess. His

---

(5) See page 473. (6) p. 474.

very grave is lost to the second generation of his family. No one knows where Jesse Hughes was buried. I have tried through every available source to locate the grave of the renowned scout, but without success.

Jesse Hanshaw, his grandson and namesake (line of Nancy), was born in 1831, at the home where his aged grandfather had died two years before. The cabin in which Mr. Hanshaw was born stood on the present site of the residence of W. S. Proctor, who still owns the farm. The place at that time consisted of two cabins, and was known as "Beggar's Town." Mr. Hanshaw declared that his mother pointed out to him the place where his grandfather was buried, and that this was on their home-farm, now owned by Proctor, and above Turkey Run, on the upland in the old orchard. He believes that he might be able to locate the spot, though no stone marks the grave. In 1893, while digging a post-hole near his residence, Proctor found a human skeleton, which may have been that of Jesse Hughes. The location where this skeleton was found — on the high ground back of where the Hughes cabin stood — corresponds with that given by Mr. Hanshaw, as pointed out by his mother.

There is an old burial ground between the road and the river, on the lower part of A. J. Rolif's farm, which adjoins that of Mr. Proctor, where repose the remains of some of the oldest settlers of that region, and it has been suggested that Jesse Hughes might have been buried there. Another tradition says that he was buried near "Hughes' Eddy," (7) below Ravenswood. But I am inclined to believe that Mr. Hanshaw is right in his location of the grave of the old scout. There is no doubt that Mrs. Hanshaw knew where her father was buried, and her son should know, within a reasonable degree of accuracy, the location of the grave.

After the death of Jesse Hughes, his wife lived with her daughter Massie, at Gandeeville, Roane County, (now) West Virginia, where she died in January 1842. She was buried at Gandeeville, and at this writing her grave is shown only by a crude stone. It is hoped that the numerous descendants of this pioneer mother will mark with an enduring and appropriate monument her last resting place, before it, like that of her renowned husband, is lost to the world forever.

A few years ago, the old rocking-chair that belonged to Mrs. Jesse Hughes was still preserved by some of her immediate descend-

---
(7) See page 474.

ants in Jackson County, West Virginia. What became of this chair is not known to me, but it is, in all probability, still in possession of some of the family in that region.

Mr. Samuel Alkire of Hacker's Creek, was once in possession of an old gun charger that belonged to his great-grandfather, Jesse Hughes. This charger was finely carved from a prong of the antler of a deer, and evidently measured out death to more than one Indian in the wilds of the Monongahela. Unfortunately, this interesting relic, perhaps the last memento of the great scout, was lost about thirty years ago, by a squirrel hunter, on lower Hacker's Creek, which had been the theatre of the most turbulent scenes in the wild life of Jesse Hughes.

CHAPTER XXIII

THOMAS HUGHES, SENIOR — Settled on Elk Creek, in (now) Harrison County, (West) Virginia, and killed by Indians on Hacker's Creek in 1778. It is not known where he was born, but the evidence is cogent that the most of his life was spent on the border, (1) and that his removal to the Upper Monongahela was from the Wappatomaka. The majority of the pioneers of the country in which he settled came from that region, and there is strong proof, in the birth of his son, Elias, that he resided there in 1757.

It is not certainly known whom Thomas Hughes, Senior, married. I have been unable to find any record touching that phase of his life. Some of the older descendants of his son Elias think that his wife's maiden name was Baker.

The number of children, their names, and the dates of their births, are not with certainty known. The names of some of them, however, are known.

JESSE HUGHES was born in 1750, settled on Hacker's Creek in 1771-72; married Miss Grace Tanner the year of his settlement there; became one of the most famous scouts and Indian fighters of all the west; moved to the Wabash in the fall of 1797 or 1798; moved thence to eastern Kentucky the following fall, exact location not known; moved thence to western Virginia in the following spring, and settled at the mouth of Turkey Run, in what is now Jackson County, West Virginia; afterwards settled on Sand Creek, same county, near where Sandyville was afterwards built; died at the mouth of Turkey Run, just above the town of Ravenswood, in the Autumn of 1829.

THOMAS HUGHES, JUNIOR, was born about 1754; settled on the West Fork about 1775; was an active scout during the entire border wars, and was Lieutenant of a Company of Spies. He afterwards settled in Jackson County, West Virginia, where he died in October, 1837. His wife died three months previous. Her name is unknown to me. They left one child, Thomas, born 1774, who was still living in 1854.

ELIAS HUGHES was born in 1757, in now Hardy County, Virginia. He was called "Ellis" Hughes by many of the early

---
(1) See page 474.

settlers, the name "Ellis" being applied as the result of the inattention of the pioneers to the exactness in speaking names. (2) He came to Harrison County while only a boy and grew up to be a scout and Indian fighter second only to his brother Jesse. Was in Battle of Point Pleasant and subsequently commissioned a Captain of Spies. He married Miss Jane Sleeth. In 1797, moved to the Muskingum in Ohio, and the next year to Licking County, Ohio. Was Captain of Militia and commissioned Second Lieutenant, Col. Rennick's Regiment Mounted Ohio Volunteers, War 1812. Died near Utica, Ohio, December 22, 1844. His wife died in 1827.

SUDNA, daughter of Thomas Hughes, Sr., married Colonel William Lowther, who settled on Hughes' River, and was a pioneer in Northwestern Virginia, and active in the protection of the settlers from the attacks of the Indians.

JOB HUGHES — History of this son not known to me. He married Mary Hamm, 1791, in Harrison County, (West) Virginia. Died and was buried in Jackson County, now West Virginia.

ANOTHER SON was killed by the Indians. His name is not known, nor can it at this time be determined where or when the tragedy occurred, but it must have been on the western waters.

ANOTHER DAUGHTER, name not known to me, was married to Joseph Bibbee, who settled on the Ohio River below the present town of Ravenswood, in what is now Jackson County, West Virginia.

A marriage license was granted in Harrison County, Virginia, in 1795, to William Bibby and Deborah Hughes. William was a brother of Joseph Bibbee; Deborah may have been the daughter of Thomas Hughes, Sr. Tradition among the descendants of William Bibby, or Bibbee, in Jackson County, West Virginia, says that the Bibbee brothers either married sisters or cousins. William Bibbee was a noted hunter and killed the last buffalo in now Jackson County, West Virginia.

In the same year (1795) Benjamin Cox and Mary Hughes were married in Harrison County, Virginia.

DESCENDANTS OF JESSE HUGHES.

MARTHA, born in December, 1773, captured by the Indians, December, 1787; returned from captivity, December, 1790; married Jacob Bonnett in 1792, a brother to John Bonnett who was

---
(2) See page 474.

killed on the Little Kanawha, and lived all her life near West's Fort, now Jane Lew, just below the main road and opposite the present Methodist Episcopal Church, where she died in December, 1834, and was buried at the old Harmony Church Cemetery on Hacker's Creek. Her grave is marked by a plain sandstone slab, on which is the following inscription:

> MARTHA, DAUGHTER OF JESSE HUGHES
> BORN DECEMBER, 1773
> MADE PRISONER BY THE INDIANS DEC., 1787
> RETURNED FROM CAPTIVITY, 1790
> MARRIED JACOB BONNETT, 1792
> DIED DEC., 1834
> AGED 61 YEARS.

Martha left a long line of descendants on Hacker's Creek. Some of the best families of the valley, including the Bonnetts and the Alkires. To the late Elias Bonnett, a grandson of Martha, and to his son, Henry G. Bonnett, I am especially indebted for some of the incidents in the life of Jesse Hughes.

RACHEL, married William Cottrell; lived on Hacker's Creek near the mouth of Life's Run until the death of her husband, when she moved to Spring Creek, six miles from Spencer, Roane County, West Virginia, where she died; buried near Spencer. The old Cottrell cabin of hewed logs is still standing on Hacker's Creek, just below the pike, and near the bridge spanning the creek, on the road leading up Life's Run.

SUDNA, married Elijah Runner; lived and died near Sandyville on Big Sand Creek, Jackson County, West Virginia.

ELIZABETH, married James Stanley; lived and died on Mud Run, a tributary of Big Sand Creek, Jackson County, West Virginia.

MASSIE, born on Hacker's Creek, in 1786 or 1787; married Uriah Gandee; lived for a time near Sandyville, Jackson County; in 1824 moved to where Gandeeville now is in Roane County, West Virginia; her husband died in 1855, when she went to live with her son, J. S. Gandee, where she resided until her death, May 30, 1883. She was buried on the home farm near Gandeeville.

NANCY AGNES, married George W. Hanshaw; lived at the mouth of Turkey Run, above Ravenswood; later moved above the mouth of Straight Fork on Big Sand Creek, Jackson County.

LOURANEY, married Uriah Sayre; lived at the mouth of Groundhog Run, on the Ohio River, in Meigs County, Ohio. (3)

THOMAS, lived on the Ohio River below Ravenswood, where he died. I do not know who he married.

WILLIAM, married a Miss Statts; lived and died on Mill Creek, three miles below Ripley, in what is now Jackson County, West Virginia.

JESSE, married Susana Mock in 1800. His history is unknown to me.

THE WILLIAM COTTRELL CABIN
Photographed 1909

Originally this cabin stood near the right-hand bank of Hacker's Creek, on the opposite side of the valley. The logs were hewed after they were placed in the walls. A spacious fireplace occupied nearly the entire right end of the room. A narrow vent, not unlike a porthole, is concealed by the conspicuous board just to the right of the only door. There are no other openings or windows.

The above are the children of Jesse Hughes, the scout, ranger, pioneer, and famous Indian fighter.

It is said that in size, features and complexion, William Hughes was almost an exact counterpart of his noted father.

Massie, the daughter of Jesse Hughes, who married Uriah Gandee, had twelve children, to wit: Sarah, Jesse, William, George, Cynthia, Grace, Lucinda, Samuel, Mary (who died when nine years old), a child unnamed that died in infancy, Martha, and James Stanley. Of this family ten lived to maturity; but two are now living: Samuel, born February 24, 1824, and James Stanley, born July 27, 1832.

---
(3) See page 475.

The Gandee children, like those of many other post-pioneer families of Northwestern Virginia, were reared in the woods without the advantages of education. James Stanley, the youngest, named for the husband of his Aunt Elizabeth, did not attend school more than ninety days all told. He learned to write, and the rudiments of arithmetic, after his first marriage. He was married twice, and true to the traditions of his forest clan, reared many children to the honor of his country — twenty-one in all — eighteen of whom are still living. Mr. Gandee has filled many positions of trust in his county, from constable to high sheriff, and was for several years president of his township Board of Education. He laid out the town of Gandeeville on the old home farm in Roane County, West Virginia.

To Mr. Gandee, more than any other person, am I indebted for facts and incidents connected with the life of Jesse Hughes. Pertaining to genealogy and family history, Mr. Gandee is the best informed of any of the immediate descendants of the celebrated scout. His opportunity for obtaining data regarding the biography of his grandfather was, perhaps, unsurpassed, by any person now living. His grandmother made her home with his parents from 1827 until her death, January 1842, and his mother resided with him during the last quarter century of her life.

DESCENDANTS OF ELIAS HUGHES.

ELIAS HUGHES married Miss Jane Sleeth. I am unable to give the names of their children in the order of their ages, but will set them down as furnished by Mrs. Pansy Hall Thatcher, a descendant of Elias Hughes. The names are as follows:

Margaret (married Jones), *Mary* (married Foster), *Susanna* (married Leach), *Sudna* (married Marlin), *Jane* (married Hight), *Sarah* (married Davis), *Kate* (unmarried), *Thomas*, *Henry*, *Job*, *Elias*, *David*, *John* and *Jonathan* (the youngest). Two others died while quite young.

Mrs. L. Bancroft Fant, of Newark, Ohio, writes me that one daughter married ———— Ratliff.

Records in the U. S. Treasury Department show that the pension due Elias Hughes at the time of his death was paid to his children as follows: Susanna Leach, Margaret Jones, Sarah Davis, John, Elias and Jonathan Hughes, and Sudna Marlin.

JONATHAN HUGHES was born January 14, 1796, in Harrison

County, Virginia, and came with his parents to Ohio in 1798. In 1815 he was apprenticed to a carpenter and joiner in Mt. Vernon, Ohio. On June 9th, 1817, he married Lavina Davis, who was born June 14th, 1800. They had five children: Clarinda, born December 7th, 1818; Louisa, born November 17th, 1820; James M., born March 31, 1827; Adaline N., born December 7th, 1829. James moved to Indiana.

Jonathan Hughes "never drank whiskey as a beverage, never tasted tobacco but once, never smoked a cigar, never voted the Democratic ticket but once, and that was for Jackson. Mr. Hughes is a strong prohibitionist." (4)

(4) See page 475

CHAPTER XXIV

ELIAS HUGHES survived his two noted brothers, Jesse and Thomas, several years, and was among the last of the Virginia frontiersmen. As a scout, he excelled in some respects either of his two brothers. He rose to the rank of captain and was the recognized champion rifle shot on the western waters. Like many of his contemporaries, the border annals contain but little of his early life. *Withers* mentions him in connection with four incidents only; three of these are quoted in the preceding pages of this volume, and the other will be given in the course of this sketch. More is known of his subsequent life in Ohio, where he moved soon after the Treaty of Greenville.

In many instances historians have dealt confusedly with his personality. I have had occasion to mention that while his given name was Elias he was generally known as "Ellis." Under this double sobriquet he went through life to the grave and passed into history. For even a vague conception of the deeds of this great borderman, various historical works must be consulted, where the reader becomes mystified by this diversity in his name. Owing to these conditions, it has been deemed desirable to reproduce here in a concise form, all that could be gathered concerning his life. *Lewis* says: (1)

"Belonging to General Lewis' army was a young man named Ellis Hughes. He was a native of Virginia, and had been bred in the hot-bed of Indian warfare. The Indians having murdered a young lady (2) to whom he was very much attached, and subsequently his father, he vowed revenge, and the return of peace did not mitigate his hatred of the race. Shortly after Wayne's treaty with the Indians in 1795, he forsook his native mountains, and in company with one John Ratcliff removed north of the Ohio, where they became the first settlers in what is now Licking County, in that State. Hughes died near Utica, that County, in March, 1845, at an advanced age, in hope of a happy future, claiming and accredited by all who knew him, to be the last survivor of the battle of Point Pleasant. He was buried with military honors and other demonstrations of respect."

The following paragraph is found in connection with the Battle of Point Pleasant:

"The admittedly last survivor of those who personally participated in this memorable fight was Mr. Ellis Hughes, one of the remarkable family of border

---
(1) See page 475. (2) p. 475.

settlers and Indian fighters of that name. After Wayne's treaty, he and a neighbor, Radcliff, removed to Ohio, and were the first to settle in (now) Licking County. Hughes died in 1845, near Utica, aged in the nineties." (3)

The Last Survivor.

"It is admitted by all that the last survivor of the battle of Point Pleasant was Ellis Hughes, who died at Utica, Ohio, in 1840, aged over ninety years." (4)

The Last Survivor of the Battle of Point Pleasant.

"The assertion has been made, and I have never heard it disputed, that the last survivor of the battle of Point Pleasant was Ellis Hughes who died in 1840, at Utica, Ohio. This is clearly a mistake. There was certainly a soldier in that battle who survived Ellis Hughes several years, and who died in February, 1848, in that portion of Randolph County which became Tucker County in 1856.

"Samuel Bonnifield was born April 11, 1752, where Washington City now stands. * * *

"In the summer of 1774 Samuel Bonnifield went on a visit to Fauquier County, Virginia. At that time Governor Dunmore was preparing for a campaign against the Indians in Ohio, and Bonnifield joined the army, although he was not a citizen of Virginia. When the march began for the west, he found himself under General Lewis. They marched to Lewisburg in Greenbrier County. Here Bonnifield first met Isaac Shelby, with whom he formed an intimate acquaintance, and of whom he afterwards frequently spoke. The army proceeded to the mouth of the Gauley, and from that point a portion made canoes and went by water to the Ohio. Among these was Bonnifield. His reminiscences of the battle of October 10, contain a few minor details which I have never seen published. He relates that he and Isaac Shelby were behind the same log, and had, for some time, been trying to discover the spot from which occasional bullets had been coming which apparently had been fired at them whenever they showed themselves. Finally Bonnifield made the discovery; but at that moment his gun was empty, and he therefore pointed out the head and face of an Indian some fifty yards distant, protruding from behind a log. Shelby took careful aim, fired, and when the Indians yielded ground shortly after, they found the warrior lying behind the log, shot through the head.

"None of the published accounts of the battle which I have seen mention the fact that the retreating Indians were observed while in the act of crossing the Ohio. Bonnifield speaks particularly of seeing them crossing in large numbers. To him the sight seems to have furnished amusement; for he related with much merriment how a dozen or more Indians would set out from shore on a single log, how the log would roll and careen despite their efforts to steady it; how one by one they would fall off, and strike out swimming for the Ohio shore, while the log perhaps would float away without a passenger." (5)

"Ellis" Hughes, of the foregoing citations, and Elias Hughes, the scout, were one and the same person. In the Census of Monongalia County, Virginia, 1782, he is listed as Elias Hughes at the head of a family of five. In the Census of Harrison County,

(3) See page 475. (4) p. 475. (5) p. 475.

Virginia, 1785, he appears as Ellis Hughes at the head of a family of six. Both enumerations included parents. (6)

Elias Hughes came early to the western waters. The record of homestead entries in Monongalia County, 1781, shows that he was granted "400 acres on West Fork [river] adjoining lands of James Tanner, to include his improvement made in 1770." (7) He assisted in the building of Nutter's Fort and was closely identified with the border wars, which intervened from the Battle of Point Pleasant to the Treaty of Greenville. We get a glimpse of his career during this period, from the evidence which he submitted with his claim for pension as a Revolutionary soldier, heretofore unpublished.

In his deposition, executed August 23, 1832, he states that as near as he could recollect he was then about seventy-five years old. He entered the service at the commencement of the war, and was commissioned a captain of spies under Col. Benjamin Wilson, and served as such for about two years. Col. Lowther then took command, and he was under him with the rank of captain for over a year; when it appears that Col. Lowther left the service. Hughes was under the impression that the colonel resigned, but was not positive. Col. George Jackson then took command of the scouts and Hughes continued in service until the close of the war.

Hughes states that when Col. Jackson assumed command, owing to some new arrangement in the disposition of the Indian spies, he did not retain his commission as captain. According to the then regulation, the services of the spies were no longer required in companies. They were separated in bodies of two, and boundaries assigned over which they were to scout. They met at certain points, reported their observations and carried any appearance of the enemy to the nearest stations.

In his petition, Hughes was vouched for by Jacob Riley and Stephen McDougal, but he was not granted a pension.

In 1834, Hughes made a second declaration, which is so fraught with historic interest that I give it in full:

"THE STATE OF OHIO }
LICKING COUNTY }

"Personally appeared before me, the undersigned, a Justice of the Peace within and for the County aforesaid, Elias Hughes, who being duly sworn deposeth and saith that by reason of old age and consequently loss of memory, he cannot

(6) See page 475. (7) p. 475.

minutely enter into a detail of his services in the Revolutionary War. Deponent saith, however, without fear of contradiction, that he served as a ranger and spy during the whole of the Revolutionary War, from the year 1775 to the year 1783, and also prior and subsequently thereto, that his first engagement against the Indians was at the battle of Point Pleasant on the Big Kanhawa in the year 1774, that his last services were performed in the year of Wayne's treaty with the Indians, in the year 1795 (as he thinks), in the neighborhood of Buchannon against a party of 22 Indians by pursuing them and giving the alarm to the settlement—that said Indians succeeded in getting off with Mrs. Bozarth (wife of John Bozarth) and two of the children as prisoners, who were delivered up to General Wayne after the treaty.

"Deponent saith that after the declaration of war in 1775, he volunteered in the service in the Virginia States troops (he thinks), under one Captain James Booth under whom, to the best of his recollection, he continued to serve up to the year (in the spring) of 1778, when his father Thomas was killed by the Indians on Hacker's Creek, Va. Deponent states that about that time one Stephen Ratcliff or Ratlift who held a commission as Captain (under Col. or Major Lowther) left the service and went back on to the south Branch of the Potomac. Deponent saith that he was then commissioned by Col. Benjamin Wilson as a captain to supply the vacancy occasioned by reason of the said Ratcliff leaving the service. Deponent states he well recollects that his commission was printed but by whom it was signed he cannot say, but under the impression that it was signed by the Gov. of Va. Deponent states as he has before stated in his original declaration that he served not less than three years as captain of the Rangers or spies, that he may perhaps he mistaken (from the great length of time which has elapsed and from loss of memory which he is sensible has failed him very materially), in the order and disposition of arranging Col. Benj. Wilson and Col. Wm. Lowther as officers of the Rev. at the time he was so engaged and serving under them as aforesaid, he is, however, satisfied that they were the two principal leaders in the commencement of the Revolution in West Augusta Co., Va., and whether they did or did not at that time hold commissions under the Government as Col. or Major he cannot say positively (they have at least subsequently acquired those titles); he is satisfied however that they either assumed or had in fact such authority delegated to them by the Government that they took upon themselves the organization and disposition of the troops in that section of the country and of paying off the soldiers, recommending the appointment of officers, etc., and that he did in fact hold a commission and served as a captain in the Rev. for not less than three years as before stated. (Deponent states on having his memory refreshed that he is mistaken in saying (as stated in his original declaration) that he was commissioned as captain at the commencement of the War, that it was not until the spring of 1778 (as he thinks).

"Deponent states that from his youth, he always had a fondness for his gun and that his principal occupation was that of hunting from the time he was able to carry a gun up to the time of the Rev., that a number of years before the time of the Rev. (does not recollect the year) he removed with his father in the neighborhood of Clarksburg, Va., together with several other families, John Hacker, Wm. Hacker, Samuel Pringle, Wm. Ratcliff, John Cutright & John Hacker with their families, that on the breaking out of war, his services being required, he of choice volunteered his services as he has before stated, that his name is mentioned in the Border Warfare, a work published by Alex. Withers, at Clarksburg, 1831, and in which a part of his services is detailed (though not generally or particularly). Deponent states that his services may be computed as follows, viz: as a private from the year 1775 up to the year 1778, as a captain, from 1778 up to the year 1781, and from the year 1781 up to the year 1783 as a private. Deponent states he has sent on to Virginia in order to prepare the testimony of witnesses who served with him and by whom he expected to be able to prove his services both as a private and as captain in the service, but in consequence of the death of Alexander West and the absence of David Sleith, his most important witness, he has not been able to establish his services as satisfactorily as he expected to be able to do. Deponent states positively from his own knowledge that he has actually served as above stated, that he did service faithfully during the whole of the Rev. War without any interruption, and that he also served after the peace of 1783 up to the year of 1795. Deponent states that he is unable to say whether he will be able to procure any further testimony in regard to his services than that which is attached to his original declaration, to wit, the testimony of Wm. Powers, Esq., and Jesse Lowther—that he does not know at this time of any person living within his knowledge (except David Sleith) whose testimony will be material. Deponent states that for three years past, he has been entirely blind and from his limited means he is unable to be at further expense in order to establish his services. He hereby proposes to submit to the Department his original and amended declaration with the testimony accompanying the same with a view that the same may be acted upon giving the department a discretionary power to grant him a pension as captain or private, as the evidence in the case may in their discretion seem to justify.

his
ELIAS X HUGHES
mark

"Sworn and subscribed to Dec. 5, 1834.

M. M. CAFFER, *Justice of the Peace*."

The foregoing declaration was followed by several lengthy testimonies among them one from Tarah Curtis, a clergyman, all speaking highly of Hughes as a man of veracity and whose statement could be relied upon. Some of these affidavits are of more than passing interest, of which a full synopsis is here given.

Under date of September 8, 1834, before John Mitchell, J. P., William Powers, of Harrison County, Virginia, states that he was then sixty-nine years old, and that he first became acquainted with Elias Hughes in 1774 at the building of Nutter's Fort, near where the town of Clarksburgh now is; that he thought Hughes was then seventeen years old, and resided with his father at a place now called Westfield, in Lewis County, Virginia. From that time to 1796, he was more or less acquainted with Hughes, and for a portion of the time participated with him in the scenes of warfare then going on between the whites and Indians on the western frontier of Virginia.

Powers could not state from personal knowledge of Hughes service from commencement of the Revolution, 1776 to 1783, as he was not in the same company of spies, but frequently met him in connection with the discharge of his duties during that period. He states that he was present at one time in the spring of 1781, when Colonel Lowther with sixteen others, of whom Elias Hughes was of the number, returned to Clarksburgh with five Indian scalps, a great quantity of plunder and two prisoners, whom they had taken and rescued from the Indians. Powers further states that after the peace between Great Britain and the United States in 1783, the war with the Indians did not subside for a number of years; consequently a force was necessary to be kept up for their mutual defense against the Indians. He states that by this means he and Elias Hughes were thrown together on numerous occasions (from the year 1783 up to the year 1795), and he had an opportunity of forming a pretty good opinion of the character of Hughes as an Indian warrior; that he believes the country in those days did not contain a more vigilant, brave and efficient soldier; that from all that he had seen and heard of Elias Hughes, he was, when his services were needed to go on an expedition, at all times ready to go at a moment's warning.

September 10, 1834, Jesse Lowther, before John Davis, J. P. for Harrison County, Virginia, states that he was then sixty-one years old; born in Harrison County, Virginia, where he resided ever since, and was well acquainted with Elias Hughes from the time that he was capable of knowing any person, and the most that he could relate respecting said Hughes as an Indian warrior was information derived from his father, William Lowther, and others; that during the Revolution he was too young to participate in the scenes of warfare then going forward on the western frontier of Virginia. Lowther states that he well recollected at one time that Elias Hughes was engaged with his father, William Lowther, then a Major, in March 1781, with fifteen others pursuing a party of fourteen Indians, who were then retreating from Randolph County, where they had been murdering and plundering a number of inhabitants. His father and other men pursued the Indians from Arnold's Fort, sometimes called Lowther's Fort, to Indian Creek, a tributary of Hughes River, where they overtook and killed five of the Indians and returned with their scalps to said fort, having rescued two of the white prisoners, Daugherty and Mrs. Roney, whose son was accidentally killed during the attack on the Indians. Mr. Lowther well remembered that the plunder taken from the Indians at that time, when shared to each man, amounted to £14 17 s. 5 d.; that amongst the plunder taken were nine guns, six silver half-moons, one whole moon and one war club and spear, a number of "Tom Hawks" and scalping knives, silver arm bands, earrings and nose jewelry, one cap containing 44 silver broaches, a number of (as he thinks) Kowaknick pouches (of otter skins) and paint bags.

Lowther states that as far back as his recollection extends, and from information derived from his father and others, Hughes was from the first among the foremost to go forth against the Indians when his services were required, and understood that he was Captain of Spies, but at what period he could not tell. He further states that he has been at Hughes' house in Ohio since he left Virginia, and is satisfied that he is the same identical Elias Hughes mentioned in his original declaration made in Licking County, Ohio, August 23, 1832, now here exhibited No. 4776.

Mr. Davis, Justice, adds that Jesse Lowther's statements are entitled to credit.

In an affidavit, February 25, 1842, before John Moore, J. P., Licking County, Ohio, General Thomas W. Wilson, son of Colonel Benjamin Wilson, deceased, who figured prominently in the border wars of western Virginia, states that he was then 38 years old, and up to the time he was twenty-two years of age he continued to reside with his father in Harrison County, Virginia. He had frequently heard his father relate many incidents relative to border warfare, in which Elias Hughes played part. His father always spoke of Hughes in the highest terms, as a brave and efficient soldier and spy, and in whom he had the most implicit confidence; that from his peculiar sagacity and knowledge of the Indian character combined with his personal activity, perseverance and bravery he ranked him amongst the foremost of the Rangers and Spies of his day.

General Wilson stated that he had often heard his father say that Hughes was appointed Captain of the Rangers and Spies in place of one Ratcliff, who was discharged, as he understood, on account of his cowardice; that it was necessary for the safety of the country that said Ratcliff be removed, and Hughes appointed in his place; that said Ratcliff was a careless, trifling, cowardly dog and not to be depended upon. Hughes received his appointment, as the General thought, on Sunday morning before daylight, and started upon the scout and pursuit of Indians, and thought it was the same trip that he returned with the scalps of seven Indians.

The General had heard many circumstances and anecdotes told of Hughes by those of his acquaintances, in relation to his encounters and exploits among the Indians in the time of the Revolution, and that from the character given him by all he was highly distinguished for his bravery, and must have contributed much to the defense of the country during the war of the Revolution.

The pursuit and defeat on Hughes River of the warriors who desolated the Leading Creek settlement in 1781 had no parallel on the western waters. The number of Indians killed has been variously estimated. *Withers*, as previously quoted, placed this loss at five, which number is confirmed by the testimony of Jesse Lowther, Gen. Wilson, who got his information from Col. Benjamin Wilson, states that the number slain was seven. This tallies with the report of John Cutright, who participated in the affair. (8) The Indians were so adroit in their movements, that they were seldom anticipated, or punished in these border forays.

Comparatively few incidents in the Virginia frontier life of Elias Hughes have been preserved. I am indebted to Rev. Daniel G. Helmick for that which immediately follows:

Elias Hughes and one Brown, for whom Brown's Creek in Harrison County, West Virginia, was named, were hunting in the vicinity of Lost Creek near the West Fork River, when Hughes shot and wounded an elk, which made off. There was a rivalry between the two men as to their personal endurance; to settle which it was agreed that they give chase until the game was overhauled, or one, or both of the hunters ready to say "quit." They immediately started at a swinging trot, but the proverb that a "stern chase is a long chase" was to be amply verified. Hour after hour went by with no let-up to that relentless trot.

The quarry was finally overhauled on lower Turkey Run, or Peck's Run in (now) Upshur County. Hughes did not suffer materially from this remarkable run; but not so with Brown. The tendons of his lower limbs were badly strained, which contracting into corded knots, disabled him for several days.

---
(8) See page 475.

CHAPTER XXV

The memory of Elias Hughes in later years is inseparably connected with that of his kinsman and associate, John Ratcliff, who accompanied him to Ohio. The following biographical sketch of these two bordermen is by *Isaac Smucker*: (1)

OUR PIONEERS
Capt. Elias Hughes and John Ratcliff.
1798.

"Elias Hughes and John Ratliff were our first settlers, and closed their lives here, hence their names are as much interwoven with the history of Licking County as is the name of General Washington with the history of the United States, or as are the names of the Presidents, Lincoln and General Grant, with the history of the late rebellion. And to attempt the production of a history of our country without making Hughes and Ratliff prominent actors therein would manifestly issue in failure.

"Elias Hughes was born near the South branch of the Potomac, a section of country which furnished Licking County many of its early settlers and most useful citizens. His birth occurred sometime before Braddock's defeat in 1755. Of his early life little is known, until in 1774, we find him a soldier in the army of General Lewis, engaged in the battle of Point Pleasant. Gen. Lewis, you are aware, commanded the left wing of the army of Lord Dunmore, who was then Governor of the Colony of Virginia, and successfully fought the distinguished Shawanese Chief, Cornstalk, who had a large force of Indians under his command. One-fifth of Lewis' command was killed or wounded, but Elias Hughes escaped unhurt in this hard fought battle, which lasted an entire day. At the time of his death, which occurred more than seventy years after the battle, he was, and had been for years, the last survivor of that sanguinary conflict.

"We next find Hughes a resident of Harrison County, in Western Virginia, where his chief employment, during the 21 years that intervened between the battle of Point Pleasant and the treaty of Greenville in 1795, was that of a scout or spy, on the frontier settlements near to or bordering on the Ohio River. This service, which was a labor of love with him, he rendered at the instance of his State and of the border settlers that had been for a long time greatly harassed by the Indians, who had murdered many of the whites on the frontiers, their women and children included, under circumstances of atrocity but seldom paralleled. Hughes' father and others of his kindred, and also a young woman to whom he was betrothed, had been massacred by them. These acts of atrocious barbarity made him ever after an unrelenting and merciless enemy of the whole race of Red Skins, and in retaliation for their numerous butcheries his deadly rifle was brought to bear fatally upon many of their number in after years. It is but an act of simple justice to the memory of this veteran pioneer, who was well known as an

---
(1) See page 475.

Indian hater, and an Indian killer, that the provocations he had, be fully presented, and properly understood. Born and raised on the frontiers, among a rude and unlettered people, and untaught and wholly uncultivated and unenlightened as he was, it is not surprising that, under all these circumstances, considering, too, the horrid aggravation he had, he should have given rather full play to strong and malignant passions, and that he should have cherished, even to old age, the harsher and more revengeful feelings of his nature. His vindictiveness or sense of justice led him to keep accounts about balanced between the whole race of red men and himself. This he did fully, so long as the Indians maintained a hostile attitude towards the whites—perhaps a little longer. He owed them nothing at the final settlement.

"The treaty of Greenville, commonly called 'Wayne's Treaty,' made and ratified in 1795, terminated Indian hostilities, or rather the defeat of the Indians the previous year, by General Wayne, in the battle of the 'Fallen Timbers,' near the rapids of the Maumee, brought about that result, and hence scouts were no longer required. Elias Hughes, like the Moor in Shakespeare, when he reached the conviction that 'Othello's occupation's gone,' now finding his services as a scout no longer in demand, surrendered his commission of Captain of scouts, and directed his attention to more pacific and less hazardous pursuits. And here it may be stated that he had been commissioned by that distinguished frontiersman, Col. Ben Wilson, the father of our fellow citizen, Daniel Wilson, and of the late Mrs. Dr. John J. Brice, as a captain of scouts.

"In 1796 Hughes entered the service, as a hunter, of a surveying party, who were about to engage in running the range lines of lands lying in part, in what is now Licking County. The fine bottoms of the Licking were thus brought to his notice, and he resolved to leave his mountain home in the 'Old Dominion,' and locate himself and family on the uncultivated and more fertile lands of the Licking Valley, beyond the white settlements. Accordingly, in the spring of 1797, he gathered together his limited effects, and with his wife and twelve children started for the mouth of the Licking, most of them going on foot, and the remainder on pack horses. This point had been made accessible to footmen and horseback travelers by the location and opening in the year before, by Zane and others, the road from Wheeling to Maysville; and also of a road previously cut out from Marietta up the Muskingum River. (2) John Ratliff, who was a nephew of Hughes, came with his wife and four children, with the latter, and in the same manner to the mouth of the Licking. Here they remained one year, and in the spring of 1798, both families, numbering twenty-one persons, moved in the same style to the 'Bowling Green,' twenty miles up the Licking from its mouth, and there made the first permanent white settlement in the territory now forming Licking County. They erected their cabins near the mouth of the Bowling Green Run, about four miles below Newark, on the banks of the Licking, and about half a mile, or less, apart. They found the 'Bowling Green' a level, untimbered green lawn or prairie, and they at once proceeded to raise a crop of corn. Whether the 'Bowling Green' was a natural prairie, or had been cleared by the Indians or some white persons, remains an unsettled question. The nearest neighbors of Hughes and Ratliff, for two years, lived about ten miles down the Licking, one of whom was Philip Barrick, who, in 1801, moved up the valley and located near the 'Licking Narrows.'

---

(2) See page 475.

"The Hughes and Ratliff colony subsisted mainly on the meat of the wild animals of the forest, and on the fish caught and 'gigged' in the Licking, although a considerable crop of vegetables and corn was raised the first and subsequent years. The elk and buffalo had disappeared, but bear, deer, wild turkeys and a great variety of the smaller game, as well as fish, were in such abundance as to supply the full demands of these early settlers. Berries, wild fruits, nuts and other spontaneous productions of the earth also contributed for many years, in no inconsiderable degree, to the subsistence of the pioneer settlers.

"Ratliff, in some particulars, was a different style of man from Hughes. He was much more given to the peaceful avocations of life, and for one reared on the frontiers, had not been largely engaged in border warfare; although he as well as Hughes, was considerably devoted to the chase, to fishing, trapping, bee hunting, as well as to the pursuit of the ferocious animals of the forest, and the birds of prey that tenanted this wilderness.

"In 1799, a son was born to Elias Hughes, and he was the only accession to the Bowling Green colony in that year. * * *

"In the year 1801, an event of no inconsiderable importance transpired at the 'Bowling Green.' Two Indians came along one night and stole four horses. They belonged to Elias Hughes, John Ratliff, John Weedman, a recent emigrant (from Pennsylvania), and a Mr. Bland, who lived at the mouth of the Licking, but who was at that time visiting Hughes. In the morning after the horses were stolen, their owners determined to pursue and kill the thieves, feeling assured that they were Indians. Weedman backed out, but Hughes, Ratliff and Bland, being well armed, started in pursuit. They were enabled to follow the trail, readily tracking them through the grass and weeds. Overtaking them on Owl Creek, they shot them. Bland's flint did not strike fire, but Hughes' and Ratliff's did, and those Indians stole no more horses. When the Indians were overtaken and it was evident that the horses would be recovered, Bland and Ratliff relented, and feeling less sanguinary than when they started on the pursuit, they suggested to Hughes to let the thieves escape, after the horses were obtained, but the latter was not that style of man. He negatived their proposition in such emphatic terms, and in use of such forcible expletives of the profane order as were common among frontiersmen in those days, as to soon bring them to the determination with which they set out. When Hughes said a thing must be done, and he could do it, or cause it to be done, it was done. This was one of the cases—he had his way—they had agreed to kill the Indian horse thieves—and they did. Hughes knew them and believed them to have been engaged in stealing horses and then returning them to their owners for a compensation in skins and furs.

"This sanguinary transaction necessitated the erection of a blockhouse on the 'Bowling Green' as a means of protection against the infuriated friends of the defunct horse thieves, who were greatly incensed against those they suspected of killing them, but it never became necessary to defend it, the Indians finally deciding it inexpedient to assault it. One evening, however, after the excitement had nearly subsided, two well armed Indians entered Hughes' cabin, and in a menacing manner introduced the subject of killing those Indians. Mrs. Hughes seeing that trouble might be had with their visitors, quietly sent for Ratliff, who readily responded, rifle in hand. Hughes, in those days always carried a butcher knife in his belt, and he also had a rifle at hand. Bloody work seemed imminent, but the Indians, after remaining face to face with those veteran back-woodsmen all night, sometimes in rather spirited discussion, deemed it wise, in the early morning, to retire without any hostile act. * * *

"In 1802, Elias Hughes was elected captain of the first company of militia raised within the present limits of our county. This company he commanded a number of years. They had to go to Lancaster to attend battalion drills. Captain Hughes had four children born to him after he settled at the 'Bowling Green,' making the sum total of his children sixteen. Jonathan is the only one of the sixteen now living in Licking County. He was born in Harrison County, Virginia, in 1796, was brought to the mouth of Licking in 1797, and was two years old at the time of his father's removal in 1798 to the 'Bowling Green.' The older children had to walk, on their removal up the Licking, but Jonathan and his brother David (who also was too young to walk), were brought up in a salt sack thrown across a horse. Jonathan was put in one end of the sack and David in the other, openings being first cut in the sack for their heads to go through. The sack was then slung across the pack saddled horse, and a rider or two, with the other loading, put upon him and then started for the 'Bowling Green,' while the others walked or came up in a canoe. It would, indeed, be an interesting picture that gave us, on canvas, an accurate view of this original colony of emigrants while in motion. Jonathan, the salt sack boy of 1798, is now more than seventy-six years old, and is the oldest settler of our county—emphatically, our Pioneer.

"Ratliff's wife died in 1802, and was probably the first white adult person that died within the present limits of our county. * * * Ratliff married again, his second wife being the daughter of a pioneer by the name of Stateler, who lived near the mouth of the Rocky Fork. He also raised a considerable family but none of them now live, if living at all, in our county. He had a son in the army during the War of 1812, who, after his return from the army, removed to Louisiana. He also had a daughter, Mary, who intermarried with a Mr. Evans. Some of the issue of this marriage, being grandchildren of John Ratliff, are still living in our county, principally, I learn, in Perry Township.

"Ratliff finally removed to the south side of the Licking near the mouth of the Brushy Fork, where he died about the year 1811. He, no more than Hughes, seems to have had much success in the acquisition of property. Indeed, it is not probable that either of them ever had much ambition in that direction.

"Capt. Elias Hughes, on all other subjects except Indian warfare, was generally of a taciturn disposition, but he was fond of relating his exploits and successes as a scout; sitting up whole nights, sometimes, to relate to willing interested listeners his hair-breadth escapes and adventures, and the thrilling stories, heroic acts and deeds of renown in which he had borne a part. He was unassuming, temperate, honest, mild-mannered, unpretending, unambitious, but firm, determined, unyielding, and some thought him vindictive. When he resolved on a certain line of conduct he commonly pursued it to success, or failed only after a vigorous effort. Fond of adventure, he displayed in border warfare, in battle, in pursuit of Indians, and in explorations of new countries, and in the pioneer settlement of them, the energy, bravery, self-sacrificing virtues, that so conspicuously distinguished the early pioneers of the Great West.

"In the War of 1812, Capt. Hughes, notwithstanding his age, volunteered for the defense of Fort Meigs. On the formation of a company for that service, he was elected to conduct the men to headquarters at Worthington for organization. At the election of company officers he was made a Lieutenant, the late General John Spencer being elected Captain. He was patriotic to the core and so were his sons, not less than three of them being engaged in the same war. One of them contracted disease while in the service of his country, of which he died. (3)

"Elias Hughes lived many years on the North Fork, a few miles above Newark, and also for several years at Clinton, in Knox County, from whence he removed to Monroe Township, near Johnston. Here, in 1827, Mrs. Hughes died. (4) She had the qualities which admirably adapted her to discharge the duties of a pioneer wife and mother. Her training had been in the Presbyterian faith, and the instruction to her children was in accord with it. Upon her death, most of his children having married and removed from the county, Capt. Hughes became a welcome inmate of the house of his son, Jonathan, who lived in Utica. He, you remember, was introduced to you as the salt sack emigrant of 1798.

"For many years Capt. Hughes was a pensioner, regularly receiving from his beneficent government the means to enable him to spend his declining years in the full enjoyment of all the blessings of life, kindly ministered unto by Jonathan and his family, with whom he spent the last seventeen years of his life.

"Capt. Hughes was the subject of more varied vicissitudes, adverse fortunes and experiences more diversified than usually fall to the lot of man, but he met them in the heroic spirit of those who are determined to encounter them successfully, and meet the stern realities of life like men. Enduring as he did, for the last sixteen years of his life, the terrible affliction of total blindness, he was, of course, deprived of the enjoyment afforded by views of the glory and grandeur of the Creator's works, but he was resigned to this afflictive dispensation of Providence, feeling disposed to endure all meekly, calmly, patiently, and to trustingly, hopefully 'bide his time.'

"In his declining years his attention was directed to religious subjects to which he gave much thoughtful and serious consideration, and for many years he cherished the cheering hopes of a happy future inspired alone by the Christian's faith. He died in December, 1844, and was buried with military honors and other demonstrations of respect. His age is not certainly known, but the best information obtainable makes him at the time of his death about ninety years old.

"Such was the life and career, thus imperfectly sketched, of one of the most remarkable men that ever lived in our county. His was a life full of privations, adventures, hardships, toils, exposures, excitements, anxieties—a life providentially preserved through so many years of constant peril, and of exposures to unusual hazards and dangers. It is one of our chief duties, as a Pioneer Society, to preserve from the oblivion the recollection of the heroic deeds and achievements of our pioneer settlers, and to keep fresh and green in our memories, and in the memories of those who are to come after us, the sufferings and noble deeds of the self-sacrificing men and women who first settled in these forests, erected cabins, cleared the land, and converted the wilderness into fruitful fields, and made comfortable and pleasant homes for their descendants, the men and women of the present generation. And none of all the meritorious pioneers of our county are better entitled to this service at our hands than Capt. Elias Hughes and John Ratliff, and their wives and children, who composed the colony of twenty-one that made the first settlement in the territory that now forms Licking County."

(3) See page 476. (4) p. 476.

"In 1820 an Indian squaw of the Stockbridge tribe was shot near the county line, between Utica and Martinsburgh. She was taken to Mt. Vernon where she died. One McLane shot her, and was sent to the penitentiary for it. He and four others named McDaniel, Evans, Chadwick, and Hughes (not Elias) were engaged in chopping, when this squaw and others of the tribe came along and camped near them. The diabolical proposition was made and accepted that they should play cards, and that the loser should shoot her. McLane was the loser, and did the shooting. His confederates, or at least some of them, were tried and acquitted. In Norton's History of Knox County it is stated that 'Hughes shot this squaw, simply to gratify his hatred of the Indian race.' How an intelligent man, writing history could justify himself for making such a gross mistake, regarding a matter on which he could easily get correct information from a thousand residents of this county and of Knox, it is hard to conceive. Elias Hughes had neither part nor lot in the matter, directly or remotely, but condemned the outrage in unmeasured terms. He was not guilty, and this emphatic denial is deemed an act of simple justice to Mr. Hughes." (5)

Howe (6) says Licking County, Ohio,

"* * * was first settled, shortly after Wayne's treaty of 1795, by John Ratliff and Ellis Hughes, in some old Indian cornfields, about five miles below Newark, on the Licking. These men were from Western Virginia. They lived mainly by hunting, raising, however, a little corn, the cultivation of which was left, in a great measure, to their wives."

Howe gives the following account of the shooting of the Indian horse thieves:

"Hughes had been bred in the hot-bed of Indian warfare. The Indians having, at an early day, murdered a young woman to whom he was attached, and subsequently his father, the return of peace did not mitigate his hatred of the race. One night, in April, 1800, two Indians stole the horses of Hughes and Ratliff from a little enclosure near their cabins. Missing them in the morning, they started off, well armed, in pursuit, accompanied by a man named Bland. They followed their trail in a northern direction all day, and at night camped in the woods. At the gray of the morning they came upon the Indians, who were asleep and unconscious of danger. Concealing themselves behind the trees they waited until the Indians had awakened, and were commencing preparations for their journey. They drew up their rifles to shoot, and just at that moment one of the Indians discovered them, and instinctively clapping his hand on his breast, as if to ward off the fatal ball, exclaimed in tones of affright, 'me bad Indian!—me no do so more!' The appeal was in vain, the smoke curled from the glistening barrels, the report rang in the morning air, and the poor Indians fell dead. They returned to their cabins with the horses and 'plunder' taken from the Indians, and swore mutual secrecy for this violation of law.

"One evening, some time after, Hughes was quietly sitting in his cabin, when he was startled by the entrance of two powerful and well-armed savages. Concealing his emotions, he gave them a welcome and offered them seats. His wife, a muscular, squaw-like looking female, stepped aside and privately sent for Ratliff,

(5) See page 476. (6) p. 477.

whose cabin was near. Presently Ratliff, who had made a detour, entered with his rifle, from an opposite direction, as if he had been out hunting. He found Hughes talking with the Indians about the murder. Hughes had his tomahawk and scalping-knife, as was his custom, in a belt around his person, but his rifle hung from the cabin wall, which he deemed it imprudent to attempt to obtain. There all the long night sat the parties, mutually fearing each other, and neither summoning sufficient courage to stir. When morning dawned, the Indians left, shaking hands and bidding farewell, but in their retreat, were very cautious not to be shot in ambush by the hardy borderers.

"Hughes died near Utica, in this county, in March, 1845, at an advanced age, in the hope of a happy future. His early life had been one of much adventure; he was, it is supposed, the last survivor of the bloody battle of Point Pleasant. He was buried with military honors and other demonstrations of respect."

This was Elias Hughes of border fame.

The pursuit and shooting of the Indian horse thieves by Hughes, "Jack" Ratliff and Bland, is given by *Norton* (7) and is practically the same as Howe's version, but not so elaborate, and closes with this statement:

"Our old townsman, Wm. Mofford, informs us that when improving his farm on Mile Run, Wayne Township, he was clearing off ground on which to build his house, and he then plowed up the two Indians killed by Hughes, and also a rusty gun barrel, brass guard and other pieces of a gun, which had not decayed. This was in 1835, and Jacob Mitchel now (1862) has the old relics.

"George Conkie gathered up the bones and buried them, and the house was built on the spot—the old Peck Place on Mile Run bottom, where Mrs. Acre now lives. In early days there was a favorite camping ground for the Indians, about where these Indians were killed."

Norton states that Hughes died in March, 1845.

Among the *Draper Manuscripts* (8) are the following communications from Col. Robert Davidson, in response to inquiries from Dr. Draper. They are here published for the first time.

"NEWARK, 10th March, 1850.
"Mr. LYMAN C. DRAPER.

"DEAR SIR, Yours of 23d Nov last to Mr. William Van Buskirk requesting information as to the adventures of his father John Vanbuskirk and others in the border warefare along the Ohio River at an early day has been handed the subscriber (as an old acquaintance of his fathers) by Mr. Wm. Buskirk to reply thereto. Last week I placed in the postoffice directed to you the Granville Intelligencer containing a detailed report of the desperate conflict of Adam Poe, his brother Andrew, and others with the gigantic Indean, Bigfoot, and brothers, five in all July 1782 and next week look for the Newark Gazett of this place containing some notes of the adventures of Jno Van Buskirk written and published for your convenience and to do some justice to the memory of a very worthy man wom I always esteemed as one of the fronteere defenders when I was too young to defend my self.

(7) See page 477. (8) p. 477.

Elias Hughes

"If you shall desire it, I can send you a more detailed account of Elias Hughes who at the age of 18 was in the battl at Point Pleasant October 10th 1774 and continued from that, employed in hunting, spying, and killing Indeans until after Gen. Wains Treaty 1794 [1795].

"You will pleas excuse my friend Wm. Buskirk in not writing you. In the first place he thought the information would come with a better grace from one of the early aquantances of his father than from him He is a fine young man but reluctant to write would rather attend his saw mill a day than write an hour. If you shall wish for any more on the subject the border wariors write to him.

Very respectfully yours, &c
Robt. Davidson.

Mr. Lyman C. Draper Esq
   Leverington
     Philadelphia County, Pa."

"Newark, February 22, 1851 (9)

" * * * * * * * * *

"I wrote some time past to know of jonathan Hughes where his father was born and to what religious denomination he entered But have not yet heard from him I presume he has been from home or by other means has not received my letter. As to Elias Hughes, it is something uncertain but he considered himself 18 [years] of age when in the battle of Point pleasant, Mouth of Kanawa, under Colo. Lewis—I am not positive as to the Religious denomination to which he inclined but think it was to the Methodist Episcopal Church. His daughter in law Mrs. jonathan Hughes was my informant as to his vengeance disposition not long after his death I was then (in addition to what I knew) endeavoring to collect more knoledge of his life and adventures for the purpose of writing the obituary notice which soon after appeared in the Newark Advocate which I sent last year.

"When I saw Gen. Thomas Wedsday last, he enformed me that he would [be] in Philadelphia this winter and that he intended to do himself pleasure of calling upon you—

"If I shall soon hear from Mr. jonathan Hughes I shall write again (10) I should have remarked on the other side that I think Elias Hughes was born on the South branch of Potomac Va. and that his father at an early day moved thence to Harrison county, Va. and there was held [killed] by the Indeans.

"Although I have been acquainted with Dr. Coulter many years I[t] was but lately I learned that he knew any[thing] about Capt. Bready But have not the least of his statements

Very respectfully yours &c
Robt. Davidson."

"N. B. Since writing the foregoing Dr. Coulter informs me that he thinks Capt Bready was from 30 to 35 years of age when he died. (11)

Lyman C. Draper Esq
   Leverington
     Philadelphia County, Pa."

(9) See page 477. (10) p. 477. (11) p. 477.

Last of the Border Warriors. (12)

"Died on the 22nd ult., Capt. Elias Hughes, aged ninety years, at the residence of his son, Jonathan, near Utica, O. He was buried with military honors by the military of the vicinity.

"At an early day Thomas Hughes & family moved from the South Branch of Potomac to Harrison County, North-Western part of Virginia, where his son, Elias, became one of those extraordinary, active and daring spies and soldiers of the day.

"At the age of eighteen, under the command of Col. Lewis, he was in the battle of Point Pleasant, which continued from early in the morning until near night before the Indians gave way, October 10, 1774. On returning home he joined a company of spies under Capt. Boothe, for the protection of the then exposed frontier settlements.

"At one time, being out spying with a comerade, they examined the localities near the steep bank of a run, under smoke of rotten wood to keep off the gnats & lay down upon their arms for the night, their moccasins tied to the breech of their guns. (13) Some time after, hearing something like the snapping of a stick, & looking in the direction, saw at a distance three Indians approaching. Instantly the whites sprung to their feet, leaped down the bank and over the run. The Indians in pursuit, not knowing the place so well, fell down the bank. The whites, hearing the splash, stopped an instant, put on their moccasins, raised a yell & put off at full speed, leaving the Indians to take care of themselves.

"Capt. Boothe in time being killed by the Indians, Joseph Ratliff succeeded to the command, but lacking, as a soldier, the confidence of the men, left the country, and Hughes on a sudden emergency being appointed in his place, under Col. Lowther, put off in pursuit of Indians, found them, & returned with 6 or 7 scalps. (Date not known at present.) (14)

"In June, 1778, three women were in the field near West's Fort picking greens, when they were fired upon without effect by one of a party of four Indians. The women screamed and ran for the fort, and one Indian in pursuit speared Mrs. Freeman. Being fired upon from the fort without effect, the Indians ran off in different directions. They were soon pursued by Jesse Hughes, Elias & others. After some time, at a distance they heard the howl like that of a wolf. They ran some distance in the direction and stopping at a suitable place, Jesse howled also. He was answered, and two Indians were soon seen advancing. An opportunity offering, Elias downed one, (15) the other ran. The whites pursued, but he running into a small hazel thicket and they round on each side to take him in the outgoing, he watching them ran the back way and escaped. In the meantime he who had been shot recovered so much as to make off also, and a shower coming on prevented the pursuit by obliterating the blood on the track.

"In March, 1781, a party of 14 Indians, nearly depopulated the settlement upon Leading Creek (Taggart's Valley) and put off. They were pursued unsuccessfully by a party from Clarksburg, (16) but in the meantime, Col. Lowther & Capt. Hughes, learning by spies that the Indians had been seen near the mouth of Isaac's Creek, put off with a party of 17, and on an evening, Hughes being alone in advance for the purpose, discovered the Indians on a branch of Hughes' River, coolly putting up for the night, apparently not apprehensive of pursuit at that distance.

(12) See page 477. (13) p. 477. (14) p. 477. (15) p. 477. (16) p. 477.

"On the return to the party it became an object of interest, not to risk the lives of the prisoners, Mrs. Roney, her little son and Daniel Doherty; therefore, when it was thought the Indians might be sleeping, the Captain crawled near enough to discover the position of Mrs. Roney and Doherty, but saw nothing of the boy. Before day the whole party, in perfect order, crawled close & fired upon the Indians, one only escaping.

Mrs. Roney and Doherty were uninjured, but the boy, having been sleeping in the bosom of an Indian was killed by a ball after passing through the Indian's head. The plunder sold the 17th of the month, produced a dividend of 14£. 17s. and 5d. to each one of the seventeen.

"In September, 1785, Lowther, Hughes and others, in pursuit of a party of Indians who had stolen horses from near Clarksburg, slept near them on the third night, not knowing it. Next morning the whites parted, taking different routes. Hughes & party soon discovered the Indians, and fired upon them, killing one. The rest ran off in various directions, and one coming near Lowther's party was shot by the Colonel as he ran. They then started for home, and before going far were fired upon, & John Barnet (17) wounded so that he died before reaching home.

"At another time (date not known) Hughes and party discovering a party of Indians, fired upon them. The Indians ran in different directions: Hughes after one, was gaining upon him fast, in a piece of bottom land in which were no trees, when the Indian turning quickly about with loaded gun uplifted. Hughes' gun was empty, & no tree to spring behind. But instantly springing obliquely to the right and left, with a bound, & outstretched arm, flirted the muzzle of the Indian's gun one side, and the next moment had his long knife in him up to the hilt.

"After Gen. Wayne's treaty, Capt. Hughes & family settled upon the waters of the Licking, Ohio. The Indians having, at an early day, killed a young woman whom he highly esteemed, & subsequently his father, the return of peace did not eradicate his antipathy. In the month of April, 1800, two Indians having collected a quantity of fur on the Rocky Fork of Licking, proceeded to the Bowling Green, stole three horses and put off for Sandusky. The next morning Hughes, Ratliff and Blair, going out for the horses, and not finding them, did not return to apprise their families, but continued upon their trail, and at night discovered the Indians' fire on Granny's Creek, some few miles N. W. of where Mt. Vernon now stands; lay down for the night, and the next morning walked up to the Indians as they were cooking their morning repast. At first the Indians looked somewhat embarrassed, proposed restoration of the horses and giving part of their furs by way of conciliation, to which the whites did not dissent, but were thinking of the whole of the furs and future safety of the horses. It being a damp morning, it was proposed to shoot off all their guns and put in fresh loads. A mark was made, Hughes ostensibly raised his gun to shoot, which attracted the attention of the Indians to the mark, and was a signal. Ratliff downed one, Blair's gun flashed, but Hughes turning quickly around, emptied his gun into the other Indian's head, setting fire at the same time to the handkerchief around it. On returning, they kept their expedition a secret for some time. Many more interesting incidents might be related, but not with desirable accuracy of the present day.

"Capt. Hughes' memory failed him considerably the last three or four years. Previously his eyesight failed him entirely, but partially returned again. With

(17) See page 477.

patience he waited his coming end, firmly believing that his Redeemer lived, and that through him he should enjoy a happy futurity."—COMMUNICATED.

That Elias Hughes continued to murder Indians after going to Ohio is undeniable. He once returned on a visit to the settlements on the Upper Monongahela, and some of his old acquaintances noticing his restless movements and constant watching on every side, said to him, "Ellis, I see you're still hunting Injuns." "Yes, and I'll hunt 'em as long as I live." "Have you had any luck since leaving here?" "Not much, but I know where there are fourteen guns hid in an old sycamore in my country."

Through the kindness of Mrs. Pansy Hall Thatcher, a lineal descendant of Capt. Elias Hughes, I am enabled to give a personal description of the old scout, by two of his granddaughters, who were still living in Licking County, Ohio, in 1907.

Elias Hughes was small in size, of light build, small hands and could wear a woman's shoe. His hair was combed down smooth and cut off evenly at the shoulder. His hair showed no signs of grey, even at his death. His eyes were blue and his face was always clean-shaved. He was eccentric in his dress, at all times wearing a hunting shirt and refusing to wear a coat. This shirt was of blue trimmed in red, and with red fringe around the edge. He also refused to have a button on his hunting shirt, tying it with small pieces of tape.

A family tradition says, that "Elias Hughes was lying asleep in the house, when he dreamed that his children were in danger. When he awakened, a friend, who was in the same house, was loading his gun. Elias asked him what he was going to do. He said, "I hear a wild turkey; I am going to shoot it." Elias said, "I will get your turkey for you." He went out and returned in a few minutes with the scalp of an Indian, whom he had found in his cornfield near where his children were playing. The Indian had imitated the turkey's call in hopes of luring some one from the house."

This tradition may be the growth from Jesse Hughes' experience with the turkey at Clarksburg, and of David Morgan's remarkable dream and combat with the two Indians near Prickets Fort in 1778, cited elsewhere in this volume. It is probable that Elias Hughes was connected with the revolting sequel of Morgan's battle, which might account in part for the story.

In 1782, Elias Hughes had an adventure with Indians in a

cornfield on the West Fork River, but with different results from that of the foregoing tradition.

"In August as Arnold and Paul Richards were returning to Richards' Fort, they were shot at by some Indians, lying hid in a cornfield adjoining the fort, and both fell from their horses. The Indians leaped over the fence immediately and tomahawked and scalped them.

"These two men were murdered in full view of the fort, and the firing drew its inmates to the gate to ascertain its cause. When they saw that the two Richards were down, they rightly judged that Indians had done the deed; and Elias Hughes, ever bold and daring, taking down his gun, went out alone at the back gate and entered the cornfield, into which the savages had again retired, to see if he could not avenge on one of them the murder of his friends. Creeping softly along, he came in view of them standing near the fence, reloading their guns, and looking intently at the people at the fort gate. Taking a deliberate aim at one of them, he touched the trigger. His gun flashed, and the Indians alarmed, ran speedily away." (18)

It is claimed that Captain Hughes could read and write, although his signature appears in his declaration for pension and other statements with an "X." This, however, may have been on account of his blindness at that time. Like his brother, Jesse, Captain Hughes died in indigency. His life had been devoted to the trail and the chase; and his wants measured only by his present needs, were supplied from the forest and streams. For two-score years his supreme joy had been a saturnalia of blood, and not until the loss of his sight and when there were no more "Injuns to kill," did his thoughts turn to the "future life."

Captain Hughes is buried near the center of the cemetery at Utica, Ohio. At the interment crossed cannons were discharged over his grave, which is yearly decorated with flowers. A gray, flat stone marks the last silent camp of the "*Last of the Border Warriors.*" (19)

---

(18) See page 477. (19) p. 477.

CHAPTER XXVI

For one who figured so prominently on the Trans-Allegheny border, Colonel William Lowther has received but meagre consideration from the historian. The following brief summary of his life by *Withers* is practically the source from which all subsequent writers have drawn:

"There was likewise, at this time, a considerable accession to the settlements on Buchannon and Hacker's Creek. So great was the increase of population in this latter neighborhood, that the crops of the preceding season did not afford more than one-third of the breadstuff, which would be ordinarily consumed in the same time, by an equal number of persons. Such indeed was the state of suffering among the inhabitants, consequent on this scarcity, that the year 1773 is called in the traditional legends of that day, the *starving year;* and such were the exertions of William Lowther to mitigate that suffering, and so great the success with which they were crowned, (1) that his name has been transmitted to their descendants, hallowed by the blessings of those, whose wants he contributed so largely to relieve."

To the foregoing, *Withers* adds the following note:

"William Lowther was the son of Robert, and came with his father to the Hacker Creek settlement in 1772. He soon became one of the most conspicuous men in that section of country; while his private virtues and public actions endeared him to every individual of the community. During the war of 1774, and subsequently, he was the most active and efficient defender of that vicinity, against the insidious attacks of the savage foe, and there were very few, if any, scouting parties proceeding from thence, by which the Indians were killed or otherwise much annoyed, but those which were commanded by him.

"He was the first justice of the peace in the district of West Augusta—the first sheriff in the county of Harrison and Wood, and once a delegate to the General Assembly of the States. His military merits carried him through the subordinate grades to the rank of Colonel. Despising the pomp and pageantry of office, he accepted it for the good of the community, and was truly an effective man. Esteemed, beloved by all, he might have exerted his influence over others, to the advancement of his individual interest; but he sought the advancement of the general weal, not a personal or family aggrandizement. His example might teach others, that offices were created for public good, not for private emolument. If aspirants for office at the present day were to regard its perquisites less, and their fitness for the discharge of its duties more, the country would enjoy a greater portion of happiness and prosperity, and a sure foundation for the permanence of these be laid, in the more disinterested character of her counsellors and their consequent, increased devotion of her interests." (2)

Although an officer during the greater period of the border

---

(1) See page 478. (2) p. 478.

wars and at times, in general command of the military, and accredited with leading many of the pursuits of marauding Indians, *Withers* notes but two such occurrences. These have already been cited elsewhere in this volume. *Lewis* gives the following brief of the Colonel's life: (3)

"William Lowther—Henry, George and William were the sons of Henry Low, and were English miners; for their superior skill and meritorious service '*ther*' was added to the name by royal edict. William had a son Robert, who with his wife, Aquilla Rees Lowther, emigrated to America in 1740, and came to the Hacker settlement in 1767, accompanied by their son William, the subject of this sketch, was born in 1742. The latter married Sudna Hughes, sister of Elias, Jesse, Thomas and Job, of Indian war fame, and settled on Simpson's Creek in 1772. Many of their descendants are now living in Clarksburgh and the surrounding country.

"William Lowther became distinguished as a skillful and courageous frontiersman, and for his unselfish devotion to the good of the colonists. The population of these frontier settlements increased so rapidly that the supply of provisions became insufficient, and the year 1773 was called in the early traditions of the section, 'the starving year.' Such were the exertions of William Lowther to mitigate the sufferings of the people, and so great was his success that his name is transmitted to their descendants hallowed by their blessings. During the war 1774, and subsequently, he was the most active and efficient defender of the settlements in that vicinity, against the savage foe, and many a successful expedition against them was commanded by him. He was one of the first justices of the peace in Harrison County, also the first sheriff of Harrison and Wood Counties, and a delegate to the General Assembly of the State. He also attained all the subordinate ranks in the military service until promoted to that of colonel, and by his unassuming good qualities endeared himself to all with whom he became associated. He died October 28, 1814."

Many of Colonel Lowther's descendants deny that the name was changed by royal edict as late as set forth by Lewis. Mrs. Iva Lowther Peters, of New York, a lineal descendant of Colonel Lowther, line of his son William, after devoting several years to the study of the family history, is confident that the change, if at all, could not have been made so recent as the days of the Colonel's grandfather, Henry Lowther. That the name in its present form is ancient, and is found in connection with the nobility and lawmakers of England, cannot be gainsaid; and from a practical and social point of view, the authenticity of the story may well be questioned.

Two family traditionary accounts of the origin of the name and the migration to America are at variance, and are here given for the first time. That which immediately follows, is from the *Draper Manuscripts*, and is fraught with historic interest: (4)

---
(3) See page 478. (4) p. 479.

"Robert Lowther was born in Ireland about the beginning of the seventeenth century whose primitive name was Low the Lowther generation in Ireland and England were miners to trade and from some extraordinary discovery in the mineral business the King of England added "Ther" to their name which made it Lowther. Robert Lowther emigrated from Ireland to America he was a quaker and fled from the Storms and Persecutions incident to quakers in those Days and Settled in Pennsylvania the home of the quakers after a short stay in Pennsylvania he emigrated to Virginia and settled in Augusta County there young Wm was born who is the subject of our narrative. Wm Lowther was Born in Augusta County va who was the son of Robert the quaker he was Born Dec 22d in the year 1743 and there he receivd his education (5) and when a youth of about seventeen years of age he volunteered his services under David Scott to repel the Indians from the borders of Augusta County and he was occasionally in that service some length of time.

"we pass over several years of Wm Lowthers life and come directly to his emigration to Northwestern virginia Wm Lowther emigrated with his father Robert to Harrison County from Augusty County va in the year 1772 he had not been long in that country before he was appointed Capt of a small boddy of men to defend the infant settlement of Harrison County va from the fury of savage cruelty he defended the settlement with unexpected success with a small boddy of hardy virginians and in a short time Capt Lowthers worth and valure was known in the most parts of Virginia and the adjoining states he remained as capt several years still repelling the savages with unabating zeal untill George Rogers Clark Caled for volunteers in northwestern virginia and of this call hear the declaration or surtificate of Wm Powers co compiler of Border Warfare.

"In the year 1781 General George Rogers Clark caled for volunteers he called espesially on Capt Wm Lowther and offered him a commission if he would come and join his Legion Lowther acceded to the call and there was a company made up of volunteers and joined Clark at fort pitt and Capt Lowther was appointed Major of that company George Jackson was appointed Capt of said company and during their march down the ohio River many of the volunteers Run off Major Lowther finding his company very much weakened they had fallen below his expectation and in consequence of which Major Lowther threw up his Commission and Clark accepted of it and he returned home

"and in the year 1787 he was appointed Col of the Northwestern territory of Virginia he had the whole command and to superintend all that region I saw his commision I heard it red, and he superintended and defended it with vigilence and care, and retaind his commission untill Wayns treaty with the Indians at Granville given under my hand this 26 day of December 1850. Wm Powers co compiler Border Warefare no sooner than he had returned home from Clark's campaign than his attention was caled to the defense of his respective Settlement he had Forts of defense and Safty built in each respective Settlement he had raingers and spies imploid in reconnoitering the Country and when the faithless Deviles as he frequently caled them would commit murder in the Settlements he would follow them in person and frequently overtake them kill and disperse there company Such were his ardent zeal and perceveance that the Indians grew very cautious and were hard to follow and suffice it to say that there was nothing done in any

---

(5) See page 479.

Colonel William Lowther 249

expedition against the Indians without his presence he was fearless and undanted in all his undertakings.

"he was a man of extraordinary strength and action was of the Billious temperment his stature was five feet eleven inches commonly weighed one hundred and eighty pounds he was cherry and undismaid amidst the most trying circumstances in life

"Col Wm Lowther was caled the defender and protector of Northwestern Virginia he defended in time of war protected in time of famine and if it had not been for his energy and sympathy for his fellow beings in the year 1773 the inhabitants of the infant settlement must have perished with hunger he roamed amidst danger and alarm kiled venison elks Buffalow and Bear and thus he supplied all their wants

"Col Wm Lowther was a Lyon in time of war and famine a lamb in time of Peace and plenty he was kind an affectionate to all his friends and acquaintencies his house was the home of the widow and fatherless an asylum for the Preecher and wayfaring man the heralds of the cross would frequently call on him in time of the Indian war and be very fearful and frequently quote this passage of Scripture the wicked flee where no man persueth but the Righteous are as bold as a Lyon and they would ask Col Lowther how the passage could be true for they the Preechers were feerful but Col Lowther was bold as a Lyon

"his house was a common house to repair to for his neighbors children to have the bonds of matrimony Solemnized he gave to all sheard of his bounty he has given some, lasting habitations

"he cared not for wealth or Personal aggrandizement his purse was not his own his Neighbors sheard it with him we will give the reader to understand that when Wm Lowther Received his commission as Col his business became very extensive he was charged says Powers, to take care of the differant Stations on the Ohio River he visited each Station occasionally supplied them with ammunition and provision gave directions for defense had raingers appointed to observe the movement of the enemy and what could be done by any mortal being in person he performd with unabating zeal

"now suffer me to say in conjunction with Border warfare he was the first justice of the Peace in the district of west Augusto the first Sheriff in Harrison and wood [counties] and the first Capt, first major, first Col once a delegate to the general assembly of the states and then retired to private life

"Enough he cries I'm freed from care And toil and pain
  My countrys liberty and peace is gaind

"we see Col Lowther with peace and quietude from 1795 to the war of 1812 with Great Britian and the united States.

"I was but a boy of 12 years old and I could see him amidst the multitude Animating his country man to enlist in the cause of their country when he could do no more he would frequently Sing war Songs tel deed of Bravery and renoun all to inspire his countryman with zeal and courage to inlest in the cause of their country his youngest son embarked in the cause of his country in 1813 and 14 the old Col gave him up that he never Should See his face again and so it turned out to be for Col Lowther Died before his son returned.

"as many other men he had his favorites among his children like Jacob of old he had his Joseph and his Benjamine when he died his Benjamine was gon to fight the Battles of his country and a few minetes before he expired he caled his Joseph unto him laid hands on him and imparted unto him his Benediction

"Exhorting him to serve the true and living God he died in the full triumphs of a living faith in the Salvation of all Adams fallen race.

"your humble writer would have written more extensively concerning Col Wm Lowther but being a relative he feels a dilacy in following through all the mianderings of Col Wm Lowthers life it is enough for me to say that Col Wm Lowther was one of the first to defend his country from savage cruelty and the last to lay down his arms of defense.

"Wm Lowther Died amids the struggle with Great Britian and the united states he Died in the fall of 1814 aged 71 years and ten months.

"DEAR SIR I have gone threw with this little narrative you are at liberty to correct any errors you may perchance to see amend or abridge as you see proper, yours with due respect

Elias J. Lowther

LYMAN C. DRAPER"

MEMORANDA by Draper—This statement was mailed at West Milford, Va., January 11, 1851, and furnished at my request.

Mr. Granville S. Lowther, of West Virginia, a son of Elias J. Lowther, writes me:

"The Lowthers are of Scotch Irish descent, whose original name was Low. I cannot give dates for this, but during the knighthood days of England it was customary to appoint days for athletic sports, over which the king and his royal court presided. Pitching the quoit, or stone, was among the tests of manhood, and one day a stranger entered the arena and selecting a large stone, cast it farther than could any of his competitors. The king, astonished at this feat, had the champion brought before him and inquired his name. 'Low,' was the reply. 'Then,' said the king, 'I will add 'ther' and for your valor you shall be called Lowther.' He was afterwards appointed clerk of the King's Bench, as Sir Henry Lowther, which position has since been filled by others of his name.

"Their emigration to America dates back to the Pilgrim Fathers at Plymouth Rock, where two brothers landed. One of them died during the terrible dearth of the colony, but the other, Henry, survived, and subsequently removed to Albemarle County, Virginia. There his son, Robert, married Aquilla Rees, and was the father of Colonel William Lowther, of whom you inquire."

It is not known where Colonel William Lowther was born, further than it was within the bounds of the territory then known as Augusta County, Virginia. It is quite evident that the greater part of his life, prior to his removal to the Trans-Allegheny, was spent on the Wappatomaka. It is claimed that the birth of his son William, January 27, 1769, was at Moorefield, in now Hardy County, West Virginia. It was in that region that he met his wife, Sudna Hughes, whose parents resided there in 1757. It is safe to say that with his father, he came from that region to the Upper Monongahela, in company with Elias Hughes, Ratliffs and other settlers.

It is notable that *Withers* and *Lewis* differ in regard to the year of the settling of Colonel Lowther and his father on the western border. The error is with *Lewis*. The first permanent settlement on Hacker's creek was not until 1769, and the advent of the Lowthers into that region was in 1772, as stated by *Withers*.

In the homestead records of Monongalia County, 1781, we find that a certificate of entry was granted "William Lowther, 400 acres on Hacker's Creek adjoining lands claimed by Jesse Hughes, to include his settlement made thereon in 1772 with a preemption of 1000 acres adjoining." Colonel Lowther was a man of resources, and acquired several tracts of land by purchasing the claims, or improvements of other settlers. In this manner he secured several thousand acres on the western waters. (6)

It would be difficult to determine by the homestead records just where Robert Lowther actually settled. He must have died prior to 1781, when Colonel Lowther inherited title to 400 acres at the mouth of Hacker's Creek, "settled" on by his father in 1775. In 1781, Joseph Lowther, as "Heir-at-Law of Robert Lowther," secured a grant for 400 acres on Washburn's Run in (now) Harrison County, "to include his settlement made thereon in the year 1775." In the same year was granted to — "Samuel Rubels, Ass'e, to Robert Lowther, 400 acres on Rubels Mill Run, a branch of Cheat River, to include his actual settlement in 1770." There was also issued a certificate of title — "Arthur Trader, Assignee, to Robert Lowther, 400 acres on Roberts Mill Run, adjoining lands of Samuel Ruble, to include his settlement made in 1770." These two entries were doubtless made on the same stream, Rubels Run, and the variations in the name are due to carelessness on the part of the recording clerk. In 1800, one William Lowther was a subscriber to St. John's Parish, Brook County (West), Virginia. (7)

The census of 1782, which however, is very incomplete, shows that William Lowther and Joel Lowther, both residents of Monongalia County, constituted the only families of this name in the

(6) See page 479. (7) p. 479.

state. Joel's name reappears in the enumeration of Harrison County, 1785, but that of William does not. It is very probable that Joseph Lowther, who inherited the homestead of Robert Lowther on Washburn's Run, and Joel Lowther were one and the the same person, and perhaps a brother of Colonel William Lowther.

JONATHAN LOWTHER, killed by Indians on Hacker's Creek in 1778, was a son of Robert Lowther. Thomas Hughes, father-in-law of Colonel Lowther, was killed at the same time. This tragedy, as narrated by *Withers*, has been given elsewhere in this volume, but a tradition among the Lowthers gives a different version. Hughes and Lowther were on their way from Clarksburg to give warning at West's Fort of an Indian alarm, and were shot down within one mile of the latter post. The Indians, fourteen in number, fled, and Colonel Lowther at the head of a party of settlers, gave pursuit. They crossed the Ohio at Blennerhassett's Island and overtook the retreating warriors and surprised their camp not far from Chillicothe, and killed thirteen of them. The whites made a hurried march, and reached the settlements in safety.

This is purely a mistake. Not even the fierce desire for revenge, which would, in this case have prompted Col. Lowther and the Hughes' to great exertion, could have carried them and their followers so far into the Indian country.

By referring to *Withers*, it will be seen that when Hughes and Lowther were killed, two of the company, being intercepted from West's Fort, fled to Richards' Fort, (8) not only for safety, but to give warning as well. This last precaution was unnecessary. Isaac Washburn had been found shot and scalped at no great distance from Richards, and the alarm spread before the arrival of the fugitives. The Indians committed no further depredation, nor were they pursued by the settlers.

In a letter to the Governor of Virginia, March 22, 1793, Col. Lowther tells of a party of Indians stealing six horses within about seven miles of Clarksburg; and of his pursuing the marauders with a company of sixteen men, to the Ohio River, where, being re-enforced with five men, went down the river from Williams Station, to about four miles below Belleville, crossed the river and continued the pursuit fifty miles in the Indian country, came upon the Indian camp in daytime. "One we killed and the other got much wounded. He dropped his gun in the pursuit, which we

---
(8) See page 479.

got, but unfortunately for us he got into the thick bushy woods and we lost him. We re-took four of the horses, before we got up a party of Indians had left the camp and took off two of the horses. My men were so fatigued and our provisions exhausted that I pursued no further."

In following the "different windings taken by the Indians" the whites traveled about 186 miles, nearly the same distance to return, occupied fourteen days, Captain John Haymond, one of the party, lost a valuable horse; one other horse strayed away in the woods, which they expected to recover.

On the 26th of the same month, the colonel writes the Governor informing him of great numbers of Indians crossing the Ohio, and anticipated a blow. Indians had paid them a visit, "as you will discover by my former letter, to the proof of which I have sent you the skin of one of their heads."

The colonel was of opinion that neither "General Wayne's army nor the talk of peace can be of any safety to him."

Col. Lowther could not have remained for any considerable length of time on Hacker's Creek. No local tradition connects his residence with that settlement. He was closely identified with the region about Nutter's Fort during the earliest days of its existence. He resided on a large homestead on the West Fork River, about seven miles from Clarksburg, and near one and a half miles from West Milford. What is said to be his main original cabin is still occupied by some of his descendants. It is built of hewed logs and measures sixteen feet by twenty feet. The joists are flattened timbers, three and a half inches by seven and a half inches. The fire place is five feet and four and a half inches in height. The cabin had at some time been torn down and rebuilt. Its age is computed from 1772, the year of the colonel's advent into the settlement. This, I believe, is nearly correct. There is strong evidence that Col. Lowther did not remain on Hacker's Creek more than one year, and that he resided in the Clarksburg settlement during the *"starving year,"* 1773. The house is among the oldest, if not the oldest, in that part of the state. *Let it be preserved.* (9)

Tradition accredits Colonel Lowther, Jesse Hughes and Elias Hughes with the first actual exploration of the Little Kanawha, and its main tributary, Hughes River, in 1772, (10) at which time Jesse Hughes conferred his own name on the latter stream. The

(9) See page 481. (10) p. 481.

explorers gave such names to the principal affluents of the two rivers as were suggested by some peculiarity or object observed in connection with the stream. With a single exception, these names have all been retained. *Walnut Creek*, so named from the great number of walnut trees fringing its bank, was the scene of the surprise and defeat of Captain Bull's camp, and release of the

COLONEL WILLIAM LOWTHER'S ORIGINAL CABIN
Photographed June, 1908

Leading Creek captives by Colonel Lowther's Rangers in 1781, since which time it has been known as *Indian Creek*. (11) The explorers, it is averred, passed up the West Fork River and crossed to the head of the Little Kanawha by way of Sand Creek.

Another version of this tradition places the explorations in 1774. The party reached the Little Kanawha by way of the Indian trail up Polk Creek and down Leading Creek. After striking the Ohio, the Hughes brothers proceeded to Point Pleasant, where joining the forces of General Lewis, participated in the battle fought there in October of that year. Colonel Lowther went up the river to Fort Pitt on some business of importance.

(11) See page 481.

The following story was told Mr. J. S. Hall, by Colonel Lowther's son Jesse, some seventy-five years ago.

"When my father with several other families settled on the West Fork River," said Mr. Lowther, "grain was so scarce that it was impossible to buy corn for bread. They were compelled to rely on game for food until a crop could be raised. It was agreed that my father and Jesse Hughes, the best hunters in the party, should furnish provisions while the others cleared and cultivated the land. These two hunters not only supplied plenty of game and fish for their own people, but they gave assistance to others in need on Hacker's Creek. Before the crop matured, my grandfather visited us, bringing a knapsack of biscuit. I was then a small boy and my mother gave me one. I tasted it, then threw it down and called for 'jerk.' Mother cried at the thought of living in the wilderness so long that her children had forgotten the use of bread." (12)

This incident is very similar to that related of the Hacker family elsewhere in this volume. It could not have occurred during "starving year, " 1773, which was the year of Jesse Lowther's birth.

At one time the inhabitants were driven to the fort by Indians when provisions were extremely scarce. The inmates were on the verge of starvation, when a large turkey lit on some grapevines near the stockade and Col. Lowther shot it. Under the protection of the garrison rifles, Mrs. Lowther ran out and brought it in. She said: *"God has sent this to preserve our lives."*

Colonel Lowther did not confine his military exploits alone to the local defense of the border. In 1781 he was identified with General Clark's attempted expedition against Detroit. A rare summary of this phase of his life is the evidence submitted by his children in support of their claim for bounty land due their father as a Revolutionary soldier. This record is preserved in the Virginia State Library, and is here produced for the first time.

From an affidavit before Abner Abbott, Justice of the Peace for Lewis County, Virginia, bearing date November 7, 1832, it would appear that Jesse Carpenter, aged 70, and Thomas Cottrell, aged 73, served as Indian spies under Captain William Lowther, about 1778; when they first knew him as an officer. In 1781, Lowther went to Pittsburg as a Major and joined Colonel Joseph Crockett's Regiment, and descended the Ohio under General

---
(12) See page 481.

Clark. After his return he continued in the command of soldiers, issuing orders to Indian spies and subaltern officers; first as Major and then as Colonel until the end of Indian hostilities about 1795. He was a faithful and vigilant officer during all the years of the war that they knew him. Abbott, the Justice, vouched for Carpenter and Cottrell as "credible men and their statements entitled to full credit."

To the foregoing testimony was added that of Jacob Bush, November 24, 1832. Bush, whose declaration for pension appears in Chapter X, this volume, knew Lowther as early as 1779, at which time he was captain. He was then promoted to the rank of Major, and in 1781 was with Col. Crockett in General Clark's campaign. Upon his return was made Colonel, and so continued until the close of the Revolutionary War and Indian hostilities in 1795. He was brave and vigilant during the entire Revolution, devoting all of his time and energy to his country's service. He died in 1814, leaving children: Robert, William, Elias, Thomas and Jesse. Thomas never married and was then (1832) dead.

Michael Stump, Justice, testified to the good character of Jacob Bush, which entitled him to full credit on oath. The testimony of two of Major Lowther's men is here given in full.

"Endorsed, *Public Document*, The Executive Department for the State of Virginia, Richmond, Virginia (Weston, Virginia, 11th February), February 23, 1833, submitted to the Council of State and advice required, John Floyd.

"LEWIS COUNTY ⎫
VIRGINIA ⎬ TO WIT:

"Lewis Bonnett aged seventy-one years and Peter Bonnett aged sixty-nine years both personally appeared before the Justices of Lewis county court at the courthouse now sitting at the February term thereof. And severally declared on oath that they voluntarily entered the service of Virginia on the western waters about the year 1780 to descend the Ohio river to act for an indefinite period against the Indians that they embarked on the West Fork of the Monongahelia river, and descended it with many men from what are now Harrison, Randolph and Lewis counties. That they were under the command of Major William Lowther, captain Jonathan Coburn, Ensign Benj. Sills, they were kept a while at Red Stone fort (Brownsville now), thence to Newell's Store (Elizabeth now) and about there and Pittsburg and Mature's Island, below Pittsburg, procured boats [and] provisions for to descend the river to join General Clarke, proceeded down the Ohio as they now think in the spring of 1781. Major Lowther was attached to Col. Crockett's Regiment at Pittsburg. When the troops arrived at the mouth of the little Kachawa, [Kanawha] Capt. Coburn and these affiants and some other soldiers were stationed at Neal's Station to act as Indian [spies] and otherwise as circumstances might require to defend the frontier of Virginia here they parted with their Major who proceeded on down the river with Col. Crockett's Regiment. They saw no more of their Major till after they returned home which was in the fall of 1782. They are of the opinion that Major Lowther returned in 1783. He came back as a colonel and so continued and conducted or commanded spies, rangers and scouts until the close of Indian hostilities about 1794. They knew Col. Lowther until his death which was about 1814 in Harrison Co. These affiants were well acquainted with Jacob Bush a soldier under Capt. George Jackson and Maj. Lowther, he also went on toward Kentucky when they stopped at Neal's Station, now Parkersburg. They further certify that Major Lowther was a brave and excellent officer they knew him when he was a captain, then a Major and lastly a Col.; in this last capacity they often after 1783 acted under him as spies. Subscribed and sworn to in open court this fifth day of February 1833.

his
Lewis X Bonnett
mark
his
Peter X Bonnett"
mark

"Lewis County Court ⎱
February Term 1833 ⎰

"This day, Lewis Bonnett and Peter Bonnett, soldiers in the Revolutionary War, personally appeared in open court and signed and swore to a Joint Declaration of the Revolutionary services of the late Col. William Lowther who was a Major in Col. Crockett's Regiment, and the Court do certify that it appears to them that the said Lewis Bonnett and Peter Bonnett are respectable men, and their statement is entitled to credit.

A copy teste,
J. Talbott, C. L. C."

"At the request of the heirs of the late Col. W. Lowther, I transmit the foregoing statement of two respectable old men in this County. This is (by the heirs) offered as additional evidence of the Revolutionary services of Col. Lowther, on their applications for his land bounty. Please report to me the result of the executive deliberations on this matter as soon as practicable.

Very respectfully, your obt. servant,
J. Wamsley."

Bounty was refused Colonel Lowther's heirs, but for what cause is not known. The evidence of his service is uncontrovertible, and is the best record of his border life prior to 1792 extant. There was no application for pension in his behalf under the Act of 1806, which, however, provided for those only who incurred wounds in the Revolution. The incomplete muster rolls on file in the War Department contain no record of his military career, as evinced in the following communication in response to an inquiry:

"The name William Lowther has not been found on the rolls, on file in this office, of any organization of Virginia troops in service during the Revolutionary War. The records show, however, that one William Lowther served as a *private* in Captain Timothy Hughes' Company, Colonel James Livingston's Battalion, Continental Troops, Revolutionary War. He enlisted December 22, 1776, to serve during the war; was transferred about June, 1779, to Captain Dirck Hansen's Company, same battalion, and was mustered to January, 1782. No later record of him has been found."

In connection with Col. Lowther's military career, might be mentioned that of Sotha Hickman, one of the earliest settlers in the region of Nutter's Fort. It would appear from Hickman's first declaration for pension that he was born on the eastern shore of Maryland, June 10, 1748, and enlisted as a scout under Captain William Lowther at Nutter's Fort in 1780, and served six months, and in 1781, a tour of two months. In 1782 he enlisted for a term of six months under Captain Thomas Nutter, same region. His second declaration executed in Harrison County, July 17, 1832, is of historic value, and is here given in full.

"Sotha Hickman first being sworn, stated that he entered the service of the U. S. as a volunteer under Capt. William Louther of the Va. militia, Lieut. John Pacverz (this is very uncertain), the ensign's name not now recollected and William More being sergeant in the fall of 1780, that he continued in said service until the expiration of six months, the period for which he had enlisted. When he entered the service as aforesaid, he was a resident of Monongalia Co., that while thus engaged in the service at the time aforesaid, he was in no battle or engagement, being employed in watching the frontier and protecting it from the invasions and ravages of the combined Indian and British Canadian troops. That another time he was called into the militia service of the state aforesaid under the aforenamed Capt. Lowther on a report of invasions by the Indians and continued in said service, scouting along waters of Ten mile creek and on the West Fork river and below and around the now town of Clarksburg, then known as Nutter's Fort. That he was again called into service as aforesaid by said officers to repel an invasion of the country made by the Indians and punished them for the murder committed by them on Booths creek, that while thus out there was no skirmish with the enemy, they having immediately retreated and were not to be found and that after being engaged in burying those who had been killed, and in pursuing the Indian trail, he returned after the lapse of 5 or six days. That at another time he was likewise engaged in repelling an invasion of the country made by the Indians and under Captain Lowther, together with Daniel Daripon (?), Nathaniel Davisson, Stuffield, Baker, and others and Lieut. Powers, when considerable mischief had been effected, and when upon coming near to the enemy, they were discovered to be too numerous to be attacked by a body of troops as small as that under the command of Captain Lowther, only about 24 or

25 men, and after burying the killed, 9 or 10, they returned to Nutter's Fort for security, where they had to remain until the Indians withdrew from the neighborhood. That at several other times, he was in like manner called into service and served until the company engaged with him was ordered by the officers in command to return into fort or to their homes. He further states that although he does not remember now, the length of time which he was those several calls employed and engaged in service, yet he feels confident that, independent of his tour of duty, for six months as first stated he was nearly if not quite three months in actual service. Has no documentary evidence to prove his statements, and the last persons he knew of who could substantiate his claim, were a Douglas near the Ohio River and a Gregory in Greenbrier Co. of Va.

his
(Signed) S<small>OTHA</small> X H<small>ICKMAN</small>"
mark

Christopher Nutter testified that Hickman was a soldier under Captain Lowther at the time he (Nutter) was. Hickman was granted a pension of $40.66 a year.

The Douglas referred to by Hickman was evidently Levi Douglass, who was a boon companion of his during the border period.

These men, while trapping on the Little Kanawha, were captured and taken to the Indian towns on the Scioto River. One night they managed to elude the Indians while they were feasting and dancing and by traveling at night, succeeded in effecting their escape. Hickman was a great sportsman and came near being shot by Indians while gigging fish with others one night in the West Fork River, near Nutter's Fort. The Indians surprised them from the bank, and attempted to fire on them, but owing to a heavy fog, the priming in their guns had become wet, which caused them to "flash in the pan." The whites dropped their torch, and escaped to the opposite side of the river.

Notwithstanding all residents in the Trans-Allegheny capable of bearing arms during the Revolutionary and Border wars, were enrolled in some branch of the military, and engaged actively in repelling invasions or making expeditions into the enemies' country, local history has done but little towards preserving their identity. The names of many are lost forever. The fragmentary muster rolls of both Virginia and the War Department are woefully deficient in records of the border militiaman. The names of some of them, however, are found in the archives of the Pension Office, and in the Claims for Bounty Lands on file in the Virginia State Library. Although research in these departments is ofttimes attended with disappointment, occasionally a narration of historic value is unearthed. Such is that of Christopher Nutter whose signature often appears in evidence against those who were dropped from the pension roll subsequent to their re-examination by Singleton.

Nutter made two declarations for pension, one July 16, 1832, the other the 22nd of the following December. From these documents it would appear that Christopher Nutter was born in Sussex County, Delaware, January 21, 1760, and while yet an infant, his parents moved with him to Augusta County, Virginia, where they remained until 1769, and then removed to "Featt" [Fayette] County, Pennsylvania. In March, 1772, they moved to West Augusta, now Harrison County, West Virginia, where young Nutter lived during the rest of his life.

He was residing in Nutter's Fort in 1780 when he volunteered as a militiaman under Captain William Lowther and served six months, ostensibly as scout. In the latter part of May, or first of June, 1781, he volunteered under Captain George Jackson in General George Rogers Clark's campaign to "serve during the war." He left the village of Clarksburg and descended the West Fork and Monongahela to Pittsburg, and from there down the Ohio to its Falls, where Louisville now stands, at which point they landed August 19, 1781. He continued in service "under Captain George Jackson, George R. Clarke and Zachariah Morgan, a colonel, until after the surrender of Cornwallis," when he was discharged, as he remembered, in the same year at Louisville. He was released from further duty because of his indisposition, but all those of Jackson's company capable of service were continued on the roll until after their return to Clarksburg.

During this tour, Nutter states that he was with some continental troops, regiments not recalled, but he remembered Captain Tipton, an officer by the name of Chevay [very illegible], another of Blue, and a major, as he believed, by the name of Wales, who were considered of the regular troops. Captain Tipton and Chaplain were killed near the mouth of Bear Grass, in going to Floyds and Sullivans stations. Nutter was in no battle, but a skirmish took place at the Sandy Island below the Falls while he was in service in which Captain Johnson of the militia and Benjamin Wright were killed, and Jonathan Wright, Michael Umbels, two men named Blair and Armstrong, with others were wounded.

Nutter's subsequent military service was on the Virginia frontier. In 1782 he volunteered in Captain Thomas Nutter's Company and served six months, and in 1783 he again volunteered for a like term in Captain Christopher Carpenter's Company, during which time he was still a resident of Nutter's Fort. He was called out several times by William Lowther, first as Captain and then as Major, and served during his several enlistments as private not less than two years.

Matthias Winters, James Radcliff, Joseph Morris and Richard Hudkins testified in behalf of Nutter, and his service was proven by Jacob Bush and Alexander West who were with him in General Clark's campaign. He was granted a pension of eighty dollars a year. He died February 21, 1845.

Christopher Nutter married Rebecca Moorhead, June 28, 1785, in Harrison County, Virginia. Mrs. Nutter died October 16, 1861. The records contain no list of children.

In 1781, the Land Commissioners of Monongahela County issued to Christopher Nutter a certificate for "300 acres on Suds Run, a drain of Elk, to include his improvement made in 1772." Nutter was only twelve years old when he made the "improvement."

The Pension Office contains no record of Captain Thomas Nutter. *Withers* (13) says that in 1772 Thomas Nutter settled on Elk in the vicinity of Clarksburg, near the Forge-Mills, and that John Nutter settled on the West Fork, "near the place now owned by Adam Hickman."

Thomas Nutter was granted a certificate for "400 acres on Elk, adjoining lands claimed by Sotha Hickman, to include his settlement made in 1775." It was on this tract that Nutter's Fort was built in 1774; and Captain Thomas Nutter, whose name it bore, certainly lived there at that time; and there is no reason for supposing that he was not settled there in 1772, as stated by *Withers*. Surely are these early land records an anomaly, like unto the riddle of the Sphinx.

Nutter's Fort stood about two miles from Clarksburg, on the Buckhannon Pike, and "the trolley line now passes directly over the site of the old fort." Captain Nutter preempted 1,000 acres adjoining his settlement right, and both tracts were surveyed in 1785. The new Fair Grounds are located on this land, and some of it is still occupied by Nutter's descendants.

---
(13) See page 482.

I have not found when John Nutter was granted a homestead but the records show that he claimed lands on Simpson's Creek in 1781.

In the same year a certificate was issued to Mathew Nutter for "300 acres on east side of Elk, to include his settlement made in 1772."

The census of 1782 shows that Thomas, Christopher, Mathew and John were then residents in Monongahela County, Virginia; and all are listed in the enumeration of Harrison County, 1785, with the exception of Mathew, whose name nowhere appears.

LOWTHER COAT OF ARMS.

CHAPTER XXVII

We have a glimpse of Colonel Lowther's military service subsequent to 1791, in the following excerpts from the *Virginia State papers:* (Volume V.)

Letter of Wm. Lowther to the Governor.

"MORGANTOWN, June 7, 1792.

"D'R SIR:

"Agreeable to your request as to my part, as far as relates to my conduct, I will endeavor to give as near as my memory will serve at present, which is as followeth, to wit: I have under my command by order from the Executive (in Harrison County) one Insign, two Sergeants, two Corprils, and forty privates. I was authorized to appoint two Scouts by the Executive, which I have complyed with. And by a letter received from Capt. McMachan of Ohio country was to appoint one more in addition to the two. Capt. McMachan also appointed one in conjunction with the one I appointed by his orders, which four scouts is now under my command, two of which I have at the mouth of the Little Kanaway, the other two on the frontier of the West Fork Settlement. The Rangers, I thought proper to submit the distribution to a council of officers of Harrison, who advised me to station them in three detachments, which I have Done along the West Fork settlements, about forty miles, with a small deviation to wit: the little Kanaway, being an exposed part of the county, and a small station near the mouth, I sent a sergeant and eleven men with the two Spyes or Scouts as above mentioned. In Randolph County, I have under my command a Lieutenant, two Sergeants, two Corporals, and Twenty-five privates, the distribution of which I also left to a Council of the Randolph County Officers, which they have done as followeth: The Lieutenant and fifteen privates including the Sergeant and Corporal in the upper end of the valley, and a Sergeant and eleven men at Buchannon settlement. The two Scouts I was authorized to appoint for that county I have also made and is now under my command with the rest of the Rangers of that place, &c.

"I have the Honour to be, Sir, your most obedient and Humble Serv't." (1)

William Lowther to the Governor,

"January 25, 1793.

"D'R SIR:

"I received your commission of Captain by the Hand of Hazekiah Davison, which I do accept and find myself happy in having it in my power to render service to your excellency and my suffering fellow citizens.

"I gave the vanity to flatter myself that past services has been pleasing, which shall and ought to be motives to Induce me to gain a continuation of yours and my fellow citizen's favor.

"Notwithstanding I have been informed that complaints were to be lodged before you against Lieutenant Whitman and myself, how far the malitious haste proceeded in laying complaints before you, I know not; but is suspicious they have

---

(1) See page 482.

had some effect against Lieutenant Whitman, particularly as I hear he is Discontinued.

"We were both hard Threatened by one of our Scouts which we turned out of service for his ill conduct, and Docked him part of the time he pretende to serve. I have Reason to believe that some of our Delegates from this District were active in doing Mr. Whitman an Injury to the woundin of his carructor and Private feelings.

"Sir, should complaints have appeared before the Executive or any of the Gentlemen of your counsell, I heartily wish they may be made publick, so that Mr. Whitman may have it in his power to do himself Justice before you or a court of law. The Bearer, Mr. Wilson, is able to give you information as Touching the Premises. I presume it will be out of my Power to engage all young Experienced men as Requested by your letter and none but those that are acquainted with the use of the Rifle I wish to enlist. I wish you to Discourse with the Bearer on this subject.

"I have made some progress in the Engagement of men, but find by those who has been service last year they wish to receive their pay for past services before they make any new engagements, which Difficulty I hope will be removed upon the Return of Mr. Wilson, who by me is Empowered to settle my accounts and Receive the money for the year 1792.

"By a former letter I requested you to write if the money was Ready but as you did not write, I take it for granted you are fully prepared.

"I am with Regards, Your very Humble Serv't." (2)

John Jackson to the Governor. (3)

"BUCK HANAN, January 25, 1793.

"SIR:

"I think it my duty to Infirm you that the conduct of Capt. Wm. Lowther, extremely blamable for some time past Instead of attending to his duty, he imployed his time in Gambling, Rioting, &c. he treated the men under him in such a manner that it is thought he can git no others to ingage. Instead of paying his men thar wages would seek occasion to purchase Clames on them and then stop the money. I conceive that only the Intrust, but Reputation and dignity of the commonwealth suffers, tis certainly an Imposition to have a man in public office who disregards the public Intrust. During all the time he has been in service he has not visited the Different stations, but has Imployed himself in amusements of various Kinds If the Information which this gives is Doubted, it may be known from many."

This accusation was sent to the governor by Capt. Bogart, together with a letter commending John Jackson.

Letter of James Wood to the Governor of Virginia, June 14, 1793.

"June 14, 1793.

"SIR:

"On my arrival in the Mongelia district, I found that Capt. Lowther, Ensign Brown, and Ensign Davidson had not enlisted the quota of men assigned to them.

---

(2) See page 482. (3) p. 482.

The two ensigns declined their appointments and I nominated Johnathan Coburn and Bartholomew Jenkins to succeed them. These gentlemen have completed their quota since the men have been mustered, and are now in service. If this nomination should meet the approval of the Executive, I flatter myself, they will be commissioned after visiting all the exposed parts of the western frontier, reviewing the three companies, and mustering such as had not been mustered. I made the disposition which will appear in the inclosed instructions given to Captain Lowther, the Senior officer in the district. The scouts which have been employed in the different parts of the frontier have great merit; they have discovered and fired on several parties of Indians on their way to the Frontier at different times, and who immediately retreated with precipation, and without doing any mischief. If my proceedings should be approved by the Board, I shall think myself amply compensated for my trouble.

"I have the honor to be with the greatest respect, Sir,
Y'r mo. ob't serv't."

June 14th, 1793. Capt. James Wood's Instructions to Captain Wm. Lowther (enclosed in above letter).

"OHIO, 28th May, 1793.

"SIR:

"From my observations on the frontier of this district, I am confirmed in my opinion that to afford the best protection to the Inhabitants, will be to have a respectable force judiciously posted on the banks of the Ohio, in order to effect this purpose, I have placed Lieut. Willis' detachment of Captain Bogard's company at Hilliday's Cove, at the Mingo Bottom, and at the mouth of Shoal Creek. Captain McCollock with his company will occupy the posts on the west bank of the Ohio, above the mouth of Wheeling, opposite the mouth of Grave Creek, at the mouth of Fish Creek, and at Martin's station at the mouth of Fishing Creek. I wish it was in my power to establish a post at the mouth of Middle Island, but there is no Inhabitants, nor possibility of subsisting the men with convenience, I must be satisfied at present with posting twenty-five men at the mouth of the Little Kanawha, either Captain Bogard, Ensign Coburn, or Ensign Jenkins must take post at this place. In your quarter, I hope the scouts already appointed with thirty men to be divided and posted at the mouth of Freeman's Creek, at Salem, or at the mouth of Ten Mile Creek, will be adequate; those small Detachments you will be pleased to post immediately. A sergeant & ten men I think will be necessary to the Upper end of Tigris Valley, and the same number in the Buchannon Settlement, those you will post in the manner you may suppose most likely to render service. I have nominated Johnathan Coburn & Bartholomew Jenkins to succeed Ensigns Brown and Davidson; they both raised their quota of men, which will enable you to make the disposition I have mentioned, and which I trust will be made as soon as possible. With respect to the detachment of your company at present commanded by Lieutenant Evans, I mean them to be posted in the most advantageous manner for the protection of the exposed parts of Monongalia County; as there is no scouts employed on that Frontier at present, it will be necessary for Lieut. Evans to keep small Patrols constantly in his front—you will be pleased to direct him where to take post, and how to employ the men under his command. Ensign Morgan with his detachment is to join Capt. McColloch's company on the Ohio, where he will receive his instructions. You will be pleased to issue your orders for his immediate march; the two scouts in the valley may be discharged as soon as you appoint two others, who are to be attached to the little Kanawlia Station. To you as senior officer on this frontier, will be Confided the Command, superintending, and direction of all the Posts within the district of Monongalia; and to you the Junior officers will be directed to make their reports; and to communicate all material occurances which may arise within their respective commands. As you are the officer on whom the responsibility will be fixed, you are to take your own station at the place where you may think most likely to answer the objects of your command. A report of the State of the frontier, and of the different posts under your superintendency you will make as frequently as opportunity offers to Winchester, where your dispatches addressed to the Governor will be forwarded by the Post Master, Mr. George Norton; or if more convenient to you, forward them to the Postmaster at Pittsburg, from whence there is a regular post via Philadelphia to Richmond etc. * * * (Nothing of importance follows.)

"I have the honor to be with real esteem, Sir,

"Y'r Ob't Servant."

Col. Bogard to Col. Wm. Lowder, Harrison Co., Va.

"October 3, 1793.

"DEAR SIR:

"After my respective compliments to you, I wish to inform you that the Indains has been Near Neels Station, and has taken away 3 horses, and got three days start of us. But we persude them and they crost the Big River at the mouth of Deavil hole, and we followed them to a water called Raccoon creek, which ar alowed to be sixty miles, and all the Men Being in bad state of Health, we could not follow them any further. From thence we went across the country to the falls of Hawking, where we discovered a great deal of Indian sign, whar they had been this summer. Also I will inform you that Mr. Jenkins was taken very sick at our Return Home. I wish to inform you that the Spyes has seen Line of Indians Going up Big Elk River, and I should now be glad that you would send word to the Head of the Valley as soon as possible you can, Sir. I will inform you that there was a Spye Shot by the Indians at the mouth of Big Cannoway, this one was shot through hips, and the other through the arm; the name of the latter was Andrew Lewis, and the name of the other is unknown to us."

John McCollock to the Governor, Richmond, Feb. 8th, 1794.

"I considered it my duty to arrest Lieut. Joseph Biggs of my company of volunteer militia on the charges which I have the honor to enclose. I immediately made a report to William Lowther, Esq., as commandant of the militia in actual service, in expectation that he would Direct a Court Martial. (4)

"I have the honor to be, etc." (5)

P. 179, under date of June 12, 1794, John McCollock writes the Governor:

(4) See page 482. (5) p. 482.

(1) That the Indians "killed 4 and took three of a family at the little Canaway early in May, and killed one man at Marata the last of May. They have killed 4 and wounded 3 men on Allegheny river a few miles above Pittsburgh.

(2) "They are so lacking in ammunition they would not be able to follow the Indians if invaded." (6)

At this time there were many complaints of lack of ammunition and supplies, while the Indians were very active. Pay was more than a year in arrears.

Chas. Wells to the Governor:

"June 13, 1794.

"I am honored with your letter of the 18th of April, by Mr. Boggs, wherein your excellency conceives that I complain of Injury in furnishing provisions at the posts on the River.

"Your Excellency will please to observe that I did not mean the complaint to extend to posts on the River only, the number on the River being increased since the time of Messrs Wood's furnishing, and the Rations demanded at each post. I only wished the privilage of furnishing at the posts mentioned in my letter of the 7th of January.

"Captain Lowther's information to your Excellency respecting my construction of the contract must be very singular, as I have neither seen nor heard from Captain Lowther since I undertook the contract, nor do I recollect of mentioning my opinion to any Gentlemen on the subject.

"In March last, General Biggs mentioned to me that he had wrote to Captain Lowther to meet him at West Liberty to arange the stations before or at the time the troops were to be mustered in Ohio; on which account I attended to get instructions as to the supply, but was disappointed, and as I have not heard from Captain Lowther, or where his detachment is posted, I have drawn the conclusion that he has appointed a contractor to supply the posts under his Immediate inspection, which perhaps was the object he founded his complaint on. If so, I wish him to continue his contractor as the furnishing of his post or posts is not an object with me, and I shall account with him or any other person for Quantity of rations furnished under my contract as soon as the money comes to hand etc.

"In closing, the Indians continue depredations on our frontiers."

Cornelius Bogard to the Governor; Randolph County, Aug. 16, 1794:

"On receiving your orders I raised a Company of Volunteers for the defence of Monongalia District. On the 17th of March last I received orders from Col. William Lowther to station the troops raised in this County at the head of Tygarts Valley and Buchannon river." (7)

Sept. 4, 1794. John Haymond to the Governor:

"Mr. Stilwell, I am informed, is sent by Capt. Lowther for money due the soldiers on our frontiers."

---
(6) See page 482. (7) p. 482.

William Lowther to the Governor; Harrison Co., Feb. 21, 1795.

"I rec'd your Excellency's instructions dated the last of December and have noted the contents thereof. In conformity thereto you will herewith receive the necessary papers and documents, in order that the money may be forwarded I discharged the Scouts and Rangers immediately under my command on the first of this instant, and as Colonel George Jackson, who was appointed by the Executive to muster the rangers of Harrison was on the Assembly, I called upon Capt. John McCally to perform that duty which he did. This I thought would be more proper than to continue them in service till Colonel Jackson returned.

"I have sent you also through Thos. Wilson, Esq., Jonathan Coburn's papers as well as my own, together with the papers of eight scouts of this county, and also two ration abstracts, one for Ensign Coburn, and his men, and one for myself and eleven men including our own additional rations as officers. You will discover they are made out in our own names, as there was no person who was authorized to furnish us with rations by the Executive within one hundred miles of us, except while on the Ohio river, therefore we had to become contractors ourselves. I flatter myself the papers are all properly authenticated. If there is substance I hope your Excellency will not be so particular as to form. They are indorsed and numbered. No. 1 contains my pay abstract, muster rolls of eleven men immediately under my own command etc.

"I beg leave to mention that our scouts and rangers have received no compensation for their two last year's services whereas, those other counties in the district had received a partial payment etc.

To the Governor, 9th April, 1794.

"I am of the opinion it would be best to order the three companies destined for the defence of the Western Frontiers to the Ohio River to be posted at the best stations between Holliday's Cove and the mouth of the Little Kanawha; that Captain Lowther as Commandant of the whole, fix his own station as near the center of his command as possible. That he be instructed to visit the Different Posts, to direct the mode of performing the Duty, and to take the most effectual measures for protecting the frontier of the Monongalia District; and that he forward by post, regular monthly returns of the companies under his command."

(Signed) "JAMES WOOD."

Wm. Lowther to the Governor, April 21, 1795. Clarksburg.

"Assigning reasons for docking John Jackson 19 days pay as scout for time taken in attending to his private business and for his discharge from the service.

"Pay abstracts for scouts ordered into service under instructions from the Executive in the year 1792, Harrison County.

"Ellis Hughes, Robert Lowther, David Carpenter, Jonathan Coburn, John Hall, Thomas Herbert, Watson Clark, William Haymond, Christopher Carpenter, Obediah Davison."

Wm. Lowther to the Governor, Aug. 24, 1795, Harrison County.

"From the repeated depredations committed by the hostile tribe of Indians I have been under the necessity at sundry times to call out parties of the militia, but, by the delay occasioned by that round of order, find it still ineffectual. Therefore, by counsel of others with myself, have thought it best to call out a Lieutenant and a company for Harrison and Ensign and company for Randolph, and have also augmented the number of scouts from six to nine for Harrison and Randolph, and keep them stationed in the most exposed part of each county, to be ready at any call, and to continue while necessity may require, or until I have further instructions from your Excellency, and further I flatter myself to meet with your approbation in what I have done etc." (8)

Wm. Lowther to the Governor, Sept. 8, 1794.

"Yours by express came to hand, and I am happy to inform you that the people of this county have discovered no disposition to aid or abet the lawless Pennsylvanians, but still continue their attachment to our happy government.

"In a letter from Gen. Wood, I was desired to forward accurate returns of the situation of the Posts, etc. The posts on the river are not yet fixed. I wrote different times to Captain Bogard to march to the post assigned for his company at Newberry, a few miles above the mouth Great Hockhocking, and he has not complied, and I know not the reason, but expect it is owing to alarms in his own county. However I learn he is now on his way.

"I had appointed the mouth of Middle Island for Ensign Coburn's station." (9)

William Lowther was Colonel of Militia, Randolph County, Virginia, in 1796.

ROBERT LOWTHER, whose name appears on the Monongahela pay abstract for scouts, 1792, was Colonel Lowther's oldest son. William, his second son, also took part in some of the border forays just prior to the Treaty of Greenville. Of this son and his descendants, Rev. Granville Lowther, D. D., says:

"My great grandfather, William Lowther, was Colonel Lowther's son and was an old man when I was a child. Some characteristics of the man are as clear to me as anything of later date. In physical appearance, he was about medium height, but very muscular, high forehead, prominent nose, firm mouth, greyish blue eyes with arching brow, strong, sinewy and erect; but at times a little bent and walking with a cane. Mentally he was optimistic, proud, determined, willful, yet loving and tender as a child. He used to take me on his knee and tell stories of his Indian adventures until in my childish imagination, I could see the chase, the trail, the fight and all the realities of the border

(8) See page 482. (9) p. 482.

conflict. He would tell of how the pioneers lived in log cabins; how they dressed in flax and tow-made garments in summer, and homespun linsey in winter. He told how he used to work clearing land, plowing and hoeing corn from before daylight in the morning until dark at night, with only an hour for noon, and during that hour he would weave on the old hand loom, except what time he was at his meals. Many of the nights were spent in burning brush and logs, which tended to economize time and advance the interests of the one end in view; the conquest of the forest. His example, influence and traits largely stamped the character of his descendants.

To illustrate: "His son, John A. Lowther, was a man of superior strength, who with others were out hunting when they came upon a herd of wild hogs. The old boar showed fight and charged them as they were debating whether to run, climb trees or fight. As he came, John sprang to one side, caught the boar by an ear with one hand and beat him over the snout with a stick until he was subdued.

"John was for a time sheriff of Ritchie County, and when he got his hands on a man neither handcuffs nor other criminal appliances were necessary, for he could outrun and overcome any man he ever met. He at one time went to arrest a wrongdoer, who had taken refuge with two of his friends in a cabin. He approached the house and was about to enter, when his presence was discovered. The inmates sprang to close the door, but not until the officer had thrust his hand through the opening. The shutter was slammed against his arm and the combined weight of the three men pressed against it. With no apparent effort, Lowther flung back the door, seized his man and walked away.

"Another son, Alexander Lowther, (10) my grandfather, was in temperament nervous, quick and excitable; a man of strong will power, who scoffed at the idea of failure. He was hopeful, cheerful and sociable, with enough imagination to have been a poet, novelist or orator; but living where these powers were not in demand, he exercised his imagination in laying plans for the future of his children, building machinery and buying almost every patent device that agents tried to sell to him. He was hospitable to a fault, and for miles in every direction people knew that if they reached 'Uncle Alex Lowther's,' about meal time or night, food or lodging were as free as the water from the well. In this way, he gave to travellers hundreds of dollars, but gained in return the information and sociability they brought into his home, for it was before the days of newspapers, railroads or telegraph, and the principal source of information of a public character was gained from travellers passing from place to place on horseback. He was never a member of church, inclining to a belief in the doctrine of Universalism. When he was approaching death, he appeared for a time a little disturbed about his destiny in the future, until someone read to him the language of Christ, "I was hungered and ye gave me meat; thirsty and ye gave me drink; a stranger and ye took me in; naked and ye clothed me." When the reading was finished, he seemed at perfect ease and to rest his hope of salvation upon it. He was married twice; the first time to Miss Sarah Ireland. By this marriage, there were six sons, viz: Alexander, William I., John A., Jesse, Archibald, Robert and Jackson; two girls, Elizabeth and Sarah. He married the second time the widow Neal. There were no children by this marriage. He died at the age of 62 years.

"My father, Jesse Lowther, was a man of smaller stature, about five feet ten inches high, but very quick and muscular. He is now living at the age of eighty-four years and is still strong. (11) He, too, was of the pioneer type, who knew no defeat and acknowledged no superior. He was captain of Virginia Militia upon the breaking out of the war of the Rebellion. Excitement ran high and many reports of raids and invasions from the Confederates were rife. The colonel had ordered his regiment to West Union, West Virginia, to meet a supposed enemy and to guard the town. My father mounted a horse and rode it down, gathering his company. He rode a second one down getting equipment and necessary preparations for the journey and camp. Then they started on a forced march of eight miles across the hills to West Union. When about half way, they were met by the colonel on horseback, who in anger and excitement commanded: *'Quick step. Run into town.'* My father retorted 'Run yourself. We will be there to assist in any fight you may have on hand when we arrive.' This was insubordination, but he had inherited the spirit of his ancestors and brooked no intolerance, even from his commandant."

---

(11) See page 482.

Mr. Granville S. Lowther, previously quoted, a great grandson of Col. Lowther, line of his son Jesse, tells me that soon after the Treaty of Greenville, Col. Lowther's boys all immigrated to the Ohio, and settled about Marietta, and on the Muskingum. Chills and fever drove them back to their former home, where some of them settled on the West Fork near West Milford, Harrison County, which is known as the Lowther "Settlement." Others located on Hughes River, Ritchie County, West Virginia, and formed there a "Lowther Settlement" where many of their descendants still live.

Col. Lowther, born 1742 or 1743, died October 28, 1814, and is buried in the cemetery of his home farm, on the West Fork. His grave is marked with a rough stone, which still bears his initials (or name,) but all other inscriptions are practically defaced by time. There is a movement on foot to mark his grave with an appropriate block of granite. His wife, Sudna Hughes Lowther, survived her husband several years, and died at the home of her son, Elias, in Ritchie County, West Virginia, and lies in an unmarked grave on the Flannegan farm, on Hughes River, above Berea. Mrs. Lowther is said to have been low in stature and dark complexioned.

There is confusion regarding the relative ages of the colonel's children, but Mr. G. S. Lowther has given what is believed to be the correct genealogy. Mr. Lowther copied the record with its explanatory note from an old Bible now in his possession, which belonged to his uncle, Jesse G. Lowther:

"Robert Lowther, born ——, 1765; Thomas Lowther, born 7 day March, 1767; William Lowther, born 27 Jan, 1768; Jesse Lowther, born 21 July, 1773; Elias Lowther, born 16 Sept 1776; this was taken from Grandfather's Bible by me, Jesse G. Lowther."

Colonel Lowther's old Bible cannot be located, and is supposed to have been lost some years ago.

It has been impossible to secure a genealogy of Colonel Lowther's descendants, other than that of his two sons, Robert and Jesse.

Robert's children were: William B. Lowther, married —— Coburn; Jesse G. Lowther, married —— Switzer; Robert J. Lowther, married —— Eliza Highland; Dr. John C. Lowther, married —— Prichard; James K. Lowther, Jr., married —— Knight; "Peggy," married Thomas Ireland; Susanna, married Abraham Morrison.

The children of Jesse Lowther were: Dr. Jesse Lowther, Dr. Robert Lowther, William Lowther, Uriah Lowther, Elias Jackson Lowther, married Miss Celina McWhorter; Mary Ann, married William Hall; Sarah, married William Norris; Drusilla, married Bradley Morgan; Millie M., married Daniel Wire; Elizabeth, married Conrad Kester.

CHAPTER XXVIII

There was a settler at West's Fort who did much towards developing the country, and ameliorating the condition of the pioneers. This was Henry McWhorter who was born in New Jersey, November 13, 1760. A note in *Border Warfare* (1) states that he was born in Orange County, New York. This data was taken from his old gravestone, and is erroneous. The same note places the date of his arrival on Hacker's Creek six years too soon. Of his antecedents, but little is known. His father, a linen weaver by trade, hailed from northern Ireland (date unknown) and settled in New Jersey prior to the French and Indian Wars. The name is Scotch. J. P. MacLean, Ph. D., an authority on Scotch Highland literature and clan history, says, that the family belonged to the "Clan Buchanan," located along the eastern shores of Loch Lomond, Scotland. The Highland appellation was "Na Canonaich." The coat of arms is given in illustrated clan works. The badge was "Bilberry." The slogan was "Clare Junis," this being the name of an island in Loch Lomond.

Mr. George C. McWhorter says: "The McWhorter family is Scotch extraction. In Scotland the name is now generally written McWhirter. In this country it is now written McWhorter. The family belonged to Galloway, and at an early day formed part of a small clan which bore the name of MacWhorter. Many Scotch Lowlanders, and among them some of the MacWhorters, emigrated to the north of Ireland. One of these families was cut off in the Irish massacre of 1641, save one girl. She married a MacWhorter. Of the history of the MacWhorters, except that they were Protestants, little if anything is known prior to about the year 1700.

"In the beginning of the 18th century we find Hugh MacWhorter a prosperous linen merchant of Armagh. In 1730 he emigrated, at the solicitation of his eldest son, Alexander, to America and settled in the county of New Castle, Delaware, where he became a prominent farmer and an elder in the Presbyterian Church. By his only wife, Jane, he had eleven children. He died in 1748. Of his numerous children the eldest, Alexander, who had been educated for the Presbyterian ministry and had

(1) See page 482.

spent two years in the University of Edinburgh, died in 1734 without issue: John removed to North Carolina: Nancy married Alexander Osborne of North Carolina, and Jane married John Brevard of the same state. The descendants of John, Nancy and Jane are numerous and have doubtless found their way into various parts of the south.

"The youngest of Hugh MacWhorter's children, the second Alexander, was born July 15, 1734 O. S. He subsequently became distinguished as the Rev. Alex. MacWhorter D. D. A sketch of his life will be found in the funeral sermon preached by the Rev. Dr. Griffin on the occasion of the death of his venerable predecessor in the pastorship of the First Presb. Ch. at Newark; also in one of the Presb. magazines for 1853. Appelton's Cyclopedia likewise contains a biographical notice of Dr. MacWhorter from the pen of the late George MacWhorter, grandson of Dr. McWhorter: and corresponding member of the Historical Society of New Jersey. Alexander MacWhorter, D. D., was born July 15, 1734, O. S. Died July 20, 1807.

"In 1758 Dr. MacWhorter married Mary Cumming, daughter of Robert Cumming, of Freebold, High Sheriff of the County of Monmouth; and sister of the late Gen. Cumming of the Rev. Army. He left four children viz.:

"(1) Mary who married Samuel Beebee, a merchant of the City of New York.

"(2) Ann who married the Rev. Geo. Ogilvie, Rector of the Episcopal Church at New Brunswick.

"(3) Alexander Cumming McWhorter, born 1771, died October 8, 1808. (See account below.)

"(4) John McWhorter who married Martha Dwight of Newark, by whom he had three children, only one of whom, Margaret McWhorter, spinster, is now living. (1865)

"Alexander C. McWhorter (see above) was the first to change the spelling of the name. (2) He was a distinguished member of the New Jersey Bar and one of the most eminent citizens of Newark. Coleman, of the New York *Evening Post*, at the time of Mr. McWhorter's death wrote and published a very fine obituary of him. Alex. C. McWhorter married Phoebe Bruen of Newark, and sister of the late Matthias Bruen of Perth Amboy, N. J." (3)

"McWhorter, George Cumming, of Oswego, New York, president and compiler of the Oswego City Library, holds several prominent lay positions in the
(2) See page 482. (3) p. 483.

Protestant Episcopal Church; son of George H. of Oswego, N. Y., B. at Newark, N. J., June 18, 1795, D. at Oswego, N. Y., June 1, 1862, for many years a prominent citizen of Oswego, author of Handbook of the New Testament, Church Essays, etc., a prolific writer for the press, held several positions of honor and trust, member of Prot. Epis. Ch. (m. Feb. 9, 1819, Margaret T., dau. of John Lawrence, judge advocate-general of the Rev. Army, and conducted the trial of Andre); son of Alexander C. of Newark, N. J., b. there 1771, D. there October 8, 1808, an eminent lawyer (m. 1790, Phoebe, dau. of Caleb Bruen of Newark, and sister of Mathias Bruen, a leading citizen of Perth Amboy, N. J.); son of Alexander of Newark, N. J., b. at New Castle, Del., July 26, 1734, d. at Newark, July 20, 1807, an eminent Presbyterian clergyman, a friend of Dr. Witherspoon, and under him the First Presb. Ch. in Newark was built, he was Chaplin in Gen. Knox's brigade, was at council of war before the army crossed the Delaware, intimate with Washington, his portrait by Copley is in Yale Gallery, New Haven, Conn. (mar. Oct., 1758, Mary, dau. of Gen. Cumming of the Rev. Army); son of Hugh of New Castle, Del., the first of the name in America. The McWhorters were a small lowland clan, one went to the north of Ireland, whence a descendant, Hugh came to America." (4)

It is reasonably sure that Henry McWhorter was the son of one of the eleven children of Hugh McWhorter, the linen merchant of Armagh, who settled in New Castle, Delaware, 1730. Some of the family, as shown, settled in New Jersey and NewYork, where their descendants still reside.

Henry was one of four known brothers, all famous for their wonderful physical achievements. He was about five feet ten inches high, broad shouldered, weight about one hundred and seventy-five pounds; and was endowed with tireless energy and endurance. He was fair complexioned, had blue eyes, light hair and a Roman nose. His temperament was sanguine, but under complete self-control.

Of his three brothers, Thomas, James and Gilbert, (5) all were "mighty men" of prodigious strength and nerve. James (Jim) was of ordinary size, but a noted athlete. It is related of him, that with his fists alone he knocked out six rugged Keel Boatmen, who came to his mother's house, taking liberties which he would not tolerate.

The rivermen entered the cabin at meal-time and boisterously took possession of the table. Jim was not staying at home but happened to be there on a visit; and hoping to avoid a collision, did not interfere until a protest from his step-father, an aged and infirm Irishman, elicited from the rowdies a tirade of abuse. This was more than the fiery Jimmie could endure, and he perempto-

---
(4) See page 483. (5) p. 483.

rily ordered the men to leave the premises. He was greeted with
a chorus of insulting jeers and a combined onslaught from the
crowd. The undaunted young athlete backed into a corner of
the room and struck so rapidly and effectually that the six were
on the floor at the same time. As soon as they were able,
they picked themselves up and went away. The step-father
proudly striking the hero on the shoulder, exclaimed: "Och
Jammie an' yer the bye fer me."

Gilbert was a good-natured giant, who was never known to
lose his temper but once, on which occasion he "cleaned up the
town." So great was his size, that the calf of his leg filled the
thigh of his brother Jim's pantaloons.

Their father dying prematurely, left the family in penury,
and the boys were "bound out" to work for their board and
clothing. Henry was apprenticed to a mill-wright, and mastered
his trade when but sixteen years of age. He then joined the
Patriot Army as a "Minute Man." These troops were a potent
factor in the Revolution, and like the "Shirt Man" of Virginia,
was a unique figure. McWhorter's declaration for pension, September 4th, 1832, and his re-examination by Singleton, December 7th, 1833, depicts an interesting phase in the career of this class of troops.

He first enlisted in Capt. Wisner's Company of Minute Men,
from Orange County, New York. This was in February or March,
1776, and the men were immediately marched to Fort Constitution, on the North River, and attached to Col. Livingston's Regiment of State Militia; who also was in command of the fort. At
the end of four months, and before the term of enlistment had
expired, the regiment was disbanded.

In the last of July or the first of August, McWhorter again
enlisted from the same County, in Capt. Wisner's Company
known as The Flying Camp; and hastened to Kingsbridge, over
Spike and Devil Creek, and attached to "Col. Isaac Nichols Regiment; under Gen. George Clinton." (5½)

While at this point, several companies were detailed to Long
Island, but while on the way, McWhorter with others, under
Lieut. Langdon was stopped at Fort Washington, on the Hudson,
near New York. While here, the Battle of Long Island was fought,
after which Lieut. Langdon's men were marched back to Kingsbridge and rejoined their former companies.

(5½) See page 484.

The day that the Battle of Long Island was fought, Gen. George Clinton hurried to re-enforce the Americans, but the ensuing night being very dark, he escaped marching directly into the British lines, only by the timely discovery of the danger by his scouts. The next day Gen. Clinton returned with his forces to his old rendezvous, Kingsbridge.

Shortly after this episode, Gen. Clinton moved with his troops to the White Plains. McWhorter was present but did not participate in the battle fought there October 28, 1776. The wing of the army to which he belonged was not brought into action. After this battle Gen. Clinton moved to Peach Hills, on the North River; where McWhorter lay ill all winter. He was sent home on a furlough by Dr. Henry White, and his term of enlistment expired before he was fully recovered.

In April, 1777, McWhorter entered from his home County, Capt. Totliff's Company for one month as a substitute and served at "Peramas Mamaps"(?) (name not clear) and in May (1777) enlisted for three months under Capt. Thompkins, to work on the famous *chevaux-de-frise;* (6) "which was placed in North River just below New Windsor." Capt. Thompkins and one Gray had control of this work. Thompkins, it was said, "turned Tory and piloted the British ships through the gap that had been left."

In August, 1777, he again substituted from his home County, for a term of three months under Capt. Parsons, and was sent to Fort Montgomery, which was under the command of Gen. George Clinton. A few days before the Battle of Fort Montgomery, McWhorter was detailed to attend a ferry across the North River, three miles above the Fort; and thus escaped this engagement. Gen. James Clinton had command of Clinton's Fort, and was wounded in the British attack upon these strongholds.

Immediately upon the expiration of this term, McWhorter enlisted for one month under Capt. John Decker, of the "Insurgent" Militia of New Jersey, and was marched to Woodley, on the Delaware River; where he was detailed on fatigue duty at Red Bank Fort. While there Mud Fort was abandoned by the Americans, who set fire to the barracks. The next day the Fort was taken possession of by the British.

In March 1778, McWhorter went to Northumberland County, Pennsylvania, and volunteered under Capt. Thomas Chaplain, as a Ranger to serve against the Indians of that region. During

---
(6) See page 484.

this time he was frequently employed in guarding the boats carrying provisions to the army up the Susquehanna River.

In answer to some further questions by the court, McWhorter stated. 1. "I was born the 13th day of November in 1760 in the State of New Jersey. 2. "I have the record of my age in my Bible taken from my father's Bible. (7) 3. "When called into service I was living in Orange County, N. Y. Married in Bucks County, Pa., (8) moved from there to Hampshire Co., Va., in 1786, from thence to Harrison County, but now Lewis in the year 1790 where I now live."

Alexander West, William Powers and several others testified in McWhorter's behalf, stating that "as a man of truth he stands as high as any man." On this declaration, he was granted a pension of $73.33 a year, for twenty-two months' service in New York, New Jersey and Pennsylvania Line.

To his second declaration, Mr. Singleton gave this endorsement:

"This is a very intelligent and honest man and is entitled to all that has been awarded him."

However, his allowance was reduced to $60.00 a year, on the grounds that four months of his enlistment had been employed against the Indians. Apropos to this is the following:

"WESTON, [VA.,] April 20, 1835.
"SIR:
"My pension certificate has been required to be returned for correction and as I understand will be reduced from allowance for twenty-two months service in the Rev. War, to 18 months on the ground that four months were for services against the Indians—it is true that much time was employed against them—but whatever of the time I was not engaged against the Indians was employed on other duties and it is equally true that the officers under whom I served was employed by the Gov. either of the state General Government. I am now very old and infirm and must submit to whatever may be done in my case still it seems to me that my right to an allowance for twenty-two months service is just as clear as it is to eighteen months.

"Mr. Singleton examined me twice and each time pronounced my claim good and states he so reported. I had much rather have nothing than by a false statement of facts to receive from the government one dollar unfairly.

I am with respect, etc.,

Henry McWhorter

---

(7) See page 484. (8) p. 484.

On August 1, 1783, in Bucks County, Pennsylvania, Henry McWhorter was married to Miss Mary Fields, a noble woman, to whom he owed much for his success in life. She was born in 1760. From Bucks County they moved in 1786 to Hampshire County, Virginia. In 1790 with their little family, they sought by wagon a home in the wilds of western Virginia, and settled on McKinney's Run, a branch of Hacker's Creek, Harrison County, where McWhorter built a cabin and cleared some land.

THE HENRY McWHORTER HOUSE
Photographed by Professor G. F. Queen, 1894

Mr. Ned J. Jackson, a noted "Forty-niner," who then owned it, is seen at the door. The view is fronting the creek on the north.

Three years later, he moved near West's Fort, and on the south bank of the murky "Wiya-nipe," built a house of hewed logs, where he resided for thirty-seven years. This house is eighteen and a half feet wide, by twenty-four feet long. It is substantially constructed, and bears the marked characteristics of pioneer architecture. The chimney, like that of the Tanner house, described in Chapter XXI, is built inside of the room. This was evidently a precaution against a vulnerable point of Indian attack. If constructed on the outside it could have been demolished and an entrance gained through the opening in the wall which was always left the height of the fireplace to guard against possible conflagration. This opening was closed most substantially with stone laid evenly with the outside wall. After Indian hostilities, the cabin chimneys were built on the outside of the house; giving more room on the interior. Logs were sometimes placed upon the eaves of the cabins, to be cast on Indians besieging the door. The fireplace is six feet ten inches wide and three feet six inches high, with a stone arch. The original depth can not be determined under present conditions, as the back wall has been filled in with false work. There are now two rooms on the ground floor, and a garret room under the roof. The building is in a splendid state of preservation, and should be kept as first constructed. Built in 1793, it is the oldest house showing original construction, in the historic Hacker's Creek Valley, if not in central West Virginia. There is a fine hickory grove standing between the house and the pike on the west, grown from nuts planted by Mr. Ned J. Jackson, during the first week in October, 1857. They produce an excellent quality of fruit. Jackson carried the seed-nuts in his hat from Jackson's mill on the West Fork River.

After settling in the wilderness, McWhorter experienced many privations and hardships incident to frontier life. He often went to Winchester with pack horses for salt; and once made the trip in company with John Sims. On their return it grew desperately cold in the mountains. They were compelled to dismount and walk in order to keep from freezing. Sims was at length overcome by the cold, and sat down by the trail to rest. McWhorter, well knowing the subtle nature of the threatening danger, had been encouraging Sims to greater exertion, and now became thoroughly alarmed for his safety. He urged him not to give in, and pointed out the imminent danger of his situation, but to no purpose. Sims begged to be let alone. "I am so tired," he drowsily murmured, "and so sleepy. You go on and I will come soon." McWhorter continued to plead with him, but he rapidly sank into a state of lethargy. The death stupor was upon him, and McWhorter realized that he could be saved only by the most heroic treatment. From a beech tree he cut a keen limb, and trimming it of its branches, he applied it most vigorously to the lower extremities of his half-conscious companion. It required several stinging blows to arouse Sims, who made piteous appeals to be permitted to "take just one little nap." His pleadings were answered only by the fierce "swish" of the beech "gad" cutting the frosty air as it descended in unabated fury on the suffering victim. Finally the pain became unbearable, and Sims starting up, made at his relentless tormentor. This was the result for which McWhorter had been striving, and he dexterously kept beyond reach. Failing in his attempt, Sims again sat down, but only to feel a renewal of pain from the beech switch in the hands

A MOUNTAIN CORN CRACKER

Photographed Jan. 1910, especially for this work. Kindness of Mr. J. A. Heaton

A mountain "corn cracker," located in an unbroken forest, on Hickory Knob Run, tributary of Buffalo Creek, Clay County. W. Va. This is the oldest mill in that region, and is still in service, patrons coming twenty miles to have corn ground. Capacity about fifteen bushels a day. The "jolly miller" is Mr. William (Uncle Billy) Kyle, 74 years old.

of the obdurate Scotch-Irishman. Again did he start up in vain pursuit of the fleet-footed wielder of the effective "persuader." This drama was enacted repeatedly, and until Sims had become thoroughly "warmed up," when realizing the certain death from which he had escaped, and the danger of the situation, he required no further incentive to hasten his lagging steps. The remainder of the journey was made in harmony, and without further incident.

McWhorter crossed the mountains alone on one occasion, and camping one night, he wrapped his blanket about him, and lay down in the cavity made by the upturned roots of a fallen tree which was well filled with dry leaves. The night was cold, and he drew the cape of his great coat over his head and slept in comfort. The next morning he found that he was buried under several inches of snow.

Not of a warlike nature, there is no account of Henry McWhorter engaging in any of the border forays. His life was devoted to peaceful pursuits, and to the betterment of the conditions of those around him. There could not be a more useful artisan, nor one who was more appreciated in the new settlements than a millwright. The old sandstone hand mill manufactured a poor quality of coarse gritty meal. McWhorter as we have seen, was a skilled mill-wright, and in the same year he settled at the fort, he erected a mill on the creek, just below his residence. This mill was built of hewed logs, and the clapboard roof weighted down with poles. It was primarily for grinding corn only, but in later years, when the settlers grew wheat and rye, it was equipped for the manufacture of flour also. It was a fine structure for its day, and later it was improved by having its roof nailed on. It was the first mill built in (now) Lewis and Braxton Counties and for many years the most accessible to the Buckhannon settlement. (9)

Mills of a more primitive type are still to be met with in certain sections of West Virginia. In 1896, my father noticed one of them on the headwaters of the Gauley, in Webster County. It stood in the forest, a quarter of a mile from any residence, and had no other roof than the overhanging boughs. Although no one was in attendance, the mill was "running full blast." One or two bushels of corn poured into the hopper kept it grinding until noon, when another "turn" would last till night. The drooping bough of a neighboring tree came within such close proximity to the hopper, that a squirrel could use it as a pathway, in carrying off the grain. While the "turn" was grinding, the miller and his customer were, perhaps, in the forest hunting deer, or trout-fishing. This was one hundred and six years after the observer's grandfather had built his up-to-date corn mill on Hacker's Creek, not more than fifty miles away.

An amusing incident occurred within the present century during a court proceeding in Webster County, West Virginia, where the value of one of these "corn crackers," as they are still called, was in question. A typical mountaineer was on the witness stand.

"You have seen the mill in question, have you not?" asked the attorney.

---
(9) See page 485.

"I reckon I hev."
"You go there to mill occasionally?"
"I take co'n thar onst in er while."
"What is the value of this mill?"
"Hit aint got no valer."
"You don't mean to say that this mill is of *no* value?"
"I 'low thets w'ot I sed."
"But it must be worth something; what is its capacity?"
"Hit aint got no kerpasity."
"What? has *no* capacity?"
"I 'low thets erbout hit."
"Did you not just now say that you go there with corn occasionally?"
"I aim ter go thar onst every two weeks."
"Yet you insist that this mill has no capacity notwithstanding you have grinding done there at least twice a month."
"I 'low thats ke-rect."
"Have you not seen this mill in operation?"
"I kalkerlate thet I hev seed her a humpin' ok-kasionally."
"Well, how fast can it grind?"
"Jes' middlin."
"Will you tell just how rapidly the corn passes between the burs, or grinding stones of this mill?"
"Bout ez fas' ez a man kin eat."
"How long could he keep this up?"
"Ontil he'd starve ter death, I low."

It would appear from *Withers*, that there was a mill on Hacker's Creek in 1778, when Isaac Washburn, "who had been to mill" on this stream, was shot from his horse and killed while returning to Richards' Fort. (10)

This was evidently a "hand mill," even these rude implements for manufacturing meal were not common in the settlements. When a boy I saw a fragment of one of the stones of a mill of this kind lying by the roadside near the old residence of John Hacker, on Hacker's Creek. (11) Usually corn was crushed in crude mortars.

No patron, man or child, ever left the McWhorter mill either cold or hungry. I well remember, when a lad, listening to an old man who told how, when a little boy, he would in the dead of winter ride horseback, perched upon a grist of corn, all the way

---
(10) See page 485. (11) p. 485.

from the Upper Hacker's Creek Valley to this mill. How his breeches would "scruch" up and leave his legs bare, and by the time he arrived at the mill, his shins would be blue with cold, and so chilled and numb that he scarce could walk. The old man's voice grew tender with emotion, as he added, "Then gran-daddy McWhorter would take me to the house and get me warm, and give me some dinner."

One year there was a dearth of crops throughout the settlements, and parties from Clarksburg and other points, offered McWhorter one dollar per bushel for all the corn stored in his mill. He declined the offer, saying, "If I let this corn go, my neighbors will suffer for bread." He kept the grain, and let the needy settlers have it in exchange for labor, giving the accustomed bushel of corn for a day's work, notwithstanding wages were only twenty-five cents a day. Money in those days was not plentiful, and the virtue of such unselfish generosity by one who was as poor as the majority of the settlers cannot be overestimated. In 1790, a sacrifice of this nature was made by Isaac Williams, the founder of Williams Station, on the Virginia side of the Ohio, opposite the mouth of the Muskingum. This deed immortalized Williams. (12)

For sixty years McWhorter was a member of the Methodist Episcopal Church; fifty years of this time he was a class leader. He was conducting a meeting at West's Fort with armed sentinels standing guard, on Sunday, the day preceding the attack on the Waggoner family. During that day Tecumseh and his two warriors lay hid in a ravine near the fort. Had the sentinels given heed to the alarm of the dogs that continually barked, and dashed towards the Indian concealment, the Waggoner tragedy might have been averted. It was supposed at the time that the outcry among the dogs was caused by wolves. Evidently Jesse Hughes was not in attendance at this meeting.

Henry McWhorter was one of the appointed trustees for Weston, when that place was established a town (then Preston), in January, 1818.

In 1827, McWhorter was compelled, through financial embarrassment caused by security debts, to sell his home and mill, and return to his former residence on McKinney's Run; where he died, February 4, 1848. He was buried in the McWhorter cemetery on his farm, by the side of his wife, who died in 1834. For

---

(12) See page 485.

many years, his grave was marked by a sandstone slab, bearing this legend:

> "He first engaged in Freedom's cause,
> And fought for liberty and laws,
> Then counting all earthly things as dross,
> Became a soldier of the cross." (13)

After coming to Virginia, McWhorter lost all trace of his people in the north. It is known, however, that some of their descendants at a later day migrated to the southern states.

The children of Henry McWhorter were three in number: John, Thomas and Walter.

JOHN, the eldest, was born April 28, 1784. Early in life, he studied law and without the advantages of an education, soon became a barrister of extraordinary ability. As an advocate, his logic was hardly surpassed, and his judgment on contested points unerring. Not through his long career at the bar was he ever known to champion the cause of wrong. Although of a reckless nature during his earlier years, his respect for Christianity, even in his wildest moods, was proverbial. He has been known while at the card-table, to throw down his "hand," and in scathing words, rebuke a boon companion for irreverent reflections on Christianity. His generosity and kindness of heart were unbounded, and he was ever ready with loosened purse-strings to relieve the needy and the distressed. He was never married. From his earliest childhood he was noted for his eccentricity and absent-mindedness; and many are the amusing incidents related of him in this respect.

Like most lads reared in the forest, he was fond of the rifle. One morning he was charging his gun preparatory for a deer-hunt, when his mother requested that he first bring a pail of water from the spring near the edge of the clearing. Hastily laying aside his rifle, he snatched a bucket and forgetting his errand, strode directly past the spring. Oblivious to everything but his expected hunt, he was soon buried in the deep woods of the hillside. Cautiously wending his way, he soon discovered a buck standing partly concealed by the intervening brush. While seeking a point more advantageous for a rifle-shot, the irrepressible bucket pending from his arm came noisily in contact with a log over which he was stepping. This brought the dreamy lad back

---
(13) See page 485.

to the realities of life with startling effect, as he saw the alarmed buck bound away.

He was commissioned Captain of Militia and when the War of 1812 broke out, raised a company of volunteers (14) and with this band footed it to Parkersburg, where they embarked on flatboats for Point Pleasant. There the men were mustered into service, and on the 16th of November, 1812, he was commissioned Captain in John Connell's First Regiment Virginia Militia. They then proceeded on foot to the Maumee River and were attached to Gen. Harrison's command at Fort Meigs, until April 13, 1813, at which time their term of enlistment expired. On the return trip, which was made on foot, one of the men becoming exhausted, the Captain relieved him of his camp baggage, adding it to his own burden.

In 1814 he was in the recruiting service of the United States and March 17, 1814, he accepted a captaincy in Colonel William King's Third Regiment, U. S. Rifles; and continued in service until the close of the war. He was then commissioned Colonel of Militia, and was ever afterwards known as "Colonel," and in later years as "Judge." Although his law office was in Clarksburg, his interests were centered largely in the southern part of the county, now generally embraced in Lewis County.

With the settlers throughout this region the young Colonel was very popular, and when a division of the county was agitated, by common impulse they demanded that he represent their cause in the coming session of the Legislature. In this race, he had strong opposition, but his colleague, Dr. Edward Jackson, had a clear field. Under the old constitution of Virginia, all voting was done at the county seat, where the polls were open three days. It was very difficult to secure a full cast of the votes, scattered over so vast a region. But the Colonel was equal to the emergency, and at his call, the settlers flocked to the polls from the Kanawah, Upper West Fork, and other remote settlements; dressed in their best homespun. Each man carried a rifle, also a knapsack containing a "johnny cake" (a corruption of journey cake) and jerked venison. Money for tavern bills was not dreamed of. Hunting en route to the polls was indulged in by many, and no small amount of game secured. This was turned over to the friends of the candidates, who were expected to entertain the voters during their stay at the polls. It was understood that the

---
(14) See page 485.

Colonel was to deliver the voters, while Jackson and his friends were to see that they were cared for.

The opposition, having secured the leading hotel, the home of Dr. Williams became headquarters for the Jackson-McWhorter party. Here, for three days and three nights, the savory pot ceased not to boil, and often during this time Mrs. Williams, in doing her work, was compelled to step over the bodies of sleeping men, with scarce room to set her foot. Notwithstanding each candidate had a barrel of whiskey and tin cup at the polls, and after casting his vote, every man was at liberty to help himself, yet Mrs. Williams and her family were treated with the highest respect by these rough honest woodsmen. Many others found commodious quarters by roaring camp fires in the adjoining woods, where the appetizing venison roast, the merry jest and the wild hunter stories, regaled the passing hours.

The Colonel was elected, and in 1816, he and Dr. Jackson originated the bill that created Lewis County. Buckhannon was constituted a town the same year, and the Colonel was one of the appointed trustees. He afterwards served in the Upper House of the Virginia legislature, and was for many years Prosecuting Attorney of Lewis County and Braxton County, residing at Weston.

Mention has been made of his great absent-mindedness. This trait grew with years, and the cares of public life. Many amusing incidents are related of him in this respect. One was his "bachelor day" efforts at tailoring; after fifteen minutes spent in diligently sewing a button to his coat, he let go the button only to see it fall to the floor. By the roadside near his house, and where he had passed hundreds of times, stood a large black gum tree, whose branches hung low over the highway. In the autumn this tree was laden with dark rich-looking berries of nauseating bitterness, but in appearance not unlike the sweet palatable black-haw, of which the Colonel was extremely fond. One day, with mind deeply engrossed, he rode under this tree, when the berries hanging so temptingly near arrested his eye. He snatched some of them as he passed by, and emptying his mouth of a "quid," filled it with the supposed haws. The effect can be better imagined than described, and unlike the traditional Christian, the Colonel invoked his God after the feast.

He was passionately fond of "egg custard," and at a banquet

in Clarksburg, he helped himself liberally to what he supposed was his favorite dish. The slave-waiter, who was aware of the Colonel's weakness, approached and said politely, "Colonel, dat am not custard, it am ground hoss-radish." Humiliated at his own blunder, and irritated at what he regarded as an impertinence in the waiter, the Colonel exclaimed, "I reckon I know what I am doing." He then filled his mouth with the fiery portion. Tears rolled down his cheeks; but otherwise he endured the excruciating torture with the stoicism of an Indian warrior.

He was notorious for his bad penmanship, irritable temper, and emphatic expletives. While Prosecuting Attorney, he one day presented to the Court an indictment drawn in his own handwriting; so intricate and unintelligible to the clerk did it appear, that that dignitary's most scholarly efforts failed in deciphering its meaning. The Colonel was called upon for a "translation."

John McWhorter

SIGNATURE OF CAPTAIN JOHN McWHORTER, AS IT APPEARS WITH HIS APPLICATION FOR PENSION, MAY 27, 1781

Solemnly scanning the document for a moment, a puzzled expression came over his face. Utterly unable to read it, he was about to lay it down, when becoming irritated at the suppressed tittering of the bar, he burst forth, "Now who in hell wrote this, why the devil couldn't read it." When informed that it was his own production he bravely declared that "anybody could read it," and proceeded to do so without further trouble. Members of the bar often amused themselves, and disturbed the dignity of the court, by stealing the Colonel's papers when he was deeply absorbed in pleading. "Just to hear him rave," they said, and seldom, if ever, were they disappointed. His voice, a deep gutteral bass, was, unless provoked, low and well modulated, his language sedate and dignified, but on such occasions, he was licensed to "swear in open court," which he would do most beautifully.

A client one day asked him to fight some litigation through the courts. The Colonel listened in polite silence as the gentleman unfolded his plan, but it was obvious that he was growing indignant at the brazen duplicity of the plotter. To the anxious inquiry, "Colonel, can I win the case?" came the prompt reply, "That depends upon the jury. If you have an unscrupulous or fool jury, you are likely to win; but if you have an honorable and intelligent jury, they will see at once that the whole scheme is based upon damned rascality." The case never appeared in court.

After withdrawing from the bar, he served as Judge of the Lewis County Court under the old regime for several years. When old age compelled his retirement from public life, he was ordained a local minister in the M. E. Church. It was through his means that a small church was built on Rush Run, in Lewis County, where he often preached. He died April 14, 1880, and was buried near his home on Rush Run.

THOMAS, the second son, born July 15, 1785, inherited a part of the home farm on McKinney's Run, and was a prosperous farmer. He was a man of sterling worth to his community during his short life. He died December 28, 1815, and was the first buried in the McWhorter cemetery.

On Easter morning, 1807, Thomas McWhorter, married Delila Stalnaker, daughter of Samuel Stalnaker, Sr., an old resident of Hacker's Creek. Their children were Tabitha, married David H. Smith; Henry, married Hannah Jones; Salina, married Elias J. Lowther; Rulina married Washington Sleeth; Mary, married Hamilton J. Nutter.

His only son, Henry, was a commissary Sergeant, Company E., Third West Virginia Volunteers Cavalry. He was killed in a fight at the Gibson house on Greenbrier River, Pocahontas County, West Virginia, January 22 or 23 (near midnight), 1863. Early in the engagement, he fell mortally wounded, and congratulated himself that it was his privilege to die in battle for his country. A few moments later he was shot through the heart.

Two of his sons were non-commissioned officers in the same company and saw their father killed. One of them, Fields, was captured and sent to Libby Prison, but at the end of three months was exchanged and returned to his regiment and promoted to Commissary Sergeant.

At the battle of Sailor's Creek, Virginia, three days before Gen. Lee's surrender, he captured a confederate flag and received the guns of seven prisoners, for which he was granted a thirty days' furlough. For this signal bravery, it is said that he was awarded a special medal by Congress, but this I have not verified.

He participated in the Battle of Salem, Virginia, December 1863, and on the retreat in crossing a badly swollen stream, a four-horse team became stranded and were drowning. General Averil ordered McWhorter to swim out and cut them loose, which he successfully accomplished. The team was saved, but the health of the brave soldier was ruined forever. It was bitter cold, and within a few moments after emerging from the icy waters, his clothing was frozen stiff. He contracted a severe cold, which settled on his lungs, and ultimately caused his death in April 1877.

The other son, Rev. John S. McWhorter, M. D., was also in the Salem fight where he suffered extremely from frozen feet. While at Salem he called at a house for a lunch, for which he paid the woman fifty cents. The hungry soldier devoured this and came near dying; the food contained poison. Afterwards he contracted kidney trouble, followed by a severe attack of pneumonia. Finally he was injured by the fall of his horse, from which he has never fully recovered. He served as a corporal.

WALTER, the third and last son of Henry McWhorter, Sr., was born October 31, 1787, married Margaret Hurst in 1806. He inherited, with his brother Thomas, the homestead on McKinney's Run. Under the old military law, Walter was Major of Militia. He was a noted athlete, and never met his equal in wrestling, jumping or foot-racing. Lithe and active, and fond of daring sports, he would toy with a living rattlesnake, avoiding its quick, deadly blows with all the ease of an East Indian snake charmer. He delighted in hunting, and often engaged in this fascinating sport. (15) In one of his hunts he fired at a deer, which fell seemingly dead. When he attempted to knife it, he was "kicked so high, that when he landed from his aerial flight, the deer was bounding away."

At another time, he and his son-in-law, Samuel Stalnaker, were hunting on the headwaters of the Buckhannon, and found where a bear had gone into winter quarters in a cleft among the rocks. They succededed in routing bruin, who proved large and very fat. The entrance to the den was small, and the animal was some time in squeezing through. Stalnaker took his stand in front, with rifle levelled to fire the instant that the bear had emerged sufficiently, that when shot, it would not drop back into the den. The Major stood just over the entrance, with tomahawk raised

---
(15) See page 485.

ready to strike, should the shot prove ineffectual. Stalnaker gave warning that he was "going to shoot." The Major withheld the blow, as he afterwards said, "expecting every instant to see the fur fly, as the half-ounce of lead crashed into the bear's skull." In another moment, he did see the "fur fly," but intact with a very lively bear, which wriggled through the crevice and scampered away. After the animal had disappeared, Stalnaker was humiliated to find that in his excitement he had failed to draw back the hammer of his rifle.

There was no church in the neighborhood, and the Major's house, as with his father, was the recognized place of public worship. It was also the free home of the itinerant minister, and traveller. His wife cheerfully bore this additional hardship to the burden of caring for a large family, without murmur or complaint. It was the unenviable privilege of the Major's boys to cut and haul from the forest a store of hickory wood, for the great open fireplace, during the "winter revivals." These revivals, or "big meetings," with their "mourners bench," were regarded as an essential adjunct to the spiritual welfare of the community. Occasionally an amusing feature would bubble up at these meetings. One poor sinner who had "wrastled" at the altar night after night, and concluding that an open confession was the only road to salvation, exclaimed in a loud voice, "Lord, *why* is it that I cannot get a blessin' "? Then as if in answer to his own interrogation, he continued, "I know, Lord! I-have-cussed-and-I-have-swore; and-I-have-back-bitten-my-neighbors, and, L-o-r-d, how-I-have-l-i-e-d!" It is hoped that this penitent found that peace of mind which his honest confession merited.

Walter died August 12, 1860. His wife died December 27, 1853, from injuries sustained in a fall from the back of a runaway horse. Both were buried in the McWhorter cemetery. Their children were:

    (1) Dr. Fields McWhorter, married Miss Margaret Kester.
(16) His second wife was Sarah O. Darr.
    (2) Mary McWhorter, married Benjamin Morris.
    (3) Elizabeth McWhorter, married Samuel Stalnaker, Jr.
    (4) Rev. Eli McWhorter, married Jane Morris.
    (5) Levi McWhorter, married Eliza Alkire.
    (6) Sally McWhorter, married Nicholas Straley.
    (7) Cassandra McWhorter, married William Colerider.

---
(16) See page 485.

(8) Mansfield McWhorter, died while young.

(9) Thomas McWhorter, died while young.

(10) Rev. John Minion, M. D., married Rosetta Marple; second wife, Phoebe C. Cunningham, nee Hardman.

(11) Walter, married Ailcey Lawson.

(12) Rev. Mansfield (named for his deceased brother) married Sarah Francis; second wife, Sarah Davis.

(13) Margaret, died before maturity.

(14) Amy, died before maturity.

(15) Elsie, died before maturity.

(16) Gilbert, died in infancy.

(17) Marion, died in infancy.

Of this family, only two are now living, Dr. J. M. and Rev. Mansfield. The latter was second Lieutenant of Militia and was for sixteen years a magistrate and a member of the Lewis County Court under the old regime. Both he and Eli, the eldest son, were ministers in the M. E. Church. Dr. J. M. espoused the Universalist faith, and was the pioneer promulgator of that doctrine in his part of the State. He used to say that when a boy he spent days cutting wood for the "big meetings" held by the Methodists at his father's home and while thus engaged, the preachers were remorselessly shaking him over the fiery lake for his unrighteousness.

In May, 1909, at the age of 87, the Doctor visited his boyhood home of which he writes:

"The old McWhorter stand in Harrison County is all blotted over with dwellings, factories and one or two stores. It does not look like the home, when mother stood on the high front porch and called us boys to dinner. I took a drink from the old well, whose fountain is still pure and cold; but the noise and confusion of public life has destroyed the beauty and harmony of our old home. As the world progresses the hum and bustle of trade silences the sweet music of domestic life, and reminds us that our existence is—

'but one breath from Times old hoary nostrils blown,
As scouring o'er the spacious earth, we hear his dismal moan.'

—a short span, and we too must pass on to the great unknown, silent and mysterious." (17)

During the latter thirties and early forties, Major McWhorter held contracts for carrying the mail from Clarksburg to distant points in Lewis, Gilmer, Braxton, Upshur, Barbour and Randolph Counties. The mail was carried horseback, and J. M. and Walter

---

(17) See page 486.

did the riding. Most of the route lay through unbroken forests and was fraught with many dangers. The boys were never armed, and in a few instances met with thrilling adventures, one or two of which have been recorded elsewhere in this volume. Walter was waylaid by two highwaymen in the Cheat Mountain, and escaped capture only by his cool bravery and remarkable presence of mind. These boys often swam their horses through the waters of the West Fork, Little Kanawha and Tygart's Valley Rivers, when the "mush ice" was running. They would get up at three o'clock in the morning, in the dead of winter, and ride fifteen miles for breakfast; that too, with clothing frozen stiff with ice from fording the deep unbridged streams. They rode sixteen hours out of the twenty-four with only two meals a day. The compensation for horse and rider was one dollar per day. The savings were applied to a grinding family debt. The same spirit of energy prompted these boys, when young men, to engage as helpers in driving stock on foot to Baltimore, Maryland, at twenty-five cents per day. On the return trip they were allowed one cent per mile for walking, with two meals a day. With the money earned on these return trips, the older brother, J. M., paid for his wedding suit, resplendent with brass buttons, and the cloth costing five dollars a yard. He also engaged in freighting with a six-horse team from Cumberland, Md., to Clarksburg, (West) Va., and from Parkersburg to Beverly, (West) Virginia.

Walter was instantly killed by a passing train on April 16, 1901, at a railroad crossing near his own gate.

DR. FIELDS MCWHORTER, like his father, was a noted athlete. He later moved to Sullivan County, Missouri, and was a Fife Major in the 23d Missouri Regiment, Federal Army, participating in the Battle of Pittsburg Landing. He had two sons in the same army.

WALTER F. MCWHORTER, sergeant in Company B., 9th Virginia Regiment, was killed at the battle of Cloyd's Mountain, Virginia, May 9, 1864. He had served during the entire war, and was a soldier of more than ordinary fighting ability. It is related of him that he was not only daring on the field of battle, but was absolutely immune to fear.

A singular incident is connected with his death. Although shot through the heart, he was not instantly killed. The regimental surgeon saw him fall and hastened to his side. The dying soldier asked the surgeon to examine for the ball, which was found lodged under the skin at his back. This he requested removed. He was informed that it was useless, as he could not live. "I know that," he gasped, "but I want you to give the bullet to my brother Henry." His request was granted, and the conical minnie ball, whose concave end had collapsed, enclosing a small fragment of the dead soldier's vest, is now in the possession of the surviving brother.

HENRY CLAY MCWHORTER enlisted for the entire war, September 16, 1861, as a private in Company G, 9th Virginia Infantry and on the 30th of the same month was mustered in as Second Lieutenant of Company B, same regiment. On March 1, 1862, he was appointed Captain of Company G, and resigned September 17, 1863, on account of an accidental wound received December 8, 1862, on Patterson Creek, Hardy County, Virginia. During the balance of the war, he was Chief Clerk of Provost Marshals, Enrollment Office (for drafting) at Charleston and Point Pleasant, West Virginia. He was later Speaker of the West Virginia State Senate and Judge of the Supreme Court of that State.

JOSEPH MARCELLUS, an older son of Dr. Fields McWhorter, filled several positions of public trust. Was clerk of County Court of Roane County, West Virginia, State Auditor of West Virginia, an eminent barrister and late Judge of Circuit Court of that State.

He is the oldest great grandson now living of Henry McWhorter of the Revolutionary War. (18)

MARY MORRIS, nee McWhorter, had three sons in the Federal Army. Thomas and Walter M. enlisted September 15, 1862, in Company E, Third Regiment, West Virginia Volunteer Cavalry, and were mustered October 20, 1862.

THOMAS was Second Corporal, *Walter* was promoted Bugler, but as he could not "toot" effectively, he continued a private. Both were fearless soldiers and experienced hard service, not only on the battle field, but with *bush-whackers* in the hills of their native state. Walter has written an interesting manuscript memoir of his personal army life.

WILLIAM H. was mustered March 1, 1864, as volunteer private in Company E, First Regiment, West Virginia Light Artillery, and served to close of war. His hearing was greatly injured by the heavy detonation of his gun.

ERVIN H., son of Rev. Eli McWhorter, was also a volunteer private in the same company during the period of Wm. H. Morris' enlistment. He died soon after the close of the war.

---
(18) See page 486.

CHAPTER XXIX

The Regers were active men on the Virginia frontier during the latter years of the Revolution, and the stormy period that immediately followed. They were not of that class of bordermen, who were likely to be prominent in the recorded annals of their day. They had not that aggressive temperament which immortalized many of their contemporaries. While brave and fearless, and not hesitating to take up arms when occasion demanded, they had early learned that "Every human heart is human," and not in tradition can we find where they ever caused wanton suffering, even to the most deadly of their foes. If they shot fewer Indians than did some of their associates, they at least took out more grubs and planted more corn.

JACOB REGER, the principal founder of his family in western Virginia, came from Germany. He was married in his native country to Barbara Crites, and they with a few of their oldest children landed at some port in Virginia, probably about 1765, although it has been claimed that their arrival was much earlier. It is said that immediately after landing, the children complained of hunger and the mother purchased a loaf of bread at a nearby bakery. She gave them some of it, but was surprised to see them, after tasting it, throw it away. The parents then tasted it and they too threw it aside. It was their first experience with corn bread. They settled in the Shenandoah Valley, but later moved to the Wappatomaka, where they resided until after the close of the Revolution. They then moved to Big Run, near the village of Burnersville in (now) Barbour County, West Virginia.

In 1781, a certificate was issued to Jacob Reager (Reger) for 400 acres on Second Big Run, to include his settlement made in 1776. Reger made an "improvement" there in 1776, but it is known that he did not take up actual residence until sometime after 1782. He was still residing on the Wappatomaka, in April 1782, when Isaac, his youngest child was born. The census of 1782 shows that he was at that time a resident of Hampshire County, Virginia (now West Va.), and was the head of a family of eleven. (1) This illustrates the caution that should be exercised in fixing a positive date of an actual residence settlement, based on the date of the Trans-Allegheny homestead certificates.

---
1) See page 486.

Jacob Reger had a brother John, who was also a resident of Hampshire County, Virginia, in 1782, at the head of a family of four. (2) John Reger improved, or claimed land on Tygart's River. The date is uncertain but it was in the earliest settling of the country. In 1773, he made an "improvement" on the Buckhannon. He at that time entered 400 acres on each side of the river, adjoining lands claimed by Timothy Dorman. Leonard Reger, a sergeant in Captain William Darke's Company, 8th Virginia Regiment, Revolutionary War, was doubtless a son of this John Reger.

Jacob Reger raised a large family of children, and a notice of them, it is believed, will be of interest.

ANTHONY, the eldest son, was a volunteer in the Patriot Army, Revolution. He was commissioned an ensign, April 16, 1777, in Captain Silas Zane's Company, 15th Virginia Regiment, under Colonel William Russell. It is not known for what length of time the young ensign enlisted, nor can anything be learned of his army career. He doubtless saw active service, judging from the fighting record of his commanding officers. (3)

The date of Anthony Reger's advent into the Buckhannon country is not known. In the census of 1782, one Anthony Reger is listed without a family in the enumeration of Hampshire County, Virginia. (4) This was doubtless the young ensign of Captain Zane's Company.

The census of 1784 shows the enrollment of one Anthony Reger, as head of a family of ten, in Hampshire County. (5) This person is believed to be a brother of Jacob Reger, Sr. According to the best information Ensign Reger went to Ohio with his brother Jacob, but nothing is known of his subsequent life. He married a Widow Simmons.

JACOB, JR., the second son, was never married. He seems to have spent his time in the Buckhannon and surrounding settlements. He was a noted hunter, and during the later years of Indian hostilities, was a scout of recognized ability. In this capacity he often rendered valuable service to the settlements on the Upper Monongahela. One Schoolcraft was his associate and boon companion in these hunting and scouting excursions.

During one of their hunts, Reger's dog attacked a bear near their camp in the night. The dog could not be called off, and Reger, got up, remarking, "If I don't go and kill that bear, that

(2) See page 486. (3) p. 487. (4) p. 487. (5) p. 487.

dog will follow it all night." Taking his rifle he sallied forth, and coming near, he shot the bear through the body, but the wound was not fatal. The animal, rendered ferocious with pain, now charged his new assailant with fury. Reger was of gigantic stature and wonderful strength, but he was no match for the enraged brute. It seized him by the hip with its great jaws, and hurled him violently to the ground. It then caught him by the shoulder and "shook him as a dog shakes a rabbit." Things looked desperate for the stalwart hunter, and the fray would certainly have terminated fatally for him had not Schoolcraft hurried to his assistance, and placing his rifle to the bear's side, fired, killing it instantly. Reger was badly hurt. His hip was so mangled, that afterwards in dressing the wound, his brother used a razor freely in cutting away the hanging shreds of flesh.

Tradition says that Jacob Reger, Jr., once owned a tract of land on the Ohio, where Cincinnati now stands, but forfeited the title through unpaid taxes. He is supposed to have died there.

PHILIP, the third son, was born in Hampshire County, Virginia, in 1767. He was still a resident of that county in the spring of 1782, when at the age of fifteen he volunteered as private in Captain James Simmerel's Company, Virginia Troops, Patriot Army, and served six months or until the close of the Revolution, the following November. He was employed in guarding the Yorktown prisoners confined in the Winchester Barracks, Virginia. For this service he was granted a pension in 1832.

But little is known of Reger's life on the border. He was sometimes employed as a hunter in Henry Jackson's surveying parties, and also engaged in scouting during the last years of Indian hostilities on the border. With Samuel Jackson, he was watching an Indian trail on the Upper West Fork waters, and while lying concealed in a thicket, was bitten by a rattlesnake. Reger soon grew blind, and Jackson, a very strong man, carried him and their two guns to the nearest settlement, some ten or twelve miles distant. Reger suffered intense agony from the wound, but under the application of such remedies as were at hand, he eventually recovered.

Philip Reger was one of the appointed trustees for Buckhannon, when that village was created a town in 1816. He was the first Sheriff of Lewis County, and was a Justice of the Peace for forty years. He married twice. His first wife was Sarah Jackson.

His second wife was Mary Bozarth, a daughter of John Bozarth, Sr., whose family suffered the last attack made by the Indians on the Virginia border previously referred to in this volume. (6)

JOHN, the fourth son, who participated in the fight at Buckhannon, was born in Hardy County, Virginia, January 15, 1769. He stood six feet two inches in his moccasins, with well-rounded and muscular proportions. A veritable Hercules, he was renowned for his enormous physical strength, which was unequalled on the western frontier. He married Elizabeth West, "Little Bettie," as she was called, a daughter of Edmund West, Sr., of West's Fort. The wedding took place the year after the bride's father was killed by the Indians, December 5, 1787. At the ceremony the bride sported a "store gown" to procure which the bridegroom-elect walked from the Buckhannon settlement to Winchester and back with rifle on shoulder. During the wedding festivities, the bride stood in midair on the groom's outstretched hand. The newly-wedded couple settled near where Burnersville (Barbour County, West Virginia) now stands, where they resided as long as they lived.

John Reger's nature was as kindly as his physical strength was great. I cannot refrain from giving a few incidents in his career on the border, illustrative of the rude, happy-go-luck of those days. He could easily swim the flood-swollen rivers in his excursions, holding his gun, shot pouch and clothing high and dry in one hand. He was a noted hunter and many are the accounts of his daring feats and great endurance. On one of his hunting trips, he killed a yearling bear early in the morning and after taking out the entrails, he slung the carcass over his shoulder and carried it with him during the entire day's hunt.

As a bear hunter he excelled, and once when hunting with several others, it was agreed that he should hunt for bear, while the rest of the party went for deer. A boy who was with them decided to go with Reger; and it was not long before the dogs engaged a large bear in a dense laurel thicket, where it had its lair. Soon dogs and bear were engaged in a fierce combat, and Reger crawling on hands and knees along a narrow winding path, shot the bear, but not fatally. With the report of the heavy rifle, and the sting of the leaden missile, bruin seemed to realize that things were becoming decidedly hot at home, and that he would

---
(6) See page 487.

John Reger

"THE HERCULES OF THE BORDER"

From a Pencil Sketch, Date Uncertain
Kindness of Miss MacAvoy

vacate. With this sudden impulse, he bolted for the only exit of his domicile, which was completely blocked by the muscular form of the hunter. None but those who have attempted to penetrate the tangled depths of a Virginia laurel bed, can form any conception of its density. When bruin turned in retreat the dogs held on, and a running fight ensued. The hunter had no time to retreat, neither could "he dodge the issue" by stepping aside. His only recourse was to throw himself face down upon the ground, and let the rage of battle pass over him. This he did, and the bear was kept so busy with the dogs, that it had no time for its prostrate enemy. Reger escaped unhurt, and when he emerged from the thicket, his young companion was nowhere to be seen. Reger halloed, and was answered from a nearby gum tree, where the lad had taken refuge.

Perhaps it was during this same hunt that a bear's den was found in a rock-cliff. Reger crawled into the cave and guided by the gleam of the bear's eyes, shot it. He then backed out from the narrow passage and waiting until the death struggle ceased, re-entered feet foremost and kicked bruin on the head to ascertain if life was extinct. Finding there was no response to his most vigorous kicks, he again crawled out, only to re-enter head first. He twined a stout hickory withe about the neck of the quarry, then came forth and with the help of his comrades drew it from the den. (7)

At another time the dogs engaged a bear in a cavity made by an upturned tree, and when Reger came to the brink of the pit, the earth suddenly gave way beneath his weight and he was precipitated onto the struggling mass of bear and dogs. As he went down, he caught with one hand a bush growing on the brink, and the other arm coming in reach of the bear the enraged animal sunk its claws into the sleeve of his strong homespun hunting shirt. The dogs had fastened on the bear's hams, and were pulling with all their might in the opposite direction, while the bear, with equal energy, was endeavoring to drag the hunter's hand within reach of its fangs. The Herculean strength of the mighty woodsman was taxed to its utmost resisting the combined weight and strength of bear and dogs. At times the bear was lifted clear off the ground by the opposing efforts of hunter and dogs. More than once Reger felt the hot breath of the infuriated brute upon his hand, so nearly did it succeed in overcoming the iron sinews of

---

(7) See page 488.

the man. Human strength could not long endure the terrific strain, and the hunter felt that he would soon lose his hold upon the bush. Fortunately for him, one of the dogs let go its hold and seized upon the bear's jaw, when it released its hold on Reger's arm to box away this tormentor. Reger then soon ended the fray with his knife.

Reger went to Winchester on one occasion with pack horses for salt, dressed in homespuns and moccasins. A horse carried two bushels of salt weighing eighty-four pounds per bushel. (8) This amount (measured) was regarded as a sufficient load for a horse whose principal feed consisted of "browse" during its long trip through the mountains. While getting ready his salt, Reger was ridiculed by some of the town gentry and local toughs. The easy-going borderman deigned no reply to their coarse banterings, but when his salt was secured, he lightly slung two sacks over his shoulder, and taking one in either hand, eight bushels in all, walked leisurely to where his horses were tied. This feat gained him the admiration of his tormentors.

The fame of his strength travelled far, and one day, while sitting on his porch, a powerfully built stranger accosted him, and challenged him to fight. Reger, who was peaceably disposed, said that he had nothing to fight for. The stranger insisted and became obdurate, stating that he could whip any man that he had ever met, and hearing of Reger's prodigious strength, had come a long way to fight him and would not be disappointed. Reger would not fight, but he suddenly seized the stranger and threw him upon the porch roof. The pugilist now expressed himself as satisfied, and after partaking of refreshments, he departed without further testing the strength of his self-sought antagonist. (9)

But this good natured Titan was not always so lenient with the braggart. During those days, the militia met for muster at Beverly, and it was no unusual occurrence at such gatherings for a few "ring fights" to take place. There was a stalwart bully by the name of Kerns living in Tygart's Valley, who was the acknowledged champion of the "ring" throughout the surrounding country. At public gatherings, musters, log-rollings, house-raisings and weddings, this redoubted brave would, at an opportune moment, leap upon a stump, flop his arms vigorously and crow. This was a challenge for anyone to meet him in a "square up-and-down fight;" and woe to the hapless aspirant for pugilistic honors who

---

(8) See page 488. (9) p. 488.

had the temerity to answer with a like challenge. Kerns had never met his match. At one of the musters referred to, Reger attended with the avowed purpose of accepting the challenge of this woodstyrant, who had so terrorized his community. When Kerns learned that the "Hercules of the Border" was on the ground, he did not crow. Reger's modesty forbade any exultation over his easily-won victory.

The following incident is related of Reger, and it illustrates his good humor and gigantic strength. Reger had made bacon of some bear meat which he sold to a Mr. Black at twelve and one-half cents a pound. To pay for this bacon, Mr. Black worked for Reger in the harvest field at fifty cents a day. The weather was hot, the work heavy, and Reger would taunt Black by frequently exclaiming in broken English, "Hurrah for de bear pork." It was Reger's eighty-second birthday, and as they were returning to the field from dinner, Black and Reger's son, both large strong men, thought to take advantages of the old man, and "wallow" him. Slipping up, each caught hold of a leg, then throwing him and whirling him upon his back, both immediately sprang on him, one on either side, with arms tightly hugging the old man's shoulders. For a moment Reger lay surprised, and occasionally ejaculating, "Poys, you had better let me be," at the same time feeling for a secure hold in the waistbands of their strong homespun pantaloons. Having secured a satisfactory hold on each, he slowly lifted them from him, swung them in mid-air, cracked their heels together, then jammed their heads together a few times and cast them from him, and laughing, rose to his feet.

John Reger died May 14, 1844, and was buried in the cemetery on his home place. He left four children: Jacob, Abram, Barbara and Elizabeth.

JACOB, married Permilia Arnold. But very little is known of his life.

ABRAM, born 1793, married Leah Brake, daughter of Jacob Brake, hereafter referred to. He was commissioned lieutenant in Captain John Bozarth's Company, Virginia Troops, War of 1812. He was known as "Maje" Reger, but I do not know how he came by the title. Most likely he was Major of Militia after the war closed. Abram Reger had two sons in the Civil War. Rev. John W. Reger, D. D., who enlisted September 2, 1861, as private in the 7th Virginia Infantry, Federal Army. He was shortly afterwards appointed Chaplain, and served in that capacity with only a brief interval, until the close of the war. The latter part of his enlistment was as Chaplain of the Military Hospital at Grafton, West Virginia. The other son, Major Albert G. Reger, espoused the Southern cause, and at the commencement of the war was commissioned captain of the "Barbour Greys," recruited at Philippi, Twenty-sixth Virginia Infantry. He was soon promoted to the rank of Major, and served in this capacity until the close of the war. He saw hard service under Generals Thomas J. (*Stonewall*) Jackson and Longstreet. He was a lawyer of ability, and served in the State Senate for eight years. Another son, Rev. Alfred A., was for many years an able orthodox minister.

Of the two daughters, Barbara wedded James Teter and Elizabeth married Jacob Crislip. In the Teter family is preserved an immense German Bible brought from Germany by Jacob Reger, Sr.

ELIZABETH, the fifth child of Jacob Reger, Sr., was married twice. Her first husband was Cottrell Talbot, who settled about one mile from Burnersville on the Buckhannon River. Talbot met a tragic death. He shot and wounded a large buck, which took refuge in the river, where it was followed by Talbot's dog. The harassed buck turned on the dog, which was no match for the enraged animal in the water. Talbot went to the dog's assistance and was drowned. (10) Elizabeth's second husband was Christian Hall. She left a long line of descendants throughout central West Virginia.

ABRAM, the sixth child, was born in 1774. He also was a man of large stature and great physical strength. Although quite young, he was said to have participated in the Indian battle at Buckhannon. He was married to Miss Mary Reeder, and they reared a large family of children, whose names were: John, Isaac, Jacob, Abram, (Rev.) Hanson, Anthony, Mary, Nancy, Elizabeth and Martha.

JOHN was Colonel of Militia, and was a skilled hunter. I well remember the Colonel, a tall, venerable and kind looking old man. He had light eyes and a soft musical voice. He often visited at my parents, and it was with feelings of awe that we children listened to the thrilling hunter stories of his younger days. He took pride in demonstrating to his young auditors

---
(10) See page 489.

how supple were his joints, attributing this to his regular diet of bear meat during the greater part of his life.

The Colonel was early distinguished for his fearless nature and iron-like nerve. These qualities, coupled with an amiable disposition, won the esteem of all who knew him, and made him a favorite and a leader among his companions in their annual hunts.

ELIZABETH REGER married Jonathan Hall. Mr. John Strange Hall, of Walkersville, West Virginia, referred to elsewhere in this volume, is a son of this marriage.

ANTHONY REGER recently died in Buckhannon, West Virginia. He was ninety years old and the last grandson of Jacob Reger, Sr.

BARBARA, the seventh child of Jacob Reger, Sr., wedded Samuel Jackson. Many of her descendants still reside in the state.

ANNA and MARY, eighth and ninth children, married brothers: Anna, John Bozarth; Mary, George Bozarth. These brothers were the sons of John Bozarth, Sr., whose family was attacked, and some of them killed, by the Indians on Fink's Run, in 1795. They were the two boys mentioned by *Withers* (11) who were helping their father haul grain when the attack was made. John was a commissioned captain in the Virginia Volunteers, War of 1812. It has been claimed that George was a non-commissioned officer, same war, but I have been unable to verify this statement. Both brothers were identified with the early history of Lewis County; both acting justices. With their families they moved to Indiana at an early date, and were lost sight of by their Virginia friends.

ISAAC, the tenth child, was born on the Wappatomaka, August 19, 1782. He was married to Mary Magdaline Brake, daughter of Jacob Brake, the Indian captive. Isaac inherited the Reger homestead on Big Run, but in 1830 sold it, and settled on Upper Hacker's Creek, where some of his descendants still reside. Isaac, like his older brothers, was a great hunter, and had some thrilling experiences in this pursuit.

When a boy, he went coon-hunting one night, accompanied by two hounds, a cur, and a small fice. Most hunters kept a fice in their pack, as they proved most efficient in bear fighting. They would tree a bear when the larger dogs could not. The fice will invariably attack in the rear, and then get away before

---
(11) See page 490.

the bear can turn or seize it. Bruin can not long endure this mode of warfare, and will soon "tree." The noisy fice also excelled in treeing the dreaded panther.

On the night in question, Isaac's dogs were attacked by wolves, and getting the worst of it, they fled to their master for protection. The wolves pursued, fighting the dogs within a few feet of the boy, who stood with rifle ready to fire, had there been sufficient light to distinguish wolf from dog. Emboldened by the presence of their master, the dogs turned upon the wolves, and drove them a short distance, only to be forced back in turn. Thus the battle raged, the wolves often coming near, and with such violence that the dry leaves were thrown about Isaac's feet. Finally, the dogs, badly hurt and exhausted, gave up the fight. The hounds crawled into a nearby sink-hole, where their enemies dared not follow. The cur remained close to the boy, but the fice had disappeared. The wolves hung close around, and the boy, disdaining to abandon his hounds, remained on guard until the first rays of dawn, when the wolves fled. Isaac, with much coaxing, induced the hounds to come from their subterranean retreat. The fice was never heard of afterwards, evidently having been devoured by the wolves.

At a later time, when Isaac was about eighteen years old, he went coon-hunting, and during his rambles he reached the crest of a hill, or knob, where he paused for a short rest. Suddenly, the stillness was broken by a wild piercing scream, emanating from the hillside just below where he stood. His dogs immediately gave pursuit to some object, circling the hill, and baying furiously. Soon the chase had reached the starting point; where again there came that same wailing shriek, so intense and penetrating, that the boy, although inured to the dangers of the forest, felt the blood chill to his heart. On sped the dogs in that endless circle, and once more at the same point there arose above the deep bellowing of the hounds that awful scream. A thrill of unaccountable terror shook the boy, as again and again the gloomy hill-top was circled, and at regular intervals was repeated that frightful cry. This was more than he could stand, schooled as he was in the superstitions of the woods. He intuitively associated the mysterious being and its ominous cry with the supernatural, and calling off his dogs, he hastened from the haunted hill, under the firm conviction that they had been chasing the devil. Years after, in relating the incident, Isaac said that he had no doubt but that the creature was a panther, or some species of wild cat; but for a long time he was unshaken in his belief that the quarry was his satanic majesty himself.

Some years after Isaac had settled on Hacker's Creek, a bear killed a hog on an adjoining farm, where his son-in-law, John W. Marple, settled. Having gorged himself on pork, the bear went only a short distance and lay down. Isaac was notified, and he immediately took his rifle, and accompanied by his dogs, went to where the hog had been killed. The dogs soon routed the bear, which started for "Bear Knob," followed and worried by the dogs. When about half-way up the mountain, the bear took refuge in a poplar tree, where Isaac killed it with his rifle. This tree was felled and sawed into lumber a few years ago.

Tradition says that from the foregoing incident Bear Knob derived its name. It is claimed, however, that the knob bore its present appellation before Isaac Reger settled on Hacker's Creek. The early settlers first called it *Potato Hill*, because of its supposed resemblance to a "hill" of this growing tuber. The Knob has always been an object of interest, and the resort of Easter Sunday parties. It was originally covered with a dense forest, but has, in recent years, been cleared, and is now clothed with blue grass from base to summit. It is the highest point on the Hacker's Creek waters.

The superstitions of the early settlers is instanced in the following: Isaac Reger's son, David B., when a small boy, became the proud possessor of a young wolf, which he determined to keep as a pet. One day while feeding it, the wolf bit him. This so angered the boy that he struck it with a mallet, causing its death. David's mother, who was well versed in the occult, was standing near, and told him to hold his hand in the wolf's mouth while it was dying, and he could ever afterwards cure the "thrash" in children, by using the hand thus treated, in washing the afflicted child's mouth at a stream of running water. David acted upon his mother's suggestion, and until he was seventy-five years old, he was called upon to exercise this mysterious art of healing. He always performed this duty with reluctance, contending that there was no virtue in the operation. Strange to say, however, that in every case the treatment was followed by a speedy cure. Mr. Nicholas Linger, who resided on the Upper West Fork, acquired in a like manner this power, and was reputed to have successfully treated many cases of thrash. David Reger died in 1905, the last of seven children.

Isaac Reger's children were: Philip, died young; Ruth, married John W. Marple; Rebecca, married Nicholas McVany; Lydia, married Henry Jackson; Elizabeth, married David T. Wolf; David B., married Elizabeth Nealy; Maria, married Nimrod Scott.

CHAPTER XXX

There was a noted character living in the Buckhannon settlement at this time. Jacob Brake was captured by the Indians on the Wappatomaka when eleven years old, and remained in captivity ten years and ten months. It is said that his brother Abram was also made prisoner at the same time. Their mother was killed there by Indians in 1758 (1) and it is probable that the capture was made at the time of this tragedy, but this is not known to be true.

Jacob was adopted into a family of four brothers, one of whom was killed in a massacre, or fight, at Romney, Va., and he took the place of this fallen brother. The most of his captivity was spent in northwestern Ohio, southeastern Michigan and northeastern Indiana. After the treaty of 1763, a fur trader found him with a band of Indians on White Woman's Creek, (2) who promised upon his return to the settlements to notify his family; but failed to keep his word. During the years which ensued, Pontiac ravaged the entire western border, and not until sometime after the restoration of peace in 1765, was Jacob met by another trader who carried the news to his people. John Brake, Jr., immediately arranged to return with the trader and claim his brother under the terms of the treaty. They were to meet at Fort Pitt, but John's anxiety caused him to appear at that post a month before the appointed time. They at once proceeded to the Indian towns and found that a band of hunters including Jacob, were to leave the following day on the great annual fall hunt. There was but little difficulty in arranging for his release and Jacob returned home with his brother.

Nothing is known of his life during his captivity, only that he acquired those inevitable traits of character so peculiar to the Indian race. His step was light and noiseless, and in passing through the forest he left no visible trail. He was taciturn and would sit silently by the fireside drawing solace from his pipe. He was subject to fits of savage temper and at one time while butchering hogs, he flew into a violent rage and terrorized those near him with wild flourishes of his knife and threatening expletives in the Indian tongue.

(1) See page 490. (2) p. 490.

It is related of Jacob Brake that he knew of a lead, or copper mine, perhaps the latter, in Michigan, where the Indians resorted for supplies of that mineral. The excavation was kept concealed from the whites by refilling and building a camp fire over the disturbed spot. Brake became acquainted with the mine while a captive, and in later years agreed to pilot a party of settlers to the locality with the understanding that he was to share in all the profits accruing from a commercial development of the mineral. A company was organized with Henry Jackson as leader, whose object was to survey and "enter" a large body of land on which the mine was located.

The party left Buckhannon, and after several days travel through the wilderness, Brake one evening, announced that they were within a few hundred yards of their goal. They pitched camp, and the next morning Jackson without further preliminaries began his survey; when Brake, ever suspicious, became incensed and refused to guide them further. It was in vain that Jackson and his companions sought to allay his fears of treachery, and to get from him the location of the coveted treasure. His Indian intuition of the white man's avarice had been fully aroused, and he was obdurate and steadfast in his refusal. Jackson and his party continued the survey, but in an opposite direction; and Brake, as he afterwards declared, taking advantage of their absence, went directly to the mine. Completely foiled, the adventurers returned home in disappointment.

Jacob Brake married Miss Mary Slaughter, sister of Jesse Slaughter, and settled near where the present Baptist Cemetery is located. His cabin stood on the bank of the river, where North Buckhannon now stands.

In 1781, a certificate was granted to "Jacob Break" [Brake], assignee to Samuel Pringle, 400 acres on Buckhannon, adjoining lands of Peter Pufenglory, to include his settlement made in 1776."

Jacob Brake was a Lieutenant in Captain George Jackson's Company of Spies, or Rangers, in 1779. His knowledge of Indian character fitted him admirably for this position.

Jacob's father, John Brake, who during the Revolution resided about fifteen miles above Moorefield on the Wappatomaka, was a German nobleman, a baron, who migrated from Germany several years prior to the breaking out of the American Revolution. He was the first of the Brake family in Virginia. (3)

---
(3) See page 490.

The German element in the Colonies in general espoused the cause of freedom, but the baron remained loyal to King George and during the latter years of the war, became noted for his zeal and energy in the Tory cause. There is a tradition that the baron received from King George a royal grant for a tract of land lying along the Wappatomaka where he lived, and that this, coupled with his love for royalty, was the main or real reason for his loyalty to the British Crown. It will be remembered that King George was of German descent, and would naturally feel well-disposed towards this German nobleman.

When General Cornwallis invaded Virginia with his formidable army in June, 1781, the Tory element on the Wappatomaka became restive and manifested signs of rebellion. Under the leadership of John Claypole, a Scotchman, who resided on Lost River, a tributary of the South Branch, they raised the British flag and refused to be amenable to the Continental authorities. The home of the rich baron was the recognized headquarters for this band of loyalists. (4)

A small company of militia from Hampshire County was sent to assist the local officers in enforcing order, but finding the Tories too strong for them, they withdrew without accomplishing the object of their errand. This emboldened the Loyalists, who then regularly organized, and made John Claypole commander-in chief, and only awaited a favorable opportunity to join the British forces. To suppress this uprising, a volunteer army of four hundred wild mountain riflemen, well armed and mounted, under the command of General Morgan, left Winchester about the 18th or 20th of June and headed directly for the scene of the disturbance. The army marched by Claypole's, captured that chieftain and scattered his followers. Claypole was released on bail, and the command passed up Lost River and over the South Branch Mountain, dispersing and capturing a few Tories as they went. In some instances, the reckless troopers inflicted wanton torture on their prisoners before releasing them. One, an aged man, was killed by a drunken Irishman. John Payne was branded with a hot spade and Mathias Wilkins was threatened with hanging by having a rope placed about his neck.

General Morgan's objective point was the noble baron's, and when he reached there, he halted his army. The horses were turned into the unharvested meadows and oat fields; and for two

---

(4) See page 491.

days and nights the men revelled in the best that the splendid estate of the baron could produce. His fields were stocked with fat cattle, sheep, and hogs, with the usual complement of barnyard fowls. Possessing also a well stocked mill and a large distillery, the unrestrained troopers fared most riotously. The Tories being subdued and scattered, Morgan now marched his men back to Winchester, where they were disbanded. (5)

This incipient uprising of Tories was the only one in (now) West Virginia during the war, and it was far from serious. Evidently the most of Claypole's adherents were only half-hearted in the movement, for many of them soon after enlisted with the Patriots and marched against Cornwallis. (6)

There is a tradition which says that sometime after the suppression of the Brake-Claypole uprising, the baron, smarting from the humiliating indignities which he had suffered at the hands of his enemies, defiantly raised a large British flag over his castle-like residence. He was ordered by the Continental troops to haul it down, but with the tenacity of purpose which has made the German race famous, he refused. The troops tore it down and destroyed it. Another version is, that when the baron refused to haul the colors down, the troops destroyed his buildings and laid his fine estate in ruins. However, this may be, the episode of the flag did occur, and with the sequel, that the baron soon afterwards went back to his native country, never to return to America.

For the following genealogical table, I am indebted to Mr. Carl Reger, a great-grandson of Isaac Reger. Mr. Reger has compiled a very complete and up-to-date genealogical record of the Reger-Brake families, but the scope of this work will not permit of its insertion in full. Mr. Reger also rendered other valuable assistance in the sketch of the Reger family.

The baron, John Brake, had four children.

(1) *Elizabeth*, married Captain George Jackson, the oldest son of John and Elizabeth Jackson. (7)

(2) *John* married twice. His first wife was Elizabeth Wetherholt, who died leaving one child, Elizabeth, who married Colonel Edward Jackson, as his second wife. John's second wife was Catherine Shook.

(3) *Abram*, married Miss Davis, whose mother, Sophia, was a daughter of the "first John Jackson who settled in this country."

---

(5) See page 491. (6) p. 491. (7) p. 491.

(4) *Jacob*, the captive, married Miss Mary Slaughter, as before stated, and had five children:
(1) *Leah*, married Major Abram Reger.
(2) *Mary Magdalen*, married Isaac Reger.
(3) *Name* unknown, married Joseph Shreves.
(4) *Abram*, married Miss Elizabeth Jackson.
(5) *John*, whose wife's name is unknown to me. His descendants are numerous in the Buckhannon country.

Jacob, the captive, died in 1831. His wife died in 1830. Both are buried in the Heavner Cemetery, Buckhannon, West Virginia.

CHAPTER XXXI

Jacob Cozad, Sr., was born in 1755, and was said to have been the fourth Jacob in the direct line of the Cozad family. As nearly as can be ascertained, he came from New Jersey, perhaps with his father, and settled on Cheat River, Virginia, just prior to the Revolutionary War. The name was originally Cossart, and is Flemish, belonging to families in Rouen, France, as also in the French portion of Belgium. It was pronounced without the final "t" in France, and with the "t" made to "d" in Belgium. The name appears Cossart, Cosart, Cozard, Cosad, Cozad, and in several other forms. The Cozads first settled in this country in New Jersey, and were associated with the Suttons, who are said to have come from England, and settled in or near New York City. Some of the Suttons also migrated to Virginia, where the two families remained in close touch for many years. David Sutton, who settled at the mouth of Kinchelo Creek, now Harrison County, West Virginia, was of this family. He died there, and was buried in the Broad Run cemetery.

The following certificates of land entries were granted to Jacob Cozad, Sr., by the Land Commissioners convened at the house of Colonel John Evans, near Morgantown, in 1781.

" . . . Jacob Cazad [Cozad] ass'ee of Moses Templin, is entitled to a preemption of one thousand acres of land in Monongalia County, adjoining his settlement on Cheat River, made in 1770."

" . . . Jacob Cazad [Cozad] ass'ee to Samuel Sutton, on Morgan's Run, a branch of Cheat River, to include his settlement thereon 1770."

" . . . Jacob Cozad heir of William Drago, 400 acres on the head of Drago Run at the right-hand fork, to include his improvement made thereon."

At the time, 1770, that these entries were made, Jacob Sr., was but fifteen years old, and it is obvious that some of them, at least, were made by his father, Jacob the third, whose wife was Elizabeth Sutton.

Jacob, Sr. (or Jacob the fourth), while yet in his teens, was married to Miss Mercy Woodward. This couple, at a later day, settled on Hacker's Creek, (1) about one mile below Berlin, where Lewis Morrison now resides. Their hewed log cabin, only removed within the last few years, stood where Mr. Morrison's wash-house is now located. A large pear tree, of the sugar variety, which stands directly between the road and the site of the cabin, was planted by Jacob Cozad, Sr., soon after settling there. This venerable tree measures over sixty feet from outer branch to outer branch, and over three feet in diameter, eight feet from the ground. It is still vigorous, and produces an abundance of delicious fruit.

Jacob Cozad, Sr., was a Baptist minister, and was one of the early pastors of the Baptist church, organized at Buckhannon in 1786. (2) He afterwards moved to Fairfield, Ohio, and was minister of the early Baptist churches near there. He died in Fairfield, August 22, 1827. His wife died in 1835, aged eighty years. They had several children; among them, William, Jacob, Benjamin, John, and David; also two daughters, Mary and Mercy. William became his father's executor. If there were other children, no record has been found of their names.

While the Cozads were residing on Hacker's Creek, a tragedy occurred which made the family historic. A tolerably concise account of this occurrence is to be found in *Withers*, (3) which is deemed unnecessary to copy here.

On July 26, 1794, four of the boys, William and Jacob, with two of their brothers, said to have been "Benny" and David, were bathing in the creek a short distance below the mouth of Little Stone Coal Run, (4) which enters the creek about three-quarters of a mile below the present village of Berlin.

The creek at that time was bounded on either side by a heavy growth of forest, while its banks were lined with willows and tall weeds. The boys were enjoying themselves as only healthful boys can, and doubtless their shouts of hilarity betrayed them to some Indians lurking on the ridge just south of the creek. At this point the stream skirts the base of the hill, which rises abrupt and steep from the creek bed. The Indians could not make a direct descent upon the unsuspecting youths, without danger of discovery. They therefore descended to the stream a short distance above the bathers, and were among them before they knew of their presence. One of the Indians caught at Jacob, Jr., who, supposing that his assailant was a neighbor boy trying to surprise him, exclaimed, "Jake Sleeth, you can't catch me," and immedi-

(1) See page 492. (2) p. 492. (3) p. 492. (4) p. 492.

ately dived beneath the water. But when he came to the surface, he was seized and led ashore. In the meantime, the other boys were being secured. A small ravine, densely canopied with weeds, broke through the creek bank nearby. Into this one of the lads crawled, but was seen and dragged out by an Indian.

It was the object of the Indians, in this case as always, in either entering or leaving the settlements, to avoid the low valley

THE COZAD BEECH TREE

Photographed by Mr. Kent Reger, October 8, 1898

and travel on the high ridges as much as possible. They could move more readily, discover danger, and avoid the deadly ambuscade. They could also more effectually conceal their trail on the dry uplands, where the vegetation was less rank. But in camping, when the weather necessitated a fire, they were compelled to seek the shelter of some valley, or narrow ravine, where they were occasionally surprised by the enemy. In order to regain the ridge, the Indians with their captives proceeded up the creek to the mouth of Little Stone Coal Run. The boys carried their clothes and donned them as they travelled. At this point, the youngest of the prisoners, a lad only six years of age, cried piteously for his mother. One of the Indians seized him by the heels and killed him by striking his head against the roots of a beech tree. He was then scalped, and his body left at the foot of the tree, where it was afterwards found, and buried in what is now the Morrison Cemetery, on the old Cozad homestead. This lad's name was "Benny." Another, perhaps later son named Benjamin, survived his father in Ohio.

The evident design of the Indians in this raid was to secure prisoners. Two days previously they had captured the daughter of John Runyan but two of the band carried her away and killed her. The remaining four Indians hid in the settlements for two days, doing no further damage than shooting one or more of Carder's cattle. The little Cozad boy who was dashed to death against the tree was making an outcry which jeopardized the safety of the Indians. From their standpoint this weeping child had not the requisites of the coming warrior, and this hastened his death.

There has been some doubt regarding the identity of the tree which figured so prominently in the Cozad tragedy. Mr. J. K. P. Maxson, of Berlin, West Virginia, a grandson of Jacob Cozad, Jr., and who was raised in the immediate neighborhood, assured me that his grandfather pointed out to him, not only the tree, but the heavy spur-root against which he saw the Indian dash the head of his little brother. This tree stood in the bottom near the west bank of the run before mentioned, and not far from the creek bank. The cut here given of this tree is from a photograph made especially for this work. Mr. Maxson accompanied the photographer and designated the fatal root, by thrusting a walking-stick into the ground by its side. This stick can readily be discerned in the front, and to the side of the center of the tree. When photographed, this legend, cut in the bark of the tree could be read, "Jacob Cozad, 17—". The last two figures of the date could not be deciphered. The tree at that time was dead, having put forth its last coat of leaves the preceding year. It was a large tree, but for several years only about twenty feet of its trunk had been standing. The primitive forest had been cleared from around it, and it stood alone, a silent, decaying monument to one of the many pathetic tragedies of a century before.

After killing the little boy, the Indians turned westward, and climbed the point of the ridge facing the east. While ascending this hill, Jacob conceived the idea of possibly alarming the whites by giving a loud and prolonged whoop. This he had no sooner uttered than he was knocked senseless with a rifle in the hands of one of his captors. Jacob said afterwards, in relating this incident, that when he came to his senses, a *squaw* was dragging him up the

SCENE OF THE COZAD TRAGEDY

Photographed March 20, 1910

Hacker's Creek is to the right and the place of capture was at the base of the bluff or "first bench" seen in the distance. On the left is shown a section of the hill up which the Indians retreated with their captives.

The square block of stone marks the exact spot where stood the beech tree against the root of which the Indian dashed the head of Benny Cozad. This monument was placed March 19, 1910, by Mr. John B. Swisher of Berlin, W. Va., and bears this legend, "Benny Cozad, killed by Indians, July 26, 1794." To Mr. Swisher must be credited the first patriotic work of this kind in the historic Hacker's Creek Valley.

hill by one foot, the others of the party having gone on ahead. There were but four, some claim only three, Indians concerned in this adventure, yet Jacob declared that it was a squaw who dragged him by the foot. It is not improbable that occasionally women accompanied war parties in raiding the border. (5)

The solicitude of this Indian woman for the boy, surrounded as they were by the most deadly peril, betrays a tenderness of heart not usually attributed to the race under like circumstances

(4) See page 492.

However, the fearlessness manifested in the lad's attempt to alarm the whites would appeal strongly to his captors and win their admiration. They were not likely to deal more harshly by him than their own safety demanded. The party reached the West Fork River that night, and camped near where the old Jackson mill now stands — the birthplace of "Stonewall" Jackson.

After arriving at their town on the Scioto River, the Indians displayed a fresh scalp which the Cozad boys recognized as that of their little brother. It, with others Jacob mentioned, was sold. At no time did the prisoners dare manifest any signs of grief or bewail their condition. They were held at the different Indian towns until the Treaty of Greenville the following year, when two of them were delivered to their father. He attended the treaty in company with John Hacker and John Waggoner, as noted in a previous chapter. Cozad was recognized by some of the Indians, they having often seen him plowing in his field.

Jacob, Jr., remained with his captors until the next year, when he was found at Sandusky by his older brother and brought home. (6) He had been adopted into the family of a chief. One day while at work in a cucumber patch with his foster mother, some of the little children were playing nearby. One of them came upon a large rattlesnake and was in imminent danger from the reptile when discovered by the child's mother. These Indians held the rattlesnake in reverence and would not kill nor molest it. But the love and solicitude of the poor mother for her imperiled child overcame her superstitious veneration for the deadly serpent-god, and while she would not injure the reptile, she permitted Jacob to kill and conceal it from the other Indians. Ever after he was a favorite of the grateful mother, and it was not long until she was enabled to show her gratitude in a substantial way.

After the crushing defeat of the Indians by Wayne's army in 1794, Jacob was condemned by his enraged captors to be burned at the stake. Every preparation was made for the execution of the awful sentence, and he was permitted to bid farewell to those of his friends assembled to witness his death. While passing through the throng for this purpose, he felt a light touch upon his shoulder, and turning, was face to face with a strange Indian woman. She covertly signed him to follow her, and unnoticed, led the way to a wigwam. Here she concealed him among some

(6) See page 492.

trunks and covered him with blankets. Soon he was missed and a great commotion ensued. Diligent search was made for him, many of the Indians coming into the wigwam where he lay, even removing the blankets, but their quest was futile. Jacob afterwards said that he was fearful lest his presence should be revealed by the heavy beating of his heart, such was his anguish and dread of discovery. When the excitement had died down, two of his foster brothers secretly conveyed him to the Old Delaware Town, where he remained until after the Treaty of Greenville. He never again saw the strange woman who helped him to escape; nor was he ever mistreated again after returning to his adopted home. The sudden furious outburst against him had been prompted greatly by the baleful influence of whiskey, which the Indians had procured in quantity.

Mrs. Cecilia Pifer, of Buckhannon, West Virginia, a granddaughter of Jacob Cozad, line of his son Woodward, often heard the old man relate incidents in his captive career.

When the boys were captured, their father and mother were alone at the house. They were asked the number of men there, and answered, "Twelve." The leading warrior ejaculated, "Too many mans; too many mans."

Jacob said that his foster father was very fond of him when not under the influence of intoxicants. Both he and most of the men, if not all of them, were drinking when he was given up to die.

The captive lad often had the care of the smaller children and he learned to sing to the crying pappoose. The following is a fragment of the song as remembered by Mrs. Pifer. The last part of it is missing.

THE COZAD INDIAN SONG

It is noticeable that the last word of this song is almost, if not wholly identical with the "Pa-la-wa" of the *Turkey* clan of the Shawnees.

Jacob was instructed in the hunter's craft, and often accompanied the hunter bands in the wilderness. On these trips they sometimes suffered exceedingly from hunger. Once when reduced to the verge of starvation, a wild turkey was shot and Jacob's portion was the entrails. He always declared that this was the best feast of his life.

At another time he was made to climb a "bee tree" which they had discovered, with instructions to secure and toss the honey to the hungry band on the ground. The boy was so famished that he first sought to appease his own sufferings; at which the Indians called to him in a threatening manner. He replied by brandishing his knife at them, which so pleased them that he was greeted with laughter and exclamations of approval.

He was put through the most rigorous treatment to inure him to the hardships of the hunter and warrior.

At one time his head was shaved and then bathed in warm water; and after being divested of all clothing, he was sent into the intensely cold forest to carry firewood. He said that he never suffered with the cold so much in all his life. This seeming cruelty was not enforced through any spirit of animosity or ill will, but was a part of the schooling of the young Indian boys.

After returning from captivity, Jacob married Sarah Taylor and settled on part of his father's estate, where his son-in-law, George Lawson, now resides. The site of his first cabin is now occupied by Mr. Lawson's garden. The cabin was burned down, and Cozad then built a frame house near the site of the first. This house is still standing, and is a part of Mr. Lawson's present residence. Jacob moved to Fairfield, Ohio, and was living there in 1807 or 1808. Later he returned to Hacker's Creek, where he resided as long as he lived. By his first wife he had six children, Woodward, Jacob, Samuel, David, Mercy and Jackson, all of whom, except Samuel and David, lived to be grown, married and raised families.

Jacob survived his first wife, and married Ruby Beeman. By her he had four children, whose names were Elijah, Frank, Clerenda and Elizabeth. Clerenda married Mr. George Lawson, whose son, G. C. Lawson, of Meadow Bluff, West Virginia, rendered material aid in the preparation of this sketch. Elizabeth married Mr. John A. Maxson, the father of Mr. J. K. P. Maxson, of Berlin, West Virginia. In later years Jacob, Jr., was again left a widower, and again married. His third wife was a Skidmore. Jacob Cozad, like his father, was a "Hard Shell" Baptist minister, and preached at Buckhannon and elsewhere. He was also a "Sweat and Herb" doctor, having learned this art of healing from the Indians during his captivity. He owned slaves, but before his death he freed them, willing them one hundred dollars each when of age. Cozad died at his home in 1862, in his eighty-ninth year, and was buried in the Morrison Cemetery.

The adventure of Jacob Cozad with the rattlesnake, while among the Indians, is interesting and most significant.

With primitive man, as far back as record or myth extends, the serpent has been an object of mystery and veneration. Man in the hunter state has ever been a close student of nature. Constant contact with the living creatures upon which he preyed, or contended in the fierce struggle for existence, schooled him in the habits of all manner of life about him. His mind incapable of grasping and reasoning out the potent elements governing the actions of certain animals, birds, and reptiles, he associated them with the supernatural. This led to the individual, or tribal adoption of the creature as a sub-deity, or totem, and its worship as such. The noiseless uncanny glide of the serpent, without visible means of locomotion, and its subtile power over its prey, has doubtless been a prime factor in placing it among the chosen totems of primitive man. There are but few religious systems in the world that does not pay in some way, homage to the serpent.

With the American Indian various animals, birds and reptiles were worshiped as emblematic or representative of the Master of Life. In many localities the historic Indian has painted, or carved the images of these totem-animals upon the smooth surface of stone in the neighborhood of his abode. We also find them upon the walls of the secluded and sacred temple cave of the medicine man and prophet. These crude *pictographs* and *petroglyphs* speak plainly of mystic and religious ceremonies. They are the pathetic record of the strivings of the children of nature to solve the mysterious problems of life, and to probe the dark night of the future.

Interesting examples of the *petroglyphs* may be seen on a large flat stone on Lost Creek, Harrison County, West Virginia. Also on the walls of a small cave, or rock shelter, on Two Lick Run, same county. In 1888, I brought the existence of this cave to the notice of the Bureau of Ethnology, Washington, which culminated in a thorough examination of it in the same year by Professor W. H. Holmes of that Bureau. (7)

Of serpents, the rattlesnake was the favorite totem of the Red Man. We find the conventional form of this reptile etched on the shell gorgets, buried deep in the tumuli of the mound-building Indians. This points strongly, if not conclusively, to its totemic significance with that ancient people. (8)

It is not known by what tribe Jacob Cozad, Jr., was held captive; but it is supposed to have been the Shawnee, or possibly the Delaware. The incident of the rattlesnake implies that his captors were worshippers of that reptile. That such was the custom in vogue among the Chippeway-Ojibwas, we learn from Henry's observance of this practice while a captive with the Chippewas. (9)

This specie of worship was also observed among the Menominee, by Colonel McKenney, (10) while encamped on Fox River, Wisconsin, in 1827. In this case, however, sentiment was not so highly developed as with the Chippewas, but partook more of the nature of *Fetichism*. (11)

---

(7) See page 492. (8) p. 492. (9) p. 492. (10) p. 493. (11) p. 493.

CHAPTER XXXII

The Hurst family settled on Cheat River. The head, William or Henry, name uncertain but probably the first given, was a soldier in the Revolution and served during the greater part, if not the entire period, of that conflict. I have been unable to trace his military record, as no claim for pension was ever filed and the muster rolls in the War Department are very incomplete. From the information at hand it would appear that he came from the Wappatomaka to the Cheat River. Tradition has it that the family first lived in Hardy County; and later in Hampshire County.

Hurst died early and his widow, whose maiden name was Sims, came with her family to the West Fork country when her eldest child, John, was fourteen years old. The widow remarried and the children, eight in number, were placed in different families to work for their board and clothing. They were John, Katherine, Nancy, Daniel, Margaret, Samuel, Sallie and William. John married ——Winans; Katherine married John Shall, and moved to Ohio; Nancy married a Mr. King, and settled in Harrison County, West Virginia; Daniel married Eleanor Powers, nee Davidson; Margaret married Walter McWhorter; Samuel married —— Romine, and settled on a branch of McKinney's Run, Harrison County; Sallie married John West, a son of Alexander West, the scout, and settled on Fink's Creek, in now Gilmer County, West Virginia; William married —— Sigler, and moved to Ohio, and later to Missouri; died in 1869. His descendants are scattered through the west and Pacific slope. John and Daniel were soldiers in War of 1812.

JOHN HURST was a private in Captain John Bozarth's Company, Fifth Regiment, Virginia Militia, under Col. Isaac Booth. His service commenced August 30, 1814, and expired March 19, 1815, during which time he was at Norfolk, Virginia.

This soldier settled on Fink's Creek, in now Gilmer County, West Virginia, ten miles from any human habitation and when that region was an unbroken wilderness. He completed his cabin and moved on the 10th day of April, and carved from the heavily-timbered bottom land a corn patch the same season. He grubbed and cut down trees and piled the brush in the day time and at night would fire the brush heaps and cut the trunks into logs by the light of the blaze. When fatigued, he would lay down within the circle of light where the wild animals would not venture, and sleep soundly. When refreshed, he would replenish his fires and proceed with his chopping and ofttimes the ring of his axe resounded throughout the entire night. The field he thus cleared, Hurst cultivated in corn for thirty consecutive years, with no perceptible diminution of fertility. The back-water overflow from the creek amply replenished the soil.

Hurst cleared land and shot wild animals during the weekdays and devoted his summer Sundays killing poisonous reptiles. These latter were very numerous, and the first year he destroyed seventy of them by actual count. One night he arose to give one of the children a drink of water, and when he stepped on the loose puncheon floor, a rattlesnake sounded an alarm in the corner of the cabin. The intruder was dispatched.

Hurst's antipathy for these reptiles was augmented in an early day. When a boy and residing with his parents on Cheat River, he was cow hunting one evening during the first warm days of spring. He stepped upon a large boulder to listen for the bell. A rattlesnake crawled from under the rock, and he struck it with a stick. In its dying throes it sounded an alarm, when others made their appearance. The lad was soon kept busy knocking them from his perch, as they advanced from every side. Before realizing his danger he was surrounded, and was nearly overcome by the nauseating aroma from the loathsome angry swarm. This odor, which is always perceptible, is greatly increased when the serpent is in a state of excitement. Hurst was bare-footed, and his only means of escape was by leaping over them, which he did, and ran for a small creek only a short distance away. But he was not to escape so easily. The reptiles pursued him so closely and in such numbers, that he was compelled to continue his flight across the stream, which at this point was both narrow and shallow. Two of the rattlers swam after him, and these he killed.

The habit of the rattler and the copperhead is to congregate in dens in the fall, where they hibernate during the winter. These dens occur in favored localities, usually among the rocks on the sunny side of the hill, or mountain. During the first warm days of spring, the inmates will make their appearance and bask in the sun. In the early days of the country, and even now in sparsely settled and mountainous districts, the reptiles have been seen by the hundreds lying in tangled masses about their dens. This they continue to do for a few days before scattering throughout the surrounding country. It was such a den that Hurst happened upon. (1)

Just before moving to the West Fork, a bear came near the Hurst cabin one night and the dog chased it up a tree on the river bank. John, who, it must be remembered, was only thirteen or fourteen years of age, procured his father's gun and a torch and hastening to the spot built a fire with the intention of remaining there until morning when he could shoot the bear. In the after part of the night a terrific storm burst over the forest and the rain descending in a deluge the fire was soon extinguished. The lad sought shelter in the house but the faithful dog remained on guard. Just before daybreak, bruin came down from his perch when the dog, a strong, courageous animal, engaged it in deadly conflict. The struggle was protracted for one of its nature. The uproar was plainly audible at the cabin and the mother experienced great difficulty in restraining the intrepid boy from going to the help of the brave dog. Finally the tumult subsided and the dog came home badly hurt. Soon as it was light, the lad hastened to the scene of the fight and found the sand bar on which it had been waged, stained with blood and other signs attesting to the desperate nature of the battle. The bear had made off leaving a trail of blood. This the boy followed to the top of a bare ridge where it was lost.

After settling on Fink's Creek, wild animals and reptiles vied in making Hurst's life strenuous. Panthers were so fierce and numerous that the children were not permitted to go alone in the woods. One autumn day the father left home to secure help for a "house raising." Not returning in the evening, George, the eldest boy, went to bring the cows from the forest. He had proceeded about a quarter of a mile from home when he stepped from the path to pick up a few hickory nuts. While thus engaged, a small dog which accompanied him and had preceded him some three or four rods, gave a yelp of agony. Cautiously peering ahead, he saw the dog in the clutches of two panthers. Unobserved by the animals, he climbed a dog-wood bush, while they carried their prey a short distance up the hillside and concealed it

---
(1) See page 494.

in a small cavern in a ledge of rocks. The boy descended from the bush and ran home. The dog's body was never afterwards disturbed, but eventually shriveled away. Panthers are extremely dangerous when guarding their prey.

Hurst was hunting one day near the summit of a ridge when he discovered the partly-eaten carcass of a deer only recently killed, and buried in a mound of leaves. While examining the find, he was startled by a series of screams emanating from the lower slopes of the hill; and looking he saw a large panther charging directly toward him. A steep bluff intervened, and as the animal climbed this, it was hidden from view for a moment. Hurst sprang to the side of a large tree and raised his rifle. When the panther reached the brow of the declivity, still shrieking with rage, it paused to locate its enemy; when the rifle rang out and it fell dead.

Hurst was a splendid marksman. Once while watching a lick from a "blind," he caught the glimpse of a shadowy form approach the brow of the bluff just over the lick. It stopped and remained motionless, with only a spot of it, some four inches in diameter, visible through the dense foliage of the thicket. Hurst not knowing what the animal was refrained from firing, trusting to secure a deer. But as the sun sank behind the forest-clad hills and no other game in sight, he determined to take a shot at the strangely silent visitor on the bluff. At the report of his rifle the animal bounded twenty feet through the bushes and disappeared. Upon investigation, the hunter found a large panther stone dead. It had only made two or three leaps, the ball having passed directly through its heart. It, too, had been lying in wait for deer.

At another time while hunting with a companion, their dogs chased an immense panther which took refuge in a lofty tree. It walked upon a large limb where it crouched watching its enemies on the ground. Hurst declared his intention of shooting it in the eye. His companion remonstrated, pointing out the imminent danger of an attack should he miss, or slightly wound the animal. He should aim at the vital part of its body, where the heavy ball would be sure of disabling it. Hurst, self-confident, disregarded the warning and fired. The panther toppled from its perch and fell lifeless among the dogs. The bullet had entered the eye so cleverly that not even a lash had been damaged.

Hurst's hair was turned prematurely gray by the following incident: He often in the summer time slept alone in the woods, preferring the open air to the close cabin. He would build a "smothered" fire to "smudge" the insect pests, rake up a few dry leaves for a couch and pillowing his head on the root of a sheltering tree, sleep soundly. One night he was awakened by a stealthy creeping noise at no great distance from where he was lying, followed by a light tapping in the dead leaves. This was succeeded by the same gliding rustle as if some animal was crawling towards him. Again it ceased, when once more came that ominous: *tap, tap, tap*, like the measured toll of a funeral bell. This was repeated at successively nearer points, while Hurst lay helpless and unable to see the supposed danger. He had not the least doubt but that he was being stalked by a panther. The tapping was made by its tail as it paused in its approach. Hurst grasped his knife, which, with his rifle, was at his side, but dared not move for fear of provoking an immediate attack. After a seemingly long interval, he discerned a light spot on a dark and dimly outlined body flattened to the ground only a few feet away. This proved to be his dog, who forbidden, had followed him and conscious of disobedience, was endeavoring in its mute way to curry favor with a displeased master. It is needless to say that the faithful animal was greeted kindly. Hurst's hair from this time on turned rapidly white.

Perhaps it was this same dog, whose disobedience upon another occasion, was probably instrumental in saving his master's life. Forbidding the dog to follow him, Hurst was watching a deer lick where the dog soon joined him, manifesting great uneasiness. He was scolded down, but immediately looking up into the tree overhead, he bristled his mane and growled. Hurst's glance followed and he saw a great panther in the act of leaping upon him. Like a flash his rifle went to his shoulder and the panther came hurtling to the ground dead.

Bears were numerous around Hurst's wilderness home. One autumn while hunting his winter's meat, he came upon the trail of four bears where they had entered a dense laurel thicket, or "bed," as usually called. Hurst crawled after them on hands and knees, and after much difficulty located the game lying fast asleep in a depression made by the upturned roots of a fallen tree. Selecting the fattest he dispatched it with a single shot, when the other three scampered away. The one killed proved to be very fat, weighing some four hundred pounds. The hunter experienced hard labor in rolling it from the cavity onto ground where the carcass could be dressed. The hams cured as bacon, weighed when sold in Clarksburg the next spring, forty pounds each. The price was twelve and a half cents a pound.

Hurst had innumerable adventures with both bears and panthers but the following was, he afterwards declared, the most trying ordeal in his hunter life. He shot and wounded a bear near his home and it escaped into a nearby laurel bed. He called to his children, George and "Betsy," to bring two young dogs which he was training. The children came in haste to see the sport. The dogs took up the trail and entered the thicket but immediately came out with accelerated speed closely pursued by the enraged bear. The children ran screaming to their father and clung tightly to the tail of his hunting shirt; while the dogs with true canine instinct also sought the protection of their master. Around the hunter and children in a narrow circle raced the demoralized dogs with bruin growling at their heels. Hurst could not use his rifle with safety and the situation began to look desperate. Finally clubbing his gun, he succeeded in felling the bear and then dispatched it with his knife.

But few excelled Hurst as a hunter. The wary turkey he decoyed to its death by calls upon the hollow wing bone of this bird; and the wolf by imitating the peculiar pack-gathering howl of this animal. These feats, however, were not uncommon with the hunter.

Wolves were numerous, and Hurst, for years, could keep no sheep because of their depredations. One night a band of four of them attacked his hogs and in turn were set upon by the dog. As Hurst opened the door, a powerful wolf threw the dog at his feet. The light from the open fireplace streaming through the doorway frightened the pack away. The next morning Hurst went in pursuit and trailing them about half a mile, he discovered a single wolf standing in the brush, and fired. The animal fell, when another one leaped from the thicket and ran down the hill. Reloading his gun, Hurst howled and was answered in the distance. Repeating the call, he soon had the wolf within rifle range, when it, too, was killed. In this way he dispatched a third one and then went in search of the one he saw running. He was surprised to come upon its dead body. Unawares to him, it had stood in line and beyond the wolf first killed, and the bullet had slain them both. Four wolves with three shots before breakfast was no mean achievement even in that early day.

Hurst found a cavern in which a mother wolf had her young. He did not disturb them, but just before the puppies were old enough to leave the nest, he captured them, letting the old wolf escape. This he did for three or four consecutive seasons, realizing eight dollars a scalp, the bounty paid by the state. Later, as the number of wolves grew decimated, and the injury to the live stock industry decreased, the bounty was reduced to four dollars. It was not unusual for settlers to "breed" wolves for bounty money as did Hurst; nor was it regarded as illegitimate gain. There was a large hollow chestnut tree on the farm where I was raised, from which for two years young wolves were secured by Thomas C. Hinzeman, a local hunter. This was at a later day and when the animal was nearing extinction.

When a young man, Hurst walked through the wilderness to the salt works at Charleston and cut wood for the furnace at twenty-five cents a cord. He was very athletic and made four cords a day. It was practically the only place in the country where money was paid for labor and he remained until he had earned the munificent sum of forty dollars. When starting on his return home he was short of powder, nor could any be procured at the works. He left at noon and as he passed the last isolated cabin in the settlement, he offered the settler twenty-five cents for two loads of powder, which was refused. Hurst proceeded about a half-mile further when he shot a fawn and encamped for the night. He roasted venison for supper and soon his camp was invested by wolves. Some of them came so near that he heard them gnawing the bones which he had cast aside. A rifle shot dispersed them for the night.

Hurst lay down by his camp fire in repose. Inured to a hunter's life he was a light sleeper and far in the night was aroused by the approach of stealthy footsteps. An intuition of impending danger prompted him without rising to glide beyond the blaze of his camp fire. He took shelter behind the upturned roots of a tree and with rifle thrust over this effective screen, he watched and listened. Soon a dog came into the camp light and was recognized as one seen at the cabin where the ammunition had been refused him the evening before. Cautious steps drew nearer and presently there appeared on the opposite side of the low-burning fagots, silhouetted against the dark background of forest, the form of his friend of the powder episode. He was carrying a rifle and at his belt hung a long murderous-looking knife. The sinister design of the night prowler seemed fully manifest. In negotiating for the powder Hurst had disclosed that he was from the salt works where he had been employed and the stranger, rightly surmising that he had money, had followed him with evil intent. For a moment the man stood scrutinizing the deserted camp and then turned away. During this brief interval Hurst drew careful aim at the intruder and twice did his nervous finger touch the trigger. Reflecting, however, that he was in no immediate danger, he restrained his impulse to fire. Hurst did not return to his camp that night, nor did he see or hear anything more of his unwelcome visitor.

The next morning after a breakfast of roast venison, and preparing a steak to serve for dinner, he set out on his journey. It was forty miles to the settlement on Steer Creek, now Gilmer County, and he reached there early in the evening. Hurst lived to old age and died at his home on Fink's Creek, West Virginia.

DANIEL HURST volunteered at Clarksburg, Virginia, as a substitute for Thomas Bond in Captain John Bozarth's Company, Fifth Regiment Virginia Militia, under Colonel Isaac Booth. He was mustered in at Bridgeport, Harrison County, Virginia, about September 1, 1814. Captain John McWhorter was the United States Recruiting officer of that station at that time. Hurst with his company, was marched to Norfolk, Virginia, where he was honorably discharged in February or March, 1815. On the return trip home, which was made on foot, the soldiers suffered so intensely from lack of food, that Hurst, who was marching in the rear, came one day upon the closely picked bones of a dead horse by the road-side. He said afterwards: "I would have been glad for a piece of the meat, but those in advance had taken every scrap." Hurst afterwards received warrants for two hundred and eighty acres of Military Bounty Land.

On May 31, 1818, Daniel Hurst married Olenor Powers and settled on Duck Creek, (2) Harrison County. Later he moved to Fink's Creek, Lewis County. In his declaration for pension his wife's name is given as Ellen Davison. Hurst was allowed a

---
(2) See page 495.

pension of $96.00 a year. He died in Lewis County, West Virginia, October 7, 1872.

Daniel Hurst was a good-natured, sympathetic man but often incurred the displeasure of others by his impetuosity and readiness to decry any apparent injustice to the weak or unfortunate. Once, in company with my father, driving stock across the mountains, and while in Staunton, Virginia, they were regaled with stories of slave floggings by several rough slave overseers. One worthy loudly boasted: "I have tied up many a nigger, stripped him, and given him a hundred lashes before breakfast." Hurst sprang to his feet, his eyes flashing with indignation, and shaking a finger in the face of the blustering stranger, burst forth, "Yes, and *you* ought to be in Hell before breakfast. Why, damn you, you don't know how to treat a nigger. In our country we feed them and keep them as fat and slick as stable horses, and when the master wants to shave he calls Sambo and uses his face as a mirror. We don't whip slaves, and if you were half as decent as the meanest nigger, you would find no occasion to use the lash." The boaster quailed before this furious outburst and was content to make no reply.

In the widow's claim for pension she states that her maiden name was Eleanor Davidson, and that she married Powers who died about fifteen months later; and then she married Daniel Hurst.

CHAPTER XXXIII

In the boyhood days of my father there lived in his neighborhood on McKinney's Run, an honest, eccentric, good-natured character by the name of James Bent, Belt or Broadbelt; usually called "Jim Belt." The variation was owing to the careless mode of speaking names in certain sections of the country, and did not reflect on the good reputation of its possessor. Jim was a tall, handsome, well-proportioned specimen of the Virginia mountaineer; free-hearted and generous to a fault. His voice was like the roar of a lion and his soul embraced the universe. Not an habitual drinker, yet was he better at his cups than the accumulation of this world's goods with its accompanying worry and annoyances. His boast was: "I came into this world with nothing and I want to leave it in the same way, with all accounts squared." His hope was realized.

Jim's conscientiousness was proverbial. He decried chicanery in all of its forms; a man should live up to his word and moral obligations. When drinking, his ideas of right and wrong were ofttimes somewhat confused. John Fletcher, a neighbor, borrowed his saddle which he was to return the same evening. On that day Jim took a few eggs to Jane Lew, the nearest village, to exchange them for a pound of coffee and incidentally got drunk. The afternoon came on wet and drizzly, and Jim, ever loath to leave genial companions, did not start home until long after nightfall. By the time he reached his domicile, the rain had increased to a steady downpour, and the night was pitchy black.

Owing to the inclemency of the weather, and the fact that Jim had no horse and could make no immediate use of the saddle, Mr. Fletcher did not return it as agreed. This aroused Jim's ire, and despite the earnest protest of his patient wife, he tramped a mile back over the muddy road and calling Fletcher from his bed, berated him roundly for his negligence and lack of integrity. Fletcher took it good-naturedly, closed the door and went back to his couch.

Jim returned home, still "preaching," and on his way back was met by a belated neighbor who inquired why he was out so late in such a storm, and the cause of his perturbation. Without halting, the stickler for truth replied: "I am saying curse John Fletcher: and curse the man who would not get up at the hour of midnight to burn his shirt to see how to curse him: I will curse him 'til the end of eternity; and then, curse him, I will double my diligency on him." The next morning Jim called on Mr. Fletcher with a profuse apology and the offer of his saddle so long as he had need for it.

At a later day Jim's grey horse, Jack, the only one that he owned, broke into his cornfield, and he was drunk enough to believe that he should enforce the law against the culprit. Placing a rope about Jack's neck, he led him to the summit of Buck Knob, (1) and seating himself on a log, still holding the rope, there alone in the woods, proceeded to preach old Jack's funeral.

"Well Jack," exclaimed the self-constituted judge and moralist, "this is a damned pretty scrape in your old days. Your past life has been a credit to you and your country. For your previous good record I fain would spare you: but you have fallen. Meteor-like, you have flashed athwart the way, only to go down in the oblivion of night. All too late have you learned that the aeonian career of the tiniest atom in the Milky-way, is far preferable to that of the greatest of shooting stars. You have violated the law and the morals of the universe cry out against you. Immutable Justice demands that your life atone for your wrongdoing. In the evening of life, when homage and grandeur should be yours, here, on this magnificent mountain top, canopied with the trees of the ages, and overlooking the scenes of your youth, are you to die in disgrace. You are sentenced to be hanged by the neck until you are *dead, dead, dead.*"

Jim now fixed a running noose in the end of the rope about Jack's neck, and then bent down a stout sapling to which he securely fastened the other end. Then bidding poor Jack an affectionate farewell, he let go the bush, which in its rebound, threw the executioner over the brink of the summit and sent him rolling down the steep declivity. Scrambling to his feet he climbed back to the scene of action, but the horse was nowhere in sight. The rope breaking, Jack had decided that it was a reprieve and galloped away.

Jim gazed around awe-struck and mystified. "Why, where is Jack?" he exclaimed. "Well, now!" he mused, "perhaps I was mistaken. Jack, after all was not so bad. Like Enoch and Elijah, he has been translated."

Jim was a soldier in the War of 1812, and served from August 1st, 1814, to September 20th, 1814; as private in Captain Edward Digg's Company, Virginia Militia. He was extremely proud of his military ability and training.

At log rollings, where the ubiquitous jug always appeared, Jim would "tea up," and at the close of the day's labor muster the men as a company, armed with handspikes and march them to the house with all the dignity, pomp and precision of a true Martinet.

Like many others, Jim's courage was wanting in some respects. Napoleon, the military scourge of Europe, would pale at the sight of a cat; while our hero of 1812 stood in mortal terror of a toad.

One day at a log rolling Jim, during the noon hour, was sent to the cellar for a bucket of "hard cider." In anticipation of coming joy, he placed the vessel, and as he turned the faucet his eye fell upon a large toad ensconced by the side of the barrel. He sprang back and stood gazing transfixed at the goggle-eyed monster, until a half-hogshead of cider had gushed forth and flooded the floor. The proprietor wondering at Jim's delay, entered the cellar and in amazement inquired the meaning of such waste. Without shifting his eyes the captain of the "hand-spike brigade" pointed to the terrible batrachian now sitting "belly deep" in the sparkling beverage, and exclaimed: "Do-you-see-that-damned-thing-sitting-there-by-the-bar-*rel?*"

At another time Jim was mowing grass for a neighbor on low marshy ground, infested with numerous "spring" frogs. One of these on being disturbed sprang against the mower's scythe, which caused him to pause in considerable agitation. He resumed work, however, until his ankle was struck by another of the leaping terrors. This was more than the grim fighter could stand, and with an exclamation of dismay, he shouldered his scythe and abruptly left the field saying: "The whole earth seems polluted with the cursed things."

Jim, like many others of his day, was wholly uneducated and could neither read nor write; but was both pleasing and polite in speech and bearing. This, with his native dignity and really good character, made him a general favorite with all who knew him. When in his cups he was fond of oratory, and the village boys supplying him with a few drinks and "official documents," consisting usually of old almanacs, would mount him on a storebox in the street and call for a speech on some topic of vital importance. Jim was ever ready to respond to these patriotic appeals, and after making some extravagant statements would say: "Now, gentlemen, I will prove this by my doc's;" (documents) and proceed to quote elaborately from his last year's almanacs.

Jim possessed not an acre of ground, but when in these moods he imagined that he was very wealthy. He "owned" all the land from Jane Lew to his home, distant two miles. At such times, in his boundless joy, he would hurl his hat high in the air, giving vent to a wild throat bursting roar. Then, as he listened in ecstacy to the echoes rolling along the wooded hillside, he would bellow: *"Is it possible that we are in the land of the living and the land that flows with milk and honey?"*

Some of Jim's escapades were pathetic. One day while drinking, he conceived the munificent idea of buying a wool hat for each of his "six boys." He was, at that time childless and had no money, but the unscrupulous merchant well knowing his honesty, let him have the goods on credit. The next morning Jim went to flailing wheat at fifty cents a day to pay for the useless hats, costing one dollar each.

Jim was a magnificent horseman, and at one time rode as mail carrier on the Benjamin Bell contract. His splendid appearance on his fine cream-colored saddler was remarked by all, and was recognizable at a great distance upon the highway. He once owned a small bay pony called Sam. Unlike the recreant Jack, Sam was the joy of his master's life, sharing his light-hearted poverty and entering into his military exploits with an intelligence and equine affection that was almost human. Jim resided on a branch of McKinney's Run. He often went to Jane Lew, where he would usually take aboard a cargo of "bust head" before starting home. Whether from genuine endearment for Sam and a deep solicitude for his comfort, or from some other cause, these trips were generally made on foot. Some distance below Jim's lowly mansion was a bottom field, perhaps one-fourth of a mile in length, open to the commons. In this secluded sunlit dale, Sam was wont to while away his time nibbling at the short goose-pasture found there.

Jim, erstwhile meandering home, hilarious with "tanglefoot" and swelling with patriotism, when reaching this field, would call: "*A-t-t-e-n-t-i-o-n: To A-r-m-s:*" Recognizing the war cry of his "pard," Sam would respond with alacrity, rushing to Jim's side with every nerve tense and quivering with anticipation of the coming "fray."

Throwing himself on Sam's bare back, this grim warrior would proceed to marshal an imaginary army in battle array. In a stentorian voice that could be heard for a mile, the "general" would arrange his forces in divisions, regiments, battalions and companies. Then in tones that reverberated among the surrounding hills, would thunder:

"*C-h-a-r-g-e the E-n-e-m-y:*" With no restraining bit or rein, Sam would dash away at the top of his speed for the far end of the field. As the cavalcade reached the goal, "M-a-r-k T-i-m-e:" would resound above the thunder of hoofs and Sam would immediately "take up."

"*Right about face:*" and Sam would wheel and stand motionless while the "general" rearranged his shattered host for the counter charge. These maneuvers the "pards" would go through by the hour and ofttimes long after nightfall, with perhaps not a soul in sight. Often Jim would take Sam to the summit of Buck Knob, and there command his "army" so vociferously, as to be heard all over the surrounding country.

Peace to the memory of the "pards."

Jim died at his residence near Jane Lew, October 11, 1851, and was buried either in the Harmony Cemetery or at Broad Run.

On April 18, 1878, his widow, Mrs. Jane Scarf, nee Sims, applied for, and was granted a pension on account of her husband's military service in War of 1812. She was then residing near Jacksonville, West Virginia. In her claim for pension, she stated that she believed that her husband's name was Bent. She died April 3, 1887, aged eighty-four years.

CHAPTER XXXIV

The belief in witchcraft and auguries was intuitive with the border settler. The Witch, and the Black Wizard were mediums of evil spirits, or the Devil, to do secret injury to the human race. The baleful influence of these invidious enemies of mankind was more to be dreaded than the visible dangers besetting the wilderness home. The scout and the hunter knew not at what hour a "witch spell" cast over his usually trusty rifle, would render it impotent in the conflict or the chase. Not only the rifle, and the shot-pouch with its contents, but his own person was subject to those appalling "spells." Flagrant, or continued "bad luck" was always attributable to the malignant "witch spell." These could be broken only by negative conjury and necromancy. In every settlement there was usually a conjurer, or "witch doctor." These gifted persons, successfully combating the malevolency of the witch, were regarded as public benefactors. Their status among those believing in sorcery, was scarce below that of the *good* Indian "medicine man" with his own people.

These superstitious fallacies were so strong with our first settlers, that it is no surprise that we still find the occult among their descendants in the isolated and mountainous districts. It is no unusual occurrence at this day for the stalwart mountaineer to be saddled, bridled and ridden to some distant town and return, in a single night. One unfortunate, living on the headwaters of the West Fork of the Monongahela, was subjected to this indignity. He was galloped to Weston, the county seat, a distance of ten miles and back; but in this case the impressed steed fared most sumptuously. The gratitude of his invisible rider was attested in a generous feed: "Eight big y'ars uv yaller co'n jes' like I wus a hoss." The effects of this strenuous night journey and the bounteous "feed" were such that it was necessary the next day for the jaded "broncho" to tramp seven miles to a Witch Doctor, for the purpose of having the "spell" broken.

I remember an old Virginian, a tenant on my father's farm, who was a victim marked for the witches. He could not keep a cow: if he did, a neighboring woman, who was said to be part Indian, would draw the milk by spreading a table cloth over a hollow stump and then "stripping" at the four corners. He lost a horse through the machinations of a witch, or sorceress, whose enmity he had incurred. The long-suffering victim determined, if possible, to rid the community of this Machiavellian curse. He would kill the witch. This could be done by burning the dead body of the horse, and perforating it with a pointed stick while being consumed. Proceeding to carry this scheme into effect, and while the "killing" was in progress, the executioner was startled to see a shadowy black cat leap from the flames and vanish. This was the witch, now destroyed forever.

But there were others, and the persecution continued. The old gentleman was lamed by a "ha'r ball" shot into his leg by one of these malicious creatures. These "balls" are composed of hair and other foreign material, and are very troublesome. He thought to remove it by incision, but was deterred from further effort when he felt the point of his jackknife grate on the end of a wire. His wife, by using due caution, escaped many of the personal ills which befell her less fortunate spouse. In crossing a field, she avoided the bars, or gateway, nor would she climb the fence consecutively in the same place.

This family was not alone in misfortune. A near neighbor lost several pigs through the agency of a witch. The proof of this was apparent when the skins of the dead porkers turned dark. The half-Indian woman was the guilty party, but in this case the "execution" by fire and spear proved ineffectual. The "witch" lived for many years after.

In another instance, which came under my observation, a farmer dismantled a small log stable and burned it with the body of a "bewitched" horse that had died therein, for the purpose of annihilating the witch.

Mr. John S. Hall, who has been referred to often in the course of this volume as one well versed in local history and traditions, gave me the following story. It dates back within forty years of the close of the Virginia border, and is the same occult philosophy that swayed the minds of the first Monongahela pioneers. It is not unlike others that were told me in childhood by the mountain people, and is interesting to the folk-lore student.

"The only person exercising the occult in behalf of some of my earliest acquaintances," said Mr. Hall, "was Elkany Roby, known as 'Elky.'" He was a pioneer of Collins Settlement, in

Lewis County, West Virginia, and at my earliest recollection he had reached the zenith of his fame. His summary method of disposing of witches gave him notoriety. He shot them with a silver bullet. Roby's chief work as wizard was in removing spells from guns. The old flint locks were very subject to these spells; but sometimes the spell was on the hunter. It was the wizard's work to ascertain the cause, and apply the remedy. For this purpose, the gun was first examined, unbreeched, and every piece scrutinized and cleaned. If no trace of the witch was found, the shot-pouch was then examined, which generally proved that the spell was on the hunter. Sometimes the witch was found to be young and timid, and could be frightened away without resorting to drastic means. In other cases the depredation was so great that the owner was advised to dispose of the gun to a gunsmith for what he could get, and to buy a new one. He was not to sell or trade it to anyone in the neighborhood, under pain of the severest spell that the wizard could conjure.

"Roby's execution of a witch was weird and unique. A charcoal outline of the witch was drawn on a board, which was then set up against a tree, facing the south. Then taking his position in front of the witch-board (the witch was invisible to the uninitiated) he would load his gun. A charm which he took from his mouth was carefully pushed down on the bullet. Then muttering an incantation, unintelligible to the few permitted to witness the scene, he aimed, and discharged the weapon. Usually a splotch of blood would appear on the drawing, which indicated that the shot was fatal. Sometimes the process had to be repeated before such a result was obtained. If only wounded, the witch was liable to return when healed. No bullet mark was ever visible on the board, and that the outlined figure should flow blood was a wonder. But all is mystery in the occult.

"When well advanced in years, Roby moved to the Little Kanawha, now Gilmer County. The fame of his achievements had preceded him, and fortunately he arrived when his help was most needed. He had occupied his new home but a few days when he was called upon to slay the most malevolent witch that had ever visited the community. It was just at the opening of the sugar season, and a neighbor found a large 'turn-off' of sugar unfit for use. It had a salty taste and a disagreeable odor. Even children, so fond of sweets, refused it with disgust. Roby was summoned, and after a careful examination of the premises, pronounced it the most malicious and diabolical case that had ever come to his notice. No mercy should be shown such a witch, and he would exterminate it if in his power. If successful, he would expect a compensation of fifty pounds of sugar; this was satisfactory to the victim, and Roby proceeded to business.

"He first directed that the spiles be withdrawn from the trees, and the troughs emptied, washed, and set up to drain. While this was being done, the wizard returned home to prepare for the conflict. In the afternoon he appeared, bearing his trusty rifle, and a board on which was drawn in bold lines the figure of a witch. This was placed against a noble sugar tree near the center of the grove; then calling his patron to witness the operation, the executioner took his position in front of the image. He carefully charged his rifle, exhibiting the shining bullet before thrusting it to its place, with the secret charm added. Then invoking a 'spell,' he took deliberate aim and fired. As the echo of the shot rang through the grove, and the wizard was yet wreathed in smoke, the excited patron exclaimed, 'Begosh, yer hit 'er, old man, I see blood.' 'Yes,' was the solemn reply, 'I seed the witch drap and vanish.' The blood showed a wound near the heart, and consequently fatal.

"All hands, including the women, were then called to replace the spiles and troughs, the wizard assisting. The next morning the disenchanter was on hand to note the result. Pure sweet water was flowing and the troughs well filled. The magician took charge of the furnace while the family did the outside work. That night they had a 'turn-off' to delight an epicure. The salutary result of the incantation was complete, and the hero of the occasion was gratefully invited to take control of the furnace, and share in the 'run'.

"The late William Bennett, of Walkersville, a gentleman of intelligence and veracity, got closer to Roby's conjuring than anyone else. This he accomplished by patronage and flattery. The Bennetts were renowned hunters, and for one so distinguished to bring his gun for treatment appealed to the old man's vanity. After a long and intimate study of Roby and his 'Black Art,' Mr. Bennett expressed the belief that Roby was honest and sincere in his assumption of magical powers."

CHAPTER XXXV

Of the *carnivora* of West Virginia, the common or Black Bear, the Grey or Timber Wolf and the Panther were the principal: and the last two by far the most ferocious. Owing to the many game preserves established by the different sporting clubs in recent years, the first of these animals, which, more properly speaking, is *omnivorous*, have increased in such numbers as to become a menace to the domestic stock in their vicinity. The panther is still met with in certain remote regions, but the wolf is practically extinct. A few are said to haunt the more obscure wilds of the Alleghenies and the gloomy recesses of the Gauley Mountains in Pocahontas County, but their pack-howling has long since ceased to be a source of dread to the belated traveler. In September 1902, Mr. William E. Connelley heard them one dark night in the deep forest between Buffalo Creek and Gauley River, in Nicholas County. (1) The last one seen on the waters of Hacker's Creek, was about 1854, by Mr. Thomas Boram, on the farm where I was raised on Buckhannon Run. The last one killed in that section was by Mr. Thomas Hinzman, on the head of the right-hand fork of the same stream.

The settler pursued the wolf with rifle, trap and poison; but *Doddridge* claims that the rabies was the prime factor in their extermination. (2) But some of them, at least, escaped all enemies and died of old age. When the Hurst family was residing on the Cheat River, the children going to the spring one morning found a wolf lying dead nearby with no visible marks of violence upon it. An examination revealed that it did not have a tooth in its head, and that it had succumbed to the ravages of hunger and senile decay.

Owing to the crafty nature of the wolf, comparatively few of them fell before the hunter's aim. The strategy by which they secure their prey enabled them to flourish in vast numbers throughout this uninhabited wilderness teeming with game. Their cunning in this respect has always been proverbial; (3) and today among the western Indians, the success of the most noted hunter is usually attributable to the skill or "power" obtained from the wolf through the occult. The young Indian whose tutelary is the wolf, will be sure to excel as a hunter.

(1) See page 495. (2) p. 495. (3) p. 495.

Singly the wolf is cowardly, but when driven by extreme hunger it is then very bold. While my grandparents were living on McKinney's Run, a wolf caught a sheep in daylight and throttled it against the corner of the house. My grandmother hearing the disturbance, ran out and chased the marauder away. When banded together in hunting packs, they are exceedingly fierce and dangerous. They overran the entire Trans-Allegheny. (4) No one was safe alone in the woods at night, or at any time during the winter when the wolves were often in a starving condition.

TREED BY WOLVES.

Late one evening Henry Glaze was hunting on the right-hand fork of Buckhannon Run, near the base of the mountain and not far from the trail which led from West's Fort to the Buckhannon settlement; on land later owned by David Wilson, when he discovered fresh wolf sign. The State paid a bounty for the scalp of this animal, and with the view of decoying one or more of them within rifle shot, he uttered a howl so like that of the wolf that ere the echoes had ceased there came an answering cry from the woods. This was in turn answered at intervals from several points in the forest. Elated with his success, the wily hunter repeated the cry and was answered at closer proximity. Each successive howl brought a response more numerous and from a rapidly narrowing circle. Before the hunter realized his danger he heard the swift patter of feet among the dry leaves, and hastily dropping his rifle, he had barely time to spring into the branches of a large dogwood bush. He was immediately surrounded by a cordon of hungry beasts, which, made fearless by numbers, surged and snarled at the root of the tree. Safely ensconced in the branches of the sturdy dogwood, the hunter gazed down into the green and baleful eyes of the hungry pack. The deadly fangs of a hundred froth-covered jaws gleamed and snapped in the fitful starlight. The sanguine hunter was now himself hunted. During the entire night the wolves growled and fought beneath him. Finally they began to leave, one by one. When the last wolf had slunk into the dark thickets the hunter descended and hurried to camp, content to return without wolf scalps.

At a later day, Mrs. Edmonds, who resided on McKinney's Run, was coming home from Lost Creek late one evening, and

(4) See page 496.

just as she reached the brow of the ridge dividing those two streams, she was startled to find that she was being closely pursued by wolves. Escape by flight was impossible, so she took refuge in a beech tree. There she was held prisoner, until after dark, when her family, knowing the danger of the forest path, went in search of her with torches. At the approach of the lights the wolves vanished. Mrs. Edmonds then descended from her uncomfortable perch, and the party returned home in safety.

A Wilderness Mystery.

When *Lost Creek* was first visited by hunters and home seekers, they discovered signs of some one having been there previously, and who seemingly was lost. From this, the stream was named. Various trees on which "T. G." had been carved were found. One such stood near a brackish, or "salt" lick which the hunters found on a branch of the creek; a great resort for deer. To this day this branch is known as "T. G. Lick Run." The letters were supposed to be the initials of the unfortunate one, whose coming to that wilderness ever remained as deep a mystery as was that of his subsequent fate.

Stalked by a Panther.

The perils experienced by the early settlers from the panther cannot at this day be realized. Though cautious and stealthy to the point of cowardice, this animal, when driven by hunger or disturbed at its prey, is extremely fierce and dangerous. Innumerable adventures of pioneers with this animal in the Virginia forests could be recounted, of which the following are illustrative:

One of the Bozarths was cow-hunting near his home one evening, and, contrary to the general rule, was unarmed. For the purpose of listening for the bell, and a possibly wider view, he mounted a large rock where he was stalked by an enormous panther; which he discovered in the act of springing upon him. Knowing the power of the human intellect over the lower animals, Bozarth met its glance with a steady and unflinching eye. This cowed, but did not vanquish the foe. It began circling the rock to seek an unguarded point from which to attack, but Bozarth turned with it and at the same time called loudly for his dogs. Fortunately they heard him and coming to the rescue, the panther made off.

A Baby Saved by a Fice.

A pioneer family settled on Cheat River. One summer morning the husband started hunting leaving the wife alone in the cabin with her baby sleeping in a cradle near the open door. A full-grown panther entered the yard, and was carelessly mistaken by the mother for a calf. The animal, gaunt with hunger, thrust its head in the doorway and sniffed at the unconscious child, when a little fice which was in the room, flew at the intruder and chased it up a tree. There the little dog bayed it until the woman called her husband, who had not yet passed beyond the reach of her voice, who came and shot it.

Combat in the Dark.

Perhaps one of the most remarkable encounters with the panther in the Trans-Allegheny, occurred in the southern part of now West Virginia, in the early years of the last century. A settler was returning home from one of his neighbors in the evening just after dark. His path led over a "foot-log," which consisted of a tree felled across a stream not far from his cabin. As he stepped from the log, a large animal rose from out the shadows of the stump, and fastened one paw on his shoulder and striking him on the cheek with the other, attempted to seize him by the neck with its teeth. The man, a powerful athlete, was wholly unarmed; but he caught his strange assailant by the throat and struck it three heavy blows with his fist. It loosed its hold and with a low moaning cry sank to the ground. The man, badly torn about the face and shoulder, and bleeding profusely, made his way to the house. The next morning he returned to the scene of the combat and found an immense panther lying dead where it had dropped in the fight. The sledge hammer-like blows had landed directly over the heart, breaking three ribs and causing instant death. The animal made no resistance after receiving the first blow.

Heroic Woman.

Heroic combats with the panther were not confined to the men alone. Tradition and history abounds with the intrepidity of the pioneer women, in every phase of wilderness life. One winter day a panther entered the yard of a Mr. Gothrup, living in now Taylor County, West Virginia, and caught a sheep. In the absence of her husband, Mrs. Gothrup seized a rifle and shot the marauder, breaking its back. Disabled, the savage animal lay writhing in pain, uttering frightful growls and shrieks. Having no more powder, Mrs. Gothrup requested a neighbor who was passing, to dispatch it with an axe. This honor was declined, and the courageous woman took the axe and with a well-directed blow ended its misery.

A Mail Carrier's Thrilling Adventure.

Panthers continued to be a source of menace to the isolated settlers for many years after the border was freed from the raids of the red warrior. In 1841, my father, then a lad carrying the mail through central western Virginia, had an adventure not unlike that of Mr. Bozarth. One bright sunshiny day, while riding down Leading Creek, just below the mouth of Camp-meeting Run, in Lewis County, he saw what he supposed to be a large dog on the hillside above the road, and hallooed, expecting it to run. At the sound of his voice the animal stopped, looked around, and instead of running away, changed its course and came trotting into the road only a few yards ahead of him. There it stopped and crouched down. The boy at once saw that it was a panther, and fully realized the imminent danger confronting him. The animal was large, gaunt, and appeared very hungry, but the fearless boy, wholly unarmed, did not for a moment waver in his determination to deliver the mail on schedule time. He pressed his horse so close to the savage beast, "that I could," he afterwards said, in relating the incident, "have struck it with an ox-gad." His horse hesitated, snorting with fear and excitement. The great cat crouched low, ready for a spring. Its muzzle was thrust forward, and its ears laid close to its head. It gave involuntary notice of its intentions to spring by instinctively thrusting out its immense claws, and nervously twitching its long slender tail. With these ominous warnings, it would instantly lift its head, every muscle drawn tense. But the boy, keen, alert and well aware of his enemy's one weakness, met its fierce appalling eye with a calm unwavering gaze. The panther quickly shrank back, only to repeat the maneuvers, but at each attempt to leap, it was held in check by the lad's fearless eye. While this thrilling eye duel was in progress, the lad thought to frighten his wily enemy with loud blasts upon the post-horn, with which all mail carriers were equipped, for the purpose of heralding their approach to the postoffice. The attempt was vain; the hungry beast did not for an instant relax its vigilance, nor abate its attempt to leap upon its prey unawares. The boy was still urging his horse forward, and at length came opposite the animal. Slowly he moved on, and at the same time turned in his saddle to keep his eye on the enemy. In this fashion he rode away, leaving the panther still crouching in the road. In that position it remained until he had ridden several hundred yards and passed beyond its sight in a bend of the road.

In December, 1839, this lad was crossing the Cheat Mountain with the mail. It was about four o'clock in the morning, and very dark. He was on the summit of the mountain, far from any human habitation, and where the road on either side was hemmed with an unbroken wilderness of sombre hemlock and dense laurel. On one or two previous occasions travelers had at this point been attacked by a panther, and even in daylight the place with its gloomy tangle of impenetrable thicket was calculated to inspire the bravest with a sense of loneliness and instinctive dread. As the boy, numbed and sleepy with cold, was letting his horse plod along, he heard, only a few rods from the road, what seemed the hoot of an owl, blending gradually into the dismal howl of the wolf, but ending in a wild shrieking scream. The startled boy attempted to urge his horse, a very frisky animal, to greater speed. To his dismay, he found that the bit had slipped from its mouth. The horse was laboring through a snowdrift which reached the saddle skirts, and the rider could do nothing but let it proceed at a walk. He fully expected every instant to feel the panther's claws in his back, but from some cause he was not further molested.

A Surprised Panther.

Sometime in the first quarter of the last century, Stephen Martin, referred to elsewhere in this volume, was hunting near the mouth of White Oak Run, on the Middle Fork River, in

Randolph County, West Virginia, and camped one night by the side of an immense fallen oak tree. Gathering a quantity of the thick dry bark, he built a fire, and after eating a repast, lay down near it, and under the sheltering side of the log.

Far in the night, Martin was aroused by the stealthy movements of some animal on the opposite side of the trunk, and instinctively he knew that it was a panther. Knowing the terrible strength and savage nature of his foe, and not daring to move, he secured his knife and awaited the assault with some misgiving. The fire had died down leaving a bed of extremely hot coals, so characteristic of oak bark. This was completely masked by a covering of feathery white ashes, which showed conspicuously in the darkness. Presently the panther reared up against the log directly over Martin, whose keen ear detected in sniffing the air trying to locate its prey. Suddenly it leaped and struck the ash-hidden fire with deadly precision. There was a surprised panther, and action was decisive. Maddened with pain and fury, it filled the forest with the most terrifying shrieks and screams. The frenzied animal was a whirlwind of agility, as grappling with its mysterious foe the glowing embers were scattered in every direction. There could be but one sequel to such contest, and in a moment the vanquished cat bounded away, still screaming, into the forest. Its cries were heard growing fainter and fainter until they finally died in the distance. Martin replenished the demolished fire and then returned to his couch of leaves, knowing that he would not be molested again soon by that panther.

A Scared Darky.

Occasionally the actions of these fierce animals in attacking man, are strange and eccentric. "Black Wash," a mulatto, was a slave, born near the Blue Ridge in Virginia, and with other slaves was brought by Thomas McDonnald, to Lewis County, (now) West Virginia, about the year 1850. "Wash" was a young man, tall and muscular, trusty and a good worker. He was hired out to work for Jackson Arnold, on the "Indian Farm" referred to elsewhere in this volume. Wash lived alone, caring for the stock and doing general farm work. One autumn day he went to help a neighbor kill hogs some two or three miles distant. The work was not completed until after dark, and Wash was advised in returning home not to go over the forest path, as a panther had recently been seen there; but to travel the main road, although the distance was greater. Wash declared that he had seen "Painters" afo', and that he was not afraid of any in the woods.

Carrying a small piece of meat and his big knife, Wash started over the hill path. When in the depth of the woods, a huge panther suddenly appeared in the path in front of him. It crouched and sprang, going over Wash's head, who struck at it but the blow went wild. Thoroughly frightened, Wash turned facing his nimble assailant, which again crouched to spring. With eyes gleaming like coals of fire, it went into the air, and soared over the head of the six-foot man, who this time succeeded in plunging the long blade of his knife full length in its flying body. The animal made a peculiar moaning wail as it struck the ground, and vanished among the trees. Wash hurried home, and the next morning in company with another man, he returned to the place of the attack where, following a trail of blood, they came upon the dead body of the panther, not more than twenty steps away. The random knife blow had passed directly through its heart.

A Hunter Pursued.

In the autumn of 1878 a striking instance of the ferocious, craven nature of the panther came under my personal observation. A hunting party was rendezvoused on the waters of the Greenbrier River in Pocahontas County, West Virginia; and one dark rainy day five of its members were overtaken by night some three miles from camp. The forest at this point was a dense, pathless tangle of pine and laurel, through which no sunbeam could penetrate, even on the brightest of days. The rain was a steady downpour, and a thick fog coupled with the pitchy night, rendered the otherwise gloomy woods a veritable dungeon of blackness. Fallen timber constantly obstructed their steps, and the men became separated and considerably scattered as they laboriously climbed the prostrate trunks, or crawled under the snarls of dripping laurel. They were guided by the occasional discharge of a heavy rifle by those at the camp, which was termed: "Shooting the lost into camp."

For three hours the drenched and weary hunters struggled through this chaos of hidden dangers, and were still a half-mile from camp. Suddenly my older brother, Cyrus S. McWhorter, who was several yards in the rear, was startled by the loud crashing of brush as some large animal charging in great leaps over the laurel, came down within four or five feet of him. Several times during the evening he had detected stealthy steps following him, and he instantly surmised that it was a panther. Turning quickly he faced his invisible assailant, and thrusting his rifle towards where he knew the animal to be crouching, he fired. The lurid flash and report frightened it, and it fled noisily through the thickets. Soon after this the gleam of a torch carried by a rescue party lit up the surrounding gloom, and it was not long until the fatigued men were all gathered about a roaring log fire within the sheltering camp. The attacking animal was undoubtedly a panther, as one had been heard "yawling" in the forest during several of the preceding nights. Had the young man attempted to flee, even if such had been possible, he must have been killed.

A Startled Irishman.

Not far from this same locality and only a few months previously a young man named Coff, while hunting cattle was overtaken by darkness several miles from home. Wearied with the day's tramp, he sat down upon a log for a short rest and was soon dozing. Presently he became aware of a light measured *tap, tap, tap*, in the dry leaves just back of him; which, in his half-somnambulent condition, he attributed to a rabbit. This timid little animal has a habit while gamboling at night, of stopping abruptly and striking the ground with its hind foot with the result as described. The noise was continued at short intervals and at closer points; and Coff, realizing a sub-consciousness of impending danger, suddenly turned his head, when a huge panther leaped away and ran screaming through the forest. Its cries were heard until it passed over a distant ridge. The disturbance in the leaves was caused by the nervous twitching, or beating of the panther's tail, which invariably accompanies the movements of this animal when creeping upon its prey.

The Last Panther.

The last panther killed in Lewis County, West Virginia, was by John Riffle, on Oil Creek, nearly sixty years ago, just above where the village of Confluence is now located. The animal had committed several depredations and one day entered a field where there was a herd of cattle belonging to Alexander Skinner. The stock was in mortal terror of the intruder, while the panther seemed in the best of humor. It would crouch and sniff along the ground, gambolling and frisking like a kitten. Occasionally it would bound towards the cattle, then suddenly stop and watch the affrighted animals run away. This panther had often been hunted with the best dogs in the community, but had invariably eluded its pursuers. Finally a noisy fice chased it up a tree and it was shot as above stated. The heroic little dog was killed by having its head crushed in the jaws of the panther during the death struggle.

The Last Bear.

Perhaps the last bear ever seen on the lower waters of Hacker's Creek, was on McKinney's Run, about the year 1828. My father, who was just "old enough to hoe corn," went into the orchard one day during the noon hour, before returning to the corn field. He saw what he supposed was a large short-tailed dog climb the fence some fifteen or twenty feet away, and go into the woods. A dozen years later he saw a bear in a show and then for the first time he knew that the big short-tailed dog was a real bear.

A Daring Woman.

When Hacker's Creek was being settled, a Mrs. Wolf was out hunting cows not far from her cabin. A small dog which accompanied her, chased a bear up a tree. Having no gun and seeing that bruin was inclined to come down, the dauntless woman took a penknife, the only weapon that she had, and with hickory bark lashed it to the end of a pole and used this as an effective "prod" whenever his bear-ship attempted to descend. In this way she prevented the animal's escape until her husband came and shot it.

Humorous Bear Story.

When a boy, an old hunter and a neighbor told me about shooting a bear on the farm where I was raised, on Buckhannon Run, a branch of Hacker's Creek.

"I wus a huntin on the north side uv the hill, in yanders-cove," said the ancient nimrod, pointing to the deeply wooded hillside, "when I run onter a big bar' a raken uv the leaves fer mast. I ups with my rifle an' let him have it jest back uv the shoulder. At the report uv the gun, he rolled over on his side a clawin' at the hurtin' place an' a bellerin': 'Oh Lord! Oh Lord! Oh Lord! He didn't see me an' the win' wus ag'in him an' he couldn't git me located; but I tell yer that he made the leaves fly fer a minit. I hurried, but a-fore I could git a-nuther load down the old flint lock, that-er bar' up an' skeedadled an' I see'd nuthin' more uv him. Why didn't I wade inter him with my huntin' knife arter shootin' him? Wall, that-er bar' wus a snorter, an' he had a mighty fine hide that I didn't wanter spile; besides, I wus purty bizy jest then a ramin' a bullet down my rifle, an' I hadn't no time ter spar'. I guess, sonny, yer never see'd a big bar' all crazy with hurtin' an' a rantankerin' in the woods, did yer? Wall when yer do, I bet yer don't go a spilen' uv his hide with a knife."

The First Buck.

"An' right up yander," continued the old man, designating the south hillside, "on the Huckleberry Pint, I killed my fust buck; an' he was a whopper too. I wus a little-like shaver, an' my dad had never let me go huntin' with the gun. That day arter I had begged fer sometime, he give me the flint lock an' two loads uv powder an' said: 'If yer don' come back with a deer I won't let yer go no more.' Thar' wus snow on the ground but hit wus not cold an' the sun wus a shinin' and thawy-like an' I knowed that the deer would likely be whar' the snow wus meltin' an' all sheltered from the wind; up thar' whar' yer dad's sheep like ter stay on sich days. I wus mighty anxious ter find a deer, an' when I come on the upper bench an' looked over the bluff an' see'd four a layin' down, my heart give a jump an' I feel sorter qua'r; but I took sight at a big buck an' broke his back an' the others run away. I finished him with my knife an' I bet yer that Gineral Washington didn't feel bigger at the Battle uv Waterloo than I did when I went home ter git a hoss an' bring in that-er buck. An' I killed one arter-wards, over thar' whar' the willer tree is a growin' by the spring at the foot of the hill on the north side uv the bottom. Yer see my dad let me go huntin' often arter havin sich good luck the fust time."

A Modern Nimrod.

The following interesting letter was a reluctant compliance with the request of my father for a brief synopsis of a hunter's career. Bearing no date, it was written in April, 1907, and is the record of a typical mountaineer; a simile of the hundreds who have spent their lives in killing game throughout the ranges of the mighty Alleghenies. In 1889, my father visited Mr. Arbogast, and went with him to one of his bear traps some three or four miles from his house and up the Greenbrier River. The trap was constructed of logs, and contained a yearling bear, which was dead. The hunter had delayed his rounds one day too long.

"Dear Dr. J. M. McWhorter:

I will try to answer a few of your questions. I killed first deer in 1848 with a flint lock rifle. About 1852 I had the lock changed to percusion. I killed the majority [of deer] with [this] mountain rifle. In 1878 I got a 45-60 winchester. The first fall after I had the [flint] lock changed I killed 8 [deer] next fall 20; next [fall] 25. After that I killed from 25 to 30 every fall. 32 was the most I killed in one fall. I killed 2 to 5 Red Deer every Summer which were not counted in fall hunts at that time. I killed 2 at one shot 3 [different] times. I killed 4 a day 2 [twice] I killed 5 in half day out of six I saw with muzzle loader. I made an estimate I have killed between 6 and 7 hundred [deer] 25 was the highest number I saw in one day—I killed and caught several Bear—I shot one wolf and Poisoned and caught several others in trap. We have had 8 sheep killed in sight of house and many less numbers at different times by wolves Bear and Panthers. I killed 2 Panthers [in] one day. My father had a dog that treed 11 panthers that he killed. Dog went out on his own accord and treed one. Panther came down and killed the dog. Was snow on the ground—was a young dog along with him came back next morning wounded by the panther. Father took his back track to where the old dog was killed. The panther had carried him into a laurel thicket [and] had eat him about half up [and] was laying by the dog. When father followed the trail to where the dog was the panther walked away. Father went about 2 hundred yards in the thicket. Panther had stopped twice in that distance til he saw Father coming, so he thought. Was a soft snow in April which made things plain.

A Bear came at night when I was a small Boy father was not at home—took a small hog from where they lay at night before we had gone to bed; heard it squeal as the Bear carried it off. Must have been 200 yards away when stopped squealing. The hog bed was about 50 yards from house. Second night after, it came back caught a fat hog in pen about 30 feet from house. Father heard it squeal went out with gun was too dark to see it He hallooed [and] as it climbed over pen he shot at the noise did not hit it. I had a salt lick for deer at the root of a chestnut tree; deer and groundhogs dug down through the roots. Went thare one morning to salt it—a deer had put its head down between the roots got its head fast was dead, and warm yet. I had killed a number of deer thare before and after—I killed an eagle that had swallowed about 6 inches of a deer's rib one end was broken off slanting very sharp the other end being a joint was round. This end was in its craw the other end stuck out about $2\frac{1}{2}$ inches to one side of back bone. The part that stuck out was bleached as white as a bone that had laid on ground several years, and wore as smooth as if it had been done with sand paper. I suppose in using its wings the feathers wore it smooth.

I only had one close call in the woods that I know of. Was out hunting snow was about a foot deep commenced sleeting in a short time crust on snow bore me up and slick as glass. Feet slipped from under me was on a steep hillside. Down the hill I went feet front about 30 yards to a large log, the gun stopped against the log. I went over turned head in front about 30 yards run into a bunch of dead brush which caught in my clothes by breaking off, the snags caught which I think saved me from getting killed or badly hurt. It was about 100 yards to stream of water nothing in way to stop me. I worked my way back to where my gun stopped at log, by breaking through the snow crust with heel of shoes. Then used breech of gun to break through crust of snow, until I got down to a stream of water which led to river and home. I met Father about half a mile from home going to look for me. I was born in a cabin 20 feet from the house I now live in, 72 years ago 6th of last March 1907 lived here all the time.

I wish I had kept a statement of every day's hunt during my life taken down every evening. I give this as a true statement &ct.

Kindest Regards to any one who by chance may read this statement.

A. M. V. ARBOGAST.

Dunlevie Pocahontas Co W. Va.

APPENDIX

LORD DUNMORE
Courtesy of Wisconsin State Historical Society
Reduced from an old engraving in Wisconsin Historical Society's Library.

APPENDIX I

A published *Descriptive List of the Manuscript Collection of the State Historical Society of Wisconsin,* has only recently placed the Dr. Lyman C. Draper *Manuscripts* within the reach of the general student of pioneer history. They consist of four hundred and sixty-nine volumes, and are the most valuable of their kind extant. Research along special lines in this great mass of hitherto unclassified material was attended with such cost and uncertainty, that it was practically inaccessible to other than the local student.

Thirty-three volumes consist of data for a series of sketches on frontier wars. Two of these, Volumes XX and XXI, are devoted entirely to material for a new edition of *Withers Chronicles of Border Warfare.*

This work Dr. Draper commenced in 1890, and was thus engaged when stricken with death, August 26, 1891. The volume was afterwards completed by Dr. Thwaites, and published in 1895, by The Robert Clarke Company, Cincinnati. The correspondence here published for the first time is interesting in connection with some of the topics treated in this volume. With but two exceptions, the letters bear the date of 1891, and some of them within a few days of Dr. Draper's death. The Manuscripts were not accessible to me until 1908, and after all but chapters 31 and 32 had been written; and any reference in previous chapters to these documents has been inserted subsequent to this date. The correspondence is given under catalogue numbers.

"BUCKHANNON TOWN LEWIS CO. VA.
Febry 24th, 1849.

"L. C. DRAPER ESQR.

"SIR: I now proceed to answer your Enquires in your 3 Letters to me of October 17th, 1848 Janry 15 1849 and Janry 22d 1849. I should have answered you sooner but have been waiting to obtain some information on some points which would have been use to you in getting up the needful information you desire, but I have been unable to obtain the information desired in consequence of the advanced age of the persons from whom I expected to Learn the facts of several Transactions of importance, but their old age and doted condition of their minds has prevented me from doing so. Mr. John Cutright for whom you enquire is one. You first enquire about the Bull affair, this place is situated on the Little Kanawha River (in the County of Braxton Va.) now known as the Bull Town salt works, where Lick salt is made, David White, the brother of W^m. White was taking [taken] prisoner some time previous to the destruction of Bull Town, and was present at the taking of Stroud's family in the summer of 1772, this occurence led to the destruction of Bull Town, David White knew the property and household furniture of belonging to the family of Mr. Stroud and after White escaped from the Indians he in company with others frequently went to the settlement at Bull Town on hunting expeditions, and when he saw the goods and Chattles of Stroud, White inform{d} the settlement of Buckhannon and it was fully believed amongst them that the inhabitants of Bull Town were a harbour and shelter for the unfriendly and invading savage foe, and no doubt was the case (1) this enraged the white settlement to think that the Indians who professed friendship was a place of Refuge for the foe &c. so a party of 5 or more men went and doubtless destroy{d} the place, kil{d} the whole party & perhaps throwed the bodies in the River. Wm. White Wm. Hacker Samuel Pringle and Andrew Skidmore were four of the party, perhaps John Pringle Andrew Friend and David White and Elijah Runner was also of the party. Samuel Pringle is one of the 1st. settlers that settled on the Buckhannon River who settled at the mouth of Turkey Run about three miles from our Town. Pringle resided in this neighborhood untill he died he was upwards of 100 years of age, Hacker also died an old man on his farm on hacker's creek (you enquire) what finely became of White, White was a Terror to the Indians they had several chances to shoot at him but was afraid to do so for fear they would miss their mark and then he would retaliate, White was the stay of Buckhannon fort, and was the Leader of many of the scouting parties and the parties following and Chastizing the Indians for the depredations committed on the Citizens. White being dead when the information was gathered for Co{l}. Wither's cronicle It was therefore gathered principly from the friends of Lowther, Sleeth, Wilson, and Hacker and not giving White the Honor due him. White was taken prisoner twice By the Indians and managed so as to disguise himself and was enable[d] to make his escape at one time in making his escape he kiled an Indian feeding his Horse (2) White took the horse and flew for his safety after traveling some distance passing near Other Horses feeding one of White['s] followed after the one White was Riding so he took them both away Riding Them by Turns the Indians followed him closely for a Long distance one of their dogs over took him and the Dog knowing White followed him off also—White fought at the Battle of Point Pleasant his Brother David White fought Bled and died in that Battle, kiled several Indians on that day, he stated that he had 15 fair Shots and saw them all fall, he said 5 in One heap. Lt. frog was shot By an Indian in sight of White the Indian ran up to scalp Frog frog raising and grapling with the Indian untill White could single out the Indian from Frog, White then shot the Indian so another ran up and was Shot By White also and so on untill five Indians were laid in One heap—after the Battle was over White took some of his company of Virginians to the Spot and Shew[ed] them the Heap of Dead Bodies, Frog has by this time expired when the white[s'] examined the 5 persons kil{d}. by White the features of one of them has the appearance of a white man accordingly he was washed and recognized By his Brother Thomas Collet of Tygerts Valley This was George Collet (3) that was kiled he encouraged the Indians throughout all the fight with Loud Hussaws and was seen firing a Large Gun up into the air and crying fight on fight on we will soon whip the white Damn{d}. Suns of bitches. White was in company with John Cutright and others in capturing the Stolen Horses,

(1) See page 496. (2) p. 496. (3) p. 496.

at which time Cutright was wounded in the side as spoken of by Wither's cronicle page 210 (4)—this John Cutright spoken of was John the younger son of Benjamin[.] John Senr. I think removed at an early day to Kentucky. He was the one that fought at Point Pleasant. John Cutright the younger was a brave man and frequently accompanied White in excersions through the country spying &c at one time, White and Cutright was out on Cutrights farm weeding corn one would work and the other standing guard. in the evening when they went to Leave they Turned out their Horse and Salted him on a Rock. they then left for home, the Indians took the Horse before he had took but a few licks of the salt. they no doubt was watching White and Cutright but was afraid to attact them, on the next day when they returned to their labor they found the Horse gone and the salt yet Laying on the Rock. they followed the Trail for about 6 miles when they found the Horse turned Loose with a Bell on him, and found first sign of the Indians. they crept up to the Horse stoped the Bell and made their way off Cutright on the Horse and White on foot they had not went far when Cutright espied a Large Buck he dismounted and in spite of White would shoot the Buck, White told him the Indians would be on them before the[y] could dress the Deer, so Cutright fired and kill^d. the buck. White walked ahead Cutright dress^d. the Buck t[h]rowed him on the Horse mounted and Rode on after White the Indians follow^d. in close pursuit to within one half mile of the fort, when they arrived at the fort Cutright, White & several others returned on the trail in hopes to Meet the savages on the pursuit and thus be enabled to take them by surprise, but not going more than one half mile the[y] found they had discovered them and Left the path—no doubt but White kiled number of Indians, he at one time was arrested an[d] took to winchester Jail and there plac'd in Irons. this act enraged the friends of White they raised a company of some 100 or more and march^d. to Winchester at the break of day all Black^d. except two of the M^r. Fryes who would not paint themselves they were the commanders, they went to the Jail & demanded the prisoner the Jailor refused the[y] cocked their guns on him and told him to open the Door and Release the prisoner the Jailor gave them up the key they took him out took him to the smith shop cut off his Irons & brought him Home, last of all he was kiled by the Indians in sight of Buckhannon Fort, he was betrayed into the hands of his enemies by a white man named Timothy Dorman Dorman lived about 2 and a half miles from the fort, and while the other inhabitants fled to the fort, Dorman remained at home apparently unconcerned, saying there was no danger, (had White treated Dorman to the same severity that he did John Bull, for harboring the Indians, Dorman would have rept his reward as a traitor before the betrayal of White.) One day he professed to have fears for his safety and desired White to come down on the next day and aid himself and family to the fort. White promised him to do so, and accordingly went, and when he got there he saw signs of Indians in the yard, White told Dorman that the indians had been their and that It was a plot between him Dorman and the Indians to kill him and said he would go away and leave him with them. Dorman denied knowing that the ind^s. had been there and Beged of White not to Leave them there for the Indians would kill him and all his family White consented to remove them to the fort by a back road after they had passed on to where the two Roads run togeth[er], The Indians in ambush fired on him 3 balls passing through his body not withstanding the N^o. of Wounds he had Received he still remained on his horse for

---

(4) See page 497.

some time and It was believed that If his Horse [had] not become so frighted and Ran into the falling Top of a Tree he would have made his escape to the fort safely with his scalp, though he was wounded mortally, he fell in sight of the fort the men from the fort got to him before he was Dead he still knew his friends. the[y] had the River to cross in a canoe before they could reach him or they would of saved his scalp from the savages. (5) Dorman & family went off with the Indians, and soon returned again at the head of a party and conducted them to the dwelling of his friends and aided in the Buchery of them, he was worse than a savage—his character is Given by Col. Withers in his cronicle page 250, 251, (6) on the eight of Febry 1782, (7) John Fink was kiled while engaged in hawling rails to his farm on Buckhannon River the savages fired several guns at him and before he could unloose the Horses from the sled he fell his father was with him he mounted on one of the horses and rode of[f] making his escape. John Fink fell within a few yards from where my office now stands near the center of our Town, this occurence took place 1 month previous to the murder of White. (8) Page 229 (9) while John Jackson and his son George was returning to the fort, passing within one half mile of our town and upon my present farm the Indians fired on them but fortunately missing both, George discovered the smoke from the Indians Gun rising from behind a forked tree prepared himself and as the Indian peaked through the croch of the Tree Jackson fired at him the Ball struck too Low in Crotch and thus glancing perhaps over the savages head. Jacksons then made their way with all spead to the fort not knowing but what they were more Indians in reach, the Horse on which George Jackson was Riding Took fright and ran to the fort the Horse pass^d. out of his Girt & left Jackson & the saddle lying on the ground safely landed at the fort gate &c.

You enquire for the chief Bald Eagle the account giving By Col. Withers in his work is correct 105. (10) or at Least as much so as I can give, as I cannot find any person Living that can give any further particulars of the murder of the old chief, It is said he was kild by Jacob Scott, (11) W^m. Hacker and Elijah Runner. they are all three Dead. Runner while wrestling with a friend fell and Died in a short time after was Buryed one half or three fourths mile from this place. There are many small errors committed by the information Given to Col. Withers such as rong names &c It was David Conly that struck the Indian over the head with the Drawing knife instead of Ralston as discrib^d. by Withers. (12) Petro (13) who was taken prisoner with White was said never to be heard of after. Petro was heard of, when some of the prisoners return^d. the[y] stated that he died at detroit before peace was made. My father was but a boy in the days of invasion here. he Resided on the South Branch. at one time the Indians came to the House of John Wilson who was his step Father, after Wilson had done with the Labors of the day laid himself on his bed to rest while the wife was preparing the supper, the Dogs sprang from their slumber to an attact in the yeard the night being dark the old Gentleman knew too well the cause, he spring from his Bed the Door was standing open and throw^d. back against the wall from where the old man were. he consequently had to pass the Door way to get to the Door and shuved it shut, while he was closing the Door the Indians struck with a stick *on the Door step.* the old man making fast the Door calling to the old Lady to put out the fire, after he had fastened the Door as well as he could he took down his

---

(5) See page 497. (6) p. 500. (7) p. 500. (8) p. 500. (9) p. 500. (10) p. 500. (11) p. 500. (12) p. 500. (13) p. 500.

old rusty gun prepared her for action, while the old Lady took the axe and my father took an old rusty sword, the Indians made several attempts to forc[e] open the Door, but not being able to do so, again they would fall back to get rid of the Dogs. at every attempt they made at the Door, the old man would incourage the Dogs. they being very cross no Doubt but they took hold to the savages at every attempt they made to force open the Door, they thus continued during the night until the appearance of Day drove them off, knowing If they waited till Light that the Old man would reak his vingence on them for disturbing himself and family during the night.

I could mention a number of circumstances of the Indians making their appearance and trying to decoy persons in their hands, but not knowing whether such information is desirable to you I will therefore desist. *I mean such as the following.* at one time while my mother was a mear child (Daughter of W^m. White) was playing near the fort in the dusk of the evening, an Indian passing near them, held out to some of the smallest of the children *in his hand* some nuts in order to get them to come silently to him, but being discovered by one of the Larger children and cried out Indians the children all ran towards the fort. White always quick and ready Rushed to the gate Just in time to see the Indian pass in to a thicket of Timber, the Indian seeing White had discovered him he spring behind a large tree and kept White and the tree in a range untill he pass behind Bluff or bank. and thus made his escape, at an other time two boys went out to bring up their cows, while driving the cows homeward, they discovered some milk keelers Laying in the path which had been placed ther after they had pass^d. out. (these vessels had been taken a few days previous from a neighboring house) One of the Boys was in act of stoping to Look—while the other one cried out run. (knowing the object) as soon as the boys commenced running the Indians whistled and then call^d. stop, stop. but the boys was off homewards—Tigerts Valley *so called* is now the County of Randolph was named after David Tigert who first settled on this valley uppon what's now call^d. the Valley River[.] Tigert It seems was a trapper followed the waters for the purpose and Lastly made a Trip and never returned back to this Valley again I have no knowledge of any of his decendants—I now close my communication By saying I have not been able to obtain as much information as I had expected I should—W^m. White as I before mentioned was kil^d. and Treacherously kil^d too, and deserves more Honor for active service in defending his country against a savage foe than his memory ever received in the pages of History, White had but two children one son & one Daughter; his son W^m. W. White still lives here the Daughter Elizabeth married Joel Westfall my Father, raised a large family and died here Whites widow never married but lived to an old age and died near this place.

Respectfully yours
(Signed) HENRY F. WESTFALL (14)

"I am Col. of a Regiment of Infantry & P M at this place.
To L. C. Draper Esq
  from H. F. Westfall P M
  Lyman C. Draper Esq
    Philadelphia Pa
      Box 797 P O"

---

(14) See page 500.

(Draper MSS. 8ZZ45.)

"Harmony grove (15) April 12th 1849

"Mr Draper Sir, yours of the 16th of Jan was duly received when received I was Laying with a fevor which kept me prostrate 4 weeks then I had an attac of Cholera but I yet live this is the appology I offer for my delay.

"As my uncle W^m. Hacker & W^m. Powers of this neighborhood wrote the Borderwarfare thare is to be found all or nearly so that can be had of information as to the difficulties of this region with the Indians.

"I have been to see Jonathan Hacker (distance 20 miles) a Bro. of Said W^m. Hacker but cannot get the time that Bald eagle was kill^d. nor nothing that might be of advantage to you

"The William Hacker refer^d. to in the case of Bald Eagle was Brother to Old John Hacker first settler on Hacker's creek (as in Border warfare), his scouts & campaigns are not known it is said he was the foremost in danger the bravest in peral & the first to assist in need, When one of his comerads I understood a mr Cutright was shot through the flesh of the brest W^m. Hacker drew a piece of silk through the bullet hole to clense & then bound up the wound, & one old man says he once had the name of doctor from his attention to the wounded, he moved to the Read banks of Ohio River in Kentucky Shortly after the Death of Bald Eagle —Reports say he moved from Ky to Canady & became wealthy this by some is doubted But I believe it true—he must now be dead for I am informed he was Older than my Grandfather Old John Hacker we cant hear of any W^m. Hackers Decendants

"I am Very Sorry that I cannot give you more

"William Hacker the writer of the Border Warfare was the son of John Hacker But my Grand uncle W^m. Hacker Was the Man that assisted in distroying Bulltown &^{c}.

"This I have done I would have done more with pleasure but I can get nothing more of Use to you."

(Signed) Yours David H. Smith (16)

Addressed: Mr Lyman C Draper Philadelphia Pa
(Postmarked Jane Lew [Va] April 16)

(The following correspondence is all from the Draper MSS. 3U.)

"Green Clay Co Kan Jan 20 1891

"Mr Draper
"Dear Sir

"I received your letter yesterday after examining carefully I will proceed answer it the best I know how. my grate Grand Father come from England in 1740 and my Grand Father (John Hacker) was born about 3 weeks after landing in America near Winchester va (17) what time in the year I am not able to say (write H. M. Hacker my son Jane Lew W va he will go to the simetury & take the right date off the tomb stone) he died April 24, 1824 at the [age] of 84 years. he filled no office but Indian scout. he had 6 sons and 4 daughters his oldest son William was a Preacher a Majestrate and School teacher in that early day. as I have answered all the questions you have ask me I remain yours truly

J. T. Hacker

(15) See page 500. (16) p. 500. (17) p. 501.

"if you desire any other infermation command me I meane about the family records I am at your surves   J. T. H."

"Green Kan Jan 26 1891

"Mr Draper
"Dear Sir

"as for my Grand Father ever scouting in ohio is something I cannot say. as for the collections being facts I suppose there are no doubt; but my Grandfather did not collect any of them: it was my uncle William Hacker his oldest son & William Powers who collected the facts of the Indian troubles in W va and my uncle died before he completed the work; and his Heirs were not able nor willing to go on with it and Powers and the Hacker sold to Mr Withers. I suppose Judge Duncan had something to do in the collection of facts. I am not shore about the date of my uncles death; the tomb stone will tell; he was buried in the same semetory that my Grand Father was. (18)   if my memory serves me right he died in 1830 I suppose that what is written in the border warefare is truth but perhaps it is not all that might have been Collected and written

Yours very truly
J. T. Hacker

"an old democrat in my 79th year only 39 days till my burth day I was 12 when my Grand Father died Wm. Hacker my uncle and myself are all the Preachers of the family."

"Janelew W. Va Janua 28th/91

"Mr. Lyman C. Draper

"Sir   I received yours of the 23rd but I was not able to take the trip to the gravyard till yesturday it is 5 mls from here I send you a true coppy of the Inscription and you can use just what you want of it.   I also send you his wifes birth and death.   if you dont need it all right it costs nothing to send it

I will Just say to you if there is any more information you wish from here that I can gather up I will gladly do so.   and I will say now that I wish the agency of this State when the work is ready for sale hoping to hear from you soon I am yours

H. M. Hacker"

[Copy]

"This monument erected in memory of John Hacker Born 1st of January, 1743. Settled on this farm in Wilderness, 1769, endured innumerable privations by Indian hostilities—died April 20th A. D. 1821, (19) aged 81y. 3m. 9d. was the first intered in this graveyard.   Prepare to follow me

"Margaret Hacker, wife of John Hacker, was born in Ireland, June 24, 1747 —Came to America, 1748.   Died May 8th 1832—aged 84 ys 10 m & 14 days."

"Green Kan Feb 13 1891

"Mr L. Draper Esq
"Dear Sir

"I received you letter yesterday

"examined its contents and to my best recolections there was but two Children of my Great Grandfather and they were both Boys Wm and John. and they were the only family of that name I ever heard of being in America.   at that early

---

(18) See page 501.   (19) p. 501.

date. Wm went down the Mississippi to what was then called the Red Banks* and that was the last account as for my Grand Father ever being in Illinois I cannot say. Jacob Hardman a grand son living in South Bend Indiana (dead now perhaps) wrote to me 14 years ago for accounts of the family and I gave him dates &C he was writing a Book if he is not living some of his family may be he was to send me a Book but I never got it. all the Hacker boys went to Ind.

"all well and striving for Heaven.
"Kansas has turned upside down politically
"I say huray for Democracy

Yours trely
J. T. HACKER"

*[Note by L. C. Draper]
Red Banks or Hendersonville, Ky: Dr. Hildreth in *American Pioneer*, II, 102.

"SOUTH BEND, ST. JOSEPH COUNTY,
INDIANA, March 20, 1891

"LYMAN C. DRAPER
"DEAR SIR:

"Dr. Jacob Hardman died in this city several years ago. Was very old at the time of his death but had a good memory. He has one daughter living in this city—Miss Maggie Hardman. Hon. Wm Hacker, Shelbyville, Ind., a cousin of Dr. Hardman would be of service to you in looking up the family history. He is quite a historian and a great masonic leader and teacher.

Respectfully
ELMER CROCKETT, P. M."

"GREEN CLAY Co KAN April 13/91

"Dear Bro Draper I recd your letter a few days ago & I now will try to answer it as near as I can. Wm Powers lived on Hackers Creek 5 Ms below where Wm Hacker lived close to Jane Lew and was a farmer and owned a fine farm in the valley of Hackers Creek, and died there: as for his age I cannot tell had 3 sons Benjamin Ezeckial & Wm they moved off I know not where you can get his age and death by writing to Col James W Jackson Jane Lew Lewis Co W va as for the extent of the ade he gave my uncle I cannot inform you but I always unders[t]ood they were equal pardners. Hacker died first. as for Wm Hacker in Shelbyville of whome you wrote I know nothing: he must be a cousin of mine

yours trely
J. T. HACKER"

"GREEN KAN may 12/91

"MR L C DRAPER
"DEAR SIR

"I received your letter yesterday and I now procede to answer it 1st Wm Powers clamed an equal share with Wm Hacker and Hackers Heirs and Powers himself before his death, sold to Withers what they received I know not.

2nd of this W^m. G. Hacker of Wichita I know nothing he clames to be a grandson of Alex Hackers who says you say that his father* colected the matter used by Wethers. It cannot be true for this was all done before the oldest son of Alex was grown. Alex Hacker Wife [died] and he bound his boyes all out, and went to Ind. and married again. there were 6 Boys of John Hacker my Grand father, and Alex was the 5th one and 2 Girls before Alex. Wm was the 1st you can see the policy of it

3rd I cannot answer that whether the Indians killed Wm Hackers Wife & family or not my father had told me often that his unkle William had no family he acted as sergent in the Indian wars

4th in reference to the killing of the Indian Chief Bald Eagle I know nothing; but if the Border Warfair says so I suppose it is true. of these other Men that you write was with Hacker I know nothing

5. I was raised on Hackers Creek and lived there the most of my life: was born March 6 1812 therefore I was seventy nine March 6 last

7th Wither got the Collections for a trifle I always understood; I know [not] how much

8th I knew Withers Persanly and my idea is that he in reference to education he was limited and not strictly honest (this is confidential)

9 I cannot [say] any thing about Israel

10 W. Powers has a son living in Norton Co Kansas norton is the town his name is Wm D Powers lives in Norton Co Norton P O Kansas

I have answered the 10 questions to the best of my knowledge. My Father has often told me that his uncle William Hacker went down the Mississippi to what is called the red Banks: whether he ever had any heirs or not I am not apprised

"I am very much under obligations to you for the Magazine you sent me yours truly

J. T. Hacker

*It was grandfather, Alex^r. Hacker."

"Green Kan May 25/91

"Mr Draper
'Dear Sir

"your letter of the 19 recd will say first that I was mis informed about the address of Wm D. Powers and gave you the rong one, have learned cince that his adress is Wichita Sedgwick Co Kansas you will not be likely to hear from that letter, you say that perhaps my grand father furnished some scheches [sketches] to his nefew my uncle William my uncle was my Grand Fathers oldest son: perhaps he did furnish some; but I do not know that he did my Grandfather was born 3 weks after his Parents landed in America his Bro Wm was born in Engeland how old he was when they landed in America I cannot say. The last depridation committed in west va was in the year of 1795 after pease made Wm Hacker my Great uncle went down the Mississippi to the read banks was supposed to have died there: in reference to his family being kiled or his being wounded or fighting in Ill as I wrote before I know nothing: only what the Border Warfair says; which you can read for your self.

"as for this Dr. Wm A. Hacker in Ill know nothing there is A Wm Hacker the Mear [Mayor] of Leavensworth Kan you may get some information [from] him my uncles Hacker four of the Boys, moved in an early day to Shelby Co Ind and consiquently I lost sight of them "as for my Grandfather's Brother Wm what I said or intended to, if I did not that he came to Hackers Creek and acted as surgen and had no family tho the Indians were on the warpath before that. I said if the Border Warfair said his family were killed by the Indians it must be true but when he came to Hackers Creek he had no family so I have understood

J T Hacker

"excuse bad speling and writing for my education was gotten in the wilderness of W va in a log school House with paper window glass your friend

J T H"

"Green Kan May 30 1891

"Mr Draper Dear Sir

"I received your letter yesterday and I will proceded to answer it to the best of my judgement my memory (from what my father said) is that Wm Hacker my Grand fathers Bro was about 2½ years the oldest; but my understanding is that he never had any family. in reference to the destroying and murdering the Indeans at Bulltown it is true my father has told me often about it; and blamed his uncle much for the masacree. for they were friendly Indians and it was so inhuman they kiled Wimen and Children caught the poore little Children by the heels and nocked their brains out against there huts. this horable story has been told me by my Father and several old Indian wariers on Hackers Creek. it is horable but true. Its not worth while to deneigh it. those men said. gnits would make lice; and the Bulltown indians harbered the wariers there were several of the old wariers who scouted and fought the Indians that remained on Hackers Creek and died there so I got many Indian storyes when there would 2 or more get togather. (as for Wm Hacker of shelbyville I would love to know whose son he is an his age) as for Scott and Runner, or White I can give you no certain account: or there decendance my opinion is they went to Kentucky down about Louisville or below; this is only my opinion not from any evidence only impression. as for the cheaf Bald Eagle I have said in a former letter I know nothing but will say as I have allready said to you in other letters that that is written in Withers work is true considdered so by all the old warriors with whome I have converst Withers was not consedered strictly upright but honest in compiling the Book People thought he aught to have sined Hackers and Powers name to the Book insted of his own. tho that matter but little

"My Dear Bro I am still of the opinion that Wm Hacker my grand Fathers Bro was never marrierd my Father always told me so it has been some time since I have read the Border Warfair: I do not remember whether it is mentioned in the Book of Wm Hackers family being killed by the Indians if it is mentioned there I will beleave it and if it is not there I will think it ought not be there. I am honest and I dont want you to think otherwise

"I have done all I could to collect my mind togather to find the truth and to keep off of what I have read in withers work suposing you had it and give you what I have from memory and tradition no more at this time
but remaen your sincear friend
and bro in Christ

J. T. Hacker" (20)

---

(20) See page 501.

"Wichita Kansas March 17th 1891

"Lyman C. Draper Esq.
 Madison, Wisconsin.
"Dear Sir
   "Your letter of Feb. 25th to hand which has been delayed on account of my name being addressed Granvill Hacker. I am known in this country only by the name of W. G. Hacker I have been here in Sedgwck Co. going on 21 years. I resided in Illinois 4 years previs to that time I lived in Vª where I was borned and raised on Hackers creek now Lewis Co. West Vª You speak of the Rev. William Hacker. I do not know of such a man on our side of the house. My fathers name is Thomas S. Hacker, he was born in 1816 and died in Letart Falls* in 1885; my father's father's name was Alexander Hacker, his fathers name was John Hacker the Mary Hacker that the border of Warfare speaks of was the daughter of John Hacker and a sister of my fathers father was scalped and stabbed seven (7) times by the Indians on Dec. 5th 1787 (21) in the year 1760 (22) my great grand father John Hacker and his brother William Hacker came from the valley of Vª not far from Lexington, to the old fort Buckhannon now West Vª, our family are quite numerous and wonderfully scattered, there is a great many of them Uncle Jonathan Hacker's children reside in Indiana; Uncle Philip's are in Tennessee and Kentucky. Uncle William's in Kentucky & Indiana My great, great grandfather, John Hacker, and his brother William resided where Buchanon now stands. Some eight or ten years before the arrival of Smuel Pringle, (23) John and Benjamin Carturight and it appears that Samuel Pringle and my great grand-father John Hacker had a dispute in regard to what we call claims on land John Hacker and John and William Radicliff taken up their farms in about one and a half miles of where Jane Lew now stands, (and later) know now in later days as Powers farm on the creek what is known then as a branch of the Monongahela The creek was named after my great grand-father John Hacker as Hacker's creek in the year 1769 You speak of or asked me if I knew of any of my kinsmen furnishing any of the chronicals of the border of war fare to Alexander Withers, I beg to say while it appears on the pages of border of war fare in the beginning that Alexander Withers was the author of the Border of War Fare, or history of the settlements by the whites of North Western Vª I say he is not the author, my grandfather Alexander Hacker, my fathers father is the original writer and had the manuscript ready for publication about the year 1830 but was not able to bear the expens of publication at that time, my father informed me also my mother of who was Charlotte Hess her father Heschia Hess who went through the Revolutionary [&] War of 1812 whom I knew when I was a small boy just beginning to pry into historical writings—that Alexander Withers did make a bargain with my grandfather Alexander Hacker, if he would allow him to have a great many of the books published and have control of their sale he would bear the expences of the publication and that Alexander Hacker should have the credit of writing the book, this my grandfather agreed to, you see on the first page, under the flyleafed cover, that Alexander S. Withers did steal the right and title of the cronicles of the Border of Ware Fare, from Grandfather Hacker: and the Withers family

---

*Meigs County, Ohio. L. V. McW.

---

(21) See page 501. (22) p. 501. (23) p. 501.

is intitled to no credit for the writing of the Border of War Fare ma[li]ciously stolen away from my ancestors. I beg to give Mr. Withers credit only for having the money to bring about the publication of this valuable book now open before my eyes. I refer you to pages 93 and 105 and 280 & 281 for facts printed and published in the Border of War Fare, (24) my kinsman in V^a are numerous namly Smith's Baton's Allman's Alkires Post's Bonnet's Morrison's West's many others to tegious to mention. I will say that I myself and a cousin of Indina have traced our ancestors through North America back to England even to Colonel Francis Hacker who read the death warrant of King Charles the (1) first where he was beheaded at White hall England after the thirty years war and the end of the Romish yoke by Lord Cromwell and others. The name was then spelled previous to this, Hecker; under the old Anglo Saxon of Germany, it was spelled— Heckeredt: We go on farther to the seven high priests, that our sacred history gives an account of, long before John Knox's time when they resolved to form a band and called themselves Knight Templars and drew their swords in defence of the widows the orphans and the Christian religion from thense we came and now we stand my cousin informs me it would cost about $800 to have his manuscript published in book form, it appears that he does not want history of our people published till after his death. I persume he is waiting to add to the last days and moments of our lives, or his life while he remains with us on earth. I would be very glad to know who this H W Hacker of Jane Lew is and what age he is, if he is a man of means and moral and in good standing I could give him a position with our manufacuring astablishment would like to correspond with him. I am unable to make out who this Rev. William Hacker is perhaps he is a descendant of my great grand father John Hacker's brother William. I had a cousin John Hacker that was a preacher about Jane Lew. I beg of you in honor to the Hacker's in general not to allow the name of Alexander Wither's to bear any connection to your rewriting the Border of War Fare. I knew a Rev Mr. Clark who I think was connected with the Cincinnati Publishing Company about 42 years ago. Could this be any relation to R. C. Clarke—if so, I know him to be a good preacher. In answer to yours I could not say right now whether & where there any living children of my grandfather. I think that Jonathan Hacker my fathers brother is dead. I know that my father died in 1885 I think that William Hacker my uncle is living in Tennessee. You might write Uncle Daniel Helmick at Tenbonparise Tennessee if he is living he can give you the desired information, he married one of my fathers brothers daughters I think, or my grandfathers only sister I don't know which, there were seven children in my grandfathers family six boys and one girl. I will cheerfully do so from time to time, and hope to hear from you often. I have a better head than I have a stead[y] hand, my daughter Mary Ella H. has written this letter for me very hurridly and in a very much embarrased condition this being the first attempt of writing a letter dictated, hope you will excuse all urse and omittances and more aspecialy our paper. as I only received your letter yesterday and under the pressure of buisness have been hurried to answer your communication now approaching the "wee" hours of the night, please find enclosed two cards which one will you choose.

       I remain Yours Very Truly
         WILLIAM GRANVILL HACKER"

---

(24) See page 502.

"WICHITA, KAS, May 10th 1891

"LYMAN C. DRAPER

"DR SIR: My father was born in 1816 his name, Th⁸ S. Hacker. I was his oldest child, born in 1841, & the only one living.

"My father's father was Alexʳ Hacker, a son of John Hacker. John & his brother William Hacker settled at old fort Buchannon. John locating about a mile and a half from Jane Lew, on the road from Jane Lew to Jackson's Mill on the West Fork. (25)

"I did not say that my grandfather, Alexʳ Hacker wrote the Chronicles of Border Warfare, but by his father, John Hacker. (26) I cant help what other claim, that Wᵐ Hacker, John's son, wrote the Chronicles; or what John T. Hacker, a Methodist minister, says, that Wᵐ Hacker, a son of John, & one Wᵐ Powers did the gathering of the materials for the work. Thinks they are not old enough.

"The father of Wᵐ Powers, married into the Hacker family. I knew Wᵐ Powers when [I was] a small boy. John T. Hacker wᵈ like to have owned the whole world, but only got enough of it to lay his body on, after he came out of the Confederate army. (27) * * * *

"Sally Hacker, daughter of John Hacker, the pioneer, married David Smith— she lived to be 84 years old

"In answer to your question what did Withers pay for the manuscript he used in his work. Have no knowledge of Israel, the publisher. Have often heard my parents speak of Wither's book, that he defrauded the Hackers out of the title or authorship of the work. I have seen them shed tears over it. Withers did [not] pay anything for the work, nor promise to pay anything. There was some consideration made, I know, in regard to the publishing of the work with John Hacker. There was a great intimacy between my father & Henry Withers, son of Alexʳ Withers, who kept a store some 6 or 7 miles on Hackers Creek, handed down by his father There was something wrong about the publication of the book. I cᵈ have known more, but I left that country in 1859, when I was abt. 18 years old.

"William Hacker, brother of John Hacker that came to Hackers' Creek— there is not much known of him only as an Indian fighter. I suppose you are aware that he lost his wife in the early settlement of Virginia near old fort Buchannon—murdered by the Indians in a lull of peace, after they came to Hacker's Creek about the year 1769 or 1770. From this time on, we find him killing Bald Eagle on Hacker's Creek on the frontier with Jacob Scott & Elijah Runner. Wᵐ Hacker also took more Indⁿ scalps at Bulltown, in retaliation for the murder of his family: The family of Strode [Stroud] living on Gauley river—in company with a party of 5 men, two of whom were Wᵐ White & Wᵐ Hacker [destroyed Bulltown.]   Respectfully

W. G. HACKER
By ELLA HACKER"

"LYMAN C DRAPER   "May 18th 1891
    "Madison, Wisconsin

"DEAR SIR   I am happy to inform you that Uncle William Hacker married a Scotch lady she was murdered by the Indians about the time or some little time

(25) See page 502. (26) p. 502. (27) p. 502.

before the second coming of Samuel Pringle in the year of 1768. I know of Pringle's they with the Hacker's Jackson's and Sleath's Davis Brown's and Hughes and Radcliff's settled in and around Buckhannon, my grand father Hesicha Hess Peter Wagner my uncle David Smith Jaboc Cocad I have heard them talk this over that Wm Hacker's wife had never been mentioned in the Border of Ware Fare I have often when I was a small boy heard Peter Wagner once a captive talk about these matters when he was a very old man I used to work for him, spreading hay in harvest and have heard him tell Indian massacres and of his capture. I have also heard Aunt Math Bonnet speak of William Hacker's wife being murded by the Indians I have also heard the above parties speak of Aunt Mary Wolf being murdered. In the year according to record of Withers 1768 we find that Wm Hacker and John Hacker his brother my fathers grandfather with others let out from Buckhannon or Bushs Fort and went on to the West Fork of the Mongalia the following year now known as Hackers creek. And that Wm Hacker Jess Hugh's was the hunters with others that killed the game that supplied those that tilled the ground and give considerable service to the new settlements and once and a while take in an Indian on the sly I have heard folks speak in very sly way about parties killing Indians and tha[t] Wm Hacker was getting revenge or I should say did get revenge but there was but few people that knew it. Wm Hacker at the time his wife was murdered did not have any children or as I never heard any of his children spoken of. I seen that his brother John Hacker had a girl a sister to Edmond West['s wife] a daughter of John Hacker 11 years in 1787 this Mary Hacker was my fathers great aunt that was scalped and stabbed seven times in the body threw over the fence for dead by order of Lenard Schoolcraft a trator to the whites. you take 1768 and 1787 and deduct the lesser from the greater and you have 19 years between the time of the settling of Buckhannon by the Hacker and the massachres and captures of the daughter of Jess Hughs on Hackers creek you take the eleven years from the 19 years and you have left 8 years. now this is supposed to be the youngest daughter of John Hacker. the oldest daughter marrying the Hess and Hughs. would bring the time or the elapse of 8 years down that Wm Hacker must have got married about the time his brother John did my grandfather Hess. (28) I have heard him talk, with my father and mother about killing an old Indian up above the mill dam by Jackson mill at Jane Lew (29) and cutting him open filling him full of sand and sinking him in the water I have went to the place to see if I could see him myself when I was smal I cannot explain why Wm Hackers wife was not mentioned in the border of War Fare any more than I can tell why this Indian grandfather Hess killed was not mentioned by Withers, this is where I have heard the folks talk that Withers hadn't all of the Hacker manuscript published I can not help what honorable Wm Hacker of Shelbyville says, but I have heard Peter Wagner Jacob Corcad Richard Baton Aunt Math Bonnet maiden name Hacker (30) Uncle David Smith my father my grandfather Hess, and mother speak of the Bulltown that was named Bultown by the Indians masachred and was spoken in a way that it was Wm Hacker and the two whites and two other parties that Withers has left out that did murder those Indians for revenge now since I have written you the first letter I called to memory what is known at the North edge of Braxton and South edge of Lewis Co's a farm of plantation known as the Hacker by some Hacke flats and Hacker plantation or Hacker farm near Jacksonville not a great ways

(28) See page 502. (29) p. 507. (30) p.507.

from Sutonville talking with Mr. Law a few days ago of which he claimed relationship to me, of which I have only known him a short time less than a year Mr Laws wife was a Keth and her grandmother was a Hacker now I have no doubt in my mind but that William Hacker married the second time in amongst the children of his associates as I do know that he did associate with Jesse Hughs and that Hughs and Keth's and Slegthes and McNeamor Mackletess and Hackers are all related, with others I have not mentioned some of these a little distant relation above mentioned to somewhat some others are a distinction being between John H and Wm Hacker it is very evident that Wm Hacker has carried his side of the relationship in a se[c]ond marriage to that of John H his brother as to the Bald Eagle the old Indian cheif I am unable to say wether Bald Eagle had any hand in the killing of Wm H. wife or not. (31) In regard to Elijah Runner the associate of William Hacker and Jacob Scott as to Jacob Scott I have never seen but have heard him spoken of frequently as to Elijah Runner I have been in his son's blacksmith shop or the original Elijah Runner I don't know which many a time when I was about 8 or 10 years old Mr Runner was a very old man at that time and had his home and shop located of Jessie Run Lewis Co W V^a my father was a very intimate friend of Mr. Runner (32) I do not know of any of his family that is living I have not known anything of Mr Runner for about 40 yars I have given you the dates and all the information and what I have heard talked of when I was small in regard of the killing of Mrs Hacker Bald Eagle and others that I can it matters not what Mr Withers book has not chronocclized or has cronciklized I have only given to you what I have learned and heard before I ever saw the Border of War Fare that book I never saw until after I was 16 or 17 years old then I precured one and read it and found that it did not contain all that I knew before I saw the book as my memory from others and from old heads was my education by listening reletting and remembering was all that I had to speak of I never could write to amount to anything or read writing to our last civil war I will give you the name of a relative of ours that lives on Hacker creek West V^a Lewis Co. by the name of Nicklos Alkire who might give you information in regard to Elijah Runner or Jacob Scott's children that would give the diserd information which you request of me. I will also refer you to Iscic Jackson Jane Lew West V^a I believe that I have answered all of your questions and the facts as near as I possibly can

       Yours Respetaly

           W G Hacker (33)
             Per E"

        "Pennsboro Ritchie Co W Va
           June 5/91

"L C Draper Esqr
"Dr Sir
 "I received your letter and will try to get my daughters Husband Mr T A Brown attorney at law at Elizabeth Wirt Co W Va to attend to your request but if he cant spare the time I will consider the Proposition my self the Book was written by Grandfather Powers and a Friend at his own house I have the table uppon which it was written. Withers was only employed by him to make it ready for the Press in case Mr Brown will undertake it I will furnish him with what informa-

---

(31) See page 507. (32) p. 507. (33) p. 507.

APPENDIX I

tion I have and can collect, which I think will be considerable. Please write to him and if he cannot undertake the correspondence I will do the best I can to help you out with your undertaking.

"with the best wishes that you may sucksead in seting rite a long standing wrong to my Grandfather and his descendents to God and mankind I bid you
A Respectful adiew
WILLIAM. M. POWERS

PS—always consider me at your service Wm M. P."

"PENNSBORO RITCHIE Co W VA
June 27/91

"L C DRAPER L. L. D.
"DEAR SIR
"as I roat to you before I met with an accident that nearly cost me my life but am getting some better so that I am able to write a little agane I have written to various ones for information and I think we will soon begin to reap a rich harvest I am doing every thing I can to ade in the cause and I would thank you for any suggestion you think Proper to make you asked in your first letter if Grandfather was a Publick man yes—under the Virginia law of his day. I have understood that the madgistrate was appointed instead of elected as is now the case and after being madgistrate for so long then they served a turn of Sheriff and then Madgistrate for so long againe at any rate my Grandfather was [has] filled the two offices for a grate number of years he also held a commision as captain (34) in the Indian war and had charge of some posts on the Ohio River and was a candidate for the legislature but was defeated by one voat. He was a Freemason and was known and respected as far as any man in western virginia in his day and when he died he was buried in the honors of war the melistia was commanded by Col. D. H. Smith now dead and the general Program was arainged by Hon Blackwell Jackson of Jane Lew now dead now as to this statement I will write and find out some of the statement who of his old nabors are living and give you thare address: he drew a Pension from the U. S. Government you ask in the second letter who aded Grandfather: W^m. Hacker the first male white child born on the crick and the crick was named after this W^m. Hacker (35) to what extent did he assist whether in writing or gathering the statements I dont know but as I have always understood that grandfather was the author of the book it would be resonable to suppose that Hacker furnished infermation and grandfather did the writing as grandfather was a good scribe and a well educated and informed man for the backwoods: this would seam the true case but to as I have never herd the Hacker Family lay any clame to the authorship of the Book in such cases we only can infer from what reason teaches at what Period did your grandfather work—I dont know; but would suppose him to be from 50 to 60 years old when he done it what araingements did he make with withers I always understood that withers was only imployed by grand father to correct or rather to devide in chapters and such like, so as to be ready for the Press without delay so that the type setting could be gone on with without delay; but what Pay he was to have I dont know did withers fulfill what he agreed to do in the matter I have understood that he left out considerable that should have ben in it especially some fites with indiens which grandfather was in was this assistant of your grand father connected with

(34) See page 507. (35) p. 507.

this withers arraingement I think not I never herd so; in fact, I never herd that he lade any claim to the work. I think if he demanded any thing that grandfather must have satisfied him. what became of the manuscript statements Joseph Israel the Printer, ran of to the west and took the manuscripts with him and that was the reason always asigned by grandfathers family why grandfather didnt go to law for his property and I think he was getting old, and altho a very brave man and grate fighter, I think rather than go to law he would suffer wrong. how many Pages of them wase thare or about how many? I have no Knowledge when and whare did your grandfather die and at what age? at his home near Jane Lew June 6″ 1855 in his 90th year. dont know when born but know he was nearly 90 when he died whare was he born at what was then known as Powers foart on Simpsons Crik whare the town of bridgeport now stands in Harrison County, W. Va. (36)
and when settled in west va I dont know when his father setled in w va but he came from Hagerstown M. D. thay once owned the land that hagerstown stands on; thay decended from very welthy europeans, I belive thay ware inglish: grandfather's grandfather once owned 10 merchant ships was he old enough to take any part in the indian wars yes and did take Part and was not given credit with it in his own book on p 105 (37) of withers work is given an account of the deth of Bald Eagle what was it led to his murder I dont know but will try to find out on p 106 (38) the destruction of Bulltown is it correct I dont know but will try to find out do you know when and whare Jacob Scott & Elijah Runner died & thare ages & descendants do not I know a Elijah Runnion perhaps he is one L C Draper a man I gratly respect let me apoligise for this delay I could have got others to write in fact made the trial but met with such Poor success that I stoped untill I could write myself now kind old friend be sure and write all you want to and ask all questions you want and he assured I will gladly do my best to answer them correctly as I can of course I know nothing only by tradition but of course that is all you can expect and to dont send stamped envilopes to me I will not put you to that expense in your old days altho a Poor Enjinear & inventor yet it dos me more good than you think to correspond with a man of your integrity lerning and such—now may you live to complete all your works and to enjoy the fruits of your labors and when you go hence as we all must may you find the Peas which Paseth understanding

Kind Friend fair the well
WM. M. POWERS"

"PENNSBORO RITCHIE CO W VA
July 4″/91

"L C DRAPER
"DR SIR

"I received your letter a day or two ago and will try to answer your inqurys the best I can

"1st Grandfathers Fathers name was John; dont know when he was born or when he died or his age: he owned a farm at Westfield on the West fork river 5 or 6 miles below weston the 1st site of Lewis Co but the site was moved to weston and the town dwindled to nothing I think thare is where he died Father moved to Kans and took his Grandfathers large Family Bible with him a large planly engraved

(36) See page 507. (37) p. 507. (38) p. 507.

Bible costing $17 dollars at that time would cost about $3.50 only now Father is dead and I fear I cant find the record of Great Grandfathers birth but at any rate I have wrote to day to my Brother in Kansas to send me the records of Grandfather and his Father and a copy of Grandfathers commission as captian of the post on the ohio river if he can find them I have understood from outside partys that the name of the Fort at Bridgeport was Powers fort; (39) I never herd our family call it by that name; but I dont doubt but that was the name of the fort I have herd Grandfather say he knew when the city of Clarksburg was all in the woods and that is only 5 miles west of Bridgeport now Joseph Johnson was once Govner of Virginia and a relation of Grandfathers he was living a few years ago but is very likely to be dead by this time but his children might know all about the Powers Family while they lived at Bridgeport he had a soninlaw by the name of English who used to visit Grandfather often, some years before he died. I am satisfied If he is living he could give you very valuable information: 2d yes, Father and me Placed a marble Headstone at his grave in 1861 that will give the dates in full & it may be his Father was buried there (at Broad Run Graveyard) also 3d I have understood he had the office of sheriff several terms. I recollect the last time he had it when he was eighty odd years old and could not ride the County and sold the office to other partys: he has a Grand Son by the name of Levi Bond at Lost Creek Postoffice Harrison Co W Va who must be about 70 I expect he knows how often he had the office and mite have other valuable information but if you address him dont mention my name as we ar not on good terms

"4 never saw Joseph Israel he must have Run off soon after publishing the Border warefare 5 Elija Runnion died (40) about 1858 aged about 60, thirty years or more younger than Grandfather was a renter & laborer; lived in Lewis & Harrison Countys and liked a dram; has a son Wm Runnion at Jane Lew or Buchanen I dont know which

"Wm. D. Powers was my father he is dead I have written more letters of inquiry & will write some more be assured your letters is always welcom

Your True Friend

WILLIAM M. POWERS"

"PENNSBORO RITCHIE Co W VA
July 20/91

"LYMAN C DRAPER
"DR SIR

"I have ben wating to hear from the letters I wroat to difron Parties for information in regard to Grandfather & his works but have received no answer as yet I have written to the P M in Kansas to find my Brothers address as I havent got no answer from the letter I sent my Brother he must have moved I have written other leters of enquiry and hope to gane some information from some of them I have lerned from enquiry that Luther Haymond the Cashier of the 1st National Bank of Clarksburg is still living he is as Honerable Man as West Virginia affords he was an old friend of Grandfathers I believe if you would write to him he could give you more information about Grandfather & his Book & his Indian fighting than any other man now living I recollect of hearing the old folks talk of two fights that Grandfather had with Indians one was with Elis & Jess Hughes & Alex West Grandfather & others the indeans had taken a lot of Prisoners and these

(39) See page 507. (40) p. 508.

men folowed them and overtook them at night and wated till in the nite and the attacked Indians and recaptured the Prisoners John Rony a white Boy captive was I believe the only white one kiled in the battle he also was in the fight with them I think some whare in the country in company with Col Lowther and others and one of thare Party one John Bonnet I think was kiled in the fight and they caried his remanes as long as thay could and rapt him in a blanket & buried him in a cave in the rocks.

Your Tru Friend
Wm. M. Powers"

"Pennsboro W Va Aug 12/91
Ritchie Co

"Lyman C Draper
"Dr Sir

"I have just received a letter from my Brother giving old family records &c he says thare is no exact record of the birth of our grate grandfather John but will suppose he was born between the years 1740 & 1745 since the record of the birth of his eldest son Thomas is 1763 John Powers the husband of Prudence was born Probably about 1742 and deceased Oct 26 1823 his son William the 2nd son of John and Prudence and the Husband of Hannah was born Nov 9" 1765 and deceased June 6" 1855 he say he cant find Grandfathers commission as captane in the Indian war but has sean his land warrent for 160 akers of land entitled to him as a soldier I have written several letters of enquiry about Grandfather but only Part of them have been answered and such as was was not of any value if this had only ben begun some 15 years ago before some of those who knew about old times died it would have ben an easy mater to find out about it but now it seam nearly impossible to obtain much information on the subject I have ben informed by one who I wrote to for information that Miss Withers a grandaughter of the Clament of Border warefare is at work overhawling hur grandfathers Book with the intention of having it republished I understand that Noah Flesher of Weston Lewis co is Prepareing a similar work for Publication I wish to keep you informed about such matters as well as I can

"You wrote me in your last letter that your Lady was very sick Pleas receive my sympathy for you & hur we have had sickness in our family at times I know the trouble and the sorrow of it and if what we see with the hewman eye was all it would be sad indead but when we look through sickness sorrow Pane and death with the eyes of the spirit upheld by our Savior then we have hope of eternal safety beyond the river that we all must cross may she be upheld by his Spirit that he Promised to send us all and when she starts over the Jordan that Jordan that we all must cross may she cross not with sadness & regret but with the Joy of the blest

From your ever Gratefull
Friend
Wm M Powers"

"Jane Lew W Va May 26/91

"Mr Lyman C Draper

"Dear Sir I Received yours of 9" and in Reply I do not know very Much a bout the Early Settles of this Country all Though my Grand & Greate Grand

Fathers was a most the first Settlers of this Country tha Emigrated her[e] from New Jersey 1st you wish to know How the Work of Withers Border War Fare Was goten up and How the People Regarded it. I think Withers Wrote it and W^m. Powers gave Him the Most of the Sketches I was acquainted With Both that is Withers & Powers and they Were Good Men and I think Whot Sketches thay give were very Corect as far as I know; I never Read it but understand it to be only a few of the Many accurences With the Indians in this Section of the Country I Supose thar is no person here that knows anything about the killing of Indian Bald Eagle tha is a Mr Cutright (41) at Hinkle's Ville Upshur Co W V^a I under Stand he is 91 years old he mite give you some good infermation I do not know any descendants of Jacob Scott or Elija Runnen W^m. Powers Has a Grand Son Lives at Pennsborough Ritchie Co W V^a Martime Powers the Reason I did not Write Sooner is I thought I Mite git Some More infermation but I do not know of any More I Have Heard My Grand Father Jackson & other Old People Tell a good deal about the Early days of this Country but I was young then and tha ar all pased a way and thar is but few that can give Much account of the Indian Times in this Country Now. So I Give you all the Infermation I cold

Yours &C

J. W. Jackson" (42)

(41) See page 508. (42) p. 508.

APPENDIX II

The former presence of the Buffalo, or American Bison, has been traced as far east as Cavetown, Maryland, and records show that it was not unknown in the proximity of the Georgia coast,

THE BUFFALO OF GOMARA
Courtesy of Smithsonian Institution

but no remains of it has ever been found adjacent to the Atlantic seaboard. *Handbook of American Indians*, Part I, p. 169.

While the animal was known to some of the inland valley Indians east of the Appalachians, and where its presence in historic times is attested by an occasional geographical name, it was not common in that region. This mighty mountain range was a

barrier to eastern migration, broken only by a few passes. It was crossed by buffalo and Indian trails at —
 Cumberland Gap, Kentucky and Tennessee.
 Head of the James River, Virginia.
 Head of the Potomac River, West Virginia.
 Head of the Juniata River, tributary to the Susquehanna, Pennsylvania. Hulbert's *Washington and the West*, New York, 1905, pp. 17, 18.

Wagon roads, then railways have been built through all of these passes, practically following the old paths, or trails in question.

The great range of the buffalo was between the Allegheny and the Rocky Mountains, with general migrations North and South. While a recognized plains animal, it was more widely diffused throughout the Trans-Allegheny and western Virginia, than has been supposed; but never in extensive herds. This, in a measure, was owing to the great dearth of grasses in the dense forests; which, however, was more open then than at a later period. Especially is this true in those regions where this animal and droves of deer and elk were wont to feed. *Clear Creek*, Clearfield County, Pa., was so called by the Indians because of the extensive aeries there cleared of underbrush, destroyed by buffaloes. *On the Border with Colonel Antes*, p. 67.

In dealing numerically with the Trans-Allegheny buffalo, there was one factor that has never been properly considered. The animal, a lumbering beast, lived there the year round, and its numbers, especially in winter, must have been greatly decimated by the innumerable packs of timber wolves which infested this vast wilderness. Young calves and isolated individuals fell an easy prey to this voracious, fleet-footed carnivora. Escape by flight was impossible. *Doddridge*, p. 104, speaks of the destructiveness of the wolf to the cattle of the early settlers. *Waddell* testifies to their former great numbers, their scourge to the western settlers and bounty paid for their scalps. — *Annals of Augusta County*, pp. 22, 42.

Easily hunted, the buffalo became practically extinct soon after the advent of the white man on the western waters, and allusion to it by the chronicles is casual. It was a century before the more wily, tenacious elk was exterminated in the alpine-like regions of the Alleghenies. The following data on the subject is from the *Draper Manuscripts*, LBB46-49, Wisconsin State Historical Society. *"The Buffalo or Bison in West Virginia," "From Geological Survey of Kentucky," "The American Bison,"* by J. A. Allen, 1876.

"Warden also refers to the former existence of buffaloes in the western part of Pennsylvania and to their early extinction there and in Kentucky. (1) Gallatin says: The name of Buffalo Creek, between Pittsburg and Wheeling, proves that they had spread thus far eastwardly when that country was first settled by the Anglo-Americans. (2) Further to the southward, in West Virginia, in the Vallies of the Kanawha and its tributaries, as well as thence westward, the former abundance of the buffalo is well attested.

"One of the earliest references to the existence of the buffalo in West Virginia is that contained in the Journal of the Rev. David Jones, who in 1772, made a journey to the Indian tribes west of the Ohio River. (3) Under date June 18, 1772, he writes: 'Went out to view the land on the east side [of the Little Kanawha] to kill provisions. Mr. Owens killed several deer, and a stately buffalo bull. The country is here level, and the soil not despicable.' In speaking of that part of the Valley of the Ohio near the mouth of the 'Great Guiandot,' he says under date of January, 1773: 'In this part of the country even at this season, pasturage is so good that creatures are well supplied without any assistance. Here are great abundance of buffalo, which are a species of cattle, as some suppose, left here by the former inhabitants.' In describing the country about Wheeling he says: 'The wild beasts met with here are bears, wolves, panthers, wild cats, foxes, raccoons, beavers, otters, and some few squirrels and rabbits; buffaloes, deer and elk, called by the Delawares moos.' (4)

"Buffaloes are well-known to have existed on the Monongahela, and (5) throughout the region between this river and the Ohio, over the area drained by the Little Kanawha, Buffalo, Fishing, Wheeling, and other small tributaries of the Ohio, where it is said to have been much interval or open land, (6) and thence southward to the Great Kanawha. As already noticed, there is abundant evidence of its former existence on the sources of the Kanawha, extending to the head of the Greenbrier Rivers, in Pocahontas County, and thence eastward, at times at least, over the sources of the James.

"Gallatin states that in his time (1784-85) 'they were abundant on the southern side of the Ohio, between the Great and Little Kanawha. I have during eight months lived principally upon their flesh.' (7). The following additional testimony, contained in a letter written by Dr. Charles McCormick, dated Fort Gibson, Cherokee Nation, August 18, 1844, is furnished by Dr. Elliott Coues. Dr. McCormick says: 'I have just seen Capt. [Nathan] Boone, and he promises to write and tell you all about it.' In the meantime, he says, he killed his first buffalo somewhere about 1793, on the Kanawha in Virginia. He was then quite a small boy. He has also killed buffalo on New River, and near the Big Sandy, in Virginia in '97 and '98. (8)

"The Bison Americanus, or wild buffalo, had retired from Western New York and Pennsylvania to the Ohio Valley.

"H. T. Wiley's *Hist. of Monongalia Co., W. Va.*, p. 26, says: 'A mile or so

(1) See page 508. (2) p. 508. (3) p. 508. (4) p. 508. (5) p. 508. (6) p. 508. (7) p. 508. (8) p. 508.

380 APPENDIX II

from Stewart-town is the 'Buffalo Pond'—a long, narrow hollow, with high rocky sides running back from Cheat River, and terminating in a wall ten or twelve feet high. It is asserted that the Indians used this as a trap for buffaloes. They drove the bison up into it from the river, and then shot them."

"Buffalo Creek in Logan Co., W. Va.—on scrap of W. Va., in Mitchells' Atlas of 1884.

"1756—Buffalo killed on Shawnee expdn. on Sandy Tug Fork:—*Withers*, 63-64 [p. 83, new edition]. (9)

"1767-69: Buffalo on Buchanan R.—Barbour Co.—Water of Monongahela: *Withers*, 91-93 [pp. 120-122, new edition]. (10)

"In 1784, in descending the Ohio, Gen. Muhlenberg first mentions killing buffalo, below Hockhocking.

"In Oct. 1785 Gen. Butler mentions first buffalo killed at Big Sandy.

"1770—In the autumn of 1770, when Washington made his Ohio Tour, he went as low as the Great Kenhawa and up that stream about fourteen miles, finding 'buffaloes and other wild game in great abundance.' *Sparks' Washington*, I, 121, II, 524, 525, 528.

"In 1780, buffalo were so plenty on the Little Kenhawa that Col. Brodhead sent hunters there for a supply of buffalo meat for use of his troops at Fort Pitt. (Hist. of Fayette Co. Pa., p. 86.)

"1773—Rev. D. Jones' Journal mentions buffaloes—p. 30.

"Doddridge is indefinite as to buffaloes in Monongahela country—pp. 83, 123, &c.

"About 1742, in Augusta Co., Va., *Withers*, 43 [p. 50, new edition]. (11)

"Between 1763 and 1774, there were some buffaloe and elk to be seen in the Greenbrier country. Kercheval's *Hist. of the Valley*, 2nd edn., 230.

"Range of the bison: see *The Nation*, Aug. 16, 1877, 105." (12)

This history of the bison in western Virginia is far from complete.

Christopher Gist, who was sent into the Trans-Allegheny by the *Ohio Company* in 1750-52, saw droves of forty to fifty buffalo on the Little Miami River, Ohio. *Gist's Journals*, Pittsburg, 1893, p. 55.

Killed one barren buffalo cow on the Little Miami River, Ohio, p. 56.

Killed two buffalo on the Little Kanawha, p. 60.

Killed a buffalo on the Big Kanawha, p. 64.

1752, Killed two buffaloes on the waters of Monongahela River, p. 73.

1752, Killed four buffaloes while camped at mouth of Lawwellaconin Creek (Pond Creek, Wood County, West Va.), p. 76.

1752, Molchuconickon, or Buffalo Creek (Middle Island Creek, in Tyler, Doddridge and Pleasants Counties, West Va.,) p. 76.

---

(9) See page 508. (10) p. 508. (11) p. 508. (12) p. 508.

1752, Neemokeesy Creek, "saw signs of buffalo, elk and deer, which frequented a large cave to lick a kind of saltish clay which I found there in the cave" (cave 50 by 150 feet wide), p. 76. Gist speaks of killing a black fox at this place.

173–, John Macky hunts buffalo on the Shenandoah and James Rivers, in Virginia. Note by Draper, *Withers*, p. 50.

1738-40, John Salling, a captive with the Cherokees, kills a buffalo at the Salt Springs in Kentucky. *Withers*, p. 48.

176–, The Pringles purloin jerked buffalo meat from Indians on Buckhannon River. Chapter IX, this vol.

1769, John Hacker kills buffalo cow on waters of Great Kanawha. Chapter VI, this vol.

1788, Buffalo in Kentucky. *Withers*, p. 373.

1796, Buffalo on Fishing Creek. (Wetzel County West Va.) *Withers*, p. 374. *DeHass* gives the date 1786, p. 294.

Buffalo killed in (now) Jackson County, West Va., by William Bibbee, date unknown. Chapt. XXIII, this vol.

1772, In a hunt on New Year's day settlers kill seven buffaloes on Elk Creek, in (now) Harrison County, West Va.

1790, Buffalo bull killed in autumn, on Hughes River, in (perhaps) now Ritchie County, West Va.

1791, Two buffaloes killed in March, on the West Fork of the Little Kanawha River.

1792, Two buffalo hunters killed by Indians while canoeing on the Little Kanawha.

Haymond's History of Harrison County, West Va., pp. 21, 122, 359, 360.

1774, May 17, 300 buffaloes seen at a "salt spring" on Kentucky River.

1774, Aug. 4, "a gang of Buffaloes" met on the Kentucky River, two killed.

1774, Oct. 17, Indians seen hunting buffaloes on the lower Great Kanawha River.

1774, Oct. 26, buffalo "sign" observed on the Ohio side of the river opposite Point Pleasant.

Dunmore's War, pp. 122, 133, 286, 369.

1805, last buffalo seen in the region of Huntington, Cabell County, West Va.

"The last buffalo killed in Kanawha County, West Va., was in 1815, on the waters of the Little Sandy Creek of Elk River, about twelve miles from Charleston.

The last elk killed in that country was in 1820 on Two Mile Creek of Elk River, about five and a half miles from Charleston." *Trans-Allegheny Pioneers*—p. 62. The same authority continues "It is said that vast herds of buffalo summered in the Kanawha Valley, 'in an early day,' within reach of the Salt Spring, or 'Buffalo Big Lick,' as it was called, and in the fall, went to the grass regions of Ohio and Kentucky, and the cane brakes of the Kentucky streams. Their routes were—for Kentucky, down through Teay's Valley, and for Ohio, down Kanawha to Thirteen Mile Creek, and over to Letart, where they crossed the Ohio River. Colonel Croghan, who came down the Ohio in a boat in 1765 encountered a vast herd crossing at Letart."

"In 1825—at least as late as that—a buffalo cow and her calf were killed at Valley Head, near the source of Tygart's River, * * * * About 1830 the wife of Thomas B. Summerfield shot an elk at a lick near the head of Sandy Creek, a branch of the Dry Fork of Cheat River. Five years later Abraham Mullenix killed another elk at the same place. In 1840 another was killed on Red Creek, in Tucker County. In 1843 three hunters from Dry Fork, Joab Carr and two men named Flannagan, killed three elk on the Black Fork of Cheat River, near where the present town of Davis now stands. So far as known these were the last elk killed on the soil of West Virginia, but the animal was not extinct for fifteen or twenty years later. Hunters were not able to bring any in, but they knew their haunts, and spent considerable time chasing them, almost as late as the beginning of the Civil War. The animals last range was in the Canaan Valley in Tucker County, and one of the last hunters to pursue them was William Losh of Tucker." *Trans-Allegheny Historical Magazine*, pp. 200-201.

In 1867 an elk was killed by an unknown hunter at Elk Lick on Middle River, Pocahontas County. I heard it related in a hunter's camp on Greenbrier River in 1878, that only a few years previous, the enormous antler of an elk, recently cast, had been found in the mountain fastness of Pocahontas County. Tracks of the animal had also been seen near the headwaters of the Cheat River, no later than 1873.

Buffaloes the maker of "McColloch's path," (Preston County, West Va.) mentioned in Washington's Diary of Sept. 1784. *Washington and the West*, Vol. I, p. 67.

Buffalo and Indian path, or trail followed by the Baltimore and Ohio Southern Railway, Doddridge, and Wood Counties, West Va. *Hulbert's Historic Highways*, Cleveland, 1904, Vol. I, p. 138.

"Granny's Creek," in Braxton County, received its name when Henry Jackson commenced a survey thereon and one of his hunters named Loudin, killed a buffalo cow, which was so old and tough that the men declared her to be the grandmother of all buffaloes.

The low gap between Rover's Run and Buckhannon Run,

just east of my boyhood home on the last named stream, was known as a "Buffalo Wallow, or Stamping Ground." The soil is a stiff red clay, and over an area of perhaps a quarter of an acre, there was a depression of from one to two feet, devoid of timber. I was familiar with this "wallow" while the ridge was yet covered with forest; but it has since been practically obliterated by the plow. There was also a small "bear wallow" on the opposite high ridge next to Bridge Run, which was visible only a few years ago.

A slightly brackish or saline spring, on Bone Creek, a tributary of Hughes River, Ritchie County, West Virginia, was evidently a resort of buffalo and other large animals. The spring, or lick, is on the old Somerville farm near Auburn, and is located at the head of a shallow marshy ravine in the creek bottom. The deep paths worn in the banks of the ravine by the hoofs of the animals were still visible when I visited it in 1879. The Creek derived its name from the numerous bones and teeth found at this "Bone Lick." Some of the teeth were very large. One seen and described by Captain John Somerville as a "double molar" was evidently that of a mastodon. Another remarkable specimen was a "tusk" which, when "placed with either point on a table, described an arch through which a large inverted teacup could be passed."

Evidence of an occupation of this bottom by the aborigines were not lacking. A grooved, well-polished, hard stone axe, about six inches in length, was ploughed up just above the lick. In another part of the same field, and near a living spring, stood an oak, not less than three feet in diameter. This tree was made into rails, and when cut, it was found to have been ineffectually girdled when only about five inches in diameter. The girdling was about two feet from the ground and was a series of bruises from a blunt implement, such as would be produced with a stone axe. The injury caused a swelling, or ridged growth, in which at one point a small cavity had formed. In this was a sandstone, one inch in thickness — other dimensions not given.

In 1886 Captain Somerville in digging a fish pond about fifty feet below where the last mentioned spring now comes to the surface, at a depth of three feet took out a quantity of stone where the spring had at some former time, been systematically walled. Flint implements and other relics of primitive industry have often been unearthed by the plow contiguous to these springs.

Appendix II

Buffalo Geographical Names of West Virginia.

For assistance in the following compilation, I am indebted to Mr. David B. Reger, Assistant State's Geologist of West Virginia. Gannatt's *Gazetteer of West Va.* (Bulletin No. 233, U. S. Geological Survey, 1904) was also consulted.

Buffalo Creek, tributary to the Little Kanawha; Braxton County.

Buffalo Creek, rising in Pennsylvania and flowing west through Brook County, into the Ohio.

Buffalo Calf Fork, branch of Middle Island Creek, Doddridge County.

Buffalo Creek, small tributary of Meadow River; Fayette and Greenbrier Counties; so named from quantities of "buffalo grass" found there by first settlers.

Buffalo Fork, affluent of Meadow River; Fayette County. This stream is called "Buffalo Lick Branch," in Col. Fleming's Orderly Book, where "Camp 5th" was pitched by Gen. Lewis' Army on the night of Sept. 15, 1774. *Dunmore's War*, 321.

Buffalo Creek, small tributary to New River; Fayette and Summers Counties.

Buffalo Creek, tributary to North Branch of Potomac; Grant County.

Buffalo Creek, tributary to Monongahela River; Harrison County.

Buffalo Creek, Jackson County.

Buffalo Lick, tributary to Mill Creek; Jackson County.

Buffalo Lick, small affluent of Elk River; Kanawha County.

Buffalo Fork, small branch Hughes Creek; Kanawha County.

Buffalo Fork, branch of Smither's Creek; Kanawha County.

Buffalo Lick, small unchartered stream entering Hacker's Creek from the south, just east of the John Hacker homestead; Lewis County.

Buffalo Creek, small branch of Mud River; a tributary of Guyandot River; Lincoln County.

Buffalo Creek, small left-hand tributary to Guyandot River; Logan County.

Buffalo Creek, small right-hand branch of Guyandot River; Logan County. (Noted by Draper.)

Buffalo Mountain, Logan and Wyoming Counties; elevation, 2000 to 2500 feet.

Buffalo Creek, small branch of Tug Fork of Big Sandy River; Mingo County.

Buffalo Creek, large tributary to the Monongahela River; Monongalia and Marion Counties.

Buffalo Creek, tributary to Elk River; Nicholas and Clay Counties.

Buffalo Hills, elevation, 2000 to 2500 feet; Pendleton County.

Buffalo Run, now called "Trout Run," near Franklin; Pendleton County.

Buffalo Run, former name of a small tributary to Cheat River; Preston County.

Buffalo Creek, large tributary to Cheat River; Preston County.

Buffalo Mountain, spur-ridge near where the Staunton and Parkersburg Pike scales the Allegheny Mountain; Pocahontas County. So named because of its resemblance to the profile of an enormous buffalo. Rev. William T. Price, of Marlington, West Va., writes me: "From a point of view one or two miles to the southwest, the contour of this spur is suggestive of the 'American Spread Eagle.'"

Buffalo Ridge, summit in Marthas Ridge; Pocahontas County.

Buffalo Fork, tributary to East Fork of Greenbrier River; Pocahontas County.

Buffalo Run, small branch of Deer Creek, tributary to North Fork of Greenbrier River; Pocahontas County.

Buffalo Creek, tributary to the Great Kanawha; Putnam County.

Buffalo Ridge, Putnam County.

Buffalo, post-village, named from Big Buffalo Creek; Putnam County.

Buffalo-lick, post-village; Roane County.

Buffalo Fork, small tributary to Clear Fork of Coal River; Raleigh County.

Buffalo Run, two small branches, having the same name, of Middle Island Creek; Tyler County.

Buffalo Lick Run, small unchartered branch of Bull Run; Upshur County.

Buffalo Bull Knob, summit in Webster County.

Buffalo Run, tributary to Right Fork of Middle Fork of Little Kanawha; Webster County.

Buffalo Lick Great, forks of Elk River; Webster County. See Chapter VI, this vol.

Buffalo Fork, tributary of Back Fork or Right Fork of Little Kanawha; Webster County. See Chapter VI, this vol.

Buffalo Run, branch of South Fork of Fishing Creek; Wetzel County.

Buffalo Creek, small branch of Little Huff Creek; tributary to Guyandot River; Wyoming County.

Buffalo ——, tributary to Pond Creek; Wood County.

There are a number of streams within the State which bear the name "bull;" such as bull creek, bull run, bull fork and bull lick. It is more than probable that the most of these, if not all of them, were named from some incident connected with bull-buffaloes. The majority of our watercourses were named in the earliest settlement of the country; and these names can hardly be associated with our domestic cattle. This deduction will also hold when applied to the several geographical appellations denoting "cow," and "calf."

BUFFALO IN VIRGINIA EAST OF THE ALLEGHENY MOUNTAINS.

Buffalo Gap; middle branch of the Shenandoah River. *Withers*, p. 50.

"The buffalo roamed at will over these hills and valleys, and in their migrations made a well-defined trail between Rockfish Gap, in the Blue Ridge, and Buffalo Gap, in the North Mountain, passing by the present site of Staunton." *Annals of Augusta County*, p. 7.

A section of a buffalo path is still to be seen one mile north of the bridge crossing the Cowpasture River, on the Harrisonburg and Hot Springs Pike; in Bath County.

Old hunters reported that buffaloes frequented the salt licks at (now) Saltville; in Smythe County.

Buffalo Run; Amherst County.

Buffalo River; Amherst and Nelson Counties.

Buffalo Ridge; Amherst and Nelson Counties. Elevation 1,000 feet.

Buffalo Hill; Augusta County.

Buffalo Branch; tributary to Shenandoah River, Augusta County.

Buffalo Gap; caused by Buffalo Branch, in Little North Mountains, Augusta County.

Buffalo Gap; post village, Augusta County. Altitude, 1,882 feet.

Buffalo Creek; affluent Roanoke River, Bedford and Campbell Counties.

Buffalo Creek; tributary Roanoke River, Botetourt County.

Buffalo Gap; tributary James River, Buchanan County.

Buffalo Creek; tributary Roanoke River; Halifax County.

Buffalo Lithia Springs; post village, Mecklenburg County.

Buffalo Junction; post village, Mecklenburg County. (Named from Buffalo Lithia Springs.)

Buffalo Creek; tributary James River, Nelson County.

Buffalo Station; post village, Nelson County.

Buffalo Springs; r. r. station, Nelson County.

Buffalo Ridge; post village, Patricks County.

Buffalo Creek; branch of Appomattox River, Prince Edward County.

Buffalo Creek; right-hand tributary James River, Rockbridge County.

Buffalo Creek; left-hand tributary James River, Rockbridge County.

Buffaloforge; post village, Rockbridge County.

Buffalo Mills; post village, Rockbridge County.

Buffalo Ford; crossing the North Fork of Holston River, Russell County. Consult *Gazetteer of Virginia*. (Gannett.)

APPENDIX III

At various times human bones have been found at Indian Camp, described in Chapter VIII, this vol. These consisted of fragments of bone, among them pieces of skull. Some of the latter have been thrown up by woodchucks burrowing under the wall at the north end of the camp. Such instances were noticed by me on several different occasions when making observations there. An occasional tooth was found but they were not plentiful.

The Indians frequently resorted to this shelter. It was a favorite location, if we are to judge from the amount of camp refuse and potsherds found. The abundance of these last would indicate that women were largely identified with its occupancy. Pottery is seldom associated, and never in quantity, with camps occupied by men exclusively; such as war parties or members of the priestcraft. A few fragments of steatite vessels have been secured, mistaken by treasure seekers for "crucibles." A piece obtained by me in 1883, was of superior workmanship. This ware is more properly identified with the tribes of the South; the Catawbas, Cherokees, Creeks and others. It was in vogue on a smaller scale among some of the Northern tribes, while in California its usage was considerable.

In 1892, Prof. G. F. Queen and myself made a hurried examination of Indian Camp. Bones, or kitchen refuse; shells of the mussel, shreds of pottery and rude and broken arrow points; a bone awl and the rim-fragment of a solid sandstone pot or vessel were found. The outside surface of this last relic shows a series of long, rasp-like marks of uniform depth, while the interior is smooth. The top was finished with a slightly projecting rim. The contour of the vessel rounded and narrowed towards the bottom, but its capacity could hardly be determined by the fragment obtained; but perhaps about one gallon, maybe less.

In 1893, with Mr. Ernest Phillips, I made a thorough investigation of the floor debris of the Camp; with the indisputable proof of both remote and recent occupation by the aborigines. Six separate fire-hearths were discovered at various depths. The principal one used by the Indians was at the north end of the

Camp and measured four feet by four feet. It was six inches thick and was buried under ten inches of vegetable mould. It was near this hearth that the woodchucks unearthed the several pieces of human skull. A smaller hearth found nearby evidently antedated it many years. It was twelve inches by twelve inches across, three inches thick, and was beneath a bed of what appeared to be clay burned to a bright reddish color, free from sand or grit. This deposit seemingly had been systematically arranged and was of the same size of the underlying ash bed; and was one and a half inches thick. Beneath the clay and hearth, at the depth of two feet three inches was found the bone from the foot of a bear. Just back of the large altar-like stone at the entrance of the Camp, at the depth of eighteen inches was found a human skull crushed into fragments. While the cavern had for several years been used as a stable, there had been no rapid accumulation of vegetable mould. On the contrary, Mr. Lothan Phillips, the owner, had hauled considerable of the original rich debris and ashes and scattered them on an adjoining "truck patch;" and in all probability the skull was not then covered deeper than when first buried. It was here that the old hunter had many years previously uncovered the eighteen skeletons.

Near the center of the Camp and at a depth of sixteen inches, on a rough block of stone, seemingly the natural floor, was found a quantity of a substance which we could not entirely identify. This deposit was three inches thick in the center, six inches wide and twenty-four inches long; tapering to an edge on every side. It extended in a southeasterly and northwesterly direction. In color it combined all the hues of the rainbow. It resembled ochre, or a paint-pigment and was probably a mass of decorative paint in preparation by the Indians. The different mineral ingredients had not yet been thoroughly kneaded or mixed. In texture it was free from grit, soft and pasty. Unfortunately the large sample secured was, through accident, lost before it could be analyzed. The Yakimas tell me that their old people used to obtain a clay-like substance from a cavern in Mt. Adams, which they made into war-paint, first subjecting it to a burning process. Doubtless this deposit had been so treated; and that which was overlaying the fire-hearth mentioned, was found as placed in the method of baking.

A few hundred yards south of this Camp, about 1881, Mr.

Burton Phillips unearthed with his plow, twenty perfect flint implements of the spear-head class. There was also one common polished stone celt and an ordinary water crystal. I was fortunate in securing thirteen of the spear-heads in perfect condition, also the stem or base of another one which had been broken after discovery. The others were scattered or destroyed before I learned that they had been found. Those obtained are nicely chipped thin blades of chalcedony or jasper. They vary in color from pure white to black, while some are translucent. With but one exception they are of the leaf-shaped pattern with notched base. One is un-notched. They are of medium size and show a similarity of workmanship; and are doubtless the handiwork of the same artisan. Mr. Phillips declared that they were found some ten or twelve inches below the surface, planted point downward, in a circle about two feet in diameter. They are a finished product, and the manner in which they had been buried precludes the idea of the ordinary "cache" so often noted in preliminary chipped or unfinished flint implements.

Some eighteen inches below these spear-heads was a heavy slab of sandstone in its natural condition. It measured about four feet by six feet across, and some twelve inches thick. In his search for treasure, Mr. Phillips uncovered this stone, carrying the excavation down one side to a point below and under it. Not having at hand the means of lifting it, a charge of blasting powder was exploded beneath it which cracked it into two or three pieces. These were not removed. I saw the stone in its original position after it had been broken, and evidently it had not been placed there by man nor had it any connection with the flint implements buried over it. (1) Such a find of relics is unusual in that region.

Ash Camp, four miles east of Indian Camp, on the waters of Ten Mile Creek, tributary of the Middle Fork River, was so named from its vast accumulation of ashes. The estimate was several hundreds of bushels when I first saw the camp in 1883, and old settlers claimed that the quantity had greatly deteriorated within their recollection. It was a noted rendezvous, and was much frequented by the red men, as was also a rock-shelter on French Creek, affluent of the Buckhannon River. In a visit to Ash Camp in 1892, I noticed traces of human remains mingled with broken pottery and other refuse. There were a few other rock-shelters scattered throughout that region, but Indian Camp,

(1) See page 508.

and Ash Camp, situated as they were on an Indian trail or warpath, were preferred haunts of the tribesmen until about the opening of Dunmore's War in 1774. It is not at all probable that these resorts were ever used by the Indian hunter-bands after the Bull Town and Indian Camp massacres.

Near Indian Camp until a few years ago, there stood a beech tree on which was carved the outlines of an Indian warrior in full costume. This work was old and was supposed to have been the handicraft of some of the first settlers on the Buckhannon; or possibly "Snath," of whom, more anon.

About Indian Camp there hovers an interesting tradition of a "Lost Mine," and buried treasure of fabulous richness. Its origin antedates the Revolution, with some apparent foundation of truth; although this region is not alone in its claim to the scene of original operations; but covers portions of Kentucky and Tennessee as well. The mine was worked by a party of Spanish and English adventurers, who were subsequently nearly exterminated by their Indian allies. It appears that there were Spaniards by the name of Petro, or Pedro, on the Upper Monongahela as early as 1777, whose descendants are still living in Randolph County. (2) Nothing is known of their previous history. Their presence in the settlements may, perhaps, be traced in the tradition. There were Petros in Hampshire County, Virginia, in 1782, if not earlier. It is believed by some investigators that straggling bands of the early Spanish explorers of the Southern tide water, penetrated the Virginia and Kentucky wilderness. It would have been in keeping with the traditions of these insatiable gold seekers to have done so.

Near Indian Camp, in 1883, I was shown the ruins of the "ancient mine," and also a small polished stone relic, resembling a disc, and a fragment of drossy lead, claimed to have been taken from the debris or waste of this mine. With these relics were found pieces of basketry and a buckskin moccasin. I also examined an interesting figure carved on a large sandstone boulder in a nearby grotto, known as the "Chimney Rocks." Owing to the porous nature of this boulder, the figure had been nearly obliterated by vandals, and its outlines could not be accurately deciphered. In appearance, it rudely represented the compasses. The trace of a camp fire was observed in the smoke-tinged wall at the back of the grotto.

An interesting volume could be written from data at hand,

---
(2) See page 509.

regarding the "mine." The wild legends relating to its discovery and working; its subsequent forced abandonment through the hostility of the Indians, brought about by the reckless deed of one of the miners; the burial of vast treasure; the battle; the massacre, and final flight and escape of but two of the party, — all are fraught with thrilling romance.

On July 15th, 1867, Dr. L. S. S. Farnsworth, resident dentist of Buckhannon, brought to light some legendary rock inscriptions on the head of Stone Coal Creek, which were supposed to have connection with this mine and its disastrous tragedies. These had previously been found by a squirrel hunter named Calvin Smith, who determining to seek a home in the west, revealed to Dr. Farnsworth the location of his discovery. In company with Mr. Valentine Lorentz, Dr. Farnsworth repaired to the region indicated by the hunter, where they found in the woods on a high ridge, an immense flat stone bearing the inscription shown in Fig. 1.

WAS FOUGHT FOR
THE RICH MINDS
SWARTUS CNANCU
1555
RITEN BY SNATH
DONE WHILE THE BATEL

FIG. 1

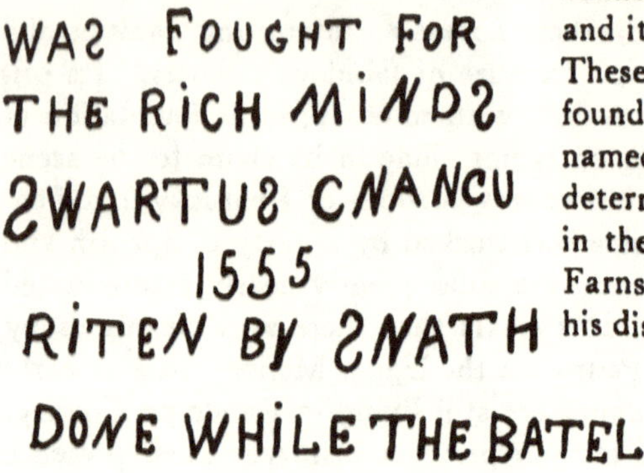

About three-fourths of a mile northwest of this mysterious monument, was found an upright stone, "resembling a tombstone" bearing the legend shown in Fig. 2.

The solitary "S" is supposed to signify Silver.

Dr. Farnsworth had this relic in his office for several years, where it was seen by a number of persons.

Three-fourths of a mile further northwest was found a small cave, or shelter formed by a rock projecting some

1555 LBS
OF GOLD AND
S. SEPERAT
ED FROM
SNATH
1777
THE OAR

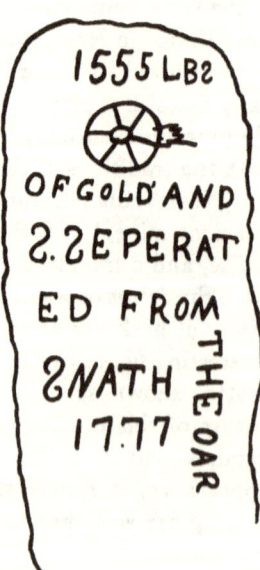

FIG. 2

ten or fifteen feet from the hillside. This grotto had at some time previous been occupied as a camp. Back from the entrance and lying on the floor was a heavy slab of stone, measuring several feet across, which had in more recent years fallen from overhead. Carved in the roof of the cave was a rude circle, with the four cardinal points of the compass designated by the usual alphabetical characters. Across the surface of this circle, extended a well-defined "pointer," not unlike the needle of a compass. The fallen fragment of the roof had evidently carried away an inscription, as shown by the accompanying cut. (Fig. 3.) This stone could not be overturned for the purpose of de-

FIG. 3

ciphering the full inscription, but it required but little imagination to determine that *Gold* and *Snath* were largely its component parts.

By the aid of his compass Dr. Farnsworth writes me, it was apparent that the "pointer" at this cavern and the finger of the inverted hand on the upright stone, indicated lines which converged at a point on the Buckhannon River just below the crossing, or ford at the village of Sago. Afterwards four other stone "pointers or guides" were found near the Sago ford, which apparently had connection with those on Stone Coal.

My brother, C. C. F. McWhorter, who was for many years County Clerk of Upshur County, saw and examined the inscribed stone, in Dr. Farnsworth's office. It appeared very old and weather worn, the lettering evidently had been done with a small pointed steel instrument, and, while crude, was very legible.

Mr. McWhorter has a copy of an inscribed stone, made by the late Col. Henry F. Westfall, local historian of Buckhannon. This inscription is very nearly that which Dr. Farnsworth says was on the large immovable stone (Fig. 1), but its contour is very much that of Fig. 2. The accompanying cut (Fig. 4) is from a photograph of the Westfall copy, which is made on the discolored fly-leaf of an old book, with no attempt at imitating the handicraft of the mysterious Snath. The Colonel, it should be noted, places the discovery of this stone in January 1866. This may perhaps be the discovery by Smith referred to. It is proper to state that Figures 1, 2 and 3, are from copies which Dr. Farnsworth made from memory; not having at hand the originals which he carefully executed at the time of his discovery.

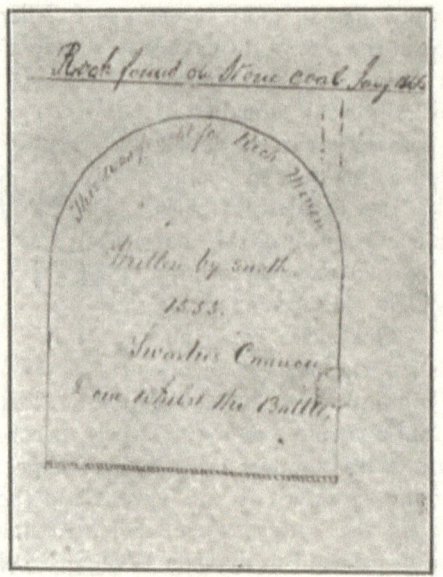

Fig. 4

Cutright says in connection with Indian Camp:—

"There is other data pointing to this rock as the rendezvous of the Indians. On the Buckhannon river west of Sago and Ten Mile, certain stones are planted in the shape of a spearhead, whose sharp end points in the direction of Indian Camp Rock. These rock or pointers the author himself has observed and there may be others which aim in the same direction, evidently for the purpose of telling wandering bands of Indians where they might find a safe seclusion, sheltering protection and a temporary home." (3)

Whether or not Mr. Cutright's theory in regard to the pointed rocks is correct, it is certain that speculation relative to the "mine" and buried treasure ran high; and not all of which was confined to local circles. Parties from across the water made fruitless quest with "chart" and "key" for the secreted bullion. There are those still living who have not abandoned the search, and who believe that success will yet be theirs.

Mr. Cutright gives a narrative of three Frenchmen who

---
(3) See page 509.

crossed the mountains at an earlier period, perhaps in the forties, in quest of gold and camped for many years under a shelving rock on the waters of the Little Kanawha, near Rock Cave Postoffice, in Upshur County. One of them eventually died and was buried by his comrades, under the rock which had sheltered them so long; and where a century later a Caucasian skull was unearthed. (4) The two survivors recrossed the mountains never to return. It is not known that these adventurers were in any way connected with the later achievements of Swartus Cnancu and Snath, but their dreams of wealth in the western wilderness were never realized.

Legends of the celebrated "Swift Mines" are linked with Indian Camp and its connecting stories of "buried treasure." One version of the original discovery of the mine, or mines, is that an Indian appeared in Jamestown, Virginia, wearing arm-bands and other ornaments of silver and when interrogated, offered to pilot a party across the mountains where there was "plenty" of such metal. This he afterwards done, and on the sequel hangs the wild, weird story of Swartus Cnancu, the resourceful Snath and their unfortunate companions, in the wilderness of the Buckhannon.

While working the "mine" at Indian Camp, so runs the tradition, the Indians were friendly until late in the season and after a large quantity of the metal had been smelted, one of the adventurers, in an altercation with an Indian while hunting, struck the red man, which precipitated hostilities, fatal to the expedition. To avenge the insult, the Indians attacked and killed several of the miners and held the camp in a state of siege. The survivors foreseeing their probable doom, attempted to obliterate all visible traces of the mine by blasting great fragments of stone from the overhanging cliff and letting them drop into the opening of the shaft, or tunnel. While this was being done and while the battle still raged, Snath managed to extricate himself from the beleagured camp, and at various places set up stone "pointers," and constructed a "key" and "chart" by which a return to the mine could be accomplished.

A lull in hostilities induced the belief that the Indians had abandoned the wilderness and the miners prepared to return east of the mountains. They buried vast quantities of bullion and set up additional "markers" by which it could be subsequently located. In the meantime they were again set upon by the Indians and only

(4) See page 509.

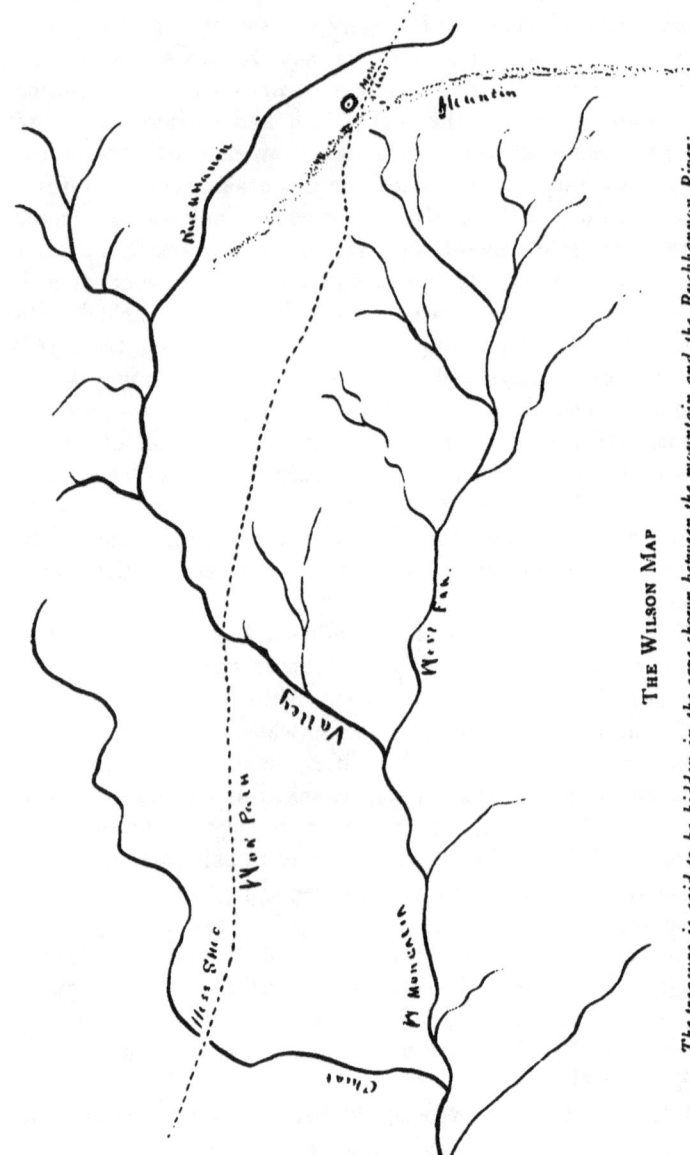

THE WILSON MAP

The treasure is said to be hidden in the cave shown between the mountain and the Buckhannon River; and where they are crossed by the "War Path."

two, with the "chart" and "key" escaped. These instruments have been variously deciphered and seemingly applied alike to different localities.

The old "drill marks" which I examined on some blocks of stone at this "mine," appeared to resemble certain fossil imprint belonging to the carboniferous period. The same can be said of the "frying pan" done in intaglio on the face of the cliff where the blasting had been done. However, the lapse of more than one hundred years might have a tendency to produce in the porous sandstone the noticeable irregularity of surface in both the "drill" cuts and the "frying pan;" this last a supposed "marker." A large "drill" groove was also observed on the front of this cliff.

In 1883, report came to me that a few ancient looking tools, supposedly those of the "Mound Builders," had been discovered in a small cave on Grass Run not far from Indian Camp. Upon investigation it was learned that the implements, whatever they were, were of iron and very rusty; and ignorant of their importance, the finder had taken them to a local blacksmith, who hammered them into articles better fitted to modern domestic use. They were described as "strange looking tools," and no one knew how they came to be placed there.

I have an old map done in ink on parchment, which tells of money or mineral in a cave on the Buckhannon River. It was given me by the late Joseph M. Wilson, of Berlin, West Va., in 1891, who found it among some papers left by his grandfather who died a few years after the close of the Civil War. Mr. Wilson could tell but little about the map, further than that when a boy in his early teens, he accompanied his grandfather to Marion County, to obtain a companion paper, or "key" to the map; and the old gentleman said to him on the return trip: "I now have the paper that I wanted and I can go directly to the cave and find the money." The old man was soon afterwards taken ill and never recovered. I remember him distinctly.

It was more than a year after his death that the map and "key" occurred to Mr. Wilson, and he went to his step-grandmother and asked her about them. She produced a bundle of papers and among them was the map. The most diligent search failed to reveal the other paper and the inference was that it had been destroyed. The old lady was very illiterate and acknowledged that she had "burned a lot of such trash," deeming it of no value.

Mr. Wilson in commenting, said: "My grandfather had no doubt about the authenticity of these papers and their import; otherwise he never would have ridden across two counties, nearly, to get one of them. He told me that the map was given him during the Civil War by a party whose name I do not recall, in Monongalia County; and who was then on his way to secure the treasure, but was deterred on account of the dangers encountered. Not only were contingents of both armies to be met with, but the dreaded "bush-whacker" infested every mountain pass. He informed my grandfather where he could find the "key" with the party in Marion County, and promised to return after the close of the war, when they would go together and find the hidden money. The man then rode away never to be seen again."

The map locates this treasure or mine, near the head of the Buckhannon River, and adjacent to a mountain on the right-hand side of the stream. It is on a "Wor Path" which crosses the Cheat River at the "Hoss Shoo." Both Indian Camp and Ash Camp are on an old Indian war path, or trail.

Of the Swift Mines in Kentucky, the following contribution from Mr. Connelley is apropos. The mystery is only deepened by this anomalous written record, added to the unaccountable stone inscriptions of the mountain fastness. It is hoped that some writer will enter this romantic field and rescue from oblivion the fascinating legends of the "Lost Mine" and "Buried Treasure" of the Trans-Allegheny.

Swift's Journal—The Apperson Copy

BY WILLIAM E. CONNELLEY.

The first account of Swift's Silver Mines that I ever saw is the following Journal. It was put into my hands when I was eleven years old. The constant reading of this paper developed in me a desire to learn and preserve all obtainable information concerning John Swift. It was the momentary impulse of a good man that placed this copy of Swift's Journal in my possession.

At the close of the Civil War the Hon. Richard Apperson, of

Mount Sterling, Kentucky, was, for a short time, the Judge, or the acting Judge, of the Circuit Court of Magoffin County, where my father, Constantine Connelley, Jr., then lived. When in our village Judge Apperson always stopped with William Adams, the founder of the town and the pioneer settler in that part of the county. Mr. Adams had three sons near my own age, and we were inseparable companions. Judge Apperson possessed a deep love for children; I think I can truthfully say that he made an acquaintance and friend of every boy in the village during the first week of his sojourn. He was an excellent conversationalist and an entertaining story-teller, as well as an able and popular Justice. He told stories by the score of the adventures of Kentucky pioneers. And I remember that he enjoyed our juvenile sports, and that he never failed to join our game of marbles when he had a leisure hour; we looked upon him as a friend and regarded him as a companion.

At the end of one of his terms of Court, one of the Adams boys and myself were assisting him to gather up his books, papers, and a few articles of clothing. We were stuffing these into a pair of saddle-bags preparatory to his departure for the next county in his circuit. We requested that he tell us one more story before leaving; he readily complied. I remember that he told of Mrs. Hannah Dennis, and her escape from the Shawnees by concealing herself in a hollow sycamore log on the bank of the Scioto River. When leaving the room some one of us found this copy of Swift's Journal. Whether he did not wish to re-open his crowded saddle-bags to stow it away, or whether he did not care for the paper, I do not know. He looked it over a minute, then handed it to me, telling me to keep it, and not to destroy it nor lose it. I never saw Judge Apperson after that day.

I kept the paper twenty-nine years, and valued it much; I lost it through the stupidity of an inexperienced typewriter to whom I entrusted it to copy. I did not then know of Judge Apperson's death, and wrote to him to enquire if the copy the typewriter made was accurate, and to ask him where he had obtained the paper. His brother replied, informing me of the Judge's death several years before. I received the intelligence of his death with deep regret.

I believe the copy made for me is an exact copy of the original. It follows:

Appendix III

Started on the 25th of June, 1761, from Alexandria, Virginia, and came to Leesburg; thence to Winchester; thence to Little's; thence to Pittsburg; thence to the headwaters of Wheeling; thence to the Little Kanawha; thence to the Big Kanawha; thence to the Guyandotte; thence to Great Sandy Creek; and from thence to the Great Ridge bearing in a southwesterly direction; and from thence to a large river the name of which was unknown to us; and from thence to a large and very rocky creek; and from thence to the mines, where we remained from the 18th of July to the 26th of October, 1761, when we left them and returned over the same way we had taken to come out. And on the 28th of October our scouts discovered six savages; by altering our course we avoided them. On the 30th we were pursued by savages, but we esccaped from them. We saw no more of the savages until the 9th of November, when they fired on us and shot a hole in our lading which soon enlarged and spilled the silver. We fired in return and they must have fled for we saw no more of them; we did not camp this night until after we had crossed the Kanawha. We arrived at the settlements without further conflict, December 2nd, 1761.

April 15th, 1762. We this day started back to the mines. We arrived there on the 10th day of May without accident except the spilled rum.

August 1st, 1762. We this day left the mines to return home. We came to a sudden halt and camped a short time on the 2nd of August when we were alarmed by savages. We escaped from them and camped on our creek. We were greatly pestered but came through safe; we left a valuable prize on the south of the big Gap where we marked some trees with our names and curious marks. From this place we went to Cassell's Woods, and from that place we went to Virginia, where we remained until the next spring, 1763.

We then started on the 1st day of May, 1763, and came to New River; and from thence to the Holston; and from thence to the Cumberland Valley.

Here we set our course and went to the place where our mines are situated, arriving there the 2nd of June, 1763.

We remained here until the 1st of September, when we set out for home. We went through Cassell's Woods, and stopped with Cassellman for five days. From Cassellman's we went to the settlements, and arrived home October 12th, 1763.

We started from home on the 1st of October, 1767, and got to the mines on the 4th of November, 1767. We stayed until the 1st of April, 1768, when we set out for home. We went by the way of Sandy Creek, meeting with nothing material on the way to the settlements.

We left Alexandria on the 4th of June, same year, 1768, and arrived safely at the mines on the 1st of July. We remained here till the 26th of October, 1768. Arrived at home on the 24th of December. Our horses stolen by the Indians was a great loss to us as we were compelled to conceal and leave their lading at the mouth of a large creek running due east.

We left our homes in North Carolina on the 16th day of May, 1769, and started for the mines. We went by the way of the door in the Cumberland Mountains and arrived at the mines safe and sound 24th of June, 1769.

We stayed at the mines until 19th October, 1769. On that day we started home, and went by the way of Sandy Creek. At the Forks of Sandy we lost two of our horses, stolen by savages, and here we concealed their lading, a great loss to us, but we escaped with our lives, and got safe home 1st December, 1769.

I was at the place again, and came by the place where we left the two-horse loads, and the valuable prize, and found all things as we left them in 1762 and 1763. [1768]

On the 1st September, 1769, we left between $22,000.00 and $30,000.00 in crowns on a large creek running near a south course. Close by the creek we marked our names, Swift, Jefferson, and Munday, and other names on a large beech tree with compasses, square and trowel. About twenty or thirty poles from the creek stands a small rock, and between it and the creek you will find a small rock of a bluish color with three chops made with a grit-stone by rubbing it on the rock. By the side of this rock you will find the prize. We left prizes here at three different times. At no great distance from the place we left $15,000.00 of the same kind, marking three or four trees with marks. Not far from these trees, we left a prize near a forked white oak, and about three feet underground, and laid two long stones across it, marking several stones close about it.

At the Forks of Sandy, close by the fork, is a small rockhouse which has a spring in one end of it, and between it and a small branch we hid a prize under the ground. It was valued at

$6,000.00. We likewise left $3,000.00 buried in the rocks of the rockhouse.

Directions to Find Swift's Silver Mines in Kentucky.

The furnace that I built is on the left-hand side of a very rocky creek at a remote place in the West. To find the best ore, climb up the cliff at the left-hand side of the furnace and go a due south direction until you strike a small branch nearby. Go to the head of the branch without crossing, and you there see my name on three beech trees. From these trees go due east to the top of the low ridge. Pass a small knob on top of the ridge to the right-hand when you will see a big rock which has fallen from a high ledge. Behind this fallen rock we got our best ore. This vein runs northeast and southwest, lying and being in latitude 37 degrees and 56 minutes N. And ore is also found in latitude 38 degrees and 2 minutes N. By astronomical observations and calculations you will find the location of both these veins of silver ore to be on the 83rd meridian of longitude or very close to it.

Description of the Country.

The creek heads southwest and runs northeast. It abounds with laurel. It is so cliffy and rocky that it is nearly impossible to get horses to the furnace. So extremely rough is the way that we rarely took our horses nearer than six or seven miles of the place.

There is a thicket of holly a quarter of a mile below the furnace and a small lick a mile above. There is a large buffalo lick two miles from the small lick on another creek that we called Lick Creek. The creek forks about three miles below the furnace and the left-hand fork is the furnace creek. Below the forks the creek is a small stream of water running generally in a northeasterly direction.

Between the forks and holly thicket you will find my name on a beech tree, cut in the year 1767, and about one mile below, you will find Munday, Jefferson and Swift's names in the year 1762, 1765 and 1767.

Between the small lick and the furnace is a remarkable rock; it hangs out quite over the creek, and the water runs under it.

The mountains and hills are covered with laurel and watercourses so much that a man can not get along without much difficulty where paths are not cut. Most of the mountains and hills have but little timber and are poor and barren. North of the furnace about three miles is a larger hill seven or eight miles long upon which there is good timber of different kinds, but south of it there is little timber worth notice.

Furnace Creek forks about three miles above the lick, and in the forks upon the foot of the hill you will find three white oaks growing from one stump. On each of them is cut a small notch with a tomahawk. We sometimes went to a salt spring up the right-hand fork, and came this way back which was the cause for our marking the trees.

From the door in the Cumberland Mountains, on the top at the north, you will run north, forty degrees west, we supposed forty-one miles, and if on the right course you will find trees marked with curious marks all the way. In the course we crossed many creeks and one river.

The first company in search of these mines was composed of Staley, Ireland, McClintock, Blackburn and Swift.

We concealed much silver in bars and crowns in the Indian cave. Set your compass on the west side of the furnace under the rockhouse, and go due west fifty poles, when you will find a tree in this form ——————— Set your compass at the second turn and go south twenty poles and you will find a large tree and a limb growing out of the south side near the ground; under this limb we buried four ten-gallon kegs full of crowns.

Set your compass on the south side of the furnace and steer south two hundred poles and you will find a tree that grows in this form——————— Set your compass at the second turn and go south twenty poles. Under the large limb of a big tree which leans down the creek you will find ore. You cannot miss finding the furnace if you find the ———————————.

The Journal ends abruptly, and I do not know whether it is because I never had all the Journal in my possession or not. A part of the paper may have been mislaid by Judge Apperson, or he may never have completed the copy which he gave me.

This copy is evidently an amplification of the preceding copy, or the original from which that one has deteriorated. The arrangement is somewhat different, but it seems clear to me that the two papers are closely related. A more logical arrangement appears in this paper; and still it has the unfortunate tone of insincerity and want of cohesion at more than one place. I do not value it highly.

(PUBLISHED BY PERMISSION)

CHENUTE, KANSAS, September 20, 1903.

MY DEAR MR. MCWHORTER.

Complying with your request, I am sending you the Judge Apperson copy of *Swift's Journal.* I doubt if the riddle of this *Journal,* and your rock inscriptions, of which you wrote me, will ever be solved. The secret has vanished with the mighty wilderness, which knew and gave it birth. The mystery will deepen as the years go by.

Just this time last year I was going through Braxton, Clay, and Nicholas Counties, West Virginia, portions of the regions referred to in the *Journal.* I found much of it covered with primal forest, as when these mysterious adventurers pierced its awe-inspiring solitudes nearly one hundred and fifty years ago. I was entranced with the charm of the "everlasting hills." I stood on Powell's Mountain and looked far over the valleys and lower hill-ranges. The blue haze of Indian Summer hung aloft. The woods took on every hue of known color. I could see the smoke from the cabins in the valley of the Gauley. At my feet was the little gem, the valley of the Muddlety. Cattle fed on a hundred hills. To the north I supposed that I discerned the outlines of the Elk River Valley. I saw the saucy squirrel as he shook down brown chestnuts in my path. I thought of the simple folk living in happy content in these romantic woods. I envied them. Man disquiets himself and runs to and fro in the earth. He seeks pleasure — a vain pursuit. The West Virginian or the Kentuckian who is content in his beautiful valley with its clear water, entrancing forests, mild and healthful climate is wise — much wiser than I have been in striving to carve a name on the tablets of fame. My only recompense is the thought that the old blood of the Celts has girdled the world and been the pioneer stock in every country now known to civilization; and that I was urged on by the energy developed by my ancestors and yours when they were dwellers on the shores of the Baltic and Black Seas. That must be your solace in your new home and western environments.

I have seen the vast, arid plains of the Columbia; and the deep forests of Oregon and Washington. I have looked into the green waters of the great Sound. I have gone up the most beautiful of Western valleys, the Willamette. I have been tossed on the bosom of the mighty Pacific; but there was ever with me a remembrance of the blue hills of old Kentucky. Such memory is put into the soul of every mountaineer.

Duty calls us to strange places, and while we may be strangers in a strange land, we can do our duty there. I have often looked at the full moon swung in the heavens and imagined that my friends on the Southern hills might be gazing there, too. God's providence hedges us about whether we are on the dark rolling Columbia or the romantic Monongahela. Man is worth nothing without an ideal, and one of mine is the old home-land where the beech nuts drop, the waters are blue and the folk generous and honest without the destructive lust for wealth so characteristic of the modern American. It is the background of my life and my inspiration.

But I will tell you of my journey. I left Clarksburg on a cloudy morning in October. At Weston it was raining; and it continued to rain all the way to Sutton, as it only can in the foothills of the Alleghenies in the autumn. The following day was cloudy, but one of those days when you know that it will not rain. I worked at Little Otter, in Braxton County, and that night I stayed at Frametown, on Elk River. This village consists of a mill and a small hotel, named in memory of old man Frame, once a Justice of the Peace, and who first settled there. He became famous for punishing a constable for summoning witnesses to attend his court on the day there was a shooting-match for beef. He had proclaimed all shooting-match days holidays.

From Frametown I started at daylight to the home of Abner Ramsey, near Enoch, in Clay County, guided by Hughes, a great-grandson of Jesse Hughes, the pioneer and Indian fighter. Ramsey lived on the top of a crag seemingly a mile high and overhanging Buffalo Creek; on which stream the father of my guide had once owned a mill and where he died. It was the pension claims of two surviving widows, which I was investigating for the

Government Bureau of Pensions. It appeared that he had married one without getting a divorce from the other.

It was five o'clock before I was ready to descend from the crag on which Ramsey dwelt, and I had to get to Nicholas Court House or Summersville, that night. Hughes left me at Ramsey's, and I had for guide my driver, a rather rough customer by name of Thayer, a boy of nineteen, who had already killed his man. When we were leaving Sutton he came armed to the teeth and with two quarts of bust-head. I prevailed on him to leave both behind, telling him that I would protect him. He insisted that he had enemies who would kill him and demanded to know "what kind uv weepins yo' totin'." I told him that I only carried a small pocket-knife and had no expectation of needing to use even that. He was skeptical and I had much trouble in getting him off without his artillery, but finally succeeded in having him discard both weapons and whiskey.

Thayer was familiar with most of the roads, but was appalled when I told him that I should go to Summersville yet that night. The road is through a ninety-six thousand acre tract without a stick amiss. It was darker than Egypt, and I had to walk and feel for the road several miles over the mountains; but we struck the Gauley at the mouth of Muddlety at midnight. From that point to Summersville it is a beautiful country with good roads.

The next day we drove from Summersville to Sutton, crossing Powell's Mountain on the way. The day was grand, and I would give much for a photograph of the view from the mountain looking west; a finer view I have not seen. They had recently erected a monument on top of the mountain in honor of some Confederate officer who fell there in the Civil War, but I had not time to get the facts. Do you know about the circumstances? I should like to have the particulars. (5)

I shall not forget this trip to my dying day. The smoky haze drifted idly, and the blending of a thousand hues made the day ideal. At Birch River, or Big Birch, at the foot of the mountain, we had dinner. The hotel was kept by a widow. The daughter cooked our meal and waited on the table. In all my travels I have not seen a fairer girl nor one of more native intelligence and modesty. She said she often thought she would like to see more of the world, and knew that she should like a good education and be able to fit herself for a higher sphere; but her

(5) See page 509.

mother needed her help in the "tavern" and she must remain. She was content and happy in this duty to her mother, though she had full confidence in her ability to make her way in the world and secure a good education; but she was willing to forego all, that the burden might be lightened for her parent. Her self-sacrifice is but a single one of the tragedies being enacted in the far-off mountains we both love so well.

We passed through Little Birch and over mountains and reached Sutton before sundown. That night I walked a mile to interview William Carpenter, of whom I have written you. (7) He wanted me to remain over night and go with him to Scott's Mountain to shoot wild turkeys. He also promised me some rare sport trailing a famous coon which had eluded all the dogs in the country for some years. He assured me that I should shoot a bear if I desired, as there were many in the woods.

I saw a number of deer on the trip and heard wolves in the forest between Buffalo Creek and the Gauley. I heard witch and ghost stories and more folk-lore than I could gather in the west in a lifetime.

Your friend,
WILLIAM E. CONNELLEY.

APPENDIX IV

Correspondence favoring executive clemency for John Claypole and his adherents, in the Tory uprising in Hampshire County, Virginia, 1781.

"HAMPSHIRE COUNTY, April 14th, 1781.

"Enclosing "Return" of Two Battalions in that county — Instructions had come from Genl: Clarke not to march the militia until further Orders — He has issued the order for the full number required by the Draft, but, adds, "I am afraid they will not be complyed with, by Reason of the disaffected people amongst us. (A Collector of one of the Divisions for making up the Cloathes and Beef was Interrupted in the execution of his office.) A certain John Claypole said if all the men were of his mind, they would not make up any Cloathes, Beef or Men, and all that would join him shuld turn out. Upon which he got all the men present, to five or six and Got Liquor and Drank King George the third's health, and Damnation to Congress, upon which Complaint was made to three Magistrates. Upon which there was a warrant Issued for several of them, and Guard of Fifty men with the Sheriff. When they came to the place they found sixty or seventy men embodied, with arms — After some time they capitulated. the Sheriff served the precept on the said John Claypole, but he refused to come with him or give up his arms; but agreed to come such a time, which time is Passt — Inclosed you have a Copy of a Letter they sent me, and the answer I sent them — I was informed there was one hundred and fifty of them to Gether the next day. I am informed there are several Deserters amongst those people, Some from the English Prisoners. Some Eighteen Months men, and some Eight Months men which they support and conceal." Refers his Excellency to Mr. Woodson the bearer for further particulars."

The letter enclosed, with reply—

"SIR,

"Having consulted the Majority, it is the Desire of them that their Conduct that has past Lately may be forgiven, as a great part of it was occasioned by Liquor, and as there is things that is Laid to the Charge of Sum, that is clear of the Charge. but moreover we acknowledge our behavior was not Discreet. if you would Please to pass it by, we will submit to pay our Tax as the Law directs; and are willing to pay our District tax or Beef and Clothing if they can be purchased, and likewise to Complyable to the Laws of the State, as far as our ability will allow. the Request of the majority I have hereunto set my hand —

From Sir, yr: humble Servant
JOSIAH OSBURN."

To Colo. Van Meter — April 3d 1781.

Reply—

"April 4th, 1781.

"SIR,

"I rec'd yours dated the third Inst: and am very Glad to hear the Mutineers Begin to see their Folly. they may Depend I shall shew them all the Lenity the circumstance of the Case will admit of, but those chargable with breaking the Law I cannot clear, as I am but an Individual, unless they who are in the warrant Comes in and Clears themselves — from your friend, while you are friends to yourselves and the United States.

GARRETT VANMETER."

To Josiah Osburn—

Letter from Garrett VanMeter Co. Com: to Governor Jefferson—From *Calendar of Virginia State Papers*, Vol. II, pp. 40-41.

"ROCKINGHAM COUNTY, August 2nd, 1781."

"SIR,

"I have the honour to enclose to your Excellency a petition from John Claypole and others, concerned in the late Insurrection in Hampshire County; which I wish from motives of good policy, as well as humanity may have the desired effect. As I apprehend it would be attended with pernicious consequences to hold out pardon to those who denied to surrender themselves to Justice, or delayed to submit to the Laws of their Country, untill they were sure of escaping punishment; and at the same time to prosecute those who readily submitted the Investigation and punishment of their crimes, to the Laws of the Land: since it would certainly operate as an Encouragement to future offenders to stand out untill they were assured of Indemnity.

"Another political reason I beg leave to assign, is the many relations & connexions that the Claypole Family have in that part of the Country: as there is the Father & 5 sons, with many grand children, who by inter-marriages are connected with the most considerable Families on those waters, and the strongest friends to our present Constitution, and to prosecute him with vigour, whilst the ringleaders have evaded Justice by flight, and those in similar circumstances of Guilt are pardoned, would probably sour the minds of his numerous connexions, and perhaps be reguarded by them as pointed and partial.

"I must also add, that he has a letter from General: Morgan engaging to procure his pardon, on his returning to his Duty—Humanity also pleads strongly in their behalf, for on my attending the intended Court of Oyer the 10th ult: for the Trial of those Miscreants, as directed by your Excellencies Letter, I had the opportunity of viewing the distressing Scenes of aged mothers, wives, & children crowding to the Court House to take the last Leave of their unhappy Sons, husbands & fathers, apprehending that Execution would be immediate on the Sentence of Death, which in spite of all my aversion to Tories, strongly affected my feelings — I need not mention to a Gentleman of your approved Goodness of Heart, the maxim of a celebrated Writer "that it is the Enormity, or dangerous Tendency of a Crime that alone can warrant any Earthly Legislature in putting him to Death, that commits it." And tho' the crime of the petitioners was of the most dangerous Tendency, yet they transgressed more thro Ignorance than Design; and their offence proceeded rather from Error & prejudice, than any deliberate Intention of Injuring the State, or disturbing Government: from all which considerations I would humbly presume that the honble Board will extend the Act of Indemnity, as well to the petitioners

herein referred to, as to all those, who were by the Examining Court, bound over
to be indicted at the next grand Jury for the County" &c &c

* * * * * * * *

" I have the honour to be, Your Excelly's
                  most obt & very humble Servt."

Letter from Peter Hog to Governor Nelson, containing petition from John Claypole and others—From *Calendar of Virginia State Papers*, Vol. II, pp. 284-285.

"HAMPSHIRE COUNTY, November 26th, 1781.

"Having been examined by a called court "hath been set for further trial," but in as much as "the same ignorance and unaccountable infatuation" seems to extend to this unhappy man "that actuated those deluded people, and although he was the worst of them, he hopes, if it be consistent with wisdom that he may also "experience the lenity of the Legislature" — A few of "the deluded wretches" still remain out, particularly a certain John Woolf, who had broken Jail, and has never been seen since — He has taken every means to have them all apprehended — He will at the command of His Excellency call a Court of Oyer & Terminer for the trial of Smith and others, but hopes the Legislature may "incline to pass an act of indemnity for the whole of them."

Is much in need of a copy of the new Militia Law and the Articles of War, not being able to "try delinquents" in consequence — Asks for a number of blank commissions to supply the new nominations made — His declining health forces him to resign his commission as Co. Lieutenant, but as Mr. Joseph Nevill who has been recommended to succeed him cannot act until commissioned, he will endeavour to act until Mr. Nevill qualifies, especially as Col: Cresap, next in command lives in so remote a part of the Country. He sends this by Mr. Woodrow, as an Express, as neither of the Delegates are going down, and hopes his expenses will be allowed.

Letter from Colonel Garrett VanMeter to Governor Nelson, — Informing him, "that Robert Smith one of the Ringleaders of the late insurrection in this County hath voluntarily surrendered himself."—From the *Calendar of Virginia State Papers*, Vol. II, pp. 624, 625.

TO HIS EXCELLENCY THOS: NELSON ESQR. GOVERNOR &C AND THE HONORABLE
    COUNCIL OF VIRGINIA.

The petition of John Claypole, Thos: Denton, David Roberts, Jr., Mathias Wilkins, and George Wilkins, Inhabitants of Cacapon in the County of Hampshire
                                                            Humbly Sheweth

That your petitioners living in an obscure and remote corner of the State, are precluded from every Intelligence of the State of affairs, either by Public Papers or from Information of Men of Credit and Veracity, and at the same time infested by the wicked Emissaries or pretended Emmissaries of the British who travel through all parts of the Frontiers, and by Misrepresentations and false news poisoned the Minds of the Ignorant and credulous Settlers: That your petitioners from narrow and confined notions, & attached to strongly to their Interests, conceived the Act of laying the enormous Tax of Eighty Two Pounds paper Money on every hundred pounds of their property, rated in Specie, and a Bounty for the Recruits of the Continental Army, and the Law subjecting them, at the same time to be draughted for the said Service, and the further Act for Cloathing the Army, as unjust and oppressive after paying such a high tax on their Assessed property, and those wicked and designing men by their artfull insinuations & false Intelligences industriously propagated to delude & seduce your petitioners, too readily prevailed on them to oppose the Execution of the said Acts, and take up Arms in defence of what those wretches called their Liberty and property. But your Petitioners Humbly shew that they never concocted or conspired the destruction of Government, or the hurt of any Individuals, further than to defend themselves when attacked or compelled to yield obedience to those Laws. And when your petitioners were made sensible of their Error, by the Gentlemen from the Adjacent Counties, who marched a body of men sufficient to have put all the disobedient & deluded crew to the Sword, but from motives of humanity & prudence attempted the more mild method of Argument to dispel the delusion, and bring them back to their duty, your Petitioners, ready to receive information, and open to correction readily gave up their Arms and engaged to deliver themselves to Justice and submit to the Laws of their Country when called for; which they have since done and stood their Trials in the County Court of Hampshire, and were by that Court adjudged to stand a further Tryal before a Special Court of Oyer and Terminer, appointed to meet at the Court House on the Tenth Day of July last, but the Gentlemen nominated as Judges by the Hon'ble Board failing to attend, the prosecution was postponed. And your petitioners were then Informed by a Proclamation under the hand of the County Lieutenant, that the Executive, ever prone to adopt the most lenient measures to penitent offenders, offered pardon and Indemnity to all those concerned in the late insurrection, if they would return to their duty, and behave as good Citizens in future. And your petitioners impressed with a deep Sense of the gracious Intentions of your Excellency and the Hon'ble Board, towards the Ignorant and deluded, were encouraged to sue for pardon; and that the same Act of grace might be extended towards them, since they humbly conceive their Conduct has been more Consonant to the Duty of good Citizens, who conscious that they have Transgress'd against the Laws of their Country, readily delivered themselves to Justice and to Tryal by their Peers, to suffer the punishment due to their crimes, tho' committed thro' Ignorance and misguided zeal; Whereas those who have availed themselves of the said Proclamation, tho' equally guilty, did not come in until their safety was insured to them by the promise of pardon.

Wherefore, your Petitioners humbly hope, from the known Clemency of your Excellency, and that Equianimity that governs the Councils of the Hon'ble Board, that they will be graciously pleased to pardon their past offences, and include them in the Act of Indemnity so mercifully held out to offenders under the like circumstances, and they engage, on the Faith of honest Citizens to Act a true and faithful part to the State in future, if they are released from further prosecution, and restored to the privileges of other Citizens: which your petitioner John Claypole is more encouraged to expect, from a letter of Genl: Morgan's to your said Petitioner, wherein he promises to procure his pardon, on his returning to his Allegiance and becoming a Good Citizen; this he humbly conceives his behavior has done since he was convince of his Error, and freed from those mistaken prejudices that seduced him from his duty —

Wherefore, in deep contrition for their past misconduct and sincere promise of conducting themselves as good citizens for the time to come, they humbly pray for Pardon, and that the Hon'ble Board will save their innocent wives and children from ruin and misery, which they must necessarily be involved in, for the crimes of their deluded Husbands and Parents,

And your Petitioners shall ever pray &c."

Papers relating to the pardon of John Claypole and others.— From *Calendar of Virginia State Papers*, Vol. II, pp. 682, 683.

PETITION OF CITIZENS TO THE EXECUTIVE, FOR THE PARDON OF JOHN CLAYPOLE, ON ACCOUNT OF HIS PREVIOUS GOOD STANDING AS AN "HONEST, PEACEABLE, WELL MEANING MAN."

HAMPSHIRE COUNTY, 1781.

Numerously signed, the following names appearing among the signatures — Vandeventer, Ruddell, Hutton, Bullett, Bird, Hite, VanMeter, Randall, Vause, Lynch, Ashby, Harris, Shanklin, and many others.— From *Calendar of Virginia State Papers*, Vol. II, pp. 683, 684.

"HAMPSHIRE COUNTY, 1781.

"PETITION OF JACOB BRAKE (1) AND OTHERS, for pardon for having through ignorance, and the persuasion of others, joined in the late 'Conspiracy against the State the object of which was to refuse payment of Taxes, and to oppose the Act of Oct: 1780 for raising Troops for the Service" —

"Setting forth the same reasons given in John Claypole's application, why they should enjoy Executive Clemency, and adding, that they 'have been instrumental in detecting and bringing in some of the Principal Conspirators to Justice &c.

"Signed by —JACOB BRAKE, Adam Rodebaugh, John Mace, Michael Algrie, Isaac Brake, John Mitchell, Saml: Lourie, Leonard Hier, Jacob Hier, George Peck, John Casner, Jacob Yeazle, Thos: Nutler, Thos: Stacey, John Rodebaugh, Henry Rodebaugh, Jacob House, Jeremiah Ozburn, Jacob Crites, Anthony Reager, Josiah Ozburn, George Lites, Charles Borrer, Jacob Pickle, John Wease, Adam Wease, & Adam Wease, Jur: — "

From *Calendar of Virginia State Papers*, Vol. II, p. 686.

---

(1) See page 506.

NOTES

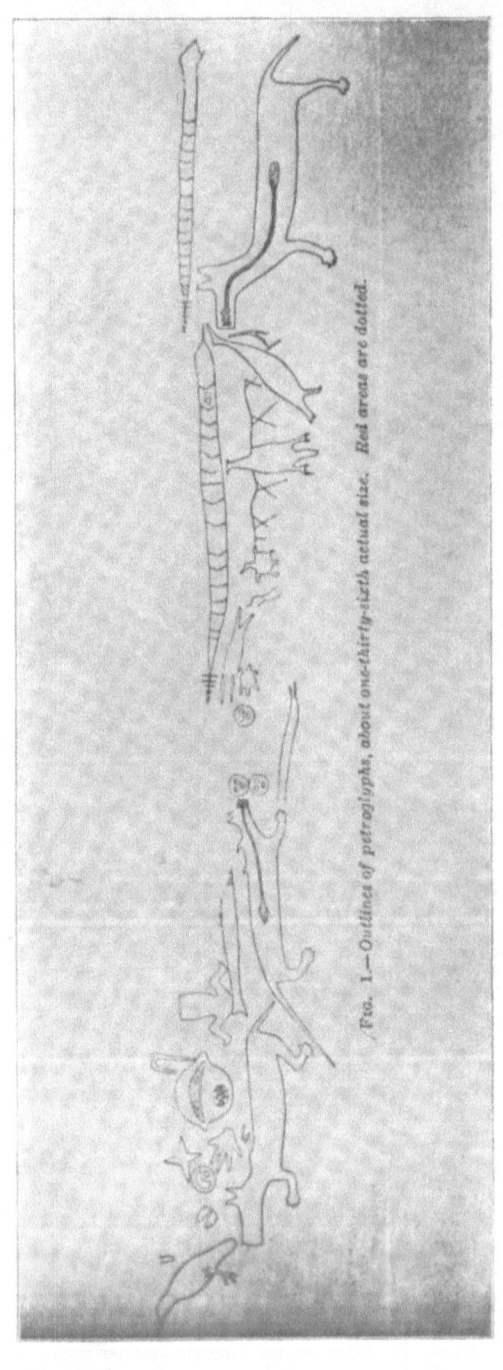

Fig. 1.—Outlines of petroglyphs, about one-thirty-sixth actual size. Red areas are dotted.

PETROGLYPHS—INDIAN TEMPLE-CAVE. LOCATED ON TWO LICK RUN, HARRISON COUNTY, WEST VA.

Courtesy of Hon. Henry Haymond

With the exception of the serpents, the figures are all done in Intaglio; the excavations, from 1-8 to 1-4 inch, are smoothly finished. See p. 322. and Note 7. Chapt. XXVI. Also History of Harrison County, West Va.: pp. 396 to 398; where Prof. Holmes' observations on this cavern are fully set forth.

NOTES ON CHAPTER I

(1) WAP-PA-TO-MA-KA: also spelled, *Wa-po-tom-i-ka:* the Indian appellation for the South Branch of the Potomac River. I have adhered to this aboriginal cognomen, which was bestowed by some tribe of the Algonquian family; most probably the Leni-lenape (Delaware), or the Shawnee. On a map of Virginia, 1769, it is written "Wappocomo, or South Branch of Potowmac R." Other forms of the name are met with in the earliest records. The meaning has been interpreted by some writers: "river of wild geese;" which I am inclined to doubt. The name contains the Delaware and the Shawnee root, *wap*, or *wamp* (white). It is very similar to Wah-pi-ko-me'-kah (white waters), the Delaware and the Miami name for the White River of Indiana. Other names of corresponding import might be mentioned. Wakatomika, Shawnee town on Muskingum River.

A village of the Munsee branch of the Delaware nation, located on White River where Muncie, Indiana, now stands, was called *Wapicomekoke* (Wah-pi-ko-me-kunk) "White-river town."

WAPEMINSKINK (Wah-pi-mins-kink), was a Delaware town on the west fork of this stream at the present site of Anderson, Indiana. It has been erroneously identified with *Wapicomekoke*.—*Hand Book of American Indians:* Bureau of Ethnology, Washington, 1910, Part 2, p. 912.

WAPPATOMICA was the "upper Shawnee village" on the upper waters of the Great Miami River, Ohio, during the Revolutionary War. The name has gone into history in, perhaps, a dozen different forms. Butterfield's *History of the Girtys*, Cincinnati, 1896, p. 74.

WAPAKONETA (Wa-pa-ko-ne'-ta), "White-jacket," was a small contemporary village of the same tribe on the waters of Mad River; and after the Treaty of Greenville, 1795, on the Auglaize River, Ohio. *White-jacket* was a Shawnee chief.

The South Branch was known to the Iroquois by the name usually spelled *Cohongononita*. In this is found the Iroquoin root for *wild-goose*, "kohank;" and if the interpretation: "river of wild geese" is applicable to this historic stream, it is through this name and not the *Wappatomaka* of the Algonquian, Delaware-Shawnee. Unfortunately most of the Indian geographical names recorded by the colonists are greatly corrupted; and often the rendition, at best, can only be a surmise.

(2) WITHERS—*Border Warfare;* Cincinnati, 1895, p. 117.
DEHASS—*Indian Wars of Western Virginia;* Wheeling, 1851, p. 75.
MO-NON-GA-HE-LA: by far the most pleasing, euphonic geographic name within the Trans-Allegheny. On some of the old maps and early records it is spelled: *Menangihilli, Mohengeyela, Mohongeyela, Mohongaly, Monongalia,* and a few other forms. Of Algonquian origin, the meaning is uncertain. That which is generally accepted, and as interpreted, implies: "falling-in-banks," or "sliding-banks." The peninsula formed by the junction of this stream and that of the Youghiogheny, was called by the Delawares: *Meh-non-au-au-ge-hel-ak,* "place of caving" or "falling banks," from which, doubtless, the present name, *Monongahela* was derived.

For some of the Indian names of streams in West Virginia, see Hale's *Trans-Alleghany Pioneers;* Cincinnati, 1886. Report of *Archives and History of the State of West Virginia;* Charleston, 1906.

THE PRINGLE SYCAMORE OF TODAY
Courtesy of Mr. M. C. Brake

(3) TURKEY RUN — This beautiful little valley, made historic by the Pringle Camp, received its name from the vast numbers of wild turkeys found there by the first settlers.

The spot whereon grew the Pringle Sycamore, is on the land now owned by Mr. Webster Dix; on the west side of Turkey Run, about twenty-five feet from the stream and some forty to fifty feet from the bank of the Buckhannon River. *Withers,* p. 119, speaks of the stump of this tree as still standing in 1831. The late Hon. William C. Carper, of Buckhannon, remembered seeing it about 1848. The cavity was not less than twelve feet across.

This stump disappeared many years ago and a second sycamore sprang up from the roots of the parent tree. This tree grew quite tall and straight. About the year 1880, it was blown down and washed away by a flood. But as if reluctant to fail to mark the site of the first primitive home of the white man in that region, the roots shot forth a second sprout and this grew into a bushy tree. It has a cavity in its trunk that will shelter two or three men from an ordinary storm. Mr. Dix has promised me that this historic land mark shall be protected.

(4) Prof. A. L. Keith, of Carleton College, Northfield, Minn.; a great great grandson of John Pringle and Rebecca Simpson, is confident, after exhaustive research, that the two John Pringles are identical, and that Simpson the trapper and Simpson the slave holder were one and the same person. This, however, has not been truly verified. Several of the Kentucky Pringles were in the War of 1812.

(5) See *Chapter IX,* this Volume.

(6) For a further sketch of the Pringles, see *Border Warfare.*
Also, Chapter XVIII, *History of Upshur County, West Va.,* 1906.
All references herein to the several County Histories of West Vigrinia, have been added since this volume was practically completed.

(7) See *Chapter XXXIV,* this Volume, for notice of the belief in witchcraft.

(8) DODDRIDGE, in his *Notes on the Settlement and Indian Wars of Virginia and Pennsylvania;* Albany, 1876, pp. 140, 141, gives this description of the hunting shirt.

"The hunting shirt was universally worn. This was a kind of loose frock, reaching half way down the thighs, with large sleeves, open before, and so wide as to lop over a foot or more when belted. The cape was large, and sometimes handsomely fringed with a raveled piece of cloth of a different color from that of the hunting shirt itself. The bosom of this dress served as a wallet to hold a chunk of bread, cakes, jerk, tow for wiping the barrel of the rifle, or any other necessary for the hunter or warrior. The belt, which was always tied behind, answered several purposes, beside that of holding the dress together. In cold weather the mittens, and sometimes the bullet-bag, occupied the front part of it. To the right side was suspended the tomahawk and to the left the scalping knife in its leathern sheath. The hunting shirt was generally made of linsey, sometimes of coarse linen, and a few of dressed deer skins. These last were very cold and uncomfortable in wet weather."

See also the *History of the Valley, by Kercheval;* an old edition, p. 338. *DeHass*, pp. 94, 95. *Annals of the West;* Pittsburg, 1857, p. 339.

At a later day the hunting shirt was of a different pattern, a sort of long sack coat or "wammus," minus the cape and belt. The material was homespun linsey, usually colored red. The back was cut in one piece, with the front corners long and pendulous. These corners were tied together in front, drawing the tail in a close-fitting belt about the waist. This formed the body of the coat into a capacious bag, extending entirely around the person of the wearer. In this handy repository the hunter carried his food and small necessaries.

Several years ago a settler in Gilmer County, West Virginia, named Wilson, was digging ginseng. In the back of his wammus he carried a ration of corn bread and jerk. He was accompanied by his two dogs, and in the course of the day came upon a bear. One of the dogs immediately fled to camp. The bear soon threw the man, and was proceeding to "chew him up." Fortunately the bear got hold of the corn pone, and while demolishing that savory morsel, the dog which had remained faithful seized the bear about the head, causing it to release its hold on both man and pone to deal with this canine adversary. Wilson, now free, sprang to his feet and dispatched the bear with his rifle. Upon his return to camp, he promptly shot the recreant dog, swearing that he would not keep a dog that would desert him in time of danger.

The origin of the word "jerk," as applied to dried venison, was thus humorously explained by Abram Reger and Stephen Martin, two old hunters of the Buckhannon region: "The hunter often takes a bite of dried venison without cutting it with his knife; and it requires a strong quick *jerk* with both hands and teeth to sever it—hence the name."

(9) The following is part of a note written by me for the recent (1895) edition of *Wither's Chronicles of Border Warfare.*

"Hughes was a noted border scout, but a man of fierce unbridled passions, and so confirmed an Indian hater that no tribesman, however peaceful his record, was safe in his presence. Some of the most cruel acts on the frontier are, by tradition, attributed to this man. While he was a great scout and Indian trader [trailer], he never headed an expedition of note. This, no doubt, was because of his fierce temperament and bad reputation among his countrymen."

"Want of space alone," says Mr. Thwaites, the editor, "prevents me from giving Mr. McWhorter's narrative of Hughes' long and bloody career. In studying the annals of the border," continues the editor, "we must not fail to note that here and there were many savage-hearted men among the white settlers whose deeds were quite as atrocious as any attributed to the red-skins. Current histories of Indian warfare seldom recognize this fact."

(10) *Border Warfare*, pp. 121, 122. DeHass, *Indian Wars*, pp. 77, 78.

(11) *Border Warfare*, p. 122.

(12) See Chapter XXV, this Volume.

(13) *History of Upshur County, West Va.*, p. 183.

NOTES ON CHAPTER II

(1) *Border Warfare*, Editor's Preface, p. 5.

(2) Draper's Memoir of Withers, *Border Warfare*, p. 11.

(3) This was William Hacker, Jr., the eldest son of John Hacker, the first settler on Hacker's Creek. William Hacker, Sr., the scout, and John Hacker the settler, were brothers. There was a sister named "Betsy," who, tradition says, was Mrs. Merrill, of Kentucky border fame; while another version of this tradition has it that she married a Mr. Freeman, although crediting her with the terrible achievements of Mrs. Merrill with an axe and a featherbed.

For an account of this occurrence, see *Border Warfare*, pp. 405, 406. *DeHass*, pp. 297, 298. McKnight, *Our Western Border*, Chicago, 1902, p. 698.

(4) This was Elias Hughes. See Chapters XXIV, XXV, this Volume.

(5) Since writing this chapter I have come in possession of several interesting letters on this topic, which are given in Appendix I, this Volume.

(6) I cannot refrain from here giving a few incidents of Mrs. Cunningham's captivity as told by my step-mother, a granddaughter of Mrs. Cunningham; and who often heard her grandmother tell the story of her adventures.

While concealed in the cavern, the searching party of whites came upon the rock overhead so closely that Mrs. Cunningham said, "Not only were their voices plainly audible, and I recognized some of them, but the slight rustle of their shot pouches was borne to my ear. I was in mortal terror lest my baby should cry, knowing full well that swift death would follow."

A pole which lay in the cavern showed for many years the cuts where the Indians had hacked it with their tomahawks during their involuntary delay.

When Simon Girty was negotiating for her release at the Maumee Rapids in the autumn 1788, the Indians seemed reluctant to let her go and haggled for some time over the amount which they were receiving in exchange. Finally one of them seized her roughly by the shoulder and shoving her towards Girty, exclaimed fiercely: "*Take* her, we have nothing for *our* flesh and blood." He was referring to the warrior who was mortally wounded by Edward Cunningham when she was taken prisoner.

Simon Girty was instrumental in restoring Mrs. Cunningham to her friends after a captivity of more than three years; but McKee, the British agent, furnished the goods that were given in exchange.

In the Autobiography of Rev. James L. Clarke, it is declared that Mrs. Cunningham, whose Christian name was Phoebe, embraced religion while on her way to the Indian towns. She died in 1845, near Freed, Calhoun County, West Va., and was buried there.

For a general account of the Cunningham tragedy, consult: *Border Warfare*, *DeHass*, *McKnight* and Chapter VI, Lowther's *History of Ritchie County, West Va.* DeHass and McKnight both state that the attack on the Cunninghams was in June 1785; but Lieut. Duvall who was in command of the Harrison County Militia at that time, gives the date "31st August," of that year, when he reported Mrs. Cunningham killed. See Note 4, Chapter XVII, this Volume, for notice of Lieut. J. P. Duvall.

Mrs. Cunningham in depicting domestic pioneer life, gave facts which I do not recall ever seeing in print. Horse collars were made from the soft fiber obtained from the linden tree. When the sap was in full flow the bark was stripped from the trunk in long sheets and thrown into the water and left there until the sap-fiber became loosened; when it could be separated from the rough outer coating in thin ribbon-like layers. This was plaited into thick pads and used as horse collars. Grape vines, or hickory bark twisted into ropes, answered for traces.

There was among the Cunninghams, one Joe, captured by the Indians when a small boy and retained by them until grown. The traits of his forest life were indelibly fixed. He wore large rings in his ears and in many ways retained the Indian dress. A heavy hunting knife always hung at his belt, and he had an unpleasant way of slipping upon persons unawares and suddenly whipping out his knife, feign stabbing them, accompanying the motion with a gutteral "*Whou.*" He was known as "Indian Joe."

(7) *Border Warfare*, pp. 309, 310.

(8) *Border Warfare*, p. 290.

(9) *Border Warfare*, pp. 247-258.

(10) *Border Warfare*, p. 370.

(11) The "Messrs. Bonnetts" were Lewis, Peter and Jacob; brothers to Samuel and John Bonnett, referred to elsewhere in this Volume. They came from Hardy County, Virginia. Lewis and Peter were granted pensions for services as Indian spies from 1779 to 1783. Their narratives are interesting, setting forth at length their services along the Ohio River and country adjacent to the upper Monongahela settlements.

Lewis states that "In April 1783 in a skirmish with a band of Indians, had a brother John killed, we put his body in a well known cave in Lewis Co. where his bones are yet to be seen." (1833.)

John Bonnett was killed in September 1778.

Lewis Bonnett was born in Hardy County, Va., in 1762.

The declaration of Peter Bonnett is practically the same as that of his brother Lewis, and both were granted pensions.

Jacob Bonnett was pensioned for services as private in Col. Crocket's Virginia Regiment. He died in Lewis County, Va., in December, 1847. His wife, Martha, a daughter of Jesse Hughes, died in December, 1834. They left the following children: Martha; Delilah, married Abram Hess; Eliza, married Fleming Sprouse; Lucinda, married Jesse Butcher; Samuel, Gracie, Elizabeth.

All but the last three children were still living in Lewis County, Va., in April 1860. Samuel, Gracie and Elizabeth had died previously, leaving descendants.

Adam Flesher secured a pension for two years alleged service in Col. Duvall's Regiment, but upon the recommendation and evidence secured by W. G. Singleton, both Flesher and the Bonnetts were dropped from the pension roll as being too young to have served in the Revolutionary War.

Flesher's declaration is of interest, setting forth in detail his experiences during the War. He was the son of Henry Flesher, the first settler at Weston, and he states that in October, 1781, he went with his father and family to the Buckhannon Fort where he engaged in a five days scout for Indians. The Flesher family remained there until the following spring. There were no disturbances during the winter, but "in February the Indians came within 2 miles of the Fort, and killed John Finch, [Fink] the alarm was given the men of the fort including myself; we went out, found the body and buried it. I was engaged in this matter two days."

Henry Flesher was born July 29, 1764; making him seventeen years of age at the time of his service at the Buckhannon Fort. Many served in the Revolutionary War at that age and even younger. On February 22, 1792, Flesher married Elizabeth Staats, who was born October 12, 1776. Flesher died November 4, 1854.

Jesse Carpenter and Thomas Cottral were also granted pensions for military services on the border, but were subsequently stricken from the list for the same reason as were the Bonnetts and Flesher. Cottral claimed to have served through the seasons of 1779, 1780, 1781 and 1782. His declaration is barren of incidents. He was born in Pennsylvania, January 22, 1762. Singleton was instrumental in having several others of that region eliminated from the pension roll, mostly on the same grounds as the foregoing cases. In many instances his rulings appear very arbitrary and unjust.

(12) For a notice of Col. John McWhorter, see Chapter XXVIII, this Volume.

(13) Now deceased. See Note 17, Chapter XXVIII.

(14) *Border Warfare*, p. 366.

(15) *Border Warfare*, pp. 217, 218.

(16) *Border Warfare*, pp. 135, 137.

NOTES ON CHAPTER III

(1) The reader will hardly fail to notice the striking similarity of the two preceding incidents and those related of *Lewis Wetzel*, by the same author, *DeHass*, pp. 349, 353.

These sketches of *Hughes*, and *Wetzel*, are also found in McKnight's *Ou Western Border*, pp. 330-332, 669-671.

(2) Without doubt this incident occurred at West's Fort. It is briefly mentioned in *Border Warfare*, pp. 287, 288. A full account of the transaction will be found elsewhere in this Volume.

(3) Local tradition says that two of the garrison at Fort Jefferson, Ohio, were lured into the woods just west of the Fort and there killed. In this manner, in the summer of 1792, Capt. Shaylor, the commander of that Fort, with his son, "a lad of fine promise," were decoyed from the fortress and the latter killed. The Captain escaped closely pursued and wounded in the back by an arrow. See Burnet's *Notes on the Northwestern Territory*, Cincinnati, 1847, pp. 112, 113, where Shaylor is ranked as Major. Also, Howe's *Historical Collections of Ohio*, Volume I, pp. 529, 530.

Samuel Drake, a youth and a rifleman in Gen. Harrison's Army, War of 1812, used to relate that while in camp where Detroit now stands, he heard turkeys calling for two mornings back of his tent. Early on the second morning he stepped outside and was examining his rifle for the purpose of going to shoot the turkey, when an old woodsman with a rifle on his shoulder called: "Sammy where are you going with that gun." Just then there was another call from the turkey and Drake replied: "I am going to shoot that turkey." The old borderman heard it, and then carefully stationed Drake at the rear of the tent and told him to stay there and watch and he would "go shoot the turkey and give it to him." The scout then went about a half mile down the river and disappeared in the woods. While Drake was watching the place from where the cries issued, he heard the report of a rifle and saw an Indian throw up his hands and fall across a log. Soon the old rifleman came back and told Drake to "go get the turkey and cook it."

(4) *History of Augusta County, Virginia;* Staunton, 1882, p. 353.

NOTES ON CHAPTER IV

(1) C. V. Woodson, in his memoranda of the *Hughes Family, of Powhatan County* (Virginia), p. 208, Volume V, *Virginia. Magazine of History*, 1897, says:

"Record (as far as now known) of the Hughes family, who originally owned Hughes' Creek, in Powhatan, Va.

"Jesse Hughes and his wife (French Huguenot) came from the mother country in company with a large number of other Huguenots, and settled in this State while yet a colony of England. With others who obtained grants of land from King Charles II, of England, Jesse Hughes settled Hughes' Creek, on James River, in Powhatan, Va., and on this place he and his family lived and died. No record of births, deaths or marriages extant. Hughes' Creek was entailed, according to the English law. Continued in the family through four generations. Martha Hartwell Hughes, who intermarried with Francis Goode (son of Robert Goode, the third), of Whitby, was the last owner, when it fell into other hands.

"Jesse Hughes' son, Robert Hughes (first) married and left sons and daughters. No record of births, marriages and deaths of himself and family now extant.

"Robert Hughes (the second) son of Robert Hughes (the first), married Ann Hartwell, of New Kent. They had three sons, Jesse Hughes, Robert Hughes (the third) and David Hughes; also two daughters, Fanny Hughes and Temperance Hughes. She married Henry Watkins, of Bush River, Prince Edward County. They had five sons and two daughters. No record of family now extant as to births and deaths.

"Jesse Hughes, son of Robert Hughes (the second), was a pioneer and explorer of the mountains and the west of Virginia. He was a man of energy and bravery. He died on one of his expeditions to the mountains. Died unmarried, and from him his brother, Robert Hughes, inherited Hughes' Creek. See DeHass for an account of Jesse Hughes' career in West Virginia as Indian fighter, etc.

"Robert Hughes (the third) served in the Revolutionary War as captain of a volunteer company; married previous to the war, Mary Mosby, a daughter of Littleberry Mosby and his wife. Elizabeth Netherland was a daughter of his first wife.

"Robert Hughes (the third) died soon after the close of the Revolutionary War, leaving three daughters, Martha Hartwell Hughes, Elizabeth Netherland Hughes and Ann Hartwell Hughes. No sons."

It is very probable that Mr. Woodson errs in stating that Jesse Hughes was a French Huguenot. During the terrible persecution of the Huguenots in France, many of them migrated to England, Germany and other European countries, while others settled in Africa and the North American Colonies. It is not improbable that the wife of Jesse Hughes, the founder of this family in Powhatan, was a French Huguenot and that they were accompanied by others of her countrymen to Virginia. It is hardly necessary to note that Mr. Woodson has confounded Jesse Hughes, who died in the mountains, with Jesse Hughes, the scout of border fame.

(2) Albache's *Western Annals*, Pittsburgh, 1857, p. 174.

(3) *Border Warfare*, pp. 89, 118.

(4) Following is the version of this tragedy as narrated in *Border Warfare*, pp. 240, 241:

"In the last of April, a party of about twenty Indians came to the neighborhoods of Hacker's Creek and the West Fork. At this time the inhabitants of those neighborhoods had removed to West's Fort, on the creek, and to Richard's Fort on the river; and leaving the women and children in them during the day, under the protection of a few men, the others were in the habit of performing the usual labors of their farms in companies, so as to preserve them from attacks of the Indians. A company of men, being thus engaged, the first week of May, in a field, now owned by Minter Bailey, on Hacker's Creek, and being a good deal dispersed in various occupations, some fencing, others clearing, and a few ploughing, they were unexpectedly fired upon by the Indians, and Thomas Hughes and Jonathan Lowther shot down; the others being incautiously without arms fled for safety. Two of the company, having the Indians rather between them and West's Fort, ran directly to Richard's, as well for their own security as to give the alarm there. But they had already been apprized that the enemy was at hand. Isaac Washburn, who had been to mill on Hacker's Creek the day before, on his return to Richard's Fort and near to where Clement's mill now stands, was shot from his horse, tomahawked and scalped. The finding of his body, thus cruelly mangled, had given them the alarm, and they were already on their guard, before the two men from Hacker's Creek arrived with the intelligence of what had been done there. The Indians then left the neighborhood without effecting more havoc; and the whites were too weak to go in pursuit, and molest them."

It was claimed by the old settlers, that Isaac Washburn was shot on the river bank, and feeling his wound mortal and to save his hair which was long and luxuriant, he leaped into the deep water just above the mouth of the run which still bears his name. The crossing was on a ripple a little further down.

Mr. Clark W. Helmick of West Milford, West Va., writes me that he often talked with Jesse Lowther, a lad of about ten years at the time of the Washburn tragedy, who lived in the Richard Fort, and if Washburn was scalped at all it was while he was in the water.

Several years ago a party while seining this same hole, brought to light an old rifle supposed to have been Washburn's. The barrel is octagon, measuring forty-three and three-fourths inches in length, and partly rusted in two. Most of the stock was gone but part of the heavy wood and the lock are in a fair state of preservation. The flint was missing from the lock. Mr. D. B. Rider, one of the seiners, carefully preserved the relic. It is now in the possession of Mr. W. M. Bird of Lost Creek, West Va., who also has the bullet with which the gun was loaded at the time of Washburn's death. It weighs half-ounce, and is oval at the point and flat at the base. (*See cut and Note 6, Chapter XVI, this Volume.*)

Jesse Lowther narrated that when Washburn was killed some of the men were out hunting and came near being ambushed. Thomas Hughes fled for the fort, hotly pursued by three Indians. As the scout drew near the stockade one of the men perched on the wall near the gate kept halloing: "*Run Tom, run Tom, er they'll ketch ye.*" This constant urging annoyed Hughes, who, as soon as he came up exclaimed: "Shut yer damned hollerin'; do ye s'pose a man would run booby with three Injuns after him?"

There were five brothers of the Washburns, and like the Schoolcrafts, the family was nearly exterminated during the border wars.

Benjamin was the only one to escape, and he in company with Benjamin Shinn and William Grundy, was fired upon in 1778, when returning from a deer lick on the head of Booth's Creek, near Baxter's Run, Grundy was killed. *Withers* p. 247.

Later in the same year while gathering pine knots from which to manufacture shoemakers wax, preparatory to leaving the country because of Indian hostilities, James and Stephen were fired upon and the latter killed and scalped. James was taken to the Indian towns and beaten to death while running the gauntlet the second time. *Withers* pp. 250, 251.

It is tradition that a few nights previous to his death, Stephen dreamed that he was scalped, which filled his mind with gloomy forebodings of coming fate.

In June 1782, an Indian shot and scalped Charles Washburn, while he was cutting wood near his own dooryard. *Withers*, p. 345.

Tradition says that a sister was carried into captivity and adopted into an Indian family. One day two scouts, one of whom was Lewis Wetzel, came upon two squaws near the banks of a river in the Indian country and they determined to drown them. One of these was the Washburn woman, who making herself known was rescued and brought home by the scouts, but her campanion was drowned.

This adventure is very similar to that of the scouts, Robert McClellan and one White, in 1790, as told in *Our Western Border*, p. 563.

The scouts had been sent out from Fort Gower, on the Hock-hocking River, in Ohio, and were spying on the Indians from an eminence since known as Mount Pleasant. White went to a spring for water near the river bank and was discovered by two squaws, who came within a few feet of him. The surprise was mutual; but the elder woman recovering, gave the alarm halloo. The scout seized them both and rushed into the river and attempted to drown them. The older squaw soon succumbed, but the younger one made a stout resistance and spoke to him in English. White released her, when she informed him that she had been a captive for ten years, was taken with her brother below Wheeling, but the brother had effected his escape on the second night. With the girl, White hurried back where McClellan lay concealed, and where they immediately had a fight with pursuing Indians, in which the girl took an active part. Under cover of night, the party eluded their enemies, and in time reached the fort. The rescued girl's name was Washburn; her mother and a sister were killed at the time of her capture.

McClellan was a noted frontiersman, and was identified with many stirring events on the border. Was in the battle of the Fallen Timbers, and subsequently a trader among the western tribes, and eventually drifted to Astoria, Oregon, in the interest of the Astor Fur Company. With a few comrades, he started to return to the States, and the entire party had nearly perished of hunger and hardships encountered on the desert and in the mountains. This was in 1812. McClellan died two years later.

(5) For a biographical sketch of Elias Hughes, see Chapters XXIV, XXV, this Volume.

(6) Henry Flesher settled on the present site of Weston, in 1776, or soon after. He entered and secured certificate for 400 acres. It is said that his flailing, or thrashing floor was where the court house is now located. His cabin stood about fifty yards from where the Bland Hotel was afterwards erected, and at the head of Main Street. At the time Flesher was attacked by Indians, he was hauling logs for a stable.

(7) See *Chapter XX*, this Volume, for a sketch of Adam O'Brien.

(8) The report of Mr. Singleton and the ruling of the Pension Office in Hughes' case are most singular. In many of his conclusions regarding the service and status of the border militia scouts, it is difficult to believe that Singleton was not swayed by a spirit of uncharitable discrimination. In a few instances his charge of dishonesty is based upon the testimony of men whom he, in other cases, branded as frauds. He decried others, whose good character was vouched for by men of unquestionable integrity. This inconsistency is painfully manifest in more than one case.

The Act of Congress, June 4, 1832, pensioning soldiers of the Revolutionary War, are the clauses under which Hughes and most of the militia or border scouts applied for pensions. See *Statutes at Large*, Twenty-Second Congress, First

Session, Chapter CXXVI. The limitation contained in Section 2 was removed by Act, Frebuary 19, 1833, and construed not to embrace invalid pensioners.

(9) In 1757, the privates in Capt. Hogg's Company of Augusta County, Virginia, rangers were paid twenty pence (about fifteen cents) a day, and they found their own clothing. *Annals of Augusta County*, Richmond, 1886, p. 100.

But if the scout's temporal wants were poorly provided for, his spiritual welfare was certainly not neglected. In October of the same year, Governor Dinwiddie wrote to Major Lewis: "Recommend morality and sobriety to all the people, with a due submission and regard to Providence. Let swearing, private quarrels, drunkenness and gaming be strictly forbid."

The Virginia General Assembly of October, 1782, enacted:

"And whereas, the allowance to scouts employed for discovering the approach of Indian or any other enemy on the frontiers is inadequate to their fatigue and trouble. Be it enacted, that every scout who shall hereafter be employed, as by law directed, shall be entitled to receive for every day he shall be so employed, the sum of five shillings per day, to be audited and paid in the same manner as the militia in this Act is directed to be paid."—Hening, "*Statutes at Large*," Vol. II, p. 181.

In 1791 scouts employed at the forts along the Ohio were paid by the government, "five shillings, or eighty-four cents a day."

(10) *Border Warfare*, p. 246.

(11) Abridged from William Hanford, in *The West Virginia Historical Magazine*, Volume 4, pp. 220-223.

(12) *Border Warfare*, p. 123.

(13) Saffell's *Records of the Revolutionary War*, New York, 1858, p. 242.

(14) *The Conspiracy of Pontiac*, Boston, 1888, pp. 40, 41.

For advocacy of the use of bloodhounds in Indian warfare, see *Bouquet's Expedition Against the Ohio Indians*, Cincinnati, 1906, p. 41.

(15) It is claimed by the immediate descendants of Jesse Hughes that he at one time owned all the land on Jesse's Run. If he claimed lands other than the 400 acres acquired by settlement, it must have been under the questionable right of "tomahawk improvement." I have been unable to find of record that he even acquired by preemption the 1,000 acres to which his homestead entitled him.

"There was at an early period of our settlements, an inferior kind of land title, denominated a *tomahawk right*, which was made by deadening a few trees near the head of a spring, and marking the bark of some one, or more of them with the initials of the name of the person who made the improvement."—*Doddridge*, p. 130.

The land laws of Virginia were very crude and inefficient. Kentucky inherited them and had endless trouble as the result. One law allowed a settler four hundred acres for building a cabin and raising a crop, and this gave him the right to preempt one thousand acres additional. Another law allowed anyone who planted a patch of corn, one hundred acres of land for each acre in his corn patch. This was called a *Corn Right*. In 1779, Virginia enacted a law which provided for the land entries made by the Trans-Allegheny settlers, securing to them a sound title. Those who had not actually settled, but at their cost had sent others to settle on public land, were entitled to four hundred acres for each family settled, at a cost of two dollars and twenty-five cents for each hundred acres. Each settler having the above right could preempt one thousand acres additional at forty cents an acre.

Tomahawk claims, while not legal, were usually recognized by newcomers, who, if desirous of settling on one of them, preferred to pay the claimant something rather than enter into a quarrel, as friendship was essential for mutual protection against a common foe. Occasionally, however, some stalwart borderman, endowed with a pugnacious disposition, would take forcible possession of a tomahawk claim, and if the former claimant was too annoying in his importunity for a compensation he was sometimes given a "laced jacket," that is, a flogging with hickory switches.

If the virtue and efficiency of the "tomahawk right" was vested solely in the fighting qualities and the physical abilities of the claimant to defend his holding against violent invasion, Jesse Hughes had what was the equal of a warranty deed to his wooded domain.

Jesse Hughes' tomahawk claims will be referred to again in the course of this Volume.

(16) On page 285, *Trans-Allegheny Historical Magazine* (1902), Prof. Hu Maxwell, in writing of the "Pioneers in Monongalia County," claims that there were permanent settlements made in this region as early as 1766, and that one of these was in (now) Braxton County, as follows:

"In the same year James Workman penetrated to the region now forming Gilmer County and built his cabin and became a settler. His cabin stood on the west bank of the Little Kanawha. He sold his claim to William Stewart."

Professor Maxwell bases his conclusions on the following certificate of homestead entry, granted in 1781.

"William Stewart, assignee of James Workman, 400 acres on the Little Kanhaway, on the west side of said Kanhaway, in right of said Workman's residence to include an improvement made in the year of 1766, with a preemption to 1,000 acres adjoining thereto."

I have the highest regard for Professor Maxwell as a historian, but I doubt seriously if there is sufficient ground for asserting that James Workman actually settled in that remote region as early as 1766. While Workman is credited with a "residence," it must be borne in mind that this certificate was not issued until 1781. Nor does it imply that such "residence" was made in 1766. It is significant, however, that the certificate was worded to "include an improvement made in 1766."

As previously cited, a few trees girdled near a spring were, in those days, a recognized "improvement." Indeed, as I shall have occasion to show elsewhere in this Volume, land claims were sometimes recognized by the establishment of a hunter's camp only. In the case of Workman, the logical inference is that his "improvement" of 1766 consisted of a "tomahawk improvement," and that his residence, if otherwise than that of a hunter, was made at a later period.

For additional data regarding the early "claims" and homestead grants on the western waters, see Chapters XII, XVII, XXVI, XXIX and notes in Chapters XXIV and XXX, this Volume.

(17) Poisonous reptiles were not the least of the dangers which beset the early settler. *Doddridge* devotes an entire chapter to this plague. Their proneness to crawl into the cabins made them the more to be dreaded. A small child of a pioneer on the Cheat River was playing on the sunny side of the cabin one morning, when she came running to the door and exclaimed, "Mamma, there is a big yaller worm in the side of the house; come and kill it." The mother, thoughtless of danger, replied, "You kill it." The child soon returned, declaring that she could not kill it. The mother went out and was dismayed to find an immense yellow rattler ensconced between the logs of the cabin. So comfortable was the reptile in the warm rays of the sun that the child's light blows with a stick had not disturbed it. But the rattler was not always so gentle mannered. See Chapter XXXII, this Volume.

NOTES ON CHAPTER V

(1) Probably named for John McKinney, or McKenney, who was among the earliest, if not the first to claim land or settle on this stream.

(2) This was Hacker's homestead, for which he received certificate "for 400 acres on Hacker's Creek adjoining lands of John Sleath, Sen., [Sleeth] to include his settlement made in 1773." *Withers* says that Hacker settled on Hacker's Creek in 1769. *Border Warfare,* p. 122. This is correct, but Hacker was one whose first crop was destroyed by buffalo, and he did not bring his family permanently from the South Branch until the winter of 1770, or later. A few years ago the hewed log house built by Hacker was still standing, though in a ruined condition. In the later years of Indian hostilities this house was used as a fort or blockhouse, by the immediate settlers. It has now been removed, and some of the logs used in building a stable nearby. The foundation of the capacious stone chimney has been left intact by Mr. David Swisher, the present owner of the farm. When the chimney was torn down, the date, 1787, was found cut on the surface of one of the stones. This stone is now in the foundation of Mr. Swisher's house. But this was not Hacker's original cabin. He first settled about one-fourth of a mile east of where this more pretentious house stood.

John Hacker was granted certificate for "400 acres on Buckhannon, adjoining lands of George Jackson, to include his settlement made in 1774." In these early land grants, the term "settlement" was synonymous, and applied alike to actual settlement, settlement by tenant, and settlement by "improvement." This should be borne in mind, otherwise the reader is likely to become confused. The laws governing these land-cedings were very plastic.

Hacker was also allotted 108 acres in the "Clark Grant," in Indiana, for service as private in Colonel Clark's Illinois Campaign, 1778. See English's *Conquest of the Northwest,* Volume II, p. 845.

(3) See *Chapter XXXI,* this Volume.

(4) This little valley, while yet covered with an unbroken forest, was named from the following incident: My grandfather, Walter McWhorter, and John Edmonds, were there hunting; and the latter seeing at a distance through the

woods what he supposed to be a wolf, fired and killed his favorite dog, "Rover." The stream has ever since been known as *Rover's Run.*

(5) After the examination of this mysterious monument, the excavation was re-filled and the stones carefully placed in their former position. This policy was strictly adhered to in the many investigations that were made among the remains of the aboriginal inhabitants of the valley.

(6) All relics obtained through many years of field collecting, with full data, were placed permanently in the Museum of the *West Virginia Historical and Antiquarian Society,* Charleston; since created the *Department of Archives and History.*

(7) ROOTING CREEK was named as early as 1781, but the origin of the name is unknown. The traditional account is, that in the settlement of the country, hogs, escaping from their owners, became wild and frequented this stream, and hunters found the surface of the rich bottom lands widely disturbed by the rooting propensity of these long-nosed porkers, hence the name. This explanation is perhaps correct.

(8) Many of the old "Indian Fields" have their legends of hidden treasure and weird tales of supernatural visitations. A gentleman who had lived all his life in close proximity to the ash-circle on Rooting Creek, gave me the following "well authenticated" story. It fully illustrates the tenacious hold of superstition on succeeding generations of the native hill and mountain people.

From the time of the earliest settlement of the little valley, said the narrator, there was a tradition of buried treasure of unknown richness. This was guarded by the disembodied spirit of the former owner, or, as was more probable, that of some unfortunate victim sacrificed when the treasure was deposited, and whose spirit was forever doomed to hover about the fatal spot until released from its vigils by the removal of the trove. Oft in the evening twilight, the lone hunter by his camp fire, or the belated passerby would be startled by plaintive and ghostly callings from the gloomy forest. Emanating from a certain point, the wild weird sounds—like a voice from the sepulchre—would wail, "*Come here! Come here! Come here!*" Then, as the last cadence of that mysterious cry died in the distance, the darkening shadows on every side re-echoed, "*Come here! Come here! Come here!*" until the entire surrounding forest would be filled with an uncanny indistinct murmur of ghostly voices, ending in a broken sob of despair. Many times had the hardy hunter or straitened settler, mastering superstitious fear, sought diligently for the treasure, but without success. Years passed into the endless cycle of time. Settlers cleared the stately forest from the rich bottom and the lower hillslopes of the valley. The calling of the wilderness spirit was still heard at regular intervals from out the gloaming; but succeeding generations ceased to regard the supernatural disturbance with that same degree of awe as did their simple-minded ancestors. Indeed, some of the inhabitants came to observe the "spooky" visitations with resentment. A climax was reached one evening, when a foolhardy settler seized his rifle and discharged it in the direction of the wood-crowned hill, from whence the voice proceeded. Instantly the cries ceased, and at the same moment, from beneath the floor of the offender's cabin, there came a terrible uproar, mingled with demoniacal shrieks and stifled groans; succeeded by the oppressive stillness of death. The frightened, awe-stricken settler dared no further molestation of the woodland ghost. Soon afterwards the uncanny disturbance ceased. A few days later, some parties passing near where the mysterious callings had emanated, were startled to find a deep excavation near the roots of a large tree. Peering into the depths of the newly-dug pit, they beheld the imprint of a large iron pot evidently but recently removed. Here had been buried the long sought treasure. The lucky finder was never known, but the guardian spirit, now released from its odious task, had departed forever.

A similar story was told and believed by the early settlers regarding a small earthen mound situated near an old Indian village site, on bottom land owned by the late William Bargerhoof, on Saul's Run, near Lorentz, Upshur County. This mound, when examined by me in 1880, measured from fifteen to twenty feet across, and about two feet six inches in height. At that time it showed a shallow pit in the center, where, a few years previous, some farmers one night sunk a shaft to the original surface of the ground. They were searching for treasure, but met with the usual disappointment. Two of the party informed me that in the excavation they found numerous flint chips and arrow points; while near the bottom of the mound were "several poles resembling hand-spikes." These were in a fair state of preservation, which would induce the belief that the mound could not lay claim to great age. Parties who lived near the mound all their lives said that before it had been degraded by the plow, it was very symmetrical in contour, and about six feet in height.

The story in question averred that if a stick were thrust into the mound and left there until nightfall, unearthly shrieks and screams would issue therefrom, until the perpetrator of the outrage, unable to endure the frightful disturbance, repeated nightly so long as the stick remained in place, would remove the stick and fill up the hole. This done, the unaccountable noises would instantly cease. It is needless to say that the experience was seldom repeated. This story, religiously believed in by the first settlers, for more than two generations, secured the mound from the obliterating influence of the plow. It is regrettable that it ever lost its prestige. See *The Archaeologist*, Volume 1, No. 5, p. 96.

NOTES ON CHAPTER VI

(1) This legend of the sly hunter was told me by Washington Alkire, a great grandson of Jesse Hughes, and well versed in local traditions.

When a boy, I often heard the story of John Bozarth, the pioneer, and his son George, "gen-senging" on Turkey Run, of the Pringle camp. George, a lad in his teens, knelt to quench his thirst at a spring or rivulet, and noticing a peculiar looking stone protruding from the bank, chipped it with his hoe and was surprised to see revealed by the fracture, a dull metalic surface. He called to his father who was some distance away, that he had "found a mine." The old gentleman, who was of a brusque nature, ordered him to his work, adding "you are always finding something." The boy obeyed but first detached two or three small fragments of the stone and placed them in his wallet. That night after returning home, the specimens were examined and found to be rich in lead. A diligent search was instituted for the strange spring, but the quest proved fruitless. George could never identify the spot, and the "mine" eventually became a tradition of the wilderness.

(2) Drake's *Indians of North America*, Alden, New York, p. 623.

(3) Hatch's *A Chapter on the War 1812*, Cincinnati, 1872, p. 89.

(4) The Shawnee belonged to the Algonquian linguistic stock of Indians. They have been the greatest wanderers among the North American tribes. They were fierce and always ready for war, and were driven from place to place by those tribes with which they warred. They have lived in most of the country east of the Mississippi, first in one locality and then another. They were pushed westward about 1727 to 1730 with the Delawares. In the Ohio Valley in historic times, their chief seat was what is now the southern part of Ohio. They lived on the Lower Muskingum at the time the Wyandots had their towns on the upper waters of that stream. The last of their Muskingum towns were destroyed by the campaign of Col. Angus McDonnald, in Dunmore's War. They went to the Scioto.

The Shawnees were called younger brothers by the Delawares, and between the two tribes there was always a strong attachment. They moved westward before the advancing whites, and began to cross the Mississippi at the close of Pontiac's War. They lived in Missouri, and about 1828 were located on the south bank of the Kansas River from its mouth to a point beyond Shawnee County, in a country unsurpassed for fertility and beauty. They live now among the Cherokees and Senecas in the Indian Territory. Some of the greatest Indian captains, orators and statesmen were Shawnees; among whom were Cornstalk, Paxnous, Blue Jacket and Tecumseh.

The Shawnees were plundering and murdering on the frontier settlements of the colonies. Western Virginia and Kentucky suffered more from them than from all other tribes. There are among them now families founded by captive men and women from the best families in Virginia, Maryland and Pennsylvania. The Shawnees were called by the French, *Chaouanons*. They called themselves the *Shawano*.—William E. Connelley. *All subsequent notes written by Mr. Connelley will be signed with his initials only.*

(5) Shawnee blood is found among the various tribes from the Mexican Border to the British Line. Both they and the Delawares were known in the Treaty between the Republic of Texas and the Cherokees and their Associate bands, February 23, 1836. It may be noteworthy that in this treaty there is mention of the "Younger Brothers" of the Cherokees, a name by which the Shawnees were recognized by the Delawares.

The only known son of Chief Tecumseh was a signer of this treaty; but I have been unable to identify him among the seven other signers. (See *Texas Library and Historical Commission, First Biennial Report*, XX, p. 36.) His name as known in history was *Pugeshashenwa*—"cat or panther in act of seizing prey," or "crouching" or "watching his prey." He was also known among his tribesmen as *Nah-thah-way-nah*, "who is it?" as generally used in reference to some person approaching or standing near. Neither of these names are connected with the treaty in question. This, however, may be accounted for in the Indian plurality of names. Indians frequently changed names, ofttimes commemorative of some event in their lives, but not always from such caprice or fancy. Should a warrior signalize himself by inflicting loss or humiliation upon an enemy, it was expedient, at times, to assume another name in order to better escape retaliatory vengeance. Many of the old tribesmen have explained this phase of tribal life to me.

PUGESHASHENWA was born about 1796. *Mamate*, his mother, was divorced by Tecumseh, after the Indian custom, but she cared for the child until he was seven or eight years old. He was then taken over by *Menewaulakoosee*, or *Tecumsapeas*, the only sister of Tecumseh, for whom he had great affection, ofttimes making her costly presents. It is said that this boy afterwards became an officer in the British military. He was presented with a sword and was given a pension by the British, in honor of his father's service to the Crown.

PUGESHASHENWA had a son, *Wapameepto:* "giving light as he walks," better known as Big" Jim," corrupted from "Dick Jim;" born on the Sabine Reservation, Texas, in 1832. In 1872 he became Chief of the *Kispicotha;* known as Big Jim's Band of Absentee Shawnees. He died in August, 1900, of smallpox, while in Mexico, on a mission of procuring a place for his people where they would be free from the influence of the white man. He was succeeded by his only son, To-tom-mo, or "Little Jim," born about 1875. His name is given by some writers as To-no-mo; but Mr. O. J. Green, Superintendent of the Absentee Shawnees, Oklahoma, writes me that he is known by the name as first given.

THOMAS WASHINGTON, whose mother was a sister of *Wapameepto*, was also Chief of the Absentee Shawnees.

Tecumseh had other wives than *Mamate;* the last of whom was *Wa-be-le-gane-qua:* "white wing." He lived with her from 1802 to 1807, but it is not known that he had other children than the one son; but there may have been others. There is living among the fourteen Confederated Tribes, known as the Yakimas of Washington, a tall, spare, sinewy man just past the meridian of life, who differs in some respects from the tribesmen about him. This is *Chief Tecumseh Yak-atow'-it*, who gave me this fragment of his family history.

"Mine," said he, "is an inherited name on my father's side. I am descended from a long line of warriors. My father was Yakatowit, Chief of the Klickitats. My grandfather, whose name I cannot recall, was a noted warrior who came from far to the east, I know not the locality. His father was a great chief named Tecumseh, who was a mighty warrior. I know but little of his history, nor am I certain of his tribe. I only know that my father told me that he fell in battle fighting with King George's soldiers against the Americans. This was a long time ago. I know not how many years. It has been long since that battle was fought."

While Tecumseh enjoys but slight education, he is a man of strong mentality and high moral integrity. He has always been a leading spirit in tribal affairs, and on March 18, 1912, was chosen "Head Chief of all the Yakimas." This, however, was in a factional fight and being a man of sensitive honor, he has never pressed his claim. I have often met with him in tribal councils and visited at his home. When I first met him, he had never read of this most renowned Shawnee; nor does he know the meaning, or interpretation of his own name. He explained that "Tecumseh," in Klickitat, has no primal rendition, but is "only a name." He is proud of his traditional lineage, and justly.

CHIEF PUKEESHENO: "I light from flying," the father of Tecumseh, was killed in the Battle of Point Pleasant, October 10, 1774. His eldest son, *Cheeseekau*, fought with him.

MEETHEETASHE or *Methoatask:* "a turtle laying eggs in the sand," the mother of Tecumseh, is said to have been a Creek woman. She died among the Cherokees, where she went soon after the death of her husband, *Pukeesheno*. Tecumseh was then but six years old, and *Cheeseekau*, a great warrior and a man of high integrity, took him under his care and gave him the training which, perhaps, largely moulded his future meteoric career. *Cheeseekau* was killed in battle with the whites on the Tennessee border in 1788 or 1789. A younger brother, *Sauwaseekau*, a brave warrior, was killed in the Battle of Fallen Timbers, August 20, 1795, while fighting at Tecumseh's side. Some place this tragedy at Harmer's defeat, 1790.

Tecumseh was killed in the battle of the Thames, Ontario, Canada, October 5, 1813. His son, *Pugeshashenwa*, fought with him in this battle, and *Wasegoboah:* "stand firm," a valiant warrior and the husband of *Menewaulakoosee*, was slain. The body of Tecumseh was not fully identified by the American troops, but that which was supposed to be his was flayed, in part, and the cuticle carried away as mementoes and made into razor strops and other objects. Although the body was lying within the light of the camp fires of the victors, it was recovered the following night and carried off by his surviving warriors. Eggleston's *Tecumseh and the Shawnee Prophet*. New York, p. 318.

Drake gives the Indian and British loss in this battle, 100 killed and 200 wounded. American loss, 18 killed and 58 wounded. Drake's *Indians of North America*, 15th Edition, p. 622.

At the onset of the battle, the British, under Gen. Proctor, fled, leaving their brave Indian allies to stem the brunt of the fray. Tecumseh fell in the thickest of the fight, at the head of his warriors of whom 120 were left on the field. *Drake's Indians*, p. 620. The great chieftain had a premonition that this was to be his last battle, and just before the engagement he discarded his British uniform of Brigadier General, and donned his Indian buckskin shirt. He gave his sword to one of his chiefs and said: "When my son becomes a noted warrior and able to wield a sword, give this to him." This incident should not be considered as evidence that *Pugheshashenwa* was not with his father in this battle. Only seventeen years old, he was not regarded as a "noted warrior," nor entitled to wear the sword, which in Tecumseh's case was an emblem of authority. This greatest of Shawnees was rightly dominated by the English, "*King of the Woods.*" Consult Hatch's *A Chapter of the History of the War of 1812*. Drake's *Life of Tecumseh*. Wood's *Lives of Famous Indian Chiefs*, and many other histories of the western border.

(6) BUCK KNOB, so named from the incident of an early settler killing a buck thereon. It is the highest elevation in the vicinity and a prominent land mark. Its summit is pointed and stony. In one of the graves opened in this burial ground, I found a small ornamented stone pipe with the characteristic funnel-shaped orifices of the ancient, or pre-Columbian period. With it was a rather irregular water-worn pebble of a few ounces, highly polished and of granitic texture and pleasing hue. It evidently came from the glacial drift of the Northwest, probably Ohio. It is very similar to some which I have observed cherished by modern Indians, and supposed to possess talismanic virtues. Such charms or fetish, are always prized very highly.

(7) *Border Warfare*, p. 122.

(8) See *Appendix II*, this Volume, for notice of buffalo in Western Virginia.

NOTES ON CHAPTER VII

(1) *Border Warfare*, pp. 136-138.
Thwaites says that Stroud resided on Elk River.
GAULEY RIVER—This name is French, which some writers contend signifies "The River of the Gauls." This definition is far fetched and fanciful. The stream was named for *Gauloise*, a French trapper who haunted its banks in an early day. The present appellation is an English corruption of the original.

It is said that this stream was called by the Miamis, Chin-qou-ta-na, and by the Delawares To-ke-bel-lo-ke, or water of the falls. It has the clearest water, and is one of the most widely picturesque streams of the Great Kanawha system.

(2) The Delawares were one of the principal tribes of the Algonquian family, and were divided into three sub-tribes: the Minsi, Monseys, Munsees, or Minisinks; the Unami, or Wonameys; and the Unalachtigos. The Minsi lived on the head-waters of the Delaware River, their territory extending down to the mouth of the Lehigh. The country of the Unami was the valley of the Delaware from the mouth of the Lehigh southward. The Unalachtigo country was about the mouth of the Delaware River, and extending southward. The Delawares did not extend west of the valley of the Delaware until after contact with Europeans. The valley of the Susquehanna was occupied by the Susquehanocks, Iroquoians, and the Delawares were forced into it by pressure of English settlements. The Minsi had no part in the treaty with William Penn.

The upper valley of the Delaware, however, was pre-eminently the home of the Minsies (the historic Minisinks), where they built their towns, planted their corn and kindled their council fires, and whence they set out on the hunt or on the war path. The Minsies, Monsies, or Muncys, were the most warlike of their people, and proverbially impatient of the white man's presence in the Indian country. The murder of one Wright at John Burt's house in Snaketown, in September of 1727, was the act of Minsies, and subjects are told of Kindassowa, who resided "at the Forks of the Susquehanna above Mechayomy." The following notice of the physical peculiarities and traits of these mountaineers, is copied from a paper, in the hand writing of Mr. Heckewelder. "According to my observation and judgment of Indian tribes, the Minsies have a peculiarity which signalizes them from other nations or tribes; and I have seldom failed in pointing them out among a crowd, where they, Delawares and Mohicans were together. The principal distinguishing marks with me, are—robust or strong-boned, broad faces, somewhat surly countenances, greater head of hair and this growing low down on the foreheads, short, round-like nose, thick lips seldom closed, or rather having their mouths generally somewhat open, which I am inclined to believe, may be owing in some measure to an awkward custom of this people, who, instead of pointing to a thing or object with their hands or fingers, as other Indians do, generally draw out their mouths or lips in the desired direction. They are averse to manners, prone to mischief, and friends of war. Their natural complexion is dark, more so than any Indians I have seen yet, but being within these twenty years much mixed by inter-marriages with other tribes, their color has become lighter or fairer."—*Transactions of the Moravian Historical Society*, 1, pp. 255, 256.

The matter which the author refers to in his *History of The Indian Nations*, and to which attention is called in his note, is that transaction in the history of the Delawares and the Six Nations whereby the latter induced the former to become women in order to better conserve the peace among the Indian tribes. In the work above referred to the author treats the subject at great length, and has received the disparagement of critics who know nothing but fault-finding. Both the evidence and the probability are in favor of the account given by Heckewelder. And the matter does not rest solely upon the Heckewelder account. In the edition of his *History of the Indian Nations*, published in 1881, edited by the Rev. William C. Reichel, who was himself an authority on the history of the Delawares and other tribes, may be found the following note (pp. 59, 60):

The following is the passage from Loskiel, which that historian copied from David Zeisberger's "Collection of Notes on the Indians," compiled by the missionary during his residence in the valley of the Tuscarawas about 1778. "According to the account of the Delawares, they were always too powerful for the Iroquois, so that the latter were at length convinced that if they continued the war, their total extirpation would be inevitable. They therefore sent the following message to the Delawares: 'It is not profitable that all the nations should be at war with each other, for this will at length be the ruin of the whole Indian race. We have therefore considered a remedy by which this evil may be prevented. One nation shall be the *woman*. We will place her in the midst, and the other nations who make war shall be the man, and live around the woman. No one shall touch or hurt the woman, and if anyone does it, we will immediately say to him, 'why do you beat the woman?' Then all the men shall fall upon him who has beaten the woman. The woman shall not go to war, but endeavor to keep with all. Therefore, if the men that surround her beat each other, and the war be carried on with violence, the woman shall have the right of addressing them, 'Ye men, what are ye about? Why do you beat each other? We are almost afraid. Consider that your wives and children must perish, unless you desist. Do you mean to destroy yourselves from the face of the earth?' The men shall hear and obey the woman.' The Delawares add, that, not immediately perceiving the intention of the Iroquois, they submitted to be the *woman*. The Iroquois then appointed a great feast, and invited the Delaware nation to it; when, in consequence of the authority given them, they made a solemn speech containing three capital points. The first was, that they declared the Delaware nation to be the *woman* in the following words: 'We dress you in a woman's long habit, reaching down to your feet, and adorn you with earrings;' meaning that they should no more take up arms. The second point was thus expressed: 'We hang a calabash filled with oil and medicine upon your arm. With the oil you shall cleanse the ears of the other nations, that they may attend to good and not to bad words, and with the medicine you shall heal those who are walking in foolish ways, that they may return to their senses and incline their hearts to peace.' The third point, by which the Delawares were exhorted to make agriculture their future employ and means of subsistence, was thus worded: 'We deliver into your hands a plant of Indian corn and a how.' Each of these points was confirmed by delivering a belt of wampum, and these belts have been carefully laid up, and their meaning frequently repeated.

"The Iroquois, on the contrary, assert that they conquered the Delaware and that the latter were forced to adopt the defenseless state and appellation of a *woman* to avoid total ruin.

"Whether these different accounts be true or false, certain it is that the Delaware nation has ever since been looked to for preservation of peace, and entrusted with the charge of the great belt of peace and chain of friendship, which they must take care to preserve inviolate. According to the figurative explanation of the Indians, the middle of the chain of friendship is placed upon the shoulder of the Delaware, the rest of the Indian nations holding one end and the Europeans the other."—*Wm. E. C.*

(3) *Border Warfare*, p. 136.

(4) On page 137, *Chronicles of Border Warfare*, is the following statement by the Editor, R. G. Thwaites, in a note made up from information furnished him by me:

"Mr. McWhorter writes me that two others were Jesse Hughes and John Cutright (corruption of Cartwright?), both of them settlers on Hacker's Creek. * * * The massacre of the Bull Town Indians was accompanied by atrocities as repulsive as any reported by captives in Indian camps; of these there had long been traditions, but details were not fully known until revealed by Cutright upon his deathbed in 1852, when he had reached the age of 105 years." * * *

It is to be noted that Mr. Thwaites is mistaken in saying that Cutright was a settler on Hacker's Creek. He was a settler on the Buckhannon. See Chapter IX, this Volume. Not only was Cutright's confession made on his deathbed, but the details had been narrated by him when he was in full possession of all his faculties, on more than one occasion and to more than one person.

Col. Henry F. Westfall says that "Wm. White, Wm. Hacker, Samuel Pringle and Andrew Skidmore were four of the party, perhaps John Pringle, Andrew Friend and David White and Elijah Runner were also of the party." See Westfall's letter, *Appendix I*, this Volume.

There was in the settlements a man named Reeder, from the Wappatomaka, a notorious renegade, who is believed by some to have been in the Bulltown massacre. His hatred for the red race was insatiate. He killed peaceable Indians secretly and by the most inhuman method. He first plied his victims with whisky until helplessly intoxicated, and then thrust his ramrod full length up into their intestines, causing death, but leaving no visible marks of violence. He is known to have killed no less than fifteen in this way, and four of these at one time.

(5) Those who would find excuse for the retaliation by the borderers in the Stroud murder, should bear in mind that, viewed in the same light, the Shawnee had just provocation for aggressive vengeance, and the tragedy at Stroud's was of that nature.

"The last news we have had here is the killing of nine Shawanes Indians in Augusta County, Va., who were passing this way to the Cherokee Nation, to war against them, and had obtained a pass from Col. Lewis, of that county. Yet, notwithstanding a number of county people met them a few miles from Col. Lewis' and killed nine, there being but ten in the Company."

Extract from a letter from Fort Loudoun, 1768, *History of Augusta County, Virginia*, Staunton, 1882, p. 143.

(6) *Border Warfare*, p. 136.

(7) *Appendix I*, this Volume.

(8) A parallel to this pathetic incident is found in the Kennebec Indian, who, prompted by the same motive that drove Captain Bull from his Kanawha home, exhumed the body of his child and carried it two hundred miles to his people in Canada.

NOTES ON CHAPTER VIII

(1) *Border Warfare*, p. 137.

(2) For a further notice of Indian Camp, see *Appendix III*, this Volume.

NOTES ON CHAPTER IX

(1) *Border Warfare*, p. 122.

(2) *Appendix I*, this Volume.

(3) See letter of David H. Smith, *Appendix I*, this Volume.

(4) *Withers*, p. 247, gives the date of Booth's death, June 16, 1778. He was killed on Tuesday. *Cutright* places the tragedy one year later, which is erroneous.

The Draper Manuscripts, 100, 79, contains the following pension statement of John Cutright:

"John Cutright, Lewis Co. Va., Dec'n Aug. 7, 1832. In May, 1778, volunteered in Capt. James Boothe's company, at West's Fort on Hacker's Creek, for 18 months. In June, 1779, Capt. Boothe was killed by the Indians, on Boothe's Creek, in now Harrison Co. Va. &c."

(5) See *Chapter XXX*, this Volume.

(6) From 1777, the *bloody year of the border*, to 1780, Virginia was hard pressed for troops and drafting became necessary. An act of the State Legislature, May, 1777, ordered that unless the number of men required were enlisted by the tenth of August, they should be drafted. In the interval, the Virginia troops suffered considerable loss, especially at the Battle of Germantown; and in October of that year another act was passed for recruiting the regiments by drafting unless the quota was enlisted by the twelfth of February, 1778. Only unmarried men were liable to this impressment. *Annals of Augusta County*, p. 163.

An act of October, 1778, required each county, except Illinois, to furnish the "one twenty-fifth man" of its militia for the Virginia regiments by May 1, 1779, to serve for three years, or during the war. The war spirit had cooled considerably, and volunteers not forthcoming, it was ordered by Act of the Legislature, May,

1779, that the "one twenty-fifth man of the militia" be drafted for eighteen months. *Annals of Augusta County*, p. 167.

An act of the Legislature, May, 1780, provided that the several counties, exclusive of the *County of Illinois* and the territory in dispute between Virginia and Pennsylvania, should furnish one fifteenth man of the militia to serve in the Continental Army until December 31, 1781. Staunton was place of rendezvous. In October, 1780, the Legislature called for 3,000 men drafted for eighteen months if not furnished by volunteering. This was the last enactment on the subject during the war. *Annals of Augusta County*, p. 174.

Destitution among the Virginia troops during this period was appalling. An inventory of the "arms, accoutrements and clothing" of fifty-three men commanded by Major Isaac Beall, 4th Virginia Regiment, when returned June 21, 1778, consisted of: 46 muskets, 39 bayonets, 39 b. slings, 47 cartouch boxes, 14 hats, 46 coats, 28 vests, 11 pairs breeches, 19 pairs stockings, 38 shirts, 46 pairs shoes, 32 blankets, 20 knapsacks, 30 overalls, 3 camp kettles and 3 canteens.

In some instances a soldier could boast a pair of stockings but no shoes, while others possessed a blanket but neither hat, breeches nor overalls. One, Gallent Crosbay, was fully armed, while his wearing apparel was accounted for in a pair of shoes and a knapsack. William Lipscomb's *exclusive* possessions consisted of a musket, bayonet, b. sling and cartouch box. *Virginia Magazine of History and Biography*, Volume 1, p. 207.

Under date, "Camp Charlotte, 7 December, 1780," Major-General Nathanial Green, wrote General Washington: "Nothing can be more wretched and distressing than the condition of the troops, starving with cold and hunger, without tents and camp equipage. Those of the Virginia line are literally naked; and a great part totally unfit for any kind of duty, and must remain so until clothing can be had from the northward. I have written to Governor Jefferson not to send forward any more until they are well clothed and properly equipped." Sparks "*Correspondence of the American Revolution.*" Volume III, p. 166.

Under these conditions, coupled with the uncertainty of a moneyed compensation it can hardly be a wonder that the discouraged Virginians refused to leave their homes and their woods to engage in a cause which appeared well nigh hopeless.

The territorial dispute between Virginia and Pennsylvania at this time waxed warm, and was also a great drawback to the state enlistments and the American cause. The following interesting letter found among the *Draper* manuscripts, and here published for the first time, portrays the temper of the Virginia border colony relative to this trouble.

"Monongalia April 10th 1780

"Dear Wm

"I have Started John of to Wms Burg for the Surveyors Comn. which I Could not get for him without his appearing there in person (how ye. lad will make out I Cannot tell for he Drives on partly in ye. Old Way) But let that be as it will it has taken all the money I Could spare to fitt him out for the trip Besides Given Richard Orders to Draw on you for £300 to help out with his expences which Ricd. is to Borrow from some one and you must by no means refuse the Order in Case he should Draw one on you—I shall leave this place in a Day or two for the falls—there is Certain Accounts Brought to pitt of the Indians taken 2 Boats and that they are very thick on the River the passage without great Care will be Daingerous—the people is in great Confusion heare on account of the Disputed line and is Determined to Declare them selves a Separate State which will be Done before the Last of this Month George Rooks is at the head of it.

I am y^r. Aff^t B^r

GAB^L MADISON

I shall rite to you
by the first op^y from
the fals if I G^t the.
Addressed: To M^r. William Madison Botetourt
Endorsed: Letter Gab. Madison 80." *Wis. Hist. Soc. 5zz73, A. L. S.*

(7) Among those dropped from the pension roll in Lewis Co., was Patrick McCan, of McCan's Fort. He was awarded $95 a year for alleged two years' service as private and sergeant in Col. Broadhead's Regiment, Revolutionary War. It afterwards appeared that McCan was too young for service in the Revolution, and his pension was stopped. He had a brother killed in the Patriot Army.

The McCans came from Ireland, and in 1785 were residing on lands owned by John Powers. Patrick was noted for his eccentricity and self emulation. Be it said, however, that his stories were of a harmless nature, usually bordering on the miraculous. He was once hunting, and reaching the brow of a hill, he beheld a great commotion among the tall weeds growing on a lower flat. Supposing that the disturbance was caused by a deer, he silently approached in order to get a shot. On coming to the place he was amazed to behold a *log* rolling back and forth, so crooked that it could not lie still. This gave rise to the proverb still current in that region, "Crooked as McCan's log."

(8) This was, perhaps, in 1780, when Cutright was wounded on Laurel Lick, a branch of Hacker's Creek, and not far from Berlin, W. Va. See *Border Warfare*, p. 290. On that occasion, Cutright displayed most reckless courage and was admonished by his comrades to exercise more caution, but to no purpose. When shot, Cutright was in the little valley, and the Indian fired from a laurel bed some distance on the hillside. At the report of the rifle, Cutright leaped into the air and screamed, "*I'm shot.*" Tradition says that the ball took effect in his arm.

(9) The Virginia militia organized under the Convention ordinance, July 17, 1775, were constituted "minute men" and each was required to "furnish himself with a good rifle, if to be had, otherwise with a tomahawk, common firelock bayonet, pouch, or cartouch box, and three charges of powder and ball." They were subject to military service from the age of sixteen to fifty, and if shown by affidavit that a militiaman was unable to furnish arms he was supplied at public expense. "The officers were required to equip themselves, and officers and men were liable to a fine for failure in this respect." *Annals of Augusta County*, p. 157.

The militiaman of the Virginia border was a unique figure in the Revolution, Proud, arrogant and wholly self-reliant, these wild, deadly riflemen chafed at restraint and military discipline. Like the Indian, whose warfare he emulated. he could not at all times be relied upon in open battle; but when left to his own resources, and native tactics, he was sure to win the respect, but hardly the admiration of his more methodical adversary. Clad in the picturesque hunting shirt, he was regarded with mingled scorn and dread by the gorgeous "Red Coat," who derisively dubbed him "Shirt Man."

A letter among the *Draper Manuscripts* (45 J. 101 A. L.) from Lieut. Gov. Henry Hamelton, to Gen. Guy Carleton (British), dated at Detroit, Dec. 4th, 1775, says: * * * "The Virginians are haughty Violent and bloody, the savages have a high opinion of them as Warriors, but are jealous of their encroachments, and very suspicious of their faith in treaties, the Virginians having furnished them with frequent cause, seizing their chiefs & detaining them as hostages, during which time their treatment has not been as mild as good policy should have dictated. In the inroads of the Virginians upon the savages, the former have plundered, burnt and murdered without mercy." * * * *Revolution on the Upper Ohio*, Madison, 1908, p. 129.

(10) *Lossing*, Volume 1, pp. 331, 332.

(11) See Westfall's letter, *Appendix I*, this Volume. *Dunmore's War*, Madison, Wis., 1905, p. 422.

(12) *Border Warfare*, pp. 288, 289.

(13) For additional mention of Cutright, see Col. Westfall's letter, *Appendix I*, this Volume, also *Border Warfare*, and *History of Upshur Co., W. Va.*

NOTES ON CHAPTER X

(1) Kercheval's *History of the Valley*, pp. 129, 130, 132, 140, 141.

(2) It is thought by some that Lieutenant John White, who was killed and scalped in Tygart's Valley in 1778, was of this family, but I have not looked up his antecedents.

Lieut. White was a leading man in his community, and his death was deeply deplored. It was generally supposed that he was not slain by Indians, but was ambushed and shot by two deserters from the American Army, who were hiding in the mountains and suspected White was seeking their apprehension. *History of Randolph County*, 1898, p. 184.

That many outrages on the border then, as in later years, were committed by renegade whites and charged to the Indians, cannot be denied. *Kercheval* gives an instance, where, in 1758 two white men disguised as Indians were mistaken for such and were pursued and killed by the settlers near the present site of Martinsburg, Virginia. Their intentions were robbery. *Kercheval* adds: "The Indians were frequently charged with outrages they never committed." *History of the Valley*, p. 114.

(3) See *Kercheval*, pp. 140, 141. *Dunmore's War*, p. 422. Also Col. Westfall's letter, *Appendix I*, this Volume.

Col. John Sevier's military career did not end with the battle of Point Pleasant. He served as a Commissary and Colonel of North Carolina Troops during the Revolutionary War, and was one of the Colonels in command at the Battle of King's Mountain, and conducted two campaigns against the Cherokees. He was the first militia general of the territory of Tennessee and the first Governor of that State. He was made a Brigadier General of the United States Army, July 19,

1798, and was honorably discharged June 15, 1800. He died near Fort Decatur, Alabama, September 24, 1815.

His son James served under him during 1780, 1781 and 1782.

(4) *Border Warfare*, p. 136.

(5) *Kercheval*, pp. 140, 141, 142.

(6) *Border Warfare*, p. 135.

(7) For notice of the earliest military organization of the Buckhannon settlement, see Chapter XVII, this Volume.

(8) *Withers*, pp. 232, 233, gives this account of the capture of White and Petro:
"In September of this year (1777) Leonard Petro and Wm. White, being engaged in watching the path leading up the Little Kanawha, killed an elk late in the evening; and taking part of it with them, withdrew a short distance for the purpose of eating their suppers and spending the night. About midnight, White, awaking from sleep, discovered by the light of the moon, that there were several Indians near, who had been drawn in quest of them by the report of the gun in the evening. He saw at a glance the impossibility of escape by flight; and preferring captivity to death, he whispered to Petro to lie still, lest any movement of his, might lead to this result. In a few minutes the Indians sprang on them, and White raising himself as one lay hold on him, aimed a furious blow with his tomahawk, hoping to wound the Indian by whom he was beset, and then make his escape. Missing his aim he affected to have been ignorant of the fact that he was encountered by Indians, professed great joy at meeting with them, and declared that he was then on his way to their towns. They were not deceived by the artifice; for although he assumed an air of pleasantness and gaity, calculated to win upon their confidence, yet the woeful countenance and rueful expression of poor Petro, convinced them that White's conduct was feigned, that he might lull them into inattention, and they be enabled to effect an escape. They were both tied for the night; and in the morning White being painted red, and Petro black, they were forced to proceed to the Indian towns. When approaching a village, the whoop of success brought several to meet them; and on their arrival at it, they found that every preparation was made for their running the gauntlet; in going through which ceremony both were much bruised. White did not however remain long in captivity. Eluding their vigilance, he took one of their guns and began his flight homeward.—Before he had traveled far, he met an Indian on horseback, whom he succeeded in shooting; and mounting the horse from which he fell, his return to the Valley was much facilitated. Petro was never heard of afterwards. The painting of him black, had indicated their intention of killing him; and the escape of White probably hastened his doom."

See Westfall's letter and Note 5, *Appendix I;* and Note 2, *Appendix III;* for death of Capt. White, and further notice of Petro.

(9) Mrs. White witnessed the shooting of her husband and saw the Indian when he attempted to secure the scalp of his victim. She soon afterwards became a mother, and the child developed unmistakable Indian traits of character. Not only his swarthy features, but his movements and habits were those of an Indian. He grew to manhood and became a great hunter, remaining in the wilderness alone

for days and weeks at a time. He could scarcely be induced to perform physical labor, nor could any influence that was thrown around him ever constrain him to adopt the higher ways of civilization. Some of the present generation remember seeing him with his rifle and hunter garb, a wild reminder of an era of the past. He was a "poet," and often composed satiric verse against those who incurred his displeasure.

Captain White left but one other child, Elizabeth, who in 1798, married Joel Westfall.

(10) *Border Warfare*, p. 340. See note 5, *Appendix I*, this Volume.

(11) *Border Warfare*, pp. 340, 341.

(12) John Fink was the son of Henry Fink, who came to the Buckhannon settlement at an early day. In 1781 a certificate was issued to "Henry Phink [Fink], assignee to Henry Rule, 400 acres on Buckhannon River, adjoining lands of David Wilson, to include his settlement made in 1770."

Tradition says that when Henry Fink first came to the settlement, he with his family made their abode in the cavity of a large sycamore near the mouth of Fink's Run, just west of Buckhannon. I remember seeing the stump of this tree, but the tradition is without foundation. See Col. Westfall's letter and Note 5, *Appendix I*, for further account of Fink.

(13) Under the auspices of the Elizabeth Zane Chapter of the D. A. R. of Buckhannon, on July 4th, 1912, a fitting granite monument was dedicated to Capt. William White and John Fink. The cost ($600) was raised by popular local subscription, and a contribution from the County of Upshur, under a late State law permitting such patriotic use of the public funds.

(14) The treaty of Fort Stanwix in 1768 by which the Six Nations ceded all *their* "rights" to the vast region west of the Allegheny Mountains and south of the Ohio River, was *not* an extinguishment of the full Indian title. The Delawares and Shawnees refused to sign the treaty; and the rights of the Ohio Indians, the true owners, were wholly ignored. Their title was "extinguished" by Dunmore's Conquest six years later, of which the sequel was the Battle of Fallen Timbers in 1794, after twenty years of incessant border wars.

Delaware Indians on the Monongahela River

"Mr. Walker being sworn—says—That he was app^{td} a Com^r & attended at F: Stanwix—Genl: Lewis, other Com^r was called off—Sir Wm Johnston had a state of Virg^a claim—who said the Indians acknowd Vir^a claim—refused a copy of minutes—promised auth^{tc} documents—gave deed of cefsion—deferred giving any other papers—got a copy of Treaty from Gents at bar—Com^{rs} of any State only asked Questions abt respective claims—No Comrs held any conference with Indians—Considered himself in signing In^a claim—not as Com^r but as witnefs—beleives if he had been called in as Com^r, he should have signed it in that character as he was informed the Lands could only be had on those terms. In F^t. Stanwix treaty, Indians complied with V^a claim—Pamphlet of India^s claim a perfect record of the transaction"— * * * * *

"Nothing said of any land lying west of Ohio—On Ex^{on} of deed, thinks Indians were called to table & acknowledged it, and believes marked it—Custom for Indians to treat by cheifs—one cheif generally signing for his nation—Saw Indians who s^d they lived at Squirrel Hill, hath heard that Delawares lived on Monongahala—Shawanese had towns opposite Mouth Scioto in year 1756—at this purchase, considered territory as delivered up on Ex^{on} of Deed, as far as Deed went—Letters from Mr Stewart claimed part of this land for Cherokees—Indians always bound lands sold by natural boundaries—Remembers North^{wd} Indians with Braddock, supposes they were invited by him. Had Conver^{on} with Sir W^m on treaty of Lancaster—thought in finishing treaty at fort Stanwix that the affair was concluded."—From *Calendar of Virginia State Papers;* Volume I, pp. 297, 298.

For notice of Indian habitations on the Upper Monongalia, refer to Chapters V, VI, and XV, this Volume.

NOTES ON CHAPTER XI

(1) Cornstalk and Logan.

(2) *Winning of the West,* Sagamore Edition, New York, 1900, Volume 2, pp. 33, 34.

(3) *History of Randolph County, West Va.,* 1898, p. 42.

(4) *Border Warfare,* p. 143.

(5) *Winning of the West,* Volume 1, p. 184.

(6) *Winning of the West,* Volume 1, p. 182.

(7) *Border Warfare,* p. 143.

(8) *Winning of the West,* Volume 1, pp. 236 to 238.

(9) The character of these Kentucky interlopers was strongly attested in 1778, when, on the 12th of November, Col. James Wood of the 8th Virginia Regiment, wrote Gen. Washington from Williamsburg, attributing the prevalence of desertion among the troops raised on the border, to the: "pernicious measure of sending a body of men for the protection of the settlement on Kentucky, which does not consist of more than sixty men, most of whom are land robbers and runaways from different states, which has formed a harbour for deserters and every other species of villains. Besides, the idea was ridiculous to think of extending our territory, when we ought to be making use of every exertion to secure what we already occupy." *Sparks Correspondence of the American Revolution,* Boston, 1853, Volume II, pp. 229, 230.

See Note 2, Chapter XXI, this Volume, for additional information on the Long Hunters.

(10) *Border Warfare,* p. 136.

(11) *Border Warfare,* pp. 135, 136.

(12) Indirectly the whites stand charged with the responsibility of this conflict in an indictment by Benjamin Franklin, who, after stating that the Indians "have no intoxicating liquors but what they have received from us," continues:

"The dreadful war in 1774 between the Shawanese, some of the Mingoes, and the people of Virginia, in which so many lives were lost, was brought on by the consequences of drunkenness. It produced murders which were followed by private revenge, and ended in a most cruel and destructive war." Quoted from *On the Frontier with Colonel Antes*, Camden, N. J., 1900, p. 127.

(13) *Border Warfare*, pp. 135, 136.

(14) *Monongahela of Old*, Pittsburgh, 1858-1892, p. 88.

(15) *Border Warfare*, p. 135.

(16) At no time during the interval from the closing of Pontiac's War in 1765 to Dunmore's Conquest in 1774, did the whites cease in acts of aggressive bloodshed. The annals of the Virginia border are lurid with such crimes. A letter dated Winchester April 30, 1765, contains this passage:

"The frontier inhabitants of this colony and Maryland are removing fast over the Alleghanies in order to settle and live there. The two hunters who killed the two Indians near Pittsburg, some time ago, are so audacious as to boast of the fact and show the scalps publicly. What may such proceedings not produce? One of these hunters, named Walker, lives in Augusta County, Va."

Extract of a Letter from Carlisle

"A number of men from this settlement went up to Shamokin (Fort Augusta) to kill the Indians there, which caused them all to fly from that place."

From Lord Botetourt, 1770

"I send the body of John Ingman, he having confessed himself concerned in the murder of Indian Stephen. You will find there never was an act of villainy more unprovoked and more deliberately undertaken."

From Fort Pitt, 1771

"I take the liberty to enclose for your perusal the copy of an affidavit relative to the murder of the two Seneca Indians. I have had several meetings with the chiefs, who seem well pleased with the steps taken in the affair."

Peyton's *History of Augusta County, Va.*, p. 143.

The letter quoted in Note 5, Chapter VII, this Volume, should be included in the foregoing list.

(17) The circumstances attending the treachery by which the Indians of Logan's camp were induced to cross the Ohio to Baker's house, where they were murdered, are now well known and universally condemned. Accounts of this tragedy may be found in *Western Annals*, p. 219; *Appendix* to *Jefferson's Notes; Drake's Indians of North America*, pp. 537, 538, and many other works on the early history of the States in the Ohio Valley.

(18) Hildreth's *Pioneer History*, pp. 93, 94.

(19) On April 18, and May 5, 1778, the County Court of Rockbridge County, Virginia, sat for the examination of Captain Hall and Hugh Galbraith: "upon a charge of suspicion" of being guilty of the killing of Cornstalk and two other Indians in November, 1777, and they denying their guilt, and no one appearing against them, were acquitted. This farce of justice was fully carried out on both occasions by the sheriff making proclamation at the door of the court house for

all persons who could give evidence against the accused, to come forward and testify. No one volunteered, and the murderers went free.

Annals of Augusta County, Va., Richmond, 1886, p. 164.

(20) *Border Warfare*, pp. 245, 246.

This was evidently John Sleath (Sleeth) to whom a certificate was issued in 1781, for "400 acres on Hacker's Creek, adjoining lands of John Hacker to include his settlement made in 1777.'"

The same year David Sleath (Sleeth) secured a grant for "200 acres on the waters of Hacker's Creek, adjoining lands claimed by Samuel Bonnett, to include his settlement made in 1770."

David W. Sleeth was an enlisted scout on the western waters during the Revolution. From his declaration for pension made Aug. 7, 1832, it would appear that he was born in Frederick County, Va., May 18, 1762.

He was a member of Capt. James Booth's Company of rangers and spies in 1777-78; place and time of enlistment, West's Fort on Hacker's Creek; May 1777, term of service eighteen months. After the death of Capt. Booth in June, 1778, the company was under the command of Lieut. Edward Freeman, for the remainder of his enlistment, or until November, 1778, who went to Kentucky without giving the men their discharges. Immediately after the expiration of his enlistment with Capt. Booth, Sleeth joined Capt. George Jackson's Company of scouts at the Buckhannon Fort, and served until the latter part of 1780. The sub-officers of this company were Jacob Brake, Lieut., Timothy Dorman, Ensign. Sleeth states that he was in several skirmishes with the Indians during this enlistment and often acted as scout in subsequent years. Sleeth's declaration is followed by sworn affidavits from John Talbott and Henry McWhorter, testifying that Sleeth's statements were corerct and that he was a reliable man. John Cutright and Jacob Bush also vouched for Sleeth's veracity.

Sleeth was granted a pension, but on October 3, 1834, he was re-examined by W. G. Singleton, Special Pension Agent, who, it appears received from him a correct repetition of his former declaration. The result of this examination was forwarded to the Pension Office with the following note by the examiner:

"This man Sleeth is the same who as magistrate certified such a number of declarations from Lewis County, it is currently stated (and no doubt of the fact) that he received from $10 to $20 for each and every declaration of his certifying through his corrupt means, many frauds have been committed. The narrative of service here detailed by him, you will, I presume, compare with his declaration, whether they be the same or not is wholly immaterial. There is no doubt of his being an imposter."

(Signed) W. G. SINGLETON.

This report was, however, accompanied with statements from William Powers and Christopher Nutter saying that Sleeth's declaration was in part erroneous, that Freeman never succeeded Booth in command, and that there was no such thing as an eighteen months' enlistment.

It should be borne in mind that Sleeth's declaration tallies with that of John Cutright, that Capt. Booth's Company was organized for an eighteen months' tour, although one places the date of enlistment May, 1777, the other, one year later, but concur that Freeman succeeded Capt. Booth in command and that he subsequently went to Kentucky. Usually the scouts were enlisted for a term of nine months, but the latter 70's was the most stormy period of the border, and it is probable that the eighteen months included two continuous enlistments of nine months each.

Everything considered Mr. Singleton was unnecessarily severe in his denunciation of Sleeth, who had previously been well vouched for. It is noteworthy that the pension agent did not produce any evidence in support of his assertion that the old scout had openly certified to fraudulent declarations.

Subsequently we find a sworn statement from one of Sleeth's old associates in arms, who says: "to the best of his recollection it was in 1778 or before that time that David Sleeth enlisted under Capt. Booth, and says that he was out under him, Elias Hughes, on one excursion when he, said E. Hughes, had the command of a company of spies."

his
(Signed) ELIAS X HUGHES
mark

Dated Dec. 20, 1838, Licking County, Ohio.

Sleeth is well spoken of in connection with his testimony for Jacob Bush, and perhaps others, and he seems to have stood well with the settlers in general.

Mrs. Elizabeth Butcher, John Cutright and Mrs. Phoebe Cunningham testified in behalf of Sleeth. Mrs. Butcher was the widow of Paulcer Butcher, a member of the same company of spies with Sleeth.

David W. Sleeth was a resident on Leading Creek in Lewis County, 1834. There is no mention of him by *Withers*.

(21) *Border Warfare*, p. 275.

(22) *Border Warfare*, pp. 287, 288.

(23) See *Border Warfare*, p. 287, for note on Beech Fort.

(24) In the still nights of the Appalachian forests, the notes of the great horned owl can be heard a long distance. No benighted traveler of that land can ever forget the cries of these night-birds heard while traversing the mountain roads. Sometimes he will be startled by the uncanny, goblin-like laughter of a group of owls gathered on the dead branches of some large tree deep in the forest and far from danger. These peculiar cries can be heard for more than a mile. The owl hoot, like the howl of the wolf, was a favorite signal call of both Indian and white scout.

(25) See Chapter XXXV, this Volume.

(26) There was a block house about three miles west of Bush's Fort, on Fink's Run, where Jesse went to loose the stock. It was built by some of the Jackson's on land now owned by Mr. Martin Reger. Prof. Maxwell refers to this building as "Jackson's Fort." *History of Randolph County, West Va.*, p. 414. It could hardly be termed a fort, in the sense of that word. It was only a block house, or a strongly built two-story log dwelling without a palisade; and never figured as a defensive stronghold.

NOTES ON CHAPTER XII

(1) *Border Warfare*, pp. 310-313.

(2) "The moccasins in ordinary use cost but a few hours labor to make them. This was done by an instrument denominated a moccasin awl, which was made of the back spring of an old clasp knife. This awl, with its buckshorn handle, was an appendage of every shot pouch strap, together with a roll of buckskin for mending the moccasins. This was the labor of almost every evening. They were sewed together and patched with deer skin thongs, or whangs as they were commonly called." *Kercheval*, pp. 338, 339. *Doddridge*, p. 141.

In 1905, I saw an exact counterpart of the awl here described, in the hands of a Warm Springs Indian woman, who, with a piece of buckskin and thong, was deftly repairing a badly worn moccasin.

(3) See Chapters XXVI and XXVII for sketch of the Lowthers.

(4) *Border Warfare*, pp. 376-380.

(5) Dr. Thwaites, *Editor*, adds the following note:
"Another case of border superstition is related to me by McWhorter. Alexander West had been doing sentry duty most of the night before, and on being relieved early in the morning, sat with his back to a tree and, rifle across his lap, fell asleep. On awakening he sprang to his feet and cried, 'Boys, look out! Some of us will be killed today! I saw the *red doe* in my dream; that is the sign of death; I never knew it to fail!' When Bonnett fell, it was considered in camp to be a verification of the 'red sign.' Bonnett was carried by his comrades on a rude stretcher, but in four days died. His body was placed in a cleft of rock and the entrance securely chinked."

West claimed that often in their scouting expeditions, or in times of imminent peril, he would have a premonition, or warning, of danger by seeing a red doe passing before him in a dream. This startling vision was invariably followed by the immediate death, or fatal wounding of some of his associates. West, it is claimed by those who knew him, was of a religious or devotional nature.

(6) Conditions on the border have practically been the same from the Pequot War to the massacre on the Wounded Knee. A horrible story of retaliatory vengeance on a cattle-raiding band of California Indians, in 1852-53, was told me by one of the participants, Mr. Ned J. Jackson, a noted "Forty-niner."

"We had," said Jackson, "a small herd of cattle which we expected to butcher for the mining camps. Our herd, we estimated, would dress about 20,000 pounds of beef, worth one dollar per pound. One day Chief Padocia's band of Indians, known as the Cotton Wood Creek Tribe, numbering about eighty-five persons, all told, came upon the cattle in the hills, killed several and feasted upon the meat. Going in search of our cattle we found the Indian encampment deserted, and the slaughtered beef strewn around. Enraged at our loss, we gathered the meat and burned it upon a pile of logs. We, however, preserved one quarter of a beef and thoroughly saturated it with strychnine, leaving it in the camp. Strychnine was used by the miners against wolves and other predatory animals. The Indians returned and devoured this, from the effects of which sixty-five or seventy of them died. Terror-stricken, Padocia complained to some of the whites of the mysterious power that had swept away so many of his people, who from no apparent cause fell dead upon the trail, women and children not being exempt from the terrible plague. The chief was upbraided for stealing the white man's cattle, and was warned that the white man would not stand such conduct, and that he had power to kill an Indian at any distance, whether in his presence or not. The simple minded Padocia excused the theft by declaring that his people were starving, and that they did not deem it wrong to take the cattle, as they were found on the Indian's own land."

(7) *Border Warfare*, p. 240.

(8) *Border Warfare*, p. 246.

(9) The original certificate of this appointment is in the possession of Miss Minnie McWhorter, a daughter of Judge H. C. McWhorter and a granddaughter of the old postmaster.

Fields McWhorter, M. D., son of Walter and a grandson of Henry McWhorter, was an all round athlete. For several years, when a young man, he was "miller" at the McWhorter Mill, and it was his set rule to "wrastle" with every able-bodied man who came for grinding. He never met his match until he measured strength with Benjamin Morris, who hailed from New Jersey. Morris only weighed one hundred and twenty pounds at maturity, but he threw the doughty miller and held him supinely until he acknowledged himself vanquished. Morris afterwards married the miller's oldest sister, Mary.

(10) Spark's *Washington*, Volume VII, p. 343.

(11) "Sir, "Fort Pitt, May 30th, 1781.

"This will be delivered to your Excellency by Ens. Tannehill, Paymaster to the 7th Virga. Regt., whom I have sent Express to Richmond in order to procure the 4 months pay allowed by the Hon: the Assembly of Virga. towards the Depreciation of their former pay, &c—I hope when your Excellency is Assured that they have not received a single shilling for these twenty months past, you will interest yourself in their Behalf &c—* * *

"Inclosed is also my Acct: Expenses in forwarding the Powder from Carlisle to this place for Genl: Clarke &c. * * *

"Genl: Clarke will write your Excellency by this opportunity, and I make no doubt give you every information relative to the intended Expedition—I am much afraid he will not be able to get many of the militia from this quarter, as I have just heard that three hundred men from the Counties of Monongahela and Ohio, have crossed the Ohio at Wheeling, and are gone to cut of the Moravian Indian towns; if so they will hardly turn out on their return—Indeed it appears to me they have done this, in order to evade going with Genl: Clarke—the Moravians have always given the most convincing proofs of their attachment to the Cause of America, by always giving in Intelligence of every party that came against the frontiers; and on the late expedition, they furnished Colo. Broadhead and his party with a large quantity of provisions when they were starving—For the news of this post, permit me to refer Your Excellency to the Bearer Ens. Tannehill—

I have the honour to be Your Excellency's
most obedient Humble Servt.,
Jno: Gibson Colo. Comd. F. Pitt"

Letter from Colonel John Gibson Comdt., at Fort Pitt, to Governor Thomas Jefferson.

From *"Calendar of Virginia State Papers,"* Volume 11, p. 131. See *Note 4, Chapter XXX, and Appendix IV,* this Volume.

"On the breaking out of the Revolution, Gibson was the Western agent of Virginia, at Fort Pitt. After the treaty held in October, 1775, at that post, between the Delawares and representatives of the Shawanese and Senecas on the one part, and the Commissioners of the American Congress on the other part, by which the neutrality of the former tribe was secured, he undertook a tour to the Western Indians in the interest of peace. Upon his return, he entered the service, rising, finally, to the command of the 13th Virginia regiment, being sent back to Fort Pitt as indicated by Washington, in the above letter, in the summer of 1778. He remained at that post until the close of the war. He was a member of the convention which framed the Constitution of the State of Pennsylvania in 1790; and subsequently, was a judge of Allegheny county, that State; also, a major-general of militia. He was Secretary of the Territory of Indiana until it became a State. He died in Fayette county, Pennsylvania, April 10, 1822."

"Washington Crawford Letters," p. 69.

(12) *Border Warfare,* p. 288.

(13) *Heads of Families,* Virginia, pp. 36-90.

NOTES ON CHAPTER XIII

(1) *Border Warfare,* p. 290.

(2) *Border Warfare,* p. 246.

(3) *Dellass,* p. 257.

(4) There were many pigeon roosts throughout the mountain regions of Virginia. Men and boys would go to these roosts at night, and by the light of torches slaughter the birds by the thousand. The last great flight of pigeons occurred in 1873. I well remember this never repeated scene, as they passed over the little valley where my father then lived. One autumn morning a deep roar was suddenly heard, and a great cloud of pigeons swept over the woodcrested hill on the north. For an hour, with brief intervals, the sky was darkened in every direction as flock after flock, in countless myriads, poured southward.

It has been supposed that this bird once so numerous, is now extinct, but I see by the local press that in October, 1907, a flock estimated at about five hundred was seen hovering about the tree tops near Addison, West Virginia; and from their movements appeared to be foraging.

(5) *Withers,* p. 310, *Dellass,* pp. 256, 257.

Col. Westfall claimed that when attacked the Schoolcraft boys were on the Buckhannon River, below Bush's Fort.

(6) In the first census of Virginia, 1782, the name of John Schoolcraft appears in the enumeration of Monongalia County, but not in connection with a family. *Heads of Families, Virginia,* p. 35.

(7) *Border Warfare*, pp. 282, 284, 310, 377 and 379.

(8) Perhaps it was the "phantom deer" that Mr. Isaac Posy, an old nimrod of the upper West Fork, had an experience with when a boy. Posy related the story to Mr. Hall, as follows:

"When about eighteen years of age, I crossed over to one of the upper branches of the Sand Fork to visit friends and hunt where game was more abundant than nearer my home. The next morning, with a cousin younger than myself, we started on the hunt. When leaving, I told my aunt that we would come back with a deer and would have venison for breakfast. But the old lady shook her head and replied, 'No, Isaac, you will see no deer today.' Notwithstanding the augury, we struck out with glowing anticipations, though we knew the old lady was generally regarded as a witch. Strange to say though sign was abundant, we tramped all day through the snow without seeing a single deer. Next morning I determined to go home. My aunt told me that it would be best, but added, 'You will see a deer today.' 'Well,' I replied, 'if I kill one before I cross the ridge I will come back and we will have our venison yet.' 'Never mind coming back, Isaac, but you will see a deer today, and it will be a big one,' was the answer. I left, and on approaching the gap in the ridge a magnificent buck stood before me, not fifty yards distant.

"Well, did you get it?" Hall asked, as Posy hesitated. His reply was: "These things make a body feel mighty queer. I just shook all over. I could hardly hold the gun in my hands. For an instant I turned my head away, and when I looked again, it was gone. I never felt like huntin' in them woods any more."

The solitude of the wilderness was productive of mystery. It engendered in the untutored mind of the Indian and woodsman a belief in the supernatural. That which could not readily be accounted for by natural deduction, appealed to him strongly, and intuitively it was associated with the occult. He was guided by omens, signs and auguries.

Walter McWhorter, with others, was hunting on the Little Kanawha. One day their dog passed swiftly and silently near them, seemingly on the trail of some creature. He vanished, and the unnatural actions of the animal surprised the hunters. They waited long for his return, and followed his trail a great distance, calling loudly, but he was never again seen or heard of. Whether he had been lost on the trail of the "Phantom Deer," or had met a tragic death in conflict with some wild animal, was only conjecture. Such incidents made visible impressions on the mind of the hunter, and was the foundation for many stories of the supernatural.

An old hunter of marked intelligence, who in an early day frequented the wilds of the Buckhannon and Middle Fork region, told me in all sincerity, the following story:

"My pardner and I were hunting on the Buckhannon, and camped at Indian Camp. One evening, just after nightfall, while reclining near our fire, we were startled by hearing from the canopy of laurel which crowned the brow of the overhanging rock, the soft notes of a melody, strange, weird and entrancing. As the music floated down through the darkness, I was enthralled. Never had I heard cadence of such mingled sadness and joy. It was the voice of a woman, but not of earth; the carol of a bird, from Paradise. It seemed everywhere; it filled the recesses of the cavern, it stole through the thickets and flooded the forest with melody sweet and unreal. I was enraptured, transported, lost. I laughed, I wept. My comrade, unable to control his feelings, sprang upon the large rock in the entrance of the cavern and danced in mad abandonment. How long the song lasted, I never knew. It died away as mysteriously as it came, and left us wondering what it could be."

(9) At the time of this siege, Simon Girty, Indian name, Katepacomen—was still loyal to the American cause and was then acting as interpreter for Col. George Morgan, Indian Agent at Fort Pitt, for the Middle Department. Not only Schoolcraft, but *Withers*, and many other writers have fallen into the error that Simon Girty led the Indians against Fort Henry. Girty did not desert from Fort Pitt until March 28, 1778. See Hildreth's *Pioneer History*, pp. 129, 130.

The number of Indians engaged in this raid has been variously estimated and as high as 400. *Butterfield*, a recognized authority, makes it 200. *History of the Girtys*, p. 43. The loss sustained by Mason and Ogle, was 15 killed and 5 wounded; although the computation has been placed at 23 killed. The Indian casualty was one killed and 9 wounded. The rescue party of which Schoolcraft was a member, numbered 14, all of them volunteers.

(10) "Gane," uncertain and evidently intended for *Zane*. For a notice of Col. Silas Zane, see *Note 3*, Chapter XXIX. this Volume.

(11) Schoolcraft, like *Doddridge* and *Withers*, errs in the date of Col. Broadhead's Coshocton expedition, which took place two years after his campaign on the Allegheny River, when the Seneca village Buckaloons was destroyed in 1779, referred to in Note 14, Chapter XV, this Volume.

COSCHOCTON: corrupted from the Indian name: Goschachguen, or Goschochking: "completed," or "finished," was located on the north side of the Tuscarawas River, at its junction with the Muskingum. It was a village of considerable extent; composed of log huts and a large council house. It was the chief town of the Turtle clan of the Delawares, and the capitol of the tribe.

The atrocities attending the reduction of Coshocton is a substance of history and forms a dark page in our border annals. It also instances the lawlessness of the borderers, and their supreme contempt for restraint and discipline, if indeed their commander was not a party to their acts. The village was surprised and destroyed, and all the Indians captured "without firing a single shot." Chief Pekillon, a friendly Delaware who accompanied the army, pointed out fifteen or sixteen warriors among the prisoners who were suspected for their activity and cruelty against the settlements. That night a council was held to determine the fate of these accused, and the sentence was death. They were bound, taken a short distance below the town and were tomahawked, speared and scalped.

The next morning a splendid looking chief came from the opposite side of the flood-swollen river, under a pledge of protection for the purpose of making peace. While he was talking with Col. Broadhead, a militia man, named Wetzel, came up behind him, and whipping a concealed tomahawk from the bosom of his hunting shirt, he dealt the unsuspecting chief a fatal blow on the back of his head. *DeHass*, p. 181, alone of the chroniclers, gives the murderer's first name, John. In the *Draper Manuscripts* (2 E 8), it is stated that Lewis Wetzel did the killing.

The same day of this outrage, the army, about 300 men, started on its return to Fort Pitt, and the prisoners, numbering about twenty, were placed under the tender care of the militia. After proceeding a short distance, these were all massacred with the exception of a few women and children, who were taken to Fort Pitt and afterwards exchanged for an equal number of white prisoners. Accounts of Col. Broadhead's achievements can be found by consulting *Heckewelder, Doddridge, DeHass, Drake, Withers,* and many other works pertaining to the early history of the Ohio Valley.

(12) Schoolcraft was granted a pension. He died March 6, 1850. Mrs. Nancy Schoolcraft, whose maiden name was Brown, was, as her deceased husband's beneficiary, vouched for by Washington Bailey, Henry McWhorter and Carr Bailey. She was not granted a pension, evidently abandoning her claim of her own accord. She was married to John Schoolcraft July 18, 1805.

(13) See Butterfield's *History of the Girtys.* Also Thwaite's Notes, *Border Warfare,* pp. 224, 225.

(14) *Indian Wars of Northwestern Va.,* pp. 280, 281; *Our Western Border,* pp. 525 to 527; *Field Book of the American Revolution,* Volume II, p. 498; *Annals of the West,* pp. 356 to 358.

(15) *Border Warfare,* pp. 356 to 357.

(16) In addition to *Withers,* see *DeHass,* pp. 269, 270, 280, 281, where both the Zane and the Scott claims are fully set forth. Also *McKnight,* pp. 525 to 527.

(17) *Washington Irvine Correspondence,* p. 312.

For notice of Capt. John Boggs, and the Boggs family, see *Frontier Defense on the Upper Ohio,* pp. 65, 67, 68.

(18) *Washington Irvine Correspondence,* pp. 397, 398.

The Indian army numbering 238, was led by Capt. Andrew Brandt (usually spelled Pratt) with his forty rangers. James Girty (Indian name Swatswih) was along but had no command. *History of the Girtys,* p. 201. *Roosevelt* in speaking of the siege of 1782, without any foundation whatever, says: "Simon Girty with fife and drum, led a large band of Indians and Detroit rangers against it, [Wheeling] only to be beaten off." *Winning of the West,* Volume 2, p. 274. In a foot note on the same page, this writer avers: "we do not know which of the two brothers Girty was in command, nor whether either was present at the first attack." (1777) *Roosevelt* seemed to be ignorant of the fact that there were three of the Girty brothers who acquired fame by affiliating with the Indians. They were captured with others at the taking of Fort Granville on the Juniata in now Mifflin County, Pa., in July, 1756. Simon, born 1741, was adopted by the Senecas. James, born 1743, was adopted by the Shawnees. George, born 1745, was adopted by the Delawares. They were returned from captivity in 1759. James and Simon deserted to the British in the Spring of 1778, while George remained loyal to the American cause until the following year. An older brother, Thomas, born 1739, was rescued when the Delaware town Kittaning on the Allegheny was destroyed by Col. John Armstrong in September, 1756. The mother and a half-brother were retained by the Delawares and delivered up with the other brothers in 1759. The stepfather, John Turner, was burned at the stake at Kittaning soon after the capture in 1756.

(19) Gen. Clark's Expedition against Vincennes was in 1778. His Campaign of 1781 was an attempt against Detroit.

Capt. John Floyd was shot and fatally wounded by Indians in ambush near Floyd's Station, Jefferson County, Ky., April 12, 1783. He was brave and valiant, and his death was a blow to the settlements of that region.

NOTES ON CHAPTER XIV

(1) *Withers*, p. 287.

(2) The conquest of the primitive races by civilized man has been practically the same the world over. The early settlers of Australia, acting upon the principle of economy, "killed the native black men because they were cattle thieves, the women because they gave birth to cattle thieves, and the children because they grew up to be cattle thieves." An old Australian ranger, in conversation with me said, "I went from England to Australia in 1850, and settled in Queensland, and engaged in the cattle business. The native blacks were born cattle thieves and were very treacherous. It was lawful to shoot them wherever found, as they were not susceptible to civilization, and were regarded as vermin. The settlers often banded together and formed a 'ring hunt,' a general 'round-up' of the natives. On such occasions, the hunters, well armed and mounted, would enclose an area some fifty miles in extent, and drive the blacks to a common center, where they were all killed—men, women and children. Usually the men would die game. I saw one of them armed only with a wooden spear, who after receiving eight rifle balls in his body, charged madly at the cordon of well-armed men who hemmed him in. Ofttimes a village or settlement would be surprised and the entire population captured. On such occasion, the prisoners were forced to dig a trench sufficient to hold the bodies of the dead. Then all would be killed but one stout buck, who after being compelled to inter his dead tribesmen, was shot to death by his captors."

(3) One such case is set forth in *Conspiracy of Pontiac*, Volume II, pp. 39 to 41.

NOTES ON CHAPTER XV

(1) "A correspondent asks where, when and why the Buckhannon River gets its name. The editor does not know. The river was named very early, at least as early as 1781, as is mentioned in records of that date. The spelling has not always been the same as now. There were persons of that name living in the region as early as one hundred and six years ago." *Trans-Allegheny Historical Magazine*, Volume II, p. 71, 1902.

Prof. Hu Maxwell in response to an inquiry on this topic says: "I am reasonably sure that the name Buckhannon will never be found in records as early as 1779. That name was first written 'Buck-Hannon's Creek' as is shown by the Monona records. I believe that the name comes from some man whose surname Hannon, and whose given name was Buck."

A letter from John Jackson to the Governor dated Jan. 25th, 1793, was written at "Buck-Hanan." See biographical sketch of Col. Lowther, this Volume.

BUCKHANNON RUN was evidently so named because the trail from West's Fort to the Buckhannon settlement led directly up this stream, which heads against the ridge dividing the Hacker's Creek and Buckhannon waters: hence the name Buckhannon, or "Hacker's Creek Mountain."

Since writing this chapter, *Mr. Cutright's History of Upshur County, W. Va.*, has been published. On pages 274, 275 the author endeavors to show that the Buckhannon River bears the name of a "poor old Scotch clergyman, named John Buchannon," who resided in Richmond, Virginia, in 1785. Mr. Cutright says:

"* * * John Buchannon was a missionary minister and teacher for several years after his arrival in this country, * * *. On one occasion his bishop sent him to the headwaters of the Monongahela on a tour of inspection and a mission of help. He crossed the mountains to Tygart's Valley and from thence was going to a mission which he learned was on the West Fork near the town of Weston. We are unable to find whether he made more than one trip, as we are also unable to possess facts of his discovery and exploration. Our personal opinion is that he thought that the river which runs from south to north through Upshur County had not been discovered, named and explored by any white man thoroughly. He assumed to do both and being desirous of perpetuating the dead, called the river after his own name."

The mere fact that a mission on the West Fork was visited by this clergyman subsequent to 1785 which is apparently the earliest notice that Mr. Cutright found of him in Virginia, will hardly connect his name with the Buckhannon River, which had been named at least four years previously.

While Mr. Cutright expresses his satisfaction with this "origin of the name of our county seat and the principal stream in the county," he suggests that the name may have been derived from that of the Earl Buchan, who was a friend of General Washington, through whose instrumentality he became interested in Rev. Byron Fairfax, who was heir to the great Virginia Fairfax Estate.

This hypothetical origin of the name in question is too chimerical to seriously engage the attention of any student of border annals.

(2) *Border Warfare*, p. 40.

(3) *Border Warfare*, p. 75.

(4) *Border Warfare*, p. 119.

(5) Evidence of more remote occupancy of the Buckhannon Valley by the Aborigines has been met with. Traces of an Indian village are found where Buckhannon now stands. Flint chips and arrow points are still picked up at a point just below the town, and on the opposite side of the river, while a few years ago the fragments of a large steatite pot were unearthed at a depth of about four feet in a brick yard not far from the river bank. A few pieces of a similar kind were uncovered at Indian Camp. Steatite implements found in that region are of southern origin. Occasional fragments of such vessels have been found on Hacker's Creek, one by a ditcher just below Berlin. In the year 1893, I plowed up a small fragment along with a pitted hammer stone, near the roots of what had once been a large black walnut tree, on my father's farm on Buckhannon Run. With these relics were the traces of a camp fire, not extensively used.

In a small mound opened at Sago on the Buckhannon a few years ago, was found a finely carved stone pipe. From the bowl projected the well shaped head of some animal, ostensibly that of the wolf or fox. In general outline the pipe resembled some of the ancient mound types met with in the Mississippi Valley. A stone pipe of the more modified Indian form was taken from a grave on the Buckhannon River, near the mouth of French Creek, and was placed by me in the Museum of the *West Virginia State Historical and Antiquarian Society*, Charleston.

(6) BUCK-ON-GA-HE-LAS (breaker-in-pieces). The name is spelled in various ways, among others, *Buokongahelas, Bukongahelas* and *Bokongehelas*. The first form, however, has precedence. See *Hand Book of American Indians*, Volume I.

This renowned chieftain was also known as *Pachgantschihilas*, and *Petchnanalas*. According to *Heckewelder*, his name signified: *"a ful-filler,"* or *"one who succeeds in all he undertakes."*

Plurality of names is common with the Indian, especially the warriors. I have a close friend in a Warm Springs warrior, who fought the Modocs in the Lava Beds, War 1872-73, and who joined the Bannock uprising in 1878, who is known by eight distinctive names. A contemporary warrior of the same tribe, boasted fifty-two names.

(7) BUCKONGAHELAS, in a speech to his tribesmen, the friendly Moravians of Gnadenhueten, prior to the massacre of those unfortunates, gave just grounds for his siding with the British. The many wrongs suffered by his people at the hands of the "Long Knives" drove him to war. For this speech and a biographical sketch of its author, see Drake's *Indians of North America*.

(8) *Western Annals*, pp. 656 to 661.

(9) *Border Warfare*, pp. 428 to 430. For a further account of the Bozarth tragedy, see Chapter XXIX, this Volume.

(10) Dawson's Life of Wm. Henry Harrison; quoted from English's *Conquest of the Northwest*, Volume II, p. 791.

(11) Excerpt from letter of Mr. John Johnston, former Indian Agent at Fort Wayne, Indiana, to Dr. L. C. Draper, April 27, 1849. *Draper Mss*. 11YY35.

(12) From letter of John Johnston to Dr. Draper, Dec. 1, 1850. *Draper Mss*. 11YY38. *Frontier Defense on the Upper Ohio*, pp. 117, 118.

(13) Data obtained from Mr. John Johnston by Dr. Draper, in June 1843. *Draper Mss*. 11YY9.

(14) See *Life of Mary Jemison*, Buffalo, 1877, p. 186.

BUCKALOON OR BUCKALOONS, was the name of a Seneca village on the Allegheny River, in Warren Co., Pa. It was destroyed by Col. Broadhead in 1779, the Indians fleeing upon his approach. It was called *Kachuiodagon*, 1749. *Washington Irvine Correspondence*, p. 43.

NOTES ON CHAPTER XVI

(1) *Border Warfare*, p. 342.

(2) *Border Warfare*, p. 342.

(3) *Border Warfare*, p. 428.

(4) *Indian Wars*, pp. 389, 390.

(5) Such confessions and revelations of plots and intended forays were not uncommon among the Indians. That of Fort Miami in 1763 is a typical illustration. *Conspiracy of Pontiac*, Vol. 1, p. 198. Captured Pottawatomie and Shawnee warriors revealed to General Wayne at Fort Greenville important facts relative to the strength and intentions of the enemy then marching against him. *Western Annals*, pp. 639-642.

(6) I am the owner of an old flint-lock rifle, said to have been used in this skirmish, either by John Reger referred to, or his younger brother Abram, or Abraham. The rifle is full stocked with hard maple, and has the old-fashioned brass tallow box in the side of the stock. On the lid of this box, in large Spencerian capitals are the clear cut letters, "A. D. R." On the barrel, near the breech, in Roman figures and small English capitals, is this inscription:

105 Va. REGt. WASHINGTON.

The lettering is plain and legible, though crudely executed. The gun weighs nine pounds, fourteen ounces, and measures full length fifty-six and one-fourth inches. The barrel is forty inches. It was, doubtless, originally some two or more inches longer but was subsequently shortened at the breech on account of being "burned out." It takes a ball one-half inch in diameter, and carries about twenty bullets to the pound. Rifles of that period that carried more than forty-five bullets to the pound were not "thought sufficiently heavy for hunting or war."—*Doddridge*. The rear sight is extremely fine, and formerly was eleven inches from the breech, but has at sometime been set back on the barrel four inches. The bead or front sight is silver. The original lock is not on the gun, but it still retains a typical flint-lock, and is in prime shooting order. It was supposedly the property of an elder brother, Anthony Reger, who was an Ensign in the Thirteenth Virginia Regiment, Revolutionary War. The regimental number, if such, on the barrel does not correspond with that of Reger's regiment, but it is not known that he owned it during the war; nor can it at this time be determined that the number is regimental. It may be an enrollment number.

There are no printed rolls of the Revolution extant, showing the number of regiments in the Continental Army, or the number that served from the State of Virginia. Virginia is supposed to have furnished 26,678 regulars to the Continental Army, and 30,000 militia, or state troops, which would not suffice to make one hundred and five regiments.

Perhaps the most authentic estimate on this topic is that of Gen. Knox in 1790, when Secretary of War:

In 1775 he credits Virginia with no continental troops, but estimates 2,000 men as serving in the militia of that State.

In 1776 he gives Virginia 6,181 men in continental pay, and does not conjecture the number of militia.

In 1777 Virginia had 5,744 continentals, 1,269 militia, and in addition, a conjectured estimate of 4,000 more militiamen.

In 1778 Virginia had 5,230 continentals, with a conjectured estimate of 2,000 militiamen.

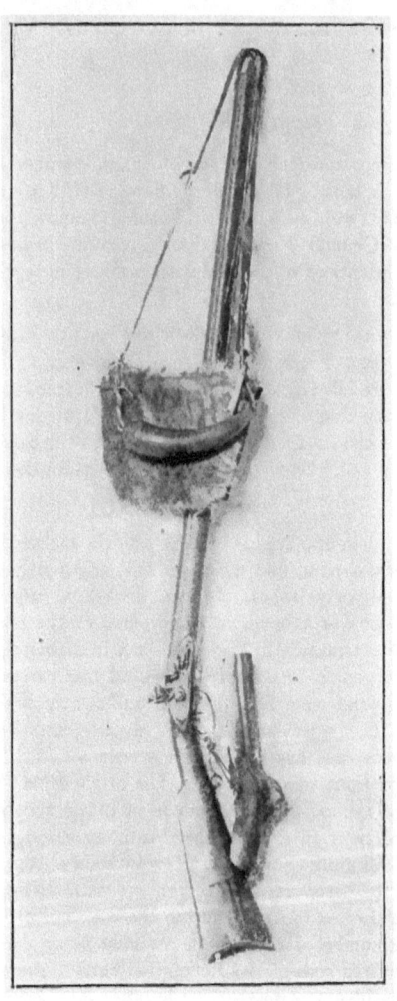

THE REGER RIFLE AND McWHORTER SHOT POUCH
(See Note 6, Chapt. XVI; and Note 15, Chapt. XXVIII.)

Tied to the trigger guard of the rifle, is the leathern cap, universally used by the scout and hunter for the protection of the lock from rain and dampness. These were made by stretching the green, or wet hide from the hock of a beef, elk or deer, over the lock and breech of the gun and letting them dry there which gave permanent shape. Those from the elk and deer always retained the hair; but the beef skins, as in the one here shown, were often tanned in the usual way, and kept well greased, making them more impervious to dampness. They were always attached to the guard with a thong of sufficient length to permit easy removal from the lock, as here depicted. These lock shields were often used long after the percussion caps came into use.

The original red-buckskin "flap," or cover of the McWhorter shot pouch, was lost in the latter nineties, and has been replaced with a similar one of Indian tan.

In 1779 there were 3,973 continentals and an estimate of 3,000 militia.
In 1780 Virginia had 2,486 continentals and an estimate of 1,500 militia.
In 1781 the state furnished 1,225 continentals, 2,894 militia and in addition, about 2,000 more militia.
In 1782 there were 1,204 continentals and about 1,000 militia.
In 1783 Virginia had 629 continentals.
See *Amer. State Papers.* Military Affairs, Volume 1, pp. 14-19.

A very light percentage of Virginia's enrolled militia was ever in the Continental service. They were, more often, engaged in state and frontier guard duty, and in desultory campaigning and foraying against the Indians. From the returns of 1780, 1781, *Jefferson* in his *Notes on Virginia*, Boston, 1829, pp. 93-95, estimates that Virginia then had 49,971 militiamen enrolled. Of these 4,458 were west of the Alleghenies. Greenbrier County's enrollment was 502; that of Monongalia County 1,000. The estimate for the last named county were from returns a little earlier than the dates given. All free males between the ages of sixteen and fifty were enrolled militiamen.

The militia regiments increased in number as new counties were formed, and regiments were organized in these counties. Beginning shortly after the Revolutionary War with less than one hundred regiments, there were nearly two hundred regiments in the militia before the Civil War. In 1792 the regiment of the highest number was the One Hundred and First in Spottsylvania County.

In 1799 the 105th Militia Regiment was formed in Washington County, Virginia, to which many of the commissioned officers of the old 70th were transferred. The militia were generally armed with muskets but the supply was inadequate for the men enrolled, and had to be passed from company to company for drill purposes; consequently all sorts of guns were pressed into service. It is more than probable that the rifle in question was owned by some militiaman of the 105th, and was carried by him to the county militia musters. However, it was in service during the Revolution, and the troublous period on the Virginia border, immediately following. It is reputed to have killed the last Indian slain in the Buckhannon settlement, near the mouth of Fink's Run. This may have been the warrior killed by John Reger in the fight referred to.

Roosevelt claims that the frontier rifle of the Trans-Allegheny was of small bore, and generally carried "a ball of seventy, more rarely of thirty or forty, to the pound; and was usually of backwoods manufacture." *Winning of the West.* Volume 1, pp. 149-196. Volume 2, p. 59.

This is in contradiction to *Doddridge*, who on p. 177 states:

"Rifles of former times were different from those of modern date; few of them carried more than forty-five bullets to the pound. Bullets of a less size were not thought sufficiently heavy for hunting or war."

The same author on p. 176, says:

"A wellgrown boy, at the age of twelve or thirteen years, was furnished with a small rifle and shot pouch. He then became a fort soldier, and had his port hole assigned him. Hunting squirrels, turkeys and raccoons soon made him expert in the use of his gun."

Roosevelt seemingly bases his theory on the measurement of one of Daniel Boone's squirrel rifles; which, of course, was of greater length than the boy rifle described by *Doddridge*. The frontier rifle was made to meet the requirements

OUTLINE OF BULLET
Found in the Breech of the Isaac Washburn Rifle. Full size; weight ½ oz.

of the day, and such was the Reger rifle and the old rifle with its half-ounce ball dragged up in a fishing net from its ancient river bed near Richards' Fort; and described in Note 4, Chapter IV, this Volume. Bullets which I have picked up near the home sites of the border settlers, seldom weighed less than a half-ounce.

It would appear from *Doddridge*, p. 281, that it was customary with the experienced frontiersman, to cut off the neck of the bullet very close and when expecting an attack or a battle, to scrape them for the purpose of reducing their size a little, and to use "patches" half the ordinary thickness so as to avoid the possibility of "choking," or "jamming."

(7) For further account of the Regers, see Chapter XXIX, this Volume.

(8) See Chapter X, this Volume.

(9) *Border Warfare*, pp. 341, 342.

(10) *Border Warfare*, pp. 396-397.

(11) *Hist. of Upshur County, W. Va.*, pp. 202, 203.

(12) The land records of 1781 show that Gee Bush owned land near, or on Gee Lick, a branch of Freeman's Creek, and that George Bush owned lands on the West Fork River. One John Bush preempted 1,000 acres on Decker's Creek (now Monongalia Co.), which included his settlement made in 1770.

NOTES ON CHAPTER XVII

(1) *Border Warfare*, p. 342.

(2) One of the active scouts on the western waters was Edward Jackson, son of John Jackson, settler at Buckhannon in 1769. He was a commissioned captain of militia in Randolph County, in 1787, and was also a surveyor. In the *Calendar of Virginia State Papers*, Volume 4, p. 299, is found this record:

BOND OF EDWARD JACKSON

"As surveyor of Randolph County, commissioned such by the Governor of Virginia in the penalty of Two Thousand Pounds lawful money, June 25th, 1787."

Another scout, ——— Roy, given name unknown, resided near West's Fort. He was a very resolute man, often making the journey to Pendleton County alone. He discovered an Indian taking a hive of bees from his yard one day, but the Indian fled and escaped.

(3) The scouts in their first visits to the Little Kanawha region, went by way of Sand Fork. They soon learned that the Indian path on Leading Creek was the shorter route, and that it led direct to the Little Kanawha and thence to the Ohio; therefore the name "Leading Creek."

"Polk Creek" along which this trail passed, derived its name from a poke stalk that the scouts saw growing in a cavity at the top of a large sycamore tree that had been broken off. This tree stood in the bend of the creek near the present railroad depot at Weston. The stream bore this appellation in 1781, and is a corruption of *Poke* Creek.

(4) The contiguousness of the navigable waters of the Monongahela and the Little Kanawha, was brought to the notice of Gen. Washington in 1784; whose information was: "that the Portage does not exceed Nine Miles—and that a very good Waggon Road may be had between—That from the Mouth of the River Cheat to that of the West Fork, is computed to be about 30 Miles, & the Navigation good—as it also is up the West fork." Hulbert's *Washington and the West*, New York, 1905, p. 57. A railway now pasess over this "Portage," or low gap.

This "Indian Carrying Place" was evidently where John P. Duvall was granted a certificate for "400 acres at the Indian House on the waters of the West Fork, to include his settlement made in 1776." The mention here in this early record of the "Indian House" is significant, and the inference is that there was some structure erected there and used by the Indians when the country was first settled by the whites. It strengthens the claim that this was a thoroughfare of importance, and that the "House," built of poles, bark or other light material, was a regular stopping place for any band of Indians passing through that region. The plow still unearths evidences of an extensive village or camping site, and in the ravine leading down to the Kanawha side, the base of a low cliff shows the charred discoloration of continued camp fires. A mound of considerable magnitude, for that locality, is still to be seen; as is also one on Canoe Run, referred to later in the text.

John P. Duvall who home-steaded at the "Indian House" was prominent on the border; in both civil and military affairs. He was one of the Commissioners appointed to adjust land claims on the western waters, at Clarksburg in 1781; and was subsequently County Lieutenant of Harrison County, Va. He was in command of the County Militia when the Indians raided the Flesher, and the Cunningham families in 1784-85; mentioned in Chapter II, this Volume. In reporting the Cunningham tragedy to the Governor, Duvall stated that the militia was not organized, and ammunition very scarce; that he had sent out fifty men and six spies. The effective force in the entire County was about "two hundred and fifteen men, and about one hundred and thirty guns." In addition to ammunition, which he was sending for, Lieut. Duvall requested of the Governor, that if "there is any Rifles Belonging to the State in any of the Back magazines, to wit, Alexandria, Winchester or Fredericksburg, should acknowledge it as a singular favor to send an order for about Two Hundred of them." *Calendar of Virginia State Papers*, Volume IV, p. 53.

(5) *History of the Girtys*, Cincinnati, 1890, p. 54.

Tradition says that a stranger came to the home of a Mr. Morris, a settler on Peters Creek in (now) Nicholas County, and stayed there a part of one winter. Morris visited the Kanawha settlement, and described his visitor, who had a peculiar scar on his face. He was told that he was harboring none other than Simon Girty, the notorious renegade. Morris returned home and drove his guest away. Shortly after this the Indians attacked Morris' home and killed two of his children. A tree growing where the victims were buried is still pointed out by the inhabitants of that neighborhood. Peters Creek was named for a slave owned by Morris.

(6) This was in the region where Frenchton now stands in Upshur County. This village was originally called *Beech Town*, which name dates to the great hunt described. Jesse Hughes, when he saw the disturbed condition of the leaves by the bears in search of beech nuts, exclaimed, "All the bears in the country must have come to Beech Town."

The legendary version of this name as given by Cutright (*Hist. of Upshur County, W. Va.*, p. 323), is that the Indians when making forays into this section of Virginia. had, for self protection, erected of beech logs and poles at this point a number of huts, is purely mythical. These predatory war parties did not build villages, and the environments of *Beech Town*, so far from any prominent water course precludes the idea of an Indian village being located there.

(7) It was not unusual for the foraying warriors to carry the bow for use on such occasions as depicted in the text. With this silent though effective weapon, game could be killed in close proximity to the settlements without betrayal of their presence.

(8) George Jackson Arnold was a successful farmer, a noted hunter, a surgeon and an able lawyer. He succeeded Col. John McWhorter as Prosecuting Attorney of Lewis County. Mr. Arnold was born in Fauquier County, Virginia, in 1815, and died at his home on "Indian Farm," previously referred to, in 1899.

An Incident of the Seneca Trail

(9) Mrs. Heavner, a widow, with her two sons and four daughters, crossed the mountains over the Seneca Trail and settled on the head of Abram's Run, on the upper West Fork; named for Abram Bennett the first settler on the stream. In recounting some of the incidents on the trail, she said, "I walked the entire heavenly road with Mamie, then one year old, on my hip."

(10) There was a Joseph Hall residing in Harrison County in 1818-1820, who in the spring of 1776, enlisted as private in Capt. David Stephenson's Company, 8th Va. Regt., commanded by Gen. Mulhenberg, and served two years. Part of this time, however, he was attached to the 12th Va. Regt., under Col. Bowman. His declaration for pension in 1820 shows that he was in indigent circumstances and had one child, Sarah, aged 28.

(11) *History of Kanawha County, West Va.*, pp. 119, 120, 121. See also Hale's *Trans-Allegheny Pioneers*, pp. 276, 277.

(12) Lewis *History of West Va.*, p. 523.

NOTES ON CHAPTER XVIII

(1) *Border Warfare*, pp. 399, 400.

(2) "Soon after the establishment of Marietta, a rude wagon road was opened through the forest between that colony and Redstone (Brownsville Pa.). This was the road Carpenter was following." Note, *Withers*, p. 399.

(3) *History of the Ohio Valley*, pp. 300, 304.

(4) This is the first account we have of Tecumseh leading a war party against the white settlers. Drake, in his *Aboriginal Races of North America*, p. 616, cites the Waggoner massacre, in the Spring of 1792, as Tecumseh's initiatory exploit as a young warrior. Tecumseh is said to have received his first baptism of fire in 1786, when Col. Benjamin Logan led a band of four hundred or five hundred mounted Kentucky riflemen against the Shawnee towns on Mad River. The fight took place near where Dayton, Ohio, now stands. Some writers place Tecumseh's first fight at Gen. Harmer's defeat, in 1790; which is evidently a mistake.

(5) This instance of abstinence from food while on a forced march in the Virginia wilderness, was repeated by Tecumseh the following spring when retreating from his successful raid on the Waggoner family on Jesse's Run, near West's Fort. The children who were taken captive related, after their return, that during the rapid retreat from the scene of blood, both Indians and prisoners had no food of any sort until after they had gained the fastness of the wilderness beyond the Ohio River. Here the Indians killed deer and roasted venison. Peter declared that even in his famished condition, the meat "tasted like rotten wood," because of the absence of salt.

For the *menu* of the Indian warrior when on the warpath, see the *Heckewelder Narrative*, pp. 163, 164.

(6) The Indian garb was peculiarly adapted to a life in the woods; and the hunter and scout assumed it with but slight modification. For comfort and sanitation the Indian dress cannot be excelled. It is well described by Dr. Doddridge in his *Notes on the Settlement and Indian Wars of the Western Parts of Virginia and Pennsylvania*, Albany, 1876, p. 142. Also Kercheval's *History of the Valley*, p. 339.

"In the later years of the Indian war our young men became more enamored of the Indian dress throughout, with the exception of the match coat. The drawers were laid aside and the leggins made longer, so as to reach the upper part of the thigh. The Indian breech clout was adopted. This was a piece of linen or cloth, nearly a yard long, and eight or nine inches broad. This passed under the belt before and behind leaving the ends for flaps hanging before and behind over the belt. These flaps were sometimes ornamented with some coarse kind of embroidery work. To the same belts which secured the breech clout, strings which supported the long leggins were attached. When this belt, as was often the case, passed over the hunting shirt the upper part of the thighs and part of the hips were naked."

(7) Hildreth's *Lives of the Early Settlers of Ohio*, Cincinnati, 1852, p. 149.

(8) For a sketch of the life of Isaac Williams, see Hildreth's *Early Settlers of Ohio*; also his *Pioneer History of the Ohio Valley*.

(9) Lewis, *History of West Virginia*, pp. 657, 658.

NOTES ON CHAPTER XIX

(1) It is not known at what date John Waggoner came to the Hacker's Creek settlement; nor is it certain where he hailed from. The records of Monongalia County, 1779, show that one John Waggoner assigned his claim to 4,000 acres of

land on Buffalo Run, a branch of Cheat River, which included his "settlement made in 1774."

The Census of Virginia, 1782, shows only one John Waggoner in the state, residence Hampshire County, with four in family. There is but one John Waggoner listed in the Census of 1785, residence Harrison County, five in family. In all probability this was one and the same party.

(2) For an instance of this kind, see *Life of Grey Hawk*.

(3) See *Bouquet's Expedition Against the Ohio Indians*, Cincinnati, 1907, pp. 62, 67, for a graphic description of such scenes as depicted in the text.

(4) Drake's *Indian Captivities*, Buffalo, 1853, p. 183.

(5) Drake's *Indian Captivities*, pp. 185, 186.

(6) *Border Warfare*, pp. 408, 411.

(7) In an editor's note, p. 410, *Border Warfare*, Booher's name is given as "Baker"; a typographical error.

PAINT CREEK: a tributary of the Scioto, in Ross County, Ohio. It was the former home of the Chillicothe branch of the Shawnees. Their village, "Old Town," stood on the banks of this stream, near the present Chillicothe, in 1774. It was laid waste by the Kentuckians in 1787; but the Indians were in possession of the country until after the War of 1812.

One tradition says that the Delawares were the despoilers of the Waggoner family. There may have been some member of that tribe with the marauders, but the Shawnees were the authors of the tragedy.

(8) Drake's *Indian Captivities*, p. 190.

NOTES ON CHAPTER XX

(1) *Border Warfare*, p. 414.

(2) Adam O'Brien, to whose carelessness must be attributed the Carpenter tragedy, was an eccentric man, who seemingly had been driven to the wilderness because of some trouble in the settlements. He came early into the Trans-Allegheny, and revelled in a life of freedom, "untrammeled by laws" and the restraining influences of society.

The following is taken from *The West Virginia Historical Magazine*, Volume III, pp. 307, 308.

"One of the first settlers of the Trans-Allegheny country was Adam O'Brien, if his roving disposition and movements would entitle him to the name of settler. He had a cabin on Elk River at the mouth of Holly River; a long time he owned two tracts of land, held by patents, in Randolph county; he lived on the Little Kanawha and he lived and died on the Big Sandy of Elk in Kanawha county. He seems to have been engaged in making settlements on good lands for others and that he had made many. He said that all he had to do was to cut his initials "A. O. B." on some trees, cut down a few saplings and plant a hand full of corn and he secured a right to four hundred acres of land, though it afterwards cost a good deal of hard swearing.

"When asked how he came to seek the wilderness and encounter the perils and sufferings of frontier life, he answered that he liked it and did not mind it a bit and in further explanation said, that he was a poor man and had got behind hand and when that's the case, there is no staying in the settlements for those varments, the sheriffs and constables, who were worse than Indians, because you could kill Indians, and you dare not kill the sheriffs. That after the king's proclamation for all settlers and surveyors to remove east of the big ridge, from off the western waters, there was no people on the west side except those who had run away from justice and here they were as free as the biggest buck agoing, and after the peace of sixty-three, it was all quiet in the back woods. That there was a settlement at Dunkard's bottom, and a small one where Clarksburg now is, and some squatters here and there, that had their cabins, their corn and potatoes and their guns with which they kept themselves in bear meat and venison, and while they had no money, they had skins with which they could secure powder and lead and such things as they had to buy. He said that they lived quite happy before the Revolution, for then there was no law, no courts and no sheriffs and they all agreed pretty well, but after a while the people began to come and make settlements and then there was need for law; and then came the lawyers and next the preachers and from that time they never had any peace any more, that the laywers persuaded them to sue when they were not paid, and the preachers *converted* one half and they began to quarrel with the other half because they would not take care of their own souls, and from that time, they never had any peace for body or soul, and that the sheriffs were worse than the wild cats and painters, and would take the last coverlit from your wife's straw bed or turn you out in a storm, and I tell you, mister, I would rather take my chances and live among savages than live among justices and lawyers and sheriffs, who with all their civility, have no natural feeling in them. The settlers had to go to the field with their gun and ofttimes their wives had to keep watch with rifle while they were at the plough."

In 1781, Adam O'Brien was granted a certificate for "400 acres on the West Fork, to include his settlement made in 1775;" also for "400 acres on Lost Creek, to include his settlement made in 1781."

O'Brien and a man named Fink were fired upon by Indians while watching a deer lick on Fink's Creek, a branch of Beech Fork of the Little Kanawha, wounding Fink in the heel. The hunters fled up the creek, and when reaching the low gap between this stream and Hardway's Run, Fink could go no further, and finding that the Indians were pressing them close he advised O'Brien to abandon him to his fate and seek his own safety. This, O'Brien was constrained to do, and Fink concealing himself shot and killed one of his pursuers as they came up. He in turn was killed. The Indians, evidently fearing an ambuscade, fled leaving their dead comrade where he fell. When O'Brien with others returned a few days later they buried the two bodies on the low ridge, where their graves can yet be seen. An account of this tragedy is given in Col. D. S. Dewee's "*Recollections,*" 1904, p. 68.

(3) In the latter part of September, 1902, I was sent by the Bureau of Pensions to investigate some claims in central West Virginia. I was a Special Examiner, and I arrived at Sutton, the county seat of Braxton County, the 30th of September.

From that town I journeyed to make my investigations. The country is a lean one so far as soil goes, or it looked so to me, after seeing the rich, black prairies of the West. But the country fascinated me, for I was born and brought up in a country very similar to it in eastern Kentucky. I had been in Clarksburg over night; Monday morning (as I now remember, though I am not sure it was Monday) I took the train for Sutton. The morning was dark and lowering, and the train had not been long on the road until it began to rain; it rained more and harder as the day advanced. The country had the peculiar drowned appearance common to that land during heavy rains in the fall; the ravines in the hillsides ran bank full, carrying down the soil, often eating down the rock. The trees were dripping in their straggling foliage, now browned by the frosts, and much of it on the ground —dead leaves drifted by the overflowing brooks, "branches," as they say there.

While the landscape was dreary, I had a ride of enjoyment. The large timber on the rocky hillsides and the huge fragments of sandstone lying about the bases of cliffs reminded me of my native country.

Of my travels while in the discharge of my duties I shall not speak at this time. But while at Sutton I heard of an old hunter who lived in the village. I went to see him one dark night while I was there. My work was not done until late, and I found him in bed. His name was William Carpenter. He told me the following concerning his family:

William Carpenter was born at Centralia, fourteen miles from Sutton, Braxton County, West Virginia, April 17, 1827. His great grandfather came from England and settled in the Big Bend of Jackson's River, given name of ancestor and date of coming to America not now known with certainty. His grandfather, Jeremiah Carpenter, was born at the Big Bend of Jackson's River. *Withers* would seem to incline to the opinion that the Carpenters came from Bath County, Va. (*Border Warfare*, 414.) When nine years old Jeremiah was captured by the Shawnees, who made a raid into the Big Bend country, and by them carried to their country where he was adopted by the tribe; he lived with them until he was eighteen. Once during his captivity the Chief's squaw became enraged at him and tried to kill him; she struck him on the head with a hoe. Her daughter rescued him and took him to the Ohio River where she washed his head and dressed his wounds, all the time weeping over the unfortunate boy, who never forgot her; it was even supposed that he was to have married her had he remained with the Shawnees. He remembered her as a gentle young woman of many personal charms and much modesty, who spent most of her time trying to make people as happy as their condition would warrant, a work which she received little enough encouragement in the Indian village. The place of the captivity was Oldtown, opposite the mouth of the Kanawha.

When young Carpenter was exchanged, an action which he regretted, so complete an Indian had he become by habit, he returned to the Big Bend, where he married. After he married he moved to the site of the present town of Centralia, Braxton County, building his house about one-fourth of a mile above Dry Run. This settlement must have been prior to the year 1792 (*Withers*, 414), though Mr. Carpenter could not give me the exact date. He was the first settler in what is now Braxton County. Adam O'Brien was the second settler, and he came in the spring of 1792. (*Withers*, 414.) O'Brien settled on the town site of Sutton, or rather on the bank of Elk River opposite the present town site, where he lived in the hollow of a great sycamore tree. He blazed a trail from his house to Saltville or Bulltown on the Little Kanawha, where he went to make salt. Bulltown was named for Captain Bull, an old Indian, tribe Carpenter did not know; it was so named by the Indians, and was their gathering place in that part of the country, and was a ford on the Little Kanawha. O'Brien made other trails through the country, and they endangered the lives of the settlers. The Indians came up the Elk River every spring on their raids into the settlements. They came also up the Little Kanawha, the various bands met at Bulltown for the last consultation before the descent upon the settlers then beginning to come into that country. One spring (Carpenter could not give me the date, but *Withers* says it was in 1793) the Indians discovered the trail blazed by O'Brien; perhaps it had been made the preceding winter. They followed it to the Elk River, to Sutton, the house of O'Brien, though they did not find him or his family. He had gone back to the settlements, because he could not raise grain for his family until he had made a clearing. (*Withers*.) Carpenter had built a house on the river bank, and some of the chips from his axe had floated down and were found in the Elk River by the Indians when they arrived there. They immediately surmised that someone was living further up the stream, the banks of which they followed up with great caution. Jeremiah Carpenter was accompanied by his brother Benjamin when he came into that wilderness. Benjamin had gone back to the settlements and married during the previous winter—some four months before this raid. He had built his cabin on the bank of the Elk River, at the mouth of Holly Creek, about twelve miles above Sutton. The father, mother, and sisters of the Carpenters had now moved to the Elk River settlement.

In March Ben Carpenter had killed a large red buck (male deer). It was very unusual to see a buck with his coat red at that season of the year. They do not get red until June or July. Jeremiah told Ben that something awful was to befall them, something terrible; the killing of the red buck foretold it. Ben said he would wear moccasins made from that deer's hide, and he put it in the river to soak to take the grain off, as they do in dressing deer skins.

There were two of these Indians. On the day they discovered the chips floating on Elk River, Ben's mother and little sister came to visit him. They went across the river to assist Ben in firing some log heaps in his clearing. Mrs. Carpenter (Ben's wife) was sick and was left in bed. When Ben had worked awhile he told his mother and sister he would go back to the house and help his wife prepare dinner, and left them in the field still at work burning the great log heaps. Ben crossed the river, but before going into the house took the hide of the red buck from the stream and began to take off the grain. He had just put it on the graining block and commenced work when one of the Indians who was concealed behind a log fired on him but missed him. There was one large Indian and one small one. The small Indian had shot at Ben. When the Indian fired Ben ran into the house to get his gun. Now, the big Indian had gone into the house and tomahawked Mrs. Carpenter while she was in bed, perhaps sometime before Ben had returned from his clearing. After killing the wife he concealed himself in the house to wait for Ben, should the little Indian fail to kill him. Ben's gun was in the rack over the cabin door. When he ran in he reached up to get it and as his arm was up the big Indian shot him and killed him. His mother alarmed by the shot of the little Indian, was looking towards the house at the moment, and saw the flash of the Indian's gun go under Ben's arm and saw him fall back dead. She immediately concealed her little daughter in the hollow of a large stump, covering it with a large flat stone, and ran for her husband, first telling the child to make no noise under any circumstances. Ben's father came from his cabin and went to Ben's cabin, and found the Indians gone, having carried off Ben's gun and shot pouch and powder horn.

Jesse Hughes was the famous Indian fighter of that part of Western Virginia. He roamed the whole of the country, and he had many places of temporary abode in the wilderness—hunting camps, where he spent much time or little as the mood might incline him. His home, so Carpenter said, was on Spring Creek, somewhere on the Ohio. He told me, also, that Hughes died on Mill Creek, on the Ohio, but he did not know where that was nor when he died. One of the favorite places of Hughes was in Braxton County, and he had many points of "lookout" from which he could observe the coming of Indians. He had also many places of safety to which he fled when there was danger from Indians. The case I had for investigation was one of contesting widows of one of his descendants. The fall following the raid on Ben Carpenter's house, Hughes killed a big Indian and a little one. The big one had Ben's gun, powder horn, and shot pouch, and it was supposed he slew Carpenter's murderers. The circumstance of the killing is of interest.

It was after the settlers had gathered into their forts in the fall on account of some Indian invasion. The fort was on the West Fork of the Monongahela River. Hughes lived in the vicinity. He had a fine cow on which he put a large bell and allowed to range the woods about the fort. The bell had not been heard for some days, and Hughes knew that the Indians had killed his cow. One day, towards sundown, the bell was heard in the woods approaching the fort in the way a cow would come—in a roundabout way as though the cow was returning, stopping to browse, then coming on, etc. Hughes was accosted with, "Hughes, there goes your cow," and replied, "Yes, my cow is dead, but I will make that bell ring in the morning."

During the night he painted and dressed himself like an Indian and went out into the woods to the head of a "hollow" down in the depths of which the bell was heard in the dusk of the preceding day. Here he concealed himself. As soon as it was light he heard the bell begin to ring. After some time in creeping softly about he saw a big Indian with his gun in position to shoot and the little Indian with the bell on his neck walking about on hands and knees like a cow feeding. Hughes shot the big Indian, then ran and got the gun of the dead warrior and pursued the little Indian and finally came up with him and shot him with his companion's gun, which was the gun of Ben Carpenter. Hughes was so furious when he recognized the gun of his friend that he cut strips of hide from the backs of the Indian and after tanning them used them for belts.

Carpenter's grandfather once discovered the presence of Indians in his neighborhood. He knew he would be killed if he remained at home. He took his family up Elk River to Laurel Creek and up this creek to Camp Run—waded all the way. They went into a cave very difficult to find and lived there until the Indians left the country. Carpenter's father was born in this cave while the family were hiding there from the Indians. Once the Indians came into the cave and remained a considerable time while Carpenter and his family were also in there, but they did not discover the whites.

(4) A similar case is reported as tradition by *Kercheval* p. 143, which occurred near Furman's Fort, east of the mountains, at an early date. A Mr. Hogeland went out from the fort one evening in pursuit of the milch cows. He heard the bell rattle continuously in the glen and suspecting the cause, ascended a ridge overlooking the ravine, and saw an Indian with the bell attached to a small sapling, which he was gently shaking, causing the bell to rattle, hoping to decoy the owner of the cattle to death. Hogeland shot the Indian through the body. Another Indian started up, fled, and escaped. Another version of this tradition, narrated by the same author, states that a young man with Hogeland shot the second Indian. This, like the turkey call, was a favorite mode of decoy with the red warrior. By it, fourteen men fell into ambuscade and were killed at Fort Laurens, in 1793.

In 1790, "the Indians killed some cows on a creek in the upper end of Kanawha County, and hung the bells on swinging limbs, so they would ring as the wind blew. When the citizens went out to bring their cows home they were shot down. The creek was named, from this circumstance, 'Bell Creek.'" Hale's *Trans-Allegheny Pioneers*, pp. 275, 276.

(5) *Pioneer History*, p. 300.

(6) This was in July, 1791, when a body of Indians lay in ambush one morning in a cornfield at Marietta for the purpose of attacking the laborers in a flax and oat field adjoining. The workers were delayed in going to the field, and the enemy despairing of success, left their place of concealment, where their tracks were afterward found.

(7) Joshua Fleethart was born on the frontier of Pennsylvania, and grew up immured to the dangers of the forest. Standing over six feet in height, and possessed of remarkable strength and dare-devil courage, he was one of the most noted scouts on the Ohio border. For a time he lived on Blennerhassett's Island, but subsequently removed to Farmers Castle (Belpry), where he was employed as a hunter and scout. See Hildreth's *Pioneer History*, pp. 391, 401 to 405.

(8) *Annals of Augusta County*, Virginia, p. 174.

(9) *Dunmore's War*, pp. 407, 408, 409, 419.

NOTES ON CHAPTER XXI

(1) This was the farm owned by the late Benoni Mitchell, whose father purchased it from Tanner. The large two-story hewn log house still standing in a good state of preservation, was erected but not completed by Tanner. It is a fine specimen of the fort-like residence of Virginia border days. The crevices between the heavy oak logs are still firmly chinked with stone and mud. The massive stone chimney built inside the west end of the house is the most remarkable feature of this interesting relic of an era forever past. It is made of irregular cobblestone laid in clay mortar, and measures sixteen feet wide at the back. On the ground floor, it is built in the shape of a half-diamond, each angle measuring ten feet across. In each of these is a huge open fireplace, each facing a separate room. The largest of these fireplaces is four feet high by five feet wide; the other

The Tanner House
Queen, 1894

is four by four feet. They are about two feet and six inches in depth, but evidently were much deeper when first built, false backs having been built in. The spans, or arches, are composed of stone. On the upper floor the shape of the chimney was modified to that of a half hexagon. The two side walls measure each five feet across, while the center face is six feet, in which is a good sized fireplace. The chimney is twenty-eight feet high and carries its width of sixteen feet to the garret, where it narrows to eight feet. At the top it measures six feet by two and one-half feet.

The original front door was removed only a few years ago. It was a massive affair, made of black walnut boards crossed diagonally and fastened together with hammered nails. The boards had been cut with a whipsaw, or, as some declared, hewed with an axe only. The door was three inches thick, and was hung on ponderous iron hinges that reached nearly across its entire width, and were secured in place with heavy hand-forged iron clinch-nails. The house, as it stood for many years, has three rooms on the ground floor and two on the second floor. It is now owned by Mr. John A. Mitchell, a son of Benoni, and who gave me the above measurements. The house has not been occupied for the last few years. It is in a splendid state of preservation; if steps are not taken to continue this, it will soon go the way of all such landmarks. Hacker's Creek would do well to organize a society looking to the perpetuation of not only this, but many other objects of historic interest in the valley. Places where known tragedies in Indian warfare occurred should be marked with appropriately inscribed stones. Indian village sites and burial grounds should also be located and marked. The graves of old pioneers, not now properly designated, should have attention. Unless this is done, every trace of primitive life, romance and tragedy in this beautiful valley will soon pass into oblivion.

LAMENT—Since this note was written, the Tanner house has been dismantled.

(2) There was a Hughes among the "Long Hunters," but his given name is not known. This hunter could not have been Jesse Hughes; but there is reason to believe that it was a member of his family, perhaps his father.

In 1761, a number of hunters came into what is now Carter's Valley, in east Tennessee, to hunt. There were nineteen men, the company being composed of parties of men from different localities: some from several adjoining counties of Virginia, some from Pennsylvania, and one party from the Yadkin, in North Carolina, seemingly, for Daniel Boone was at the head of it. He, however, left when the company of hunters reached the place now occupied by the town of Abington, Virginia. These hunters remained several months in that region, and gave their present names to Powell's Valley, Powell's Mountain, Clinch Mountain, Clinch River, Copper Ridge, Newman's Ridge, Wallen's Ridge, and Scagg's Ridge. It is said they entered Kentucky through the Cumberland Gap, and terminated their western journey fourteen miles beyond, at Laurel Mountain.

They returned year after year in larger and larger companies, and penetrated further each year into the interior of the continent. In 1762, they came in by the way of Flower Gap, in the Blue Ridge, Jones Ford on the New River, and Blue Springs Gap, in Iron Mountain. They spent most of that year in what is now Hawkins County, Tennessee. In the fall of 1763, they went through the Cumberland Gap and hunted on the Cumberland River. In 1764, they hunted on the Rock Castle River and about the Crab Orchard, in Kentucky. Daniel Boone came among them to learn the geography of the western country. One of these hunters, Scaggs, was employed by Boone to explore the Cumberland River country, which he did. This visit of Boone must have been in some subsequent year, though it is set down by Judge Heywood as having been in 1764. This party continued to hunt in the western wilderness every year, sometimes numbering forty hunters, with pack horses. In 1771, they numbered twenty-two, among them—

"James Knox, Henry Knox, Richard Skaggs, Henry Skaggs, Isaac Bledsoe, Abraham Bledsoe, James Graham, Joseph Drake, John Montgomery, —— Russell, ——Hughes, Wm. Allen, Wm. Lynch, David Lynch, Christopher Stoph, and others—twenty-two in all, with several horses. They were so successful in getting skins they could not pack them all back; and as their hunt was prolonged, they built what they called a skin house, at a common center in what is now Green County, upon the Caney Fork of Russell's Creek, almost upon the very spot now occupied by the Baptist meeting house called Mt. Gilead. Their hunt extended into the barrens of Green River. One of the hunters named Bledsoe wrote on a fallen poplar which had lost its bark, near where Creed Haskins lived until his death in 1851: '2,300 Deer Skins lost; Ruination by God.' Part of the company returned to the settlements in February, 1772, but others remained . . . . . The party returned late in 1772, some of them having been out from home for between two and three years; they have been known ever since as the '*Long Hunters.*'" Collins' *History of Kentucky*, p. 418.

Among these hunters were Henry Scaggs, Richards Scaggs, Matthias Harman, several named Belvins—all of whom lived afterwards in eastern Kentucky, on the Big Sandy River. Tradition in that country says that Jesse Hughes came there to hunt with these bordermen. They were all famous Indian fighters and explorers. In some way Jesse Hughes must have become acquainted with them before they settled in eastern Kentucky. There were long periods when we have no account of Jesse Hughes.

Such scouts as Jesse Hughes were not developed in one generation on the wilderness. It required two or three generations on the border to develop a man with the qualities of Hughes. As we find this Hughes family scattered from eastern Virginia to the Rocky Mountains, we must conclude that they were ever in the van of civilization from their first arrival in America, and that the hatred of the Indian which reached its supreme development in Jesse Hughes was the result of warfare against the race for several generations. As we find no other family of this name in all the annals of the border, of enough prominence or experience to be a member of the company of Long Hunters, it is but reasonable to believe it was some member of this family. The evidence is all in favor of it. Refer to Chapter XI, this Volume, for notice of the Long Hunters.

—*Wm. E. C.*

(3) *Ohio Valley in Colonial Days*, Albany, 1890, p. 190.

(4) *Border Warfare*, pp. 276, 277; *DeHass*, 247, 251.

The story of the flaying of the two warriors disabled by David Morgan near Pricket's Fort in 1779, and the manufacture of their skins into belts, shot pouches, razor strops and saddle coverings, is well known to students of border history.

A very concise account of this occurrence is found in the authorities referred to, also *Our Western Border*, but not so replete. Mr. W. A. Morgan, of Petroleum, W. Va., writes me that he remembers seeing a piece of this Indian cuticle in the possession of his father, Charles A. Morgan, a son of Morgan Morgan, of Morgantown, W. Va.

A striking example of hereditary depravity is instanced in the following which is taken from Wiley's *History of Monongalia County, West Virginia*, pp. 496, 497.

"The Oregon War, called in official records the Yakima and other wars, began in 1854-5 and continued nearly three years. It was the result of a general outbreak of the Indians along the Oregon and Washington frontiers. They had over 3,500 warriors engaged in the contest. Colonel Frank W. Thompson of Monongalia, commanded Company A, 1st regiment Oregon mounted volunteers, which was afterwards re-organized as Company C, Battalion Oregon and Washington mounted rangers. Dallas Price and Oliver Price, two brothers who were descendants of the old Indian-fighting Morgans, and who were born and reared in Monongalia County, were in Thompson's company.

"Among the hottest contests of this war was a four-days' fight on the Walla-Walla River, at the point where Fort Bennett now stands—which fort, it is said, was named in honor of Captain Bennett, of Marion County, who was killed in that battle. The Indians were commanded by Peopeomoxmox, or Yellow Serpent, one of the most famous Indians ever on the Pacific Coast. During the fight, Colonel Thompson saw this chief killed by a Missouri soldier named Sam Warfield, who knocked him in the head with his gun and afterwards scalped him, in retaliation for outrages committed by his warriors. After the chief had been scalped, Oliver Price cut a piece of skin from his back, had it tanned, and made a razor strop of it—another illustration of the savage hostility existing between the Morgan blood and the Indian race."

While the battle of Walla Walla fought November 7, 1855, has no connection with the Virginia border narrative, it is only proper to state that Peo-peo-mox-mox was not in command of the Indian forces on that occasion. Two days previous this noted Chief of the Cayuse and Walla Wallas, with a few of his followers, came under a flag of truce to Colonel Kelly who was then marching against their village, and stated that he and his people did not want to fight and that they would come the next day and have a talk and make a treaty of peace. The Chief's sincerity was doubted and the peace delegates were informed that they could remain as hostages, or return to their people, in which latter case their village would be immediately attacked. With this alternative they showed good faith by accepting imprisonment, but one of the party was permitted to return to the village with a message of the agreement.

Colonel Kelly stated that when he moved against the Indians, that the latter began the fight, but Mr. A. P. Woodward, an eye witness declared that to his knowledge, one Jont, of Company B, committed the first hostile act. During the battle the peace delegates were all massacred by their guards with the exception of one, a Nez Perce boy, who had accompanied them. It was claimed by some that the Indians were killed while endeavoring to escape but others stated that the guard attempted to tie them and met with resistance, which provoked the massacre.

Creditable eye witnesses declared that there was no effort on the part of the prisoners to escape, and only one, *Wolf Skin*, an athletic Williamette, made any resistance. When attacked, he drew a concealed knife and slashed desperately at his slayers. Whatever the deduction, the damning fact remains that these Indians entered the hostile camp under the sacred pledge of a flag of truce, and in the end were forcibly detained and murdered. In point of atrocity, this crime is a parallel to the massacre of the Shawnee hostages, Chief Cornstalk and others, at Point Pleasant, 1777, alluded to in a previous chapter. For a similar outrage in 1873, Kintpuash, or Keintpoos (Captain Jack), the Modoc leader of Lava Beds fame, and three of his followers were hanged. There was no hanging at Point Pleasant, or Walla Walla.

One gentleman, who was an early frontiersman and Indian fighter on the Columbia River, stated to me in connection with the Walla Walla incident: "I knew Warfield, the soldier who killed Yellow Serpent. He was a 'cultas' [worthless] cuss, and capable of such deeds. Personally I know just how those soldiers felt. We all believed that no Indian should live and we worked to that end."

When questioned about the flaying of Yellow Serpent, he replied: "I have heard that story; it was talked of, but I never knew the trooper who did it."

Yellow Serpent had on previous occasions proven his friendship to the whites in various substantial ways. He was a warrior possessed of many noble traits of character.

(5) Civilization is a growth, an evolution, and no people in their primitive purity and simplicity of nature has ever survived a sudden and continuous contact with the higher order of life.

The moral debauchery by the whites of the Northwestern Indians was assured in their defeat by General Wayne, in 1794. Before that time, the constant wars so long waged on the border prevented a social mingling of the two races; but with the signing of the Treaty of Greenville, this barrier was removed, and the rum-steeped civilization of the Pale Face soon got in its deadly work.

The latent cause of the rapid degradation of those splendid tribes is graphically set forth in the twenty-first chapter of that most rare work, Burnet's *Notes on the Northwestern Territory*, Cincinnati, 1847. See also Hatche's *War of 1812 in the Northwest*, Cincinnati, 1882, pp. 99, 110.

(6) This cavern was named for John I. Haynes. It is on the property now owned by his daughter, Mrs. C. B. Howes, and is located at a narrows, or defile on Sand Creek, one-half mile from Crow Summit. At this point, the valley is not more than one hundred and fifty feet wide; is flanked by high and abrupt cliffs, and was an admirable place to watch for game. A few years ago, a branch of the Baltimore & Ohio Railroad was built through this defile, and the cave completely obliterated, the stone being removed for bridge building.

Mr. C. S. Wilcox, of Crow Summit, who has resided within one mile of the cave for the past thirty years, gives me the following sketch of this local landmark:

"This cave was a great watering place for teams from the interior counties of Roane, Calhoun, Gilmer and Braxton. The cave proper extended back for about thirty feet from the entrance, then forked, one fork running north fifty or sixty feet, the other nearly due west for one hundred feet or more. In each fork there was a stream of clear cool water, both of which are still running. Just

BORDER SETTLERS OF NORTHWESTERN VIRGINIA   473

above the mouth of the cave was a fine old elm tree with three large roots, one of which ran up the bare face of the rock to the soil; another to the right over the barren rock to its edge and then down to the soil; the third ran nearly perpendicular down the naked rock, tapping the ground at its base. The cave showed evidence of having been used for camping purposes. Under the overhanging rock, and to one side of the entrance, was a fire hearth, and still further back in the cave were several boulders, the size of a water pail, which showed traces of having been in contact with fire.

While this cave was never scientifically examined for the purpose of determining the nature of its occupancy, it cannot be questioned that it was an Indian resort, or camping place."

It is lamentable that one by one those historic landmarks, the silent reminders of primitive life, of stealthy hunter and warrior fierce, of a wild people's heroic struggle for existence in their own land, of the pathetic disappearance of an outraged race into the shadowy twilight of oblivion, are being swept away by the remorseless hand of greed-crazed commercialism.

(7) The keen perception which enabled Hughes to recognize this Indian from the imprint left by the deformed foot is remarkable, but in this accomplishment of the trailer the white man never surpassed the Indian, and perhaps never became his equal. Many remarkable instances are mentioned in history, one in the *Conspiracy of Pontiac*, Volume I, p. 160.

NOTES ON CHAPTER XXII

(1) As shown elsewhere in this volume, the father of Jesse Hughes settled on Elk Creek, near Clarksburg, and was killed by the Indians on Hacker's Creek, in 1778.

(2) This is a mistake. Hughes' River is not a navigable stream. But it was named for either Elias or Jesse Hughes, probably for Jesse.

(3) This would imply that Jesse moved to the Wabash before General Wayne defeated the Indians in 1794, which is error. As previously shown in this volume, he did not leave Hacker's Creek until the autumn of 1797 or 1798. Jesse Hughes never settled on the Muskingum, nor did he ever "make peace" with the Indian.

(4) Sand Creek.

(5) There is a striking similarity in the financial reverses which overtook these three great scouts, Boone, Hughes and Kenton, in their old age. Boone and Kenton, however, had some of their lands restored, while Congress granted Kenton a small pension.

It is quite probable that these three men were close associates during part of the border wars. Boone settled in the Great Kanawha Valley about 1786, and lived there some ten years. Kenton, with two companions, Strader and Yager, entered this valley in 1771, where they trapped and hunted until the spring of 1773; at which time their camp was attacked by Indians and Strader killed. Kenton and Yager narrowly escaped without guns or blankets. It is said that the hunters confined their operations to the Elk River region with headquarters at the mouth of Two Mile Creek, the scene of the tragedy. They disposed of their furs to a French trader, who was located at the confluence of the Elk with the Great Kanawha. Kenton afterwards returned to his old haunts where he remained until the breaking out of Dunmore's War in 1774. For a sketch of Boone and Kenton, see *Our Western Border*.

About twenty years ago (this, 1909) Joseph Druillard or Drouillard, died at Gallipolis, Ohio, when nearly one hundred years old. He was a man of marked intelligence, with an extraordinarily strong memory. He said that his father was a French trader in the Northwest Territory, and that he had often heard him speak of saving Kenton, when the Indians had him bound to the stake. Capt. Drouillard of the U. S. A. is a son of Joseph Drouillard, Sr.

Pierre Drouillard was a French trader among the Northwestern tribes, and interpreter for the British. Simon Girty prevailed on him to furnish the goods, worth $100, with which to redeem Kenton at Sandusky, in 1778. After the war Kenton took his benefactor into his Kentucky home and presented him with a piece of land. Drouillard subsequently entered the service of the United States in negotiating with the Northwestern Indians. In 1776 he married Angeline Labadie. He died in April, 1803, leaving several children; among them George, who was with Lewis and Clark in their Expedition to the Pacific in 1803-06. *Revolution on the Upper Ohio*, Madison, Wis., 1908, p. 128.

Some writers give the name of Kenton's rescuer: *Druyr*, a captain in the British Northwest service.

A Joseph Drouillard was an interpreter in a council of the British and Indians, at Detroit, June 14, 1778. *History of the Girtys*, p. 63.

(6) Turkey Run.

(7) Hughes' Eddy is said to have been named for Thomas Hughes, a reputed cousin of Jesse Hughes. I believe that it was named for Jesse's brother Thomas.

NOTES ON CHAPTER XXIII

(1) There can be little doubt that Thomas Hughes, Sr., was an experienced woodsman and hunter, and that he came of a family that had been in the van of the advancing settlements a generation or more before his birth. American history teaches that the most successful hunters and border settlers, scouts, rangers and Indian fighters come of families that had been in contact with the Indians far in advance of the settlements some generations. The qualities which produced their success were necessarily hereditary to some degree.—*Wm. E. C.*

(2) Names often went through a process of transformation on the border. In one family graveyard in Pennsylvania, the tombstone of the first comer from Ireland bears the name of O'Flannigan; the monuments of his children bear the name of Flanigan; while those of a later generation bear the names of Flanikan and Fleniken.—*Wm. E. C.*

(3) Lewis in his *History of West Virginia*, gives the name of this daughter as Lucinda.

(4) *History of Licking County, Ohio*, pp. 696, 697.

NOTES ON CHAPTER XXIV

(1) Lewis, *History of West Virginia*, p. 135.

(2) A tradition handed down in the Hughes family in Ohio, declared that the Indians made prisoner the young lady here mentioned, and in their flight were so closely pursued by Elias Hughes and others, that they not only killed their captive, but severed the lifeless body and hung the fragments to the boughs of trees. This outrage was the prime factor for Hughes' hatred of the race. The same tradition avers that in later years the Indians killed two of his brothers-in-law.

(3) Hale's "*Trans-Allegheny Pioneers*," p. 223.

(4) *West Virginia Historical Magazine*, Volume II, p. 35.

(5) Prof. Hu Maxwell in the *Trans-Allegheny Historical Magazine*, Volume I, pp. 234, 235.

Gen. Lewis' army camped at the mouth of Five Mile Fork of Kelly's Creek, a tributary of the Great Kanawha, in Kanawha County, W. Va. In 1874 a party of surveyors, among them Mr. Wesley Mollohan, a great grandson of George Mollohan, whose tragic death is given in Chapter XVII, this Volume, while endeavoring to locate an early survey, blocked one or more beech trees at this old camp, and discovered on one of them, axe marks covered with just one hundred annular growths.

The advance of the army camped in the midst of a fine beech grove at *Ruffner's Hollow*, near where Charleston now stands. On the bark of one of these trees was engraved the names of several of the officers in command, with dates. This tree was cut down about sixty years ago by a party ignorant of its historic value. It is claimed that when the main column came up, it encamped about a half mile lower down, on the banks of the Elk River.

(6) *Heads of Families*, Virginia, pp. 35-90.

(7) Elias Hughes was born in now Hardy County, West Virginia, about 1757, and was approximately thirteen years old when he made his first "improvement" on the West Fork River in 1770. For a confirmation of this, see his second declaration for pension and the testimony of his vouchers, this sketch.

(8) See Chapter XII, this Volume.

NOTES ON CHAPTER XXV

(1) *Licking County, Ohio Pioneer Pamphlets*, Newark, O., 1872.

(2) The following statement was made by Elias Hughes' son, Jonathan, who resided south of Utica until 1890:

"My father came to Muskingum County in 1797 in a vessel made of a large poplar tree. He started for Licking County in 1798, coming on foot and horse back, travelling as fast as their geese could walk. He was 97 when he died, was soldier in 1774 and was not married until he was 25. My father was a remarkably smart man in old age. When he was 80 he started from Utica after sunrise, and arrived at his daughter's in Muskingum County before sunset the same day, a distance of forty miles, he resided with me from 1828 until 1844 when he died. He had been blind in one eye before he made the walk spoken of, but found he was totally blind when he reached his daughter's. Outside of this he was in perfect health until he died."

(3) It is shown by the records in the War Department, Washington, that Elias Hughes, Sr., served as Second Lieutenant in Capt. John Spencer's Company, Col. Renick's Mounted Regiment of Ohio Volunteers and Militia from May 5 to May 25, 1813. This included six days allowed for travelling home at twenty miles per day, from Lower Sandusky. One Elias Hughes, Jr., served as a private in the same company from May 5 to May 27, 1813, including eight days to return home from the Lower Sandusky, allowing fifteen miles per day. This private Hughes was evidently a son of Lieutenant Hughes, although the earlier records of the war show that one Elias Hughes served as a Corporal in Capt. John Spencer's Company, 3rd (Cass') Regiment of Ohio Volunteers and Militia, from June 1, 1812, to June 1, 1813. We could readily believe that these were one and the same person, did not their terms of enlistment overlap. A granddaughter of Capt. Elias Hughes, who was still living in Licking County, Ohio, in 1905, says that two sons contracted "camp fever" while in the service and both died after returning home. An inquiry to the War Department elicited the following reply:

"The records in this office show that one Thomas Hughes (name also spelled Hughs) served as a private and a corporal of Captain John Spencer's Company of Infantry, 3d Regiment (Cass') Ohio Volunteers and Militia, War of 1812. His service commenced June 1, 1812, and he is reported on a roll from June 1, 1812, to January 1, 1813, died October 24, 1812; and on a roll from June 1, 1812, to May 31, 1813, died on — of November, 1812. No more definite information as to his death has been found.

"The name David Hughes has not been found on the rolls, on file in this office, of any organization, of Ohio or regular army troops in service during the War of 1812."

It is impossible to harmonize the term of service of this soldier, as evidenced by the foregoing record with the date of his death. Even if there were two volunteers of the same name, there is still a discrepancy in the dates. Elias Hughes, Jr., was still living in 1844, and was one of the beneficiaries in the last payment of his father's pension.

The memorable siege of Fort Meigs, Ross County, Ohio, by the combined forces of Chief Tecumseh and Gen. Proctor, endured from the fifth to the ninth of May, 1813, consequently Lieut. Elias Hughes must have participated in the defense of that fortress.

(4) Miss Jane Sleath married Capt. Elias Hughes about the year of 1780 or 1781. Her remains lie in an unmarked grave at Johnstown, Licking County, Ohio.

(5) *History of Licking County, Ohio,* Newark, 1881.

(6) *Historical Collections of Ohio*, Cincinnati, 1902, Volume II, p. 65, 66.

(7) *History of Knox County, Ohio*, Newark, 1862, pp. 18, 19.

(8) *Draper MSS*. Catalogue number 8NN37.

(9) Extract) *Draper MSS.*, 8NN38.

(10) It would appear that Col. Davidson received no reply from Mr. Jonathan Hughes. Owing to the many conflicting stories circulated concerning his father's life, Jonathan Hughes eventually refused to give any information on the subject.

I am reliably informed that Elias Hughes was not identified with any church, but he had strict religious principles; was a total abstainer, refusing wine or other intoxicating stimulants even when very old.

(11) Evidently *Capt. Samuel Brady*, soldier of the Revolution, and renowned scout of the Upper Ohio River. He was the son of Capt. John Brady, of the Twelfth Pa. Regt. Revolutionary War, who was killed by three Iroquois warriors in ambush on the West Branch of the Susquehanna River, April 11th, 1779.

Samuel was one of six stalwart brothers, of whom James, a magnificent looking young man, was shot, speared, tomahawked and scalped by Indians on the same stream, August 8th, 1779, and died five days later. These two tragedies imbittered Samuel against the Indians, and like his contemporaries, the Hughes, he swore eternal enmity against the entire race.

According to *DeHass*, p. 381, Capt. Samuel Brady was born at Shippensburgh, Pa., in 1756. *Heitman's Historical Register*, p. 96, states that he died Dec. 25th, 1795; while *Our Western Border*, p. 442, gives as the date of his death, about the year 1800, at West Liberty, West Va.

(12) From the *Newark* (Ohio) *Gazette*, January 30, 1845; in the *Draper MSS.* 8NN30.

(13) "Buckskin moccasins kept on at night have a tendency to rot."—L. C. D.

(14) The sequel of the Leading Creek massacre in 1781.

(15) It was Jesse Hughes who shot this Indian. See Chapter XI, this Volume.

(16) As previously shown in this volume, the unsuccessful pursuing party was organized in the Tygart's Valley settlements under Colonel Wilson.

(17) Bonnett, John.

(18) *Withers*, p. 345.

(19) Since the foregoing was written, Mrs. Fant informs me that through the auspices of the Daughters of the American Revolution, Hughes' grave has been marked with a marble slab, and two bronze tablets commemorative of his services in the Revolution, and the War of 1812.

For a brief of Elias Hughes, see *Tenth Ohio Annual Conference Daughters of the American Revolution*, 1908, p. 68.

NOTES ON CHAPTER XXVI

(1) It is claimed in a family tradition that Colonel Lowther owned slaves, by which means he was enabled to produce larger crops than the other settlers, and was thus prepared to mitigate the sufferings of the colonists during the "starving year," 1773. This doubtless is true notwithstanding nine years later, 1782, the census showed eighty-one blacks in Monongalia County, but none of them owned by Colonel Lowther.

Mr. Granville S. Lowther writes me that he often heard his grandfather (Col. Lowther's son Jesse) speak of these slaves, whose names were Dick and Job. They were kept at work in the fields while some of the settlers stood guard on the lookout for Indians.

Col. Lowther was not a hard taskmaster and the attachment between master and slave was mutual.

The time-honored custom of burning the *yew log* during Christmas festivities was sacredly observed. In the spring when the sap in the timber was heavy, the blacks would cut a large gum "back log" and bury it in a swamp until Christmas Eve, when it was resurrected, hauled to the cabin door and rolled into the capacious fireplace. Until this soggy "back log" burned in two, the slaves were free to come and go without restraint. This holiday invariably lasted until after New Year and was looked forward to with anticipated joy by the poor blacks.

Dick and Job would never permit sassafras to be burned in the house. If any of the Colonel's family had the temerity to place a stick of this timber on the fire, they would immediately throw it outdoors, exclaiming, "Yo' b'un dat wood an' dar'll be a fuss in de fambly afo' night."

On one occasion the Colonel sent Job to a distant part of the farm to make rails. To reach the timber it was necessary to cross a field in which was a pugnacious ram. This "lord of the flock" resented all intrusion on his grassy domain, but the peace-loving Job had hoped to pass unobserved. He reached the middle of the field when he was discovered by the enemy. The wily black knew from experience the utter futility of attempting to stand before that maddened avalanch of horn and wool, and had recourse to stratagem. He hastily drove his iron wedge into the side of a stump letting it project a few inches, on which he hung his hat. Then springing to the opposite side he bantered the enraged animal until it rammed the decoy with a force that proved self destructive. With some misgivings Job returned home and informed the Colonel of what he had done. "Well," said the Colonel, "go take his hide and then make some rails, I guess he will bunt you no more." The appreciative Job always averred that this was far better than a whipping. Such considerate acts endeared the Colonel to the blacks who on more than one occasion during Indian incursions, risked their lives for him.

Mr. Lowther writes further: "These slaves are buried in the Lowther cemetery two miles below West Milford, where all the old set of Lowthers are buried. Uncle Robert J. Lowther fell heir to this part of the estate and always cared for the graves of Dick and Job as he did those of his ancestors. He has often pointed their graves out to me."

(2) Withers' *Border Warfare*, pp. 127, 128.

(3) Lewis' *History of West Virginia*, pp. 548, 549.

(4) *Draper Manuscripts*, 36 J., 151-157.

(5) It is apparent that Col. Lowther was well educated for his day; but none of his posterity, however, to the second generation, had the same facilities for learning as he. If the early Trans-Allegheny pioneer was kept busy fighting Indians, he also reveled in a forest teeming with game, where his wants were easily supplied and for the first few years was practically exempt from any arduous agricultural pursuits. These were the conditions which in most cases lured the hunter settler across the mountains; but they soon passed, entailing on the two succeeding generations a life of unmitigated toil with but few and inferior educational advantages. "Book larnen" was considered of secondary importance. Vast forests were to be cleared, hemp and wool manufactured into wearing apparel, and the able-bodied boy or girl could, at most, be spared for only a few weeks of schooling during the mid-winter. Attainment to poor spelling, reading and writing, with a slight degree in mathematics, were deemed sufficient.

The log cabin school house with its split rail benches, oiled paper windows and great open fireplace has been too often described for repetition here. Indeed so tenaciously did this isolated region cling to its pristine life, that my first school days, one hundred years after its first settling, were spent in just such a building with the sole improvement of a single *glass* window. With the rapid opening of the richer country beyond the Ohio, the mighty wave of emigration swept onward leaving the upper Monongahela isolated, wild and primitive, which romantic life was destined to be broken only by the commercial development of the great mineral resources, a century afterwards.

(6) Miss Minnie Kendall Lowther, of Fonze, West Virginia, a lineal descendant of Colonel Lowther, has a deed executed to the colonel, in 1786, for land in Harrison County, Virginia. It is written on parchment, and is almost illegible. The deed calls for 220 acres, located on the west side of the West Fork River, given by the Commonwealth, "In Consideration of the ancient Composition of one pound five shillings Sterling, paid by Wm. Lowther * * * Asse. of Robert Parks," and is signed by "P. Henry," then Governor of Virginia.

(7) Doddridge's *Settlement and Indian Wars of Virginia and Pennsylvania*, p. 12.

(8) See Note 4, Chapter IV this Volume, for full citation from *Withers*.

This is the only instance where Richards' Fort is mentioned by *Withers*, p. 241. *DeHass* speaks of it once, p. 240. It is occasionally referred to by the scouts in their declarations for pension.

Brown's Fort, McCan's Fort, Jackson's Fort, Arnold's Fort, sometimes called Lowther's Fort and Powers' Fort, were probably only strategic and strongly built dwellings or block houses, where the immediate inhabitants fled on occasion of sudden alarms, and where scouts had regular places of meeting. It is known that some of these were of this character.

Bush's Fort, West's Fort, Nutter's Fort and Richards' Fort were the only stockade strongholds on the Buckhannon and West Fork Rivers.

The location of Richards' Fort has been a matter of dispute. By some it is thought to have stood on the west side of the West Fork River, near the mouth of Sycamore Creek, some six miles from Clarksburg. It was at this point that

Jacob Richards was granted a certificate for "400 acres on Sycamore Creek to include his settlement made in 1771." Mr. Henry Haymond, author of *The History of Harrison County, West Virginia*, writes me:

"Richards' Fort was undoubtedly located near the mouth of Sycamore, although it is claimed that it was two miles further up the river."

In 1781 Charles Stewart received a certificate for "four hundred acres on that branch of West Fork called Buffalo about three miles from Richards' Fort, to include his settlement made in 1771." Buffalo Creek is some three or four miles above Sycamore Creek.

Mr. C. W. Helmick of West Milford, who has resided all his life in that region writes me in response to an inquiry:

"Richards' Fort stood about two and a fourth miles, or two and a half miles *above* the mouth of Sycamore Creek. I have walked over the route many times. The mouth of Buffalo Creek is about one and a half miles above the Fort site, but the land on this Creek is rough for the first one and a half miles, and then opens out very fine. The homestead of Charles Stewart was certainly on this good land, which is two and a half or three miles above where the fort stood. From the center of West Milford (a short half mile above the fort site) it is three and a quarter miles to the mouth of Sycamore by the pike, and fully as far by the county road down the river, as there are two large hills between the fort site and the mouth of the last named creek, where the Richards' homestead is located and the road makes considerable detour for grade. The fort stood on the old Clarksburg Pike, nearly nine miles southwest of that town, and about a third of a mile north of the river.

"The site of Richards' Fort is marked by the spring which was inside of the palisade and now known as the *Fort Spring*. It would furnish water for all domestic purposes, including stock. Furthermore a slight ridge embracing perhaps half an acre still shows the contour of the stockade. I have often traced its boundaries, and in former years it was plainly visible, but now it is nearly obliterated by the plow. The enclosure was an oblong square, extending east and west.

"A point three or four hundred yards further south would have been more strategic, had there been water. As it was, the fort was overlooked by a hill some two hundred and fifty or three hundred yards north. This distance, however, was beyond the effective range of the guns used in those days, especially against a stockade, and if the undergrowth was cut from the hill side, it would have been difficult for an enemy to approach without being seen. The valley here is about a half mile wide.

"Clemen's Mill referred to by *Withers*, was not built until after 1800, on the West Fork River, and was the beginning of West Milford. It continued in good running order until destroyed by a flood in 1888. It has since been rebuilt on the same site."

This statement from Mr. Helmick, who, when a boy, had the ruins of the old fort pointed out to him by Jesse Lowther (who was residing there as a boy at the time of the Washburn tragedy), should settle for all time the location of Richards' Fort.

There were other Richards than Jacob on the border, mostly in the immediate vicinity. Arnold Richards owned 300 acres on the West Fork adjoining lands of William Lowther (1773). Paul Richards 400 acres adjoining Arnold Richards

(1774). Conrad Richards, 400 acres at the mouth of Lost Creek (1774), with preemption of 1,000 acres adjoining. Henry Runyon, assignee of William Richards, 400 acres on Lost Creek (1775). Adam O'Brien, assignee to John Richards, 400 acres on Lost Creek (1781). Isaac Richards, 400 acres on the waters of Elk Creek (no date). Henry Richards 400 acres on Cheat River (1776) with preemption of 1,000 acres adjoining.

Of these men, Conrad's house was attacked by two Indians in October 1778, who scalped, but did not kill a little girl playing in the yard. Richards barred the door and shot and wounded one of the warriors, when they fled. *Withers*, pp. 251, 252.

In August 1782, Arnold and Paul Richards were both killed within sight of Richards' Fort. An account of this incident is given in Chapter XXV, this Volume.

(9) Mr. J. M. Lowther, of Auburn, West Va., owns an old cross-cut saw, which his great-grandfather, Col. Lowther, purchased in Winchester, Va., and carried to the Clarksburg settlement on a pack horse. With this saw was cut the timbers for Nutter's Fort, which was built in 1774.

(10) Miss Lowther, previously referred to and who has spent many years collecting pioneer lore of that region, writes me in regard to the Hughes-Lowther exploring party: "I am satisfied that there is truth in this tradition. I have it verified from various sources. *Hardesty*, in his history of this section, speaks of it, but in many respects his statements are incorrect."

(11) *Border Warfare*, pp. 311, 312, 313.

INDIAN CREEK, a tributary of Elk River, in Kanawha County, derived its name from a similar occurrence. A small party of Indian warriors captured a boy in the Greenbrier County, and were pursued by the settlers. They were surprised in camp on this stream, one of their number killed, and the boy rescued.

(12) Bread was not always found on the domestic board of the pioneer. The inroads of wild animals on the meagre "corn patch," or other causes often left the lonely cabin with no sustenance save the products of the wilderness. But the resourceful settler found a substitute for the "Staff of Life," in jerked venison, the rabbit and the breast of the wild turkey; while the flesh of the bear often smoked and baconed, supplied the genuine meat. Pure bear oil was freely drunk by the early settler, who contended that it made his "jints supple, kept out the rheumatiz and made him longwinded." One old hunter boasted that he could "drink a pint of bar ile and it would stay down like warm coffee," and that he drank it till his "skin wuz as 'ily as a bacon rine," and his "close smelled jis like a bar." Maple syrup and sugar were sometimes eaten with the lean and dry meats. Many of the pioneer dishes were a counterpart of the Indian menu.

In 1832, George Catlin was feasted by Mah-to-toh-pa (the four bears), Second Chief of the Mandans, upper Missouri River. The principal dish consisted of pemmican and marrow fat. Pemmican was made by drying buffalo meat very hard and pulverizing it in a large mortar until nearly as fine as sawdust. It was then packed in bladders, or sacks of skin for future use. Marrow fat was collected by breaking buffalo bones and boiling out the fat and pouring it into distended buffalo bladders. After cooling, it became quite hard like tallow, and had the appearance and very nearly the flavor of the richest yellow butter. This pemmican and marrow fat were eaten as bread and butter, and were highly relished by Mr. Catlin. Catlin's *North American Indians*, Philadelphia, 1891, pp. 189-191.

The Caughnawaga Indians mixed rendered bear's fat and maple sugar until the fat was almost as sweet as sugar, in which they dipped their roasted venison. Drake's *Indian Captivities*, Buffalo, 1853, p. 198.

(13) *Border Warfare*, p. 127.

NOTES ON CHAPTER XXVII

(1) *Virginia State Papers*, Volume V.

(2) *Virginia State Papers*, Volume VI.

(3) The four following letters are from *Virginia State Papers*, Volume VI.

(4) Lieut. Biggs brought counter charges against Capt. McColloch and a general court martial was ordered by Brigadier General Benjamin Biggs, but the *Virginia State Papers* contain no record of the results of such order.

The findings would have to be approved by the Council of State and it is possible that a record of the proceedings is to be found in the *Council Journals*.

(5) *Virginia State Papers*, Vol. VII, p. 28.

(6) *Virginia State Papers*, Volume VII, p. 179.

(7) *Virginia State Papers*, Volume VII, p. 260.

(8) *Virginia State Papers*, Volume VII, p. 298.

(9) *Virginia State Papers*, Volume VII.

(10) From his widow's claim for pension, admitted December 15, 1879, it is shown that "Alexander Lowther, when twenty or twenty-one years old, was drafted from Harrison County, Virginia, in Captain John Bozarth's Company, Virginia Militia, War 1812, and served from August 30 to December 10, 1814. Was on duty at Norfolk, Virginia, occupation farmer, born in Harrison County, Virginia. Personal appearance: height, five feet, nine inches, hair light, eyes blue, fair complexion. Died April 30, 1864. Widow's maiden name, Rachel M. Neel; married Alexander Lowther June 6, 1842." Widow was granted eight dollars a month from March 9, 1818, the date of the approval of the act.

This is the only military record of any of Col. Lowther's family that my copyist has been able to find in the Government Pension Office.

(11) Jesse Lowther died at his residence in Chrisman, Illinois, Oct. 21, 1909, two years after Dr. Lowther's letter had been written.

NOTES ON CHAPTER XXVIII

(1) *Border Warfare*, p. 288.

(2) The changed mode in spelling the name by Alexander Cumming McWhorter, born in 1771, evidently applies to the first syllable only, when, perhaps, "Mac" may have been abbreviated to "Mc." In all records which have come to my

notice, including a few *prior* to the Revolutionary period, the name is spelled with "o" and in identically its present form:"McWhorter." Usually in most records "Mac" in any name appears as "Mc." In Scotland, as in this country, it is not only spelled McWhorter and McWhirter, but also McWherter. Hugh McWhorter of Armagh who died in 1748, left but four known children from a family of eleven, whose descent is followed in the text quotation from George C. McWhorter. Others of his family may have left descendants, but I have been unable to trace them with certainty.

(3) *Proceedings of the New Jersey Historical Society*, 1865, Volume X, p. 66.

(4) *American Ancestry*, Volume III.

See Heitman's *Historical Register* for notice of Alexander McWhorter, Chaplain of Knox's Artillery Brigade, Revolutionary War.

That the McWhorter was a "Lowland Clan" is obviously a mistake. "Mac," or "Mc," meaning "son," is purely *Gaelic* and is foreign to the *Sassenach* or Lowland Saxon.

(5) In 1790, Gilbert, John and Thomas McWhorter, resided in Warwick Township, Orange County, N. Y.; two in each family. The only other of the name listed in that State at that time was Matthew, with eight in family, who lived in Washington County. *Heads of Families, N. Y.*, pp. 147-193.

It is claimed that Matthew McWhorter came from Balibay, Armagh, Ulster, Ireland, with Rev. Thomas Clark and his congregation, and landed at New York, July 28th, 1764. This colony settled in then Charlotte County, N. Y., and erected a town, naming it New Perth, now Salem. A Presbyterian Church was founded, of which Alexander was an Elder and a staunch contributor. He was active in the Revolutionary War, and received a soldier's land grant. He was also a member of the State Legislature at Albany, Kingston and Poughkeepsie, 1780-81-82. He had several children, those known being Matthew, John, James, Jane and Rebecca. Matthew, Jr., born 1767, it is claimed served in the Washington County Troops, Revolution, and was given a land grant; but I have found no record of his service. He died in Salem, N. Y., Feb. 15th, 1812.

The Virginia branch of the family has it that Henry had other brothers, among them John and Robert.

It is found from regimental muster and payrolls, that James and Matthew McWhorter were enlisted in the Charlotte County, N. Y. Militia, Revolutionary War, and were granted 500 acres each Land Bounty Rights.

James McW[h]orter and John and Thomas McWhorter served in the Orange County, N. Y. Militia, 4th Regiment, Col. John Hathorn. This Regiment was called out "on an alarm of Minisink," July 1777.

John McWhorter served in Capt. William Jackson's Company, Col. Henry B. Livingston's 4th Regiment New York Line, from May 5th, 1778, to February 5th, 1779.

Thomas McWhorter enlisted in the New York, "The Levies," Col. Lewis Duboise.

As "The Levies" were drafts from the different militia regiments and the people direct, the two several enlistments of John and Thomas McWhorter, may, perhaps, have been by the same men.

William McQuarter was enlisted in the First Regiment New York Line; Col. Goose VanSchaick, Revolutionary War. Evidently this soldier's name was McWhorter, and the difference in spelling was due to the peculiar pronunciation. By act of May 10th, 1779, Congress voted the officers and men of this regiment its thanks "for their activity and good conduct in the late expedition against the Onondagas."

A private of the New York State Troops was paid $6.66 2-3 a month.

(5½) This was evidently Lieut. Col. Richard Livingston's First Canadian Regiment, of which Isaac Nichols was First Lieutenant.

(6) The "chevaux-de-fris" was placed across the Hudson, or North River, at Plum Point, at a cost of over a quarter million dollars, continental money. It was an iron chain eight hundred feet in length, buoyed up with heavy spars and rafts of timber. The work was surveyed in the autumn of 1776, but it was completed only a short time when the British destroyed it, October 7th, 1777.

Lossing's *Field Book of the Revolution*, Volume II, pp. 114, 164, 168.

(7) Henry McWhorter's old Bible is preserved by Judge J. C. McWhorter, of Buckhannon, West Va., in a fine mahogany case made especially for that purpose.

(8) The census of 1790 shows that Robert McWhorter, with seven in family; and Wm. McWhorter, eight in family, were then residents in Cumberland County, Pa.; and that Hugh McWhorter, nine in family, was a resident of Northumberland County, same state. *Heads of Families, Pennsylvania.*

One Robert McWhorter and Sarah Johnston were married in Philadelphia, Pa., December 15th, 1743. There is but little or no doubt that this Pennsylvania family were descendants of Hugh McWhorter who came from Armagh, in 1730. However, this has not been verified.

One Robert McWhorter served in the Revolution. It would appear from his declaration for pension, that in 1777 he was drafted at Middleton, Pa., for two months in Capt. Crouche's Company, Col. Elder's Regiment Pennsylvania Militia; and was engaged in scouting throughout the country about Wilmington and Newport; and assisted to pull up and destroy a bridge over Whitley Creek, at the time Gen. Washington was encamped on the hill near by. This was done for the purpose of retarding Gen. Howe, then in pursuit of Washington.

McWhorter was discharged after serving only fourteen days but was immediately drafted for two months in Capt. John Ruthaford's Company, Tenth Battalion, Col. Alexander Lourey's Regiment Pennsylvania Militia. He served his full term and was released; but in two months after, was again drafted for the same length of time, in the same company and regiment and with no change of officers. During this term he was in the fiercely contested battles of Brandywine and Germantown. It will be remembered that in the first of these, the raw militia distinguished itself in repelling the onslaughts of the British regulars. After serving this tour and in the fall of the same year, McWhorter joined Capt. James Colier's Company, Col. Robert Elder's Regiment Pennsylvania Militia, as a substitute for his brother William, who had been drafted for two months. During this enlistment he was in several skirmishes but was subsequently marched to Redding, and encamped at Perkyoming Creek for some time.

Afterwards, and near the close of the war, he was employed for six months to take provision boats up the Susquehanna River, for Gen. Sullivan's army. The boats, —— in number, went from Middleton to Sunbury, where he was discharged, having served three and a half months.

Robert McWhorter was born near Philadelphia, Bucks County, Pa., Feb. 16, 1747. He resided in Bucks and Lancaster Counties until about 1809, and then moved to near Brownsville on the Cumberland River, Kentucky. He lived there until about 1827, when he moved to Washington County, Indiana; and was still residing there in November 1832, at which time his application for pension was made. He was granted a certificate for twenty dollars and fifty cents a year.

(9) In a former magazine article, I state that the McWhorter mill was the first in (now) Lewis and Upshur Counties, which is a mistake. In this same article and a subsequent brief of *"Henry McWhorter and Descendants,"* there appear several errors, mostly typographical, which are here corrected. See *West Virginia Historical Magazine*, Volume I, No. 3, Volume II, No. 1.

(10) *Border Warfare*, p. 241.

See Note 4, Chapter IV, this Volume, for a full account of the Washburn tragedy.

(11) The Harrison County records of 1784 refer to "Edmund West's Mill," which evidently was only a water power hand-mill. It is tradition that John Hacker's hand-mill was rigged to run by water power. Many of the settlers possessed only the mortar and pestle for crushing grain, and had often to go considerable distance for the luxury of a hand-mill.

(12) Hildreth's *Lives of the Early Settlers of Ohio;* pp. 486-488. Also, *Pioneer History of the Ohio Valley*.

(13) In 1906, through the instrumentality of Dr. J. M. McWhorter, the graves of Henry McWhorter and wife were marked with a modest, though substantial granite monument.

(14) This company was mustered on the Alkire farm on Hacker's Creek, below the mouth of Life's Run. Nicholas Alkire, Sr., was a member of this company.

(15) Walter McWhorter was Major 137th Regiment, 20th Brigade, 3rd Division, Virginia Militia. His commission on sheep skin, bearing date May 9, 1831, is signed by John Floyd, Governor, and is in my possession. The pocket of the Major's old shot pouch with knife scabbard, powder horn and gun charger is owned by his grandson, L. D. McWhorter of Buckhannon, West Va. The charger, neatly carved from buck-horn, measures a "squirrel load" only.

(16) Margaret Kester was the daughter of a Revolutionary soldier. From his two declarations for pension made at Clarksburg (West) Va., August 21, 1832, and May 18, 1835, it would appear that Joseph Kester was born in Pennsylvania, 1753, and when nine years old removed with his parents to Brock's Gap, Virginia.

In 1780 he entered the militia as a substitute for Conrad Kester, on a three months tour under Capt. Biddell, Major Hamilton and Col. Nalls. The command was marched from Augusta County to Richmond, Edmunds Mill and a creek called Hot Water, where they were engaged watching the movements of the British.

Shortly after his discharge and return home from this service, he was called out for a second term of three months in Capt. George Huston's Company, Col.

Benjamin Harris, Virginia Militia. They went from Brock's Gap to Richmond, thence to Hot Water near Williamsburg, where his regiment was sent in pursuit of the British, who had taken some cattle belonging to Americans. The command came up with the enemy about four hundred strong, and an engagement of two hours ensued in which some seventy or eighty of the British were killed. The American loss was light.

Soon after this occurrence, Kester was included in a detail of about four hundred men who were placed on the road near "Old Jamestown" to cover the retreat of the Americans who were defeated there under "Generals Wane and Millenburgh." (This was evidently the battle fought near Jamestown Island on the evening of July 6, 1781, where the American forces under Generals LaFayette and Wayne were led into an ambuscade and defeated by Cornwallis. *Field Book of the Revolution*, Vol. II, p. 466-468.)

The Americans fell back to the main army and Kester was afterwards marched down the river to Portsmouth, thence back to Petersburg, where he was discharged two weeks prior to the surrender of Gen. Cornwallis, Oct. 19, 1781, and twenty days in excess of his enlisted time. Kester stated that he was not given a written discharge, nor was it usual for the militia to receive such. He was vouched for by Hamilton Gass, D. Morris, John Hoff and John C. Lowther, and was granted a pension of $30.00 a year, which was afterwards reduced to $22.22 a year. Singleton, special pension agent, who re-examined Kester, gave him a favorable report.

Joseph Kester came from Brock's Gap, Rockingham County, Virginia, to (now) Harrison County, (West) Virginia, about 1787, where he was still living in 1835. He died a few years later in Marion County, Ohio. He married Miss Morrison, whose family resided on Hacker's Creek. Among their children were Alexander, Joseph, Conrad, Archibald, Mary, Susan who married a Jenkins; Margaret, and another daughter who married Cupp.

Joseph Kester was the brother and half-brother of twenty-seven children, twenty-four boys and three girls.

He was a great wrestler, athletic and quick in movement. Once while at a house raising and when the building was nearing completion, he was pitched head first from the top of the wall, but caught with the instep of one foot over the projecting eave-pole. He hung for a moment, and then purposely loosing his hold, whirled in mid-air and landed on his feet.

(17) Since writing this chapter, Dr. J. M. McWhorter died at the residence of his daughter, Mrs. Leni L. (McW.) Jenkins, in Buckhannon, West Va., November 9, 1909. For a brief sketch of his life see *History of Upshur County, West Va.*, pp. 512 to 515.

Rev. Mansfield McWhorter died at the home of his only child, Mrs. E. R. Dyer, near Philippi, W. Va., January 5, 1915.

(18) Judge Joseph M. McWhorter, and his brother, Judge Henry C., have both died since this writing.

NOTES ON CHAPTER XXIX

(1) *Heads of Families*, Virginia, p. 25.

(2) *Heads of Families*, Virginia, p. 25.

(3) Colonel Russell was an able officer in the Revolution, and was actively engaged on the border during the long Indian wars immediately following. He is often mentioned in the border annals. He volunteered as a private in Colonel James Wilkinson's Company of mounted Kentuckians in an expedition against the Wabash Indians in 1791. He distinguished himself by leading the charge as a non-commissioned volunteer in the only fight during that expedition. *Burnet's Notes*, p. 121.

Captain Silas Zane was an active partisan during the Revolution and the border wars. He was commissioned First Lieutenant, 13th Virginia Regiment, December 28, 1776; and was promoted to the rank of Captain, February 9, 1777, and served until February 12, 1778. Captain Zane participated in the defense of Fort Henry when it was besieged by the Indians and British in September, 1782. Beach's *Indian Miscellany*, p. 59; *Border Warfare*, p. 357. *Lossing* says that Captain Silas Zane was in the defense of Fort Henry when invested by Indians, August 31 and September 1, 1777. *Field Book of the Revolution*, Vol. II, p. 498.

Refer to Chapter XIII, this Volume, for notice of the sieges of Fort Henry.

(4) *Heads of Families*, Virginia, p. 25.

(5) *Heads of Families*, Virginia, p. 69.

(6) *Withers*, pp. 428-30, says that the Indians "took Mrs. Bozarth and two boys prisoners." The names of these boys were Lot and Zed.

Zed was a "jolly fool" and seemingly did not fully comprehend the fearful work done by the Indians. While the warriors were engaged in killing the children, Zed came up to them and demanded to know what they were doing. He cursed them roundly, called them "Damned black rascals." This strange conduct led the superstitious Indians to believe that the child was demented and was an object of Divine commiseration and protection. Gently stroking his head, they ejaculated, "Brave boy, brave boy." After reaching the Ohio country, the marauders were safe from pursuit and they proceeded with leisure often camping and hunting. They killed game and dressed some of the choice pieces to carry home to their families. These epicurean morsels Zed would steal and devour. His captors, in real or feigned anger, brandished their tomahawks over his head, threatening him with instant death; but the half-witted lad cursed them loudly, answering deadly threats with vituperative abuse. His mother, stricken with grief, fearing the exasperated Indians would slay the child, urged them to "whip him soundly and make him behave." Tenderly patting the boy's head, they would answer, "Him too brave; him too brave. No hurt. Great Spirit." Zed once escaped from his captors and took refuge in a hollow log. The Indians in their search for him came so near that the boy heard them, and betrayed his place of concealment by hurling at his pursuers a volley of calumnious epithets.

Tradition says that two of Bozarth's daughters were also carried off in this raid, and that they returned from captivity with their mother and the two boys. Philip Reger's second wife was the younger of these daughters. Elizabeth, the older, became the second wife of Uriah Forenash and after his death, she is said to have married James Morrison. She died 1862. Both Forenash and Morrison were in Lord Dunmore's expedition against the Indians in 1774. Morrison was an apprenticed cooper in England, but ran away before he had worked his allotted time. His ocean voyage was paid, for which he worked after landing in America.

The "Forenash plantation" referred to by *Withers*, p. 121, was the farm of Jacob Forenash. Jacob was an easy going, honest man, content with his lot and not over zealous in procuring either riches or renown among men. His "plantation" consisted of fifty acres, mostly hilly land, and was a part of a tract which had been abandoned by a former settler. Jacob bought the land of his friend, Mr. Joseph Hall, and paid for it in work. He fixed up the abandoned cabin, cleared a "corn patch" and lived in contented poverty. His improvement was such a marked contrast to the large farms around him, that in time it was dubbed the "Forenash Plantation" and as such went down in history.

The Bozarth homestead, the scene of the Indian massacre—the last committed by the Indians on the Virginia frontier—stood east of the present railroad station of Lorentz, south of the pike and opposite the residence of the late Valentine Lorentz, the old homestead of Jacob Lorentz. *Maxwell* places the scene of this tragedy on the Buckhannon River, and within the present bounds of Barbour County, which is clearly a mistake. See *History of Barbour County*, W. Va.

(7) As daring as was Reger's feat, it was eclipsed in a later day by Robert Somerville, in (now) Gilmer County, W. Va. A party of settlers, among them Somerville, were seeking new homes on the waters of the Little Kanawha, and while passing over the bridle path leading along Bloody Run and Horn Creek, they saw, after reaching the latter stream, the tracks of two large panthers in the snow. The men followed the trail to a crevice in a ledge of rock, where the beasts had entered. A fire was kindled in the mouth of the lair, with the purpose of "smoking out" the game, but this was not accomplished. For some cause the smoke did not enter the den. It was then suggested that some one go in and dispatch the fierce cats; but one after another of the party found from actual trial that the entrance was so *small* that it would not admit the passage of his body. Finally Mr. Somerville, the last man of the party, who was also the *largest*, weighing over two hundred pounds, entered the cavern and shot the panthers. In point of daring, either this or Reger's feat surpass that of General Israel Putman's celebrated achievement of entering the wolf's den.

BLOODY RUN derived its name from the following incident: Some hunters in an early day had their rendezvous on this stream. Two of their number quarrelled and so serious was the disagreement that they had recourse to arms. Each with drawn knife sprang behind a tree, and from these sheltered positions fought a bloodless duel. In derision of this farcical battle the stream was called *Bloody Run*.

(8) Kercheval's *History of the Valley*, p. 344.

(9) A similar, though more ludicrous incident occurred in the same region at a later day. Lewis Collins was widely known for his unsurpassed physical strength; and one evening a tall muscular stranger mounted on a very diminutive mule rode up to his gate and calling Collins from where he was lounging on the grass near his cabin door, announced tha the was a "Kain-tuck-ian;" and while passing through the country had heard of him as the strongest man in "these shur parts;" and that he had ridden several miles out of his way to fight him. Collins, who was noted for his peaceable disposition, demurred; but the Kentucky "colonel" explained:

"I hev nev'r met my match in a fight and if thar's a better man on Gwads green airth than me, I want ter know hit; an' yo' must fight."

During this colloquy, Collins had passed into the road and was now standing near his strange caller; and noting the striking disparity of the rider and his mount, a humorous thought came to him and he said:

"Stranger that's mighty purty meul yo'r a ridin'."

"Y-as:" was the whimsical reply, "an' he thinks a lot uv me; and I'm jes' sot on him. Fact is we'r mos' like brothers an' when one's 'nsulted tother'n kicks."

"I see thar's quite a 'semblance;" rejoined Collins, "but I didn't s'pose yo' wus so close kin."

"Looker hyre stranger:" flashed the giant as a scowl of anger darkened his brow, "don't cast no inflections on this shur brigade; or 'Ill git down an' do wot I come fer."

"I meant nuthin':" placated Collins, "I wus a complimentin' yo' both an' if the meul kin stan' hit, I cain't see whar yo' hev any right ter flar' up."

"Wal' be kerful:" was the half doubting yet ominous warning.

"He has the trimest laigs thet I ever seed on a meul," said Collins stooping as if to make a closer inspection. "Will he kick?"

The Kentuckian lounged lazily in his saddle as he drolled.—

"He don' kick nuthin'; gentler'n a dawg."

Collins bent lower and getting his ponderous shoulder under the mule, he gave a mighty upward heave, when both mount and rider was lifted clear of the ground and sent sprawling over the low rail fence into the yard.

"Why I thought yo' said thet he wus gentle," exclaimed Collins in feigned surprise as the discomforted pugilist extricated himself from the struggling mule; "I hope yo' haint hurt none."

The giant got on his feet and was, at first, inclined to anger; but as the ludicrousness of the situation dawned upon him, he burst into a loud laugh and exclaimed:

"An' I hope yo' haint hurt stranger: That's an ol' trick uv hisn an' I only wanted ter s'prise yo'. I reckon we wont fight none this time, an' if yo' air willin' we'll shake han's an' call hit squar'."

"Sartin:" exclaimed Collins as two brawny hands met in a hearty clasp across the fence; "but yo'r not goin' yit. We'll put yo'r brother in the shed an' give him some co'n an' yo'll go in an' stay all night."

(10) The attachment of the early settler for his faithful dog was affectionate, and often as strong as life itself.

The Hurst family (see Chapter XXXI, this Volume), while residing on the Cheat River, owned a magnificent dog, which had often protected the children from the attacks of wild animals, and was no small factor in keeping the table supplied with meat.

One day this dog chased a deer near the cabin, and the animal hard pressed, dashed for the river, which was frozen over to near the center, where the water ran swift and cold. When the deer struck the ice, it fell and slid into this open channel and instantly disappeared. The dog following, went also into the water, but reappearing caught with its front feet on the edge of the ice, but could not climb upon it. The family soon gathered on the bank but owing to the frail nature of the ice, which also sloped materially to the center, none could venture on it. The dog whined piteously, and Hurst wanted to attempt to go to him, but his wife, knowing that he would meet with certain death, prevailed on him not to do so. Finally the poor dog became exhausted, and losing its hold, was swept from sight by the icy current, while the entire family stood weeping on the shore.

(11) *Border Warfare*, p. 429.

NOTES ON CHAPTER XXX

(1) *Kercheval*, p. 121.

(2) A small branch of the Muskingum River, so named from a white woman prisoner, Mary Harris, captured by the French and Indians when about ten years old. She was, when Gist saw her there in 1750, upwards of fifty years old, and had an Indian husband and several children. There was a small Indian town on *White Woman's Creek* when visited by Gist. *Gist's Journal*, p. 41.

(3) It is shown by the Census of 1782 and 1784, that both a senior and junior Jacob Brake were at that time residents of Hampshire County, Virginia. In 1784, Jacob, Sr., represented a family of nine, an increase of one over 1782. The family of Jacob, Jr., numbered four each enumeration.

In 1782-84, John Brake was a resident of Hampshire County, Virginia, with three in family. This is supposed to have been John Brake, Jr., a son of the baron. It is claimed by the descendants of the baron that he was the founder of the Brake family in America. I have not looked up his antecedents, but it would appear that another member, or branch of the family, was represented in Jacob Brake, Sr., perhaps a brother to the baron. These are the only parties of the name appearing in the Census of Virginia from 1783 to 1785. There was, however, one Isaac Brake living in Hampshire County in 1781.

The first government census of the United States was made in 1790, but unfortunately the schedules for Virginia are missing, having been destroyed when the British burned the Federal Capitol, August 25, 1814. This loss is irreparable. *The Heads of Families* of Virginia as published by the United States Government, 1907, is compiled from some manuscript state enumerations of 1782, 1783, 1784 and 1785, and the tax lists of Greenbrier County from 1783 to 1786. Only thirty-nine of the seventy-eight counties are represented in these schedules, which are, as there is reason to believe, incomplete.

The early Census Enumerator met with difficulties now unheard of. It was a new phase in the life of the settlers; many imagined that its design was an increase of taxation, while not a few opposed it from a superstitious belief that it would incur Divine displeasure. See *Heads of Families*, p. 5.

Jacob Brake, Jr., who is listed in the enumeration of Hampshire County, may have been the returned Indian captive. The fact that the land records of Monongalia County show that he made a "settlement" on the Buckhannon in 1776, is not proof that he resided there at that time. There is evidence that many more of those, who early secured homesteads in the Trans-Allegheny under the lax land laws of Virginia, were not actual residents of that region until after the close of the Revolutionary War. The case of Jacob Reger, Sr., noted in the preceding chapter, can hardly be regarded as a solitary instance of its kind. Nor should Brake's military service at Buckhannon in 1779 be accepted as positive proof of a local residence. It was in that year that Augusta County militiamen were on duty in the settlements, and it is not improbable that soldiers from Hampshire County were also in such service.

(4) "HAMPSHIRE COUNTY, May 22, 1781.
"DEAR SIR,
"We are under the disagreeable necessity of troubling you for your assistance immediately. I received an Express just now from the Commanding Officer of this County, for as many men as can be had, not at any Rate, less than three hundred from Frederick County. Col: Vanmeter recommends that they who can, be mounted, may immediately mount & come & the Foot to follow as quick as Possible. We look upon it, that our lives & Fortunes are in danger of being taken, we don't know how soon — Yesterday the militia of this county march'd to Capt. Stumps; there made a halt, and sent a party of light Horse to see what Discoveries they could make about Jacob Brake's Mill on the South Fork. they were repuls'd by a fire & got off without any Loss, & brought with them two prisoners — they can't make any Discovery of the number of the Enemy. I understood by one Powel who came from Claypoles, on the Lost River (the Commander of the Tories), that he expected by last night to command one thousand men — Col: Vanmeter, in his Express, has left the proceedings in a great measure to my judgment, & I think the only sure Remmedy to apply, would be to prevail upon Genl: Morgan to take a Tower amongst them, which seems to be their chief Resin — they are daily dareing him. The People of the County, who are our Friends, are so much connected, as well as related, that they are, on these accts very bacward to turn out, so that the welfare of our wives & children seems greatly to depend upon your Immediate Assistance. they threaten, if successful, to kill Men, Women & Children. I shall leave you to consider the deplorable situation of your Suffering Friends & Neighbors — "

"N. B. Let the men be officer'd & well arm'd"

"Capt: Beall, the Bearer, has seen the Express & can inform you more particularly the contents thereof. — "

LETTER FROM COL: ELIAS PASTON TO THE COUNTY LIEUTENANT OF FREDERICK —   "PR: EXPRESS."

From *Calendar of Virginia State Papers*, Vol. II, pp. 113, 114. See note 1, *Appendix IV*, this Volume.

(5) *Kercheval*, pp. 121, 195 to 199.   Lewis *Hist. of W. Va.*, pp. 139-144.

(6) See *Appendix IV*, this Volume.

(7) Cutright says that the name of the eldest son of John Jackson was Joseph. This is a mistake. *History of Upshur County, West Virginia*, p. 181.

NOTES ON CHAPTER XXXI

(1) Jacob Cozad was a resident in Monongalia County, Virginia, in 1782, six in family. *Heads of Families;* Virginia, p. 35.

(2) *History of the Rise and Progress of the Baptists in Virginia*, by Robert E. Semple, Richmond, 1810, p. 336.

(3) *Border Warfare*, pp. 419, 421.

(4) This stream is also locally known as "Lawson" Run, but in a note on page 421, *Border Warfare*, it is called "Lanson" Run, a typographical error.

(5) It is not at all improbable that women sometimes accompanied the warriors in their incursions into Virginia. I have been told by the Yakimas, Warm Springs Indians and other tribes that very often their women, usually two or three in number, would voluntarily go with war parties even to distant parts. They performed the ordinary duties of the camp; the preparation and cooking of food, keeping moccasins and other wearing apparel in repair and looking to the general comfort of the men. None but the bravest of women would venture on such expeditions, and when fortunate enough to return they were ever afterwards entitled to sit in all councils and participate in the war dance with the most valiant warriors of the tribe.

The Indian *Amazon* will compare favorably with her sister of any race. History is not lacking in instances of her prowess. De Smet gives a vivid account of Flathead women assisting in the repulse of a superior band of Crow warriors on their camp in 1846. *Early Western Travels*, Cleveland, 1906, Volume 29, p. 333.

Two Moon, a Nez Perce warrior of note, told me that at the Battle of the White Bird, Idaho, which was the opening fight of Chief Joseph's War, 1877, he shot down a soldier and his wife ran to the wounded man and while he was raising to his knees she unbuckled his cartridge belt and then went to another fallen trooper and secured his belt and also a box of cartridges, and ran back with them to her husband, who was still exchanging shots with the enemy. Later, at the Battle of Big Hole, Montana, when the camp was broken and the Indians were retreating, this same woman stopped and took from a wounded soldier not only his cartridge belt but a box of ammunition which he had been carrying and was holding close in his arms. With some of the other women she stood guard over this coveted prize until Two Moon came and took charge of it. The former of these feats, especially, will compare with that of Elizabeth Zane, or Mollie Scott, at the Siege of Fort Henry, one hundred years before.

(6) *Border Warfare*, p. 420.

(7) An interesting illustrated description of Prof. Holmes' observation on this cave can be seen in the American Anthropologist for July 1890, also *Tenth Annual Report of the Bureau of Ethnology*, Washington, pp. 475-478.

(8) *Art in Shell of the Ancient Americans*, Holmes, *Second Annual Report of the Bureau of Ethnology*, Washington, pp. 289 to 293.

(9) *Travels and Adventures in Canada, 1760-1776;* by Alexander Henry, New York, 1809; pp. 175, 179. Drake's *Indian Captivities*, Buffalo, 1853; pp. 330, 331.

(10) *Memories, Official and Personal;* Thomas L. McKenney: New York, 1846. Volume 1, pp. 100, 102, 107, 114.

(11) I have found unmistakable evidence of reverence for the rattlesnake among the Yakimas of Washington. Shut-to-mon-en, "sheared-head" so called from the peculiar mode of cutting the hair as practiced by his father and grandfather, who were noted warriors and whose name he inherited: as one of the head men of the tribe gave me this bit of lore on the subject.

"Long time ago Injun no kill Wah^k-puch [rattlesnake] only when some man die from bite of him snake. Then Injun kill some [rattlesnakes] for dead man. Wah^k-puch once talk same as people: but all Injun no understand him. You see *ke-nute'* over there?" pointing to an ancient land slide in the barren and rocky hillside near Toppenish Creek: "Lots Wah^k-puch live there. Long time ago woman see big Wah^k-puch there near creek. Maybe fifteen feet long. Him had horns. Wan'-tah, big medicine man, tell me he once see this snake. Him horns tipped with black; and red band across forehead. Him Head Chief all Wah^k-puchs. Some his people live at Selah Gap [twenty-eight miles away] some live over in Rattlesnake Mountain. Chief have to run too much, him get headache. So him send one his boys to be chief at Selah Gap; and one to be chief at Rattlesnake Mountain. Him then leave one other boy to be chief at *ke-nute'*: while him go live at Dry Creek, over towards Bickleton Mountain: where, maybe, him now stay."

"Do the boy-chiefs still live at the places where they were sent by the Head Chief?"

"I don't know: maybe so. Maybe him go 'way. Train make too much noise at Selah Gap. Make um head ache. Maybe all go 'way from there. I don't know."

Many of the older Yakimas have declared to me that they would not kill a rattlesnake. If they did, the Wah^k-puch Chiefs would know of the crime and immediately determine in council what should be done with the offender. If he was to be punished, one of their men [snakes] would be delegated to bite him. There could be no escape; for the Wah^k-puch is possessed with power to find an enemy under any and all conditions. I have been told wonderful stories of such occurrences. Only certain medicine men who have received occult power from the Chief Wah^k-puch, can anticipate the intentions and movements of these terrible emissaries and forestall them. This sometimes has been done.

Formerly the Wah^k-puch were very numerous; but with the advent of the white man they greatly disappeared. The teamsters and cattle men waged incessant warfare against them, using their long-lashed whips; and the Chiefs held council and said: "No use: can't fight him. We quit." Since that time the Chiefs have lived deep in the caverns of the earth and are seldom, if ever, seen. Death speedily overtakes any person, other than the medicine men referred to, who chances to look upon a Wah^k-puch Chief. There is only one such medicine man now living who has seen one of these Chiefs. This man understands the language of the Wah^k-puch, and often hears them talking and laughing; and calling to him from out the desert, while his companions can detect no noises breaking on the stillness. With the "power" conferred upon him by the Chief Wah^k-puch, he can overcome the deadly poison of the rattlesnake's fangs, which he has twice done upon his own person. His skill as a healer, however, covers the scope of human ills. He cannot be induced to speak of the source of his "power," only when practicing the occult. To do so idly would be to destroy the potency of his magic. This gift from Wahk-puch is sacred, semi-divine, and must be referred to solely when invoking its aid.

A Japanese gentleman recently told me that some of the old men in his country declare that there is a monster serpent in the mountains where they go for nuts, which, if seen, is swiftly followed by the death of the unfortunate one.

NOTES ON CHAPTER XXXII

(1) Before the country was settled, the rattler grew to a fabulous size.

A hunter on Cheat River saw what appeared to be the trail of some object dragged through the weeds. He followed it to the river, where he found near the water an immense rattlesnake with the body of a small fawn between its distended jaws. The reptile had undertaken more than it could manage, and not being able to disgorge, had made for the water but died before reaching it.

THE DEADLY RATTLESNAKE
Photograph from Life.

As late as 1841, two small boys named Waldeck, were setting "dead-falls" for squirrels about a corn-field on the Butcher farm on Leading Creek, in Lewis County. While one of them was on his knees fixing a trap, he was struck in the side between the hip and first rib by a large rattler. Its fangs entered his body through homespun tow pantaloons, and shirt of the same material. Before the child could be carried home, his body was entirely swollen. In the greatest of agony, he survived only a few hours. A measurement of the wounds left by the fangs of the reptile, showed a jaw expanse of six inches. The following year, near this spot, a rattler was killed that measured a little over eight feet in length.

The white man — many of the Indian tribes would not molest the rattlesnake — was not the only enemy of these terrible creatures. The blacksnake pursued both the rattler and the copperhead to the death. Eagles and hawks preyed upon them in common with other varieties of reptiles: the wild hogs devoured them wherever found, and even the timid deer was their most deadly foe.

Henry McWhorter, Jr., was hunting on Cove Creek, in Gilmer County, West Virginia, and from the brow of a hill he saw on a neighboring ridge three deer standing in an attitude of alertness, gazing intently at some object near them. Suddenly, one after another they sprang upon the object and off again with such agility that no perceptible pause could be noticed between leaps. This they repeated two or three times, and then went away. McWhorter went to the place and found a large rattler cut in pieces by the sharp hoofs of the deer.

The copperhead, in one respect was more to be dreaded than the rattler. The latter seldom, if ever, makes an attack without first giving notice of its presence by a warning whir-r-r of its tail; while the former is as silent as it is vicious, and strikes with deadly precision at every moving object within reach. As "Ill-natured as a copperhead" is a mountain proverb still in vogue in the Trans-Allegheny. The pain attending the bite of this reptile is indescribable, as I can attest from personal experience when a boy. A person accustomed to them can detect their presence by the odor, which is not unlike that of green cucumbers.

Owing to their ease of detection, the rattler has been wholly exterminated within the thickly-settled regions, while the copperhead is still more or less prevalent throughout the hill districts. In the earlier days, forest fires destroyed vast numbers of these poisonous reptiles. They will not flee from this danger, but will coil and strike until killed by the heat.

(2) DUCK CREEK — The first settler on this stream shot a wild duck which was so tough that it could not be eaten, hence the name.

NOTES ON CHAPTER XXXV

(1) See *Connelley's Letter, Appendix III,* this Volume.

(2) *Settlements and Indian Wars,* p. 104.

(3) While riding across a sage-brush plain with a Yakima Indian hunter, his dog "jumped" a jack-rabbit, which headed for a low place in a small ridge in front of us and slightly to our right. The Indian remarked that if a coyote was after the "jack," it would not follow as the dog was doing, but would go over the high ground to our left and pick up its prey on the other side of the raise. I asked him how he knew that the rabbit would turn that way. He answered: "Him always go that way. But he no fool coyote." The dog was baffled at the point where the Indian had predicted the change in the course of the "jack," and when the trail was again found the truth of his assertion was verified.

At another time when sitting with this same hunter close to a camp fire in a wild canyon on a cold night, suddenly the frosty stillness was broken by the long quavering howl of a distant timber wolf; mingled with the treble notes of a coyote or prairie wolf. The Indian listened attentively and said: "Wolf, him lickin' poor coyote. Coyote have two children [cubs] and she put um over hill away from wolf: then fight um wolf so he no ketch um little coyote children." He had, during the day, pointed out to me the tracks of a large timber wolf along with those of a coyote. He then told me this story of the savage sagacity of the timber wolf.

Years ago when some of his people were crossing the Cascades and when near one of the big lakes far up in the mountains, they saw a large herd of deer, no less than forty, surrounded by a cordon of wolves and being singled out and devoured at leisure and as hunger impelled. From all appearances the slaughter had been going on for some time, perhaps days, they could not tell. They saw some of the corraled deer attempt to escape, but they were always throttled by the alert and nimble sentinels. In those days the Indians did not dare attempt to cross that part of the mountain, only in large bodies. Often small parties would disappear, being destroyed by these dreaded animals. From some cause the wolves afterwards became decimated in numbers.

(4) *Annals of Augusta County*, pp. 7, 20, 22, 42.

NOTES ON APPENDIX

NOTES ON APPENDIX I

(1) The claim that David White "was present at the taking of the Stroud family" can hardly be accepted as reliable. He may have had connection with the Bull Town massacre, but evidently his captivity was during Pontiac's War, and long prior to the Stroud tragedy. It must be conceded that Colonel Westfall was a partisan, who sought excuse for the sanguinary deeds of his ancestor. But no amount of pen veneering can ameliorate this crime of crimes. The massacre was premeditated, and wholly unjustifiable. The friendly Delawares had nothing to do with the Stroud murder.

(2) This was the time when Captain White and Leonard Petro were captured while scouting on the Little Kanawha, Sept. 1777.

See *Note 8, Chapter X, this Volume.*
Border Warfare, pp. 232, 233.
DeHass, pp. 234, 235.

(3) This is the first account of George Collet that I have ever found. On page 422, *Dunmore's War*, his name appears along with those of Tovenor Ross and John Ward, as whites who fought with the Indians in the Battle of Point Pleasant; but it is taken from Col. Westfall's letter.

Early on the morning of the battle (Oct. 10, 1774) Joseph Huey and James Mooney were hunting about one mile from the camp, when they were discovered and fired upon by the Indians. Huey fell, but Mooney escaped and gave the alarm, and within a few moments the general engagement was on. Ross may be accredited with firing the first fatal shot of this memorable battle. It was his shot that killed Huey. Mooney went down later in the fight. *Dunmore's War*, pp. 271, 272.

Captain or Lieutenant John Frogg, also spelled Frogge, was a handsome, dashing young man of Staunton, Virginia, who, it is said, accompanied General Lewis' army as a sutler. Courageous, generous and gay, he seemed a great favorite with the entire command. His fondness for display was, doubtless, his undoing. Before going into the battle, he arrayed in gaudy attire, donning a brilliant red coat or jacket, and his hat decorated with feathers and ribbons. Such garb was sure to attract the fire of the Indians, who evidently regarded him as a great leader. This accounts for the desperate courage displayed in the attempt to secure his scalp.

" * * * Amongst the slain were many brave men, both officers and privates; and a Magistrate of this place, Mr. Frog, a very worthy Gentleman, was also killed, so eager were the Indians for his scalp, that one man shot three of them over him, endeavoring by turns to scalp him." Extract from a letter written at Staunton, Virginia, November 4, 1774. *Draper MSS. 14 J57. Dunmore's War.* p. 296.

It is narrated that about noon in Staunton on the day of the battle, Frogg's little girl awoke from sleep, screaming that the Indians were killing her father. Her mother quieted her, and she again fell asleep, only to be aroused, crying, by the same terrifying vision. This was repeated the third time, which so overcame the mother, that she, too, cried out in anguish. Her neighbors were attracted by the distress, and upon learning the cause, joined in the lamentations, "until all Staunton was in a state of commotion." — *Annals of Augusta County,* pp. 136, 137.

(4) Old edition: new edition, 290.

(5) This version of the killing of Capt. White, varies somewhat from that given in Chapter X of this Volume. The only material difference, however, is the number of Indians engaged. White was doubtless betrayed by Dorman, but he was killed by one Indian only, nor was he scalped. *Withers:* pp. 340, to 343, gives the following account of the death of White, and Dorman's part in the tragedy.

"On the 8th of March [1782], as William White, Timothy Dorman and his wife, were going to, and in sight of Buchannon fort, some guns were discharged at them, and White being shot through the hip soon fell from his horse, and was tomahawked, scalped and lacerated in the most frightful manner. — Dorman and his wife were taken prisoners. The people in the fort heard the firing and flew to arms; but the river being between, the savages cleared themselves, while the whites were crossing over.

"After the killing of White (one of their most active and vigilant warriors and spies) and the capture of Dorman, it was resolved to abandon the fort, and seek elsewhere, security from the greater ills which it was found would befall them if they remained. This apprehension arose from the fact, that Dorman was then with the savages, and that to gratify his enmity to particular individuals in the settlement, he would unite with the Indians, and *from his knowledge of the country, be enabled* to conduct them more securely to blood and plunder. He was a man of sanguinary and revengeful disposition, prone to quarrelling, and had been known to say, that if he caught particular individuals with whom he was at variance, in the woods alone, he would murder them and attribute it to the savages. He had led, when in England, a most abandoned life, and after he was transported to this country, was so reckless of reputation and devoid of shame for his villainies, that he would often recount tales of theft and robbery in which he had been a conspicuous actor. The fearful apprehensions of increased and aggravated injuries after the taking of him prisoner, were well founded; and subsequent events fully proved, that, but for the evacuation of the fort, and the removal of the inhabitants, all would have fallen before the fury of savage warriors, with this abandoned miscreant at their head.

"While some of the inhabitants of that settlement were engaged in moving their property to a fort in Tygart's Valley (the others removing to Nutter's Fort and Clarksburg) they were fired upon by a party of savages, and two of them, Michael Hagle and Elias Paynter, fell. The horse on which John Bush was riding, was shot through; yet Bush succeeded in extricating himself from the falling animal, and escaping though closely pursued by one of the savages. Several times the Indian following him, would cry out to him, '*Stop, and you shall not be hurt — If you do not, I will shoot you*,' and once Bush, nearly exhausted, and in despair of getting off, actually relaxed his pace for the purpose of yielding himself a prisoner, when turning around he saw the savage stop also, and commence loading his gun. This inspired Bush with fear for the consequences, and renewing his flight he made his escape. Edward Tanner, a mere youth, was soon taken prisoner, and as he was being carried to their towns, met between twenty and thirty savages, headed by Timothy Dorman, proceeding to attack Buchannon Fort. Learning from him that the inhabitants were moving from it, and that it would be abandoned in a few days, the Indians pursued their journey with so much haste, that Dorman had well-nigh failed from fatigue. They arrived however, too late, for the accomplishment of their bloody purpose; the settlement was deserted, and the inhabitants safe within the walls of other fortresses.

"A few days after the evacuation of the fort, some of its former inmates went from Clarksburg to Buchannon for grain which had been left there. When they came in sight, they beheld a heap of ashes where the fort had been; and proceeding on, became convinced that the savages were yet lurking about. They however, continued to go from farm to farm collecting the grain, but with the utmost vigilance and caution, and at night went to an outhouse, near where the fort had stood. Here they found a paper, with the name of Timothy Dorman attached to it, dated at the Indian towns, and containing information of those who had been taken captive in that district of country.

"In the morning early, as some of the men went from the house to the mill, they saw the savages crossing the river, Dorman being with them. Thinking it best to impress them with a belief that they were able to encounter them in open conflict, the men advanced towards them, — calling to their companions in the house, to come on. The Indians fled hastily to the woods, and the whites, not so rash as to pursue them, returned to the house, and secured themselves in it as well as they could. At night, Captain George Jackson went privately forth from the house, and at great hazard of being discovered by the waylaying savages, proceeded to Clarksburg, where he obtained such a reinforcement as enabled him to return openly and escort his former companions in danger, from the place of its existence.

"Disappointed in their hopes of involving the inhabitants of the Buchannon settlements in destruction, the savages went on to the Valley. Here, between Westfall's and Wilson's forts, they came upon John Bush and his wife, Jacob Stalnaker and his son Adam. The two latter being on horseback and riding behind Bush and his wife, were fired at, and Adam fell. The old gentleman rode briskly on, but some of the savages were before him and endeavored to catch the reins of his bridle, and thus stop his flight. He however, escaped them all. The horse from which Adam Stalnaker had fallen, was caught by Bush, and both he and Mrs. Bush got safely away on him.

"The Indians then crossed the Allegheny Mountains, and coming to the house of Mrs. Gregg (Dorman's former master) made an attack on it. A daughter of that gentleman, alone fell a victim to their thirst for blood. When taken prisoner, she refused to go with them, and Dorman sunk his tomahawk into her head and then scalped her. She however, lived several days and related the circumstances above detailed."

In Morton's *History of Pendleton County, West Va.*, 1910, p. 64, is this item touching the career of Timothy Dorman:

"In 1781 took place what seems the last Indian raid into this county. A party of redskins, led by Tim Dahmer, a white renegade, came by the Seneca trail to the house of William Gragg, who lived on the highland a mile east of Onego. Dahmer had lived with the Graggs, and held a grudge against a daughter of the family. Gragg was away from the house getting a supply of firewood, and seeing Indians at the house he kept out of danger. His mother, a feeble old lady, and with whom Dahmer had been on good terms, was taken out into the yard in her chair. The wife was also unharmed, but the daughter was scalped and the house set on fire, after which the renegade and his helpers made a prudent retreat. The girl was taken up the river, probably to the house of Philip Harper, but died of her injuries."

To *Withers'* account of the killing of Capt. White, *Thwaites* adds the following note:

"L. V. McWhorter informs me that White, who was a prominent settler, was once with others on a hunting expedition, when they surprised a small party of Indians. They killed several, but one active young brave ran off, with White close at his heels. The Indian leaped from a precipice, alighting in a quagmire in which he sank to his waist. White, with tomahawk in hand, jumped after him. In the struggle which ensued, White buried his weapon in the red man's skull. The victim's father was among those who escaped, and for a long time — McWhorter says 'several years' — he lurked about the settlements trailing White. Finally he succeeded in shooting his man, within sight of the fort. Mrs. White was an eye-witness of the tragedy. McWhorter claims that Withers is mistaken in saying that White was 'tomahawked, scalped and lacerated in the most frightful manner.' The avenging Indian tried to get his scalp, but an attacking party from the fort were so close upon him that he fled before accomplishing his object. McWhorter reports another case, not mentioned by Withers. One Fink was 'killed by Indians in ambush, while letting down a pair of bars one evening, just in front of where the Buckhannon court-house now stands.' "

Fink, here mentioned, is undoubtedly the John Fink who was killed just one month prior to the death of White, and as depicted by Col. Westfall. *Withers*, p. 318, says of this tragedy:

"On the 8th of February, 1782, while Henry Fink and his son John, were engaged in sledding rails, on their farm in the Buchannon settlement, several guns were simultaneously discharged at them; and before John had time to reply to his father's enquiry, whether he was hurt, another gun was fired and he fell lifeless. Having unlinked the chain which fastened the horse to the sled, the old man gal-

loped briskly away. He reached his home in safety, and immediately moved his family to the fort. On the next day the lifeless body of John was brought into the fort — The first shot had wounded his arm; the ball from the second passed through his heart, & he was afterwards scalped."
See Chapter X, this Volume.

(6) Old edition — new edition pp. 340, 341, 342.

(7) Old edition — new edition, pp. 313 — See Chapter X, this Volume.

(8) Colonel Westfall evidently wrote the date of young Fink's death from *Withers'* work. Refer to Chapter X, this Volume, for inscription on Fink's gravestone.

(9) *Withers* — new edition, p. 313.

(10) *Withers* — old edition; new edition, pp. 135, 136. There is considerable reference to the Bald Eagle tragedy throughout this correspondence. For the date of the death of this historic chief, see Chapter XI, this Volume.

(11) Jacob Scott came to the western settlements early. In 1781, he was granted a title to "400 acres on Scott's Run adjoining land claimed by David Scott, to include his settlement made in 1771." Scott's Run flows into the Monongahela in Monongalia County.

(12) The incident here referred to, occurred, according to *Withers*, in 1794, in Tygart's Valley, where a few families were gathered for mutual protection. Mr. Canaan and three of the children were killed and Mrs. Canaan made prisoner. The Indian, who shot Canaan, was struck on the head with a drawing-knife and brought to the ground by a young man named Ralston, who, with the other inmates, fled into the darkness and escaped. Mrs. Canaan was afterwards redeemed from captivity by her brother. — *Border Warfare*, p. 422.

Maxwell shows clearly that it was Joseph Kinnan and not Canaan, who was killed, and the time of the tragedy was May 11, 1791. The warrior's nose was severed by the blow from the drawing-knife in the hands of young Ralston, or David Conley. The Indians retreated to the middle fork of the Buckhannon, where they lay concealed several weeks, until the wounded warrior had recovered, when they proceeded on uninterruptedly. *History of Randolph County, West Virginia*, pp. 186, 187.

(13) *Border Warfare*, pp. 232, 233. Refer to Note 8, Chapter X; and Note 2, Appendix III; this Volume, for further notice of Petro, or Pedro.

(14) *Draper Manuscripts* 8XX, 70, 71.

This letter, perhaps the only one extant of its class from Colonel Westfall, conveys a fair idea of the nature and value of his original manuscripts destroyed by fire several years ago.

(15) Harmony Church, the first built on Hacker's Creek. It was constructed of hewed logs, with a gallery, and stood on a slight eminence a short distance above the mouth of Jesse's Run. Since this writing it has been dismantled.

(16) *Draper Manuscript*, 8ZZ45.

David H. was a son of David Smith, referred to elsewhere in this Volume.

David Smith married a daughter of John Hacker, the pioneer; was a Captain of Militia and officiated at the military funeral of William Powers, the soldier and scout. He was tall and very erect at eighty.

(17) Mr. Hacker is evidently in error as to his great-grandfather's arrival in America. John Hacker was born during the ocean voyage, or within a few weeks after the landing of the parents.

(18) A careful search of the cemetery in question failed to disclose the grave of any William Hacker.

(19) John Hacker died April 20, 1824, and such is the date given on his gravestone. The error made by Mr. H. M. Hacker in copying, is doubtless responsible for Dr. Draper giving the year 1821 as that of John Hacker's death. *Border Warfare*, p. 121.

The stone, which formerly marked Hacker's grave, bears this inscription:

"1 8 2 4
J . H .
A G E D 81 Y .
3 M. 9 D.
J O H N   H A C K E R
B O R N
J A N U A R Y 1st
1 7 4 3 . O . S .
D I E D   A P R I L 20th
1 8 2 4 "

This monument was in later years supplanted by the present, more pretentious one, though both are slabs of native sandstone. The old one is now placed at the head of a grave in the same row with Hacker and his wife, with three or four graves intervening. These are doubtless some of their children, but they are unmarked.

Some of John Hacker's descendants maintain that he was born on sea, during the ocean voyage of his parents: and that the letters "O. S." appearing in conjunction with the date of his birth, denote "on sea." This may be true, but it is also probable that they stand for *Old Style*, or the Julian method of recognizing the time prior to September 3, 1752, at which time the English statute went into effect, adopting the Gregorian, *New Style* Calendar.

(20) The foregoing letters from Mr. Hacker, and all subsequent correspondence in this Appendix are from the *Draper Manuscripts* 3U.

Rev. John T. Hacker was born on Hacker's Creek, (West) Virginia, March 6, 1812. He lived there the greater part of his life, and for many years was a minister of the M. P. Church. In later years he moved to the middle west, and died at Green, Kansas, December 13, 1896.

(21) This occurred at the time of the West tragedy on Hacker's Creek, noted elsewhere in this Volume.

(22) This was 1769 instead of 1760.

(23) A mistake — the Hacker's came with the Pringles.

(24) Old edition — See pp. 122, 135, 136, 137, 378, 379, 390, new edition.

(25) John Hacker settled on Hacker's Creek, some five miles above West's Fort, now Jane Lew, and in an opposite direction from "Jackson's Mill on the West Fork." This is not the only mistake current with the residence of this early pioneer. *Cutright* states as tradition, that after John Hacker settled on Hacker's Creek, "he began the trade of a blacksmith. * * * * * So great became the demand for his services, both in the Buckhannon river settlement and Hacker's creek settlement, that business judgment advised him to open up a shop at Lorentz, a small place four miles west of Buckhannon town on the summit of the divide between the waters of Hacker's creek and the Buckhannon river." *History of Upshur Co., West Virginia*, pp. 181-82.

No evidence has been found in support of this statement. The distance between Jane Lew and Buckhannon is about sixteen miles and there could be no business motive in Hacker removing his shop to the Buckhannon settlement. Lorentz is situated about two miles east of the divide between the Buckhannon River and Hacker's Creek, as the trail ran, and in the early settling of the country it was unknown as a village. John Hacker, however, was not a blacksmith. He "tinkered" at gun repairing only. One of his sons was a blacksmith in later years.

J. K. P. Maxson, of Berlin, West Virginia, owns an old grindstone, said to have belonged to John Hacker and Jacob Cozad, Sr. I remember seeing the date, 1770, that had been cut on the side of the stone. Long use in Maxson's blacksmith shop has worn away that part of the stone on which this date was cut. Beyond question, this was the first grindstone brought to Hacker's Creek Valley. It should be placed in the Museum of that State.

(26) The obvious mistake in Mr. Hacker's preceding letter, that Alexander Hacker was the author of *Border Warfare*, was due to a misunderstanding of his daughter, who was receiving the dictation while "very much embarrassed." John Hacker, the pioneer, supplied no small amount of the manuscript material for *Border Warfare*.

(27) John T. Hacker did not serve in the Confederate Army, Civil War. He was refused enlistment on account of age.

(28) This was Hezekiah Hess, who, with others from Lewis County, was dropped from the Revolutionary pension roll. From his declaration for pension, made September 19, 1833, it would appear that Hezekiah Hess was born October 9, 1756, in Dutchess County, New York, and was brought to Hampshire County, Virginia, when but seven months old, where he continued to reside, exclusive of his military service, until 1822. He then moved to Lewis County, Virginia.

In June, 1776, Hezekiah Hess with eleven other men volunteered from Hampshire County (now Hardy County, Virginia), as a private Indian spy under Captain Pogue, of the Twentieth Battalion of Augusta Militia, who was then recruiting men to act as border spies. The Twentieth Battalion was commanded by Colonel Hugart, but Colonel Sampson Mathews had general command of the Augusta Militia. With his men, Captain Pogue immediately marched to the fort in the Little Levels on the Greenbrier River, in now Greenbrier County, West Virginia, and entered on the duties of spying throughout the wilderness on the headwaters of Jackson River, Back Creek, Greenbrier River, New River, Kanawha, Gauley and Elk Rivers; Stoney Creek, Locust Creek, Mill Creek and other contiguous streams. The scouts reported from time to time at the fort in the Little Levels until November (1776). Cold weather setting in, they were disbanded and retired to the fort at Warm Springs for the Winter. During this term of service, the Indians committed no other mischief in the settlements, than merely to steal a few horses, which occurred in September. The scouts immediately gave pursuit and came up with the marauders, descending Ten Mile Creek. A few shots were exchanged, but no lives lost on either side. The Indians fled, abandoning the horses, which were recaptured and restored to their owners.

In March, 1777, at the Warm Springs Fort, Hess again volunteered for the season as Spy and Ranger under Captain Pogue and Lieutenant Kennison, for service principally in the same territory as the preceding year, with headquarters at Pogue's Fort, in the Little Levels. During this Summer, the scouts made one excursion down the Gauley River to the mouth of Birch River, from thence back to the mouth of Meadow River, ascending this stream to Donnelley's Fort in the Big Levels of Greenbrier. Here they met Captain Stewart and Donnelley with some of their Rangers of Donnelley's Fort. Captain Pogue with his spies continued up Meadow River to Pogue's Fort.

In August of this year, "a large body of Indians, supposed to number upwards of one hundred warriors, appeared on Locust Creek, near the lower end of the Droup." (Locust Creek is in Pocahontas County and flows into the Greenbrier, north of Droup Mountain.) Captains Pogue and Chain formed a junction of their men and marched to attack the enemy, who were found concealed among rocks and fallen timber. The Indians were routed with the loss of eleven warriors killed, and were pursued to the Gauley Mountains. The whites suffered no fatalities, but five of their number were wounded. This was the only occurrence worthy of note during the season. The spies continued in the field until December, when they retired to the fort and spent two months in repairing and fortifying their stronghold.

In February, the company under the same officers were again placed in the field, and continued spying until the following December. During this time of service, in spite of the vigilance of the spies, the Indians would enter the frontier settlements and steal horses, but generally the thefts were detected and the property retaken before the warriors could get out of the country.

In the month of July of this year, a family on the head of Tygart's Valley were massacred by a band of straggling Indians, and Captain Pogue hastened to the scene with his Rangers, but the Indians had fled beyond pursuit. Some men from Warwick's Fort had buried the dead and then given chase to the foe.

In March, 1779, at the Little Levels, Hess again enlisted as a private in Captain Pogue's Company of Spies, and served principally under Lieutenant Kennison until the last of the following November. In May of this year, a small party of Indians made their appearance on Anthonius Creek (evidently Anthony Creek), a tributary of the Greenbrier River, and killed a part of two families, burned their dwellings and outbuildings and destroyed their cattle. The perpetrators of this tragedy then bent their way across the Greenbrier River, over the mountains to Gauley (River), thence to Peter's Creek (in now Nicholas County), where they were overtaken and surprised by Lieutenant Kennison and eight men, including Hess. A volley from the scouts brought down three of the warriors, when the others, twelve or fifteen in number, precipitately fled, leaving three captive children and some stolen horses, which were returned to the proper persons.

In July of the same year, Hess in company with five others, under Lieutenant Kennison, was scouting on Big Elk River near the Fork Lick, and while making preparations to camp for the night they were surprised and fired upon by a party of Indians, slightly wounding one man in the shoulder. The scouts were vastly outnumbered, and immediately took flight and were closely pursued until nightfall closed the chase. The fugitives eventually reached the fort in safety. These were the only occurrences of note during the season. Alarms were frequent, and neighborhood horses stolen, but were usually recaptured.

Hess, in his first declaration, claimed never to have received any discharge paper, but was merely dismissed by his captain; and that he was not under any regular field officer, but his captain was subject to orders from Col. Hugart, Commander of the 20th Battalion Augusta Militia; and of Col. Sampson Mathews, Commandant of the whole County of Augusta. For sketches of Sampson Mathews, see *Annals of Augusta County*, pp. 109, 148, 161, 166, also Peyton *History of Augusta County*, p. 173.

Hess, it would appear, saw no further service as an enlisted scout. His declaration was drawn by James Bennett, and he was vouched for by Abram Whetsel and Jacob Wymer. In November 1833, Hess was allowed eighty dollars per annum to begin March 1831. Subsequent statements from John Mitchel, Samuel Bonnett and William Powers, to the effect that they being acquainted with Hezekiah Hess, knew that he was too young to have been a soldier in the War of the Revolution, with the sequence that the soldier's name was stricken from the pension roll.

Under date July 14, 1834 or 1836 (date very indistinct) W. G. Singleton examined Hess and sent the following report of his age and Revolutionary service to the United States Pension Office:

"* * * , 72 years old July 18th but has no record of his age, — sometime during the Revolutionary War (as he thinks, cant say in what years) Capt. William Pogue inlisted 10 men including himself at Morefield, Hardy Co. Va for 18 months, and marched them to the Warm Springs, Bath Co. Va. marched from Hardy Co. about Mar. 1st got to Bath the last of March remained there until the next spring then went to Cloverlick in latter ———————— (very illegible and maybe a county name) county remained there until Dec. following. There were upwards of a hundred men at Warm Springs, this was all the service he done and all he gave unto James Bennett who wrote his declaration before Thomas Heneman. Bennett said he must have the first draw. he replied it was too much. Bennett got all but $5. Since his pension was granted has been to Weston the county seat of Lewis several times, distant 11 miles to see after his money,—always walked.

Benjamin Copelan aged 82, Christopher Nutter aged 74 both gave Hess a very bad name stating that he is the greatest liar in the vicinity and are of the opinion that his statement is a fabrication."

(Signed) W. G. SINGLETON.

Evidently there were then, as now, scores of patriots (?) who felt no compunction in defrauding their beloved country, for which they had so valiantly offered their lives; but in justice let it be remembered that the majority of these old frontiersmen, Hess included, as evidenced by the familiar "X" in his signature, were very illiterate and were victims of conniving mercenaries, who drew up and had them sign mendacious "declarations," of which they were wholly ignorant. Admittedly a boaster, it is hard to conceive that Hess would, in so short a time, make two declarations of such varying import. Charity would suggest that like John Cutright, his illiteracy and credulity were imposed upon, his honor ruthlessly sacrificed for a selfish motive. This undoubtedly is true. J. Wamsley was actively engaged in writing fraudulent declarations on contract, and usually received as compensation all the first money drawn. Some were signed knowingly, others were not. He wrote those of the "Messrs. Bonnetts," who could neither read nor write. He offered to write declarations for Abram Reger, a son of Jacob Reger, Sr., and Samuel Bonnett, who were too young for service in the Revolutionary War; but the offer was spurned. Many of the old soldiers fled to distant parts to avoid prosecution, while others were financially ruined in their efforts at restitution. James Bennett, a young man of ability, who wrote Hess' declaration, was inveigled into this business by Wamsley, and became a fugitive in Texas. He was afterwards pardoned and permitted to return home.

With no means of proving his military service, Hess' name was never restored to the pension roll; and his last years were marked with penury and suffering. He survived his wife, and lived with his daughter, Charity, on Hacker's Creek, where he died October 4, 1848. The descendants of Hess claim that he served in the War of 1812, but I have found no record of such service. No claim for pension was ever filed.

Hezekiah Hess left the following children: Charity (married Thomas Hacker), Mary (married Thomas Parsons), Matilda (married ———— Stanley); Melissa, and Abraham. He is known to have had another daughter, Nancy, who married Isaac Williams and went west about 1840, and of whom nothing more was ever heard.

Hess' declaration was sworn to before Thomas C. Hinzman, born in Harrison County, Virginia, March 2, 1797. Near the close of the War of 1812, he enlisted with some Virginia troops, and was sent to Norfolk, Virginia, but saw no active service. He lived on Buckhannon Run, Lewis County, the greater part of his life, and was Justice for more than thirty years. He is reputed to have killed the last wolf slain in that country.

His father, Henry Hinseman (as then spelled), was a Revolutionary soldier, who settled on Simpson's Creek, Harrison County, sometime after the close of the war, but removed to Hacker's Creek, about 1799, where he died December 24, 1827. It would appear from the evidence on the claim for pension made April 4, 1859, by his widow, Charity Hinseman, nee Coon, that he enlisted or volunteered, at Philadelphia in the Summer of 1779 or 1780, for six or nine months and was attached to the artillery. At the expiration of his term, he re-enlisted for three years in a Pennsylvania Regiment and served till close of the war. His regiment was commanded a part of the time by Col. Butler and one of his Captains was Gray or Kenneda. This second enlistment was "about the time of the Revolt of the Penna. Line at which time several of the Regts. were consolidated." This was the famous revolt of thirteen hundred troops under Gen. Wayne, January 1781, at Morristown, Penn. The widow stated that she married Henry Hinseman in Harrison County, Va., Sept. 16, 1794, by John Loveberry, a Baptist preacher; and that she received Bounty Land from the U. S. under Act March 3, 1855. Henry Hinseman's name appears on the December 1780 Muster Rolls, Capt. Grey's Company, late Line of Pennsylvania.

Records in the Comptroller General's office May 31, 1791, show that the "State of Pennsylvania is indebted to Henry Hinseman, late of the New Levies in the sum of seventeen pounds, ten shillings with the lawful interest from the first day of July, one thousand seven hundred and eighty-three. The same being due up account settled in the office. Pursuant to Act of Assembly passed the first day of April, 1784."

(Signed)   JOHN DONNALDSON.
Reg. Gen. Office.

In October 1859, a certificate was granted to Charity Hinseman for $23.33 per annum with back pay from March 4, 1848. On Sept. 4, 1860, her name was dropped from the pension roll, but was re-instated June 16, 1866. In her petition made May 26, 1865, at the age of one hundred and five years, in the County of Roane, State of West Virginia, Charity Hinseman testified that she was unable to labor on account of her advanced age and that she had not "in any manner encouraged the rebels or manifested a sympathy with the cause of the rebellion." She died March 13, 1872, at the home of her son-in-law, Stephen Starcher, near Spencer, Roane County, West Va., when one hundred and twelve years old. Records in the Treasury Department show that at the time of her death Mrs. Hinseman was receiving $10.27 per month and the last payment was made to Stephen Starcher, Administrator, and pension left children were Thomas C. and John Hinseman, Mary Rains, Elizabeth Hughes and Rebecca Whitzel.

The following genealogy is copied from four leaves torn from the old family Bible as testified to by J. M. McWhorter, Clerk of Roane County, and submitted as evidence in Mrs. Hinseman's claim for pension. The name Charity, however, appears on the margin, near the center of the list, but it is here placed in its proper order:

"Henry Hinseman and Charity Coon was married in the year of our Lord 1794, Sept. 16th.

Abraham Hinseman was born the 29 day of June 1795.
Thomas Hinseman was born the 2nd day of March 1797.
Sarah Hinseman was born the 6 day of february 1799.
Massey and a
Elizabeth Hinseman was born the 19 day of March 1801.
Henry Hinseman was born the 20 day of March 1803.
William Hinseman was born March the 19, 1805.
David Hinseman was born May the 10, 1807.
Mary Hynman was born the 29 Jan. 1811.
John Hynman was born 11 July 1813.
Rebecka Hinseman was born the July 19, 1816.
Charity Hineman was born the 25 of february 1819."

It has been claimed that Henry Hinseman was a deserter from the Hessian troops; but his grandson, Mr. David B. Hinzman, line of his son Thomas C., writes me that such tradition is without foundation, and that his grandfather served six years in the Revolution, part of this time under Gen. Morgan, and was wounded three times.

(29) The McWhorter Mill at West's Fort, was afterwards owned by the Jacksons. In later years, there was a mill further up the creek, on the David Smith farm, and in my earliest recollections was known as the "Boram Mill." It was in the creek above where the dam for this mill was afterwards built, that the body of the murdered Indian was said to have been sunk.

The killing of the Indian and sinking him in Hacker's Creek, must have been perpetrated by another than Hess, who did not settle on the western waters until 1822. Tradition says that this Indian was killed on the David Smith farm, some distance above the West Homestead, and was one of the party engaged in the West tragedy in 1787 and who, on that occasion stabbed and scalped the little daughter of John Hacker. It is probable that the warrior met death at the hands of some of the Hackers, when visiting the settlements during peace in after years.

(30) Mr. Hacker writes me, "When a lad, I was often at the house of Aunt Martha Bonnett, widow of John Bonnett, who was killed by Indians in 1787. She was quite aged, and I sometimes did chores for her. I frequently heard her speak of border times and Indian forays. She resided three or four miles south of Jane Lew. There was a ledge of rocks, where the Indians once sat and repaired their moccasins. You certainly remember the old 'Bug-a-boo Hollow.'"

(31) Bald Eagle was murdered about 1772, just prior to the Bull Town massacre. If William Hacker's wife was killed by the Indians, it must have been after these events. The Mrs. Hacker, who was attacked by the Indians near West's Fort in June 1778 (*Border Warfare*, p. 245), is claimed to have been the wife of William Hacker. (*History of Upshur County*, West Virginia, p. 182.) I have been unable to find any other data touching the case.

(32) This could not have been Elijah Runner, of notorious border fame. See note 40, this correspondence.

(33) Rev. William Granville Hacker was born on Hacker's Creek, West Virginia, 1841, and like his kinsman, Rev. John T. Hacker, grew to manhood without the facilities of obtaining an education. In September 1862 he enlisted as a private in the Fifteenth West Virginia Regiment and served to the close of the war. He participated in nineteen regular battles and twenty-seven skirmishes; and was wounded three times, the most serious being in the right thigh, received during an engagement near Richmond, Virginia.

Mr. Hacker was a clergyman for years, living in Wichita, Kansas. Since the writing of this note, he died April 13, 1911.

(34) Powers was ensign of a company of scouts under Colonel Lowther in 1783, but he never held the commission of captain.

(35) A mistake: This stream was named for John Hacker, the father of the William Hacker referred to.

(36) William Powers was born in Frederick County, Virginia, November 9, 1765.

(37) Old edition — new edition, pp. 135, 136.

(38) Old edition — new edition, pp. 136, 137, 138.

(39) Bridgeport is on Simpson's Creek, about six miles from Clarksburg. Here was located Power's Fort alluded to in *Border Warfare*, p. 247.

(40) This inquiry of Dr. Draper was in regard to Elijah Runner, who was connected with the murder of the Delaware Chief, Bald Eagle. (*Border Warfare*, pp. 135, 136.) There was a family of Runyons living in the vicinity of Jane Lew at this time, who were confused by Dr. Draper's correspondents with the Elijah Runner of historic renown.

(41) James W. Jackson was a grandson of Stephen Jackson, a son of Captain Edward Jackson, who settled on the Buckhannon with his father, John Jackson in 1769. Stephen Jackson was a scout during the later years of Indian hostilities on the border.

(42) Christopher T. Cutright, who died July 15, 1897, aged 93.

NOTES ON APPENDIX II

(1) "Warden's Statistics &c., I, 250."

(2) "Trans. Am. Ethnol. Soc., II, I."

(3) "Journal of Two Visits, 17."

(4) "Jones' Jour. of Two Visits, 30, 84."

(5) "Trans. Am. Antiq. Soc., II, foot note 139, 140."

(6) "Hutchins' Top. 1 Description, 4."

(7) "Trans. Am. Ethnol. Soc., II, p. 1."

(8) "Am. Naturalist, V. 720."

(9) This was at the Burning Springs. Two buffaloes were killed and their hides suspended on the limbs of a beech tree. When retreating over this route a short time later, the starving soldiers, who were not permitted to kindle a fire at night although it was dead winter, cut these hides into long strips, or *tugs*, and roasting them in the flames of the burning spring, ate them. From this incident *Tug River* derived its name. *Withers*, p. 83. — For another version of the origin of this name, consult the *First Biennial Report of West Virginia State Archives and History*, pp. 262, 263. — *L. V. McW.*

(10) Alluding to the buffalo killed by Samuel Pringle while camped in the sycamore tree in (now) Upshur County; and the destruction of the corn crop of the settlers in 1769. — *L. V. McW.*

(11) Both *Withers* and *DeHass* give the date 1736, when Benjamin Burden presented to Gov. Gooch of Virginia, a buffalo calf which had been caught on the waters of the Shenandoah River, and tamed. — *L. V. McW.*

(12) Consult also *Hand Book of American Indians*, Part I. p. 169. — *L. V. McW*.

NOTES ON APPENDIX III

(1) The spear-heads secured, were, at a later day, along with other relics, placed by me in the *Museum of the West Virginia Historical and Antiquarian Society*, Charleston: since converted into *State Archives and History*.

(2) Prof. Maxwell says: "The Petro family (sometimes spelled Pedro) were said to be Spanish. They were dark of complexion, and of spare build. When and how they came to Randolph has never been certainly ascertained. They are frequently mentioned in the earliest county records, and their descendants are now numerous in Randolph and adjoining counties." *History of Randolph County, West Va.*, p. 183.

Refer to *Note 8, Chapter X.*, and Westfall's Letter, *Appendix I*, this Volume, for mention of Petro.

(3) *History of Upshur County, West Va.*, pp. 331, 332.

(4) *History of Upshur County, West Va.*, pp. 332 to 335.

(5) Powell's Mountain is in the Northern part of Nicholas County. The monument noted by Mr. Connelley, who got his information from his guide who was ignorant of the facts, is one erected to Henry Young, a civilian killed by the van guard of Gen. Rosencrans' troops sent from Clarksburg to dislodge Brigadier Gen. John B. Floyd, Confederate, who was encamped in the southern part of the County. The Federals came upon Young near the summit of the mountain, then a wilderness, and disregarding the order to halt, was killed. A Federal officer appeared at the Young homestead and reported the particulars of the death of the husband and father. Young was buried there and the monument afterwards placed with funds secured by partisan subscription.

After the killing of Young, Rosencrans continued his march and on the 10th of September, 1861, came upon Boyd's forces at Carnefix Ferry, where a severe engagement ensued. The Confederates were defeated, and made a hurried retreat into Virginia.

Judge Wm. S. O'Brien of West Virginia, who is well versed in local history, writes me that partisan feeling ran high in that sparsely settled region because of the killing of Young, which was done by Ohio troops. His friends claimed that he was a harmless man, and the victim of "bush-whacking" methods, so prevalent throughout the mountains during the entire Civil War. On the other hand Union sympathizers averred that Young was a "bush-whacker." The Judge is of opinion that neither report is correct; and that Young, startled by the sudden appearance of the Federals, fled, as he supposed, from certain capture or death; which hastened his undoing. A negro who claimed to have been with the troops and witnessed the shooting, gave Mr. Frank Scott, of West Virginia, practically the same version of the tragedy as obtained by the family from the reporting officer.

NOTES ON APPENDIX IV

(1) It is noteworthy that *Kercheval* and subsequent writers speak of the mill owned by John Brake, a "German of considerable wealth," whose residence was the rendezvous of the Tory element. It is very probable that Jacob Brake was a brother to John, and the mill in question was joint property. It is significant that the name of John Brake does not appear in any of the petitions for executive clemency with that of Claypole, Jacob Brake and others. Perhaps he was among those who had already fled the country.—Refer to Note 4, Chapt. XXX, this Volume, for notice of Brake's mill.

www.ingramcontent.com/pod-product-compliance
Lightning Source LLC
Chambersburg PA
CBHW021845300426
44115CB00005B/22